A-Z
of
KIT CARS

DEDICATION

For Carol, Natalie and Michelle. Without you three there'd be nothing.
Thank you for everything. Plus, I can't forget my late,
much-missed mate, Peter Coxhead. I did it, Pete!

Peter Coxhead

Steve Hole

First published in February 2012

A catalogue record for this book is available from the British Library

ISBN 978 1 84425 677 8

Library of Congress catalog card no. 2010927389

Published by Haynes Publishing, Sparkford,
Yeovil, Somerset BA22 7JJ, UK

Tel. 01963 440635 Fax 01963 440001
Int. tel. +44 1963 440635 Fax +44 1963 440001
E-mail: sales@haynes.co.uk
Website: www.haynes.co.uk

Haynes North America, Inc.,
861 Lawrence Drive, Newbury Park,
California 91320, USA

Designed and typeset by James Robertson

Printed in the USA by Odcombe Press LP,
1299 Bridgestone Parkway, LaVergne, TN 37086

A–Z of KIT CARS

The definitive encyclopaedia of the
UK's kit-car industry since 1949

STEVE HOLE

Haynes Publishing

Acknowledgements

I would like to thank more people than I can remember. Sincere thanks (in no particular order) to Gary Axon, Robert Daniels (www.1950sspecials.com), Chris Rees, Peter Filby, James Hale, Dave Perry, Terry Sands, Tim Dutton, Sipko Postuma, Jem Marsh, Tom Hamblin, Barry Collyer, Richard Porter, Stephen Turner, Ken Baker, Alexander 'Sandy' Fraser, Richard Heseltine, Danny Lockstone, Marcos Heritage, Enzo Michelini, Arunas Racelis, Paul Robinshaw, Martin Chisholm Collectors Cars Ltd, Jim Dudley, Gerald Dawson, Dave Malins (Tornado Register), Jeremy Phillips, Marcus Potts (Latham Register), Bill Woodhouse, Philip Ivimey (Gilbern Owners Club) and Den Tanner, and to a chap called Alan Morgan who gave a young, fresh-faced 'me' a job on a magazine called *Kit Cars & Specials* way back in the '80s. It's your fault, Al!

I mustn't forget, either, Martin Foster, the best editor I ever saw (and *Sportscar* magazine should've been huge, mate!) Also Terry Grimwood, the best boss I ever had...

Finally, I salute every single person who has ever tried to be a car manufacturer. Whether you succeeded or flopped, God bless you.

Foreword

By Roger Cook,

Britain's best-known investigative journalist,

and motoring enthusiast

It seems that Britain has produced more niche and kit car manufacturers than any other country on Earth. There's something admirable about the British spirit of engineering innovation, even when some of the results didn't last long, and, on occasion, didn't deserve to. Nevertheless, this has resulted in a very long list of manufacturers (over 2,000) and an even longer list of products. Obviously imbued with indomitable spirit himself, the very knowledgeable Steve Hole has undertaken to compile an authoritative A–Z of the whole lot, from 1949 onwards. If it was ever made for sale to the motoring public, it's in this weighty tome.

Steve has achieved his goal with an interesting and exhaustive survey of everything from potting shed projects to small but serious manufacturers of cars capable of taking on the world's best in terms of handling, overall performance and sometimes even styling. I've owned two such vehicles myself – a Spyder Silverstone and a Grinnall Scorpion. Building and driving your own handiwork can be strangely addictive – and judging by the number of firms catering to that addiction there are rather a lot of addicts out there. This book is for you.

(Photo courtesy Rex Features)

Preface

Kit and specialist cars have pretty much been my life. From a very young age growing up in Croydon, I'd walk past the Trojan factory every day going to and from school, where my formative senses were treated to rows of bubble cars, Elvas and, later, a small number of McLaren road cars built by the firm in the '60s. Such sights made a big impression, which evolved into buying car magazines with every bit of pocket money I had. The writings of Tony Bostock and Peter Filby in *Hot Car* were consumed eagerly, while dedicated kit car magazines also rated pretty highly.

A magnet must have led me to a job at Link House

magazines in Dingwall Avenue, Croydon, in the '80s, and a stint working for *Kit Cars & Specials* magazine was manna from heaven for me, and sowed the seeds that led to a freelance career working for *Kit Car* magazine, *Sportscar* magazine, the subsequent founding of my own publications – *totalkitcar.com* and *tkc mag* and, ultimately, this book!

To all of the thousands of people who have set out on the path to produce their own car in component form, regardless of whether or not they intended to be the next Henry Ford, whether the car was good, bad or terrible, I salute you for having the verve, the guts and the creativity. Here's to you...

The intention of this book is not to judge or even to rate the cars within. It is intended as a guide to every make of specialist car ever made in the UK since 1949. A task of this magnitude has never been attempted before. Some will set out to try and catch me out with a model or piece of information I've missed or got wrong. However, this isn't *Masquerade* and there's no puzzle to unravel, let alone a golden hare to dig up! If you discover an anomaly or a model I've left out then bully for you, but hey, I'm sorry! All the same, it would be good to know if you find any errors or omissions.

I've not included every single 'special' ever made, as that would take up a huge tome in its own right. However, I have included body conversions and the odd fully-built low-volume model for the sake of completeness.

The entries are arranged alphabetically as far as they sensibly can be, but note that in cases where model names include numbers, these precede the alphabetical sequence – *eg* the entry for the Banham 130 Spyder will be found before that for the Banham Bat. Where model 'mark' numbers occur, these are listed in numerical rather than alphabetical order (*ie* 'MkVIII' is treated as 'Mk8').

I've tried to be as accurate as possible with production dates and figures, but kit car manufacturers have often been notorious for exaggerating – the stickleback that became a shark, and all that! – so in many places I've had to rely on educated guesswork. Also, be aware that the figures for models currently in production are as accurate as possible up to June 2011.

I hope you enjoy what I believe to be the most in-depth single-volume A–Z of UK kit cars ever produced...

Steve Hole
Warlingham, Surrey
June 2011

Introduction

The father of the modern day kit car industry was a chap called Derek Buckler, for it is he who is credited with having, in 1949, commercially supplied a rudimentary form of what we now know as a kit car. But more on Buckler later.

There's always been a history in the UK of tampering with and modifying cars, aided in part by many of the early purveyors of the automobile supplying little more than chassis, leading to a raft of coachbuilders creating the bodies. One only has to look at the early days of Rolls-Royce and Bentley to see this in action.

The English Mechanic

The first real kit car in the UK was probably a design created by engineer Thomas Hyler-White (1871–1930) in 1896 that later appeared in a magazine called *English Mechanic & World of Science & Art* in January 1900. His series of articles entitled 'A Small Car and How to Build It', based on a Benz Velo, appeared in 56 parts before the *English Mechanic* turned its attention to DIY pianolas!

The avid home car-builder of 1900 was left to fill in a lot of blanks, such as sourcing engines, from a de Dion 1¾bhp – which could be steam-powered or petrol – and layout (three or four wheels!) and there are still two English Mechanic 'cars' in existence. Hyler-White suggested the use of second-hand parts wherever possible. Incidentally, in 1936 another publication, *Newnes Practical Mechanics*, ran a series of articles dealing with how to design and build a three-wheeler with a suggested build budget of £20.

The de Dion Bouton

This French company was founded in 1883 by Comte Albert de Dion, Georges Bouton and Charles Trépardoux, and rapidly became the largest car manufacturer in the world, producing 400 cars per year by 1900. They were known for their high quality, reliability and durability, attributes not that abundant in those formative years of automobiles.

Nevertheless, many enthusiasts rebodied or altered existing de Dion Bouton vehicles, again proving that the temptation to modify cars isn't a new thing…

Cyclecars

The next notable enthusiast-led motoring development was the appearance of cyclecars, which were internationally classified as such in 1912. Probably best described as a cross between a motorcycle and a car, they were usually powered by single-cylinder or V-twin engines, with J.A.P units being particularly popular.

The first cyclecar was produced in France by a company called Bédélia, although it was GN that popularised them in the UK. Founded by H.R. Godfrey and Archibald Frazer Nash, GN settled on their first commercial design, called the GN Car, in 1910, operating from a base in Hendon, North London. They used J.A.P engines at first before making their own 1,100cc unit from 1911. Around 200 were sold before the outbreak of World War 1.

Production restarted in 1919 and before long the company was bought out by British Grégoire Ltd and moved to a new factory in East Hill, Wandsworth. Chassis were quickly changed from wood to steel and initially sales were good, although the popularity of the cyclecar was beginning to wane.

GN went into liquidation in 1921 and was bought by a Mr Black. Godfrey and Frazer Nash left in late 1922 and the company ceased making motor vehicles in 1923, before closing its doors completely in 1925. Godfrey went on to set up Godfrey-Proctor and then HRG, while Frazer Nash founded his own eponymous marque and developed his chain and clutch transmission system, also known as the chain-gang.

Why did cyclecars go out of popularity? Well, many were a bit primitive, and by the dawn of the 1920s major

DOOSTER

KOUGAR SPORTS

manufacturers such as Ford had worked out ways of making their models more affordable and more appealing to the general car-buying public of the day.

The Austin 7

Another major contributory factor (if not *the* reason) for the downfall of cyclecars was the introduction of the Austin 7 in 1922, designed by Stanley Edge and Herbert Austin. It really shouldn't be underestimated just how important a car the Austin 7 was, with 290,000 being produced before it went out of production in 1939, with a large percentage of them later being used as 'donor' vehicles for a variety of specials.

The 'Chummy' – so-called due to the closeness of the occupants – had a 696cc engine that was soon increased to 747cc. Even from the early days owners were modifying their Austin 7s, with the factory introducing Ulster racers, while (Sir) William Lyons, co-founder of Swallow Sidecar Company, launched his Cyril Holland-designed Swallow in 1927, of which some 3,500 were sold before production ceased in 1932, when Lyons set up SS (later Jaguar) Cars.

It wasn't hard to see why the Austin was so popular. It had all the trimmings of a large car wrapped up in a compact, affordable design.

Bentley specials

The 1930s saw the 'specials' movement gather momentum, with the products of Bentley – the MkVI or R Type – being used as 'donors'. The large unwieldy bodies, fine for spirited cruising, were dumped in favour of rakish two-seat sports-style replacements. Many were one-offs, although there were some specialist companies around who could offer you an 'off-the-peg' number. However, no two were ever the same.

The Rytecraft Scootacar

Talk of the '30s means that we must mention another quirk of British specialist motoring – the Rytecraft Scootacar. Unbelievably, it started life as a fairground bumper car, but

made it to the public highway in 1934, manufactured by Rytecraft, run by Tom Shillan.

The Scootacar remained available until 1940, powered by a 98cc Villiers engine, upgraded in 1936 to a 249cc unit. Unbelievably tiny, it didn't have springs, gears, brake pedal, lights or a windscreen, although it did later gain some of these items as well as a reverse gear and two seats! It cost just £80 and around 1,500 were sold during its six-year lifespan. Even King Zog of Albania owned one.

The little vehicle was revived in 1965 when a chap called Jim Parkinson drove around the world in a 30-year-old example that he'd just refurbished. The eventful and amazing journey took him 421 days.

The 'specials' era

By the mid-1940s Britain had emerged from the horror of war and the euphoria of victory to face the fact that there was a seriously weakened economy to rebuild, with shortages, rationing and pretty austere times for everyone. As a result, the government introduced a policy of exporting to gain as much hard currency income as possible, and thus cars were only available to a lucky small minority.

Lying around, however, were literally thousands of old Ford Pops, Austins, Morris Eights and the like, from which you could simply chuck away the moth-eaten parts, keep the inevitably sound chassis and put a rakish sports car body on to it. One chap who could see the potential was Derek Buckler, a motorsport enthusiast from Berkshire.

Synthetic resinoids

Glassfibre is one of the key materials in the production of kit cars and its introduction delivered all sorts of possiblities for fledgling car manufacturers. Soon there were swoopy, rakish looking bodyshells appearing that wouldn't be viable in aluminium.

Fifties *specials* were initially clothed in aluminium bodies, which even back then were pricey; often twice as expensive as a rudimentary replacement chassis. Unless you got yours from one of the better purveyors – artisans such as Williams & Pritchard or Rochdale Motor Panels – your bodyshell could be pretty basic, looking like it had seen a knife and fork rather than crafted on an English Wheel.

Synthetic resinoids, more commonly known today as glassfibre, fibreglass or GPR, were long overdue. America was the world leader in the material. Resin technology, glass matting and chopped strand fibres appeared commercially in 1938 thanks to a company called Owens-Corning Fiberglass™ Corporation of Ohio. DuPont and Cyanamid were leading players in advancing the use of resins in 1942.

The first car body made from glassfibre was the Glasspar G2 made by boat-builder Bill Tritt, although the mainstream manufacturers weren't far behind with General Motors launching the Corvette at the Detroit Motor Show in January 1953, closely followed by Kaizer-Frazer and their Henry J.

The UK also weren't far behind, and a company called Microcell exhibited a one-piece fibreglass body they had developed for Allard in July 1953, although both Singer (SMX Roadster) and Jensen (541) were the first UK makers to use it in mass production, reorganising the importance of this then new-fangled material.

The first fibreglass body for proprietary kit car use appeared as early as spring 1953 and came from RGS Automobile Components run by Dick Shattocks, which was loosely based on the pre-war JAG Atlanta project that his company had acquired. At £90 it was on a par with the aluminium bodies it was meant to replace, but remember that at this stage its supply and manufacture was in its infancy. The body wasn't actually made by RGS, rather by the North East Coast Yacht Building and Engineering Company Ltd (rolls off the tongue doesn't it?) and supplied in two halves with separate doors. A crude but exciting development for the fledgling UK kit car industry.

The efforts of some early pioneers were a bit hit and miss. The day of the specialist laminator was coming, but in the meantime, some were more skilled than others in using the new material. An old Fairthorpe engineer told me years ago that their efforts often resulted in foul-smelling globby messes on the workshop floor. They made their bodies in the evening and quite often were a bit wayward in mixing the ingredients. Several occasions saw the accelerator (hardener) omitted by accident, meaning the GRP didn't go 'off'!

That man Derek Buckler, as you'd expect, was right at the forefront of fibreglass. Late 1953 saw him launch his own Mk X body, which was made for him by Galt-Glass.

One of the 'old-school' panel-beaters, Rochdale Motor Panels, more comfortable walloping aluminium, were also right in the mix as far as GRP was concerned. Co-founders Harry Smith and Frank Butterfield could see that this material was going to change the face of their business very quickly. In the spring of 1954 their Mk VI was launched, followed 12 months later by the C and F types.

By the middle of the decade, GRP bodies were swarming

LOMAX 223

onto the market and the *special* builder was spoilt for choice. Quality was rapidly improving and prices were becoming more reasonable. Major companies, such as Shell, were heavily involved at the time, producing and developing more sophisticated resins that were fire and acid resistant.

Other well-known companies involved in fibreglass body supply included Bonglass and Martin Plastics, and as mentioned earlier, it didn't take long before people started to cotton on to the skills required to laminate GRP rather than crudely daub it on. Another very notable company of the *specials* period were Micron Plastics, later known as Microplas, who started from a simple shop selling fibreglass matting and resin in Rickmansworth in 1954 founded by Sandy Wemyss. They pretty rapidly started selling their own bodies for either Ford or Austin use, and names such as Stiletto and Mistral became well known, and by 1955 they had opened another factory to cope with demand in Mitcham, Surrey, not far from where I grew up, in fact. As a young boy I used to regularly walk past the factory and vividly recall the heady aroma of epoxy resin. Perhaps that's where my grounding in kit cars came from! Their range of bodies sold in droves from 1954, when the Bill Ashton-designed Toledo for Austin 7 appeared, costing just £49. Later designs included the Stiletto, Scimitar and the most popular of all, the Mistral, of which over 500 found eager homes. Indeed it was also used as the prototype shell for the Fairthorpe Electron in 1958.

While it's true to say that fibreglass began to dominate the *specials* market very quickly, aluminium bodies didn't completely disappear. Several manufacturers, including Sid Hamblin, kept their bodies firmly in the metal camp.

Early donors

1950s *specials* builders usually resorted to two main donor vehicles – the Austin 7 and the Ford 8 or 10. We've dealt with the Austin, but what about the blue oval?

Much like the A7, the special builder of the '50s could choose from a whole raft of clapped-out pre-war Fords,

MALONE SKUNK

classed as Ford 8 or Ford 10, but in layman's terms this meant the Ford Model Y (1932–37) '8' with 23½bhp or the E93A Prefect (1938–49, with 7ft 10in wheelbase) '10' with bigger 30bhp version of the ubiquitous 1,172cc sidevalve gasper.

Other post-war Fords to be pressed into donor service included the E493A, 100E series (1953–59, 36bhp, 7ft 6in wheelbase) and the later 105E Anglia.

The swinging '60s

By the turn of the decade, customer expectations had begun to rise and they simply weren't satisfied any more with a lashed-up Pagoda-shaped bodyshell that they had to bash and smash on to an outdated Austin 7 chassis. By this time mainstream sports cars like the Triumph TR2 and MGA were affordable on the second-hand market, while the 1959 launch of the iconic Mini and little 'Frogeye' Sprite had also changed things considerably.

Similarly, almost overnight consumers turned away from the proprietary bodyshells of the late '50s and wanted complete kits with an engine and all the running gear included in the package price.

The death knell of the bodyshell also piped in the arrival of the 'proper' kit car, although this was also aided by the swingeing purchase tax applied to new cars, which was 50% in 1956, reduced to a still hefty 33% from 1958. Manufacturers such as Lotus, however, could supply the same car in component form without any tax, which was an attractive proposition to many purchasers.

From a complete kit point of view, Colin Chapman's Lotus were one of the early pioneers of such packages, supplying their Seven model complete with a spaceframe chassis, double wishbone suspension and a Ford 1172 engine with gearbox, all for £526, and Chapman claimed it could be built in just 75 hours. I recall a great advert showing Chapman in dapper black suit and a pointer stick, which proclaimed: 'He designed it, now you build it'. Buying the Seven in kit form represented a purchase tax saving of £346. By comparison,

the ageing Ford Popular cost £443 while the exciting Frogeye wore a price-tag of £670.

The arrival of the Seven in complete kit form prompted other manufacturers such as Fairthorpe, Gilbern, Rochdale, Turner and TVR to follow suit.

The dawn of the MoT test

In 1961 *Car Mechanics* magazine estimated that there were over 22,000 specials on the road in the UK, although inevitably many were deathtraps that were unregulated. It was May 1961 when the British government introduced the 'ten-year test', the forerunner of the modern-day MoT, which was intended to check the roadworthiness of the one million old cars on the UK's roads.

Of course, the majority of the specials failed this test, miserably, and suddenly there was a rush to replace the decrepit Ford Pop and Austin chassis with off-the-shelf replacements, and companies like Buckler, Littabourne, Regent, Victory, Mercury, Watling, Buroche and big daddies Halifax made hay for a time.

As already mentioned, by 1961 the bodyshell companies were struggling. Some, like Falcon Shells, concentrated on hardtops, others switched to garden ponds, and things had got so bad for many others that you could buy an EB50 shell from Edwards Brothers for under 30 quid. Others, however, moved with the times without wishing to get involved in complete kits, and Convair and Ashley Laminates started to actively offer chassis on their price lists. This hybrid supply method rescued several bodyshell manufacturers from oblivion.

Microcars

For those that didn't fancy a rakish, low-slung sports car, the parallel universe of microcars started to boom in the late '50s and quickly turned into a craze. Some well-known manufacturers within this movement also offered their products as complete kits, the first to arrive being the Opperman Unicar, followed by the Nobel 200 and Frisky Family Three, but although the exact number of micros sold as kits isn't known, it wasn't many.

Mini-fun

The advent of the Mini in 1959 had quite an impact on the kit car world, and although initially seen as a threat it wasn't long before some ingenious characters worked out its potential for kit car use, and it went on to become as important a donor as the VW Beetle. The distinction of being the first Mini-based kit car belongs to the Butterfield Musketeer, launched in 1961.

Impishness

The Hillman Imp first hove into view in 1955, designed by Michael Parkes and Tim Fry. Like the Mini it was a logical kit car donor vehicle, especially with its Coventry Climax-derived 875cc aluminium engine. From the outset the Imp had kit car potential written all over it, and in 1963 Paul Emery emerged with his Emery GT, although it wasn't until 1967 that the two best Imp-based kits arrived. First came Ginetta with their G15, which was quickly followed by the Davrian marque.

As the '60s developed it was time for the industry to take stock. We'd already seen a shift from the specials craze of supplying basic bodyshells, to proper body/chassis units and then to complete kit packages, but several other things also impacted on the industry during the decade and had a considerable influence on the manufacture of kit cars. The aforementioned ten-year test of 1961, which by 1962 had developed into the annual MoT test, had quite an effect, most of it positive, as it abruptly stopped deathtraps, built by bodgers, in their tracks. Next came the big cut in purchase tax in 1963, which had a devastating impact for a time. Suddenly getting your spanners out in a single garage to save hundreds of pounds in tax became unattractive and, of course, unnecessary to many kit buyers, and also put production sports cars like the Sprite within the reach of typical kit buyers. Hot rod kits were also extremely popular in the late '60s.

The beach buggy cometh

Other really great specialist cars of the 1960s included the Piper GTT of 1967 and the beautiful Trident Venturer, while that flower-power trippy year also marked the onslaught of the Beetle-based beach buggy. Definitely not performance orientated, the buggy did however offer FUN, FUN and – yep, you've guessed it – FUN, for very little outlay, and their humble Beetle underpinnings meant they were robust and pretty reliable.

The buggy pioneer was Bruce Meyers, whose American Manx buggy fathered thousands of bastard sons, including the GP Buggy, which is credited as the first UK bug but was actually beaten to the punch by Warren Monks of Volksrod in 1968. Mind you, the GP must be the most copied UK buggy, with loads of erstwhile agents suddenly offering their 'own' beach buggy kit!

For those that wanted more than asthmatic flat four air-cooled Veedub power, there were some experimenting with mental Porsche engines, a Corvair V8 (!) and other such units.

Suffice to say, ponderous stock Beetle handling was only exacerbated when extra power was added.

The 1970s

If the '60s had been a mix of excitement and recovery, then the '70s were totally bonkers. Beach buggy popularity was huge for a couple of years but was on a downward spiral by late 1972. It wasn't long before other manufacturers started creating 'Prof Pat Pending', Wacky Racer-looking designs mainly based on the humble Beetle.

But the biggest factor of the early '70s was the introduction of VAT in 1973, which pretty much stopped the kit car production of Ginetta, Lotus and TVR almost overnight. In fact you could actually buy a Lotus in kit form until 1974, but the launch of the new Elite marked the end of that particular road for the Norfolk firm.

Caterham Cars

1973 was also the year that Graham Nearn of Caterham Cars purchased the rights to the Lotus Seven, lock, stock and two smoking barrels, and rapidly made a decision that will go down in motoring annals as an inspired one. He purchased the rights to the angular Series IV, but soon decided to relaunch the classic Series III, and the rest, as they say, is history. The Surrey-based firm have never really looked back, and although the shape is pretty much unchanged, each year sees a new tweak and/or a more potent power unit, and it sits proudly at the top of the specialist car pecking order, shifting some 500 units per year, around 40% of which are kits.

The rest of the '70s pretty much marched by without any further significant developments save for the regular arrival of a wacky design or two. The industry was yet to see the rise of the replica, and two models in particular would go on to shape the whole industry. I'm talking, of course, about the replica Cobra and the Lotus Seven. The latter part of the decade also saw a fledgling operation run by a young chap called Tim Dutton-Woolley, and his products would go on to create a lasting legacy, but more on him later.

GTM COUPÉ

F27 CLUBMAN

STIMULATOR

The 1980s...let's get serious

The '80s saw the arrival of the first dedicated kit car magazines on the news-stands, produced by a young Peter J. Filby, whose magazines grew out of columns in *Hot Car* and a series of books published by David & Charles, such as *Fun Car Explosion*. The first dedicated kit car title was *Alternative Cars* in 1979.

Anyway, I digress. The early '80s saw the arrival of prolific manufacturers, such as Worthing-based Dutton Cars and their near neighbours Eagle Cars, commence on a path that would lead to literally thousands of sales. Tim Dutton very cleverly decided to concentrate on the budget end of the market, offering a very low kit price, and a whole raft of models saw many kit car builders cut their teeth on Dutton products.

The decade also saw the dawn of other prolific manufacturers such as Robin Hood Sportscars and Pilgrim Cars.

Robin Hood Sportscars, founded by Richard Stewart, initially began by selling Ferrari Daytona replicas based on the Triumph and, later on, Rover SD1, before settling on a path of various Lotus Seven-inspired sports cars, selling many thousands of kits.

Likewise, Pilgrim, founded by Den Tanner and Bill Harling, latched on to the Dutton idea of selling budget-priced kits, starting with their Bulldog model, a traditional roadster design that could be built very inexpensively. Thousands of these were sold before Pilgrim added the Family Tourer and Hawthorn models to their range. The latter two weren't as prolific sales-wise as the Bulldog, but the model that came next was – and how. It was called the Sumo.

1981 saw the first stirrings of a Cobra 427 frenzy that would see no end. After the initial wave of anticipation when DJ Sportscars, Unique Autocraft, Metaline and Gerry Hawkridge (making a 427 for Beribo Replica Automobiles) were racing to offer the first UK fake snake, a battle which DJ won – just, by a matter of days. There truly hasn't been another replica that has stirred the passions like Shelby's '60s

hero. In 1986 Pilgrim Cars threw their hat into the ring with their budget Sumo version, which gave people the shape without the grunt, utilising Cortina running gear at a fraction of the cost of Jaguar-based rivals. Since then the Sumo has moved upmarket a little and nowadays is usually fitted with a V8 of Chevrolet or Rover origin, but it was a gamechanger when it arrived in 1987.

Meanwhile, DJ Sportscars has also done massively well with their Tojeiro, as it subsequently became known, named after John Tojeiro, creator of the AC Ace and involved with original Cobras, and they've now taken the whole concept a step further by introducing a de Dion rear axle version, complete with their patented camber compensation system designed by the company's technical guru Peter Walker. The old warhorse may be 30 years old but it's still as fresh as a daisy and every bit as attractive. In 2009 its name was changed to DAX 427.

The 1980s marked a hugely prolific period for the kit car industry with each week bringing new models, some of which were the most hideous and laughable things ever, ever seen, and didn't do a particularly good job of promoting the industry to a wider audience – far from it in some cases, with the mainstream press treating us like a laughing stock, a stigma that's been hard to shift.

Also the Countach replica arrived on the scene, and there was much mayhem when the early appalling efforts appeared. Once the first, as-original, shape kit was announced all hell broke loose. Mind you, it should have been a close copy, as a real Lamborghini was hired from a car rental company called Town & Country, and 'splashed' over the course of a weekend in a dodgy backstreet warehouse in Manchester. Others quickly appeared, such as Conan, Venom, Sienna, Silhouette, Broadbest, etc etc etc. This was certainly the decade of the Italian exotic replica.

The traditional roadster also saw huge popularity with NG Cars, Marlin and Pilgrim – with their cheaper Bulldog alternative – all securing big sales. We also saw the JBA Falcon and Marlin unveiled and both would be prolific sellers.

The decade also saw the first work of the creative mind of one Lee Noble. His Ultima arrived in late 1985 and caused a massive stir. His demo car, registered NUT 602P, captured people's imagination, as it was the first real Group C lookalike in kit form, and although the original wasn't as pretty or sophisticated as the current-day Ultima products from the company, it was still bloody capable. Lee, of course, has also been responsible for such kits as the Noble 23 (Lotus 23 replica that later became the Auriga and Mamba), the Noble P4 and the Midtec Spyder among others, before finally gaining mainstream acceptance with the glorious M12.

Other notable arrivals in the '80s were Sylva Autokits, NG, GTM, Autotune and the dawn of kit car racing, which goes from strength to strength. A man called Dave Bradley from the 750 Motor Club came up with the idea for the Kit Car Challenge Series and those early days were crazy and exciting, with grids of Duttons, O&C Sprints and even a humungous and unlikely Atlantis Convertible, piloted by Chris Godkin, keeping the crowds entertained. Only the names have changed during the intervening years, as the various series containing kit and specialist cars are still overseen by the 750 Motor Club.

The 1990s

The '90s dawned, and euphoria welcomed their arrival, with the industry in buoyant mood and the sales figures for most UK manufacturers very encouraging. This was quickly shattered by the economic depression that soon gripped the country. Some manufacturers fell by the wayside as what is ultimately a leisure industry was hit hard, and people kept what spare cash they had and hoped that they could also keep their jobs. Even prolific products like the Pilgrim Bulldog, of which nearly 2,000 had found homes since the mid-'80s, was struggling to make headway. As surely, though, as night follows day, pips stopped squeaking and things began to settle down again.

One notable change was the chucking out of the really wild and horrid designs – and suddenly the whole industry was trying to shake off this Wacky Racer image that had given everyone such a good laugh over the years, and finally started to realise that to make real progress, quality had to improve for the majority rather than just the 'usual suspect' handful.

By the mid-'90s there were rumblings coming from the government that things had to change and that the existing concept (albeit controlled a little by the need for an MoT test) that enabled anyone to build a kit car and drive it on the road without any real checks, had to stop. Most kits were built to an acceptable level of competence, but, and we've all seen them, there have been some shocking devices 'nailed' together by an idiot in a shed that really were clearly unsafe. The Ministry was talking about some form of regulation, which immediately had the doom-mongers sounding that old death knell again…

The dawn of SVA and now, IVA

Originally seen as some kind of spectre that would kill the industry overnight, Single Vehicle Approval, also known as SVA, introduced on 1 July 1998, helped to improve standards immeasurably. SVA has now been replaced by an amended scheme called IVA that, like its predecessor, checks things such as internal and exterior projections, ie sharp bits, and also provides a set of regulations with which all amateur-built cars that use a purpose-made or amended donor car chassis have to comply. Even three-wheelers have their own Motorcycle SVA (or MSVA) that they have to abide by, while the only kits currently exempt from the scheme are body conversions which use an unmodified chassis.

Kit cars long may they ride…

K1 ATTACK

A–Z Listing of Kit Cars Made since 1949

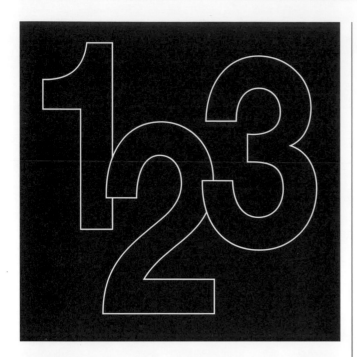

1-6-2 TURBO SPORTS

Ted Kellerman of Edmonton, North London, imported the Albar (*qv*) range to the UK and also produced his own Super Beetle-type kit called the Turbo Sports.
1-6-2 Glassfibre 1979–80
Approx 10 made

204 GT

Daytona Classics of Clacton-on-Sea was run by father and son team, Vince and Jason Phillips, and assisted by Dean Walker, who formerly worked for Dave Perry of Automotive Developments. Perry worked closely with the Phillipses. Indeed, the 204 GT replica they marketed for a time came via Dave.
Daytona Classics 1986–87
Approx 22 made

29 MODEL A FORD

Huddersfield-based company run by Paul Haigh, a well-known UK hot-rodder, who couldn't find a '29 to his requirements so set about building his own. Quality was high, with a CDS chassis and five body styles to choose from. Designed around Jaguar suspension, although alternatives were available. Power came from Rover V8. Haigh initially traded as Repro Rod Parts, and later as the Early Ford Store. The project went to Robert Taylor's Scorhill Motor Company in 1994.
Repro Rod Parts 1980–89
Early Ford Store 1989–94
Scorhill Motor Company 1994–96
Approx 35 made

34 CORNER 34 FORD

From one of the UK's top hot rodders came this '34 Ford street-rod kit based around a traditional-style ladder chassis, with Cortina or Granada front suspension and Jaguar or Volvo live rear axle. It could be ordered with coupé or pick-up style bodies. Engine choices could be anything from humble Ford 4-cylinder to V8. Chris Boyle was also responsible for the Chesil Speedster replica, which evolved from his seprate Street Beetle operation.
34 Corner 1986–91
Approx 20 made

34 CORNER 37 FORD

Hailing from Christchurch-based UK rodding guru Chris Boyle, this '37 Ford kit was similar in execution to his '34 Ford, but the body style was a convertible.
34 Corner 1986–91
Approx 8 made

34 FORD THREE-WINDOW

A Robertsbridge, East Sussex, rod maker run by Phil Ritchie, who offered this very nice '34 Ford, available with replica-style body or a 3in chopped top. Both options featured a fully-trimmed body with doors pre-fitted. The body originated from the USA and had been inspired by a famous rod called 'The California Kid' that had starred in a film of the same name.
Auto (Marine) Developments 1980–88
Approx 24 made

3GE ROADSTER

Another product influenced by the Haynes Roadster that appeared in 2007 to offer components for book buyers and subsequent car builders. This Somerset-based company, run by John Roberts, Keith Pike and Tony Due, supplies a whole range of components from wishbones to a chassis for Sierra and Mazda MX-5-based versions. Also supplies bodywork for the car from 2011.
3GE Components 2008 to date
Approx 5 made

41 DODGE

A '41 Dodge kit from Rodbodys of Three Holes, Wisbech, run by Glen Whetrans. Based on Mazda pickup with a chassis by Fenland Rod & Custom. Whetrans has a very good reputation as a fibreglass laminator.
Rodbodys 2005 to 2010
Approx 6 made

427 REPLIQUÉ

A short-lived Cobra replica (did they ever make one?) from Silverstone-based Firefox, run by Mike Todd.
Firefox 2000
Approx 1 made

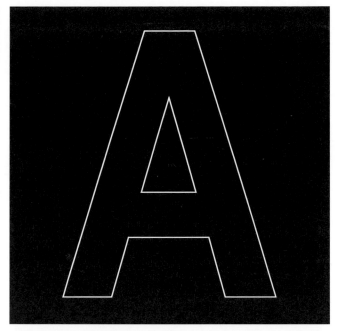

AB1/SPIDER

Alexander 'Sandy' Fraser's first attempt at car manufacturing, while based in Peterborough. He built the prototype in his kitchen using Mini front subframe, engine and running gear. Body was made out of wood with fibreglass wings. Only made one prototype before turning his attentions to the revised and improved AF1 (*qv*). *Motor* magazine described it as a 'wardrobe on wheels'!
Antique Automobiles Ltd 1971
Approx 1 made

ABC TRICAR

The Tricar was the UK's first road-going Mini-based three-wheeler, created by Ken Heather and Bill Powell, based in Kingswinford. Used complete Mini front end and reinforced floorpan that took half a Mini subframe at the rear, and retained the metal body – or part of it! After change of ownership (the company moved down the road to Brierley Hill) in 1971, body was made completely out of fibreglass.
Auto Body Craft 1969–71
Auto Body Craft 1971–73
Approx 30 made

ABS MONACO

Convertible, Countach-inspired kit from Auto Build Services of Three Legged Cross, Dorset, run by former Brightwheel employee Jon Homewood, with help from his brother Nick. They built the chassis for the Broadbest Primo; the Monaco was a development. Quite highly rated for its time. Three made. Kit cost £6,250 plus VAT in 1988.

A chap called Alan Milford had been building a Silhouette Countach replica and visited ABS, located close to his Ringwood home, for assistance. He was so impressed with the quality of the Monaco that he ditched his build and bought an ABS kit instead. During the build, Jon Homewood went bust and left him stranded.

Eager to complete his build, Milford enlisted the services of Homewood's brother, Nick, to help him, and created Prestige Sports Cars, although the company didn't last very long, leaving Milford on his own. He ceased trading soon after. The plan to market the fixed-head Scorpion (renamed Denaro) came to nought.

Moulds were spotted for sale in 1995 by Steven Potter, who decided to put the car back into production in 1999 from his base in Durham. He revised the car to run on Vauxhall Ecotec engine, mounted amidships but transversely, again this didn't last long and he only made one demo car.
Auto Build Services 1988–89
Prestige Sports Cars 1994–95
Pit Performance Vehicles 1999
Approx 6 made

ABS SCORPION/DENARO

Three Legged Cross, run by Jon Homewood, made this Lamborghini Countach replica, which evolved from the Broadbest Primo, and was the sister car to the convertible, Monaco. Kits cost £5,700 plus VAT in 1988.

When ABS went bust, erstwhile customer Alan Milford created Prestige Sports Cars, based in Ringwood. He intended to develop the now renamed Denaro but ceased trading before he could do so.
Auto Build Services 1988–89
Prestige Sports Cars 1994-95
Approx 3 made

AC CHALLENGER 2000

This Porthleven-based company had no connection to AC Cars or the Challenger (*qv*) E-type replica produced in Cornwall. The AC Challenger kit was a short-lived  Lamborghini Countach replica that appeared at the Sandown Kit Car show in 1992. Featured a chassis made by West Coast Racing of Helston, with power from a Chevy 350cu in V8. Never seen again.
AC Auto Replicas 1992
Approx 1 made

AC DONINGTON

Seen briefly in 1982, when displayed for the first (and only?) time at the Santa Pod show that year. A quirky-looking three-wheeler based on Mini mechanicals with a combination fibreglass and aluminium body.
Fraser Engineering 1982
Approx 1 made

AD 206

Dave Perry of Perry Automotive Developments, Brightlingsea, had been making a name for himself anglicising a selection of American kits to suit the UK market. One day a customer with a Lotus Europa turned up at his Essex base, wanting him to create a Ferrari 206 replica based on his Europa chassis, which he'd worked out shared the same wheelbase (4in shorter than the 246). An aluminium prototype body existed in Wales, which Perry took a mould from and gave to a couple of apprentices he had working for him at the time. They completed the one car for the customer and then did no more.

Perry's friend John Phillips, who was busy chopping the roofs off Jaguar XJ6s, was quite taken with the idea and bought the project, marketing it under the Daytona Classics banner from a unit down the coast in Clacton-on-Sea, along with his son Jason, and Perry's erstwhile employee and laminator Dean Walker. They sold around five more, coming up with a Lancia/Alfa-based version.
Perry Automotive Developments 1981–85
Daytona Classics 1985–88
JH Classics 1988–89
Deon Cars 1989–98
Approx 20 made

AD 400/MAGNUM/CHIMERA

Dave Perry created the AD 400 by stretching the Karma (*qv*) bodyshell by 4in and basing it on Ford Cortina mechanicals and his own chassis. He later chopped the roof off and created a convertible version.

After Perry Automotive Developments of Brightlingsea went into liquidation, they started up again as Automotive Design & Development, based in a block of ten sheds behind a video store in Clacton-on-Sea, before moving back to Brightlingsea and renaming the car the Magnum. Dave Perry sold four fixed-head versions and one convertible.

Project subsequently taken over by Peterborough-based Ferranté Cars, run by Robert 'RJ' Pepper, who later became Trident Autovet. He sold the car in fully-built guise, calling it the Chimera.
Perry Automotive Developments 1982
Automotive Design & Developments 1982–84
Ferranté Cars 1984–85
Trident Autovet 1985–86
Approx 11 made

AD 427

This is the Cobra replica that pretty much fathered the great majority of the UK's 427 replica projects. When Dave Perry was in America doing a deal with Classic Motor Carriages on the Gazelle kit, a makeweight in the container (to stop the rest of the consignment moving around on the long sea voyage) was the 'buck' for

the Steve Arntz Cobra replica, Perry having reckoned he might be able to do something with it. After it arrived in late 1979, he stuck it on the top of his office for over a year while he concentrated on converting the VW Beetle-based Gazelle into the Ford Cortina-based Spirit SS (qv).

He created a new chassis for the car via his own Heywood Engineering operation (based on the quay at Maldon, Essex) and also lent the mould to another manufacturer to help them create their own version of the car, which has, incidentally, gone on to sell in large numbers.

Perry sold 15 kits under the Perry Automotive Developments (and then Automotive Design & Developments) banner, although his erstwhile agent, Roger Woolley of RW Kit Cars sold more – including a batch to France that were based on VW Beetle mechanicals – when he took over the project completely (see RW 427).

Dave Perry continued making chassis for a variety of manufacturers, including DJ Sportscars, and also bodies for others, such as Gravetti, before he became disillusioned with the industry and moved into property maintenance.

He returned to the kit car scene with youngest son, Ross, in 2006, when he acquired the Auto Italia Retroforza Mazda MX-5 body conversion, the Italia (qv). Incidentally, Perry's oldest son, Lee, has worked for legendary design company Carrozzerria Bertone for many years, and has recently been responsible for the interior design of the Ferrari California.

Perry Automotive Developments 1981–83
Approx 15 made

ADAM'S BUGGY

A low-key operation run by a chap called Adam Spittle, based in Kidderminster. An off-road rail-type vehicle based on Toyota MR2 Mk1.
Adam's Buggies 2008 to date
Approx 15 made

ADAM SSK

This was the original American-spec CMC Gazelle (a Mercedes Benz SSK replica – sort of) imported to the UK by Dave Perry, who sold two before converting the car to Ford Cortina mechanicals. He moved the engine to the front, widened and lengthened the body, giving it a bespoke ladderframe chassis, and renamed it the Spirit SS (qv).

Perry Automotive Developments 1979
Approx 2 made

ADAMS ROADSTER

In the early 1980s, former Marcos and Design Probe 15 designer Dennis Adams, who had been working for American kit car company Antique & Classic Automobiles, got the idea for a big neo-classic '30s -style roadster with echoes of the Jaguar SS100. When Adams returned to the UK he set about creating it. The prototype featured a Vauxhall Monza engine, although subsequent production versions had a revised chassis and Jaguar running gear. Very well regarded, it was available as a conventional kit or as an XJ6 body conversion. Moved on to a new company in 1994, who retained the Adams Roadsters name.

Adams Roadsters 1986–99
Approx 18 made

ADJ MERLIN

Jaguar-based traditional roadster.
Company also imported US GT40
and Cobra replicas, although it's
not known if any of these were
sold.
ADJ 1989
Approx 2 made

ADR SPORT 2

Successor to the Sport 1000
(see below), the Sport 2 was a
two-seater, revised version of the
original car, with power coming
from inline four-cylinder bike
engines such as Honda CBR
1000 Fireblade. Lasted around 18
months in production before ADR
shifted to the definitive Sport 3 version.
ADR Engineering 2003–5
Approx 5 made

ADR SPORT 3

ADR is run by Adrian Daniels and
based in Touchen End, Berkshire.
This engineering and race car
orientated operation offers its
stylish ADR3 in comprehensive
rolling chassis form in addition to
turnkey guise. Power comes from
bike engines and a variety of other
units.
ADR Engineering 2008 to date
Approx 40 made

ADR SPORT 1000

The first product from Adrian Daniels Racing. It was designed primarily
for the 750 Motor Club's Formula 750 Series, which at the time ran
Reliant engines. Although the single-seat Sport 1000 retained a Morris
1000 rear axle, it featured a BMW K100 motorcycle engine. Given
stand-alone Sport 1000 series by 750 in 2002 (along with entries from
Scholar and Trevor Farrington), but grid numbers very small and they
moved on to the Sport 2, after BMW objected.
ADR Engineering 2001–3
Approx 12 made

ADRENALINE CB – *see Toniq-R*

ADT SPRINT

Revamped Mackintosh M1C (*qv*) taken over by a Saffron Walden-
based company run by Gordon Allin and Jonathan Tubb, who
switched the car to a stainless steel monocoque chassis layout
from 1991. They also ditched the Mini donor in favour of Metro
parts. Project subsequently ended up with Colin Oberline-Harris and
became the Mackintosh M3 (*qv*).
Automotive Design Technology 1991
Approx 2 made

AEON GT3/GT2 SPYDER

A drophead version of the GT3
coupé, with no roof and gullwing-
style 'doorlets'. Power for this one
is usually a Volkswagen Group 1.8
FSi turbo.

In 2011, production passed
to Doncaster-based Exceed
Autocraft Ltd, run by Matthew
Flett, and aided by former AGM
and Bramwith-man Nick Heyes,
who converted the original three-
seat central driving position to
a more conventional two-seat
arrangement.
Aeon Sportscars 2004 to 2011
Exceed Autocraft Ltd 2011 to
date
Approx 5 made

AEON GT3/GT2 COUPÉ

Innovative three-seater with central driving position from Keith Wood and John Hewat of Marden, Kent. Lots of bespoke parts, with power coming from Ford Duratec mainly, although other units can be fitted. A convertible version was introduced in 2004.

In 2011, production passed to Doncaster-based, Exceed Autocraft Ltd, run by Matthew Flett, who converted the original three-seat central driving position to a more conventional two-seat arrangement.
Aeon Sportscars 2003–2011
Exceed Autocraft 2011 to date
Approx 12 made

AERO MG3

Version of the BRA CX3 three-wheeler (*qv*) that was similar to the latter but used a Moto Guzzi engine in lieu of the increasingly hard-to-find Honda CX500 unit. Comes from Aero Cycle Cars of Ditchling, East Sussex.
Aero Cycle Cars 2007 to date
Approx 15 made

AF1

After his one-off AB1 (*qv*) effort, Alexander Fraser moved to Sleaford, where he was slightly more successful. *Motor* magazine actually liked this one, although the company still folded in 1972. Also known as AF Spider (*qv*).
A.T. Fraser Ltd 1971–72
Approx 9 made

AF GRAND PRIX

Alexander Fraser's third attempt at car making, after the AB1 (*qv*) and AF1 (*qv*). By this time he'd moved from Sleaford to Marlborough, Wiltshire. Similar in construction to the AB1 Spider, it featured mudguards rather than wings, with revised rear styling and a new windscreen.

Fraser went on to set up Lion Omnibuses, making two-thirds scale vintage buses and trucks.
AF 1969–80
Approx 4 made

AF SPORTS

Loosely based on the Burlington Berretta (*qv*), on which creator Dave Pepper formerly worked. A spaceframe chassis with Ford Cortina mechanicals underpinned the car, although Fiat and Toyota twin cam

engines could also be fitted. The body was mainly aluminium with fibreglass wings.

The first AF was a one-off built for Dave's girlfriend at the time. He often came to kit car shows in the mid-1980s straight from a gig fronting his own punk band, Blitzkrieg Zone 2020, complete with shock wig and pink nail varnish! He moved to America and the project ended up with a company called Peter Scott Diamond Ltd.

Project offered for sale in autumn 1997 although there were no takers. Resurrected when Pepper returned in 2004 and came up with a revised SVA-compliant version of the car, with a steel-tube chassis now based on Ford Sierra. Within 18 months Dave had taken off to the States again.
Auto Forge Automobiles 1987–90
Peter Scott Diamond Ltd 1997–99
AF Ltd 2004–5
Approx 40 made

AG ROADSTER

A traditional roadster, based on Triumph Herald running gear, that made its debut at Stoneleigh in 1992, although it never went into series production.
AG Fabrications 1992
Approx 1 made

AGM HAYNES ROADSTER

Similar to AGM's GRP panel set to suit Ron Champion's Locost model, their Haynes Roadster kit is designed around the later Haynes book *Build Your Own Sports Car on a budget* by Chris Gibbs, and assumes that the customer has their own chassis.
AGM Sportscars 2011 to date
Approx 10 made

AGM REVOLUTION-X

Sister car to the AGM WLR, (see entry overleaf) with which it shares a lot of the same underpinnings. First appeared in 2005 at the Newark Show.
AGM Sportscars 2005 to date
Approx 1 made

AGM RON CHAMPION

As a master of the art of fibreglass lamination, AGM-boss Alan Whitehead came up with a superb value for money body panel set aimed at builders of the Haynes Publishing book *Build Your Own Sports Car for as little as £250* by Ron Champion that spawned the Locost movement.
AGM Sportscars 2008 to date
Approx 50 made

A B C D E F G H I J K L M N O P Q R S T U V W X Y Z

AGM WLR

The work of GRP fabricator Alan Whitehead from Barnsley, South Yorkshire. A very pleasing Le Mans-inspired car with a mixture of Ford Sierra and bespoke parts. Power comes from a variety of powerplants including Rover V8 and Ford Cosworth YB.
AGM Sportscars 2002 to date
Approx 30 made

AJ4S

Tony Butler, formerly of Deon, was the man behind this one, and he offered fully-built versions of the Noble P4 from a base at Bruntingthorpe for a short time.
AJ Performance Cars 1993
Approx 1 made

AK 427

Ken Freeman ran a GRP laminating business located near Peterborough and in the mid-'90s built a Cobra replica obtained from a local company. He wasn't that impressed with the build quality so set about creating his own, along with his friend Alan Frew. It took 18 months of painstaking work before they were happy with their creation, initially known as the KF Premier before switching to the AK moniker soon after. AK, of course, stood for Alan and Ken. They worked from home for the first few years, and their Jaguar-based 427 soon became a good seller, respected for its level of workmanship and general quality, plus the friendly welcome customers received from Ken and his team, consisting of sons Dan and Jon and wife Lynda.

A move to a unit in Peterborough on the same estate as Radical Sports Cars saw sales accelerate, with the company going from strength to strength and the introduction of XK40 donors and GM LS V8 engines. Ken and Lynda retired in 2009, when Jon and his wife Wendi took over.
AK Sports Cars 1996 to date
Approx 300 made

AKS CONTINENTAL

Auto Kraft Shells of Bishop's Stortford launched the Continental, based on Ford 8 or 10 chassis (90in wheelbase), in 1959. Subsequently available in hardtop and fastback guises until the company ceased making bodies in 1962 following the advent of the comprehensive kit and the 10-year test.
Auto Kraft Shells 1959–62
Approx 400 made

ALBA ELEVEN

Announced in late 1997, this was a Ford Sierra-based Lotus Eleven replica from a Chichester, West Sussex, company, complete with Ford power between 150 and 225bhp. Spaceframe chassis was a close copy of the original Lotus item with double wishbone front suspension and a 'live' rear axle located by radius arms and a Mumford link. Only one prototype built.
Alba Automotive 1997
Approx 1 made

ALBAR BUGGY

Hailing from Alois Barmettler's operation, this buggy was basically a reworked GP Super Buggy (long wheelbase) aimed at the Swiss market, where Barmettler was a GP agent and the car was called the Albar E. It was further revised into the 'ES', and between them the two models sold over 400 units in Europe (the 'S' was the dominant seller) before, much to GP's irritation, the Albar buggy found its way to the UK. 1-6-2 Engineering of Edmonton, run by Ted Kellerman, marketed them, although sales were slow.
1-6-2 Engineering 1983–86
Approx 11 made (UK)

ALBAR JET

Imported to the UK from Switzerland by Ted Kellerman's 1-6-2 operation. Usual '80s faux exotic fare with VW Beetle mechanicals, although a Ford Pinto or VW Golf unit could be fitted instead. Incidentally, the Jet was originally made in Austria from 1970, when it was known as the Custoca Strato.
1-6-2 Engineering 1983–86
Approx 3 made (UK)

ALBAR SONIC

Swiss entrepreneur Alois Barmettler was a contemporary of Franco Sbarro. His Sonic, based mainly on the VW Beetle, was a bonkers child of its time with seven headlights, which, in an era of mock exotica, made all the rest look quite ordinary! Ted Kellerman of 1-6-2 took over the rights to the car, modifying it for the UK market with a more, ahem, modest six headlight arrangement that now sat behind a panel to comply with Construction & Use Regulations. Kellerman sold about four Mk1s.

Kellerman introduced a VW Golf-based 2+2 Mk2 version with mid- rather than rear engine in 1985 and sold six – all ordered by one Arab customer. Meanwhile, in Switzerland, Barmettler later came up with a Sonic GT that had a separate spaceframe chassis and more powerful engine. This never came to the UK, however.

1-6-2 Engineering 1984–86
Approx 10 made (UK)

ALBO

Beautifully made all-aluminium Lotus Seven-inspired sports car made in small numbers by a chap called Alan Beaumont, based in Batley. Every car was different and tailored to the customer's requirements. Used Ford parts and had a live rear axle.

Albo Engineering 1993–99
Approx 8 made

ALEAT

A slabby aluminium-bodied Jaguar-based roadster based on a Kougar Sports (qv) chassis made by an artisan of aluminium called Dicky Dawes. Kit cost £12,000 in 1992. Short-lived project, the company soon switched on to their Tri-Pacer (qv) three-wheeler.

Classic Car Panels 1992
Approx 2 made

ALFA PLUS

Designed by Tim Cooksey soon after he bought the FibreFab business – and changed the company name to FF Kitcars & Conversions in the process. FibreFab used to do GRP fabrication for the exhibition company that Tim worked for, where he learned that Tony Hill wanted to sell the business. The Alfa Plus was an Alfasud-based body conversion that could be fitted to two- and four-door Alfasuds. Many saw the benefits of a stylish body conversion for the rust-prone 'Sud, replacing the rusty panels with fibreglass ones while retaining the superb handling characteristics and boxer engine. Mike Rutherford of Mako Fibreglass made the bodies.

FF Kitcars & Conversions 1982–85
Approx 3 made

ALFASTYL

Alfasud-based body conversion from company run by Steve Everitt. Similar concept to the rival Alfa Plus (qv).
Alfastyl 1984–89
Approx 17 made

ALLARD J2 REPLICA

American kit by Hardy Motors imported to these shores by Bob Egginton. As per original had a ladderframe chassis and a good reputation for quality. Not many – if any – sold here, though.

Automotive Systems Developments 1990–91
Approx 1 made (UK)

ALLARD J2X REPLICA

Harpenden-based company run by Geoffrey Eke, who had connections with the American Hardy Allard operation. However, the UK version soon had a chassis and body worked on by Dennis Adams. The Allard name was used under licence.

The original thirties Allard was powered by a Lincoln Zephyr V12 engine, although Eke's version had American V8 power.
Allard Replicas 1994–97
Approx 3 made

ALLISON MG

The attrition rate for US imports to the UK is massively high, with the vast majority failing miserably. The Allison was a VW Beetle-based MG TD replica imported here briefly by a Jersey-based company, run by Christopher Davies. The intention was to sell six per annum in the UK; sadly they only ever sold one. The Allison was of high standard, its fully trimmed bodyshell with structural steel inner frame being supplied ready to fit to an unmodified VW Beetle floorpan. Would have come in a choice of six original MG colours.
Replica Car Imports Jersey 1980
Approx 1 made (UK)

A
B
C
D
E
F
G
H
I
J
K
L
M
N
O
P
Q
R
S
T
U
V
W
X
Y
Z

ALLORA

Mid-'80s Lancia Stratos HF replica created by Stuart Gross, who built one of the first KVA GT40 replicas with V8 power (chassis by Barrie Purkett). Based on a heavily revised Lancia Beta chassis, which was effectively a semi-monocoque.

Bodies were made for the company by Bridport-based Loxton Laminates, who also marketed the Harbron Special in the mid-'80s, before passing to Bulldog makers Pilgrim Cars, who were owed a fair amount of money when Handmade Cars went bust after selling just 13 kits.

Greenwood, a former race car engineer, had been chief mechanic on René Arnoux's F5000 car and also worked for Tony Kitchener's Race Developments operation in 1973. He had also built his own clubman's car, and further kit car teeth were cut with the purchase of a GB 5000S Countach replica. Around 45 were sold by Litton cars.

Hugh Carson, based in Skipton like Litton, was the next custodian and this clever engineer, although keeping a low profile, further developed the product and sold 20 kits. In 2000, Hugh moved on to pastures new, and Lionel Gooch of NapierSport and SuperStratos took over.

Handmade Cars 1985–91
Litton Cars 1991–93
Carson Automotive Engineering 1993–2000
SuperStratos 2000 to date
Approx 113 made

ALTAIR 1172

A Ford-based *Specials* era recreation by expert Tony Weale of Reigate, Surrey. Based on Ford Popular mechanicals.

Altair Engineering 2001–5
Approx 5 made

ALTO

Peerhouse Cars was a Surrey-based company which came up with a sports car that bore a strong resemblance to the Avante and was also based on VW Beetle mechanicals. After a four-year hiatus a company called Cardo Engineering planned to put the car back into production with a mid-engined Alfasud-powered version, complete with separate spaceframe chassis option designed by Terry Sands. Nothing more was heard, though.

Peerhouse Cars 1983–84
Cardo Engineering 1988
Approx 3 made

ALTO BOXER

Mini-based conversion from Alto Duo (*qv*) creator David Gornall, who ran the fibreglass company Alto GRP (who also made the bodies for Beauford) in Preston, Lancashire. Nearly 10 years after that first attempt at car manufacture, he came up with this pretty model that used Mini

subframes and running gear (with more than a passing resemblance to the Broadspeed GT), that used Peugeot 205 rear light clusters.

Alto Component Cars 1994–97
Approx 12 made

ALTO DUO

Superb Mini-based city car created by David Gornall of Alto Cars, which was taken over by Portsmouth-based engineer and journalist, Alexander Graham Pipe, in 1987. The Duo was years ahead of its time, and if it had been launched in the mid-'90s it would perhaps have sold in the thousands.

A period of inactivity eventually saw the car relaunched by Rhino Engineering of Bewburgh, Lancashire, although they didn't enjoy much success before it finished up with Anthony Offord of Duo Cars, again in Lancashire.

Alto Component Cars 1985–87　*Automotive Concepts 1987–88*
Rhino Engineering 1995–96　*Duo Cars 1996–98*
Approx 12 made

AMALFI PASSERO

Developed by Basingstoke-based Amalfi Sportscars, run by Paul Sparrow, who came up with a Fiat X1/9-based Countach replica that was 13in shorter and 5in narrower than the original but still looked pretty cool. He was inspired by

a Prova replica that he sold in 1989 – bought, incidentally, by Larry Webb of Sovereign Cars. Sparrow later moved to Ammanford, Dyfed.

Later he developed another version with a spaceframe chassis that used Granada/Scorpio suspension. When Webb saw the Amalfi he commissioned Paul to build him one. Passero part of name quietly dropped in 1997.

Amalfi Sportscars 1994–2000
Approx 2 made

AMERICAR MODEL A

After leaving Ford SVO, where he had been a design draughtsman, Terry Sands set up the American operation in Southend-on-Sea, Essex, and imported a brace of rod kits hailing from Keith Harvey's PAW US operation. Only a handful sold.

Americar 1971–72
Approx 3 made

AMERICAR MODEL B

Second of Terry Sands' Keith Harvey rod kits.
Americar 1971–72
Approx 4 made

AMICA

Also known as the Delta (*qv*), imported quite separately by Pageant Motor Co of Hornsey, North London. The original Beetle-based version of the American CMC Mercedes SSK replica, also

known by umpteen other names, including Gazelle (*qv*), Osprey (*qv*) and Phoenix (*qv*). None succeeded in the UK.

Pageant Motor Company 1980
Approx 1 made

AMPHIBIOUS SURF

Succeeding the Amphijeep *(qv)*, Tim Dutton announced his all-new Surf in late 2010, sharing only windscreen and soft top with the previous model. Based on Suzuki Jimny, meaning four-wheel drive capability on land that of course can take to the water when desired. Tim's website mantra is 'no beach out of reach'…

Tim Dutton Amphibious Cars 2010 to date
Approx 3 made

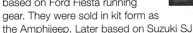

AMPHIJEEP

Amphibious car produced by Tim Dutton from his base at Littlehampton Marina. Sold in fully-built guise as the Dutton Commander then Mariner and based on Ford Fiesta running gear. They were sold in kit form as the Amphijeep. Later based on Suzuki SJ before switching to Suzuki Jimny for the Surf model.

Amphibious Cars 1994–2010
Approx 120 made

AMX ASTONISH

An Aston Martin-inspired body conversion based on Mazda MX-5, and a very easy kit to build with no cutting or welding required. Originated in Australia, created by a Russian, and imported into the UK by Jason Kemp in 2008, with manufacturing beginning here in 2010.

K Sportscars 2008 to date
Approx 18 made (UK)

ANDERSEN CUB

Founded by Liverpool-based brothers, Charles and David Anderson. Charles had bought a Scamp but wasn't impressed with its looks or refinements. When he decided to launch his own utility kit car, the styling of a friend's restored Mini Moke inspired him, although not its rigidity.

The Anderson Cub was Mini-based and had a Moke-type styling but was a very innovative package with a very rigid quadruple rail type galvanised chassis, which gave the interior a practical flat floor layout. They even offered a six-wheeler option for a time. Anderson ceased producing Cubs in 2003 when he went off to work in the furnace industry. A cracking kit car.
Relaunched in August 2011.
Anderson Motor Company 1985-2003/2011 to date
Approx 450 made

ANGLEBUG

Weird beach buggy based on Ford Anglia, complete with 997cc engine. Company based in Stockport.
Paul Haigh Autos 1971–72
Approx 7 made

ANIMAS

Came from the French hillclimb and race car preparation expert Georges Queron, and marketed for a time in the UK by Quantum Sports Cars. Renault power originally before switching to Honda VTEC, although ultimately ended up using Renault again.
Quantum Sports Cars 2005
Approx 1 made (UK)

ANNE'S BUGGY

A GP copy that was around for about as long as the average mayfly.
Anne's Buggies 1970
Approx 1 made

APAL AU-KI – *see Renegade T*

APAL BUGGY

One of the first all-original beach buggies, the Apal was a Belgian kit that first appeared in the UK in 1971, imported and distributed by VW tuning firm Cartune from their base in Middlesbrough. Often badged as the 'Cartune-Apal'. Kits cost £195 in July 1971, which was typically about £50 more than most rival products of the day. Cartune sold the buggy as a complete kit. The agency was taken on by Magenta makers Lightspeed Panels in 1972, before the 'baron of beach buggies', James Hale, and his GT Mouldings operation, took over. It ended up with Country Volks who allegedly destroyed the moulds when they went out of business in 1993.

Cartune (Teesside) Ltd 1971–73
GT Mouldings 1985–90
Country Volks 1990–93
Approx 60 made

APAL CORSA

Sister model to the popular buggy from Belgian company Apal (see above). Quirky, removable gullwing-equipped sports car based on the VW Beetle, in two-seat (chopped floorpan) or unmodified four-seater formats.

Cartune 1970–71
Approx 1 made (UK)

APAL SPEEDSTER

Belgian company Apal SA licensed the Canadian Intermeccanica for sale in Europe and from 1983 sold several, very quickly. The UK, however, has always been a tougher nut for them to crack and several companies have had a go, starting with Tim Dutton under the Starborne banner. The Speedster was launched at the 1981 Frankfurt Motor Show and even had official approval from Ferdinand Porsche, who thought the car on their stand was a restored original. Some 700 were sold before Apal ceased production in 1994. A German firm bought the rights to the Apal marque in 1998 and still make the Speedster.

In the mid-'80s the Speedster was marketed in the UK by TPC of Stratford-upon-Avon run by John Finchman (sold around 20), where a chap called Paul Woodward test-drove one. He liked it so much that his company, Speedsters of Tunbridge Wells, took it on and sold a few. He commissioned Paul Hinchcliffe and Jack Marland (now running JMA) of TRACE, who had built some superb GP Spyders, to build a demo car for them. Paul's wife Sandie, a former fashion store manager, ran the company on a day-to-day basis and sold 12.

The last UK company to sell the Apal Speedster was the Mallory Park-based Classic Carriage Company, run by Derek Moore, who in a roundabout way later became Caterham Cars' Midlands operation.

Starborne 1981–82
TPC 1985–88
Speedsters 1992–93
Classic Carriage Company 1993–94
Approx 700 made (approx 55 UK)

APOLLO

Beetle convertible conversion aping the Californian look.

Autos International 1984–85
Alternative Vehicle Centre 1985–86
Approx 5 made

APOLLO

This proposed sports car with mid-mounted Austin Maxi engine appeared for the first and only time at the Hindhead Show in 1984. It hailed from a Southampton-based company.

Highton Motors 1984
Approx 1 made

APOLLO GT

The Apollo was the brainchild of Allen Pearce of Hornchurch, who created a swoopy Chevron Can-Am-inspired gullwing 2+2 coupé, which featured a spaceframe chassis over a Beetle floorpan. For some reason it was never produced. A stillborn prototype.

Apollo Cars 1971–72
Approx 1 made

AQUARIUS

Another GP copy that wasn't very successful, nor around for very long for that matter. The Reading-based company would build you a buggy from £450 or sell you a kit for £100.

They nicked and adapted the Monty Python line, 'and now for something completely different – a BUGGY!' as an attempt at ironic humour for their adverts.

Aquarius Beach Buggies 1971–72
Approx 10 made

AQUILLA

A chunky two-seater fixed-head sports car built for ex-Aristocat Owners' Club secretary, Dave Edwards. Car based on Ford Sierra mechanicals. Cologne V6 was suggested powerplant, although Rover V8 was an option.

Autotune (Rishton) Ltd 2004
Approx 1 made

ARA LE MANS ROGUE

ARA, run by Anthony Anstead, followed up their Lowcost (see next entry) with the former ASD DBR1/DBR2 replica, of which Bob Egginton had made five. Jaguar XJ-based version of the Aston Martin DBR1 (made 1956-59) that had competed at Le Mans, with the DBR2 a 'sprint' version, of which just two were made in this period. Project acquired by AS Motorsport in 2007.
AS Motorsport 2007 to date
Approx 12 made

ARA LOWCOST

This budget-orientated LSIS package was the first model from ARA Racing. Used familiar Ford running gear.
ARA Racing 2005–6
Approx 12 made

ARIES STM LOCO

Former Stuart Taylor Motorsport Loco range made by former STM employee Steve Huckerby, of Ilkeston, Derbyshire, who continued to develop the superbly affordable range of Lotus Seven-inspired sports cars that could be powered by car and bike engines. In 2008 he announced a Mazda MX-5-based donor option.
Aries Motorsport 2007 to date
Approx 350 made (including STM)

ARKLEY S/SS

John Britten was a famous historic racer and a Morgan – later TVR – dealer based in Arkley, Hertfordshire. Back in the day, his Arkley, created in association with Lenham Motor Company, was a very popular way of converting a Midget by adding new front and rear ends. The S model featured narrow wheel arches for standard Midget wheels, while the much more popular SS had a wider stance, although the latter became the standard body in time.

Peter May Engineering acquired the project and still supply Arkley SS bodykits from £870 inc VAT (in March 2011). They have supplied over 100 since taking over. Preferred donor is the MG Midget 1,275cc, but other members of the 'Spridget' family can be used.
John Britten Garages 1970–87
Arkley Sportscars (Peter May Engineering) 1987 to date
Approx 1100 made

ARKON

Came from Purley, Surrey-based Richard Moon, assisted by his friend, Neil Morgan. It was just 33in high – or low, depending on your viewpoint. Heavily inspired by the Adams Bros' Probe 15 (*qv*), including the Hillman Imp mechanicals and 875cc engine. Had a backbone chassis from Triumph Spitfire with a rear subframe. An intended production run never materialised.
Arkon Developments 1971
Approx 1 made

ARTEESI

Austin 7 bodyshell made from steel, intended for, er, Austin 7 chassis.
Arteesi Engineering 1977–79
Approx 3 made

AS427/BOA

Cobra replica formerly made by Fiero Factory and then Euro 427 Sportscars, run by restaurateur Nigel Ramsey. The AS427 subsequently came back under the control of Keith Kirk and Steve Briddon under the Fiero Factory banner. When Keith split from Fiero Factory he marketed this car under the Venom Sports Cars banner before joining forces with Jon Harris to form Auto Speciali. After Keith passed away it lay dormant for a time until Vindicator Cars were appointed to market Auto Speciali's products in early 2010, renaming the car the Boa at the same time.
Fiero Factory 1998–2002   *Euro 427 Sportscars 2002–3*
Fiero Factory 2003–4   *Venom Sports Cars 2004–6*
Auto Speciali 2006–10   *Vindicator Cars 2010 to date*
Approx 1,000 made

ASCOT

Ford Sierra-based take on the NG TF, offered for a time in the 1990s by Pastiche Cars. See NG Cars.
Pastiche Cars 1990–91
Approx 200 made

A
B
C
D
E
F
G
H
I
J
K
L
M
N
O
P
Q
R
S
T
U
V
W
X
Y
Z

ASD HOBO

A Mini-based utility obviously inspired the Moke. ASD (Automotive System Design) was run by skilled engineer Bob Egginton, who in addition to his own projects got involved with the development of many other cars over the years, including the Tripos R81 (qv), the ex-Gravetti Cobra that became the CK Cobra or 427 (see Gravetti 427), and the American Hunter, while latterly he was making turnkey – and delightful – Maserati 250F and Aston Martin DBR2 replicas mainly for the US market. The latter was purchased by ARA Racing and is now offered by AS Motorsport (see ARA Le Mans Rogue).
Automotive Systems Design Ltd 1987–91
Approx 4 made

ASD MINIM

Excellent if quirky-looking sports car from Bob Egginton that he described as being a modern-day Sprite. The styling might not have been to everyone's taste, but by crikey, the Minim was a fine-handling, affordable little number.
Automotive Systems Design Ltd 1984–96
Approx 6 made

ASHLEY LAMINATES

Peter Pellandine had been building 'specials' since 1954 and went into business with Keith Waddington in 1955 to form Ashley Laminates, based at the Robin Hood Garage in Loughton, Essex, at local landmark the Robin Hood Roundabout. The fibreglass was laminated at a facility in Upshire, close to Epping Forest. The company made a couple of moves over the years to larger premises, firstly to Harlow, and then Bishop's Stortford. Pellandine left in 1956 to set up Falcon Design, leaving Waddington to continue on his own until the advent of the MoT test in 1962, which along with the fashion for complete kits put paid to the humble bodyshell. Waddington would relaunch his company as Ashley Auto Improvements Ltd, offering a variety of detachable hardtops and replacement front ends for such as the Spridget and Triumph Herald, before finally going bust in 1972.

ASHLEY 750

Launched in 1956, the 750, based on Austin 7 chassis, was pitched directly at the clubman '750 racer'. Pellandine took this project with him to Falcon, where it became the Falcon Mk1 (qv).
Ashley Laminates 1956–57
Approx 500 made

ASHLEY 1172

After Pellandine's departure from Ashley Laminates it took Keith Waddington quite a while to recover. The 1172 was the first post-Pellandine Ashley product, launched in 1958. Initially only available as a bodyshell designed around the Ford E93A Prefect, although a comprehensive kit package was introduced from 1959. Main engine choice was the Ford Sidevalve 1,172cc – hence the moniker – although plenty of others could be used.
Ashley Laminates 1958–62
Approx 300 made

ASHLEY GT SPRIDGET CONVERSION

Once the 'specials' market had dwindled for Ashley, Waddington reinvented his company in 1962 as Ashley Auto Improvements Ltd, specialising in a nice line in detachable GRP hardtops and rakish replacement front and rear ends for Triumph Herald and notably 'Spridget' (Frogeye Sprite and MG Midget).

Ashley weren't the only company involved in this market, and others included Williams & Pritchard, Peasmarsh, Dyna Plastics, Speedwell and Lenham, but unlike some there wasn't any body cutting involved with the Ashley conversions. It's hard to quantify exactly how many of these were sold, as customers could pick and choose what they wanted, be it a front end or a hardtop, rather than just taking the whole kit.

After lying dormant for some 38 years, the Ashley conversions for Sprite and Midget are available again, via a Surrey-based operation called Motobuild Racing, run by Darryl Davis, brother of well-known historic racer, Rae Davis.
Ashley Auto Improvements Ltd 1962–72
Motobuild Racing 2010 to date
Approx several hundred made

ASHLEY SPORTIVA

Initially based on the Ashley 1172 (see above), the Sportiva was later revised and ended up as quite a pretty car with a shorter nose and square grille.
Ashley Laminates 1960–62
Approx 12 made

ASHLEY SPORTS RACER

Another racy shell from Ashley, designed to suit wheelbases from 83in to 87in. Another one that Pellandine took with him to Falcon Designs, where it was renamed the Falcon Mk2 (qv) before becoming known as the Competition (qv).
Ashley Laminates 1956–57
Approx 20 made

ASPIRE

This kit was a body conversion for the Mazda MX-5 Mk1 that was inspired by Aston Martin, but was definitely not a replica. Made its debut at the Exeter kit car show in October 2010. The Aspire was the work of marketing experts Alex Shaw and Peter Mileham of Chard, Somerset.

Aspire Kit Cars 2010 to date
Approx 12 made

ASQUITH AUSTIN 12 VAN

Founded in 1981 by Bruce West and Crispin Reed and based in Braintree, Essex, the Asquith Motor Carriage Company's main business was making reproduction furniture, although they ventured into vehicle manufacture with their Austin 12 period van using Ford Transit donors and chassis. At one time there were 30 staff. Other vehicles produced were of the same vintage styling, although most were not available in kit form.

In 1984 the company was taken over by Hunnable Holdings of Great Yeldham, although West stayed on and worked on an officially approved London cab, launched in 1991. In 1997 Mike Edgar took control of Asquith, with new designer Paul Keegan and engineer Eddie Parsons. Further production facilities were opened in Poland and Spain before the company changed hands when Simon Rhodes took over in 2003. Other versions on the same theme included the Mascot coach, period-style London Taxi and the Cob chassis cab.

Asquith Motor Carriage Company 1981–84
Hunnable Holdings 1984–97
Asquith Motors 1997–2003
Asquith Motor Company 2003 to date
Approx 1,000 made

ASTRON GT

Short-lived, brick-like, Cortina-based four-seater from a Telford company, run by Hugh Llewellyn and Les Staines. Spectacularly made the front cover of *Kit Cars & Specials* magazine in 1985. Wasn't around long.

Astron Motors 1984–85
Approx 1 made

ATLANTIS/ATLANTIS ALCAEUS

Incredible 1930s-style tourer that wasn't a replica of anything but was clearly inspired by the ostentatious Figoni & Falaschi-designed Delage roadsters of that period. It was created by Norfolk-based radio and TV engineer Michael Booth. First appeared in July 1982. Tony Holmes of Classic Specials did a lot of promotion, while a chap called Chris Godkin memorably raced a V8-powered convertible version in the 750 Motor Club's Kit Car Challenge series in the mid-'80s. A handful were built as convertibles. The convertible/racer was officially known as the Atlantis Alcaeus and named after an ancient Greek poet. Moulds passed to Arthur Wolstenholme of Ronart Cars for a time before he sold them to the car's creator, Michael Booth.

Atlantis Motor Company 1982–86
Approx 14 made

ATOMIC

Created by Stuart Mills of MEV Ltd in 2008. It's a lightweight two-seater that features a Yamaha R1 bike engine located where the passenger seat would normally be found, thus giving a perfect 50:50 weight distribution. Acquired by Road Track Race Ltd, part of the Smarts'R'Us operation, in 2009.

Mills Extreme Vehicles 2008–9
Road Track Race 2009 to date
Approx 100 made

AURIGA 23

Formerly a Lee Noble product, when it was known as the Noble 23 (qv), Colin Strauss of Chelmsford was the man behind the Auriga. (He had been the first customer for the Noble Mk4, incidentally.) It featured a fully triangulated spaceframe suspension based around Cortina uprights. Strauss sold around 10 examples. He changed the company name to Espero in 1998, although the project lay dormant for a couple of years before being taken over by John Bridge of Mamba Motorsport, who sold a further dozen or so as the Mamba C23 (qv).

Kit Deal 1987–90
Auriga Developments aka Espero Ltd 1990–2000
Mamba Motorsport 2000 to date
Approx 110 made (includes Noble and Manta total sales)

AUSTIN SOMERSET – *see Tri-Pacer*

AUTECH C-TYPE

Aluminium-bodied Jaguar C-type replica from a Bromsgrove-based classic car specialist.
Autech Classic Cars 1985–88
Approx 20 made

AUTO IMAGINATION C-CAB

Created by Nick Butler this was basically a replica shell of his legendary hot rod, *Revenge.* Underpinned by a twin-rail steel chassis, designed to (ideally) accept a Jaguar rear end with either dropped or straight tube axles at the front end. Brilliant.
Auto Imagination 1978–80
Approx 8 made

AUTO IMAGINATION MODEL T

Nick Butler offered replicas of his superb *Andromeda* in the form of a GRP bodyshell for a time in the late seventies. He was one of the pioneers of the brief UK craze for 'Fad-Ts'.

Butler is an artisan of his craft and his replica of *Andromeda* was set up to accept Jaguar XJ6 running gear, with chassis costing £205 in 1980, sectioned GRP bodies at £140 and rolling chassis from £850. For those that wanted realism, Butler could also offer customers a large range of genuine hot rod parts imported from America.
Auto Imagination 1978–80
Approx 12 made

AUTO MILAN

Vic Minay's Dorset-based company took over the former PACE Quadriga (*qv*) project in 1992 after he'd sold the Stardust D-type (*qv*). Very Italianesque styling but not a replica, the mechanical base changed by Minay from Lancia to Ford Escort, powered by Zetec E engine. He sold the project to Welsh firm DC Mouldings (Darren Jones), who did very little with it.
Auto Milan 1992–2000
DC Mouldings 2000–1
Approx 40 made

AUTOBEE PACEMAKER

More sophisticated development of the Mk1/Mk2 body (see next entry) with four seats and revised styling. Autobodies was based in Oldham, Lancashire.
Autobodies 1960–62
Approx 30 made

AUTOBODIES Mk2

Two-seater based on 90in Ford Popular chassis. Autobodies marketed the same shell in two guises: the Mk1 featured a Jaguar C-type-style grille, while the Mk2 had an E-type-esque front end.
Autobodies 1958–60
Approx 80 made

AUTOCOM BUGGY

A Mini-based beach buggy, based on a spaceframe chassis with a GRP body from a Combe Martin, Devon-based operation.
Autocom Engineering 1987–94
Approx 5 made

AUTOCULT COBRA

Little-known Cobra replica from Tigress makers Autocult, run by Raymond Craig.
Autocult 1982–83
Approx 1 made

AUTOTUNE (RISHTON) LTD

Anthony Taylor did his apprenticeship at Rootes before becoming tuning manager at Mangoletsi's in Cheshire and moving to Lancashire to found his own company, Autotune (Rishton) Ltd, which built and tuned race engines for cars and boats. Gained a hard-earned reputation for his work on Jaguars. Built an XK children's car and followed this up with his first kit model, the Aristocat.

AUTOTUNE ARISTOCAT

Autotune's first kit, an XJ6-based replica of the Jaguar XK with un-modified Jaguar XJ rear end. Not a replica but very effective.
Autotune (Rishton) Ltd 1983 to date
Approx 300 made

AUTOTUNE ARISTOCAT SPORTS

This fixed-head version of the basic Aristocat copied the XK140's styling. Narrower and therefore more true to the original in shape.
Autotune (Rishton) Ltd 1995 to date
Approx 60 made

AUTOTUNE CAN-AM

Anthony Taylor of Autotune, a well-known historic racer, launched his take on the McLaren M1 in 1992. The Autotune Can-Am features a purpose-made chassis with input from F1 and sportscar race engineer Paul Brown. Engine choice encompasses a range of V8s from Chevy to Rover, with Hewland ZF, Renault UN1 or Porsche G50 transaxles.

The original McLaren M1 was announced in 1965 and was devised primarily for the Can-Am Challenge Cup and Group 7 sportscar races that began in 1966. The Can-Am cars were big, ground-shaking bruisers, said to be as fast as the Formula One cars of their day, attracting top drivers such as John Surtees, Bruce McLaren and Denny Hulme. McLaren's first effort was the M1A of 1965, followed by M1B the following year, designed by well-known motorsport artist Michael Turner. This was the version that McLaren entered in the Can-Am series. The cars were built by Trojan Ltd in Croydon, who had taken over the Elva concern in 1961. In 1967, the McLaren 'works' team unveiled the monocoque M6. Privateers were able to purchase the M1C, basically an upgraded M1B with a stiffer spaceframe chassis and revised suspension.

Autotune (Rishton) Ltd 1992 to date
Approx 45 made

AUTOTUNE GEMINI

Basically a reworked '50s Elva Courier Mk2. Autotune based it on Ford Escort Mk2 running gear before switching to Sierra in 2002, giving rear-wheel drive and five-link rear suspension with 'live' axle. Very affordable and fun.

Autotune (Rishton) Ltd
1988 to date
Approx 80 made

AUTOTUNE MIRAGE

Autotune acquired the old Marcos Mantis M70 (qv) project in September 1985 and converted it to Ford Cortina running gear.

Autotune (Rishton) Ltd 1985–88
Approx 4 made

AVA K1

Designed by Frome-based Nick Topliss, assisted by Ian Hunter, the K1 was a capable original design two-seater based on Escort XR3 or RS1600i mechanicals, with a slippery drag coefficient of 0.295. Relaunched in late 1990 by Bristol-based John Burton, who offered the car for a while before selling the whole project to a German operation. After which it was never heard of again.

Ava Cars 1986–88, 1990–91
Approx 16 made

AVALON S350/250LE

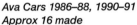

Originally known as the Curtana, the S350 (later 250LE) was underpinned by a spaceframe chassis and a combination of Ford Escort Mk3 and Cortina parts with power coming from a CVH engine and came from a Sheffiled-based company. Design by Richard Ashby of The Works Design Studio, who later designed the Savant/Quantum Xtreme.

Never seen again after its initial – and only – show debut.
Avalon Automotive 1990
Approx 1 made

AVANTE

Created by Melvyn Kay of Clewlow Motors in Longton near Stoke-on-Trent and based, like so many 1980s faux exotics, on the VW Beetle floorpan. Unlike many, though, the Avante had nice styling. It shared the same windscreen and dashboard as the Eagle SS and had a Terry Sands-designed 'Alfa-chassis'. The windscreens were originally expensive items made by none other than Royal Doulton, for some reason.

This version was briefly resurrected by Blackpool-based Paul de Roma in 1987 of Top Hat Coachworks, who also offered a BMW M1 replica briefly, too.

Avante Cars 1982–86
Top Hat Coachworks 1987
Approx 25 made

AVANTE +2

Basically a Mk2 Avante that was longer and taller to allow for an extra row of seats in a 2+2 layout, and was available alongside the original version and used 1302 or 1303 VW Beetle. +2 arrived in 1983, launched rather grandly at the Earl's Court Motorfair, which had a revised front, wider roof section, lowered rear wheel arches and was longer, taller and had a 2+2 configuration. This one could also accept Volkswagen water-cooled engine from either Golf Mk1 or Scirocco.

Avante Cars 1983–86   *Top Hat Coachworks 1987*
Approx 5 made

AVC 550 SPYDER

Became the Legend 550 Spyder (*qv*) some years later.
Alternative Vehicle Centre 1985–90
Approx 3 made

AVELLE GT

Originally known as the GTA and based on Renault Alpine A610 power, but was subsequently converted to Ford Duratec V6 mounted amidships. Car designed by Jeff Ashton. Motion Car Developments was run by James Hodds.

Motion Car Developments 2004–7
Approx 3 made

AVON SPRINT

This was a budget-orientated Lotus Seven-inspired sports car developed by his Le Mans Sportscars' boss David Yoxall's stepson, Leon Sansom, who created his own company, Avon Coachworks, to sell the kit. The model was quickly taken over by Tiger Racing, revised, and renamed the Tiger Avon (*qv*). Powered by Rover K-series when made by Avon Coachworks, although Tiger converted it to Ford Sierra mechanicals.

Avon Coachworks 1997–99
Approx 16 made

AWE ROADSTER

AWE was run by a chap called Alan Wilkinson, based in Yeovil, Somerset, who ran a GRP laminating business.

There were two versions of the Triumph-based traditional roadster, the Pintail, with front cycle wings, and the Redwing which had flowing 'clamshell' type wings.

AWE Engineering 1990–98
Approx 15 made

AWR

Short-lived three-wheeler.
Classic Images 1990
Approx 1 made

AYRSPEED SIX

Jaguar XK120 replica created by kit car journalist and author Iain Ayre, based, unsurprisingly, on Jaguar XJ6 mechanicals.

Ayrspeed 1994–98
Approx 3 made

AZTEC

An American VW Beetle-based kit made by Fiberfab, imported to the UK (briefly) by Sandbach of Cheshire.

Sandbach Replica Cars 1981–82
Approx 1 made (UK)

A
B
C
D
E
F
G
H
I
J
K
L
M
N
O
P
Q
R
S
T
U
V
W
X
Y
Z

BADSEY BULLET

After establishing himself in South Africa (see next entry), Bill Badsey built a bonkers three-wheeler called the Bullet based on the Suzuki GSX-R750 motorbike. A scheduled UK marketing deal with UVA never materialised.
Bill Badsey 1981–83
Approx 1 made

BADSEY EAGLE

Promising two-seater from the pen of Bill Badsey that was based on Austin 1100/Morris 1300 mechanicals. Nothing really came of the car, however, as Badsey emigrated to South Africa just before it could be launched.
Bill Badsey 1978
Approx 1 made

BADSWORTH LANDAULET

Vintage vehicle kit from Alan Beillby of Vintage Motor Company. Sold under a variety of names and companies during its lifespan, several of which involved Beillby. Bramwith Cars was based in Doncaster and ceased trading in 2010.

Project acquired by John and Gill Ford of AWS Ltd from the Wirral, in spring 2011.
Vintage Motor Company 1999–2010
AWS Ltd 2011 to date
Approx 15 made

BAJA GT

Speed Buggys (their spelling!) was based on a farm in Chichester, West Sussex (next door to Barry Stimson, in fact), and was run by Patrick Sumner and accountant Roger Penfold. Like many others, their fledgling business started by acting as agents for GP, hiring the buggies out, although as this seemed doomed to failure they soon became agents for Manta Ray (*qv*) manufacturers Power On Wheels.

In 1970, they devised plans for their own buggy, which unsurprisingly, was based on a GP and a hacksaw, and used a VW Beetle floorpan chopped by 16in. One of their first demo cars had a Corvair 2.3-litre engine delivering 160bhp that Sumner rejoiced in 'wheelying' at every opportunity. The one-piece bodyshell made it fairly easy for the customer to build, although this did mean that the petrol tank was notoriously difficult to fit. At launch the kit cost £185, with the body available separately at £58.

Sumner and Penfold became fed up selling buggies, and in April 1971 the project moved to Richard Park of nearby Rodding Scene, Geoff Jago's business partner, and after selling around eight more kits Park was quoted as saying 'we chucked the moulds into a hedge and forgot about them'. Alan Warren, of boat builders Audy Marine, based on Hayling Island, had other ideas and pulled them out of said hedge, relaunching the Baja in 1977. However, when he won a large boat contract in 1978, necessitating a move to larger premises in Milton Keynes, the Baja's days were numbered. Warren had, however, tidied up the kit during his tenure, and was selling kits at £180.55 inc VAT. Incidentally, he was based opposite Malcolm Wilson, creator of Seta/Zeta.

It subsequently passed through a few hands including, inevitably, James Hale, who developed the Baja into his own Sahara, on a long-wheelbase floorpan, before ending up at Horsham-based Budges Buggies in 1987.

Incidentally, the company's old farm premises is now Chichester Crematorium, while Patrick Sumner went on to enjoy a successful motor racing career and Roger Penfold became a property developer.
Speed Buggys 1970–71
Rodding Scene 1971–73
Audy Marine 1977–79
Special Car Components 1979–81
GT Mouldings 1981–87
Budges Buggies 1987–89
Approximately 55 made

BANDIT

Big things were expected of this quirky, open-top four-seater that combined buggy, sports car and hot-rod styling. It comprised a spaceframe chassis with a GRP body and either Rover K-series 1.4- or Peugeot 1.5-litre diesel power. Andy and Chris Mynheer (ex-Hornsley College of Art graduate), ran the Oxford-based company, and their prototype version was known as the Urbanizer before the name was changed to Bandit. Promoted as a 'hyper-micro' car.

The official launch took place at the 1995 Frankfurt Motor Show, although before long they were offering it in kit form at £10,668, with a memorable Mexican theme on their stand at Stoneleigh in 1996.
Concept Car Company 1993–97
Approx 5 made

PAUL BANHAM CONVERSIONS

Paul Banham was running an MG-breakers and was also a serious car enthusiast, specialising in producing conversions for owners of cars such as the Ferrari 400i, Aston Martin DBS and Rolls-Royce Corniche, and others on a commission basis. He also had the biggest collection of Jensens in the UK, owning 66 at one time. A meeting with Bob Waterhouse led to them joining forces to form Paul Banham Conversions, and their first model was a restyled Jaguar XJS, inspired by a roof-chopping procedure that Paul had been doing for some time.

For a period in the late '90s and early '00s, Paul Banham Conversions was one of the most prolific kit car manufacturers in the country. Banham is a talented and innovative designer who finds it very satisfying to do things that people said couldn't be done, and, in his own words, likes to create jewels from pieces of rubbish, in his case using humble and disregarded donor vehicles to conjure up big-selling kits. Ever the creator, he has even created Cobra replicas on Triumph and Jensen chassis.

BANHAM 130 SPYDER

Škoda Estelle-based replica of the Porsche 550 Spyder. It had been a long time since anyone had based a kit car on a Škoda and the marque hadn't become cool when Banham's kit was launched in 1998. Donors could be picked up for nothing, although once the 130 Spyder started selling in big numbers this soon changed. Was originally going to be sold under the BIS Automotive Developments banner and called the Kömet.

Project went to Colin Gontier of Watford-based 356 Sports for a short time before ending up with New Addington-based Spyder 550 Motors Ltd, run by Martin and Rowena Allen.
Paul Banham Conversions 1998–2004
356 Sports 2004–5
Spyder 550 Motors Ltd 2000-9
Approx 500 made

BANHAM NEW SPEEDSTER

Conventional thinking reasoned that a Porsche 356 replica had to be rear-engined and based on the VW Beetle. Paul Banham, unsurprisingly, didn't adhere to such notions and based his version on the Austin Metro/Rover 100 and retained a front engine configuration. It was, as Banham said, a 'new' Speedster, not a replica...

Project was taken over by 356 Sports of Watford in 2004, but wasn't offered by them for long.
Paul Banham Conversions 2002–4
356 Sports 2004–6
Approx 40 made

BANHAM PB200

Paul Banham was never afraid to push boundaries, as he showed with this Ford RS200 replica. Although correct visually – as Banham owned one of the three sets of original moulds for the car – he made his version a full four-seater using the an Austin Maestro retaining the engine in the front. Came about when Banham swapped one of his Spyder kits for the moulds, which someone had found in a skip! Like his Spyder 550 replica, the PB200 attracted many orders. Passed to Rally Sport Replicas of Northampton in 2004.
Paul Banham Conversions 2001–4
Rally Sport Replicas 2004–6
Approx 100 made

BANHAM BAT

Another innovative creation from Paul Banham that was a development of his X21/X99 (*qv*) design that made the tail fin cool again. Fiendishly clever concept with removable roof panel and rear screen. Based like the X21/X99 on Austin Metro/Rover 100 donors. Who was the bright spark who reckoned it was a Bugatti Veyron replica? It came out four years before that car, for a start.
Paul Banham Conversions 2003–4
Approx 50 made

BANHAM REDINA

Škoda Rapide-based four-seater that wasn't produced, due probably to the success of the 130 Spyder (*qv*).
Paul Banham Conversions 1999
Approx 1 made

BANHAM ROADSTER

A Mini given the Speedster treatment. Stylish.
Paul Banham Conversions 2002–6
Approx 40 made

BANHAM SPRINT

If the Rapide/Estelle-based 130 Spyder (*qv*) was imaginative then the Sprint of 1999 was revolutionary. Paul Banham had discovered that the Frogeye Sprite was originally going to be based around Mini mechanicals and so based his replica around such components, which meant that his version came complete with a boot and a huge interior with a flat floor. Sold in large numbers. Taken over by Rally Sport Replicas in 2004.

Paul Banham Conversions 1999–2004
Rally Sport Replicas 2004–6
Approx 300 made

BANHAM SUPERBUG

Paul Banham's idea of a modern beach buggy and again based on Metro mechanicals. This proved a popular kit.
Paul Banham Conversions 1999–2006
Approx 300 made

BANHAM X21/X99 CONVERTIBLE

Convertible version of the X21 Coupé (see below) that appeared in 2000. It offered similar styling albeit in roofless guise. Another strong seller.
Paul Banham Conversions 2000–6
Approx 250 made

BANHAM X21/X99 COUPÉ

Inspired by an Audi concept that Paul Banham saw in a design book. Originally known as the X99, although revised in 2000 to become the X21, a car for the 21st century. Based on Austin Metro/Rover 100 mechanicals this was a diminutive and pleasing little two-seater. One of Banham's strongest sellers.
Paul Banham Conversions 1999–2006
Approx 250 made

BANHAM XJSS

Though he had been coachbuilding since the 1970s, this Jaguar XJS body conversion was the first product from Paul Banham Conversions. Launched at Stafford Show in 1994.
Paul Banham Conversions 1994–99
Approx 40 made

BANHAM XK180

After ceasing work on his kit projects and selling most of them on, Paul Banham displayed his next idea at Goodwood Festival of Speed in 2007. It was a replica of Jaguar's stunning XK180 concept that never saw production in original guise.

Paul Banham Conversions 2007 to date
Approx 12 made

BANSHEE – *see MK GT2*

BARCHETTA 595

Stunning little roadster created by famed designer Peter Stevens (McLaren F1 and Jaguar XJR-15 among others), via his company Simpatico. It was and sold by the Dove Car Company run by Colin Jones (who also made the bodies for the Jaguar XJ220). It was based on a Fiat 126 floorpan and also used the rest of that car's mechanicals. Never really intended to be a kit car, it was, however, picked up and highly rated by the specialist press of the day.
Simpatico/Dove Car Company 1996–97
Approx 12 made

A
B
C
D
E
F
G
H
I
J
K
L
M
N
O
P
Q
R
S
T
U
V
W
X
Y
Z

BARNARD

Mercer replica from a well-known race car constructor of the day.
Barnard Sportscars 1972
Approx 1 made

BARNSDALE SALOON

Ford-based vintage-style kit from Vintage Motor Company of Doncaster. Project acquired by husband and wife team, John and Gill Ford, of Wirral-based AWS Ltd in spring 2011.
Vintage Motor Company 1998–2006
AWS Ltd 2011 to date
Approx 25 made

BAS 308

A Ferrari 308 replica from a chap called Peter Collins that made its debut at Stoneleigh Show in 1993. Unusually, it wasn't a body conversion for Pontiac Fiero or Toyota MR2, rather it featured a separate spaceframe chassis and Ford Scorpio running gear with a Rover V8 engine. Didn't last long.
BAS Developments 1993
Approx 1 made

BATTMOBILE – *see e-Trike*

BDN S2/S3

A track-orientated kit car from Herefordshire-based Baldwin Sportscars run by Ian Baldwin.
Baldwin Sportscars 2004 to date
Approx 5 made

BEACH BUGGY

Er, a beach buggy kit. Another one heavily inspired by the GP Buggy (*qv*), with round, faired-in headlights.
Beach Buggies of Southport 1971–72
Approx 10 made

BEAM BUGGY

A South African product made by Cape Town-based Beamish Buggies and briefly imported to the UK by Beetle Bits (UK).
Beetle Bits (UK) 2000–1
Approx 12 made

BEAMAN

Jaguar Mk10-based traditional roadster.
Beaman Cars 1984–85
Approx 6 made

BEARDALLS BUGGY

A fully built, well-appointed beach buggy from a GP agent based in Nottingham.
Beardalls 1971–73
Approx 6 made

BEAUFORD FOUR-DOOR

Public demand dictated that a four-door version of the Beauford (see next entry) was launched, especially as the car was eagerly grasped by the wedding hire trade and it was a lot easier for the bride to embark for the church via her own door.
Beauford Cars 1992 to date
Approx 300 made

BEAUFORD TWO-DOOR

First appeared in 1985, created by an engineer called Gordon Geskell who had built a succession of *specials* and one-offs, including a Mini van-based mobile church that was exported to Africa. The Beauford name was a conflation of 'Beautiful Ford'! Geskell originally sketched the idea in 1983 but filed it away for 18 months or so. He liked the notion of using a Mini body on long flowing wings and bonnet. Initial kits needed two donors – a Mini, and a Cortina for the mechanicals – before the process was simplified.

Company was taken over in 1996 by David and Charles Young, who initially traded from Geskell's workshop before moving to Biddulph, Staffordshire.
Beauford Cars 1985 to date
Approx 1,500 made

BEAUFORT

Another mayfly kit of which there have been many. The Beaufort was a mid-'80s traditional roadster based on the Austin 7.
Beaufort Cars 1985
Approx 1 made

BEAUJANGLE CAN-AM

Manchester-based company run by Nik Sandeman-Allen and well-known drag racer, Phil 'Ziggy' Smith. The pair were passionate hot-rod enthusiasts and ran separate operations (Smith as Mr. Beaujangle) until they amalgamated their businesses, becoming known for building all manner of bonkers vehicles from their lock-up in Salford, under the Beaujangle Enterprises name.

They turned their hands to beach buggies, chopper bikes, custom cars and drag racers, while Smith had built a sand-rail called 'Mr Beaujangle', the first in the UK, which went down a storm at the Custom Car Show at Crystal Palace, January 1971. Around this time they also introduced their T-Bucket shell (*qv*). When they launched the Can-Am, a chap called Kendrick Gough soon joined the company. As a result, they changed their name to Beaujangle Sales Ltd.

Smith had previously built a monster V8-powered Opus HRF he called 'Anomalous'.

The Can-Am was inspired by a similar American Group 7 kit and based on a VW Beetle floorpan shortened by 5in. Beaujangle produced it as a successor to their low-budget Model T, and it was (very) loosely based on sixties Can-Am racers. Sort of. A hardtop with gullwing-type doors was an option although the base kit cost just £150.

The fellas went to the trouble of organising an impromptu press launch at Mallory Park in April 1972, which ended up in chaos with spinning journalists all over the place and rumours that one had even ended up in the Mallory lake, although this was never confirmed.

Resurrected for a time by Lemazone in the mid-'80s. Didn't last long…
Beaujangle Sales Ltd 1972–73
Lemazone 1985–87
Approx 6 made

BEAUJANGLE T-BUCKET

Very obscure first product from Beaujangle Enterprises (priced at just £30), which they imported from the USA, before they concentrated on the Can-Am. Very cheap and very basic. Well-known drag racer Phil Elsom built a famous one with a hemi V8, known as 'Sneaky-T'.
Beaujangle Enterprises Ltd 1971
Approx 5 made

BEAVER

Richard Oakes was involved with the design but not the final end product. The concept came from an idea by Gordon Summers, and John Ingram was responsible for the fibreglass. Kit Cars International was based in Barnsley, and Summers ran a hardware-type shop. Later custodians Beaver Coach Works, run by Steve Barwell, hailed from South Woodham Ferrers, Essex. The project was last heard of advertised for sale in 1997 for just £2,000.
Kit Cars International 1984–85
Beaver Coach Works 1991–92
Approx 48 made

BEDOUIN

'Snowdonia' and 'Ranger' were other names used for this car, which was inspired by the Citroën Mehari. The man behind the Bedouin was Bob Williams, a joiner by trade, who was also at the time the only repairer of Panhards in the UK. Early Beavers were made entirely from marine ply with GRP introduced later on. Passed to CVC Ltd of Rempstone, Leicestershire, in 1987.
RW Services 1985–87
CVC Ltd 1987
Approx 20 made

BEETLE GEMINI

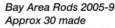

Auto Services of Redditch offered this Beetle body conversion.
Auto Services 1988–91
Approx 17 made

BEETLE ROD

After selling the Dooster (*qv*) project in 2004, Gary Janes set up Bay Area Rods, and his first project was a Beetle Rod. Hardcore, old skool. Extended wheelbase Veedub, without fenders.
Bay Area Rods 2005-9
Approx 30 made

BEETLE SALOON

A conversion kit for VW Beetle from Veedub guru Peter Cheeseman, founder of Wizard of Rods. Available in '50s and '70s styles.
Wizard Roadsters 1992–2000
Approx 50 made

BELARO BERLINETTA

Created in America. The work of a university technical lecturer called Tom Bellaw, it was imported to the UK by Steve Briddon, Roy Morris and Terry Sands, of the Fiero Factory. Based on Pontiac Fiero GT V6.

Briddon was running a successful garage repair business. Sands, meanwhile, had been involved with the kit car industry since the early seventies with Southend-on-Sea-based Americar, then Deals on Wheels, Muscle City, Sandwood, Sheldonhurst and Alternative Vehicle Centre (AVC), although by trade he was a trained technical draughtsman, having learned his craft at Ford Motor Company. Morris had run a successful tuning company in the sixties called Morspeed Conversions, before moving to Germany for 17 years, then settling in Orlando, Florida. He had been a kit car enthusiast for years before finding the Belaro. He decided to bring it to the UK.

The car was an evocation of the Ferrari Testarossa, which later passed to Dave Fuell of Lakeside Carriage Company.
Fiero Factory 1991–92
Specialist Performance Mouldings 1992–93
Lakeside Carriage Company/SPM 1993–2003
Approx 25 made

BELGRAVIA

Traditionally styled saloon. In the proven manner purchased by Essex-based Fleur de Lys.
Fleur de Lys 1983–94
Approx 15 made

BELL T70 COUPÉ

Lola T70 Spider replica derived from the GTD T70. The company was run by Derek Bell (no, *not* that one!).
Bell Performance 2000–7
Approx 5 made

BELVA

Also known as the Tipo 16, the Belva was perhaps pasta-meister John Raffo's best design of all. A chunky two-seater passed to Mike Phillips of Harlequin Autokits once John retired. One that got away.
Raffo Cars 1996–2000
Harlequin Autokits 2000–5
Approx 7 made

BELVETTA

Also known as the Tipo 17, this was John Raffo's last design before retiring, and like the Belva passed to Mike Phillips of Harlequin Autokits.
Raffo Cars 2000
Harlequin Autokits 2000–5
Approx 2 made

BERKELEY BANDINI

A recreation of the three-wheeled Berkeley T60, produced in Biggleswade in the fifties, that had been powered by Anzani, Excelsior or Royal Enfield engines. The latter-day version was was based on ubiquitous Mini mechanicals. The man behind the project was Anthony Argyle of Syston, Leicestershire. The project passed to Dave Ratner in the mid-nineties.

The company offered a Lamborghini Countach replica body to fit a VW Beetle floorpan for a time in the early '90s.
Berkeley Motor Company 1991–96
Berkeley Developments 1996–2002
Approx 7 made

BERKELEY CAMEROTTA

Created by Berkeley enthusiast Dave Ratner, the Camerotta was inspired by the British Leyland ADO35 MG prototype, which was intended as a replacement for the Midget, and was also clearly influenced by the Berkeley Bandini.
Berkeley Developments 2000–2
Approx 6 made

BERRIEN ROADSTER T

One of several US Berrien models imported to the UK by the wonderfully-named Billy Bob's Buggy Shop of Cotford St Luke, run by Helen Bowden. The Berrien range is one of the best-known of the American beach buggies.
Billy Bob's Buggy Shop 2005 to 2010
Approx 12 made (UK)

BILMAR BUCCANEER

Early Dutton rival made in Portland, Dorset, that didn't last very long at all. Had a widened Lotus Seven-style body that featured a mix of Triumph Spitfire and Ford Corsair components.
Bilmar Engineering 1971–72
Approx 10 made

BIOTA Mk1

Innovatively named Biota, from *bi* (equals 'two') and *iota* (equals 'small'). It was the brainchild of John Houghton, who made his prototype in 1968. To produce the car he joined forces with Bill Needham of Coldwell Engineering – the company that had been responsible for the Coldwell GT (*qv*) – and created a joint venture called Houghton Coldwell Ltd based in Dinnington, North Yorkshire.

Specialised Mouldings was contracted to make the fibreglass bodies, which were complicated and consisted of over 20 separate mouldings. In 1970, Houghton and Needham fell out, with the Biota sold under the Houghton Developments Ltd banner (Biota Products, run by Needham, sold 'go faster' parts).

This Mini-based kit car became an icon and did very well in hillclimbs and sprints – Houghton's own car won the BARC Hillclimb Championship in 1972. It was also notable for having a stirrup-type arrangement for brake and accelerator!

The Biota Products operation launched an intriguing 'foldaway' gullwing top at a show in Amsterdam in March 1971 that came complete with sliding windows and hinged sidescreens!

Houghton Coldwell Ltd 1969–70
Houghton Developments Ltd 1970–76
Approx 25 made

BIOTA Mk2

Styling was revised although it retained the Mk1's stirrup brake pedal. Also now featured Biota's own bespoke seat, created specially for the car, and a larger cockpit, with a de Dion back-end. A Biota CA estate version was stillborn. Jeff Williamson bought the project when Houghton emigrated to Argentina, of all places.

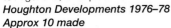

Houghton Developments 1976–78
Approx 10 made

BIRCHFIELD SPORTS

Legendary metal-basher Shapecraft is world renowned for their high-quality bodywork skills. Run by ex-Panther employee Clive Smart, they were initially based in Leatherhead, Surrey, before moving to Northamptonshire.

The Birchfield was reminiscent of the Jaguar SS100 but was an original design created by (then) GPO engineer Nick Topping. It featured a hand-formed aluminium body, in 18-gauge aluminium sheet, atop an ultra-strong spaceframe chassis made from 40mm square tube in 12-gauge steel, and was the last of four *specials* created by Topping. One of the best kits ever. In the mid-'80s held the mantle of most expensive kit car ever! It was marketed for a time from late 1991 by Challenger (*qv*) makers Car Craft Clinic. Last heard of in Australia.

CV Shapecraft 1985–91
Car Craft Clinic 1991–95
Approx 22 made

BIRKIN S3

Birkin Cars was founded in 1982 in South Africa by John Watson and named in honour of famed Bentley boy Sir Henry 'Tim' Birkin, a distant cousin. Watson was born in Wales but his parents moved to Zimbabwe (then known as Rhodesia) when he was very young. John restored a Lotus Seven S2 as a teenager.

After finishing National Service, political uncertainty in Rhodesia saw him relocate to South Africa. He considered importing the Caterham Seven but ultimately decided to create his own car, and what began as a hobby soon turned into a serious business. It was his mother who suggested the 'Birkin' name for his company.

The S3 was launched in the UK in 1998 via Watson's son Stephen, who at the time was test driver for the Arrows F1 team. The car was sold under his engine component company, Tradelink International, before they changed their name to Birkin Cars UK. A Lotus Seven-inspired sports car with square and round tube spaceframe chassis, live or IRS rear axle, double wishbone front end, with an aluminium body with GRP nose, wings and nosecone.

After several years away from the UK, 2010 saw the marque make a comeback to these shores with famed bike tuner, motorcycle race-team manager and creator of the RST V8 engine Russell Savory's RS Performance operation, based in Stow Maries, Essex; the only surviving World War One airfield in the UK.

Birkin Cars 1998–2005
Birkin Cars/RS Performance Engines Development Ltd 2010 to date
Approx 1,000 made worldwide (estimated 50+ in UK thus far)

BLACK PRINCE

William Towns-created replica of the Invicta model of the same name that he based on a Reliant Kitten, although it was made for Cornish company Invicta Cars. It never reached production, and Towns had the prototype in one of his barns for several years after.

Interstyl 1985
Approx 1 made

BLACKJACK ZERO

After his success with the Avion (*qv*), Richard Oakes wanted to develop the three-wheeler concept further, creating a more performance-orientated trike, which resulted in the equally delightful Zero, first shown in 2005. Power originally came from a VW Beetle air-cooled engine before a Moto Guzzi option was introduced, becoming standard.
Blackjack Cars 2005 to date
Approx 15 made

BLACKJACK AVION

Famed kit car designer Richard Oakes had created a leaning three-wheeler for a professor of music back in the '80s, which wasn't intended for production. Oakes subsequently fancied making his own three-wheeler and so came up with the superb Avion in 1996, which was based on Citroën 2CV mechanics and engine. Never the most powerful vehicle, it was, however, one of the most stylish.
Blackjack Cars 1996–2005
Approx 70 made

BLAZE F

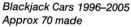

Similarly styled to the Blaze R but John Hewat cleverly came up with a body conversion kit package for the MGF.
Blaze Motorsport 2007 to date
Approx 25 made

BLAZE RR

When John Hewat left Aeon Sportscars he took the Blaze RR with him and set up Blaze Motorsport. The car was originally spawned from the Pell Genesis Evo (*see Pell Genesis*).
Blaze Motorsport 2006 to date
Approx 20 made

BLOND MOTO X190/X190 RVS

A Fiat X1/9 body conversion with power from Fiat Uno 1.3-litre turbo. Company was run by Ashley Boxall and based in St Leonard's-on-Sea, Sussex, and changed its name to Jevron Motorsport in 2000, revising the car's name slightly to X190 RVS in 1.3-litre (125bhp) or 1.4-litre (150bhp) form. Introduced an Alfa Romeo V6-powered version in 2003 called the X190 GPR V6, which had more aggressive, rounded styling, while a Lancia Monte Carlo-based example was also introduced.
Auto Elite 1998–2000   *Jevron Motorsport 2000–2008*
Approx 13 made

BM BUGGY

Yet another kit inspired by the GP Buggy (*qv*) but with a Kamm-style tail, which came from Mick Mahoney of Basingstoke. Short wheelbase kits cost £95 with a long wheelbase version at £105. Fully built examples cost from £395 in March 1971.
BM Car Things 1971–72
Approx 36 made

BMW-7DE – *see W7DE*

BOBTAIL

Launched at Stoneleigh Show in 1985, the Bobtail utility kit was the work of Westcliff-on-Sea-based Jim Peters, Nick Rogers and Steve Ahern. All Capri parts bolted straight to Lynx's ladderframe box section chassis.
Lynx Kit Cars 1985–87
Approx 8 made

BOLER T-BONE

Lancastrian David Boler, who ran an exhaust centre in Oldham, was behind this weird rod-inspired creation. Boler had previously raced an Elva Courier MkIII (*qv*) and a Cox GTM (*qv*). Early T-bones were built on the first floor of the exhaust business and had to be hoisted to the ground, although the company moved to larger premises nearby in Greenfield, in 1972, which was the same site later occupied by D&H Fibreglass, who made the Midas range. Body was made from steel, with GRP wings, underpinned by a rugged ladderframe chassis and Ford Cortina mechanicals.

Apparently the late comedian Bernard Manning owned one, as did sword-swallower and fire-eating entertainer *The Great Stromboli,* who decked his out with fireman's ladders and buckets, as you do.

David Boler Engineering Ltd 1971–74
Approx 30 made

BONITO

The Bonito had its origins with Fiberfab in America before a German company of the same name took it over under licence in 1969. It was then imported to the UK in 1981 by Poole-based ACM (a fibreglass boat-building operation), who relocated to a huge 20,000sq ft quayside factory in Torpoint, Cornwall. ACM was run by Alan Bradshaw (mechanical engineer) and Dutchman Hans Alma (international race mechanic), who was originally impressed by the car at Amsterdam Motor Show in 1971. He was reminded of it when he saw an image in *Alternative Cars* magazine and tracked it down. Graham Keane of Bristol-based AED International took over production in 1983.

A revised Bonito came to rest at John Grossart's Seraph Cars, who ditched the VW Beetle floorpan and introduced a bespoke spaceframe chassis based around Ford Cortina mechanicals.

The Bonito also inspired Clive Clark's Excalibur Crusader (*qv*).

ACM Ltd 1981–83
AED International 1983–84
Bonito Performance Centre 1984–85
Seraph Cars 1985–87
Approx 63 made

BONITO CONVERTIBLE

Created by second UK custodians of the hardtop Bonito project, AED. Didn't inspire many to get the cheque-book out.

AED International 1987
Approx 1 made

BONNEVILLE ROADSTER

Appearing for the first and only time at Newark Show in June 1992, the Bonneville Roadster was intended as a pastiche of a thirties-style hot-rod salt-flats lakester, which was based on nothing more exotic than a Sherpa van! The South Scarle-based company offered a body kit at £1,950. There couldn't have been many takers, if any, as nothing more was heard of it.

DRB Coachworks 1992
Approx 1 made

BOOM TRIKES CHOPPER RANGE

Manchester-based operation run by Ian Roberts, who imported the acclaimed German Boom trikes to the UK from 2002. In addition to the Chopper model other variants included Low Rider and Family.

Boom Trikes 2002 to date
Approx 50 made (UK)

BOUNTY HUNTER

Created in California by Brian Dries in 1969, this really is one of the classic buggies. Imported to the UK by Mel Hubbard of Manxbuggies from 1999. VW Beetle-based floorpan chopped by 14½in. Passed to Rob Kilham's East Coast Manx in 2003.

Manxbuggies 1999–2003
East Coast Manx 2003 to date
Approx 8 made

BOXER SPRINT

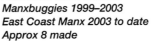

Mini-based two-seater built by Ian Shearer, who had earlier been responsible for the Nimbus Coupé (*qv*). He based his Boxer Cars operation in Rye, East Sussex. Wasn't around for long. The company's adverts of the day claimed that the car was 'alternative technology', which isn't quite *durch sprung technik*!

Boxer Cars 1986–87
Approx 1 made

BRA 289

Based in Doncaster, Beribo Replica Automobiles was founded by John Berry, an accountant, and Peter Ibbotson, who ran the Wheatley Hills Garage. The pair had been friends for 30 years before they set-up Beribo (a conflation of their surnames) in 1984. Their 289 was moulded from John Atkins' competition 289 and based on MGB mechanicals. Originally called the BRA 1800-V8.

Public demand saw a V8 option introduced in 1982 with a Mk2 chassis from 1988. Just prior to the project being sold to boat-builders Tyler Industrial Mouldings of Hoo, Kent, BRA relocated to Castle Donington.

David Wiles of BRA Motor Works acquired the project in 2005 but due to pressures of other work, shelved it – for now!

Beribo Replica Automobiles 1981–95
Tyler Industrial Mouldings 1995–98
BRA Motor Works 2005-7
Approx 480 made

BRA 427

Created for Beribo by Gerry Hawkridge before the project was sold to a German company.
Beribo Replica Automobiles 1981–82
Approx 12 made

BRA CV3

A less expensive Citroën 2CV-based version of the CX3 (see below), created by BRA Motor Works during the cold winter of 1997 and launched at the Stafford Show in March 1998 to a great fanfare, the company taking six orders during the weekend. It

shared a visual similarity to the CX3 and also had aluminium body and steel tube chassis, but had front-wheel drive with a heavily-revised Citroën 2CV rear suspension arm for the single rear wheel. BRA Motor Works sold 425 units (400 kits, 25 fully-builts) before selling the project in 2002 to Maidstone-based Leighton Cars, who were taken over by Stuart Soutter in 2006. Passed to Ditchling-based Aero Cycle Cars in 2007, the same company who had taken over the CX3 earlier.
BRA Motor Works 1998–2002
Leighton Cars 2002–7
Aero Cycle Cars 2007-9
Approx 460 made

BRA CX3

Three-wheeler created by John Berry and Peter Ibbotson with aluminium body and a 16swg steel tube chassis, with power coming from either a Honda CX500 or CX650.

Taken over by James Mather of BRA Motor Works of Flint in 1996, who made several revisions to the kit, the most notable of which was adding 4in to the length for added cockpit space. He was later joined by friend David Wiles, and the duo also created a Moto Guzzi-powered version (the MG3, five sold) and a Honda Pan European variant. They sold around 100 of their 'Mk2' long version.

In 2002 the CX project was sold to Arthur Fairley of Aero Cycle Cars of Ditchling, Sussex, who continues to market and refine the car.
Beribo Replica Automobiles 1990–96
BRA Motor Works 1996–2002
Aero Cycle Cars 2002 to date
Approx 130 made

BRA J-TYPE

Beautiful cycle-winged roadster that was inspired by '30s MGs. Aimed squarely at the NG market. Quite expensive to build, though.
Beribo Replica Automobiles 1984–92
Rodney Rushton 1995–2002
Approx 45 made

BRA MR3

The MR3 was actually the development of a James Mather Mini-based one-off from 1994 known as the 'Mini Plug'. It was revised in 1999 to use Rover Metro running gear. Only two of this three-wheeler were produced, the second of which was a high-performance version.
BRA 1999–2000
Approx 2 made

BRA P-TYPE

Like its J-type sister car, the P-Type looked to the buoyant NG market. Differed from the J-Type by having flowing, rather than cycle, wings.
Beribo Replica Automobiles 1985–92
Rodney Rushton 1995–2002
Approx 15 made

BRA Q4 CHALLENGER

A very unusual vehicle for BRA Motor Works, the Q4 was an all-terrain-type kit that used a mixture of Classic Mini and Rover Metro parts, with a MIG-welded spaceframe from 42mm x 3mm CHS structural steel, partly panelled in Zintec.
BRA Motor Works 2003
Approx 2 made

BRADLEY S61

Featured elements of Ashley and Falcon and sold by a Whalley, Lancashire company run by Tony Place, who initially based the S61 on Vauxhall Viva HB/HC parts before switching quickly to Escort

Mk2 and underpinned by a beefy square section spaceframe chassis. Place claimed that it was a Frazer Nash replica and had nothing to do with Ashley or Falcon, until Peter Pellandine stepped onto his stand at Stoneleigh one year!

Regardless of all that, the S61 was actually a very good car and should have sold in good numbers.

A Blackburn-based company marketed the car from late 1994, quoting kit prices of £2,702 inc VAT in November 1995.
Bradley Motor Company 1990-94
Thor Conversion Services 1994-96
Approx 2 made

BRAMWITH LIMOUSINE

Made by the company founded by Alan Beillby in 1996 as Heritage Vintage & Classic Vehicles, before subsequent changes saw them become the Vintage Motor Company and then Vintage Replicas. After ceasing trading in 2004 they were rescued by Asquith Motors and traded as Asquith Vintage Classics for a time before evolving into Bramwith, under new ownership.

After Bramwith Ltd ceased trading, the projects lay dormant for a time until AWS Ltd, run by husband and wife team John and Gill Ford, acquired the Bramwith Limousine and its Badsworth sister. They set about creating new moulds and an exciting new start for the projects.
Vintage Motor Company/Vintage Replicas/Asquith Vintage Classics/Bramwith Motor Company 1998 to 2010
AWS Ltd 2011 to date
Approx 125 made

BRANTON BOX VAN

Vintage van from Alan Beillby of Vintage Motor Company.
Vintage Motor Company/ Vintage Replicas/Asquith Vintage Classics/Bramwith Motor Company 1997 to 2010
Approx 60 made

BRETSA

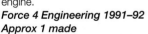

Hailing from King's Lynn and sounding like a coffee machine, the Bretsa was an ISO Grifo replica based on Jaguar XJ12 mechanicals complete with V12 engine.
Force 4 Engineering 1991–92
Approx 1 made

BRIGANTIS

A 1970 one-off by Bill Dobson. This was a convincing visual replica of the Bertone-designed Lamborghini Marzal concept car. Saw it looking a bit forlorn for sale at Stoneleigh in 1998. Never reached production.

Bill Dobson 1970
Approx 1 made

BRIGHTWHEEL CR6/STINGER

One of the better efforts on the Lamborghini Countach replica theme. Featured a strong multi-tubular perimeter spaceframe. It was made by former Sheldonhurst agents Brightwheel Replicas of Christchurch, Dorset, run by father and son team Ken and Chris Cook. CR6 stood for 'Countach Replica number 6'.

Brightwheel Replicas 1988–89
Approx 25 made

BRIGHTWHEEL VIPER

Ken and Chris Cook of Brightwheel took over the Viper and budget-orientated Viper 4 after the demise of Sheldonhurst and sold many. See also Classic Replicas Viper and Viper 4 (*qv*). An underrated car.

Brightwheel Replicas 1986–89
Approx 260 made

BRIT 2+2

Evolved from Bill Harbron's pretty and capable little Fiat-based roadster, the Harbron Special (*qv*). The Brit 2+2 featured Ford Cortina running gear in an attempt to attract a wider audience. It didn't catch on. The adverts of 1986 proclaimed: 'Buy the best and say goodbye to the rest.' We soon said goodbye to this!

Loxton Laminates 1986–87
Approx 2 made

BRITTON HAZELGROVE

A beautifully made Triumph Herald-based interpretation of a Lotus Seven Series One made by car restorer and ex-Lyncar Engineering man Bruce Hazelgrove, from his base in Wooburn Green, Buckinghamshire. Featured aluminium body panels.

Britton Hazelgrove 1987
Approx 2 made

BROADBEST PRIMO

One of the many Countach replicas around in the '80s. Promising start, as it was originally devised and intended to be sold by GT Developments, although it never appeared under their banner due to the success of their GTD 40 (*qv*). The company's GRP suppliers, Broadbest – another Poole-based company, run by Dave Andrews and Mark Ross – marketed it instead. It was allegedly the UK's first drivable Countach replica. After Broadbest's demise the car formed the basis of the ABS Scorpion (*qv*).

Broadbest Ltd 1987–88
Approx 10 made

BROCKMORE TR

A Triumph TR2/TR3 replica originally sold under the Grand Illusions banner. Passed to Brockmore of Brierley Hill in 1993, and featured a revised chassis and suspension set-up. Ford based, but with a large choice of engines available up to Rover V8.

Brockmore Classic Replicas Ltd 1993–94
Approx 4 made

BROOKE 245

Antique furniture expert Toby Sutton designed this 1950s-inspired single-seat three-wheeler based on the Renault 5 Gordini. Hump behind driver could be removed to give tandem second seat.

Hurricane manufacturers Caburn Engineering began gathering up old, out-of-production kit cars such as the Hadleigh Spring and Elysee Sprint, with the intention of putting them back into production. These included the Brooke 245, renamed the Caburn GP57.

Brooke Cars 1991–93
Caburn Engineering 2010 to date
Approx 4 made

BROOKE ME190/BROOKE 190

After the 245, Norwich-based antique furniture expert Toby Sutton turned his attention to the ME190, which really hit the performance spot. Early cars had a right-hand gearchange and Vauxhall power. A London company took over the project for three years before it ended up with Lotus and Ginetta specialist Jack Davis, at Brooke Kensington. Sold on again in the early '00s to a Devon-based operation run by Alex Munday before another Devonian partnership took over. They only offer the modified Brooke 190 with Duratec power and in fully-built guise.

Brooke Motor Company 1991–93
Brooke Cars 1993–96
Brooke Kensington 1996–2002
Brooke Cars 2002-8
Approx 43 made

BROOKLAND SWALLOW

Kit car journalist Iain Ayre's first effort at car manufacture, the Swallow was a four-seat, three-wheeled, Mini-based device. He soon moved on to a replica of Jaguar's XK120, the Ayrspeed Six (qv), under the Ayrspeed banner.

Brookland Motor Company 1993–94
Approx 1 made

BROOKLANDS

Tyler Industrial Mouldings, who were at the time marketing the BRA 289 (qv) and SP350 (qv) Daimler Dart replicas, unveiled a slightly revised Calvy Mitchel (qv), which they renamed the Brooklands at the 1997 Sandown Park Show. Wasn't around long.

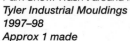

Tyler Industrial Mouldings 1997–98
Approx 1 made

BROOKLANDS 500

A very obscure three-wheeler made in 1997 by a chap called Lloyd Pennington, based in Chorley, Lancashire. Inspired by the F-Type Morgans of the thirties, but with modern mechanicals, the trike was underpinned by a steel-tube chassis and double-wishbone front suspension, with either Honda CX or Honda Pan European power.

Heyes Cycle Cars 1997
Approx 1 made

BROOMSTICK BS120

Classic car buff, historic racer and haulier Michael Moore of Ivinghoe Aston, Bedfordshire, was the man behind the superb Broomstick Jaguar XK120 replica, based on XJ6 mechanicals.

Moore had started racing in 1962 in a Falcon Sort (ex-Alan Mann car), competing in hillclimbs and sprints, initially. Moore built up a good reputation for car set-up (particularly AC Cobras) and also became well known for supplying replacement Jaguar XK120 parts. He then spent 2½ years tooling up to make his own replica of Sir William Lyons' iconic car.

The Broomstick name is connected to Moore's first Clubman *special* called *Witchcraft*. The company still exists, specialising in Jaguar parts and classic car sales.

Broomstick Cars 1993–99
Approx 36 made

BS ROADSTER

Cortina-based and derived from the EWM Brigand (qv), which had been created by Edward Waddington and inspired by the Dutton Phaeton (qv). By the time it reached Ben Sparham's Birmingham-based B&S Sports cars the Roadster's days were well and truly numbered.

Edward Waddington Motors 1984–85
B&S Sports Cars 1988–89
Approx 6 made

BS SPRINT

Evolved from the EWM Buccaneer (qv), which had been inspired by the Marlin Roadster (qv), this Ford Cortina-based kit sold in even fewer numbers than its Roadster brother. And like the Roadster, when it arrived at Ben Sparham's B&S Sports cars it didn't do any better.

BS Sports Cars 1988–89
Approx 2 made

BT7

Jaguar-based Austin Healey 3000 replica that made its debut at the Newark Show in 1988 and was heard from no more. The man behind the project was Suffolk-based Ray Bradford. Great company name.
Beccles Robotics and Automotive Developments 1988
Approx 1 made

BUCCANEER

Made by a Penge-based company. This was a type of off-road rail. Sort of!
Klasse Chassis 1994
Approx 1 made

BUCKLAND B3

Superb three-wheeler created by electronic control engineer Dick Buckland, who lived very close to the Llanwern steelworks near Newport, South Wales. Much like his contemporary, Tony Divey of Triking, Dick was a keen – and successful – Morgan F-Type racer, and his Buckland B3 was his take on that theme.

This excellent car made its debut at Stoneleigh kit car show in 1985. Unlike most kit-form trikes, the B3 was based on handling and performance, and its Ford Crossflow 1,300cc engine gave it around 90bhp and – due to its Type 9 gearbox – a reverse gear! More than enough to have fun with. Dick Buckland made them while a chap called Laurie Weeks marketed the product, until sales were taken in-house by Buckland in 1988.

A unique forward-hingeing GRP body gave unique and clever access to the rear wheel, all underpinned by Zintec steel backbone channelled chassis. Clever folded Zintec frame at front end that housed lower wishbones and upper rockers, with rear drive via a chain through Reliant Robin crownwheel and pinion and bespoke propshaft to sprocket and chain. Dick supplied 12 B3s before ill health forced production to cease.

In January 2011, it was announced that well-known UK hot-rodder John Wilcox, of Flintshire, North Wales, had acquired the project, and was going to put the car back into production, retaining Buckland as a consultant.
Light Car & Cycle Restoration Company 1985–88
Buckland Cars 1988–99
Penguin Speed Shop 2011 to date
Approx 13 made

BUCKLER CARS

Reading-based company founded by Derek Buckler, who is seen as the father of the kit car movement in the UK after he started building replicas of his Colonial chassis in component form. It was based around his own *special* that enjoyed much success in trials, autotests, sprints, circuit racing and hillclimbs from 1947. Although he never classed himself as a kit car manufacturer – the term wasn't even invented back then – Derek influenced a lot of people with his *specials* and go-faster equipment.

A very shrewd character, he managed to get around the fact that it was nigh impossible to buy a 'domestic-market' car as everything was being made for export, spurred on by a government eager (desperate?) for funds after WW2. The only modern cars available were those that servicemen bought abroad and brought back with them when they were repatriated. Indeed, the Morris 8 Series E was nicknamed the 'demob car'.

Inevitably, enthusiasm for motoring was massively high but the vast majority of cars on the road in the late '40s were old pre-war Austin 7s and Ford 8/10s, which, due to the fact that new mechanicals couldn't be had, the canny Mr Buckler used these as donor vehicles for essential components. Ever the innovator, he could offer a renovation and reconditioning service for old parts. Of course, the government also aided the growth of the kit car, as there was no stringent purchase tax to pay if the car was supplied in bits.

The first Buckler adverts appeared in *Motor Sport* magazine in 1949 and, contrary to popular belief, Buckler did offer bodies for his cars – standard-fit, of course, on factory-built cars, optional on component versions. Most Buckler bodies were hand-beaten out of wooden moulds by C.F. Taylor, a skilled panel-beater who worked in the Buckler premises (a chap called Jonnie Offord did the later aluminium work).

When GRP came along, Buckler didn't get involved. Instead they bought batches of the day's popular bodies, mainly from Microplas. If the customer preferred, they could source their own bodyshells. This is the reason why no two Bucklers ever looked the same.

The first MkV was built at Buckler's factory in Caversham and Derek himself tested it before delivery to the customer, a service offered for all factory-built cars.

Buckler was certainly a character. His first chassis was called the MkV not because it was his fifth product but because he didn't want people to think it was his first and that he was a novice! Meanwhile, customers were only given a *Buckler* bonnet badge if he personally liked their car. It's not known how many he 'awarded'.

Buckler was renowned for his range of tuning and go-faster accessories, much like LMB, and he also sold engine components, manifolds, close ratio gears, suspension conversions and wheels.

After Derek Buckler became ill in 1959, employee Peter Hilton ran the company on a day-to-day basis until it was taken over completely by Frank Fletcher and Mike Luff, who traded as Buckler Engineering until May 1965, when the company went into liquidation.

BUCKLER MkV

This underpinned Buckler's own *special*, which was a cycle-winged two-seater for 90in wheelbase that customers usually tried to replicate. Officially known as a 'Replica Special of DDP201'. From the mid-'50s could be had with a Versil GRP body.
Buckler Cars 1949–60
Approx 125 made

BUCKLER MkVI

A longer wheelbase (94in) version of the MkV, based on Ford E493A.
Buckler Cars 1952–60
Approx 50 made

BUCKLER MkVI-4

A four-seater version of the MkVI.
Buckler Cars 1953–60
Approx 35 made

BUCKLER MkX

A three-seater, line-astern configuration for a 90in aluminium body that was made in-house by C.F. Taylor and then later, from 1952, by Jonnie Offord. From 1953 could be had with a GRP body usually supplied by Galt Glass division of Durasteel Ltd or Versil of Liversedge.
Buckler Cars 1950–56
Approx 20 made

BUCKLER MkXI

As per the MkX but for 94in wheelbase with the same C.F. Taylor (or Jonnie Offord) aluminium bodies.
Buckler Cars 1951–56
Approx 35 made

BUCKLER MkXV

Had a Jonnie Offord hand-rolled aluminium body or, from 1953, a Microplas Mistral fibreglass shell option.
Buckler Cars 1951–55
Approx 40 made

BUCKLER MkXVI

Designed around MG TC/TD.
Buckler Cars 1954–58
Approx 22 made

BUCKLER MkXVII

Designed for an Ashley GT shell with 94in wheelbase.
Buckler Cars 1955–58
Approx 35 made

BUCKLER BB100

'BB' stood for 'Buckler Backbone'.
Buckler Cars 1958–60
Approx 50 made

BUCKLER DD1

Featured de Dion rear suspension and designed for Coventry Climax engines, with a body very similar to the Buckler Ninety (*qv*).
Buckler Cars 1955–56
Approx 3 made

BUCKLER DD2

As per the DD1 but designed around Microplas Mistral glassfibre body and featuring a more straightforward chassis.
Buckler Cars 1956–58
Approx 4 made

BUCKLER GT1/R

Designed primarily for the Rochdale GT bodyshell.
Buckler Cars 1958–60
Approx 18 made

BUCKLER MODEL 53

A trials type model for 84in wheelbase.
Buckler Cars 1952–55
Approx 10 made

BUCKLER NINETY

The Ninety was a dual-purpose road-racer and was one of the most successful 1,172cc racers. Usually came with hand-rolled aluminium body. Ford 100E-based from 1955.
Buckler Cars 1954–62
Approx 28 made

BUCKLEY V8

Monster Rover V8-powered trike made by Brighton-based Trike Tek run by Mick Buckley and Tim Nevill. Mental!
Trike Tek 1998–2002
Approx 18 made

BUGLE BUGGY

Heavily inspired by the US Bugetta kit, although it was an original design. Roland Sharman of Sharman Drag Company Ltd was the man behind it, although prior to the Bugle he built bespoke turnkey GP Buggies under the Bugle Beachbuggies moniker, although this operation went bust in 1970.

He then formed a company called Lotusmere, trading as the Bugle Automotive Traction & Manufacturing Company of London Ltd, based in the crypt of St Jude's Church in Fulham, West London, after a £30,000 loan from a merchant bank gave much-needed capital, which was just as well, as the operation looked as if it might have gone bust, like his first venture.

Based, unsurprisingly, on ubiquitous VW Beetle mechanicals and floorpan, and inspired by the American Bugetta (designed by Jerry Eisert), although it was actually an original Sharman design, based on a 78½in shortened floorpan. The Bugle did very well from the start, with King Hussein of Jordan ordering four well-appointed examples and Sharman sending 75 kits to Rocket Wheel Industries of California. Real 'coals to Newcastle' stuff! But there were no doubts that the Bugle was created for cruising London's King's Road rather than the beach, as it was bigger and more practical, which was part of its appeal. The buggy was apparently christened by Sharman's wife, who reckoned that the exhaust pipes looked like bugles… Bodies were made by a company in Sheerness, Kent.

The Bugle was expensive by comparison to rivals (kit priced at £160) but customers didn't seem to mind and they loved the integrated headlights and wider stance, with bigger wheels than the norm, a deliberate move by Sharman as he hated narrow buggies on narrow wheels. One chap was so desperate to get his hands on one he even swapped his two-week-old Radford Mini DeVille!

Roland also got good exposure from TV appearances, with a Bugle featuring in adverts for Lentheric cosmetics, de Beers diamonds and Ingersoll watches, although a planned role in TV's *Doctor Who* didn't materialise after a BBC researcher pranged it prior to filming! When Airfix was looking for a buggy to use for one of their glue-together kits they chose a Bugle as the subject. Possibly the trendiest buggy of a trendy scene, it even appeared at the Geneva Motor Show in 1970, and also on the front cover of *Motor* magazine.

A move to a 15,000sq ft unit in Reading, Berkshire, and a retail site in Battersea, was necessitated when the crypt premises in Fulham burnt down. The wheels came well and truly off Sharman's operation in 1971, though, when the bank wanted their loan back – in one go! Sharman staggered on until 1972, when production ceased. He almost hit the six he was looking for however, as a deal with Volkswagen for worldwide distribution failed at the last minute. So near, yet so far…

Sharman had one final attempt, trading from September 1971 as Bugle Developments & Marketing Ltd, who enthusiastically entered the Senior Service Hill Rally the same month, while they started developing a van version, too, which ultimately didn't appear. They raised kit prices to a whopping £297, which probably did for them. Mind you, they had commissioned designer Peter Stevens to come up with an intended special Bugle GT capable of 150mph, powered by a mid-mounted Chevy V8 engine, which came to nought when the Sheerness laminator's factory burnt down in 1972, taking the GT prototype with it. The official Bugle story ended soon after…

In the early 1970s Stephen Foster of Fibresports acquired some Bugle moulds and sold his version via adverts in *Custom Car* magazine between 1972 and 1979. One of these sets ended up with Yorkshireman Chris Watson, who carried on offering Bugles for six years before he too packed up.

When buggy guru James Hale of GT Mouldings relaunched the Bugle in 1995 he didn't get the Watson moulds, as many thought; rather he was offered an original set, long thought lost. These were in a sorry state, unsurprisingly, so Hale pulled two bodies from them, made one good one and then moulded from this to create the Bugle 2, which had an 82½in wheelbase. He also took the opportunity to revise the styling a little, and it now only required a 12in shortening of the Beetle floorpan. By this time he was concentrating on the launch of his own all-new GT Buggy (*qv*), and so the Bugle went on the back burner, by which time he'd sold around ten Bugle 2s.

Brothers Tony and Rob Armstrong, based in Chelmsford, Essex, then took over and have further revised the Bugle, even making one in 2005 for Channel 4 TV's *T4 On The Beach* programme. They also plan a long wheelbase Bugle 3 version.

The Bugle can lay claim to several buggy 'firsts'. It was allegedly the first 100 per cent street legal beach buggy in the UK, it had the first weathergear AND was the first to feature a Metalflake finish!

Lotusmere 1970–71
Bugle Development & Marketing Ltd 1971–72
CW Autos 1979–85
GT Mouldings 1995–2003
Bugle Buggies 2003 to date
Approx 871 made

BUGLE BUGGY PLUS 2

Lotusmere proprietor Roland Sharman came up with a long-wheelbase version of the standard Bugle, based on an unmodified VW Beetle floorpan. Despite a high-profile launch at the Custom Car Show at Crystal Palace, it didn't sell anything like as many as the original.

Lotusmere 1970–72
CW Autos 1979–85
Approx 20 made

BUGRAT – *see SV2000*

BULLOCK B1/B

Best described as a quirky 2+2 from Shepperton-based Andrew Ainsworth. Based around Ford Anglia running gear, the first B1 had bulbous headlight 'pods' to enable them to clear the front suspension, while the Mk2 'B2' was amended and featured Triumph Herald suspension and less obvious headlights.

Ainsworth Engineering 1972–73
Approx 36 made

BURGHWALLIS

A vintage limousine-type kit from Alan Beillby of Heritage Motor Company/Vintage Motor Company of Doncaster.
Heritage Motor Company/ Vintage Motor Company 1996– 2002
Approx 6 made

BURLINGTON ARROW

If you were turned on by NG's products in the early '80s and couldn't afford one, but were a dab-hand mechanically, then Haydn Davies could sell you a set of plans to build one of his Arrow roadsters. The plans cost around £15 and you could then set about

creating your alloy-skinned plywood body before fitting it to a Triumph chassis (either Spitfire, Herald or Vitesse), although an MGB-based version was available later. Burlington could supply radiator surround, scuttle panel, front wings, rear differential and running boards. Haydn estimates that he sold around 6,000 sets of plans for the Arrow and Berretta, although it's believed about 10 per cent were actually built.
Burlington Motor Company 1982–92
Approx 600 made (including Berretta)

BURLINGTON BERRETTA

As per the Arrow (above), although this one had flowing wings and used Burlington's own steel chassis if you didn't want to recommission a Triumph one. Haydn can still sell you a set of plans now if you want to build one, although these days blueprints have given way to CD-ROM.
Burlington Motor Company 1985 to date
See Burlington Arrow

BURLINGTON CENTURION

Plans-based kit from America, offered there by Quincy-Lynn Enterprises while it was imported to the UK briefly by Burlington Motor Company's Haydn Davies. Some 80,000 sets of plans were sold Stateside.
Burlington Motor Company 1985–87
Approx 1 made (UK)

BURLINGTON CHIEFTAIN

Another plans-based kit. If you wanted a short-wheelbase version you used a Triumph Spitfire; if you had a long-wheelbase requirement you used a Triumph Herald. Plan sets cost a tenner. Some 500 sets were sold.
Burlington Motor Company 1983–92
Approx 150 made

BURLINGTON SS

Haydn Davies' Burlington SS was underpinned by Triumph mechanicals, and it didn't just look like a Morgan either, as it used the Malvern company's nosecone and flowing wings! A combi plywood and GRP body was skinned in aluminium. Doors arrived in 1982, as did alternative chassis options for Ford Escort, MGB and Morris Marina. Although it looked nothing like the Gentry, Haydn was inspired by that car. Burlington sold 120 kits.

Project was taken over by Dorian Motor Company in 1986, run by father and son team Brian and Martin Doran. They were asked by Haydn Davies to make a centre body tub mould for the car and eventually took over the project completely when it became the Dorian SS (qv). Resurrected briefly in 1990 by Neil Duncan of Dorchester.
Burlington Motor Company 1980–86
Dorian Motor Company 1986–88, 1990
Approx 200 made

BUROCHE

The Buroche, from a St Albans company, was a short-lived aluminium bodyshell with cycle wings that was designed to fit the Ford E93A chassis. Its styling was similar to a front-engined Ferrari GP racer of the time.
Buroche Components Ltd 1954
Approx 4 made

BUTTERFIELD MUSKETEER

Created by Richard Butterfield, who based himself at his father's business (Dovecote Nursery) in Nazeing, Essex. The Musketeer has the distinction of being the first Mini-based kit car. Don't forget, the Mini was very new back then and Butterfield's project was offered as a coupé or a convertible and used all-new Mini engines (either 850cc or 1,000cc) and components, which were mounted in a strong multi-tube chassis. Only four were sold, mainly due to price – at £848 it cost twice as much as a new Mini! Genius! It was left to later kits to fully cash in on the Mini's obvious appeal.
Butterfield Engineering 1961–63
Approx 4 made

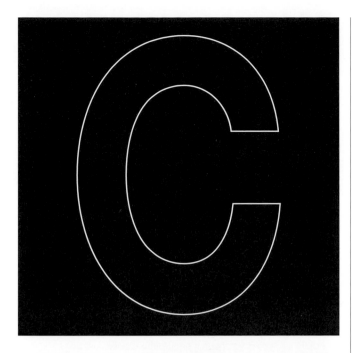

CABURN ROADSTER See HADLEIGH SPRINT

CALVY MITCHEL

Calvy, run by deep-sea diver Richard Calvy, began life as NG agents and general kit car builders, known as Constructacar and based at Southend Airport. So when they launched their own car in 1983 that bore more than a passing resemblance to an NG TC (*qv*), NG boss Nick Green was not best pleased. Indeed, NG took their grievances through the courts and Calvy was forced to redesign the Mitchel, underpinning it with a ladderframe chassis and revising the styling too, although it remained based on MGB mechanicals.

A fire devastated Calvy's factory in 1984 and he sold the project to father and son team, Michael and Liam McGivern, later that year. Incidentally, the latter would later become the landlord of The Bell Inn, located in Stilton, Cambridgeshire.

Kidderminster-based John Jones was the final custodian of the Calvy Mitchel. He introduced a 2+2 version, with rear suspension changed from MGB to Fiat 131.
Calvy Car Company 1983–84
Calvy Motor Company 1984–92
Calvy Motors 1992–95
Approx 53 made

CAMBER GT

Designed by George Holmes, an agricultural engineer based in Camber Sands, East Sussex. His friend Derek Bishop, from Greenwich, had previously run Heron Plastics and had been responsible for the Heron Europa (*qv*). The Camber GT was

underpinned by a square tube steel chassis with Mini subframes and mechanicals while the body was a hefty GRP affair reinforced with steel, with a bulbous front-end dictated by a front engine installation.

The car was launched at the Racing Car Show in 1967. Manufactured by Camber Cars of Rye and marketed by car accessory specialists, Checkpoint Ltd. The headlights were found to be illegally low, although Checkpoint did modify the sixth (and final) car built with rectangular units.

Holmes fell out with Checkpoint and revised the car back at his East Sussex base, where it became known as the Maya GT (*qv*).
Checkpoint Ltd 1967
Approx 6 made

CAMBRIDGE BODYSHELL

Cambridge Engineering was a well-known tuning and accessories company founded by Bill Williams and based in Kew, West London. The company also offered their own MG-inspired

two-seater shell for Austin 7 chassis. Purchased the Speedex range of cars and accessories in 1962.
Cambridge Engineering 1958–67
Approx 150 made

CANDY APPLE FINALE

The brainchild of Danbury-based ex-Formula 1 driver Peter Ashdown. A swoopy body conversion for the Pontiac Fiero. Eurosport made the GRP panels and Tony Claydon did the design.
Candy Apple Cars 1991–2000
Approx 32 made

CANDY APPLE FINO

More of the same from Candy Apple Cars. Another body conversion for the Pontiac Fiero, it was Ashdown's last model before emigrating to America.
Candy Apple Cars 1999–2001
Approx 8 made

CAPRICORN

Curious Mini-based Willy's Jeep lookalike from a Wakefield company that wasn't around for long.
Capricorn Cars 1985
Approx 1 made

CAPTAIN BEETLE

As the name implied, a VW Beetle conversion package.
Captain VW Ltd 1987–89
Approx 1 made

CAR 289

Bridlington-based company offered a range of imported kits for a time in the 1980s.
Classic Automotive Reproductions 1983–84
Approx 1 made

CAR 427

Imported US Cobra replica.
Classic Automotive Reproductions 1983–84
Approx 2 made

CAR COUNTACH

American import.
Classic Automotive Reproductions 1983–84
Approx 4 made

CAR D-TYPE

Jaguar replica imported from America.
Classic Automotive Reproductions 1983–84
Approx 1 made

CAR SSK

American kit imported to the UK by Bridlington-based Classic Automotive Reproductions. Based on VW Beetle.
Classic Automotive Reproductions 1983–84
Approx 1 made

CAR T70

Another American import from Classic Automotive Reproductions.
Classic Automotive Reproductions 1983–84
Approx 1 made

CAR TESTAROSSA

Another American kit.
Classic Automotive Reproductions 1983–84
Approx 1 made

CAR CRAFT CYCLONE

The exciting follow-up to the Noddy-like Zero (see next entry), and one of the most capable kit cars of all time, even if the styling wasn't to everyone's taste. A superb and original update on the Lotus Seven theme. Vauxhall power, usually in turbocharged C20LET 2.0-litre guise, gave it great performance.

Taken over for a very short while by Mark Lawrence and Paul Garside, who were based in Manchester. It's believed that the partners had a disagreement and that the moulds were literally chopped up. A massive shame. One of the greats.
Car Craft Engineering 1994–2000
Lawrence Garside Engineering (LGE) 2000
Approx 32 made

CAR CRAFT ZERO

Noddy-like car that put Lytham St Annes-based Car Craft on the map before father and son team, Terry and Leigh Whiteman, moved on to the highly exciting Cyclone (see above). Project purchased by Pete Magatti of the Fiat Recycling Centre in South Norwood, London, who traded as Zero Engineeing.
Car Craft Engineering 1991–95
Zero Engineering 1995–2004
Approx 21 made

CARIBBEAN CUB/COB

Designed by John Crosthwaite of Tamworth, Staffordshire, a former Reliant engineer whose little Moke-esque kit used Kitten or Fox mechanicals (although if the customer opted for Reliant Robin parts a separate ladderframe was required). Most ended up being exported to the West Indies, ideal territory given the holiday-friendly styling. The body was made from glassfibre with low step-in/out sides, while a windscreen was an optional extra. The Cub had four seats while the Cob was a two-seat pickup variant.
Reef Engineering 1981–83
Approx 46 made

CARISMA CENTURY

Created by Andy Hobbs and Glyn Ford from their base in Sandy, Bedfordshire, this was originally based on the Ford Cortina and was an approximation of the Jaguar SS100. It passed through several hands over the years and quality improved over its various incarnations. A 2+2 version was unveiled in 1991.

Taken over by Robert Taylor of Scorhill, a four-seat version called the Manhattan was introduced in 1993, while the original remained known as the Century.
Carisma Engineering 1989–92   Scorhill Motors 1992–93
Scorhill Motor Company 1993–96
Approx 35 made

CARISMA MANHATTAN

Four-seater version of the Carisma Century (see above) introduced in 1993 by Scorhill Motors. Not very popular.
Scorhill Motors 1992–93
Scorhill Motor Company 1993–96
Approx 2 made

CARLTON C400

An intended replica of a mid-sixties De Tomaso Pantera that Carlton's Stuart Allatt had taken a mould off. The car was never launched but intended for Ford Granada donor parts with a backbone chassis, double wishbone suspension and Rover V8.
Carlton Automotive 1990
Approx 1 made (but completed?)

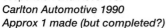

CARLTON CARRERA

Could be described as the kit car industry's attempt at Ford Capri meets Datsun 260Z, although its donor was the Ford Cortina. A true single donor vehicle. Although the styling wasn't to everyone's taste it was a sturdy and capable kit car. Highly prized by owners. First versions used four-cylinder engines before Rover V8 and Jaguar V12 options were introduced.
Carlton Automotive 1985–94
Approx 154 made

CARLTON COMMANDO

Stuart Allatt was a Barnsley-based civil engineer and got bitten by the kit car bug when he built a Nova (*qv*). He wanted his friend Dave Peasant, a mechanic, to build a utility-type kit, but by 1981 the pair had started creating what would become the Carlton Commando, which was launched in 1983. It kind of latched on to the success of the fierce-selling Dutton Sierra (*qv*), although the Commando was bigger and more practical. It was based on Ford Cortina mechanicals, including the windscreen, and a hugely strong steel tube chassis and large GRP body. Options available included pickup, flatbed and six-wheeler. Peasant built a six-wheeled version, complete with articulated trailer, which he used to deliver kits.
Carlton Automotive 1983–94
Approx 402 made

CATERHAM SEVEN

For many years, Caterham Cars' Graham Nearn was an agent for Lotus Cars before becoming sole concessionaire for the Seven. In 1973 his Surrey-based company acquired the product outright, although at the time it was in Series 4 guise. After some 35 were sold he took the bold step of reverting to the Series 3 that Lotus had stopped making in 1970. To say it was an inspired move is an understatement. Each passing year sees the cars – showroom in Caterham Valley with production in Dartford – enhanced ever further. 2005 saw the Nearn family sell out to venture capitalists, Corven, with new MD Ansar Ali at the helm.

A dizzying array of Sevens have appeared over the years from mild to wild and all points in between.

Motoring doesn't get any purer or more exciting. In 2011, Malaysian businessman Tony Fernandes (Lotus F1, Equate Energy drink, Queen's Park Rangers to name a few) became the owner of Caterham Cars. Ansar Ali remained in charge.
Caterham Cars 1973 to date
Approx 18,000 made

HIT KIT

CATERHAM SEVEN CSR

Still a Seven but different. Created by former technical director Jez Coates, the CSR was wider, with revised interior, chassis, inboard dampers and independent rear suspension instead of the S3's de Dion arrangement. First Caterham models with Ford Duratec power in 2.0- and 2.3-litre guises, initially tuned by Cosworth before Caterham's own CPT division took over.
Caterham Cars 2004 to date
Approx 250 made

CATERHAM 21

The brainchild of Caterham's former technical director Jez Coates, who created this modern two-seater with enveloping flowing body style based on the Seven's chassis equipped with outriggers launched at the same time as the Lotus Elise, which probably didn't help.
Caterham Cars 1997–2001
Approx 49 made

CAV GT

South African product instigated by the well-known entrepreneur and former manager of Sir Stirling Moss, André Loubser, along with James Fischer and Oliver McCloud. The duo had previously co-invented the Snake Board (a skateboard-type device) and were looking to invest in a new venture. Loubser had acquired one of Rudy Malan's KCC kits that itself had KVA origins and contracted a chap called Norman Lewis to rebuild it for him. There then followed an aborted tie-up with GTD before they went it alone under the Cape Advanced Vehicles banner, named in honour of Ford Advanced Vehicles.

Initially produced a GT40 underpinned by a spaceframe chassis, the first of which was completed in 2000, but in 2001 a decision was made to switch to a stainless steel monocoque.

First available in the UK via Captain Rick Chattell MBE and his Thruxton Sports Cars operation from 2003.

CAV ceased trading in 2004 and the cars were no longer available for a time until ex-CAV production manager Jean Fourie and friend John Spence formed a new company, Auto Futura, which took over and replaced the 100-series cars, as the originals have subsequently become known. The improved version arrived on these shores in 2005 under the A1 Autocraft banner before current custodians GT40 Supercars took over in 2007. Some 200 CAVs have been sold thus far worldwide.

The original cars were available in kit form, but once Auto Futura acquired the marque, fully-built only was the norm, until James Sutcliffe and Andy Waters of GT40 Supercars persuaded the factory to allow them to offer an 'all-the-bits-in-a-box' package that contains, er, all the bits in a big box!

GT40 Supercars Ltd has also recently introduced their new trackday version called the CAV GTR, which has a delightful specification including Rose joints throughout and a 400bhp Ford engine as entry-level power unit.
Thruxton Sportscars 2001–2
A1 Autocraft 2005–7
GT40 Supercars Ltd 2007 to date
Approx 25 made (UK)

CCT 7

Lotus Seven-inspired sports car aimed at the budget market. Came from Beverley-based City & County Training Ltd, with the car operation run by Joe Lord.
CCT Kitcars Ltd 2006–7
Approx 10 made

CEE VEE SPORT 602

A metal-bodied two-seater conversion on the Citroën 2CV from East Sussex-based Deux Chevaux specialist and former TV producer Andrew Gardner, initially of Bodiam before moving to South Godstone, Surrey.
Andrew Gardner Cars 2000
Approx 1 made

CERITY R

Revised and renamed version of the CHAD Supersport 4 (see below) taken over by Bristol-based businessman Arthur Thompson.
CH Automotive 1998–2000
Approx 2 made

CHAD SUPERSPORT 4

An exciting four-seat sportscar design from the talented Tony Claydon, based in Maldon, Essex, who successfully raced a variety of TVRs, Lotus Elans and Pipers in the sixties and seventies.

Tony designed building frontages, such as pub façades and also boat interiors, while he also penned several cars such as Tara 2, a design that was apparently almost picked up by Aston Martin. It reached kit production based on Ford Sierra mechanicals with Rover V8 the suggested engine.

The SS4 was a very sophisticated package featuring a steel-tube-backbone spaceframe chassis with a full perimeter frame, an integral rollcage, and steel-framed doors. The car became the Cerity R (qv).

Claydon Hamilton Automotive Design 1995–98
Approx 3 made

CHALLEMOE

Lotus Seven-inspired budget offering from a Scottish company run by a chap called Gordon Fordyce, based in Edinburgh.
Challenge Motorsport Engineers 2005
Approx 5 made

CHALLENGER

Not quite a replica of the Lotus X1 but pretty close. Created by Mark Bean of Titan Motorsport before passing to Darren George of GTS Tuning, who amended the rear suspension to his own design de Dion set-up. Not for the purists as power came from a bike engine.
Titan Motorsport 2001–5
GTS Tuning 2005-9
Approx 5 made

CHALLENGER AC428 FRUA REPLICA

An intended replica of this very rare (only four made) special-bodied AC 428 that appeared on the Triple C Challenger Cars price-lists for about six months in 1989. It's doubtful whether the company supplied any.
Triple C Challenger Cars 1989
Approx 1 made

CHALLENGER E-TYPE REPLICA

The idea for this E-type replica came over a few pints in a pub in Mevagissey, Cornwall, involving Derek Robinson and John Wilkinson. Robinson was a former maths teacher who had attempted to build a Kingfisher Mouldings Legend E-type replica, without much success.

Having left teaching in 1974, he was at the time working as a service reception manager at a car dealership, while John was an engineer at English China Clay – he'd previously built two Westfields and a Birchfield, and just happened to own a Series 1 3.8-litre Drophead Jaguar E-type, from which the Challenger was moulded (after a bit of persuasion from Derek!). A chap called Lex Bray was also heavily involved in the operation.

The duo were soon in business in St Austell as Car Care Clinic, aka 'Triple C'. They called their replica the Challenger, to which Jaguar apparently gave their blessing, even though early ones were based on Ford Cortina mechanicals, occasionally with Rover V8 power. These can be distinguished by slightly flared arches. It wasn't long before they revamped the car for Jaguar components, engineered by Goodyears Steve Green and ex-Costin employee Paul Crab.

Having tried to secure development grants to assist their growing business the pair discovered that aid wasn't available to established Cornish companies, only to attract new businesses *to* Cornwall. However, Robinson soon found out that other regions were actively looking to attract companies, so in 1987 Triple C moved to Corby, Northamptonshire, becoming Challenger Cars in the process.

Corby saw the release of the much-improved Mk2, which featured a Costin Drake Technology chassis, some 133kg lighter than the Mk1 and a considerable 334kg less than an original E-type.

1992 saw another move, to the Scottish border town of Newtown St Boswells, where they became Challenger Automotive Developments, later Reiver Motor Car Company. Due to prices of original E-types dropping at the time there wasn't really a need for the Triple C Challenger, which was a shame because it was one of the great kit cars. Reiver, incidentally, also made the AC428 and Ecosse for a time and was run by Martin Frost and Peter Gasgoyne, with a southern office in Southampton manned by Tony Cavell and Laurence Sayers-Gillen.

The Challenger was resurrected by Nick Ramsay of Avon Coachworks of Timsbury near Bristol in 1996, but a devastating factory fire in 1999 put paid to the project.

Other Triple C kits included the Malibu (qv), the Invicta Tredecim (qv) for a short while, and also the Pastiche Henley (qv), formerly the NG TF.
Car Care Clinic 1985–87
Triple C Challenger Cars 1987–93
Challenger Automotive Developments 1993
Reiver Motor Car Company 1993
Avon Coach Works 1996–99
Approx 250 made

CHALLENGER JAGUAR XJ13 REPLICA

Joining Triple C's Jaguar replicas was an intended XJ13 replica although it's not known if they actually supplied any. Formerly the Tredicim project.

Triple C Challenger Cars 1989–90
Approx 1 made

CHALLENGER LIGHTWEIGHT E-TYPE REPLICA

Inspired by the Coombs Lightweight of 1962, underpinned by Jaguar mechanicals and featuring a superb aluminium body. Expensive; just two made.

Car Craft Centre/Triple C
Challenger Cars 1988–89
Approx 2 made

CHALLENGER MERCEDES-BENZ 300 SL REPLICA

An American kit that Triple C planned to import to the UK.

Triple C Challenger Cars
1989–90
Approx 1 made

CHALLENGER PORSCHE 959 REPLICA

In addition to their core E-type replicas, Triple C also offered – or planned to offer – several American import kits, although it's doubtful if any of these were ever sold. A Porsche 959 of American origin was one of these.

Triple C Challenger Cars 1989–90
Approx 1 made

CHAMONIX 356

Brazilian-made Speedster replica that has been produced in its homeland since 1987. Sold in America for many years. VW Beetle underpinnings, although a separate spaceframe reinforcement adds rigidity. First sold briefly in the UK in 2002 by Ginetta specialist Spadge Hopkins at Cottage Classics, before Captain Rick Chattell MBE

at Thruxton Sportscars had another go. Terry Watson, boss of erstwhile Thruxton agent Tribute Sports Cars, then took over, keeping a low profile but selling a few all the same. Tribute merged with Chris Holly's Reincarations operation in early 2009.

Cottage Classics 2002
Thruxton Sports Cars 2006–7
Tribute Sports Cars 2007–9
Reincarations 2009 to date
Approx 15 made

CHAMONIX 550 SPYDER

Sister car to the Chamonix 356 (see above), their 550 Spyder has been around for just as long. There were two versions, a VW Beetle type and an 'S' variant using a water-cooled VW unit. First sold briefly in the UK by Lee Noble in the early '90s.

Cottage Classics 2002 | *Thruxton Sports Cars 2006–7*
Tribute Sports Cars 2007–9 | *Reincarations 2009-10*
Approx 10 made

CHARGER

Evolved out of the Chepeko (*qv*), which itself had been spawned by the Siva Saluki (*qv*). Embeesea was a High Wycombe company run by Mike Carlton, who had formerly worked for Neville Trickett at Siva. They changed their name to MBC in 1983, at which point Peter Dance joined the operation.

DJ Sportscars acquired the project after the demise of MBC. They kept it for a couple of years before a Welsh outfit called MDB came on the scene, renaming it the MDB Saratoga (*qv*). It subsequently moved back to Essex under the control of Viking Cars and became known as the Viking Dragon Fire (*qv*).

Embeesea Cars 1977–83 | *MBC Cars 1983–84*
DJ Sportscars 1984–86 | *MDB Sports Cars 1986–87*
Viking Cars 1987–88
Approx 420 made

CHARGER 2

Mike Carlton developed the Charger 2 as a 2+2 version of the original car, although it didn't just have an extra row of seats as the body was heavily revised. Project sold to DJ Sportscars along with standard Charger in 1984. Went to MDB, where it was known as the MDB Saturn (*qv*), before Thundersley-based Viking took over and renamed it the Viking Dragon Fly (*qv*). Confused? Phew!

Embeesea Cars 1982–83 | *MBC Cars 1983–84*
DJ Sportscars 1984–86 | *MDB Cars 1986–87*
Viking Cars 1987–88
Approx 90 made

CHEETAH GT40

Probably not the most respected
GT40 replica ever made.
Cheetah Cars 1983
Approx 1 made

CHEETAH MIRACH

The Newcastle upon Tyne
company's first model, launched
in 1983. The man behind the
operation was Kevin Mason.
Loose approximation of a
Lamborghini Miura replica. Used
a real mixture of parts from

Alfasud engine to Cortina windscreen, and was described even by the
manufacturer as being difficult to build! Dropped very quickly in favour
of the Mirach 2 (see next entry).
Cheetah Cars 1983
Approx 1 made

CHEETAH MIRACH 2

Launched at the Stoneleigh show
of 1984, this one looked a little
more like a Miura thanks to the
restyled body. Based on Jaguar
XJ6 or Ford Granada, with three
distinct versions available: mid-
engined with Alfasud engine, a
semi-monocoque with Ford XR3
CVH, or front engined with Ford V6 or Rover V8 power.
Cheetah Cars 1984–86
Approx 3 made

CHEETAH SHAMAL

Never the most critically acclaimed
company, Cheetah Cars at least
believed in offering the customer
choices. If you were tempted by
the Shamal's swoopy looks in
1984 then you could choose from
2+2 mid-engined type based on
the Lancia Beta; front-engined,
rear-wheel drive variant using Ford Escort XR3; and two-seater, mid-
engined or front-engined front-wheel drive both powered by Alfasud.
Cheetah Cars 1984–86
Approx 2 made

CHEETAH SV1

Lancia Beta or Alfasud-based convertible.
Cheetah Cars 1985–86
Approx 1 made

CHEETAH VIPER

Cobra replica that used a
combination of Triumph and Ford
Cortina/Granada components
with a galaxy of engine choices.
Had a very strangely mounted MG
windscreen.
Cheetah Cars 1984–86
Approx 11 made

CHEPEKO

Was the Siva Saluki (*qv*).
Revamped by former Neville
Trickett employee Mike Carlton.
After the revision, the basic outline
of the Chepeko was still visible.
Became the Charger (*qv*).
Embeesea Cars 1975–77
Approx 20 made

CHESIL RS60

Unveiled by the Angus McCubbin/
Jerry Baker-era Chesil operation,
the RS60 appeared briefly in late
2005/early 2006. Aimed at the
burgeoning trackday market,
it was a replica of the glorious
Porsche racers of the early '60s.
Potentially very good, weighing
in at under 500kg, powered by an Arnie Levics-prepared air-cooled
engine, with a proposed price of £26,500.
Chesil Motor Company 2005–6
Approx 2 made

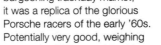

CHESIL 550 SPYDER

Always in the shadow of the company's mainstay Chesil Speedster
(*qv*) model, this is an import from German company Rudolph, whose
Karmann Ghia was also imported to the UK by Evergreen Motor
Company.
Chesil Motor Company 1996–2004
Chesil 2004–7
Tygan 2007–8
Chesil Motor Company 2008
Approx 5 made

CHESIL SPEEDSTER

A superb 356 replica created by Chris Boyle of Street Beetle, picked up by Peter Bailey of eponymous Chesil Beach-based company. Very quickly became a kit car industry icon. Bailey sold it to a new company in 2004 run by Angus McCubbin and Jerry Bailey, who ceased trading in 2007. Another operation, Tygan, took over and moved to new premises, but concentrated on fully-built cars before also ceasing trading at the end of 2008. Peter Bailey returned and relaunched his Chesil company at his former base in early 2009.

A major development came in October 2010, with the announcement of a collaboration with American company Inrekor, and the use of the advanced Composite Chassis Technology (CCT) aluminium and polypropylene sandwich construction that was offered as an option instead of the erstwhile VW Beetle floorpan. This meant that alternative engines could be used for those customers who wanted a more sophisticated vehicle with more power and performance potential.

Chesil Motor Company 1991–2004
Chesil 2004–7
Tygan 2007–8
Chesil Motor Company 2009 to date
Approx 500 made

CHEVRON B8

The Chevron B8 had originally been built by Derek Bennett back in the 1960s. Classic car racer and Chevron expert Roger Andreason, based in the wonderfully named Piddletrenthide, reintroduced it in 1992, with kit versions available from 1994. The 44 original Derek Bennett cars had used BMW power, but Andreason replaced this with Alfa or Ford twin-cams. The cars were built by Scott Ellis Racing. Andreason sold the rights and moulds in 2007 to Westfield founder Chris Smith, who has since relaunched the car – with BMW engine – in fully-built guise, with a £100,000+ price tag.

Chevron Cars 1992–98
Approx 8 made

CHEVRON B16

Roger Andreason relaunched the iconic Chevron B16 in 1990, with kit versions available from 1994. It was similar to the original and had a semi-spaceframe chassis with monocoque centre tub, aluminium sills and floors with a GRP body. Power came from Cosworth YB 2.0-litre turbo, with the V6 from the Alpine A610 an option.

Chevron Cars 1990–98
Approx 3 made

CHEVRON PICK-ME-UP

As far from the classic Chevron ethos as possible, the Pick-Me-Up was a Metro-based utility with a box-like shape and a body made from GRP and aluminium panels, all underpinned by a sturdy steel tube chassis.

THE CHEVRON 'PICK-ME-UP'
A New Concept in Multi-Purpose vehicles

PRACTICAL · VERSATILE · INEXPENSIVE

Chevron Cars 1994–98
Approx 2 made

CHIKARA

First Škoda Estelle-based kit car. Came from a Llanelli-based company but didn't last long. The only car produced was commissioned by a chap named Peter Titterton. It was brought back briefly in 1994 by a Brackley-based operation run by Alan Wilkins.

Skorpion Car Company 1986–87
SK Distributors 1994–95
Approx 1 made

CHILTON

Bugatti Type 35 replica available very briefly.

Chilton Engineering 1981
Approx 1 made

CHIMERA – *see AD 400*

CHUBSTER

From Great British Sportscars. Basically a 40mm wider Zero (*qv*) model, with a floor lowered by 30mm. Launched in October 2010, and christened by this author when the company was struggling for a name. By the time this book is published, it could well be called something different!

Great British Sportscars 2010 to date
Approx 35 made

CIPHER

Created by Professor Anthony Stevens, the Cipher is rated by many as one of the best kit car designs ever and a real 'one that got away'. Stevens had previously designed some Ford Transit-based period style vans and also the stillborn Sienna in 1979 that Bonito makers ACM looked at resurrecting in 1982.

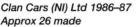

Peter Bird, later of Falcon Designs, was involved with the Cipher, which was based on a lowered and widened Reliant Kitten chassis; indeed, the Tamworth manufacturer actually built the prototype.

The chassis had an additional steel structure fitted, while there was a live axle at the rear and an aluminium 848cc Reliant engine supplying the power. Bird launched the Cipher as a kit package in 1983 before Stevens revamped it to run on Renault mechanicals, with the intention of selling it as a fully-built vehicle.

Anthony Stevens Designs Ltd 1976–80
Cipher Cars 1980–83
Falcon Design 1983–84
Stevens Cars 1984–86
Approx 12 made

CIRRUS

It was Roland Kerr who came up with this quirky-looking Mini-based beach buggy that was shown for the first and only time at the Racing Car Show of 1971.

Roland Kerr 1971
Approx 1 made

CK COBRA/CK427

Originally known as the Gravetti 427 (*qv*) before becoming the GE427. Came to rest at Bob Egginton's ASD operation in Maidstone, Kent. Quality improved greatly, but perhaps the past stigma remained.

CK Automotive (part of ASD) 1989–98
Approx 12 made

CLAN

Northern Irish resurrection of the well-known Clan marque, although one that didn't have the blessing of the original car's creator, Paul Hassauer. The man behind this project was Peter McCandless, who gave the car wider arches and pop-up headlights, with an industrial-use version of the Hillman Imp engine supplying the 'go'.

Clan Cars (NI) Ltd 1982–87
Approx 130 made

CLAN CLOVER

A mid-mounted Alfa Romeo Alfasud-based version of the Clan (see previous entry). Still clearly identifiable but heavily reworked styling, with sleek body, pumped-up arches and revised interior.

Clan Cars (NI) Ltd 1986–87
Approx 26 made

CLAN CRUSADER

Based in a huge 23,000sq ft factory in Washington New Town, County Durham, the Clan Crusader was the brainchild of former Lotus-man Paul Hassauer. It has to go down in history as one of the greatest specialist cars ever made.

Designed by John Frayling (Lotus Elite, Lola T70 and McCoy) with input from Arthur Birchall, it featured a GRP monocoque with Hillman Imp engine and running gear, and enjoyed very healthy sales at first until a problem with component supply from Chrysler caused serious damage. Project was then sold to a Cyprus-based haulage company.

Clan Cars 1971–74
Approx 350 made

CLASSIC 120

A superb replica of the Jaguar XK120 from Somerset company Nostalgia Cars UK Ltd, run by Chris Boyer, Simon Davis and Malcolm Rolfe. The latter retired in 2006, leaving Chris and Simon to continue building a superb range of cars. Their skills as classic

car restorers shine through on their replicas. Company acquired by mother and son, Heather and Matthew Ambrose in November 2011, but still based at the same Creech St Michael premises.

Nostalgia Cars UK Ltd 1998 to date
Approx 100 made

CLASSIC 140

It was a logical move for Nostalgia Cars to follow their XK120 replica with its Jaguar successor, the XK140.
Nostalgia Cars UK Ltd 2000 to date
Approx 75 made

CLASSIC 356

Martin Craven was the man behind Classic Roadsters, who imported Jürgen Möhr's range of Dresden-made VW replicas. Möhr, of course, was the creator of the Rush model, one of which was later made with great success by DJ Sportscars.
Classic Roadsters 2005-8
Approx 3 made (UK)

CLASSIC 550 SPYDER

German-made Porsche 550 Spyder replica made by Jürgen Möhr and imported by Classic Roadsters.
Classic Roadsters 2005-8
Approx 3 made (UK)

CLASSIC C-TYPE

Very well done Jaguar C-type replica available from Andy Thomas at Classic Chassis Services Ltd of Leighton Buzzard. Very close to original with aluminium body.

In late 2010, Andy Thomas stopped making C-type replicas under his own name, and joined forces with the recently relaunched Lynx Cars operation run by Tony Gott.
Classic Chassis Services Ltd 2007–2010
Approx 10 made

CLASSIC ENGLISH RACING AUTOMOBILES C-TYPE

Hampshire-based company run by John Gregson, who made a Jaguar C-type replica underpinned by Jaguar Mk2 or all-torsion bar suspension. He also made a D-type. Took over the Proteus marque in 2000 before selling it to Enduro Cars in 2006 who, despite marketing heavily and coming up with a coupé version of the C-type, ceased trading in 2008.
Classic ERA 1991–2000
Approx 45 made

CLASSIC GTO

Engineer/toolmaker Charles Wilson wanted to import an American Alpha 250 GTO replica to these shores but they would only supply their kits in bulk. Instead, Chas and businessman friend, Mike Chieseman, devised their own similar Datsun 240/260Z-based conversion. The GTO retained its original donor interior; a replica 250 GTO version was also available. Classic Sportscars was part of Lipco Engineering (founded in 1977) and was based in Ringwood, in the New Forest.
Classic Sportscars Ltd 1986–89
Approx 20 made

CLASSIC REPLICAS DINO 246 GTS

Inspired by the Deon DGT (*qv*) and, of course, the original Dino. Company run by haulier Gordon Ainsby and based in Somerset.
Classic Replicas UK 2001-9
Approx 35 made

CLASSIC REPLICAS MULE

Inspired by the Mini Moke, the Mini-based Mule was launched in 1998 by Classic Replicas, Ken Cook's next venture after Brightwheel Replicas.
Classic Replicas 1998–2002
Approx 50 made

CLASSIC REPLICAS VIPER & VIPER4

Ken Cook's Viper and its budget-orientated Viper4 sibling were good Cobra replicas with very strong chassis that sold in good numbers. Late 1995 saw the introduction of steel bulkheads, footwells and floors to the chassis.
Classic Replicas 1989–2002
Approx 150 made

CLASSIC T6

The T6 was the last derivative of the Porsche 356.
Classic Roadsters 2005-8
Approx 2 made (UK)

CN SPRINT

The CN Sprint, produced by Lotus dealers Christopher Neil Sportscars of Northwich, Cheshire, run by Christopher Dunscombe and Neil Shepherdson, used a backbone chassis and was a close replica of the Lotus Elan. Obviously, the car used Elan components, although a CVH engine could also be used. Chassis was made by Jago Automotive.

In late 1981, a full-page advert in the kit car press trumpeted the imminent launch of the National Kit Car Centre, a 10,000sq ft emporium that was intended as a general multi-marque dealership to sell a wide range of kit cars. Did it ever happen? I have my doubts…
Christopher Neil Sportscars 1984–89
Approx 120 made

COBRA SPORTS BUGGY

This was just like a GP Buggy (*qv*), and was built by the company that made the bodies for the Manta Ray (*qv*). Indeed, this was the same company's Sports Buggy (*qv*), which the Manta Ray had replaced. C&D were based in West Molesey, Surrey. Complete kits cost from £105 in March 1971, and you could choose from one of ten metalflake body colours.
C&D Automarine 1970–71
Approx 12 made

COBRETTI VIPER

Company founded by Bob and Martin Busbridge who grew up in Hampton Hill, quite close to the AC Cars factory. Bob was completely inspired by the Cobra and did his homework on what was available within the replica market. Indeed, the name Cobretti

is a conflation of Cobra and Gravetti (the first replica he looked at), and the company became agents for Brightwheel. When that company ceased trading in 1989, Cobretti maintained production. Initially based in Wallington, Surrey, moving to Morden. The Viper is available in four-, eight- or twelve-cylinder guise.
Cobretti 1989 to date
Approx 85 made

COLDWELL GT

Sheffield-based Coldwell, run by Bill Needham, was responsible for this mid-engined Mini-based two-seater.
Coldwell Engineering & Racing 1967–69
Approx 6 made

CONAN TERMINATOR

ANNOUNCING THE MOST EXACT COUNTACH REPLICA IN THE WORLD

Fully triangulated spaceframe chassis. Any V8 or V6 engine. Purpose built suspension. No large deposits.

OUR AIM IS TO HELP YOU BUILD YOUR DREAM

NOBODY DOES IT BETTER

STATE OF THE ART CHASSIS

STATE OF THE ART BODY

One of the many mid-'80s Countach replica purveyors, most of them based around the Manchester area. Conan was run by Darryl Kershaw. The Terminator was underpinned by a Lotus Esprit backbone chassis, with Rover V8 power mated to VW Beetle gearbox. If the customer wanted they could use the Veedub engine too.
Conan Cars 1986–88
Approx 12 made

CONCEPT CENTAUR

Came from a Kettering-based company run by Peter Timpson, who had been having trouble finding a chassis for a car he'd designed. A chance meeting with Marcos designers Dennis and Peter Adams resulted in him buying the body 'plug' for Probe 16 (*qv*), which he reworked, narrowing the body by 5in, giving it a new canopy-type roof and revised interior at the same time.

Timpson retained the Hillman Imp base, but with safety in mind he specified a built-in rollcage for the fibreglass monocoque for additional strength. A 2+2 version was also created, while Timpson also developed a convertible version that he named the Condor, which didn't make production.

Taken over by Biggin Hill-based Mirage Developments in 1978 before ending its days at MR Developments, Trowbridge.
Concept Developments 1974–77
Mirage Developments 1978–80
MR Developments 1980–82
Approx 25 made

CONCORD

A Barking-based company produced this nicely made bodyshell from 1960, designed for Ford 8/10 90in wheelbase. Pretty unusual for its day as it came with pre-fitted bulkheads and pre-hung doors.

Concordette Developments 1960–61
Approx 15 made

CONCORDETTE II

A development of the Concord (see above) that came with a hardtop.

Concordette Developments 1961–62
Approx 10 made

CONDESA MARQUESSA

Spanish-made version of the Siva Parisienne (*qv*), briefly imported to the UK from Majorca in 1983, and said to be 'much revised and improved'.
Condesa Cars 1983
Approx 1 made (UK)

CONTEMPORARY 427

Created by Peter Behr and originally imported to the UK by Paul Tankard from West Yorkshire. This was rated as one of the best Cobra replicas. Jim Blackburn of American Speed Specialties (initially in Beckenham, Kent, before moving to West Norwood) took over in 1991. The American manufacturer was acquired by Burt Burtis and ceased trading quite soon after, which meant difficulties for UK supply. Jim Blackburn passed away in 2000.
Contemporary Classic Motor Company 1980–91
American Speed Specialties 1991–2000
Approx 12 made (UK)

CONTINENTAL

South Shields-based Tornado Products produced this Starcraft-inspired four-berth motorhome kit that used the Ford Cortina as a donor.
Tornado Products 1989–92
Approx 6 made

CONTOUR

A trackday-orientated racer available in kit form. Designed by Suffolk-based David Dawson, formerly of Lola and Lotus, who also helped design of the Bentley Continental GT. Power came from Kawasaki ZX-12 or ZX-14 engines. Did well in the 750 MC's RGB race series.
Contour Cars 2010 to date
Approx 2 made

CONVAIR

Founded in 1955 by brothers Clive and Terry Wrenn, initially based in E2 in the heart of London's 'hard' East End before moving to Leytonstone. The Convair shell was a two-seater replacement designed to fit Ford

90in wheelbase chassis and later came with floors and dashboard pre-fitted. Became the GT in 1959 when fitted with a hardtop. Five of these were sold.

Clive went on to form Nordec Engineering, producers of the Nordec (*qv*), while Terry moved to Newark and built the TWM (*qv*), although both sold effectively the same shell.
Convair Developments 1955–59
Approx 150 made

COOL 500

Fiat 500-based little, er, Fiat fun car. Essex-based company run by Paul Miller. Not around for long before fading from view.
Cool Car Company 2004–6
Approx 10 made

COPYCATS C-TYPE

Original name for Proteus, founded by Bolton-based Jim Marland. Always a very highly-rated replica and available with either aluminium (Jaguar Mk2-based) or fibreglass (Jaguar XJ6-based) bodies. See Proteus.

Copycats 1982–87
Proteus Reproductions 1987–91
Proteus Cars 1991–99
Classic ERA 1999–2005
Enduro Cars (renamed Proteus Cars 2006) 2005–8
Proteus Cars 2009 to date
Approx 220 made

CORAM LMP

The LMP was created by Steven Turner of Coram Automotive, based in Ayrshire, and was subject to a lot of pre-launch publicity in various automotive magazines. Underpinned by a CDS, TIG-welded spaceframe chassis with Rose-jointed suspension,

and power coming from Suzuki Hayabusa, it was a stylish trackday-orientated sports car. Coram went into liquidation in October 2003.

Project was resurrected in late 2003 under the Turner Automotive banner, still run by Steven Turner, but by this time not available in kit guise. Fully-built prices started from £28,000. Power was now Kawasaki ZX-12. Turner Automotive ceased trading in 2005.

Following the 'if at first you don't succeed, try, try again' adage, the LMP reappeared again, in 2009 (with Turner still at the helm), now under the Turner Auto Design name, which is part of Glasgow-based Clyde Auto & Marine Ltd. Car said to be 20% lighter with better aerodynamics and performance. Again, not available in kit form.

Coram Automotive 2001–3   *Turner Automotive 2003–5*
Turner Auto Design 2009 to date
Approx 4 made

CORBEAU

Cool hot rod style kit based on Citroën 2CV created by Deauville Cars' Dutch agent, Danny Blaauw. Became part of the Voglie Ltd range in the Netherlands.
Deauville Cars 2007-8
Approx 3 made

CORRY CULTRA

Lisburn-based Will Corry bought the remnants of the Davrian marque. He commissioned Tony Stevens, creator of the Cipher (*qv*), to revamp its styling. Took the Davrian concept further upmarket and concentrated more on

competition (primarily rallying) use but ceased trading in 1985. Project then moved across the Irish Sea to mid-Wales and Tim Duffee's Davrian operation, where it was revised further.
Corry Car Company 1983–85
Approx 9 made

CORSE

This Lancia Stratos replica was originally known as the Allora and made by Hand Made Cars, run by Stuart Gross. Project acquired by ex-F1 engineer (René Arnoux was one of the drivers whose car he worked on) and Skipton, North Yorkshire, resident Steve Greenwood, who was later heavily involved with the Sector Three Savant (*qv*) that became the Quantum Xtreme (*qv*). He revised the Corse chassis and made many general improvements to the package before it came under the Carson Automotive Engineering banner, a company run by Hugh Carson, also based in Skipton. Subsequently passed to Lionel Gooch's Poole-based Hennessey Racing (which evolved into SuperStratos).
Litton Cars 1991–93
Carson Automotive Engineering 1993–99
SuperStratos 1999 to date
Approx 75 made

CORSE GT EVOLUZIONE

Basically a replica of the Lancia GTE Group 5 Stratos, a circuit-racing version of the Italian company's legendary rally car. Came from Lionel Gooch of SuperStratos. Created from photos and a 1/24 scale model. Nick Hennessey of Hennessey Racing was originally involved with this project.
Hennessey Racing 1999–2001
SuperStratos 2001 to date
Approx 1 made

COSTIN AMIGO

Typical low drag, streamlined two-seater from Marcos co-founder the late Frank Costin, underpinned by a plywood monocoque. Power came from a Vauxhall XE 2.0-litre. The company was based in Little Staughton, Bedfordshire.

Costin Drake Technology 1970–72
Approx 8 made

A
B
C
D
E
F
G
H
I
J
K
L
M
N
O
P
Q
R
S
T
U
V
W
X
Y
Z

COSTIN ROADSTER

Last design from the legendary Frank Costin, with input from Simon Garrett and Bill Barranco, then of IAD. After a false start intending to produce replicas of a previous Costin design, the Costin-Nathan, a new direction was taken and the first pre-production prototype appeared in 1993. The project was powered by Rover K-series engine with a triangulated spaceframe providing strength. The company was based in Wales.

Prototype number two was bought by Chris Holloway and SVA'd in 2004, with Joe Tavani of Specialist Automotive, based in Sayers Common, West Sussex, doing some work on it. He was so taken with it that he has revised it further to run on MGF mechanicals and has put it back into production.
Costin Ltd 1990–95
Specialist Automotive 2007 to date
Approx 4 made

COUNTRY CLIMBER

Short-lived, plans-built, jeep-type vehicle from Scotland that made its debut at the Scottish Kit Car Show at Ingliston in 1992.
Country Climber 1992
Approx 2 made

COUNTRY VOLKS

Bore a strong resemblance to the GP Buggy (qv) and sold in extremely good numbers.
Country Volks 1970–92
Approx 400 made

COVIN CABRIOLET

Cabriolet version of the Covin Turbo (qv) that arrived a year after the fixed-head version. Used either a VW Beetle floorpan or a bespoke spaceframe that accepted VW Variant parts. In 1992 it ended up with DJ Sportscars, who sold a further three kits. Last heard of at Grannd (sic) Performance Cars run by Richard Taylor of Luton, later of Galway in Ireland.
Covin Performance Mouldings 1985–92
DJ Sportscars 1992–95
Grannd Performance Cars 1995–98
Approx 100 made

COVIN M6 REPLICA

Less well-known Covin replica that never saw production.
Covin Performance Mouldings 1986
Approx 1 made

COVIN SE 930

It was the Porsche 935 variant of the 911 from the seventies that first saw the distinctive 'slant-nose' front-end treatment, later offered as the 930S. Covin replicated this version and based their car on the VW Type 3 Variant, using a separate bespoke backbone chassis with perimeter frame. The preferred engine option was the Ford V6 (Cologne 2.9), although Beetle or even Porsche units could be used.
Covin Performance Mouldings 1988–92
Approx 50 made

COVIN SPEEDSTER

Sister model to Covin's mainstay Porker replicas, based on VW Type 3 Variant. Always a sideline compared to their 911-inspired clones. Came to rest at Grannd (sic) Performance run by Richard Taylor, originally of Luton before he moved to Ireland.
Covin Performance Mouldings 1988–90
DJ Sportscars 1990–92
Grannd Performance Cars 1995–98
Approx 30 made

COVIN TURBO COUPÉ

Created by Essex duo Tim Cooksey and Nick Vincent (whence the 'Co Vin' name), the Covin caused a bit of a stir when it appeared in 1984. The pair exploited the fact that the 911 was out of copyright, although Porsche's lawyers were nothing if not persistent and claimed that post-73 impact bumpers and whale-tail spoiler were still covered, forcing revisions.

The Covin used a VW Beetle floorpan or a bespoke chassis with power from VW air-cooled, Ford CVH or Alfa Romeo 33 engine. The forced 'revision' had a Rinspeed-style droopsnoot.

Moved on to DJ Sportscars, where six further kits were sold before the whole lot ended up at Grannd (sic) Performance, run by Richard Taylor, in 1995.
Covin Performance Mouldings 1984–92
DJ Sportscars 1992–95
Grannd Performance Cars 1995–98
Approx 317 made

COX GTM – *see GTM Coupé*

CPC3

Originally the Noble Mk4 replica of the Ferrari P4, from Classic Performance Cars (or CPC) of Dyserth, Denbighshire, on the slopes of Hiraddug. CPC acquired the project when the Deon operation ceased trading. They marketed it as a P3 replica, which was visually identical to the P4 except that it didn't have a Perspex engine cover. Passed to Neil Foreman of NF Auto Developments in late 1995, before being sold to Dunlop Components in 2009.
Classic Performance Cars 1994–95
Approx 2 made

CR8

Years before his 164 LM project, Don Rawlson came up with a joint effort with Liberta Cars called the CR8.
Liberta Cars 1972
Approx 1 made

CR427

Superb Cobra replica from John Kerr, based on Jaguar XJ6 mechanicals. The vast majority have been fibreglass-bodied although Kerr did come up with an alloy body (one made). Regarded as one of the *very* best Cobra replicas and often powered by genuine-spec Ford FE big block V8 engine.
Crendon Replicas 1991 to date
Approx 100 made

CRS

CRS produced a box-section chassis for Ford E93A (Prefect) running gear and parts to which it was possible to fit several different proprietary bodyshells of the early sixties.
CRS 1960–61
Approx 75 made

CTR BUGGY

Very similar to the Manta Ray (*qv*) beach buggy – indeed, it was offered by a Carshalton Beeches-based company run by a former Power On Wheels customer.
CTR Developments 1971–72
Approx 17 made

CULÉBRA

American Testarossa import. Gary Roberts was the man behind the business. Did they actually bring one in? Very short-lived project.
Young Guns 1988
Approx 0 made (UK)

CURSOR

After finishing with his Bugatti replicas, Alan Hatswell of Replicar turned his attention to this quirky-looking space-age device. The majority of the production was exported to Austria, incidentally.
Replicar 1985–87
Approx 100 made

CURTANA – *see Avalon S350*

CUSTOM GLASSFIBRE C-CAB

Originally made by Ray's Rods run by Ray Christopher. When launched in 1971 was the UK's first C-Cab kit before it passed to Tom Pawley's Okehampton-based Custom Glassfibre operation.
Custom Glassfibre 1976–80
Approx 30 made

CUSTOM GLASSFIBRE FORD POP

The only Custom Glassfibre product not to have originated from Ray's Rods. This one came from ex-Marcos GRP man Pat Cuss' Fibreglass Applications operation and had been moulded from a 1953 car amended to feature wide wings and a tilting bonnet. Chassis by Hove-based Quality Rod Parts, it ran Jaguar suspension.
Fibreglass Applications 1975–78
Custom Glassfibre 1978–80
Approx 75 made

CUSTOM SPRIDGET

Conversion kit for Spridget. Came from the Derby-based company that later marketed the Shelsley Spyder (*qv*).
AG Thorpe Developments 1979–85
Approx 40 made

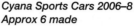

UPDATE YOUR SPRIDGET!
One-piece front in glass-fibre with flared arches for 5½J rim, Mks I-IV
STANDARD ARCH VERSION ALSO AVAILABLE

£30.00
Flares for rear £3.50 pr.

Fitting instructions supplied. Roll Cage 1⅞" O/D with Brace £9.50. Carriage 10%. Full money back guarantee.

A. G. THORPE (DEVELOPMENTS)

CWR TITAN

At the 2010 Race Retro Show, Mike Luck launched his Titan, a replica of the TVR Tuscan of 1968, using the original car's moulds for added authenticity. A spaceframe chassis with an integrated FIA-spec roll cage provides rigidity and safety, while power is provided by a GM LS3 V8 producing 480bhp. Only available fully built for about £50,000.

Mike Luck was pretty handy behind the wheel of a Westfield Eleven in the 750 Motor Club's Kit Car Challenge series back in the eighties, and in recent years has established a good reputation with his Redditch-based Classic World Racing operation, primarily restoring and preparing historic racing cars. Amalgamated with the TVR specialists David Gerald Sportscars in 2011.
Classic World Racing 2010 to date
Approx 2 made

CYANA VII

The Cyana VII was the company's first 'own' model after they had bought the Phoenix (*qv*) – previously the Sylva Striker Mk4 (*qv*) – from Stuart Taylor Motorsport and set about converting its running gear to Mazda MX-5 (see next entry). The Cyana VII was a Lotus Seven-inspired sports car created by Ian Boulton and based on Reliant Robin mechanicals.
Cyana Sports Cars 2005–7
Approx 1 made

CYANA MX-500

Derived from the Phoenix (*qv*), formerly the Sylva Striker Mk4 (*qv*), but based on Mazda MX-5 mechanicals, the MX-500 was an innovative piece of kit, using the tried and tested underpinnings of the Jeremy Phillips-derived original.
Cyana Sports Cars 2006–8
Approx 6 made

CYBERTECH

A short-lived Lamborghini Countach replica from Manchester. Made a single appearance at Stoneleigh in 1992, with a glitzy launch involving fireworks and dancing girls. Well, not quite like that but you know what I mean! After that nothing much more was heard, aside from a couple of magazine adverts.
Cybertech Developments 1992
Approx 1 made

CYGNET CYGNETINA

A stillborn convertible version of the Cygnet Monaco (see next entry). The company, based in Northampton, was run by a former Aston Martin engineer. Moved to Wootton in 1984.
Cygnet Cars 1982–85
Approx 1 made

CYGNET MONACO

Ford Cortina-based four-seater that was very angular and sadly not so exotic. Most sports cars have a 'nose-down' stance, whereas the Cygnet sloped upwards! Company based in Northampton and run by former Aston Martin engineer Peter Child. Moved to Wootten in 1984.
Cygnet Cars Ltd 1982–85
Approx 10 made

CYGNET ROADSTER

The people behind the Monaco launched their second model at the Stoneleigh Show in 1983. Shared the same Cortina underpinnings as the Cygnet. Didn't last long.
Cygnet Cars 1983
Approx 1 made

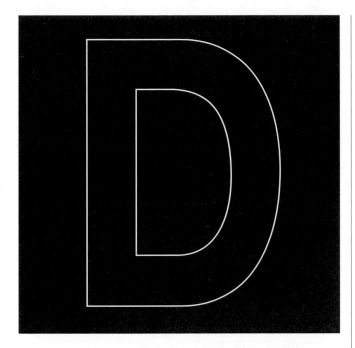

DA MONGOOSE

Short-lived three-wheeler that could be powered by a diesel engine or Honda CBR bike unit. Never reached production. Company was based in Warrington.
David Arthur 1993
Approx 1 made

DAKAR

Barry Chantler, a Kent garage proprietor, was a 4x4 enthusiast who had bought an Adams Rotrax and converted it to four-wheel drive, giving it a much beefier profile. His car appeared in the August 1990 edition of *Which Kit?* magazine. Dennis Adams was impressed and did a slight chassis redesign, then suggested that Chantler market the car as the Dakar. It really 'arrived' when Anneka Rice used one in the *Challenge Anneka* TV series.

Taken over in 2002 by Steve Bennett, who soon added a Land Rover Discovery donor option, and revitalised the kit. Steve was tragically killed in a road accident in 2007. His partner Tory Hill continues to run the company, however.
Dakar Cars 1991–2002
Dakar 4x4 Design & Conversions 2002 to date
Approx 520 made

DALESMAN

Ford Sierra-based period van range from White Rose Vehicles of Gillingham, Kent. Underpinned by a ladderframe chassis with MDF body. Models within the range included the Wharfedale delivery van and Swaledale mobile shop. Kits cost £4,995 in 1994 and included everything needed other than the donor parts.
White Rose Vehicles 1994–99
Approx 2 made

DANTE

Aluminium bodyshells of the 1950s designed to fit Austin 7 chassis. There were three models available: the Basic, the Sprint and the flared-wing Clubman. The Luton-based company was run by Robin Read, later of Lotus, who initially called his operation Robin's Sporting Motorist Agency before changing it to Dante. Jem Marsh was a salesman at the company for a time before leaving to set up Speedex and then Marcos, with Frank Costin.
Dante Engineering 1956–59
Approx 60 made

DARE G4

A relaunched Ginetta G4 from the '60s that Martin Phaff had intended to put back into production when he took over Ginetta Cars. Meanwhile, Ivor and Trevers Walklett formed DARE (UK) Ltd with Trevers' son Mark, with the initial intention to make G4s again for the Japanese market, although the car soon became available domestically, along with the G12. Trevers sadly passed away in 2000, leaving Ivor and Mark to continue. Power for this 'new' G4 comes from Ford engines.
DARE (UK) Ltd 1991 to date
Approx 150 made

DARE TG SPORT

This Ivor Walklett creation was a Lotus Seven-inspired-type car powered by Ford Zetec E and marketed by DARE (UK) Ltd. Offered in both kit and fully-built form while it remained in production.
DARE (UK) Ltd 2000–3
Approx 12 made

DARRIAN MONTE CARLO MC220 BERLINETTE

Darrian Cars was founded in 1984 by Tim Duffee, who for several years been supplying spares to Davrian customers. Their MC220 was a replica of the Alpine A110 created for a customer commission, although several more were produced, with prices from around £25,000. Sadly, although of excellent quality, they were too costly to produce and were discontinued.
Darrian Cars 2001–2
Approx 4 made

DARRIAN T9

Tim Duffee's old Davrian MkVII (*qv*) was handed to highly successful tarmac rally driver Geoff Kitney, who modified it to use mid-mounted Ford BDA power and made new moulds. The car was christened the Darrian T9. Highly successful in competition, where most have ended up. Duffee had also acquired the remnants of the Corry Cultra project. Company takes the prize for the kit car manufacturer with *the* most unpronounceable location – deep breath – Pontrhydfenigaid Ystrad Meurig!
Darrian Cars 1985–90
Approx 39 made

DARRIAN T90

A development of the very successful T9 model with input from Robin Herd, founder of March Engineering.
Darrian Cars 1990–96
Approx 26 made

DARRIAN T90 GTR

A further development of the tried and tested T9/T90. Capable car.
Darrian Cars 1996 to date
Approx 20 made

DART

Marina-based traditional roadster from a Marlow company. Had styling that wasn't for everyone, although it did have a claimed DIY build cost of just £2,000. Its magazine adverts proclaimed it was ready when it clearly wasn't!
Dart Cars 1991
Approx 1 made

DASH

Evolved from the Pelland Sports (*qv*), Ryder Rembrandt (*qv*) and Listair Dash (*qv*). Dash Sportscars of Hereford was run by Simon Parker.
Dash Sportscars 1986–88
Approx 55 made

DAVRIAN IMP Mk1

This was a convertible roadster built by Adrian Evans in 1967 that ended up spawning the Davrian marque. Underpinned by a plywood and GRP monocoque with Hillman Imp engine.
Adrian Evans 1967
Approx 1 made

DAVRIAN IMP Mk2

Adrian Evans based his new Davrian company in Clapham, South London, and the first 'proper' Davrian was basically the same car as the Mk1 except that the monocoque was now all-GRP and the headlights were pop-up units.
Davrian Developments 1968–70
Approx 20 made

DAVRIAN IMP Mk3

A fixed-head fastback with same rear-mounted Imp engine as the Mk1 and Mk2.
Davrian Developments 1969
Approx 50 made

DAVRIAN IMP Mk4

The Mk4 didn't change anything as far as the basic underpinnings went but the body was now of notchback style.
Davrian Developments 1970–71
Approx 32 made

DAVRIAN MkV–MkVII

The subsequent three versions of the Davrian differed in detail only, and all had a flip-front. Experts consider the MkVII as *the* Davrian model. Mini and VW Beetle donor options were introduced in 1973 and the company moved to Tregaron, Wales, in 1976.
Davrian Developments 1971–79
Approx 400 made total

DAVRIAN MkVIII

Another move, this time to Lampeter in 1980. The MkVIII appeared in 1980 and was completely revised with totally new styling and a Ford Fiesta engine mounted amidships.

Davrian did a deal with the Welsh Development Agency to sell the MkVIII in complete form – known as the Dragon – that ultimately led to the company overstretching itself. It sadly collapsed in 1983, with the assets bought by Corry Cars of Northern Ireland.
Davrian Developments 1980–83
Approx 50 made total

DAVRIAN DRAGON – *see Davrian MkVIII*

DJ SPORTSCARS INTERNATIONAL LTD

Founded by Derek Johns in 1968, DJ Sportscars has risen to become one of the UK's foremost kit car manufacturers. Originally made fibreglass spoilers and bolt-on 'go-faster' parts. Company was taken over by Derek's brother Brian and his wife, Pam. Made 77 bodies (in parts) and 25 complete shells for a German customer, who was fitting them to Mustang chassis. Brian and Pam retired in 2011, with their son Simon running the company with Andrew Parrish-Evans.

DAX 40

DJ purchased a set of KVA GT40 Mk1 (*qv*) moulds in 1987. Their then technical director, the late John Tojeiro, set about revising the chassis to better suit the company's purposes, which included adding 2in to the height of the body for ease of access. It effectively became a GT42! Around 36 were sold. Interestingly, KVA continued to market the original version of their car.
DJ Sportscars 1987–94
Approx 36 made

DAX 289

Seen as a perfect partner to the company's 427 replica, but didn't really catch on. It failed to capture the attention of the purists because it was really a 427 with the arches cut off, while power came from a Jaguar straight-six engine, further turning up noses!
DJ Sportscars 1983–84
Approx 5 made

DAX 427 – *see DAX Tojeiro*

DAX CALIFORNIAN

Originally produced by Sheldonhurst, the Californian was a derivative of the Porsche 356 Speedster devised by Terry Sands.
DJ Sportscars 1992–93
Approx 20 made

DAX CHARGER

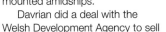

Charger and Charger 2 projects taken over by DAX in 1984 from MBC Cars. DAX sold a few before pressures of their other products resulted in both projects being sold on. Most of the kits they sold were the Charger 2 version. Project then moved on to a company called MDB Sportscars in 1986, before coming to rest as the Viking Dragon Fire (*qv*) in 1987.
DJ Sportscars 1984-86
Approx 20 made

DAX COBRA

Became famous as the '*Exchange & Mart* cars' after an advert in that paper resulted in a massive amount of interest. The kits advertised were the result of an order that a German customer never collected. Sales manager of the time Adrian Cocking, later of LR Roadsters and Ram fame, suggested offering them in kit form in the UK. Became the DAX Tojeiro (*qv*) after 77 part-bodies and 25 complete bodyshells were made.
DJ Sportscars 1979–81
Approx 102 made

DAX KAMALA

An outlandishly styled mid-engined two-seater from former Ford man and DAX technical guru Peter Walker. Superb handling with performance to match from (usually) Cosworth YB turbo powerplant. Project purchased by father and son team Mark and Tony Keen in 2000. They later developed a convertible version and alsoone with an alternative front end.

DJ Sportscars 1995–2000
Kamala Cars 2000 to date
Approx 30 made

DAX NEVADA

A cracking off-road rail-style kit championed by DJ's technical wizard Gary Sanders, who raced his version successfully in off-road events.

DJ Sportscars 1982–87
Approx 15 made

DAX RUSH

Originally a German product, part of the range of Lotus Seven-inspired sports cars created by Jürgen Mohr. Taken over by DJ Sportscars in 1991 and revised for the UK market, its larger dimensions and fierce performance have attracted many takers. The other Rush models are still produced by German company Autohaus Glauner.

DJ Sportscars 1991 to date
Approx 350 made

DAX RUSH M/C

A motorcycle-powered version of the DAX Rush, with body-styling mods, this was the first DJ Sportscars product to feature Peter Walker's patented camber compensation system. The company created a Hayabusa-powered version with turbocharger, built by Jared 'Jack' Frost of Holeshot Racing, a renowned builder of mad, high-powered bike engines.

DJ Sportscars 1999 to date
Approx 150 made

DAX SPEEDSTER

DJ Sportscars made the bodies for Covin Performance Mouldings and marketed the project themselves when Covin ceased trading, before moving on to the Californian version. Grannd (*sic*) Performance Mouldings then marketed the model for a time.

DJ Sportscars 1990–92
Grannd Performance Mouldings 1995–1998
Approx 20 made

DAX TOJEIRO

Renowned AC Ace designer and specials builder John Tojeiro joined DJ Sportscars in the early 1980s as technical director and created a bespoke chassis for this car. Officially launched at the 1983 Motorfair at Earl's Court. Developed a fierce V12 Dragonsnake version. Went on to become one of the UK's best selling Cobra replicas, and still available as the DAX 427.

DJ Sportscars 1981 to date
Approx 3,000 made

DAYTONA MIGI

An American kit made by a company in Florida called Daytona Automotive. It was originally introduced in 1971 as a nut-for-nut copy of an MG TD before they discovered in 1975 that the VW Beetle and the classic MG shared the same wheelbase and the switch was made.

Local newspaper journalist Colin Lucas lived close to the American airbases of Lakenheath and Mildenhall and liked the American way of life, and was a kit car enthusiast. One day he heard about the Migi and visited the manufacturers in the US. Although initially sceptical about a Beetle-based MG the prospect of being a car manufacturer grew on him and he formed a business with his friend, Zastava car and Yamaha motorcycle dealer Mike Richards, who ran Carter Street Garage. They based their business at Richards' premises in Fordham near Ely in Cambridgeshire. The quality of the product wasn't that bad and their first demonstrator was painstakingly built by a lovely chap called 'Old George', using a 1970 1,500cc VW Beetle as a donor. At £3,495 (in 1982) the kit was a bit pricey, and this probably did for it ultimately. They did, however, have a memorable name for their kit package – the Getaway Special!

Fordham Engineering 1982–84
Approx 27 made (UK)

DAYTONA MOYA

Not a replica, but its American manufacturer clearly took inspiration from the Bugatti Type 57/Delahaye era. Quality of the Moya was regarded as very high, although the VW Beetle base put many off. Imported to the UK by Fordham Engineering, who also imported the Fiberfab Migi II to these shores.

Fordham Engineering 1983–84
Approx 2 made (UK)

DEANFIELD T-1/T-2

Lotus Seven-inspired sports car from a Dumfries company run by Graeme Young. It was formerly made by Mark Bean at Triton Sportscars and developed further by Young, who sold a lot of his production to Northern Ireland customers. The T-1 featured a live axle using Ford Escort Mk2 parts, while the T-2 had independent rear suspension and mainly Sierra running gear.
Deanfield Motorsport 2001–5
Approx 100 made

DEAUVILLE CANARD

Canard is the French word for duck. This little car from Bognor Regis was Citroën 2CV-based. Company run by Mike Richards, father of well-known actor and singer Ben Richards.
Deauville Cars 2003 to date
Approx 40 made

DEAUVILLE CANARD 2

Launched at the Newark Show in 2010, the Canard Mk2 features a revised grille and elongated doors, with a more steeply raked windscreen and all-new boot arrangement. Donor vehicle remained Citroën 2CV.
Deauville Cars 2010 to date
Approx 10 made

DEAUVILLE CANJITO 602

Looking like a refugee from M∗A∗S∗H, this Citroën 2CV-based Willy's-style vehicle was the second product from Bognor-based Deauville Cars. It was inspired by the US MUTT kit and Citroën Mehari.
Deauville Cars 2003 to date
Approx 30 made

DEAUVILLE CORBEAU – *see Deauville Rondo*

DEAUVILLE LANDAULET

Created by Deauville Cars customer Mike Horton for wedding car duties, and is effectively a lengthened Canard with a landaulet body. Initially known as the Landaulet, but later became the Sandringham.
Deauville Cars 2007–2010
Approx 3 made

DEAUVILLE RONDO

Another neat Citroën 2CV-based car from Deauville's Dutch agent Danny Blaauw. Originally known as the Hot Rod. Later offered in the Netherlands by Voglietta Cars.
Deauville Cars 2007–8
Approx 2 made

DEAUVILLE SANDRINGHAM – *see Deauville Landaulet*

DEBONAIR

Leslie Ballamy was remarkably well-known in the 'specials' era for supplying go-faster bits and uprated suspension components. A very gifted engineer, his Guildford-based operation supplied split beam axles and IFS systems and also Rubery Owen-made LMB wheels. Jem Marsh, co-founder of Marcos, worked at LMB for a time after the closure of Speedex in 1962, although after acting as salesman for Ballamy the project was withdrawn from sale, as Marsh felt it was over-heavy and far too expensive.

Also marketed the Edwards Bros Debonair under the LMB name from 1959.
LM Ballamy (Components) Ltd 1959–63
Approx 65 made

DEEP SANDERSON DS 301

Chris Lawrence, a man synonymous with the British specialist car industry, was mesmerised by motorsport from an early age. After a career in the Royal Navy, in 1952 he became a development engineer at Rotax, working for Geoff Price, and after leaving Rotax in 1958 set up his own tuning company called Westerham Motors, based in Acton. It was here that the Deep Sanderson marque was born. The name came from a jazz band his father was in, who played a song called *Deep Henderson*, which Chris loved. His mother played a big part in getting his fledgling marque off the ground, so, in deference to her, he used her maiden name Sanderson in place of Henderson and, hey presto, Deep Sanderson!

Meanwhile, Westerham Motors closed and Chris founded LawrenceTune Engines Ltd, while he also came up with the innovative 'Lawrencelink' trailing arm suspension system.

A variety of DS Formula Junior cars (101, 102, 103 and 104) followed from 1959, until Len Bridge persuaded Chris that a range of two-seater sports cars, sold in kit form, could be the way to go. The prototype, despite being dubbed the 'Perfume Delivery Wagon' due to its styling, was a superb performer, complete with its 850cc Mini engine.

The definitive DS301 was created with design input from Andrew Wallace, while Microplas made the pleasing bodyshells that stood just 36in high. Kits were priced at £750 and around 30 were sold from 1962. Chris sadly passed away in August 2011.
LawrenceTune Engines Ltd 1962–65
Approx 31 made

DEETYPE D-TYPE REPLICA

Launched at the Speedshow in London in 1975 by an East Hanningfield company run by Bryan Wingfield, which offered replicas (tool-room copies) of Jaguar's D-type. Featured a stressed aluminium monocoque and used a Jaguar E-type as donor. Fully-built versions cost £23,000 in 1979. Incredibly well respected and sell for big money today. Incidentally, Wingfield founded the GT40 Owners' Club and made three GT40s from leftover JWA parts between 1996 and 1998.
Deetype Replicas Ltd 1974–81
Approx 22 made

DEETYPE XJ13 REPLICA

Usual top-notch Wingfield creation, this was a tool-room copy of the Jaguar XJ13. Only one made.
Deetype Replicas Ltd 1976–81
Approx 1 made

REPLICA

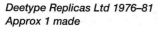

Bryan Wingfield's replica of the roadgoing version of Jaguar's D-type. Not as prolific as his D-type recreation.
Deetype Replicas Ltd 1974–81
Approx 3 made

DÉJÀ VU

Created by Ken Hadley, marketed by Lomax founder Nigel Whall, and based on Citroën 2CV running gear. Fully-built versions were offered by John Parker of JP Exhausts from 1989.
Lomax 1988–96
Approx 10 made

DELKIT CAMINO

A collaboration between ex-army officer Derek Allen, who was a manager of a boat manufacturer, when he met design consultant John Rock. Allen had attempted to get the boat maker to produce a kit car for the quieter winter months to keep the workers busy, but they rejected the idea.

In the end he formed a company with Rock, based in Telford, called Delkit GRP.

Could truly be described as a single donor vehicle using Ford Cortina Mk3/Mk4 parts with a sturdy spaceframe chassis with a backbone section built-in. Everything about the Camino was very good apart from the styling, which wasn't to everyone's taste despite the company's advertising literature describing it as 'the ultimate kit car design'.
Delkit GRP 1984–85
Approx 9 made

DELLOW

One of the big specialist car myths is that Dellow made kit cars. They didn't. A very small handful were produced in component form but the vast majority of the 300-odd produced were sold fully built. While we're here, however, we might as well give a bit of potted Dellow history.

Founded by Ken Delingpole and Ron Lowe in 1947 to produce replicas of Ron's successful trials car nicknamed 'The Flipper', Dellow (a conflation of the two protagonists' surnames) were also involved in general car preparation, tuning, and as agents for HRG and also Wade Ventor superchargers. A succession of trials cars (Mks1–7) were produced (could also be used on-road) until production ceased in 1959.

DELTA

A 1950s GRP bodyshell for 90in and 94in wheelbases. Its instigator, Adrian Evans of Worcestershire, went on to create a car called the Scorpion (*qv*) in 1979.
Glass-Fibre Laminations 1960–62
Approx 50 made

DELTA

An alternative name for the Amica (*qv*) available for a time from Pageant Motor Co of Hornsey, London N8. The car was a 1929 Mercedes SSK replica. Sort of. The basis of the Delta was a VW Beetle chassis with torsion bar suspension. Power came from a brand new 1,600cc air-cooled engine. The car was actually of high quality although far too expensive to succeed here.
Pageant Motor Company 1980
Approx 1 made

DELTA S4 REPLICA

Hailing from Blackburn-based Mick Covill, a lifelong enthusiast of Italian cars, this project is a replica of the famed Group B WRC Lancia S4 Delta, as driven by the likes of Markku Alén. The replica features a Lancia Delta body tub, with spaceframes front and rear, and mid-mounted Delta Integrale or Fiat Turbo (as per Coupé) power.
Rally Legend Replicas 2011 to date
Approx 4 made

DELTAYN PEGASUS

Very pleasing Richard Oakes design. Used a slightly revamped Hillcrest V12 chassis and was based on Jaguar XJ6/12 mechanicals. A few were produced in kit form before a French company wanted to put it into series production in 1990. Despite moving to France, lock, stock and barrel, the project didn't proceed. A restyle in 1990, after Jaguar agreed to supply brand new parts, was launched at the Geneva Motor Salon in the same year.

A 1998 reappearance in the UK saw a Jaguar-based version and one kit sale before, under the JJR Automotive banner, John Parradine launched the fully-built only – and revised Pegasus – Parradine 525S in 2000 at that year's British Motor Show, with Quantum H4 doors and roof system and a whopping, fully-built price tag of circa £130,000.
JJR Automotive/Parradine Motor Company plc 1989–90, 1998–2000
Approx 3 made (plus 22 fully-built)

DELTAYN PROTEUS

Had its origins in the AD400 (*qv*). Deltayn owner John Parradine's main line of business was importing huge industrial dumper trucks, and the Proteus, his first venture into the world of kit cars. The Proteus was a big Jaguar-based GT, complete with six headlights.
Deltayn Ltd 1985–88
Approx 2 made

DEMON – *see Diva Valkyr*

DENARO

Short-lived resurrection of the ABS Monaco (*qv*) from Nick Homewood and Alan Milford, turning it into a fixed-head. They made two.
Prestige Sport Cars 1994–95
Approx 2 made

DEON DGT

This car had formerly been made in Essex, first by Dave Perry and then by Daytona Classics. It was a 246 Dino replica based on Lancia Beta/HPE engines with Austin Allegro radiator and Carello rear lights. John Hurst, a former officer in the King's Royal Irish Hussars, had bought a kit from Daytona Classics but was not impressed, so was inspired to form JH Classics based in Shaftesbury, Dorset. JH employed the services of Swindon Sportscars to make the steel tube chassis, while Pat Cuss of Fibreglass Applications made the bodies.

Later joined by a GTS drophead coupé, sold under the Deon name, which made its debut at Stoneleigh in 1989. Deon subsequently became the company name. John Hurst returned in early 2011, under the JH Classics banner, with the DGT coupé and convertible Spyder version (GTS). The cars were now based on Toyota MR2 Mk2, with kits priced at £9,200.
Daytona Classics 1986–88   JH Classics 1988–92
Deon Cars 1992–94, 1995–98   JH Classics 2011 to date
Approx 220 made

DEON DGT LE MANS

A stripped-out lightweight version of the standard DGT, with no roof of any description.
JH Classics 1991–93
Deon Cars 1993–94, 1995–97
Approx 2 made

DEON GTS

Convertible version of the Deon DGT (*qv*).

DEON MIRABEAU

This was an original design rather than a replica but, of course, was Italian inspired. Power came from either Lancia Beta or Ford 2.9-litre V6. This car may have been named after the town of Mirabeau in France.
JH Classics 1991–93
Deon Cars 1993–94, 1995–98
Approx 63 made

DEON SCOPERTO

A convertible coupé version of the Deon DGT. The Italian word Scoperto translates as 'open top'.
JH Classics 1991–93
Deon Cars 1993–94, 1995–97
Approx 28 made

DERONDA TYPE F

Created by airline accountant Andrew Round, the Deronda Type F made its debut at the Autosport Show in 2004 as a fully-built only vehicle, but despite displaying much promise didn't really take off. Spotted in Andrew's barn by Kelvin Kinkaid of QDOS Cars, who along with his friend Alistair Courtney of Alternative Cars made the car available in kit form from the summer of 2009.
Deronda Cars 2004–7
Alternative Cars 2009 to date
Approx 2 made

DEVIL

Audi-based single-seater from Edge Sportscars of Ruislip, run by surgeon Dev Lall and designer Robin Hall, who was also responsible for the FBS Census, incidentally.
Edge Sportscars 2004 -9
Approx 14 made

DEWSBURY ROADSTER

Came from Mac McKechnie of West Yorkshire and was a traditional roadster based on the Citroën 2CV/Dyane.
Dewsbury Kit Cars 1990–91
Approx 1 made

DEZINA

Lamborghini Countach replica that was available in two versions. The original used VW Beetle parts and floorpan, albeit with a 3in shorter than original wheelbase. A later option featured a separate spaceframe chassis with correct 98½in wheelbase and mid-mounted Rover V8 engine in lieu of than air-cooled Veedub. In the original replica, the bodyshell had a separate spaceframe that bolted to the Beetle floorpan. Terry Withers was the man behind the project.
Dezina Cars 1993–97
Approx 8 made

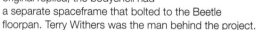

DG PHOENIX TRIKE

One of the most successful 'bike-to-trike conversions', hailing from DG Motor Services of Wellingborough, run by Dominic Gardner. The Phoenix had a VW Beetle air-cooled engine with a rudimentary box section chassis. Bikers loved it.
DG Motor Services 1982–2000
Approx 420 made

DG RAIL

Sister model to the Phoenix Trike (see previous entry), the Rail picked up on the early '80s fad for off-road sandrails made popular in the UK by the likes of UVA.
DG Motor Services 1983–89
Approx 7 made

DGT VII

The DGT Dino replica from a returning John Hurst, formerly of Deon, appeared in early 2011. The 'VII' part of the name refers to 'Version Two'. His new take on the Italian classic replica was available in Coupé GT or Targa-top GTS guises, and unlike the earlier Deon models (last available in 1998), the new versions consisted of a body conversion kit designed around Toyota MR2 Mk2, with kits priced at £9,200 on launch. Hurst was based in Hedging, Somerset.
JH Classics 2011 to date
Approx 15 made

DIAL BUCCANEER

Frank Sheen, based in Grays, Essex, was the man behind this exotic-looking creation. Featured early automotive use of carbon fibre. Project commenced in 1969 and was launched at the Racing Car Show of 1971. Based on a spaceframe chassis, this race-orientated kit car sourced its parts from a variety of cars including Triumph, VW and Ford.
Dial Plastics 1969–71
Approx 20 made

DINGBAT

Triumph Herald-based beach buggy that got lots of coverage in *Cars & Car Conversions* magazine back in the day. Created by a chap called Paul Cockburn, who had previously co-designed the Humbug VW Beetle conversion kit. Was it stillborn?
Dingbat Cars 1971–72
Approx 1 made

DIVA GT

The Diva GT was basically a modified Heron Europa (*qv*) that Tunex Conversions boss Don Sim (a former Yimkin Engineering partner) commissioned George Bishop of Heron Plastics to create for him. Power came from a Tunex breathed-on 998cc Ford engine.

The original GT was replaced by the 'B' type in 1962, which had a new spaceframe chassis and bigger windscreen, while the first Diva GTs proper were the 'C' and 'D' types (the latter having a longer

nose), most of which ended up on the racetrack, although a couple did see road use. Enjoyed over 200 race victories. However, the 10FS variant of 1966 was the first dedicated roadgoing Diva and shared many similarities with the 'D' Type. Had a heavier fibreglass body and rubber mounted engine.

Tunex became Diva Cars in 1966 and was taken over by Isle of Wight company Skodek Engineering in 1967.
Tunex Conversions 1965–66
Diva Cars 1966–67
Skodek Engineering/Enfield Automotive 1967–68
'A' type – Approx 1 made 1961
'B' type – Approx 6 made 1962–63
'C' type – Approx 13 made 1963–64
'D' type – Approx 51 made 1965–66
10FS – Approx 3 made 1966–68

DIVA VALKYR

A roadgoing Diva that was originally powered by Hillman Imp engine and known as the Demon, with a launch at the Racing Car Show of 1965. Specification was soon amended to Ford Pre-Crossflow as per Lotus Cortina-spec and the name changed to Valkyr.
Tunex Conversions 1965–66
Diva Cars 1966–67
Skodek Engineering/Enfield Automotive 1967–68
Approx 6 made

DMS ABINGDON

Intended MGA replica that was stillborn, although it was advertised in the kit car press quite heavily for a time.
Dorset Motor Services 1993
Approx 1 made

DMS BULLIT

A body conversion from Fordingbridge-based DMS, run by Derek Finlay, to turn a Ford Capri Mk2 into an Aston Martin Vantage Volante. The kit was available in coupé or convertible forms. Later taken over by Classic Replicas.
Dorset Motor Services 1990–92
Classic Replicas 1992–2003
Approx 20 made

DMS PREDATOR

Ferrari 250 GTO replica based on Datsun 240/260Z and later offered by Classic Replicas.
Dorset Motor Services 1990–92
Classic Replicas 1992–2002
Approx 20 made

DMS VENOM

Cortina-based Cobra replica that could be had with a variety of engine choices from four-cylinder to V8. Later offered by Classic Replicas.
Dorset Motor Services 1990–92
Classic Replicas 1992–2003
Approx 100 made

DNA 3SIXTY

An F360 body conversion based on Toyota MR2. Well respected. DNA Automotive are based in Birmingham.
DNA Automotive 2006 to date
A lot made

DNA 4THIRTY

Following their successful Toyota MR2-based 3Sixty, DNA has been very successful with their 4Thirty package.
DNA Automotive 2009 to date
A lot made

DNA 5SCUDO

Latest exotic replica from DNA Automotive announced in 2011. A body conversion of the F430 Scuderia. Top quality. Based on Ford Cougar.
DNA Automotive 2010

DNK/DE NOVO HORNET

Originally a 1985 one-off special built by Doug Pinchin, called the KNW2. Put into production as the DNK in 1986 in Ponterwyd, Ceredigion, before the company moved to Halesowen in 1990.
De Novo Kits 1986–92
Approx 1 made

DOMINATOR TS400

Hull-based Paul Liggott was the man behind this trackday-orientated kit. Featured on the Discovery TV show *Kitcar Crisis* in 2004. Wasn't around for long. Could accommodate all manner of engines including bike units.
Dominator Sports Cars 2004–5
Approx 8 made

DOMINO CABRIO

A Cabriolet version of the Mini on the Domino theme (see following entries).
Domino Cars 1987–91
Domino Car Co (UK) Ltd 1991–2004
Domino Composites 2004–6
Composite Designs 2006–7
DominoCars-Organisation 2008
Approx 45 made

DOMINO HT

Followed the theme of the Minus (*qv*) and was basically a GRP-bodied Mini, albeit with shortened, internally-hinged doors. An HT-ES (Evolution Sport with a carbon fibre rather than fibreglass body) was also available.

John Ingram's Domino Cars ceased trading in 1991 but continued under the control of his partner John Chapman, who ran the highly successful Fibretech division of the operation before Colin Moore took over in 2004. However, the latter's company had been liquidated by late 2007. In spring 2008 Ian E. Broadbent set up a company called DominoCars-Organisation, totally unrelated to any of the previous incarnations, and intended to put a couple of the Domino models back into production, including a diesel hybrid and electric-powered version. However, after a number of feasibility studies he didn't proceed further.
Domino Cars 1988–91
Domino Car Co (UK) Ltd 1991–2004
Domino Composites 2004–6
Composite Designs 2006–7
DominoCars-Organisation 2008
Approx 25 made

DOMINO PIMLICO

A Richard Oakes design that
hit the spot for many kit and
Mini enthusiasts when launched
in 1986. Obviously based
mechanically on the Mini, its
styling was influenced by that car
too, although its light weight, low
sills and affordable build-price
made it popular. A slightly revised Mk2 arrived in 1991.
Domino Cars 1986–91   Domino Car Co (UK) Ltd 1991–2004
Domino Composites 2004–6   Composite Designs 2006–7
DominoCars-Organisation 2008
Approx 100 made

DOMINO PREMIER

Arriving in 1988, the Premier was basically a Domino Cabrio with
lower sills, double-skinned, internally-hinged GRP doors and a
standard Mini bootlid. A Premier Plus was longer by 6in.
Domino Cars 1988–91   Domino Car Co (UK) Ltd 1991–2004
Domino Composites 2004–6   Composite Designs 2006–7
DominoCars-Organisation 2008
Approx 40 made

DOMINO PUP PICKUP

A Domino version of the classic
Mini pickup. Popular in the USA.
Domino Cars 1986–91
Domino Car Co (UK) Ltd
1991–2004
Domino Composites 2004–6
Composite Designs 2006–7
DominoCars-Organisation 2008
Approx 10 made

DOON BUGGY

A pleasing original beach buggy
design from Simon 'Chad'
Chadwick that uses VW Beetle
running gear. Available in short
and long wheelbase forms, the
latter using an unmodified Beetle
floorpan. Production and sales
transferred to Volksmagic, run by
Lee Rushton of Birmingham, in
2009. Chadwick is still involved.
Doon Buggies 2001-9
Volksmagic 2009 to date
Approx 70 made

DOOSTER 33 SPEEDSTER

Car restorer Gary Janes had been
a founding member of the UK Low
Riders Club. When he was made
redundant he turned his hobby
and passion into a business,
which he named Dooster, founded
in 2001. The Ford Granada-
based 33 Speedster was his third
product, after the Model B and Model A. In 2004 taken over by Martin
Paling of Gaddesby, Leicestershire, who continued until 2008.
Dooster 2001-8
Approx 9 made

DOOSTER MODEL A

Followed on from the Dooster
Model B (see next entry), and was
again based on Cortina running
gear. Not as popular as the Model
B. In 2004 taken over by Martin
Paling of Leicestershire who
continued until 2008.
Dooster 2001-8
Approx 3 made

DOOSTER MODEL B

Gary Janes' first project was a Model B; the ethos behind his
business as low-budget, quality rods, as he felt prices were getting
too high. His Model B used Ford Cortina running gear. In 2004 taken
over by Martin Paling of Gaddesby, Leicestershire, who continued
until 2008. The most popuar Dooster model.
Dooster 2001-8
Approx 210 made

DORIAN SS

Project taken over from Burlington
Motor Company by father and
son team Brian and Martin Doran.
Brian was an ex-Triumph test
driver at Canley and held the
honour of driving the very last
Stag off the production line. In
1986 he and Martin were asked
by Haydn Davies to make a centre body tub mould for the Burlington
SS (qv), and eventually took over the project completely. The Dorans
sold some 80 kits before ceasing trading in 1988. Resurrected briefly
by GRP laminator Neil Duncan in late 1990.
Dorian Motor Company 1986–88, 1990
Approx 80 made

DOUGLAS TF

Originally a Cypriot kit, devised by Derek Douglas, this MG TF replica was sold by the Douglas Car Company of East London, run by ex-schoolteacher Skip Pearson and import warehousing and storage company owner Reg Talbot. Used Triumph running gear and could be based on Herald/Vitesse chassis or a bespoke item, with a 20-piece GRP body with plywood floors.
Douglas Car Company 1991–98
Approx 15 made

DRAGON F1-R

Warrington-based Bill Conway was heavily involved in motorsprot and was the originator of the bike-engined Formula 1-inspired Dragon F1-R. Production ceased when Bill emigrated to the USA.
Dragon Sportscars 2003–5
Approx 2 made

DRAGONFLY

Cleary inspired by the Arkley SS, the Dragonfly came from Basingstoke-based Dan Pratt (an architect) and Steve Watson (a coachbuilder), with input during the prototype's build coming from Wincanton Engineering of Bentley.

Pratt and Watson had previously built an Arkley, and produced their take on the 'Spridget' conversion theme, which was very nicely produced, but expensive. Indeed, it cost three times more than an Arkley to build!

The donor chassis required an additional 10½in being grafted in between the front wheels and bulkhead area; a task that Dragonfly Cars was happy to carry out for the customer if required, but obviously at a price.

An acquaintance of Pratt and Watson, Mervyn Rees, a businessman who owned petrol stations and a custom trailers operation (his company had built structures for show business icons Basil Brush and Sooty!) and historic car enthusiast, came onboard as a director, but ended up taking over the company and moving down the road to Ash Vale, near Aldershot.

Rees had become frustrated that the car hadn't been marketed sufficiently, and went back to basics, re-engineering what was already a decent product into a very good one, although it was probably the high price that did for it.
Dragonfly Cars 1981–86
Approx 15 made

DRAGONFLY

Not to be confused with the Midget/Sprite-based conversion in the previous entry. This one came from a Toton, Nottinghamshire-based company run by Brendan Beirne and was an F-type Morgan replica three-wheeler, with a Z-section steel ladderframe chassis, sliding-pillar front suspension and a Reliant 848cc engine with a Honda CX500 swinging arm and Morris 8 front wheels. The car was built via a set of plans, with a body made from plywood covered in 22-gauge flat sheet steel.

Dragonfly Cars 1994–95
Approx 3 made

DREAMBIRD

Announced at the Stoneleigh Show of 1983, this two-seater came from Graham Autos, who at the time made the former Pelland Sports (*qv*) and also the Royale (*qv*).
Graham Autos 1983
Approx 1 made

DRI-SLEEVE MOONRAKER

This Bugatti Type 37 (produced 1926–29) replica was a collaboration by British-born Canadians Ryder Slone, Boris Willison and Peter Jackson, who based themselves in the former Opus factory in Warminster, Wiltshire, from 1970. The project was christened the 'Dri-Sleeve' because customers were presented with a sleeve to keep their right arm, er, *dry*! Based on a ladderframe chassis with some VW Beetle parts and a Ford Crossflow engine (which could be supercharged), with aluminium for main body and fibreglass cycle wings. For added authenticity, the customer could opt for Hartford Friction shock absorbers. The marketing and sales were carried out by one of the day's largest Lotus dealers, JA Else & Sons of Codnor, Derbyshire, where the Dri-Sleeve was looked after by Dave Whitcher. Else famously marketed their own version of the Lotus Europa for a time.

Dri-Sleeve Car Company 1971–72
Approx 25 made

DRK

Derek Roscoe and Robert Callister (from whose first names came the 'DR' element of the company name) had been well-known accident repairers for the likes of Shell, British Gas and Vauxhall (since 1957), and were based in Cheshire. Along with friend Keith Hamer (who provided the third initial), they created their own three-wheeler. Went on to make more for commercial sale. Very nicely made with painted chassis and all components pre-fitted. Customers only needed to fit the engine and gearbox.

DRK Kits 1984–98
Approx 59 made

DUCHESS ARUNVILLE

Looking a bit like a 1932 MG Magna this was advertised briefly by an Arundel-based company. Not known if they ever made one. Great name, though!
MF Cawley 1984
Approx 0 made

DUNSMORE

Wonderful creation, from a company based in Stretton-on-Dunsmore, Warwickshire, evocative of traditional 1930s roadsters, although all were different. Made by a lovely chap called Bill Hines assisted by his then (1986) 70-year-old boy 'Bunny'. Jaguar-based, although the prototype, built as a one-off, was powered by a straight six Vauxhall Ventora 3.0-litre engine with an Austin Westminster rear axle, leaf spring suspension, Andre friction dampers, non-servo drum brakes and a large string-bound steering wheel. Featured a body made primarily from steel with a GRP nosecone and plywood scuttle with steel frame. Other engines used included Rover V8 and six-cylinder Rolls Royce-built 4.0-litre Princess unit.
Dunsmore Motor Traction 1984–96
Approx 14 made

DUROW DEBONAIR

Nick Durow was an electrical engineer who made electro magnetic spray units and robot arms for a living, and lived in an Olde English pub-style house in Nottingham. The Debonair followed the usual larger-than-life theme that his vehicles promoted.
Durow Cars 1989–90
Approx 1 made

DUROW DELUGE VS

UK take on the neo-classic style of the huge Corsair, Gatsby, Doral and Desande Roadster. Inspired by a Clenet that creator Nick Durow had seen in 1982. As a fan of the MG Midget he used one for the middle section of his enormous vehicle, which used Ford Granada donor parts and was 18in longer than the donor. Underpinned by a twin-rail chassis, while the non-midget of the body made from GRP. In 1986 the basic kit cost £1,950.
Durow Cars 1985–90
Approx 4 made

DUROW STARR

If the Durow Deluge was big, the Starr was huge! Featured a steel, aluminium and stainless steel body.
Durow Cars 1986–90
Approx 3 made

DUROW VIRAGE DE VILLE

The Virage was inspired by the 1936 Chrysler Imperial and based on Ford Granada mechanicals.
Durow Cars 1992–94
Approx 1 made

A B C D E F G H I J K L M N O P Q R S T U V W X Y Z

DUTTON CARS

One of the real milestone kit car companies and a very important name in the annals of the UK specialist car industry. Founder Tim Dutton-Woolley served apprenticeships with Pressed Steel in Swindon (making bodies for Jaguar Mk10s among others), before they ceased trading and he completed his course at the Monotype Corporation in Earlswood, Surrey. Inspiration for his first commercially available kit car came from a Lotus Seven he worked on and a *special* he'd previously built for his later business partner Tony Addison behind his mum's pub in Worthing, Sussex. He decided to drop the 'Woolley' part of his name as he didn't rate the chances of a company called 'Woolley Cars'.

Dutton's philosophy was simple. In a nutshell, it was pile 'em high, sell 'em cheap, so at a time when the average kit price was quite high he brought affordable DIY motoring to the masses, with ultra-low prices. The products were often criticised, but how can you really knock anyone who's sold over 8,000 kits? Go to a party and there's a good chance that even if no one knows much about kit cars, someone will know someone who once owned a Dutton!

From the pub in Worthing, Dutton moved to a pig sty with a sloping floor in Fontwell, then a big shed in Tangmere, and then ended up employing 80 people in four factories and a showroom in Worthing… Dutton reckons that above all else the secret of his success was the fact that he was a toolmaker, rather than an engineer, which gave him an edge in production terms.

Other companies he has run over the years included Carmona Engineering (alloy wheels made in Italy), Goodwood Repair Panels, Partex Discount Ltd and a period spent selling Moke Californians under licence.

DUTTON B-TYPE

A development of the Dutton P1 (*qv*) and based on Triumph Herald running gear with a Herald/Spitfire engine, although the customer could also opt for Alfa Twin Cam and Ford Kent. Visually quite similar to the P1, though apart from the change of donor it also featured more use of glassfibre.
Dutton Sports Ltd 1971–74
Approx 250 made

DUTTON B-PLUS/B-PLUS S2

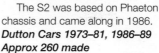

Keeping with the by now established Dutton Cars theme, the B-Plus had revised styling and a slightly larger body than the B-Type, with a beefed-up chassis too. Engine of choice was usually the Ford Crossflow, although some customers went for Ford V6.

The S2 was based on Phaeton chassis and came along in 1986.
Dutton Cars 1973–81, 1986–89
Approx 260 made

DUTTON BENETO

Development on the Dutton Sierra (*qv*) theme that tackled the then popular Rickman Ranger (*qv*) head-on. Based on Ford Escort Mk2, also using doors from that car.

When the majority of the Dutton range was sold off to Eagle and Scorhill, the Beneto (plus a drophead version) along with the Legerra and Melos (see below) remained with Tim Dutton under his Partex banner. The Beneto name was inspired by a yachting connection.
Dutton Cars 1989
Partex Discount Ltd/Mantis Cars 1989–94
Approx 12 made

DUTTON CANTERA

The Cantera differed from Tim Dutton's usual Lotus Seven-inspired theme. Although it was based on a modified B-Plus chassis it was an angular fixed-head two-seater complete with doors. The Cantera name was a mix of Porsche 911 Carrera and De Tomaso Pantera, two of Dutton's favourite cars.
Dutton Cars 1976–77
Approx 6 made

DUTTON LEGERRA

The Legerra was ambitiously intended by Tim Dutton to be a turnkey-only car, using 95% new parts, it was launched at the 1984 NEC Motor Show. It struggled to convince potential customers that it wasn't a conventional Dutton kit offering, and so was eventually released in kit form at £1,250.

When the majority of the Dutton range was sold off to Eagle and Scorhill, the Legerra along with Beneto and Melos remained with Tim Dutton under his Partex banner. Dutton's appreciation for coachbuilt limousines inspired the name Legerra from Superleggerra.
Dutton Cars 1984–89
Partex Discount Ltd/Mantis Cars 1989–94
Approx 120 made

DUTTON MELOS

Styled by Simon Saunders, then of Kat Designs and now famous for the Ariel Atom. Had a 2+2 configuration, and shared the Phaeton chassis but cost more. A Series 2 model had revised bonnet styling and colour-coded bumpers.

When the majority of the Dutton range was sold off to Eagle and Scorhill, the Melos along with the Beneto and Legerra remained with Tim Dutton under his Partex banner. The Melos (meaning 'apple' in Greek) was named after a very small Greek Cyclades island.

Dutton Cars 1982–89
Partex Discount Ltd/Mantis Cars 1989–94
Approx 1,500 made

DUTTON MALAGA

Tim Dutton went off to Spain to test the prototype and named it after the area he visited. Effectively a B-Plus (qv) with an extended rear bodywork section. A Malaga B-Plus was an option (a Malaga front body section with B-Plus rear), as was a B-Plus Malaga

(B-Plus front, Malaga rear). Chassis was B-Plus, as was the bonnet. The car was so-named after Tim nearly had an enormous car accident in – Malaga!

Dutton Cars 1974–77
Approx 200 made

DUTTON MARINER – *see Amphijeep*

DUTTON P1

Tim Dutton had built a *special* for his cousin before coming up with this inexpensive Lotus Seven-inspired kit, which was his first commercial product. Inevitably, other people wanted what he was building and so Dutton Cars was born. Based on the Austin Healey

Sprite, the body of the P1 was made from aluminium with a fibreglass nose-section and ladderframe chassis. The 'P1' name stood for 'Prototype model 1'.

Dutton Sports Ltd 1970–71
Approx 9 made

DUTTON PHAETON

The old Dutton B-Plus (*qv*) inspired the Phaeton, which also retained the usual combo of Escort donor with Triumph front suspension. It was the first of the real volume-selling Dutton models, and for a time in the early '90s Tim Dutton was selling 50 Phaetons alone per month. The Phaeton name was inspired by Tim's father's collection of coachbuilt vintage cars with Phaeton bodywork.

The Series 2 appeared in 1981 and featured a few revisions, though the big change came with the S3 of 1982, which was launched at the London Motorfair that year. An all-new spaceframe chassis provided the underpinnings with donor parts now completely Ford Escort MkI or II. Mks 1 and 2 Phaetons had Bedford CF van rear light clusters, later replaced by off-the-shelf rectangular units.

The run-out S4 of 1986 gained a new front-end styling with extra legroom and revised rear suspension. Became the Eagle P21 (*qv*).

Dutton Cars 1978–89
Approx 3,000 made

A B C D E F G H I J K L M N O P Q R S T U V W X Y Z

DUTTON RICO

Dutton's attempt at a family-style saloon. First saw the light of day in 1984, using De Lorean DMC-12 headlights, no less (although Escort Mk3 items were used later), and Escort Mk2 windscreen! A Series 2 arrived in 1985 that featured cleaner lines and flush-fitting rectangular Escort Mk3 headlights. Tim Dutton raced one of these in the 750 Motor Club's Kit Car Challenge in 1985.
Dutton Cars 1984–89
Approx 25 made

DUTTON RICO SHUTTLE

Intended as a replacement for the Dutton Sierra. Used a revised Dutton Sierra chassis.
Dutton Cars 1986–89
Approx 50 made

DUTTON SIERRA

A truly legendary kit car, offering huge space and practicality, commodities that at the time were unheard of in the kit car industry. Richard Oakes had a hand in the design. The chassis was a ladderframe with Ford Escort donor and was Dutton's first four-seater. Series 2 came along in 1984 and used the same chassis, although the GRP body was now double-skinned and the bonnet gained a ridge. Series 3 launched in 1986 enjoyed a complete revamp, featuring dropped footwells, returned edges on glassfibre, new floorpan and option of round headlights or rectangular items from Escort Mk3.

Ford didn't like the use of the Sierra name but this didn't stop Tim

Dutton, who had actually christened his car first. Dutton tested his prototype in the Sierra Nevada region of Spain, and was inspired to name his new model after the area where the engine had fallen out one day!
Dutton Cars 1980–89
Hamilton Automotive 1989–94
Approx 3,000 made

DUTTON SIERRA DROPHEAD

Drophead variant was a fun take on the Sierra theme, tackling the Eagle RV (*qv*) market with raised sides and a convertible body. The Drophead supplied the inspiration and basis for the first amphibious vehicle that Tim Dutton produced, the Dutton Mariner (see Amphijeep).
Dutton Cars 1984–87
Approx 50 made

DUTTON SIERRA PICKUP/CHASSIS CAB

Dutton could see potential in commercial vehicle markets for his Sierra variants and even advertised them in magazines such as *Farmer's Weekly*. Same chassis as standard Dutton Sierra.
Dutton Cars 1983–89
Approx 5 made

DUTTON/DSL SPYDER

Dutton's take on the Arkley SS (*qv*). Spridget conversion albeit based on Triumph Spitfire. Sold under the Dutton Sports Ltd banner, with the kit supplied in three glassfibre sections requiring the unbolting and simple replacement of the donor's outer panels.
Dutton Sports Ltd Dutton Cars 1978–81
Approx 6 made

DVT GT & DVT GTS

Announced in Spring 2011, the De Havilland Motor Company, based in Bury St Edmunds and run by Terry Groves, acquired a set of old Deon/JH Classics moulds and revised the existing DGT Coupé and Scoperto to produce the DVT GT and DVT GTS, respectively. Dispensing with the original Lancia underpinnings, the models became MG TF-based body conversion kits.
De Havilland Motor Company 2011 to date
Approx 2 made

E-KART

Similar in concept to the same company's e-Trike (next entry), but in a more conventional go-kart style, and although using modern technology is similar to the way that *specials* manufacturers offered their products back in the 1950s.
Mills Extreme Vehicles 2009 to date
Approx 20 made

E-TRIKE

Also known as the Battmobile, this tiny kart-style vehicle designed by Stuart Mills of MEV can be driven by 16-year-olds and is powered by an electric motor. Has handlebars rather than a steering wheel. Available in plan form from £50, enabling customers to go their own way with the build, although MEV can also supply a GRP body. Can be built from around £1,500.
Mills Extreme Vehicles 2009 to date
Approx 25 made

EAGLE DB50

A Daihatsu F20-based version of the Eagle RV (see below), which endowed the car with four-wheel drive capability.
Eagle Cars 1992
Approx 4 made

EAGLE M2 MILAN

Exotic styling that was a four-seat convertible based on Ford Sierra and a collaboration with German company RR Transportgerate (Dieter Rotzel). It was the first Ford Sierra-based kit. Prototype's body was made from aluminium, with the work carried out by Clive Smart at Shapecraft.
Eagle Cars 1994
Approx 1 made

EAGLE P21

Was formerly the Dutton Phaeton (*qv*). Featured cycle wings, longer body, wider cockpit, thicker GPR and a revised chassis.
Eagle Cars 1989–97
Approx 40 made

EAGLE P25

Based on Dutton Phaeton, albeit with closed wings, thicker GRP, larger cockpit, slightly longer body, and a revised chassis.
Eagle Cars 1989–97
Approx 35 made

EAGLE +2

Clearly inspired by and developed from their SS model, Eagle came up with a convertible four-seater with Ford Cortina mechanicals. VW Beetle option was not available. Didn't hit the same spot as the SS did.
Eagle Cars 1983–90
Approx 54 made

EAGLE RV

Inspired by the American VW Beetle-based Rhino (*qv*) kit Eagle acquired in 1983 from Eland Meres of Birmingham. They immediately created a new and sturdy ladderframe chassis using Ford Cortina as donor.

Its chunky off-road nature immediately attracted customers and sales took off – despite being only two-wheel drive the car displayed a pretty decent mud-plugging ability. In addition to coming up with a Sierra donor package, Eagle's Rob Budd also developed a Daihatsu Fourtrak version called the DB50, which appeared in 1992.

Tony Holmes of Classic Transport took the project over in 1997 and made some improvements to the package and build quality and generally enhanced the kit. His company was absorbed by Pilgrim Cars Ltd, who sold the project to Cumbrian Jordan Gott, who made further improvements during his couple of years in control. When he moved to Spain he passed the project on to Tim Naylor of TEAC Sportscars, who also acquired the Eagle SS from a Kent boatyard, where the moulds had been languishing. TEAC developed the Ford Sierra concept further, renaming the car the RV-2, with the 4x4 version known as the RV-4.

Eagle Cars 1983–97   *Classic Transport 1997–99*
Pilgrim Cars 1999–2004   *Jordan Developments 2004–6*
TEAC Sportscars 2007–9
Approx 1,100 made

EAGLE RV 4x4

Developed around the standard two-wheel-drive RV, Eagle's Rob Budd, a former trials motorcycle rider and keen off-roader, created a Range Rover-based version in 1985. When Eagle founder Allen Breeze left in 1986 Budd took over and ran the company until it ceased trading in 1999. The RV 4x4 passed to Surrey-based Bob May by the late '90s.

Eagle Cars 1985–96
Bob May Engineering 1996–2004
Approx 100 made

EAGLE SS

In 1980, Tim Dutton, boss of Dutton Cars, took a Concorde flight to JFK Airport, New York, with the intention of importing an exotic US kit into the UK. He created a new company, called Eagle Cars, to sell it. He took along his cousin, Allen Breeze, a graphic designer, who was installed as the boss of the company. The pair visited all the major American kit manufacturers and looked at the likes of the Kelmark GT, Sebring, Laser 917, Bradley GT and Cimbria. After a lot of deliberation, they settled on the Cimbria, made by a company called Amore Cars, and rather than becoming agents, they bought the rights to manufacture the renamed Eagle SS, in Europe.

Dutton spent some time redeveloping the package to suit the UK market, incorporating Porsche 928 pop-up headlights (Tim had a 928!), Countach-style rear airscoops, UK-spec lights, Ford Fiesta door furniture and a revised bonnet cover. New, right hand drive mouldings were created. They launched the new car at the Earls Court Motorfair in 1981.

The SS was, ironically, a loose approximation of the Richard Oakes Nova (*qv*). Standard VW-based version – as per the American Cimbria – had a tubular steel chassis. Ford Cortina mechanicals arrived in 1983. Ford versions are identifiable by a large bonnet bulge – that and the fact that the engine was in the front and not air-cooled, of course!

In 2007 Tim Naylor of TEAC Sportscars acquired the project and announced an updated and revised new version called the SS S3R, based on Toyota MR2 Mk2, and also an all-new MkIV version. Didn't stick around for long.

Eagle Cars 1981–99
TEAC Sportscars 2007–2009
Approx 605 made

EAGLE STENDETTO

A Pontiac Fiero-based Ferrari F40-esque body conversion, originally commissioned by a French manufacturer.

Eagle Cars 1991–97
Approx 40 made

EASOM MACHO

Nottingham-based Easom Engineering displayed their Ginetta G11-inspired two-seater at the Newark Show of 1988. It wasn't seen again.

Easom Engineering 1988
Approx 1 made

EASOM TOURISTA

An angular, quirky take on the beach buggy theme.

Easom Engineering 1997
Approx 1 made

EB50/EB60

Company run by John and Wilf Edwards and based in an old pottery in Tunstall near Stoke-on-Trent. A third brother, Sid, joined in 1961 to help them cope with the demand they had created via their bodyshells and 32-page 'special builders' catalogue. The glassfibre bodies were made for the Edwards' by local coachbuilders Wilson's, who struggled to keep up with sales. These were fairly basic bodyshells that came with no instructions but proved very popular and were designed around Ford mechanicals at the amazingly low price of £39. At one time they had a 16-week waiting list! The EB60 was slightly more sophisticated.

The company could supply you with a refurbished Ford chassis or their own EB93 ladderframe from 1961 that had unequal length wishbones, with coil-springs on the front with quarter-elliptic, Panhard rod and lever arm damper set-up on the rear.

In late 1962, EB amalgamated with engineering firm William Boulton Ltd, although the brothers continued their bodyshell and *specials* business. The whole concern was purchased by lorry maker ERF in 1964, for whom the Edwards produced cab bodies and front wings.

EB Bros (Staffs) Ltd 1959–64
Approx 2,000 made

EB DEBONAIR

Launched at the Racing Car Show of 1961, where the EB50/60 had been pretty basic, if effective, bodyshells, the Debonair was a complete contrast and aimed to offer mainstream quality at a cut price, but featured all the modern attributes associated with such a car, including padded leather dashboard, wind-up windows and quarter lights. Very sophisticated for its time, the Debonair was also marketed by LMB.

EB Bros (Staffs) Ltd 1961–64
Approx 55 made

EBM TAZIO

South African exotic sports car, with an original design spaceframe chassis and power from small block Chevy V8. Available in GTR (coupé) and Spyder versions. Company was based in Milton Keynes and run by Eric Booth. A comeback as a fully built supercar came to nought.

EBM Sportscars 1999–2000
Approx 3 made

ECO-EXO

Launched at Stoneleigh Kit Car Show in 2010, this is a three-wheeler with an emphasis on economy and influenced by the exo-style. Suzuki Burgman scooter is the donor vehicle with engines ranging from 125 to 650cc, enabling either 100mpg or 100mph capability. Tandem seat arrangement with a low centre of gravity. Run by father and son team Stuart and Scott Turner, and their friend Paul Turland.

Mills Extreme Vehicles 2010   *ECO-EXO 2010 to date*
Approx 4 made

ECU – *see May Corp*

EFM

Bonkers twin-engined trike from Garry Buzzelli of Ohio-based EFM Auto Clutch and imported to the UK by gearbox specialist Ron Jones.

Ron's demo car featured a pair of Yamaha V-Max engines combined for a total 300bhp, although the car could run on one engine if preferred. Performance electrifying, with a 0-60mph sprint in 2.5 seconds. Bullet!

Advico 2011
Approximately 1 made (UK)

EG ARROW

Spaniard Emilio Garcia had an illustrious automotive pedigree and had worked at Gardeners in Sutton, Surrey, before moving to Bell & Colvill before becoming half of Autokraft UK with Brian Angliss. He also owned/raced an original AC Cobra prepared by John Atkins. His name was also well known in Ferrari circles, and he did a natty line in converting Daytona Coupés to Spyders, so it's unsurprising that he came up with a replica of the car, given its renewed prominence as a result of the *Miami Vice* TV series of the late '80s.

A collaboration with Ken Atwell's son Paul, it was based on the ubiquitous Jaguar XJ12 and was originally known as the PKA V12. The car was underpinned by a backbone chassis. The Spyder model came first in 1987, with a Coupé following in 1989. Ex-KVA man Peter Jacobs, who had made the prototype bodies for the Ford RS200 and was a fibreglasser of real note, made the shells via his PLJ Special Mouldings company.

A division of exhaust specialists Custom Chrome called Swift Classics sold fully-built versions for a time.

Total sales were 73 Coupés and just seven Spyders. Garcia was the only replica maker to offer a convertible version. Kits cost £20,000 in 1988, or £25,000 fully converted.

After EG Autocraft came to a very messy ending, Norman Bond set up Arrow Spyder Ltd, based in Llanelli, although the project was finally owned by an erstwhile customer called Mr Buchanan.

PKA Marketing 1987
EG Autocraft 1987–89
Arrow Spyder Ltd 1989–91
Hillcrest 1991
Approx 80 made

EL CID

Originally known as the Oasis Scorpion, the El Cid was a Citroën Mehari replica based, unsurprisingly, on Citroën 2CV mechanicals. One of the large 1990s stable of Scorhill Motors, based in Godalming (1988–92), then Walton-on-Thames (1992–93), and finally Chertsey, where they

remained until they ceased trading in 1996. Most of their products were acquired and marketed for a time by Crestel Services, also of Chertsey.
Scorhill Motors 1988–96
Crestel Services 1996–99
Approx 11 made

ELDON ROADSTER

Formerly the Racecorp LA (*qv*), the Eldon was marketed by a company in Paddock Wood, Kent, run by Phil Surridge, a former newstrade distribution manager. He'd previously set up a general car repair business before becoming a Racecorp agent in 1991, and soon thereafter began to concentrate solely on kit car building. The Eldon moniker came from the name of the road in which the business was located. When Racecorp boss Steve Amos became disillusioned with the kit car business Surridge acquired the project and soon moved to a large new unit in Edenbridge.

Originally Ford Escort Mk2-based, although Phil came up with a Ford Sierra-based version. The company's Dutch agent sold around 45 kits but tragically died in a road accident.

Eldon ceased trading in 1999, but the car made a comeback as the Razer (*qv*) in 2003 under *Which Kit?* magazine proprietor Peter Filby.
Eldon Autokits 1993–99
Razer Sportscars 2002–7
Razor Sports Cars 2007 to date
Approx 75 made

ELLIPSE

Nice three-wheeler created by custom bike enthusiasts Alan Pitcairn and Dave Kennell of Teffont Magna, Wiltshire. Power comes from a potent S&S Racing 96ci vee-twin engine delivering around 100bhp. Two-part chassis with unequal-length front wishbones, tubular front chassis and a Ford Type 9 gearbox. Fully built price from £23,500.

In 2011 a brand-new JAP 1,300cc engine was introduced, made by JA Prestwich rights holders Dave and Les Card, and this unit is offered by Planet.
Planet Engineering 2007 to date
Approx 2 made

ELVA ENGINEERING

When Frank Nichols was demobbed from the army in 1947 he bought a general car repair business based in Westham, East Sussex, before moving to bigger premises in Bexhill-on-Sea. Nicholls was successful enough to indulge his passion for motorsport. Initially he raced a Lotus VI before commissioning Mike Chapman to build him a *special* called the CSM, a 1,172cc Ford powered cycle-winged sports car. It performed well enough to persuade Nichols and his mechanic Mac Witts to create their own car, christened the Elva (from the French *Elle va*, 'she goes').

The prototype Elva Cars product, the Courier, appeared in 1958 complete with a Williams & Pritchard body, although subsequent production versions had glassfibre bodies.

A move to a larger site in Hastings saw the company doing well supplying turnkey cars and component versions too. The latter came fully trimmed and wired with a weekend's work being enough for a customer to complete them. The company operated with 60 staff at one time, with the majority of cars going to America until one such consignment was held up in transit at US Customs resultinh in the company going into voluntary liquidation in 1961, after which this side of the business was taken over by Trojan Cars of Croydon.

Nichols, meanwhile, regrouped and with his designer Keith Marsden produced some excellent mid-engined race cars. Nichols not only managed to persuade Porsche to provide some engines but also brought BMW into sports car racing by coming up with the track-based Mk5, Mk6 and Trevor Fiore (Frost)-designed GT160.

Meanwhile, Trojan Cars formed Elva Cars (1961) Ltd and set about creating MkIII and MkIV Couriers, but by 1965 they were busy building McLaren road cars and lost a bit of interest in the Elva products, which were sold on to Shenley-based Ken Sheppard (who sold a further 26) in October of that year.

ELVA COURIER MkI

The first Courier saw the light of day in 1958 and used a ladderframe chassis and Riley 1.5 or MGA engines with Triumph suspension. It was a highly capable car on the racetrack. It's easy to tell a MkI from later models due to its split windscreen.

Elva Engineering 1958–59
Approx 50 made

ELVA COURIER MkII

Many improvements came with the launch of the MkII Courier in 1959. It featured a new chassis based around the MGA engine and a new one-piece windscreen. Taken over by Croydon-based Trojan Ltd in 1961.

Elva Engineering 1959–61
Elva Cars (1961) Ltd 1961–62
Approx 350 made

ELVA COURIER MkIII

The first 'all-Trojan Ltd' Elva, with production now switched to their Croydon factory. It was based on Triumph suspension with power from the MGA 1,622cc or Ford Pre-Crossflow engines. Early in production, Elva offered a notchback coupé complete with hardtop, but just ten of these were produced.

Elva Cars (1961) Ltd 1962–65
Approx 100 made

ELVA COURIER MkIV

Trojan developed the MkIII into a 2+2 fastback, which they called the MkIV, although this was superseded within a short time by the T-Type (not available as a kit) featuring Elva's new Tru-Trak independent suspension set-up.

In 1965 Trojan sold the project to Ken Sheppard, who continued with the T-Series 1800 (26 made), developing the Sebring Courier racer and one-off Courier 3000 Coupé (all of which were only available fully built) before ceasing production altogether in 1967.

Elva Cars (1961) Ltd 1962–65
Ken Sheppard Customised Sports Cars 1965–67
Approx 100 made

ELYSEE SPRINT

Liam Wilkinson was the man behind Gemini Cars (named after his birth sign) of Hucknall, Nottinghamshire. This Vauxhall Chevette-based car was heavily inspired by a fire-damaged Elan S1 reworked by Liam and Trevor Cook. (Wilkinson was later to become part of Road Track Race Ltd.) John Keywood of JB Sportscars in Twickenham acquired the project in 1999 and set about coming up with a Sierra-based version.

In 2010, Vincent Hurricane (*qv*) makers Caburn Engineering announced that they had acquired the project and were working on a new backbone-type chassis that would accept Ford Sierra running gear.

Gemini Cars 1991–99
JB Sportscars 1999–2001
Caburn Engineering 2010 to date
Approx 20 made

EMERY GT

Paul Emery was a very gifted engineer and racing driver, piloting his own cars – known as Emerysons – to much track success. A financier commissioned the Emery GT, launched in 1963, which was the first kit car based on the Hillman Imp. Had slightly quirky fixed head looks and glassfibre body on a spaceframe chassis.

Paul Emery Cars 1963–64
Approx 4 made

ENCORE SUPER 95

Next replica of the Lotus Elite. The original version is a genuine classic and featured a GRP monocoque tub with (usually) a Coventry Climax 1,216cc engine producing around 105bhp, and was produced 1957–63. The original car featured some ingenious touches for its day, such as the double-skinned floor, which held the differential via metalastic bobbins.

Encore Cars, run by John Hostler, was based in Duke Street, Norwich. Hostler was a Lotus enthusiast, having owned several Elans and a Europa Twin Cam and was also a former technical illustrator at *Autocar* magazine from 1962 to 77.

While looking for a new restoration project to take on, with his father David, he found a GRP laminator who could supply complete Elite bodyshells modified to fit a Spyder Engineering backbone chassis, with subframes at the front and rear to house suspension components that included double wishbones all round. Meanwhile, a Ford Sierra differential was used. The empty suspension 'turrets' of the original bodyshell that were designed for Chapman Struts now featured coil-over dampers.

Power came from a Fiesta XR2 CVH engine (although similar units from Escort Mk3 and 4, and Sierra 1.8s, could also be utilised).

Hostler was offered a job at Lotus Engineering and production of the little Super 95 ceased as a result.

Encore Cars 1992–97
Approx 10 made

ENGLISH CARS OF DISTINCTION E-TYPE REPLICA

One of the many early '80s companies offering approximations of a variety of classic cars in kit form. The difference with English Cars of Distinction was that they were Jaguar marque experts. This was a replica of the legendary E-type.

English Cars of Distinction 1980–83
Approx 3 made

ENGLISH CARS OF DISTINCTION XK120 REPLICA

Replica of the Jaguar XK120 from a company selling Classic Jags.

English Cars of Distinction 1980–83
Approx 5 made

ENGLISH CARS OF DISTINCTION XK140 REPLICA

Similar to the concept of the company's XK120 replica.

English Cars of Distinction 1980–83
Approx 2 made

ENGLISH CARS OF DISTINCTION XK150 REPLICA

XK150 replica from a Jaguar specialist.

English Cars of Distinction 1980–83
Approx 3 made

A B C D E F G H I J K L M N O P Q R S T U V W X Y Z

ENIGMA

Modern sportscar of original design based on Ford Sierra from classic car restorer, Ian McDonald of Great Yeldham, Essex.

This had a Cobra-inspired rear end, underpinned by a spaceframe chassis and unmodified MacPherson strut rear end and other Ford Sierra parts. I recall that it had a rather unique rear section that unbolted to allow an alternative coupé body to be fitted. Quite unusual, and several years ahead of the Smart ForTwos interchangeable bumpers and the like. Appeared just once, in unfinished form at the Stoneleigh show of 1999.

Whitley Sports Cars 1999
Approx 2 made

ENZO DESIGN AMILLIM XS

Aston Martin-inspired GT car, based on Mazda MX-5 and created in association with Graham Hathaway Engineering.

Enzo Design 2011
Approx 1 made

ENZO DESIGN EDF275 GTB/4

Originated by Gerry Hawkridge of Hawk Cars with around six made in 1987. Updated by Northamptonshire-based Enzo Designs.

Enzo Design 2010-11
Approx 2 made

ENZO DESIGN EDF40

A Ferrari F40 replica based on a suitable donor, a Ferrari F355!

Enzo Design 2010-11
Approx 2 made

ENZO DESIGN EDF430

Body conversion for Toyota MR2 Mk3, with kits priced around £8,000.

Enzo Design 2010-11
Approx 20 made

ENZO DESIGN RS200

Ford RS200 replica produced from a set of moulds as used by Reliant to produce the original cars.

Enzo Design 2008 to date
Approx 20 made

EPC HUSTLER

Essex-based company (initially located at Service Garage in Chelmsford, before moving to Hornchurch in 1970, ending their days in Dagenham) who enjoyed much success during the UK beach buggy craze of the early seventies. The operation was run by brothers Terry and Peter Cordingley, who had previously acted as agents for GP.

Their first attempt wasn't around for long, and the second incarnation, the Hustler, was clearly inspired by the short-wheelbase GP Buggy. Customers could pay an extra £5 and get the GT version, which had faired-in headlights and a curved Mini windscreen. The short-wheelbase example required a 12in chop of the Beetle chassis, while they also offered a long wheelbase example. A sportier-looking Hustler GT was also available, of which 50 were sold, which came with a windscreen sourced from a Fiat 500.

As soon as the beach buggy craze ended, so did EPC. They weren't helped by the fact they sold their products quite cheaply, although the Hustler was very highly regarded.

Essex Proto Conversions 1970–72
Approx 375 made

EPC PINZA GS

Less successful sister-model to the Hustler. Hybrid styling didn't appeal to many. In 1970, customers could get a painted bodyshell for £190, an extra £10 got a metalflake finish, while a hardtop to keep the occupants nice and toasty cost just £55 (plus £5 extra for metalflake). The Beetle chassis was shortened by 10in, the shell was a two-piece, and you could also choose a four-seater if the family wanted to come out with you.

Essex Proto Conversions 1970–72
Approx 11 made

EPONA

Designed by Garry Gooderham, for his final-year project at Newcastle University, and taken on as a concept by Keith Wood at Aeon Sports cars, who showed a scale model at the Detling Show of 2009. Aeon never made the model due to the success of their main business, supplying crop sprayers, and the project passed to Exceed Autocraft Ltd of Doncaster in 2011.

Aeon Sportscars 2009–2011
Exceed Autocraft Ltd 2011 to date
Approx 1 made

EQUUS – *see Estivo*

ERA 30

A Lotus 23 replica from Tiger Racing's ERA division.
Tiger Racing 2005 to date
Approx 10 made

ERA 427

Well-known American Cobra replica, imported here for a time by American Auto Parts of Thornton Heath under the 'America By Car' banner.
America By Car 1981
Approx 4 sold (UK)

ERA SINGLE-SEATER

A return to sixties single seaters from Tiger Racing's Jim Dudley and his ERA sub-division that also produced a Lotus 23 replica.
Jim worked hard to promote this delightful car and even managed to get several racing within Tiger's BRSCC-run race series, with historic racing driver par excellence, Nigel Greensall, behind the wheel on one occasion. Power for the ERA came from a Ford Zetec 2-litre with a rear-mounted Hewland Mk9 transaxle.
Tiger Racing 2003 to date
Approx 16 made

ERA TYPE 35

An obscure Bugatti Type 35 replica from the 1980s.
ERA Cars 1983–85
Approx 1 made

ES – *see Albar Buggy*

ESTEEM COUNTACH

Late 1994 Countach replica based on Fiat X1/9 from a Scottish company (Glengarnock, Ayrshire) run by American Dewayne Young. Claimed to be the 'best replica in the world'; didn't last very long. Very cheap kit price of just £1,295.
Esteem Motor Company 1994
Approx 1 made

ESTIVO

Sharp two-seater with box section steel chassis and humble Austin 1100 or Morris 1300 mechanicals, although there were intentions to produce Allegro and Maxi-based versions. Designed by ex-quantity surveyor Colin Robertson, the Estivo appeared briefly as a kit in 1983, before reappearing (again briefly) as a fully-built car in 1985 under the name Equus.
Cavallo Cars 1983
Equus Cars 1985
Approx 4 made

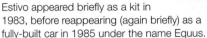

EURO 427

Formerly a Fiero Factory *(qv)* product, taken over by Hampshire-based restaurateur Nigel Ramsay in 2003 before moving to Auto Speciali and then Vindicator Cars from 2010, who renamed the car the Boa.
Euro 427 Sportscars 1999–2002
Approx 18 made

EURO LAMME

Makers ABS Motorsport are a well-known Lincolnshire GRP company who also made the Freestyle *(qv)* for a time, and offer a whole raft of Mini body conversions of which the Euro Lamme has been the most popular.
ABS Motorsport 1990 to date
Thousands made

EUROCAT MIAMI

A Ferrari Testarossa lookalike that appeared briefly in 1991. Came from an outfit in Exmouth, Devon.
Eurocat 1991
Approx 1 made

EUROCCO

Based on VW Beetle mechanicals and floorpan although an Alfa engine could also be used. Originated with a 1978 2+2 notchback design that Richard Oakes was commissioned to come up with by Mike Carlton of Charger *(qv)* manufacturer Embeesea Cars.

It was intended as a sister model to the Charger, but the success of the latter meant it ultimately didn't get into production, although it later became Steaney Development's SN1 *(qv)*. However, Embeesea kept a set of moulds and converted it to a fastback style. Once they ceased trading in 1982 it ended up with Roy Coates' S&R Sports Cars in Yorkshire, who developed it to become the SR1 *(qv)*. Did you keep up?
Embeesea Cars 1981–82
S&R Sports Cars 1982–86
Approx 5 made

EUROPA 47R

Superb Lotus Europa racer recreated from marque specialists Europa Engineering (also known as Banks Service Station), based in Southport and run by Richard Winter and Andy Short.
Europa Engineering 1992 to date
Approx 120 made

EUROPA 62S

A lightweight version of the Type 47R.
Europa Engineering 1993 to date
Approx 12 made

EUROSPORT TR40

A Triumph TR7-based Ferrari F40 replica kit from Fiat X1/9 specialists run by Gerry Brown. Company later became Tiger agents for a time.
Eurosport (UK) 1990–92 (Rayleigh)
Eurosport (UK) 1992–97 (Sawston)
Rimmer Bros 1997–98
Approx 4 made

EVANS SCORPION

Spitfire-based MG TF replica, made by the same Alf Evans responsible for the Specials-era Delta. Didn't last long.
Evans Developments 1979
Approx 1 made

EVANTÉ

Created by famed engine tuners Vegantune, run by George Robinson and based in Spalding, Lincolnshire. One of the most celebrated Lotus Elan-inspired kits. Powered by the superb VTA engine, basically a Ford Kent Crossflow block married to a twin-cam cylinder head with Ford gearbox, and available in 120bhp (1,600cc) or 140bhp (1,700cc) guises.

After the company ceased trading in 1991 the project was picked up by vintage vehicle manufacturers Fleur de Lys Automobile Manufacturing, who developed a Mk2 version.
Evanté Cars Ltd (Vegantune) 1983–91
Fleur de Lys 1992
Approx 106 made

EVANTÉ Mk2

Fleur de Lys developed the Mk2 version, which was wider, had revised styling and was powered by a Ford Zetec (a few Vauxhall-powered cars were also produced). Not as visually pleasing as the Mk1. When Fleur de Lys went pop in 1994 the Mk2 was acquired by Jeremy Snow.
Fleur de Lys Automobile Manufacturing 1992–94
Evanté Sportscars 1998–2005
Approx 15 made

EVERGREEN SPORTWAGEN

A German kit made by Rudolph, this Karmann Ghia replica was imported to the UK by Evergreen Motor Company of Lamorna, Cornwall, run by Pete Murphy.
Evergreen Motor Company 1994–99
Approx 25 made

EVO

The EVO is a gorgeous little three-wheeler powered by Suzuki GSX-R1000 bike engine, which meant fiery performance from such a lightweight bolide.

A marginal one for this book, because I had to drawline somewhere in the sand and excluded one-off *specials* and foreign kits that weren't officially available in the UK. However, a couple have crept in, and the EVO from French company Rayvolution Cars is one of them. Run by Tony La Faye and based near Paris, the company had a UK office for a time near the Channel Tunnel in Ashford, plus they actively attended UK kit car shows and sold kits here. Tony formerly worked for a major Japanese car manufacturer at their Paris design studio.

A four-wheeled Rayvolution model was under development as we closed for press.
Rayvolution Cars 2007 to date
Approx 3 made (UK)

EVO 200 – *see Evolution 200*

EVOLUTION 1 ROADSTER

Designed by Formula 27 creator Mike Ryan, it was originally available as a set of plans (£89) before being offered in traditional kit form. Taken over by Mike Gould of Evolution Sportscars, based in Bristol.

Race-spec adjustable Rose-jointed suspension with a spaceframe intended to house a Rover V8, although four-cylinder units could also be used. Had an unusual split windscreen arrangement.
Evolution Sports Cars 1997–99
Approx 12 made

EVOLUTION 200

Originally the KaRa 430 (*qv*), created by engineer Richard Sellicks and design consultant Peter Baisden. When Baisden left production continued under Sellicks at Mercury Motorsport of Shoeburyness, and the project was renamed the Evolution 200. The car was hugely capable and was based around Ford Sierra Cosworth donor parts with a spaceframe chassis and fibreglass body.

In 1998 it passed to erstwhile Mercury employee and RS enthusiast Paul Horner, trading under the RS Automotive name, and became the EVO 200. Horner was joined in 1999 by haulier Garry Campbell, and they enthusiastically marketed and exhibited the project for several years until pressure of other work saw it put on the back burner in about 2002.

Project subsequently bought by RS customer and ex-RAF man Bill Watson of Margate-based RS Motorsport in October 2008, who introduced an alternative donor to the Ford Cosworth, which by 2010 was becoming quite scarce. In 2011, they moved to new premises at Manston Airport.

KaRa Sports Cars Ltd 1991–93
Mercury Motorsport 1993–98
RS Automotive 1998–2004
RS Motorsport 2008 to date
Approx 115 made

EVOLUTION S & S2

A revamp of the Ginetta G27 (*qv*) by Peter Lathrope of Maidstone, Kent. Retained Ford Sierra donor parts and introduced a BMW option called the S2.
GKD Sports Cars 2006 to date
Approx 25 made

EW KNOBBLY

A Lister Knobbly replica from a Chesterfield company run by Eike Welhausen. Jaguar parts used throughout.
Chesterfield Motor Spares 1994
Approx 2 made

EWM BRIGAND

Produced by a Salisbury-based company run by Edward Waddington, who latched on to the success of Dutton Cars' pile 'em high, sell 'em cheap concept. The Brigand was sister model to the Buccaneer (see below) and was basically the same under the skin with alternative front and rear sections. It was clearly inspired by the Motorspeed/MFE Magic (*qv*) and Dutton Phaeton (*qv*).

In 1988 Ben Sparham of B&S Sports Cars relaunched it as the BS Roadster (*qv*). Sadly it didn't really get out of the starting blocks.
Edward Waddington Motors 1984–85
B&S Sports Cars 1988–89
Approx 9 made (including BS Roadster)

EWM BUCCANEER

Based on Ford Cortina mechanicals and pretty cheap to build, this budget traditional roadster's styling wasn't for everybody, so Edward Waddington didn't sell very many. Resurrected in 1988 by Ben Sparham of Birmingham company B&S Sports Cars, who renamed it the BS Sprint (*qv*).
Edward Waddington Motors 1984–85
B&S Sports Cars 1988–89
Approx 7 made

EX2

Redditch-based A&M Sportscars came up with this one. Company name subtly amended to AM when co-founder Adrian Morley left, leaving Malcolm Davey running the operation. A 1999 revision saw altered headlights and rear screen.
AM Sportscars 1996 to date
Approx 19 made

EXACT 308

Second offering from Scottish company Exact Replicas, run by Brian Love. Based on Toyota MR2 Mk2.
Exact Replicas 2008
Approx 2 made

EXACT 355

Toyota MR2-based F355 replica from Exact Replicas.
Exact Replicas 2006 to date
Approx 10 made

EXCALIBUR CRUSADER

Inspired by the Bonito (*qv*), the Excalibur was an attractive 2+2 based on Ford Cortina Mk3, Mk4 or Mk5. Any Ford four- or six-cylinder engine could be used, with a Rover V8 option introduced later. Creator Clive Clark was a boat-builder by trade and was based in West Looe, Cornwall.
Excalibur Cars 1985–92
Approx 32 made

EXOCET

Announced in June 2010 the Exocet is a semi-exo style modern sports car from the pencil of prolific kit car designer Stuart Mills. His first design based on Mazda MX-5 Mk1, so is therefore front-engined and rear-wheel drive and uses the complete donor drivetrain in unmodified form, the front and ear subframes, plus a whole lot more besides. A lightweight arrived in late 2011.
Mills Extreme Vehicles 2010 to date
Approx 150 made

EXTREME 355

The first model from Hull-based Extreme Sports Cars, run by Ashley Martin. An F355 based on Toyota MR2 Mk2. Features a 41-piece GRP kit.
Extreme Sports Cars
2002 to date
Approx 300 made

EXTREME 360

Extreme used a Peugeot 406 Coupé as donor for their F360 body conversion, which means an engine in the front but in return provides a four-seat capability.
Extreme Sports Cars
2004 to date
Approx 250 made

EXTREME 430

Like their F360 replica the Extreme F430 was based on Peugeot 406 Coupé.
Extreme Sports Cars
2007 to date
Approx 300 made

EXTREME 997

Body conversion from Extreme Sports Cars was a Porsche 911 997 body conversion replica based on the 996 generation.
Extreme Sports Cars 2010
Approx 10 made

EXTREME DTM

Awesome replica of the Mercedes-Benz CLK DTM AMG from Extreme Sports Cars. Based on standard CLK, and is a more than convincing clone.
Extreme Sports Cars
2009 to date
Approx 15 made

EXTREME MURCI

A very exotic Italian replica that could be based on either Toyota MR2 MkJ as a body conversion kit using the unmodified floorplan of the Toyota or on a separate spaceframe chassis devised by DC supercars. A very convincing visual impact.
Extreme Sports Cars
2009 to date
Approx 180 made

F-TYPE

Introduced by Martyn Philpott of Maidstone-based Leighton Cars alongside the BRA CV3 (*qv*) and Leighton (*qv*) projects he'd acquired from BRA Motor Works. Only available very briefly.
Leighton Cars 2005
Approx 1 made

FACTORY FIVE Mk3

Factory Five Racing, run by Mark and David Smith, based in Massachusetts, USA, are the world's largest volume seller of kit cars. Their Mk3 Roadster model has been imported to the UK since 2008 by Hunter Murrell Motorsport Ltd of Salisbury, run by Ian Hunter (no, not the Mott The Hoople one!) and Jim Murrell. They also planned to import the FFR Challenge Car and 33 Roadster.

Although FFR hasn't as yet torn up trees in sales terms in the UK the company remains the biggest selling manufacturer of latcers in the world, a R mantle they've held for over 10 years. Many thousands have been sold.
Factory Five UK 2008-9
Approx 3 made (UK)

F1-67

A beautiful single seater from Ian Gray of Stuart Taylor Motorsport. A car that wasn't a replica, but evoked memories of sixties Honda F1 cars. Power came from GM LS3 V8 with a ZFQ transaxle. Not a kit per se, but included here for the sake of completeness.
Stuart Taylor Motorsport
2008 to date
Approx 5 made

FACTORY FIVE TYPE 65 COUPÉ

Another Factory Five product imported to the UK by Hunter Murrell Motorsport from 2007.
Factory Five UK 2007-9
Approx 25 made (UK)

FAIRLITE

Essentially this was the Ginetta G3 (*qv*) available to suit proprietary chassis of the day for Ford 8/10 mechanicals.
Ginetta Cars 1959–63
Approx 40 made

FAIRTHORPE CARS

Founded by Air Vice-Marshal Don C.T. Bennett. A rather remarkable man, Bennett had served in Bomber Command during WW2 and was appointed to command the Pathfinder unit, while after the war he started his own airline and was the first man to fly a commercial airliner out of Heathrow post-war. Oh, and he was also a Member of Parliament for a time.

He found cars fascinating so decided to start his own company, Fairthorpe Cars (named after the Bennett family home in Australia) in Chalfont St Peter, Buckinghamshire.

His first model was a rudimentary microcar called the Atom, which wasn't available in kit form. Kits were introduced when ex-Daimler man John Green joined as works manager. Incidentally, a former employee of Fairthorpe was one Ken Lowe, who went on to found world-famous fan company Kenlowe.

Don Bennett passed away on 15 September 1986.

FAIRTHORPE ATOMOTA

Succeeded the Atom of 1954, which was never sold in kit form. However, *specials* enthusiasts of 1957 could put an Atomota together themselves, and it actually looked very similar to its predecessor. Had a backbone chassis and fibreglass body with a tiny BSA 646cc engine. The Atom Major was the same car but with a Standard 8/10 engine.
Fairthorpe Cars 1957–59
Approx 30 made

FAIRTHORPE ELECTRINA

Strangely-styled saloon based on Triumph Herald mechanicals and running gear. Apparently the roof section was 'splashed' from a Jaguar Mk1 and the customer could choose either an Electron or Zeta nose-section.
Fairthorpe Cars 1960–63
Approx 6 made

FAIRTHORPE ELECTRON

The Electron of 1956 was a much better effort from Fairthorpe with a sleek fibreglass body, made by Microplas. Available in kit form from 1958. A twin-rail suspension took Triumph TR2 suspension, while Coventry Climax or Standard 10 power were the most popular choices. At £734 kits were quite expensive for the day.
Fairthorpe Cars 1958–62 (kits)
Approx 20 made

FAIRTHORPE ELECTRON MINOR

Things got better still with the Electron Minor of 1957, which was by far the company's most successful model. Underpinned by a tube steel ladderframe chassis with running gear and power from the Standard 10.
Fairthorpe Cars 1957–60
Approx 300 made

FAIRTHORPE EM2

Succeeded the Electron Minor (previous entry) in 1960 and was based on Triumph Herald. A widened chassis allowed other engine options such as Ford Anglia.
Fairthorpe Cars 1960–63
Approx 50 made

FAIRTHORPE EM3

The EM3 was longer and quite stylish, with its nose section taken from the Fairthorpe Rockette (*qv*).
Fairthorpe Cars 1963–65
Approx 30 made

FAIRTHORPE EM4

Effectively the same car as the EM3 with a revised chassis to accept Triumph Spitfire engines.
Fairthorpe Cars 1965–70
Approx 10 made

FAIRTHORPE EM5

Very short-lived 2+2 version. Customers only wanted Fairthorpes with two seats.
Fairthorpe Cars 1970
Approx 5 made

FAIRTHORPE EM6

By the time the EM6 was launched its era had passed really. Notable for using a Triumph GT6 chassis instead of a Fairthorpe creation.
Fairthorpe Cars 1970–73
Approx 2 made

FAIRTHORPE ROCKETTE

Very similar to the Electron Minor (*qv*) but used a Triumph Vitesse straight-six rather than that of the Spitfire. First cars had a central third headlight *à la* Cyclops, although this was quickly dispensed with and a bonnet bulge was added instead.
Fairthorpe Cars 1962–67
Approx 25 made

FAIRTHORPE TX-GT

Donald Bennett's son Torix became heavily involved with the day-to-day running of the company and the TX-GT of 1967 was very much his work. He even created a transverse rod IRS arrangement and developed the TX-GT from the convertible prototype of 1965, basing the car on Triumph GT6 chassis and running gear. A MkII was the same but had an extra 9bhp.
Fairthorpe Cars 1967–68
Approx 7 made

FAIRTHORPE TX-S/TX-SS

Replacing the TX-GT for 1968 was the TX-S, with similar, yet more angular styling based around GT6 mechanicals and engine. Just four were sold. The main difference for the TX-SS was the fact that it had the 2.5-litre PI engine from the TR6, but this didn't make it much of a better seller with just six finding homes.
Fairthorpe Cars 1968–76
Approx 10 made

FAIRTHORPE ZETA

For their first all-out performance model Fairthorpe used an Electron Minor chassis extended by 6in, a Triumph TR3 donor and the 2.6-litre engine from the Ford Zephyr Six.
Fairthorpe Cars 1959–63
Approx 5 made

FALCON SHELLS

Based in Waltham Abbey, the company was set up by Peter Pellandine after he left Ashley Laminates in 1957. Len Terry, later of Terrier and Lotus, was employed as technical manager for a time, to give advice to customers. The company was sold to Mike Moseley in summer 1961 and moved to Hatfield, Hertfordshire.

FALCON Mk1

Pellandine brought the Ashley 750 (*qv*) shell from Ashley Laminates and renamed it the Falcon Mk1. Still based around Austin 7 parts.
Falcon Shells 1957–60
Approx 150 made

FALCON Mk2

Another refugee from Ashley, where it was known as the Sports Racer. Became known as the Falcon Competition (*qv*) in 1960 and was sold as a complete kit package. Mk2 shells cost £65.
Falcon Shells 1957–60
Approx 1,000 made

FALCON Mk3

The company's first 'own' design. Renamed the Falcon Caribbean (*qv*) in 1961. Shell designed around Ford 90in wheelbase chassis. Shells on their own cost £115, with chassis at £50.
Falcon Shells 1958–61
Approx 1,500 made

FALCON 515

Arguably the most sophisticated of the early *specials* era kits. First post-Pellandine Falcon, with design from Brazilian Tom Rohonyi. Based on Cortina Mk1.
Falcon Shells 1963–64
Approx 25 made

FALCON BERMUDA

This four-seater design was Pellandine's last for Falcon before he sold the company and emigrated to Australia in 1962. Based around Ford 10 mechanicals.
Falcon Shells 1961–63
Approx 200 made

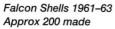

FALCON CARIBBEAN

Revised Falcon Mk3 shell sold in complete kit form from 1961. Body was used for Elva Courier MkII (*qv*). Like Ashley, Falcon also made their own chassis (Len Terry-designed), but could utilise the Ford 10 chassis too. Complete kits from £750.
Falcon Shells 1961–63
Approx 500 sold

FALCON CHASE

An early creation from Peter Bird, who also had a hand in the Anthony Stevens' Lomax and Cipher (*qv*) designs. Basically saw panels added to his Falcon Quarry (*qv*) model to give a very distinctive wedge shape.
Falcon Design 1982
Approx 1 made

FALCON COMPETITION

Basically a revised and complete kit package for the Falcon Mk2 (*qv*), with prices from £450.
Falcon Shells 1958–63
Approx 300 made

FALCON LX3

If people thought the original Sports model (see below) was bonkers then Bird's three-wheeled LX3 version was positively unhinged. Retained the Sports' Citroën 2CV donor.
Falcon Design 1984–93
The 2CV Centre 1993–2001
Became Falcon Cars (same owners but in Lincolnshire) 2001–2
Approx 60 made

FALCON QUARRY

Peter Bird's Birmingham-based Falcon Design made this strange looking sandrail with a pickup back end. Err...
Falcon Design 1983
Approx 1 made

FALCON SPORTS

An innovative idea by Peter Bird's Falcon Design of basing a Lotus Seven-inspired sports car on the humble Citroën 2CV, which might have appalled the purists but proved popular with the 200-odd customers who built one. A chap called Tony Hoderin from Rugby took over in 1987 before Bird returned in 1990 for a further three year tenure now based in Stratford-upon-Avon. In 1993 he sold the project to Mike and Paula Cooper, who ran the Frome 2CV Centre at the time. When they moved to Lincolnshire they carried on with the Falcon models under the Falcon Cars banner. The Coopers put the Sports and LX3 models on the back burner from 2002, although you may still be able to order one if you ask nicely. They also devised a tiny 'pod' trailer that could be towed behind a kit car and camped in!
Falcon Design 1984–93
The 2CV Centre 1993–2001
Falcon Cars 2001–2
Approx 230 made

FERGUS MOSQUITO

Beautiful Aston Martin Ulster replica, which was the brainchild of Fergus Engineering of Kingsbridge, Devon, run by Robert Kennedy Ping. It was underpinned by Morris Marina mechanicals with a sturdy box section ladderframe chassis. The company shut down suddenly in 1987 after just six were sold. What's not so well-known is that Kennedy Ping had originally made fully-built only nut-for-nut replicas of the Ulster that he called the Wren prior to the Mosquito.

A specialist automotive parts maker called AIMS of Union Road, Kingsbridge, run by Charles Smith, took over for a short while but didn't sell any more kits. They were succeeded by Bob Lewis' Projects of Distinction, who also acted as sole agents for Teal Cars for a time, who planned a Sherpa van donor option, although nothing much more was heard.

One of the industry's 'ones that got away'.
Fergus Engineering 1986–87   AIMS 1991–92
Projects of Distinction 1992–99
Approx 6 made

FES BRITON

FES, based in Beith, Scotland, was run by Stan Forsyth. The Briton was originally produced by Protoflight as the Kestrel (qv).
FES 1988–90
Approx 3 made

FF BUGGY

This was basically a revised FibreFab Rat from Tim Cooksey who had acquired the business from Tony Hill in 1981. A very stylish beach buggy and a very original design, which is said to have been inspired by the Balboa buggy based on 79½in floorplan, although a long wheelbase version arrived very soon after.

FF agents Stevespeed built two blue and yellow examples that were used by the BBC in the popular eighties TV series Challenge Anneka.

Cooksey returned to his previous industrial exhibition line of work in late 1985 and sold the FF projects to Steve and Martine Wilson of Country Volks.
FF Kitcars & Conversions 1983-87
Country Volks 1987-93
Approx 30 made

FF COUNTRYMAN

The customer cut the back-end of the roof section off of a VW Beetle and replaced it with a flat hardwood pick-up rear section. Created by Tony Hill and continued with Tim Cooksey, who revised it to feature a fibreglass pick-up bed section. It was available with a number of different bonnets and spoilers.
Fibre Fab 1979-81
FF Kitcras & Conversions 1981-85
Country Volks 1985–93
Approx 10 made

FIELDMOUSE

Quirky jeep-style vehicle based on Ford Popular. Not as cute as a real fieldmouse!
Fieldmouse Cars 1971–72
Approx 2 made

FIERO FACTORY

Company set up as a Pontiac Fiero and American car specialist in 1990 and run by (then) petrol station proprietor Steve Briddon and Terry Sands. They offered their own Fiero-based kits from 1991.

FIERO FACTORY EURO 427 REPLICA

A well put-together Cobra replica that sold extremely well and could be powered by a massive variety of engines including Mercedes Benz and BMW V8s. Later became the AS427 (qv) and Euro 427 (qv).
Fiero Factory 1998–2002   Euro 427 Sportscars 2002-3
Fiero Factory 2003–5   Venom Sports Cars 2005–6
Auto Speciali 2006–10   Vindicator Cars 2010 to date
Approx 1,000 made

FIERO FACTORY F282

Ferrari F355 replica body conversion for Fiero made to a very high standard, as with all of the Fiero Factory's products. Later joined by a Toyota MR2-based version called the MR3 SS but remains available.
Fiero Factory 1995 to date
Approx 400 made

FIERO FACTORY FIEROSSA

Loosely styled on the Ferrari Testarossa, the Fierossa was the Fiero Factory's next product after the Belaro Berlinetta (qv).
Fiero Factory 1991–2003
Approx 85 made

FIERO FACTORY MONZA 308

The Fierossa (see above) and Monza 308 were the company's first kit products and received well by enthusiasts and press.
Fiero Factory 1991–2003
Approx 135 made

FIERO FACTORY MR3 SS

MR2-based F355 replica that evolved from the company's successful Fiero-based F282 version.
Fiero Factory 1998 to date
Approx 400 made

FIERO FACTORY MR4T

A superb F40 replica based on Toyota MR2. Probably the kit car industry's best attempt at an F40 replica.
Fiero Factory 1999 to date
Approx 10 made

FIERO FACTORY V2

A Plymouth Prowler replica (with correct-sized 20in wheels) based on a multi-tube spaceframe/ladderframe combination, with an unstressed GRP body, double wishbone front set-up and a de Dion rear end. Donor mechanicals came from Ford Granada. Neat.
Fiero Factory 1998–2003
Approx 20 made

FIERO FACTORY VENOM

Originally a Canadian Corvette-based kit called the Vortex that Fiero Factory imported here before developing their own Granada-based version soon after. When Keith Kirk left Fiero Factory he set up Venom Sports Cars before coming under the Auto Speciali banner working with Jon Harris. Keith sadly passed away in 2008.
Fiero Factory 1995–2003
Venom Sports Cars 2003–5
Auto Speciali 2005–8
Approx 75 made

FLETCHER GT

After David Ogle was killed his eponymous SX1000 project was taken over by boat builder Norman Fletcher, along with a couple of other stillborn Ogle

Design prototypes. Fletcher amalgamated the two to create the Fletcher GT, retaining the Mini donor base. Due to the fact that only four were sold it's fairly safe to say that the buying public didn't think much of it and Fletcher soon returned to building boats.

Norman Fletcher had seen the car project as a good opportunity to create extra business when boat production was quiet, and he did in fact receive an order for 30 cars from a Swiss dealer, but ironically BMC couldn't/wouldn't supply the required components, thus the deal fell through and the Fletcher GT was abandoned.
Fletcher Boats 1967
Approx 4 made

FLITE

Interestingly named Lotus Elite (Type 14) replica from ex-RJH man, Rob Hancock, under the Phoenix Automotive Developments banner, located in South Brent, Devon.
Phoenix Automotive Developments 2011 to date
Approx 2 made

FOERS IBEX

After selling his Nomad (*qv*) and Triton (*qv*) projects to Deltech, Rotherham-based John Foers set about creating the beefier, more rugged Ibex, which reverted to a spaceframe chassis arrangement, although he employed engineering ideas from a forklift roll-over cab structure he'd produced for a customer. Based on the Land Rover Defender, the Ibex is a highly capable vehicle used by enthusiasts, and also commercially, by hill farmers and the like.

Foers sold the project to Ricardo 2004 but bought it back in 2006 and recommenced production from his new base in Northumberland, where he'd moved in 2003.

The Ibex is available in six model variations, 21 different configurations and in either 4x4 or 6x6 forms. John's son David has become part of the business and is responsible for the newly announced F8 version.
Foers Engineering 1990–2004
Ricardo Engineering 2004–6
Foers Engineering 2006 to date
Approx 110 made

HIT KIT

FOERS NOMAD

By the mid-'70s John Foers owned a Land Rover S2 and also a Mini. He reckoned that the concept of a 'Mini-Land Rover' was a good one and proceeded to build a one-off for himself. Inevitably, others saw it and wanted one, and so the fledgling Foers Engineering was born. The Nomad was the production version, based on a spaceframe chassis, and was like, er, a mini-Land Rover. After selling 172 kits Foers sold the project to fellow Rotherham company Deltech Engineering, run by Derek Chapman, who sold a further 11 before calling it a day.
Foers Engineering 1977–90
Deltech Engineering Ltd 1990–97
Approx 183 made

FOERS TRITON

John Foers launched his Triton in 1985. It was very much a more civilised and generally updated Nomad, its donor now being Metro rather than Mini. The Triton didn't take off in the same way that the Nomad did, probably due to the fact that at the time the

Metro was quite new, and it was more complicated to make and build due to the semi-monocoque. Acquired by Deltech Engineering in 1990 along with the Nomad.
Foers Engineering 1985–90
Deltech Engineering Ltd 1990–97
Approx 3 made

FORD 28/29 ROD

A Ford 28/29 replica from Ashley Markham of West Stockwith, Nottinghamshire.

Markham range acquired by Penrith-based Cygnus Custom & Classic in April 2011.
Markham Street Rods 2005–11
Cygnus Custom & Classic 2011 to date
Approx 20 made

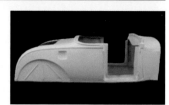

FORD 30/31 ROD

Ford 30/31 replica. Markham range acquired by Penrith-based Cygnus Custom & Classic in April 2011.
Markham Street Rods 2005–11
Cygnus Custom & Classic 2011 to date
Approx 15 made

A B C D E F G H I J K L M N O P Q R S T U V W X Y Z

FORD 34 ROD

34 Ford kit. Markham range acquired by Penrith-based Cygnus Custom & Classic in April 2011.

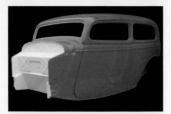

Markham Street Rods 2005–11
Cygnus Custom & Classic 2011 to date
Approx 25 made

FOREMAN P4 BERLINETTA

Neil Foreman had been an aircraft engineering apprentice at Marconi Avionics, making bits for Concorde, Nimrod, Jaguar, Typhoon and Hercules aircraft. After this he became the second employee of Guy Black at Lynx Engineering, making their first D- and C-types. He later became the second customer for Lee Noble's P4 kit (after Colin Strauss, later of Auriga), and subsequently bought the project from Classic Performance Cars, who had in turn purchased the project from JH Classics/Deon, who had – deep breath – got it from Lee Noble at Kit Deal. Phew!

Neil made several improvements, including better-fitting panels, a wider cockpit with more legroom, improved headroom, adjustable front suspension, revised geometry and more engine options, such as V12 fitment, often Ferrari 400 and Lamborghini. When Neil's Car Builders Solutions general parts business took off, he sold the P4 models to Dunlop Systems and Components, based in Coventry, although not much more was heard and the projects were offered for sale again in Autumn 2011.

NF Auto Developments 1995–2008
Dunlop Systems & Components 2008 to date
Approx 40 made

FOREMAN P4 CANAM

Convertible body for the P4 inspired by a rarer than hen's teeth version of the wondrous P4.

NF Auto Developments 1998–2008
Dunlop Systems & Components 2008 to date
Approx 6 made

FOREMAN P4 SPYDER

Revised body style for the Foreman P4 that featured no roof and a windowless tail.

NF Auto Developments 1995–2008
Dunlop Systems & Components 2008 to date
Approx 15 made

FORMULA 27 F27 CLUBMAN/MBE

Created as a plan-built Lotus Seven-inspired sports car in 1991 by Mike Ryan. Taken over in 1992 by mechanical engineer Steve Porter, who very soon introduced body/chassis kits and also a 5in wider version.

Project acquired by YKC in 2002 before moving on to current custodians Image Sports Cars, run by Peter Allen, in early 2005. Allen had done an apprenticeship at Aston Martin before becoming well known in the motorsport world, even running a Formula Ford team for a time.

One of the pioneers of inline-four bike-engined kits along with Fisher and Pell. Like the standard Clubman version, the MBE, created by Steve Porter, was available in wide- or narrow-bodied form.

Formula 27 Sportscars 1991–2002
YKC Sportscars 2002–5
Image Sports Cars 2005 to date
Approx 75 made (kits); 3,000+ sets of plans.

FORMULA 27 KR ROADSTER/MONZA

A full-bodied sports car created by Steve Porter, with power usually coming from bike engines or Ford four-cylinder car engines. Project passed to YKC Sportscars in 2002 before being revised by Peter Allen of Image Sports Cars when he took over in 2005, and the name was changed to Monza and power was amended to GM LS V8.

Formula 27 Sportscars 1998–2002
YKC Sportscars 2002–5
Image Sports Cars 2005 to date
Approx 15 made

FORMULA TR7

Could be had in Testarossa or Köenig body styles based on Triumph TR7. Short-lived kit was the work of a Pontyclun-based automotive body repair operation run by Nigel Pittard.

Formula Cars 1992
Approx 1 made

FORZARI

Jaguar restorer Paul Welch of Credington was the man behind the ambitious Group C-inspired Forzari. Styling not to everyone's taste but the innovation can't be faulted. Featured a composite/carbon fibre honeycomb monocoque, with Rose-jointed double wishbone

suspension and power from a Renault V6, although Welch said that V8s could be accommodated. Body from carbon fibre and GRP.

Forzari Developments 1996–97
Approx 1 made

FOURSTYLE

A short-lived elongated four-seater version of the Freestyle (*qv*). Retained Mini donor parts.
Funbuggies 2004–6
Approx 2 made

FRA F1

Newcastle-upon-Tyne-based Max Hall's Toyshop operation was best known for its Mini kit (see below), but in 1998 also very briefly offered this single-seater with bike power, heavily inspired by a Formula 1 car.
The Toyshop 1998
Approx 2 made

FRA MINI

The FRA (Fast Road Automobile) Mini was a GRP rebodied, de-seamed Mini conversion. The GRP monocoque was a revised version of the Sabre Sprint (*qv*) item from the mid-'80s. Hall later introduced a hatchback version and also a matching trailer.

Project passed to John Light in 2002, who created a new operation called FRA Car Company, before selling it to well-known Mini racer Dave Kimberley in 2007.
The Toyshop 1997–2002
FRA Car Company 2002–7
TDK Racing 2007 to date
Approx 35 made

FREESTYLE

Very similar to the Onyx Tomcat (*qv*) created by Dave Sewell of Fibreform, the Freestyle was marketed through fibreglass specialists ABS Group, who sold around 150 kits. Project then sold to engineer Richard Drinkell of TH Engineering in 2001, who operated the business on a part-time basis until pressure of his main occupation saw him sell it to aviation engineer Dave Smart of Wellington, Somerset, in 2004. Despite being only two-wheel drive, the 'wheel-at-each-corner' Freestyle could display decent off-road abilities when required.
ABS Group 1998–2001
TH Engineering 2001–4
Funbuggies 2004–7
Approx 325 made

FRENETTE

A Mini Moke Californian clone from Peter Frenette of St Neots, who made guns for a living. He soon shot back to that occupation.
Peter Frenette 1981–82
Approx 4 made

FROGEYE SUPERSPRITE

Exact 'Frogeye' replica made at the Simeon Motor Works in Ryde, Isle of Wight. The man behind the company was Keith Brading, who initially offered the car in fully-built guise only, before later supplying 'restoration' kits. First cars had humble A-series power, although when kit packages were launched the car was called the Supersprite, and featured modified A+-series power from the Austin Maestro (twin SU carbs instead of a single unit, and a K&N air filter), while the gearbox was a Ford MT75 unit. Around 130 of these cars were sold before the design became the IPI Frogeye, offered by Brading's erstwhile body makers, Island Plastics.

In 1989 Brading came to an agreement with Geoffrey Healey, who licensed 12 fully-built versions known as SuperSprites (note the capital 'S' on Sprite), with power coming from Rover K-series, which automatically gave the car real provenance. Fully-built cars cost a pricey £18,000 in the late '80s.
The Frogeye Car Company 1985–2000
Approx 142 made

FRS

Announced as this book closed for press, the FRS Sportscar is a three-wheeler from father and son team, Fred and Jason Reeves, both serial national speed record holders, particularly at Elvington in North Yorkshire. From their base

in Tong, Bradford, they debuted their car at the National Kit Car Motor Show at Stoneleigh in May 2011, and it's described as a roadgoing version (replica?) of a successful hillclimb car, with power coming from a Suzuki Bandit 1200cc engine.
FRS Sportscars 2011 to date
Approx 3 made

FULCRUM

Designed by Neil Williams for Hereford-based Raw Striker Ltd, the Fulcrum immediately found popularity with the trackday fraternity, while Captain Gary Goodyear won the 750 Motor Club's *Kit Car* Championship driving a Fulcrum in 2009. Project acquired in September 2010 by brothers Callum and Jeremy Bulmer, who revised the company name slightly. Fulcrum did well in competition.
Raw Striker Ltd 2007–10
Raw Engineering 2010 to date
Approx 20 made

FULGARA RTS

Essentially a Mk2 version of the Subaru Impreza-based Murtaya, with deeper doors and several styling revisions. Created by Murtaya Sports Cars of Woodbury Salterton, Devon run by Andy White and Graham Codling. Incidentally, Fulgara was the Roman goddess of lightning.

Murtaya Sports Cars 2011 to date
Approx 2 made

FURORE FORMULA ONE

A road-legal single-seater with tandem seating arrangement giving bonkers performance and a true F1-style thrill. Russ Bost of Benfleet was the man behind the project.

Furore Cars 2006 to date
Approx 6 made

FURY

One of the truly great kit cars, combining retro looks and modern mechanicals. Designed by Jeremy Phillips of Sylva Autokits in 1991, the Fury has become one of the most successful kit cars in motorsport along with its sister

model the Sylva Striker (*qv*), with which it shared the same Escort Mk2 donor, but had an enveloping body, a windscreen and doors. Name came from the Hawker Fury as a result of Phillips' love of aviation.

Sylva made about 150 before selling the project to Mark Fisher of Fisher Sportscars based in Marden, Kent, who sold several hundred during his 11-year tenure with the car before selling the project to Martin Bell's Kit Car Workshop based in Northamptonshire.

The Fury returned to Kent in 2007 under the control of Brian Hill of Cranbrook-based BGH Geartech, where former Fisher employee Steve Hughes was based.

As this book closed for press, it was announced that Steve Hughes, trading as Fury Sports Cars, had acquired the project from BGH, taking over that company's Cranbrook base.

Sylva Autokits 1991–94   Fisher Sportscars 1994–2005
Kit Car Workshop 2005–7   BGH Geartech 2007–11
Fury Sports Cars 2011 to date
Approx 850 made

FURY MENACE

A mid-engine configuration for the Menace that looked a lot like the standard Fury (see above). Created by Mark Fisher of Marden, Kent.

Fisher Sportscars 2004–5
Approx 7 made

FUTURA

This is the car that sent Fellpoint Ltd to the wall. Run by Robin Statham, they were at the time marketing the Mini Jem (*qv*) but sank all their resources into this highly futuristic two-seater. Based on the ubiquitous VW Beetle floorpan and running gear, its

wedge-like appearance was very daring for 1971, as was entry/exit, which involved the complete windscreen flipping sideways to enable passengers to climb over the nose. Featured four headlights, which were positioned behind the base of the windscreen. All brave stuff.
Fellpoint Ltd 1971
Approx 3 made

FUTURA

Stillborn project that made its debut at Sandown Show in 1992. Featured a spaceframe chassis with independent suspension all round, Renault V6 3-litre power. It was the work of ex-Prova man Barry Higgins. Company based in Darwen, Lancashire. Styling had elements of the Cizeta V16 supercar.

Devillin Cars 1992
Approx 1 made

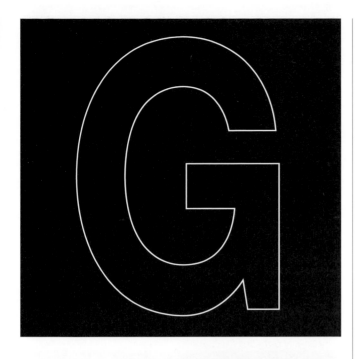

GAIA DELTOID

Created by Guy Dormehl from Dibden Purlieu and described by its creator as 'Batman meets Stealth bomber'. A spaceframe chassis into which you wheeled a motorbike, less forks, which could be reverse-engineered back to a bike if required. Taken over in 2001 by Jon Ridd, who was based just down the road from GTD in Poole, Dorset. Ridd worked closely with Crescent Suzuki (a major motorcycle dealer, who also run a British Superbike team and Suzuki's factory MotoGP effort) to develop a Hayabusa power option for the Deltoid. Not many takers.

Gaia Cars 1994–2002
Approx 11 made

GALLARGO

Exotic roadster replica based on Toyota MR2 Mk3. Originally prefixed by 'Limbo'.

Exact Replicas 2008 to date
Approx 7 made

GANDINI

Lamborghini LP400 replica also known as the Stanzani. Very short-lived. Company based in Stowmarket and run by Kevin Claydon.

The Countach Company 1993
Approx 1 made

GATSBY

Formerly known as the Spirit SS (*qv*), among other names, this American Classic Motor Carriages neo-classic kit never really made it in the UK. Originally imported to these shores by Dave Perry, it passed to Spirit Cars of London, Classic Automotive Reproductions (CAR) of Scarborough and, in 1984, Daytona Classics of Clacton-on-Sea, who used the Gatsby Cars name for this model. Next, it went to RW Kit Cars and finally faded from view as the Phoenix under D&S Engineering in 1987.

Spirit Cars of London 1983–84
Classic Automotive Reproductions 1984
Gatsby Cars/Daytona Classics 1984–86
RW Kit Cars 1986–87
D&S Engineering 1987–88
Approx 3 made

GAZELLE

Conceived as a (sort of) replica of the Mercedes-Benz SSK by American kit manufacturer Classic Motor Carriages. The original UK outfit was based in Bishopgate Street, Leeds, and was part of a company called Briton International, who specialised in airport and dockyard tractors. The UK set-up called the US Beetle-based version the Mark VR, with the domestic-developed Ford variant underpinned example known as the Mark CF. Back in 1975 a fully-built Gazelle cost £15,000, which was Porsche 911 money at the time.

Several attempts were made in the UK to get the car established here, with the Gazelle being the first effort. Over the years, it also saw the light of day as Amica (*qv*), Delta (*qv*), Spirit SS (*qv*), Gatsby (*qv*) and Phoenix (*qv*), none of which lasted long.

Classic Cars of Titchfield near Fareham had another go at selling the car here, again as the Gazelle, in 1992. That company was run by Robin Gibbs and Andy Mitchell.

Amazingly, US production only ended very recently, and not before around 3,000 had been sold there.

Gazelle Sports Car Company 1975–82
Classic Cars of Titchfield 1992–94
Approx 18 made

GB 5000 S

A Lamborghini Countach replica from GB Racing Sports, run by Andrew Grimshaw who for a time was located on the same Standish, Lancashire, site as JBA Engineering.

GB Racing Sports 1988–90
Approx 5 made

A B C D E F G H I J K L M N O P Q R S T U V W X Y Z

GB BUGGY

Another GP Buggy copy, although this was allegedly the first! The same company, run by John Cullen, later made the Invader (*qv*) buggy, a modified Desert Fox Scorpion from America.
GB Motors 1969–74
Approx 50 made

GD 427 (JAG/EURO/Mk4)

Gardner Douglas Sportscars was founded by Andy Burrows in 1990 and developed its Cobra replica kit around a backbone chassis with a GRP body with foam reinforcement. Initially available as a Jaguar-based package before an ultimate EURO version was developed in 1994 that didn't use donor parts and had all-bespoke components but still featured a choice of V8 engines. Via their LSPower division the company was one of the first to champion the use of GM's LS series of engines.

In 2005 they acquired the bodyshell that had been made by DJ David 'Kid' Jensen's motorsport operation for AC Cars, when AC sold it as the Carbon Road Series (CRS) model. One of the very best kit cars.
Gardner Douglas Sportscars 1990 to date
Approx 375 made

GD-XM – *see Griffin*

GE 427 – *see Gravetti 427*

GECKO

Tamworth-based Nick Ingram created the Gecko, which neatly crossed the divide between Mini Moke and beach buggy. Ubiquitous Mini donor supplied running gear and subframes bolted to a tough little box-section chassis to which the body, made from a mix of plywood, aluminium and fibreglass, was fixed. A variety of wheelbases were available from 50 to 100in and, if you really wanted, a six-wheeler version too. David Simmons of Simmons Design of Banbury took over in 1990.
Autobarn Fabrications 1984–90
Simmons Design 1990–92
Approx 88 made

GEM – *see Grantura Yak*

GENIE WASP

One of the relatively few Scottish kit cars, the Wasp hailed from Genie Cars of Ancrum, Jedburgh, run by Robert Taylor. Cross between a '30s-style roadster and modern sports car. A revised Sportsman version appeared in 1990.
Genie Cars 1988–92
Approx 9 made

GD T70

A second model line from Gardner Douglas that appeared in 2002. Underpinned by a square and round tube spaceframe chassis panelled in NS4 aircraft-spec 16-gauge aluminium, based on the same finely engineered principles that Gardner Douglas had created with their GD 427. Marvellous.
Gardner Douglas Sportscars 2002 to date
Approx 50 made

GENTRY

The Gentry was created by ex-Triumph worker Roger Blockley, who worked on the Spitfire production line. He built a *special* during his spare time and, as often happens in such circumstances, he soon had people asking him for a replica. Such was the response and fast sales that he set up his RMB operation in 1973, basing his MG TF replica unsurprisingly on Triumph mechanicals.

In 1989 Roger sold the project to erstwhile employees Terry Phillips and Mick Sinclair, who traded as TM Motors ('TM' standing for Terry and Mick) and developed a new Ford-based chassis option that could accept Escort Mk2 or Cortina components. Company name later changed to SP Motors, the 'SP' standing for Sinclair and Phillips.

Sinclair departed in 1997, leaving Terry (trading as TP Motors), who came up with a Ford Sierra donor package from the Barwell factory before he sold out in 2001 and went to work for then next

door neighbour Lee Noble. After lying dormant for a year or so, Alan Beillby of Vintage Motor Company took the project over and intended to offer it alongside his range of period vans. He built a demonstrator.

Enter at this stage Geoff and Ellen Beston of Nuneaton, who had purchased a Gentry on eBay in 2000. Suitably smitten, Geoff, a recently retired Chief Inspector of Traffic for Warwickshire Constabulary, found a new career and acquired the project from VMC in 2006. After a period of appraisal, Geoff and Ellen set about rebuilding the marque to a position of strength and look set fair for the future, having relaunched the car in 2008. Offered for sale in 2011 after Geoff became ill.

RMB Motors 1973–89   *TM Motors 1989–97*
SP Motors/TP Motors 1997–2001   *Vintage Motor Company 2002–6*
Gentry Motors 2008 to date   *Approx 2,500 made*

GILBERN GENIE

Gilbern's second model, the Genie arrived to replace the GT in 1967. It was a 2+2 of much larger proportions. Power changed to Zephyr 6 2.5-litre or Zephyr Zodiac 3.0-litre Essex V6. MG supplied the running gear, be it MGB or, later on, MGA.
Gilbern Cars 1967–69
Approx 202 made

GILBERN CARS

Giles Smith lived in Church village near Pontypridd, South Wales. A butcher by trade, he had a passion for cars and fancied building a *special*, as many people did in the '60s. He met Bernard Friese, an engineer, and approached him about the possibility of building him a car. Friese had been captured while serving in the German army in WW2 and after the war had set up home in the UK and had worked for Martins as a fibreglass laminator, so understood what was involved in car building. A plan was agreed to build a car for Smith completely from scratch. During the build process the project was viewed by various experts who all commented that it was far too good to simply be a one-off. So it was that Smith's *special* was the seed from which grew the Gilbern marque, the company name being a conflation of Giles and Bernard's first names.

They based themselves in a two-storey shed behind Smith's shop – not ideal, but workable. Their first car, the Gilbern GT, appeared in 1960. The intention was to offer the GT in body/chassis form, leaving customers to source their own parts, before they revised this approach in the name of quality control and began to provide all-new components in the package. The Gilbern fraternity get very upset if you use the word *kit*, but, like the Lotus Elan kits of the day, the shells came pre-painted, with the seats fitted and even pre-wired for the customer, while the body was fitted to the chassis with the doors, boot and bonnet pre-hung. The customer still needed to do a certain amount of spanner wielding, however.

Such was the buzz around the car that *Autosport* magazine tested the first Gilbern GT in spring 1960, and liked it a lot. The first handful of GTs were built in Smith's shed before production moved to the former home of nearby Red Ash Colliery, mothballed since 1921.

The first GTs were based on ubiquitous Austin A35 running gear, complete with leaf springs, although adventurous speed-hungry customers could also opt for the Coventry Climax engine. The build process was steady, if slow, and the Gilbern workforce turned out one car per month. Before long standard engine choice settled on the MGB B-Series and production increased to four units per month, the majority of cars sold having MG running gear.

There are some great stories about Giles Smith and his cars at a variety of motor shows. Memorable ones include him regularly standing on the roof of a Gilbern demonstrator and inviting others to join him to show just how strong the bodywork was, while he would also open a door and swing on it!

In spring 1968 the Gilbern marque was bought by the ACE Group, best known for manufacturing slot machines. MD Roger Collins was a keen motoring enthusiast and was eager to become a motor manufacturer. The Gilbern founders were kept on as part of the new set-up, and although Smith didn't stay for long Friese was heavily involved in readying the forthcoming Invader for production. However, he too left when ACE became part of the huge MECCA group. ACE installed a new MD, Michael Leather, and also invested heavily in the operation, tripling the workforce if not production. Summer 1969 marked the arrival of the Invader, often regarded as the archetypal Gilbern if not the most capable.

The introduction of VAT in 1973 meant that the cash-saving benefits of building a kit disappeared overnight and Gilbern, along with the likes of Lotus and TVR, deleted kit options from their range. Gilbern went into receivership later in the same year, but within three months a new investor, Anthony Peters, joined Leather and the company briefly started making cars again before stopping for good in March 1974.

For several years after its closure rumours continued to circulate that production would recommence, and the factory remained untouched, ready to go again, right up until early 1980. However, even though the odd unfinished car, still on the production line, was completed, this great British marque has never returned. Lack of funds put paid to the exciting T11 sports car project as well as a planned Invader MkIV.

A dodgy economic climate (have we been here before?) and rapid over-expansion were probably the things that did for Gilbern, but its memory is kept alive by the excellent owners' club, who own the rights to the name and moulds.

GILBERN GT

Initially the GT had either Austin
Healey Sprite or optional Coventry
Climax FWA power before MGA
engines came along in 1962, with
MGB1800 (car then known as the
GT1800) following in 1963. Running
gear was mainly Austin A35 before
moving to Morris Minor 1000.
Gilbern Cars 1960–67
Approx 277 made

GILBERN INVADER MkI

Summer 1969 marked the arrival
of the Invader, which looked quite
similar to the Genie it replaced, but
having a new chassis that didn't go
down well with press or customers,
having a 'floppy' front end. This
resulted in a MkII version in 1970
with stiffer front, while debuting the Invader Estate at the same time.

All cars had MGC suspension carried over from the Genie, with a
Panhard Rod rear end. Engine was the Zodiac Essex 3-litre V6.
Gilbern Cars 1969–70
Approx 78 made

GILBERN INVADER MkII

Exactly the same running gear and power as the MkI, but had a stiffer
front end.
Gilbern Cars 1970–72
Approx 212 made

GILBERN INVADER MkIII

A shift to Ford components
throughout was made for the Invader
MkIII of autumn 1972, with Cortina
Mk3 supplying suspension. Power
plant remained the Essex V6.
Gilbern Cars 1972–74
Approx 208 made

GILBERN INVADER ESTATE

Elegant practicality.
Gilbern Cars 1971–72
Approx 105 made

GINETTA CARS

In the 1950s the Walklett Brothers – Bob, Trevers, Doug and Ivor –
ran an agricultural structural engineering business in Woodbridge,
Suffolk. They were all motorsport enthusiasts and, helped by
brother Trevers, Ivor built a *special* based on the Wolseley Hornet,
which he subsequently wrapped around a tree. This first *special*
was retrospectively referred to as G1.

By 1962 the company had moved to larger premises in
Witham, Essex, but in 1973 moved back to Suffolk and an even
bigger site. However, with the introduction of VAT in 1973 and
the resulting collapse of the kit car industry they rationalised the
business and returned to the smaller Witham site. Ivor was the
designer, Bob handled administration, Trevers (died, aged 76, in
January 2000) styled the cars and Doug ran the works.

When the company was bought out by a consortium, led
by Martin Phaff and Mike Madiri, in 1989, Bob and Trevers
immediately retired, although Ivor stayed on for a time to help
smooth the handover period and the move to a large factory in
Scunthorpe. Martin Phaff subsequently based the company in
Sheffield and sold a steady stream of cars until the introduction
of the single-make race series – which initially used the G27 before
switching to the G20 from 2001 – at which point sales took off.

In 2005 the Ginetta marque was purchased by Lawrence
Tomlinson of LNT Automotive, a successful businessman (Times
Rich List) and race team owner, who further developed the
company's track activities but ceased kit production, with cars only
being available in fully-built guise from then on.

Meanwhile, Ivor, along with Trevers and nephew Mark, formed
DARE UK in 1990 after being commissioned to make a batch of
G4s and G12s, at first for the Japanese market before domestic
availability and new models followed.

Ginetta models that weren't available in kit form were:

G1	Was Ivor Walkett's Wolseley Hornet *Special*.
G5	A G4 fitted with a Ford Pre-Crossflow known as G4 1500 (1964 – 32 sold).
G6	Three G4 S1s fitted with DKW engines for a German customer (1964 – 3 sold).
G7	A prototype fitted with a Hillman gearbox for hill climbing.
G8	Early use of a monocoque. A Formula Three car, too costly to produce (3 made).
G9	A prototype Formula Two car based on the G8.
G12	Superb mid-engined G4 racer (1965 – 40 made).
G13	Not used for superstitious reasons.
G14	Intended as a replacement for the G4 but stillborn.
G16	Group Six sports racer (1968 – 11 made).
G17	Formula Four car – 4 sold). Hillman Imp-powered.
G18	FF1600 car developed from G17. Adrian Raynard raced on (1968 – 4 made).
G19	Abandoned Formula Three car from 1969 based on G7.
G20	Original G20 was a stillborn Formula One car fro 1969 and the last Ginette single-seater. BRM 3-litre V12 or Walkett's own 1.5-litre two stroke supercharged engine.
G22	Sports 2000 car (1978 – 2 made).
G23	A convertible G21 (1981 – 3 made).
G24	A revised G21 (1981 – 2 made).
G25	Pretty two-seater that didn't made production but was the first mid-engined Ginetta.
G29	Sports-racer powered by Mazda Wankel rotary 1986 – 1 made).
G40	G34 was renamed to celebrate the 40th anniversary in 1998.
G50	LNT-created GT car (2007-on)
G60	Revised Farbio GT5 that Ginetta acquired in late 2009.

GINETTA G2

The first Ginetta model was clearly inspired by the Lotus Six and was an affordable prospect for customers in 1958 with kits priced at around £150. A steel tube spaceframe chassis underpinned the aluminium-bodied G2 with a Ford sidevalve engine providing the power.

Ginetta Cars 1958–59
Approx 27 made

GINETTA G3

Basically a G2 with an all-enveloping body and power from Ford Anglia 100E sidevalve engine. For its day actually quite sophisticated, especially compared to some rivals. Also sold as a basic bodyshell as the Fairlite (*qv*).

Ginetta Cars 1959–63
Approx 60 made

GINETTA G4 SERIES 1

Often described as *the* classic Ginetta model and certainly their first volume seller. Power came from a Ford 105E sidevalve 997cc engine. Had a multi-tube spaceframe with double wishbones at the front and live rear axle.

Ginetta Cars 1961–63
Approx 220 made

GINETTA G4 SERIES 2

The biggest visual difference from Series 1 was the lack of rear fins, while it was also more practical, being longer with the sidevalve engine replaced by the Pre-Crossflow unit. This is the version that was revived by Ivor and Mark Walklett under the DARE banner in 1989 initially for the Japanese market.

Ginetta Cars 1963–66
Approx 300 made

GINETTA G4 SERIES 3

The Series 3 of 1966 was a much-changed car with restyled body and a bonnet that now featured pop-up headlights. Under the skin an all-new spaceframe was based around Triumph Herald front wishbones.

Ginetta Cars 1966–69
Approx 50 made

GINETTA G4 SERIES 4

After being out of production for some 12 years it was quite a surprise when Ginetta launched the G4 S4 in 1981, which followed the classic theme but was a heavily revised car, being 3in longer and 2in wider than the S3. Had an all-new spaceframe, bigger boot area and cockpit with standard engine being the Ford Crossflow.

Ginetta Cars 1981–85
Approx 100 made

GINETTA G10

With its beefy American V8 engine the G10 was aimed at the US market especially. Look closely and you can spot the MGB doors. Only a few were sold, including two convertibles, because the car wasn't eligible for any US race series.

Ginetta Cars 1964–65
Approx 3 made

GINETTA G11

The G11 was a G10 aimed at the UK market popularised by the MGB, while ironically it utilised components from that car such as doors, windscreen and 1,800cc B-Series engine. Lack of factory parts did for it before sales could develop. Two of the 12 cars sold were convertibles.

Ginetta Cars 1966
Approx 12 made

GINETTA G15

A classic Ginetta if ever there was one. A good concept with a pretty body and a bargain price. Power came from a Hillman Imp Sport 875cc engine, as did the transaxle and trailing arm rear suspension. Demonstrating Ivor Walklett's innovative mind was the lift-up rear section, allowing excellent access to the engine. In 1971, the company was producing five G15s per week, with a complete kit priced at £845.

Ginetta Cars
G15 S1 1967–68   G15 S2 1968–70   G15 S3 1970–73
G15 S4 1973   G15 S5 1973
Approx 610 made

GINETTA G20

Launched during Martin Phaff's tenure, the 'new' G20 (an earlier G20 project was stillborn in 1969) has gone on to become one of *the* classic Ginetta models. Succeeded the G27 in more ways than one as it also replaced the G27 in Ginetta's highly successful one-make race series, which was

followed by a G20 Junior series for youngsters. Kit sales ceased soon after the company was taken over by Lawrence Tomlinson's LNT operation in 2005.
Ginetta Cars 1999 to date
Approx 375 made

GINETTA G21

Underpinned by a backbone tube steel chassis. The majority of those sold were fitted with the 1,725cc engine from the Sunbeam Rapier, although some had the potent Ford Essex V6 3.0-litre.
Ginetta Cars 1971–78
Approx 70 made

GINETTA G26

This big four-seater coupé surprised a few people when it was launched in 1984. Comprised a single donor vehicle based around Ford Cortina mechanicals including windscreen, although it also featured Ford Fiesta Mk1 doors. Power came from four-cylinder engine – as per donor –

and had pop-up headlights. When equipped with a Ford V6 it had a revised front end and fixed headlights and was known as the G30.
Ginetta Cars 1984–92
Approx 280 made

GINETTA G27

Natural successor to the classic G4 Series 4. Featured a spaceframe chassis and a blend of Triumph, Morris and Ford mechanicals, with lots of different engines. Mark Walklett was very successful racing one. Continued in production in revised Series 2 form when Martin Phaff took over the company in 1989.

A Series 3 complete with head fairings appeared in 1993, and a further revised S4 version with a stylish curved windscreen was launched in 1995, based on Ford Sierra mechanicals. Superseded by the G20 and shelved until taken over by Peter Lathrope of GKD Sports Cars and, with styling further revised by Richard Ashby, it became the Evolution S (*qv*).
Ginetta Cars 1985–2005
Approx 200 made

GINETTA G28

Another sister spawned from the G26, but this one was a two-seater coupé launched at the British Motor Show of 1986. Ford Cortina-based with fixed headlights. Not a popular seller.
Ginetta Cars 1986–92
Approx 6 made

GINETTA G30

Very similar to the G26 but had revised front end with fixed headlights and Ford 2.8 Cologne or 3.0-litre Essex V6. Shared the same beefy steel spaceframe and pretty much everything else with its sister car.
Ginetta Cars 1984–92
Approx 10 made

GINETTA G31

As per G28 but designed for Ford V6 power and had a pop-up headlight arrangement.
Ginetta Cars 1986–92
Approx 70 made

GINETTA G32

The G32 was a cracking two-seater that seemed to have everything going for it. Nice styling and well made. The only trouble was that Toyota launched the MR2… The majority of G32s were coupés, with a handful of convertibles made.
Ginetta Cars 1986–90
Approx 130 made

GINETTA G33

Inspired by the G27 Series 2, the G33 was a big, hairy-chested two-seater with Rover V8-power.
Ginetta Cars 1991–95
Approx 100 made

GINETTA G34

Volvo-powered two-seater available only briefly in the UK, but did well in Sweden.
Ginetta Cars 1998
Approx 8 made (UK)

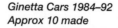

GLOBAL GT LIGHT

Created by Scotsman Phil Hazard in 1995, the Global featured a chassis made by Arch Motors. Then passed to current Lynx AE boss, Jon Lee, who introduced the 600cc engine fitment. Acquired by acclaimed racing driver Graham Hathaway in 1999. Power came from either Yamaha R6 (600cc) or R1 (1,000cc) engine.
Hazard Engineering 1995–97
Lynx AE 1997–99
Graham Hathaway Engineering 1999 to date
Approx 100 made

GLOBAL GT2

A two-seat version of the acclaimed Global GT Light (see above), designed by Bob Buck.
Graham Hathaway Engineering 2005 to date
Approx 15 made

GNAT

Wedge-shaped Mini-based buggy device with A-series engine mounted in the rear.
Gnat Cars 1974–75
Approx 3 made

GP

John Jobber had been an apprentice at Jaguar before moving to Brabham. After graduating to their F1 team in 1966 he met South African Pierre du Plessis, who was working at Lola at the time. Along with Peter Allnutt, they set up GP (Grand Prix) Speedshop in a canal-side workshop in The Ham, Brentford. Work involved race car preparation of GT40s and Lola T70s for luminaries such as Denny Hulme, Frank Gardner and Paul Hawkins.

In 1967 du Plessis went back to South Africa for a holiday and also a busman's holiday, spannering for racing driver David Piper at the Kyalami 9-hour race, and spotted a beach buggy called the Lolette, which bore a close resemblance to Bruce Meyers' Manx (*qv*). Within a few months this chance encounter resulted in a set of Lolette moulds arriving at the GP workshop.

Before very long the GP Buggy was born and was soon enjoying incredible sales. The company was regularly turning out 100 kits per month and was struggling to keep up with demand. In September 1968 they moved to the old Aston Martin factory at Hanworth Air Park. They appointed a network of agents around the UK and gave most of them a set of moulds to try and alleviate order backlogs. Although a good idea in theory all it actually did was help generate new manufacturers who made a buggy just like the GP.

A block of chicken sheds in Wallingford were converted to 'moulding' sheds to help keep up with the massive demand, with Guildford fire engine and dustcart manufacturer Dennis making bodies for GP, too.

The Super Buggy, on an unmodified Beetle floorpan, arrived in the autumn of 1969. By 1972 the interest in buggies in the UK had waned slightly, probably due to the fact that what was cool phutting along Madeira Drive in Brighton on a warm, sunny afternoon, wasn't so good in the pouring rain in Dalston High Street! The shrewd John Jobber had seen this coming and already had the Centron and LDV pickup-cum-van buggy waiting in the wings, while a stand at the Geneva salon in 1972 helped develop export markets. They also introduced the curious Water Buggy, to be used on, er, water...

All this work was seriously hindered when a fire decimated the factory at Hanworth the same year. Daunted but unbowed, the company operated from a caravan before finding temporary accommodation at Syon Hill Garage in Isleworth. Rumours abounded as to the cause of the fire: children messing around, a pure accident, maybe even jealous rivals... Soon afterwards GP Speedshop was bought out by merchant bankers, who retained Jobber as MD.

By the end of 1972 the company had moved to Worton Hall Industrial Estate, the location of the old Isleworth film studios, where movies such as *African Queen* had been filmed, and now Sky TV headquarters, where GP occupied the old canteen area, all 4,500sq ft of it.

Jobber took six months off and used the time to gain his pilot's licence. When he returned du Plessis departed and went back to live in South Africa, where he developed peritonitis and tragically died soon after.

In early 1974, a merchant bank purchased the company, although Jobber was retained as managing director. Around this time sales slowed again, but the introduction of a range of styling parts for the VW Beetle helped. That summer, GP's fibreglass laminating moved to the former Marcos factory site in Westbury, Wiltshire, and sales started to increase encouragingly once more.

In March 1975, the bankers suddenly took fright and wanted out, at which point Jobber took over ownership of the company once more, changing the name to GP Concessionaires Ltd, with the core products being the Buggy, Super Buggy (soon to be renamed Alpine), LDV and Ranchero.

The late '70s and early '80s saw the arrival of the Talon, the Rabbit (a small boat project), and the Hover Hawk hovercraft kit (of which they sold 40), the first project from the man whose name would go on to become synonymous with GP, Neville Trickett (creator of the Siva range, and MiniSprint among others, who joined the company in 1978). The 1980s dawned with the Trickett-penned Madison, which would prove to be a big seller for GP, the Turbo Beetle conversion and a go-faster kit for the Golf GTi. Incidentally, the Turbo Beetle idea was suggested by Albar founder, Al Barmettler, GP's Swiss agent at the time, and he sold over 200 in his homeland.

By the late '70s/early '80s GP was a busy operation, with a fibreglass lamination division run by Rodney Humphries, called GP Industries, based in Redditch, making stuff like fairings for police motorcycles and even AA phone boxes. Jobber also owned Special Marine, based on the Isle of Wight and was a skilled stunt/aerobatic pilot usually in a vintage Stumpe.

The chronological sequence of the company's various names and locations over the years was as follows:

GP Speedshop	1968–72	Hanworth
GP Speedshop	1972–75	Isleworth
GP Concessionaires	1975–82	Isleworth
GP Specialist Vehicles	1982–93	Isleworth
GP Developments	1993–94	Princes Risborough
GP Projects	1994–2002	Princes Risborough
GP Technical	2002–4	Helston

GP ALPINE – *see GP Super Buggy*

GP BUGGY

Inspired by the South African Lolette buggy, itself a facsimile of Bruce Meyers' Manx (*qv*). A set of Lolette moulds arrived at GP's Brentford base in 1967. Based on VW Beetle floorpan chopped by 15¾in. GP partner Pierre du Plessis competed in one, coming second in the 1969 Players No6 Championship, as did John Jobber and a well-known rally driver of the day, Mick Brown.

After Warren Monks' Volksrod, the GP Buggy was the UK's second beach buggy. Mind you, we were some way behind America, where there were estimated to be 10,000 buggies on the road at the time, with 50 manufacturers in California alone! The company's first demonstrator, a red example powered by a 1200cc Beetle engine, appeared in *Motor* magazine in August 1968.

Such was the level of enquiries that GP appointed a whole raft of agents around the UK, some of whom were entrusted with their own set of moulds in an attempt to cut delivery times. Big sellers of GP Buggies included Beardalls of Nottingham and Scottish agent Jeff Rosenbloom, an airline pilot. Sales really took off in early 1970 and John Jobber told me once: 'It was bloody frightening to be honest, there were lorries turning up regularly loaded up with buggy bodies. We used to wonder what had hit us.' The company even kept no fewer than 60 kits in stock piled eight high in a separate 5000sq/ft storage shed next to the main HQ. At one stage GP was selling over 100 buggy kits per month, every month. Before long there were – surprise, surprise – imitators.

The Brands Hatch beach buggy race of Boxing Day 1971 was a real hoot (although it only happened once), and was for buggies powered by engines up to and including 1500cc, although Jobber reckoned that nearly all their competitors were cheating with huge wheels and tyres and big-bore engines disguised as stock: 'We (Jobber, du Plessis and their mechanic, Les Smith) had standard engines and skinny tyres on our cars and we just cleared off into the distance and won by a mile. By crikey there was some cheating going on, though!' he told me years later. For the record, the festive race was waved off by Sir Stirling Moss, in a Father Christmas suit, and was won by du Plessis, with Jobber second!

About 1,700 MkIs were sold by the time a MkII version arrived in 1977, which had wider wings that enabled fitment of beefier tyres, a new bonnet design and was generally tidied up all round.

One of the most significant UK kit cars *ever*.
GP Projects 1968–92
GP Buggies (Roy Pierpoint) 1992–98
GP Buggies (David Kuschel) 1998–99
GP Buggies (Adrian House) 1999–2005
Halifax Beetles 2005–6
Kingfisher Kustoms 2006 to date
Approx 4,200 made

GP CAMEL

The Camel was only offered for a while and only really by default. It was a revised take on the Kübelwagen replica that Neville Trickett created for the Barbados Motor Company, although as they never collected it John Jobber put it into production in the UK. Wasn't around for long.
GP Projects 1977
Approx 3 made

GP CENTRON

Ever the shrewd businessman, GP boss John Jobber decided that a new model was called for just in case the rampant buggy boom went pop. So in 1970 he launched the Centron, again based on the VW Beetle, but of a more swoopy 'exotic' design complete with doors. Featured a flip-front affair that was similar to the Bond Bug in concept, if not visually. Created by GP's Pierre du Plessis and former Unipower engineer Val Dare-Bryan.

Ironically the beach buggy craze lasted longer than the Centron, which was quietly dropped in 1971. In 1983 the moulds and rights were bought by Cornish company Statestyle, although they never went into production.
GP Projects 1970–71
Approx 12 made

GP CENTRON II

Jobber had unfinished business as far as the Centron project was concerned and launched a revised Centron II in 1974, but it actually fared worse than the original version. Resurrected as the Lalande (*qv*) by Cornish company GV Plastics Fibreglass Products in 1983, to no avail, and finished its days quietly with MDB Sportscars, who renamed it the Sapphire (*qv*).
GP Projects 1974–75
Approx 4 made

GP KÜBELWAGEN

This was ex-MiniSprint and Siva designer Neville Trickett's first creation for GP. A fibreglass-bodied replica of a WW2 Kübelwagen, based on VW Beetle. Was it the UK's first four-door kit car? Several were used by the production company responsible for the war film *A Bridge Too Far*.

GT Mouldings bought the rights to the project but produced just one kit. The project ended up in Norway, apparently.
GP Projects 1976–83
GT Mouldings 1987–91
Approx 30 made

GP LDV

Nothing to do with the erstwhile van makers, the GP LDV was a beach buggy pickup, and LDV in this case stood for 'light delivery vehicle', although some were used by dudes heading for Newquay with a surfboard *nailed* to the top. Launched at the Racing Car Show in

January 1971. Most of the production went abroad, where it proved particularly popular in third-world countries where there was a real need for a low-cost commercial-style vehicle. Featured an Austin A40 (Farina) rear window used as a windscreen and a useful 11sq ft load area.

A Mk2 in 1974 saw a new dash moulding while a Mk3 in 1977 had a flat glass 'screen, wider wings and a decent rear seat moulding.
GP Projects 1970–92
Approx 250 made

GP MADISON

After the GP Talon (*qv*) came the Madison, another Neville Trickett design that was actually going to be sold via Neville's own firm, Ground Effect Developments, but John Jobber could see its potential and it became a GP product.

A modified Beetle floorpan provided the basis for Trickett's Packard-inspired body, but that long bonnet was ideal for a front engine fitment so a Ford Cortina-based version arrived in 1983. It was this variant that was taken over by a Malaysian/Australian company called Bufori, who marketed it as a fully-built car, with all memories of its kit car past glossed over. Meanwhile, the original Beetle version ended up with a company called OB&D, run by Boris Kurpill, who fitted Porsche engines and sold them fully built.
GP Projects 1980–89
OB&D 1989–95
Approx 910 made

GP MADISON COUPÉ

1983 saw the launch of the rather stunning Madison Coupé, based on Ford Cortina donor, with doors and large cycle wings. Its styling definitely tipped its hat to the Bugatti Type 57C Atalanta. Sadly it didn't sell very well at all. Taken over by Dennis Weeks' Madison Car Company in 1989, initially based near Brands Hatch before moving to Suffolk.
GP Projects 1983–89
Madison Car Company 1989–99
Approx 10 made

GP RANCHERO

GP launched their Super Buggy Estate four-seater at the ritzy Geneva Motor Show in March 1975. It was a practical four-seater that used a GP Super Buggy as a base, with an estate type hardtop, an Austin A40 rear window used as a windscreen and other glass and door furniture taken from the Hillman Imp. Kits were priced at £419.75 inc VAT.

A Mk2 version in Autumn 1977 saw the introduction of improved vacuum-formed doors, a flat-glass windscreen and wider wings. Acquired by Roy Pierpoint at the same time he purchased the GP Buggy and Super Buggy projects.
GP Projects 1975–92
GP Buggies (Roy Pierpoint) 1992–98
Approx 150 made

GP SPYDER

Another kit car classic from GP. The Spyder was a replica of Porsche's beautiful 718 RSK, based on a chopped VW Beetle floorpan and created by Neville Trickett. GP also offered a mid-engined variant that was powered by Porsche 911 air-cooled engine, while an RS60 style 'screen was on the options list too. Body was very accurate.

Project passed to Belgian Bart Aertgaerts, who based himself in Cornwall (next door to Richard Oakes' Blackjack operation, in fact) for a couple of years. He revisited the VW Golf-powered option that had been begun by John Jobber some years previously, but ceased trading in 2003.
GP Projects 1982–2001
GP Technical 2001–3
Approx 1,500 made

GP SUPER BUGGY

The Super Buggy was a long wheelbase version of the standard buggy with an unmodified Beetle floorpan. Featured a few styling revisions, notably at the rear, and could carry four people. It was launched at the Specialist Sports Car Show in London in 1970. Had the addition of a full engine cover to meet German TüV regulations. Kits were priced at £158. In an act of extreme bravery, David Stewart, Noel Hutchinson and ex-powerboat racer John Caulcutt, took part in the London-to-Mexico World Cup Rally of 1970, the same year that *Cars & Car Conversions* magazine published a build story.

A MkII came along in July 1975 with a tub more similar in style to the GP LDV, wider wings, a proper moulded-in rear seat and a revised hardtop. The MkII was very successful in the Middle East, for a reason John Jobber could never work out, and one was even used as a mobile mosque by the UAE Army. Seriously.

A MkIII in August 1977 had a new bonnet with incorporated GRP windscreen surround, meaning that the customer couldn't get the screen's rake/angle wrong. The rear seat moulding was redesigned to give real seating, plus it now folded to give more luggage space.

GP Projects 1970–92
GP Buggies (Roy Pierpoint) 1992–98
GP Buggies (David Kuschel) 1998–99
GP Buggies (Adrian House) 1999–2005
Halifax Beetles 2005–6
Kingfisher Kustoms 2006 to date
Approx 1,600 made

GP TALON

A Neville Trickett modern two-seater that appeared in 1979 and came complete with gullwing doors. Based, unsurprisingly, on unmodified VW Beetle floorpan. Around 33 Mk1s were sold before a revised Mk2 sharpened things up a bit in 1983 and gave more room in the cockpit, as a result of which it sold quite well. Project sold to Talon Sportscars in 1987.

GP Projects 1979–87
Approx 155 made

GP TURBO BEETLE

A VW Beetle given the conversion treatment, from an idea by Albar founder Al Barmettler, GP's Swiss agent at the time. He sold around 200 of these in his homeland.

GP Projects 1984–85
Approx 275 made

GRANTURA YAK/YEOMAN

Originally known as the Gem from 1968 before being renamed the Yak by the Blackpool-based fibreglass company, run by John Ward, Bernard Williams and Tommy Entwistle. Williams had been a very good dirt-track racer in the forties, and by 1955 had become a director of TVR. Ward was a fomer TVR development engineer.

Grantura Plastics was founded in 1966 in an old brickworks in Blackpool's Hoo Hill Industrial Estate, and initially made the GRP bodies for TVR, until the latter took production in-house, resulting in Grantura having spare capacity in their factory. The link with this quirky little utility vehicle wasn't so far-fetched, as they formerly made hardtops for the Mini Moke, so when that car ceased production in the UK Grantura thought they'd fill the void with their little Yak, which handled and performed very well. Its rugged, multitube chassis accepted a one-piece GRP body with Mini mechanicals, subframes and windscreen, with sills 4in lower for easier access, an 8in longer body and a drop-down tailgate and optional 'fringe-on-top' canopy! Dick Barton Ltd, BMC distributor for the West Country, was the sole distributor, calling their version the Yalk Yeoman.

The Yak was effectively done for when BMC Australia, who made Mokes for the southern hemisphere, saw it as a threat to their business and complained, at which point British Leyland refused to supply the brand-new Mini components required for overseas orders, which ultimately speeded up its demise.

Grantura Plastics 1969–70
Approx 150 made

GRAVETTI 427

Revised version of Dave Perry's AD427 and potentially a very good car in concept, with the company run by Nigel Gravett, but not so good in practise. Originally based in Sandhurst, Kent, often being known as GEL with the car advertised as the 'Brawn Again Sportscar'. Later moved to Mere, Wiltshire. Employed slick marketing and coined the 'Cob-in-a-Box' term. Quite a large operation when they went into liquidation, with 17 staff. Standard fare ladderframe chassis with GRP body reinforced by a steel supporting frame with everything bar the engine and gearbox supplied in the kit.

Bob Egginton of Automotive System Design revamped the chassis for the reborn GE Engineering (with the car by then known as the GE 427) with the company run by John Payne and Michael Hart. The GE Engineering operation didn't last long either and the project ended up with Bob Egginton as a CK Automotive (part of ASD) product known as the CK 427.

Gravetti Engineering 1983–88
GE Engineering PLC 1988–89
CK Automotive (part of ASD) 1989–98
Approx 70 made

GREGORI GPR

Created by Roger and Phil Gregory, the latter going on to form Pembleton. GPR based on Escort Mk3 with a fibreglass monocoque and showed a lot of promise, but it ultimately didn't sell. A Spyder convertible version arrived in 2001 of which four were sold.

When Phil concentrated on the Pembleton projects, Roger was joined by Mike Dowling for a time trading as Syber Sportscars before the company ceased trading.
Gregori Sportscars 1998–2000
Syber Sportscars 2000-2
Approx 12 made

GRIFFIN

Jim Finch was the man behind the Griffin, first known as the GD-XM. He was based on the same Creekmoor Industrial Estate in Dorset as GT Developments, for whom he made the bodies. Designed by Jim Clark, who later created the Manx (*qv*) and also had an involvement in Martyn Slater's Lyncar (*qv*) project.

Original GD-XM was based on Morris Minor van and dubbed the 'Post Office Express'. Relaunched as the Griffin in 1976, with a VW Beetle-based version from the following year. A company called Nomad Sales, based in Crowthorne, Berkshire, acquired the project in 1979, before Balena Cars saw the Griffin out of production.
Griffin Design 1975–79
Nomad Sales 1979–83
Balena Cars 1983–85
Approx 20 made

GRIFFON 110 DELUX

Probably the last Vauxhall Viva-based kit car. The company, based in Hucknall, Nottinghamshire, was run by Barrie Comery and John Todkill. Comery had previously worked at nearby Spartan for five years, while Todkill had been a pushbike designer at Raleigh.
Griffon Motors 1985–89
Approx 120 made

GRINNALL SCORPION III

Launched in 1991, designed by Steve Harper of Shado Design, now chief designer of Volvo. Mark Grinnall and Neil Williams developed the chassis. Power originally from BMW K1100 or K1200 motorbike engines, with a Kevlar®-reinforced fibreglass body mounted to a steel tube spaceframe. Modern styling has orthopaedic seats, with Cosworth Sierra brakes and BMW K1 suspension. A BMW K40-powered version was announced in 2010, and delivered blistering performance.
Grinnall Cars 1992 to date
Approx 250 made

GRINNALL SCORPION IV

Another Steve Harper design, the Scorpion IV was never offered in kit form but is included here for the sake of completeness. Power comes from a 225bhp four-cylinder engine.
Grinnall Cars 2001 to date
Approx 20 made

GRINNALL V8

Back in the early '80s, Mark Grinnall was earning a living as a toolmaker during the week and riding motocross bikes at the weekend for leisure and competition. As part of his hobby he also mended bikes. He'd visit motorcycle shops and salvage yards, mend their damaged bikes during weekday evenings and deliver them back, repaired, at the weekend. This venture soon became a full-time operation, such was his reputation for top-quality work. One day, while visiting a salvage yard, he came across a forlorn looking Triumph TR7, bought it, but wasn't that impressed, so set about converting it to his requirements. He sold his first to his osteopath in 1982 for £6,250, and so the Grinnall V8 was born!

It was much more than just a V8-conversion that turned a TR7 into a potent TR8. The donor car retained its steel centre section but had a revised and lightweight nose and tail, with suspension a combination of Rover SD1 and Grinnall's own components, while Mark offered his Rover V8 in 3.9-litre (225bhp) or 4.5-litre (275bhp) guises. Very highly rated.
Grinnall Moto X & Engineering 1981–91
Approx 350 made

GRINNALL TRIKE

A 30-hour job would turn a BMW or Triumph motorbike into a Grinnall Trike, available in four variants. The BMW kits are based around 1200C, R1150 R and R1200 CL, while the Triumph is the Rocket R3T, a 2.3-litre monster. A Triumph Thunderbird 1,600cc option was announced in 2010.

Design came from Steve Harper on all models except the R3T, which was designed by Steve Everitt (the man behind the Alfastyl in the mid-1980s). The end result is a stylish trike available in fully-built and kit guises, while if required the conversion can be reverse-engineered back into a motorcycle.
Grinnall Cars 2000 to date
Approx 75 made

GROUP SIX

John Mitchell of Clerkenwell in London was a Group Six motor-racing fan – so much so that he named his car the, er, Group Six. He dreamed of owning a road-going McLaren M6, which was out of reach, so he set about building his own car. It might have

looked racy but it was based on a humble VW Beetle floorpan, with a Vauxhall Cresta (later changed to Ford Capri) windscreen. Later versions gained a targa body style from 1973. The car's one claim to fame was that Radio One DJ and pretty decent drag racer, Dave Lee Travis, drove a Group Six in a film called *Wonderful Radio One*.
Group Six Fibres 1972–77
Approx 71 made

GRS TORA

A surprise came from Ginetta Cars in 1983 with the introduction of the GRS Tora, an estate type vehicle that wasn't marketed under the Ginetta brand name. Featured a galvanised steel ladderframe and based rather unusually on Hillman Hunter (or Humber Sceptre) mechanicals as were the windscreen, doors and interior. A Mk2 version based on Ford Cortina, complete with four doors, appeared just before the company was sold. See next entry.
Ginetta Cars 1983–88
Approx 360 made

GRS TORA ESTATE

Essentially a Mk2 version of the original Tora, but sufficiently different to merit its own entry. The newer version was based on a rectangular box section chassis, and was much sleeker, and was a four door with large tailgate. The Hillman Hunter/Humber Sceptre

donor was replaced by Ford Cortina Mk4. The GRS Tora Estate didn't last long as it was deleted when Ginetta Cars was sold to Martin Phaff.
Ginetta Cars 1988–89
Approx 3 made

GS EUROPA

William Towns-designed body conversion kit for the Lotus Europa, which required the removal of front and rear body panels, with new panels bonded on in their place. Project financed by Bernard Gray, owner of GS Cars of Bristol. Complete cars cost £5,250 in 1980, while £2,500 was the cost to convert a customer's own Lotus.
Interstyl 1975–80
Approx 15 made

GSM DART – *see GSM Delta*

GSM DELTA

South Africans Willie Meissner and Bon Van Niekirk decided to build their own sports car. While on a trip to England in 1956, Meissner was pretty taken with fibreglass. He told Van Niekirk, who came to the UK immediately and got a job with GRP firm Mitchell & Smith to learn more

about it. The friends got a flat in Earl's Court and worked on their plans.

They had the desire but not very good design skills, so they got fellow South African Verster de Witt, a designer, to pen it for them. The resulting car was built in a Streatham lock-up. When finished the first prototype was shipped to South Africa, where Meissner and his new Glassport Motors worked on what would become the GSM Dart, powered by Ford sidevalve engine and 100E parts.

The plan was always to sell their car in the UK, but a proposed UK investor turned out to be unreliable and the deal fell through. Then, motor racing fanatic John Scott stepped in, enabling the fledgling operation to launch the now renamed Delta at the Racing Car Show in 1961. The UK operation was based in West Malling, Kent. The cars proved very successful in motorsport during the period. The name change was caused by a bicycle manufacturer objecting to the Dart moniker.

The press ripped the car to pieces in magazine reports of the day, criticising its build quality and cost, although a last-gasp Delta Fastback was launched to no avail before the UK operation closed in October 1961. Incidentally, well-known '60s racer and Ford tuner the late Jeff Uren of Raceprooved enjoyed a lot of race success in a Delta.

Meissner and Van Niekirk returned to South Africa and resumed production of their domestic market Dart on a limited scale and also a GT version called the Flamingo (128 sold in RSA). They ceased trading for good in 1966. Several attempts at replicas have appeared over the years via Jeff Levy and John Hayden.
GSM UK 1960–61
Approx 35 made (UK)

GSM DELTA FASTBACK

As the name suggests, this was a fastback version of the Delta. Ceased production in the UK 1961 but was produced in South Africa until 1964.
GSM UK 1961
Approx 15 made (UK)

GT BUGGY

Glassfibre Techniques & Mouldings was run by the guru of the UK beach buggy scene, James Hale. Most of the well-known buggy kits had 'convalescent stays' at GT Mouldings, while over the years they also developed a couple of their own projects such as the Sahara Buggy (*qv*), basically a long wheelbase

version of the Baja GT, and more recently the GT Buggy, which was designed by Mel Hubbard. Similar to the EMPI Imp from certain angles.

Initially available in long-wheelbase form (45 sold) until 2004, when they introduced a short version. Production ceased in 2007.
GT Mouldings 1997–2007
Approx 50 made

GT SUPERCAR

This Porsche Carrera GT replica based on Porsche Boxster mechanicals came from Mark Cook of Norwich, Norfolk, and was inspired by a US kit. Actually very nicely executed. Cook is one of the top exponents in Europe of Kung Fu.
GT Supercars 2008 to date
Approx 1 made (UK)

GT-R

Formerly MK Engineering's MK GT1 (*qv*), taken over by Cheshire-based Robert Lewis. Sold 12 kits fairly quckly but wasn't around long.
Evolution Sportscars 2005–6
Approx 12 made

GTD 40 Mk1

Replica GT40 with zinc-dipped, plasti-coated spaceframe. Early cars were powered by Ford V6 engines, although this soon changed to Ford 302 V8 delivering approximately 250bhp, mated

to a GTD-spec Renault UN1 transaxle. In 1992, they announced an aluminium monocoque tub for their '40. Interestingly, GTD never used the word 'kit' to describe their products, instead using the term 'module' in their adverts. In 1987 the GTD cost £13,900, with 'turnkey-minus' examples from £26,000, less engine and transaxle.

They made four lightweight cars with an aluminium-panelled steel spaceframe and composite body.
GT Developments 1983–2000
GTD Supercars 2000–4
Approx 612 made

GT DEVELOPMENTS

Founded in Old Trafford, Manchester, by Roger Attaway, Ray Christopher and Graham Kelsey, GT Developments had for several years been heavily involved in the UK custom car show scene, running several of the nation's biggest events, including the well-known Belle Vue Show, under the Autos International banner. They had toured Europe with a selection of lavish hot rods.

Kelsey had originally met Ray 'The Rodfather' Christopher at a show in Farnborough, Hampshire, when he was looking for quality cars for his next Manchester event and Ray had the incredible V8 milk float *Past-yer-eyes* on display. One thing led to another and Ray did some TV promotion for the show and reputedly put 20,000 on the gate!

Notable Christopher rods appearing at this time included *The Helicar* and a Model T that won Ray a prestigious award in America, plus a V8 cement mixer, *C'Men'T*.

Autos International started supplying parts to KVA owners, notably suspension upgrade kits, and one particular demonstrator was known as a KVA GTD. Their intention was to co-produce this model, but ultimately it came to nothing.

They started selling beefed-up front and rear sections for KVA chassis, which accepted Ford Granada rather than Cortina parts, as Ken Atwell never supplied a build manual. His view was that if a customer needed a build manual then they shouldn't be building a GT40 replica! They also supplied KVA customers with other components that weren't supplied in the kit, such as door locks.

Ray built a two-thirds-scale Peterbilt truck used for Autos International's European trek in 1973, which ended at Le Mans, where Ray unwittingly spent several hours talking to Ford's then Executive Vice President Bob Lutz (indeed, it was he who commissioned the Ford Sierra). They got on very well, with Ray telling his new friend that he'd love to build a replica GT40. Lutz liked his idea, and told him to get in touch if he ever needed any assistance, and if he did ultimately build these cars to reserve one for him!

In the intervening period, Autos International became GT Developments in 1984, with Christopher and Kelsey moving to Ray's home town of Poole, Dorset.

A few days after his meeting with Lutz, Ray made the call that changed his life. Within a week an entourage from Ford Germany arrived at his 1,200sq ft Poole workshop to discuss the building of Ray's replica. Work began in earnest in July 1983, although detailed drawings weren't produced until 1985. In April 1986 Ray showed his first demonstrator to Eric Broadley, who loved it, forming an enduring friendship. Broadley offered encouragement and help, suggesting that they retained a spaceframe chassis rather than use a monocoque. GTD displayed the car at the British International Motor Show at Earl's Court the same year, located opposite KVA funnily enough.

In 2000 GTD was bought by Roger Marsh and David Bees, who moved the operation to Sutton Coldfield and revised the company name to GTD Supercars, although Ray Christopher's son Paul remained with the operation for a time.

A
B
C
D
E
F
G
H
I
J
K
L
M
N
O
P
Q
R
S
T
U
V
W
X
Y
Z

GTD 40 Mk2

Launched in 1992, mainly in response to demand from Japan for the car. Not an exact copy of the original Ford GT40 Mk2, it featured a Ford 302 engine rather than the original's Galaxie-sourced big block. Used a different rear body section to the GTD Mk1.
GT Developments 1992–95
Approx 25 made

GTD 250 GTO

Nothing to do with *the* GTD, this company marketed a 250 GTO conversion on Datsun 240/260Z mechanicals for a brief time.
GTD Sports Cars 1984–85
Approx 3 made

GTD SPORTSTAR

Pleasing Fiesta Mk2-based sports car that was originally commissioned by a Chinese company for their domestic market. When that order fell through GTD launched the car in kit form in the UK. Featured a unique 'Uni-chassis', which was in essence a folded and welded backbone structure with outriggers, sandwiched between an upper body and floor moulding to create a very rigid and tough monocoque. Removable rear panel converted two-seater to a 2+2. Kits priced at £4,200 on launch. One that got away?
GT Developments 1998
Approx 4 made

GTD T70

Because of the success of the GTD 40 and its reputation as a superb piece of engineering (not forgetting Ray Christopher's fine history of rod building), GT Developments had the services of top ex-Ford engineers, including Len Bailey and Pat Murphy. This led to them meeting Eric Broadley, whose son Andrew helped source parts for their '40'.

One day they got the chance to demonstrate their car to Eric Broadley, who was extremely impressed. Over a cup of coffee in his office, Ray was asked what model they'd like to do next, to which he replied a Lola T70 MkII. To his amazement, Broadley gave him his blessing. They obtained a set of genuine moulds from Specialised Mouldings and amended their GT40 chassis for the purpose. The result was another cracking replica of which GTD sold seven.

Project acquired by to Derek Bell (no, not that one!) of Bell Developments.
GT Developments 1986–99
Bell Developments 1999–2005
Approx 9 made

GTM 40TR

A GTM (RDM Automotive era) attempt at an 'exo-car'. This consisted of a revised Libra monocoque tub without front and rear sections. Launched at the Autosport Show of 2007 and in a revised form at the same event the following January. Never went into production.
GTM Cars (RDM Automotive) 2007–8
Approx 1 made

GTM BALLISTA

Formerly the Sculptural Engineering Larini (*qv*), the Ballista, as it became known, was purchased by then GTM owners RDM Automotive, and launched at the Autosport International Show in January 2007, although nothing much happened thereafter.
GTM Cars (RDM Automotive) 2007
Approx 1 made

GTM COUPÉ

Initially known as the Cox Grand Touring Mini or GTM, the car was designed by Jack Hosker and produced by Cheshire garage owner Bernard Cox in 1967. Famously, the chassis model was made from cornflake packets. It was the first mid-engined kit car. Putting the engine behind the occupants solved one of the Mini's inherent problems – its height, and as well as being pretty the GTM was a very capable little car. It's based around a steel box-section chassis, with modified Mini front subframes front and rear, and a GRP body. Gained good press due to its fine handling and looks but was difficult to build. Cox & Co went bust in 1971 after selling 55 kits.

Howard Heerey had been doing some competition driving for Cox and took over the project, coming up with a revised chassis and added a supporting frame for the engine. He also made further alterations to the interior and some subtle styling mods, such as adding a Mini front bumper and revised indicators. He renamed the Cox GTM the GTM 1-3. Heerey sold a further 155 before his operation went into liquidation.

HE Glass-Fibre took over from Heerey although they never made a car in the four years they had the project; likewise the next custodians, KMB.

One day, Peter Beck was at KMB trying in vain to buy spares for a car that he owned. Impressed by the GTM, he soon thereafter bought the project along with friends Paddy Fitch and Douglas Cowper. (The latter left shortly afterwards.)

Operating as GTM Cars, they revised the car by adding a bigger front spoiler and widening the wheel arches. The rear end also now incorporated a GRP bumper, rather than having a separate item, and new light lenses too. While at it, they added a sunroof, BL door handles and a new interior. Under Beck and Fitch GTM went on to sell around 600 units.

With the launch of their new Rossa model in 1995 the Coupé was sold to Peter Leslie of Primo Designs of Stoulton, Worcestershire, who worked hard at making the car SVA compliant such as by moving the headlights back 3in. Sadly, he did little more with the project.
Cox & Co 1967–71
Howard Heerey Engineering Ltd 1971–72
HE Glass-Fiber of Hartlepool 1972–76
GTM Cars (part of KMB Autosports) Wellingborough 1976–80
GTM Cars 1980–95
Primo Designs 1995–2001
Approx 700 made

GTM LIBRA

Brilliant mid-engined Richard Oakes design that could be powered by Rover K-series or Honda (B16 & K20a) VTECs.
GTM Cars 1998–2003
GTM Cars (RDM Automotive) 2003–7
Westfield Sports Cars 2007–10
Approx 200 made

GTM ROSSA

Richard Oakes' design featured a monocoque tub and was the Beck/Fitch GTM operation's first all-new model, being a 2+2 based on Mini mechanicals. It was launched at the Stoneleigh Show of 1986.
GTM Cars 1986–90
Approx 200 made

GTM ROSSA Mk2

Revised Rossa that featured altered front and rear panels, recessed headlights now under covers and Peugeot 205 rear light clusters, although retained Mini mechanicals.
GTM Cars 1990–93
Approx 150 made

GTM ROSSA K3

Being the Mk3 version of the Rossa, powered by K-series engine, the new Rossa, again designed by Richard Oakes, was called the 'K3'. Subframes from the donor Metro were fixed front and rear to the GRP monocoque and its smoother styling appealed to customers immediately. Project sold to Justin Gudgeon of Northlight Sportscars in 2003.
GTM Cars 1993–2003
Approx 400 made

GTM SPYDER

Superb convertible version of the acclaimed Libra (see above) by Richard Oakes. When Peter Beck passed away, Paddy Fitch carried on for a while before selling the GTM marque to David Keene of RDM Automotive of Coventry in 2003. They in turn sold the operation to Potenza Sports Cars, owners of Westfield, in 2007.
GTM Cars 2000–3
RDM Automotive 2003–7
Westfield Sports Cars 2007 to date
Approx 65 made

GTR350

Jeff Ashton, designer of the Tytan (*qv*), penned this clever scaled-down version of the classic '60s Mustang based on the Toyota MR2 Mk2.
RIDEcars 2005–6
Approx 1 made

GTS 40

A budget GT40 replica from GTS Tuning with Ford 302 power and Audi transaxle.
GTS Tuning 2009-10
Approx 3 made

GUYSON E12

When Yorkshire-based managing director of shotblas equipment manufacturers Guyson International, Jim Thomson, left the road one dark night in 1972 and smashed up his E-type S111 Roadster, he didn't just make a call to his insurers, he commissioned designer William Towns to create him a rakish body for his stricken sportscar.

Towns got the crayons and clay out and came up with a trademark angular creation that could be converted back to original spec E-type if the customer required. Only two were made; hill climb champion Thomson's car and one that William did for himself, although Guyson did offer the glassfibre conversion commercially for a time, quoting £2,000 on top of the E-type's 1974 £3,300 price tag.

Thomson's car still exists (Towns converted his back to an E-type) and featured a Ron Beatty-tuned 345bph Jaguar V12 engine complete with a triple bank of 44mm Weber LDF carburettors so big that a hole had to be cut in the bonnet to accommodate!

The project remained on Skipton-based Guyson's pricelists for three years, although there were no takers and it faded away. A superb piece of 1970s automotive ephemera.
Guyson International 1974–77
Approx 2 made

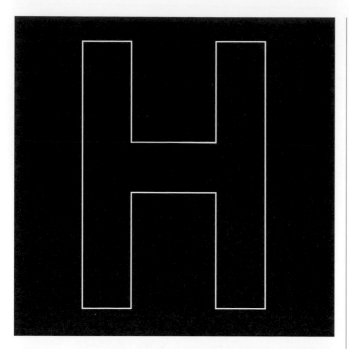

HACKER MAROC

After selling off most of his kit car models to Eagle and Scorhill, Tim Dutton carried on with the remaining kits under the Partex banner for a time before concentrating on his amphibious vehicles. He did, however, come up with the attractive Ford Fiesta body conversion (a kit package was introduced from 1993), the Hacker Maroc, which was launched at the 1991 Motor Fair in fully built only guise at a cost of £13,000. An S2 arrived in 1993 while the restyled S3 came along in 1999 and was by then based on Ford Fiesta Mk3 and designed by Simon Saunders, the creator of the Ariel Atom.

Taken over by Bolney, West Sussex-based company called The Novus Group in 2000 renamed it 'Minos', but they lasted for only a couple of years. Project acquired by a Coppull-based chap called Jim Walmsley, who intended to put the car back into production, although nothing more was heard.

Hacker Cars 1991–2000; The Novus Group 2000–2; Minos Cars 2002
Approx 22 made

HADLEIGH SPRINT/CABURN ROADSTER

More than passable Morgan lookalike marketed for a time in the '90s by a Suffolk company run by Rob Hulme, which also briefly marketed the Dash (qv) and MCA Sports Coupé (qv). Featured an aluminium-panelled spaceframe chassis with fibreglass nosecone, scuttle and wings, and used the Ford Sierra as donor vehicle. A 2+2 variant was also available.

Project ended up with Caburn Engineering, custodians of the Vincent Hurricane (qv), although they hadn't actively marketed the car by the time this book closed for press in September 2010, although plans are afoot. Now known as the Caburn Roadster.

IPS Developments 1992–95; Caburn Engineering 2007 to date
Approx 6 made

HALDANE HD100

Created by Blantyre-based John Haldane, who having built himself a Healey 100M replica using a box-section chassis and Vauxhall Chevette running gear then set about marketing it. Ford Sierra-based from 1993, in which year microlight designers Brian Harrison and Alisdair Scott, of East Kilbride, took over.

Haldane Developments 1987–93 (Blantyre)
Haldane Developments 1993–94 (East Kilbride)
Approx 100 made

HALDANE HD300

Haldane came up with a Mk2 version in 1991 with a stiffer and improved steel backbone semi-monocoque chassis. Company went into liquidation in 1994 having sold around 12 kits, and rights to the project were picked up by Den Tanner of Pilgrim Cars, who sold 12 more before selling the company to Tony Holmes in 2002, who sold a further dozen.

Haldane Developments 1991–94
Pilgrim Cars 1994–2002
Pilgrim Cars (UK) Ltd 2002–8
Approx 36 made

HAMBLIN Mk2

Three-wheeler from Sid Hamblin that used a Buckler chassis.
S.E. Hamblin Ltd 1960–62
Approx 1 made

HAMBLIN CADET

Dorset-based panel-beater Sid Hamblin's second bodyshell. Retained the Austin 7 mechanicals of the Deluxe (see below), but the cigar-shaped Cadet was made from fibreglass. It proved very popular.
S.E. Hamblin Ltd 1958–60
Approx 200 made

HAMBLIN DELUXE

The aluminium-bodied Deluxe, designed for LWB Austin 7 chassis, was Sid Hamblin's first bodyshell. It arrived in April 1957.
S.E. Hamblin Ltd 1957–58
Approx 12 made

HARBRON SPECIAL

Bill Harbron created this little roadster, which looked like a refugee from the '30s but handled like a modern Lotus Seven. Underpinned by a tubular steel spaceframe and Fiat twin-cam engine. Harbron ran a garage repair business in Bridport, Dorset.
Loxton Laminates 1986–88
Approx 12 made

HARRINGTON & KING'S SPORTS BUGGY

Prior to the Manta Ray, Connaught Cars' forecourt manager, Adrian Harrington, and his friend, Roy King, made the Sports Buggy, from their former air-raid shelter unit. Harrington owned a GP Buggy, which provided inspiration, as it did for many buggies of the period. Later resurrected by C&D Automarine of West Molesey who also made the Manta Ray bodies for Power on Wheels.
Power on Wheels 1969–70
Approx 15 made

HARRISON SPECIAL

Clearly inspired by Lotus, the Harrison Special featured a round-tube chassis, a Lotus Seven Series 2 type rear end and a Lotus VI style front, with a Ford Pre-Crossflow engine.

I pondered long and hard over the inclusion of this one because one-off *specials* that weren't intended for commercial sale aren't included within this book. What swung it though is the fact that I believe that racecar builder, John Harrison, made at least two of these in 1965.
John Harrison 1965
Approx 2 made

HAWK CARS

Gerry Hawkridge is a legend in the world of specialist cars and he set up Hawk Cars after Transformer Cars. For many years he'd been building *specials* and Austin 7 Ulsters, while making go-karts for his pupils to race during leisure time. He'd built a BRA 289 (*qv*) and later went on to create the BRA 427 for the same company. Around this time he also became involved with the Transformer project and soon found that many other people wanted his replicas.

He's one of the funniest men you'll ever meet. Hilarious things happen to you when you're in Hawkridge's company, and when it comes to automobiles not many people have a better eye for detail.

His Stratos kit was soon joined by his own take on the AC 289, and the rest, as they say, is history.

HAWK 1.8/2.6

A beautiful AC Ace from Gerry Hawkridge, which like the company's other replicas is as sympathetic a recreation as it's possible to achieve. So good it will fool many experts. Uses the same twin-tube chassis as Hawk's 289 and is powered, like the original Ace, by a straight-six engine, usually a Triumph 2.5-litre unit, or BMW, MGB or even Zephyr 2.6-litre.
Hawk Cars 1992 to date
Approx 50 made

HAWK 246 DINO

Exact replica of the Dino from Gerry Hawkridge. Two of the eight made were GTS versions.
Hawk Cars 1986–92
Approx 8 made

HAWK 275 GTB

Superb 275 GTB recreation from Gerry Hawkridge.
Hawk Cars 1987–90
Approx 6 made

HAWK 288 GTO

Gerry Hawkridge also turned his hand to the 288 GTO.
Hawk Cars 1986–90
Approx 3 made

HAWK 289 SERIES

Building a BRA 289 (*qv*) kit, Gerry worked hard to give it the utmost purity, and before long people started asking him to create his own kit version, which he launched in 1990 to great acclaim. Underpinned by MGB mechanicals, it is an accurate replica of a classic AC model.

Over the years Gerry has also added other specific models to his 289 stable, such as a nut-for-nut pastiche of '39 PH', a Le Mans version and a 289 FIA. In 2009 he extended the range further by introducing a Sebring example.
Hawk Cars 1990 to date
Approx 300 made

HAWK 427

Introduced in 2008, the Hawk 427 was a long-awaited stablemate to Gerry Hawkridge's 289 series. Definitely one for the purist.
Hawk Cars 2008-10
Approx 10 made

HAWK HF – *see Hawk Stratos*

HAWK KIRKHAM 289/427

The aluminium-bodied Kirkham models are marketed by an American company run by the Kirkham family from their base in Utah, although they are famously made in a former MiG fighter factory in Poland. Top quality and perfectly suited to the demands of Gerry Hawkridge and his customers. Hawkridge became the UK and European agent for Kirkham Motorsports in 2002. 289 and 427 body styles are available and purity is a demand, with many original parts fitting straight on to these copies. Sublime
Hawk Cars 2002 to date
Approx 30 made

HAWK/STEWART & ARDERN MINISPRINT

Superb recreation of the MiniSprint. Name came from a competition in *Kit Car* magazine, with the winning entry being Stewart & Ardern, the name of the company that had taken the project over from Geoff Thomas in the 1960s. Marketed via Metro Centre of Tunbridge Wells, run by John Mayo.

BMW objected to the use of the 'Mini' name and production stopped. Did make a reappearance with a Northamptonshire company called Rally Sport Replicas for a while.
Hawk Cars 1996–2000
Rally Sport Replicas 2002–2005
Enzo Designs 2010-11
Approx 30 made

HAWK STRATOS

Developed from Gerry's Transformer HF project, the Hawk Stratos is a glorious pastiche of the legendary Lancia rally star driven to success by the likes of Björn Waldegård and Sandro Munari. Can be ordered in several variants including Road or Stradale, and also in big-arched Gp4 in Alitalia livery. Power choices range from Alfa Romeo 3.0-litre to Ferrari 3000QV.
Hawk Cars 1986 to date
Approx 350 made

HAWK V12

A stunning Ferrari 365 GTB 'Daytona' recreation from Gerry Hawkridge. Power came from either Ferrari 400 V12 or Jaguar XJ12.
Hawk Cars 1993–94
Approx 6 made

HAWKE

Makers GCS Cars was based in Orpington, Kent. Run by Colin Puttock and Garry Hutton, who established their company as a general kit car building operation in 1993. The Hawke was a Morgan-inspired traditional roadster, based initially on Ford Cortina before a Sierra version arrived in 1997. Rover V8 power was a later option too. Chassis was a massively heavy cruciform affair.

Tiger Racing bought the project in 2000 when illness meant that GCS had to cease trading. Paul Chapman, a Pontypool garage owner, bought it from Tiger in 2003 and continued until 2007.
GCS Cars 1994–2000
Tiger Racing 2000–3
LC Developments 2003–7
Approx 135 made

HAYNES ROADSTER

Described in the *Build Your Own Sports Car on a Budget* book by Chris Gibbs, with input from Martin Keenan of MK Engineering. This was a follow-up to the massive-selling Ron Champion Locost (*qv*) book *Build Your Own Sports Car for as little as £250*. Extremely popular.
Haynes Publishing 2007 to date
Approx 150 made

HDS WARRIOR/DEFENDER

Created by Alan Hooper from his South Norwood base, this pretty 1948 Ferrari Tipo 166 Corsa Spyder pastiche was never intended as a replica, but rather to be 'evocative of', and was originally called the Lindy when powered by four-cylinder Triumph. When using a bespoke spaceframe chassis it was known as the Warrior, which also used Fiat twin-cam engine, but if the customer chose a Triumph Dolomite donor with ladderframe chassis it was known as the Defender!

When the demand became too much for Hooper he sold the project to DG Engineering based in Charlton, South London, who carried on for a while until it was taken over by Reed Motor Engineering run by Rob Askew until circa 2002. A Ford Sierra-based version was also developed.

It was dusted down by Mick Michaelides in 2005 under the Fiorano banner and renamed the Type 48 Corsa Spyder.
Hooper Design Services/Lindy Motor Services 1991–95
Hooper Creative Design Services 1996–2000
DG Motor Services 2000–1
Reed Engineering 2001–5
Fiorano 2005 to date
Approx 36 made

HEALY

No, this isn't a spelling mistake, but how the company spelt the name. Martyn Williamson was the original importer of the Sebring range in the UK, and was behind this Lamberti-created modern pastiche on the Healey theme. Granada Mk3-based, it used New Mini headlights and Smart ForTwo seats. According to marketing blurb at the time, it was apparently destined for MG Rover before they collapsed. Marketed for a while by Auto Speciali before disappearing.
Lamberti Classic Cars 2005–6
Approx 1 made

HEATHFIELD SLINGSHOT

Morgan-inspired trike with round-tube spaceframe chassis from Peter Heath of Chesterfield. Power came from Honda CX500 bike engine, with a GRP body of 'barrelback' style. Initially created as a one-off, but kits were later offered, priced at £2,150 in 1995.
Heathfield Automotive 1993–95
Approx 1 made

HELIAN

Traditional roadster from the Isle of Anglesey (Brynsiencyn, to be precise), complete with four seats, a spaceframe chassis and Ford mechanicals. Had an aluminium, steel and GRP body. Wasn't around for long.
Island Classics 1983
Approx 1 made

HELIOS

Originally known as the SP1, this exotic two-seater was a very ambitious original design created by ex-London Central School of Art & Design student Matt Ritson, based in Newcastle-upon-Tyne. Featured a backbone chassis, similar to the Lotus Europa, made by Spyder Engineering, and had mid-mounted Ford CVH power and could be had in fixed head or targa guises. Much potential.
Sagesse Motor Company 1990–91
Approx 4 made

HENSEN 427/M70

A less well-known car from Hugo Henricksen than his Hensen M30 (see next entry) was this Cobra replica, which featured what the company called a 'multi-chassis', meaning that you could start with a small engine and transplant seamlessly to a larger one later. Hensen's first demonstrator featured no bonnet scoop, had a 400ci V8 and a C6 automatic 'box.

Moved to Eagle Cars, who never marketed it. Eventually, while seeking more factory space, Eagle boss Rob Budd chopped up the moulds one day in 1986.
Hensen Automotive 1984–85
Eagle Cars 1985–86
Approx 2 made

HENSEN M30

Nightclub owner Hugo Henricksen had previously built a *special*, a wacky wild-looking thing with a massive rear wing. He'd also owned several American cars, plus a Charger (*qv*) and a Siva Saluki (*qv*). Operating from a 4,000sq ft factory in Milford Haven, his first commercially available kit was no more conventional, featuring a very angular design that some found attractive. Under the skin, the Ford Granada Mk1 donor parts and superbly engineered chassis were nicely done. Advertised as 'speed with safety' in the company's brochure, the 2in square section steel spaceframe was certainly substantial, while the double-skinned, foam-filled nose cone was a nice touch. The M30 used Ford V6 3-litre from the donor, while the M70 employed a chest-beating V8.

Hensen also pioneered the use of fire-retardant resin in his bodies. A testament to the car's high level of engineering is the fact that there are still quite a few survivors around.

Project taken over briefly by Eagle Cars, although they didn't do much with it, and in the early '90s Henricksen seriously considered putting the car back into production, but an intended American sales campaign came to nought.
Hensen Automotive 1983–85
Eagle Cars 1985–86
Approx 17 made

HERITAGE 540K LEGACY ROADSTER

A 16ft 3in leviathan out of the Silurian, Atlantis and Durow drawer. An American-made approximation of the Mercedes Benz 500K based on Chevrolet Camaro with Chevy 350ci or Ford small-block V8 power. First imported to the UK briefly by Classic Cars of Titchfield, based near Fareham and run by Robin Gibbs and Andy Mitchell, before it passed to an operation run by Ian Clitheroe based at Brighton Marina.

Just three right-hand-drive versions were made, with one sold in the UK. Rolling chassis kits cost £19,995 in 1992, which was probably the reason this giant vehicle didn't sell.
Classic Cars of Titchfield 1991–92
Heritage Motor Cars (Europe) Ltd 1992
Approx 3 made (UK)

HERITAGE C-TYPE REPLICA

Co-founder Roger Worrell described the Heritage approach as akin to 'bespoke tailoring'. Their C-type featured a multi-tube chassis, XJ6 double wishbones and Leda dampers with modified trailing arms at the rear. Raced in historic competitions by many well-known drivers including Mike Wilds and Alain de Cadenet, who competed in the gruelling Panamericana in a Heritage C in 1990.

Acquired by Adrian Cocking of Realm Engineering in 2003.
Heritage Engineering 1988–2003
Realm Engineering 2003 to date
Approx 145 made

HERITAGE 'KNOBBLY'

Lister 'Knobbly' Jaguar replica. There are still a couple to be found racing the 750 MC's Sports Racing & GT Championship. Production ended after an objection from Lister Cars.
Heritage Engineering 1992–94
Approx 3 made

HERITAGE SS100

Superb replica of the Jaguar SS100 made by Hitchin-based Heritage Engineering, run by historic racers Roger Worrell and Jack Frost. Donor vehicle was Jaguar XJ6 in Series 1 or 2 guise. Initially available in fully-built only form from £22,000 (late 1988), with a component version offered from spring 1989 from £10,000.
Heritage Engineering 1988–99
Approx 15 made

HERITAGE T70

Classic Lola T70 replica made as close to 1960s original as possible by Heritage Engineering.
Heritage Engineering 1991–2002
Approx 25 made

HERON EUROPA

After several years of producing the Heron *special* bodyshell (see next entry), George Bishop's Greenwich-based Heron Plastics launched the Europa, a kit car with a backbone chassis and a stylish fixed-head body, with power coming from Ford Anglia 997cc or Ford Pre-Crossflow 1,500cc engines. The shell was a revised version of the original *special*. It even featured independent suspension all round. However, George Bishop was quoted as saying 'I must have been drunk when I launched the Europa.'

Although the kit package provided everything you needed to build the car, its price of just under £600 was too cheap even by 1962 standards, and due to the complexity of the production process Heron lost money on each kit sold.

Swiss company MBM, run by Peter Monteverdi, sold it in their home country for a while as a fully-built car. Meanwhile, Bishop later cropped up as part of the Camber GT (*qv*) project.
Heron Plastics 1962–64
Approx 12 made

HERON PLASTICS HERON BODYSHELL

George Bishop's Heron Plastics was ideally placed when the boom for rakish bodyshells began in the 1950s. Soon evolved into the Europa.
Heron Plastics 1962–64
Approx 12 made

HGM6

Beautiful aluminium-bodied Lotus Six replica from a chap called Mark Harris, based in Scarborough, East Yorkshire.
Harris Great Marques 1998–2005
Approx 14 made

HI-TECH GT40

Hi-Tech Engineering were welding specialists based in Kidderminster, run by Pat Matthews.
Hi-Tech Engineering 1988–91
Approx 17 made

HILLCREST V12

Brynmaer, Gwent-based company Hillcrest made the former EG Arrow (although Emilio Garcia was still involved), and was joined by KVA founder Ken Attwell's son Paul, and Peter Jacobs, another ex-KVA man who had also created the body for the Ford RS200 prototype.
Hillcrest Classics 1987–88
Approx 8 made

HMS COUNTACH REPLICA

A very obscure Lamborghini Countach 25th Anniversary Edition replica from a company based near Brands Hatch. Early '80s enthusiasts could phone a bloke called 'John' as per a small ad that appeared in the kit car press for a short time in the early '90s.
HMS 1990–91
Approx 1 made

HOBO

Based in Harold Wood, Essex, the Hobo was a Mini-based Jeep-style kit with a 2in box section chassis, available in four- or six-wheel form.
Rod Penhull 1994
Approx 2 made

HOFFMANN CABRIO

Long established German convertible conversion on Citroën 2CV, imported to the UK for a time by John Ransley of Brighton-based Hoffmann Design UK.
2CV Heaven 2005–6
Approx 5 made (UK)

HOPPA

Superb modern take on the beach buggy theme created by John 'Village' Warner before passing to his father and automotive model maker Barry. Originally sold as the 'Son of a Beach' under the Fubar Factory banner, subsequently amended by Barry who reasoned that people wouldn't be happy writing out a cheque to the 'Fubar Factory' or, indeed, telling the wife that they were buying a 'Son of a Beach'.

Neat styling that married traditional beach buggy underpinnings of VW Beetle floorpan and mechanicals with a refreshing new shape.
Fubar Factory 2003–7
Hoppa Street Buggies 2007–10
Approx 5 made

HORNET

Closely related to the Locust SIII (qv), the Hornet was developed around Ford running gear by T&J Sportscars of Rotherham before passing in 1994 to Bev Evans of Barnsley-based BWE Sportscars, who introduced a Ford Sierra-based option in 2002.
T&J Sportscars 1990–94
BWE Sportscars 1994 to date
Approx 100 made

HOUNDOG

A wild and wacky conversion kit for VW Beetle that cost just £65 in early 1972, offered by this Streatham, South West London-based company.
Eagle Autos 1971–73
Approx 15 made

HOUSEHAM V8

Lincolnshire-based Bryan Househam created this Rover V8-powered Phaeton and raced it in the Kit Car Challenge Series in the 1980s. He also offered replicas of the car.
Househam Dutton 1985–87
Approx 3 made

HOWIE

Type-approved buggy that is ideally suited to off-road adventures, but can also be used on the public highway. Can be built from plans, or as a conventional kit. Power comes from a 650cc engine.
Blitzworld 2006 to date
Approx 200 made

HRB 34 FORD

HRB of Portsmouth, a company with a background in hot rods, launched this 34 Ford kit in Sedan or Coupé form in 2007.
HRB Automotive 2007–8
Approx 1 made

HRB MULSANNE

A trackday-orientated sports car far removed from their 34 Ford in concept.
HRB Automotive 2008
Approx 1 made

HUDSON KINDRED SPIRIT

As per the Free Spirit in concept but added second seat in a tandem arrangement. Large majority of sales were for this version. Retained Renault 5 mechanical basis. Creator Roy Web had a background in building hot rods, and his innovative mind came to the fore with his Free and Kindred Spirits.
Hudson Component Cars 1993–99
Wizard Cars 1999–2003
Approx 50 made

HUDSON FREE SPIRIT

Norfolk-based Roy Webb had built quite a few *specials* over the years, winning a *Custom Car* magazine competition in 1987 for an all-GRP Vauxhall Astra, while he also had a penchant for mini-motorbikes, plus he had a collection of 150 classic

motorcycles. Initially known as Webb's Wonder, the single-seat three-wheeler Free Spirit was underpinned by Renault 5 components.

Hudson Component Cars 1990–99
Wizard Cars 1999–2003
Approx 17 made

HUDSON MYSTIC

More modern take on the Free and Kindred Spirit themes with four wheels and massive rear wing. Retained Renault donor, though. Bonkers.

Hudson Component Cars 1992–93
Approx 1 made

HUMBUG

Back in the early seventies, the UK was in the grip of beach buggy mania with the likes of GP selling around 150 buggy kits per month! Also popular back then was the VW Beetle conversion kit that gave your humble veedub the rat, baja or simply just outrageous

look. The Humbug was just such a conversion and was created by Paul Cockburn and Bob King of the Design Field in Acton, although marketed through well-known beach buggy exponents Skyspeed of Heston. Compared to some, the kit was quite pricey, with £97 being the cost for your replacement front and rear ends in 1970, with essential nerf bars an additional £10.

Skyspeed 1969–72
Approx 25 made

HUNTER

A convoluted story lies behind this Triumph TR2-based traditional roadster that originated in America. Originally imported to the UK by Tripos R&D before being sold to German company Hunter RSC, from whom it remains available today.

Tripos R&D 1985–86
Approx 1 made (UK)

HUSKY

A period-type van kit package created in 1991 by the prolific John Cowperthwaite, then of Real Life Toys, from his Sheffield base. Had definite Willy's Jeep influences and featured a body made from Medite, running on Ford mechanicals. Taken over in 1995 by Gillingham-based White Rose Vehicles, run by John Richards.

A Husky II arrived in 1997 offering the customer pre-cut Medite panels, thus making it an easier build. Ladderframe chassis cost £375 in 1997.

Real Life Toys 1991–95   *White Rose Vehicles 1995–2000*
Approx 100 made

HUSTLER

William Towns' early years had involved plenty of motoring, and his father owned a Jaguar SS100, his mother an MG, while a young William drove around in a 1936 Rolls-Royce.

Towns' design career started at Rootes in 1954 where he began designing seats and door handles, although ultimately he would end up having a hand in the Hillman Hunter. Moved to Rover in 1963 working under David Bache, and styled the Rover BRM gas turbine car that ran at Le Mans in 1965. He then joined Aston Martin in 1966, firstly on seat design, but he was later responsible for the DBS and Lagonda, plus the Bulldog and Aston Martin MGB concepts.

He set up his own design company, Interstyl, and created a couple of designs that were almost taken on by British Leyland – Microdot and Minissima, plus other commissions such as a Black Prince recreation, a proposed Railton resurrection, Peugeot 205 bodykit, Pizzazz and the Guyson E12. Towns didn't just do automotive stuff either. For example, many councils used his street furniture designs in high streets and shopping arcades.

The original Hustler design was a concept for Jensen Special Projects that wasn't proceeded with, so he did it himself, under the Interstyl banner, with the first Hustler model, a Mini-based six-wheeler appearing in 1984. The Hustler really was a clever concept, and despite the angular lines that didn't excite everybody, under the skin, upper and lower chassis frames sandwiched the body panels; literally clamping them in place.

The upper section carried the sliding glass doors, windscreen and tailgate, while the lower frame enabled literally any engine to be fitted in any configuration and that, I think, encapsulated the genius of the man. He called it 'pick and mix' design! He came up with a Hustler that instead of the usual flat sheet GRP panel had a roof that could be removed and used as a rowing boat!

One of the seventies and eighties 'big three' designers, in addition to Richard Oakes and Dennis Adams. Williams sadly passed away in 1993.

A
B
C
D
E
F
G
H
I
J
K
L
M
N
O
P
Q
R
S
T
U
V
W
X
Y
Z

HUSTLER 4

Originally created for Jensen Special Products in 1978, but when they couldn't afford to produce it Towns launched it under his Interstyl banner. Simple yet effective trademark Towns angular styling. Based on Mini mechanicals, with a steel tube

chassis, upon which a metal frame was mounted for the sizeable flat glass area that included sliding side windows à la patio doors.
Interstyl 1979–89
Approx 200 made

HUSTLER 6

A six-wheeler appearing in 1981. Actually, most of the subsequent array of Hustlers could be ordered with six wheels. Similar in concept and mechanical basis to the Hustler 4 but had a second Mini rear subframe and could carry six people or a healthy payload.

Incidentally, the rear occupants sat two abreast sideways, facing each other.
Interstyl 1981–89
Approx 100 made

HUSTLER AMPHIBIAN

Towns went to Crayford Engineering of Westerham to collaborate on his amphibious Hustler. They based it on an eight-wheel all-terrain vehicle and skilfully adapted a Hustler-type body to fit. Could be driven on land and, of course, in water. Towns tested the demonstrator regularly on his own lake in Warwickshire.
Interstyl 1985–89
Approx 1 made

HUSTLER FORCE 4/FORCE 6

The Force range was a replacement for the short-lived Huntsman and was notable for the fact that Towns deleted his beloved flat glass panels, opting for proper doors and windows instead. However, the doors were massively heavy and the

windows didn't open. Could be built using Mini, Metro or Austin1100/Morris1300 donors. The Force 6 was a six-wheeler.
Interstyl 1984–89
Approx 4 made

HUSTLER HARLEQUIN

Basically the same as the Force 4 and 6 models but had an upright type grille.
Interstyl 1985–89
Approx 1 made

HUSTLER HELLCAT

Successor to the Hobo and even more basic than that model. It obviously hit the spot, because although the Hobo didn't sell this one was popular.
Interstyl 1982–89
Approx 54 made

HUSTLER HIGHLANDER

William Towns' highly versatile Hustler range could be had in a myriad permutations. He opened another avenue with 1985's Highlander, as this was a Jaguar XJ-based limousine version, aimed squarely at Range Rover demographic. A Jaguar XJ12 provided the power, underpinned by a beefed up chassis (well, Jag bits were a lot heavier than Mini stuff!), and at some 5m long the Highlander was a brute, albeit a well-appointed one with a very plush (by specialist car standards) interior, that included a space-age Clarion stereo system mounted in the transmission tunnel and a Lagonda-style LCD dashpot.
Interstyl 1985–89
Approx 8 made

HUSTLER HOBO

The Hobo was a very spartan pickup-style Hustler based on Mini mechanicals, as was the norm for Towns' range. Sadly no one ordered one, although its even more basic Hellcat successor (see above) did inspire more people.
Interstyl 1980–82
Approx 1 made

HUSTLER HOLIDAY

Possibly the most radical looking Hustler, with big, flat glass panels, a massive windscreen and a choice of Mini, Metro or Austin 1100/Morris 1300 donor. Standard version had six wheels, although four-wheels were an option.
Interstyl 1986–89
Approx 4 made

HUSTLER HUNTSMAN

As an alternative to his Mini-based Hustlers, Towns came up with the Austin 1100/Morris 1300 or Metro-based Huntsman in 1983, and as a result, the car had a more purposeful stance, due in no small part to the larger wheels. Didn't prove very popular and was soon superseded by the Force 4 and Force 6.

Interstyl 1983–89
Approx 2 made

HUSTLER SPORT

Similar in concept to the Hustler Sprint sharing mechanicals, the Sport did away with the trademark sliding flat glass panels and was a two-seater. No one was inspired enough to order one, though, as only the demonstrator was built.

Interstyl 1981–89
Approx 1 made

HUSTLER SPRINT

Having come up with the practical Hustler, a six-wheeled Hustler and also a wooden one (see below), Towns next worked on a sporty Hustler called the Sprint. Perhaps unsurprisingly. He was even moved to describe it as a Mini Audi UR Quattro. Notable for a bank of six headlights, which were sourced from a Mitsubishi Sapporo, although the rest of the mechanicals were standard Mini fare. Only three customers were inspired enough to order one.

Interstyl 1981–89
Approx 3 made

HUSTLER WOODEN

Ever the innovator, Towns came up with a Hustler made out of wood that featured a marine ply monocoque with double glazing-spec extruded aluminium frame. Again Mini-based, although in this instance a set of plans was required to create your upper body section. If you drove one of these you'd undoubtedly have heard many 'greenhouse' and 'grow tomatoes' jibes.

Interstyl 1980-89
Approx 80 made

HUTSON TF

The Naylor 1700 TF project (*qv*) was rescued by chartered engineer Maurice A. Hutson, chairman of heavy engineering company the Mahcon Group, who specialised in dock plant and quarry equipment. He installed his son, Mark, as MD of the newly formed Hutson Motor Company and renamed the car the 1700 TF.

Hutson retained the fully-built version, now priced from £15,000, preserving its hand-built nature and ash-over-steel tub. They also introduced a kit version, known as the Mahcon TF, which could also be based on Morris Marina instead of Ital if the customer preferred, and was introduced at the Newark Show of 1986. It was slightly simplified using the Marina's semi-elliptic springs and Armstrong dampers although the fully-built version's set-up of Ital live axle, located by four trailing links and Panhard rod tweaked by none other than Lotus, was also an option.

Hutson Motor Company 1986
Approx 61 made

HYDE HARRIER

The Harrier is a motorcycle, but, like the Trantor tractor, it was available in kit form so we've included it here for the sake of completeness.

The brainchild of former Triumph and Norton-Triumph engineer, Norman Hyde, it was the first kit-bike, launched in 1987 and preceded the similar but short-lived Blee Unicorn by a year.

Hyde learnt his craft from British bike pioneers Doug Hele, Bert Hopwood and Brian Jones, and he had direct involvement with a variety of Triumph and Norton motorbikes, such as the Trident, Quadrant, Bandit, Thunderbird 3 and Commando 8-valve. After selling several kits, the pretty Café Style Harrier was put on the back burner. However, in 2008, Norman joined forces with Harris Performance to create a Harrier Jubilee model and again offered the bike in kit form to a receptive new audience. The donor bike was a Triumph Bonneville (2000-on pre-EFI), which is a good choice, as the Bonneville was the Honda Fireblade of its day. Kit prices started at £4,694.13 inc VAT in January 2011.

Hyde also offers a Classic (as per 1987) version of the Harrier that also used the Bonneville donor, as well as Trident, Rocket3 and A65, and a Harris Performance chassis frame like the Jubilee version. Kit prices for the Classic started at £4,336.80 inc VAT in January 2011.

Hyde Harrier Motorcycles 1978–79/2008 to date
Approx 50 made

A B C D E F G H I J K L M N O P Q R S T U V W X Y Z

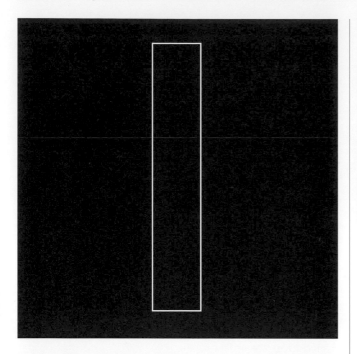

IAN'S TRIKE

Bikers' trike from, er, a bloke called Ian.
Ian's Custom Cycles 1977–79
Approx 5 made

IKON 40

A Mayfly of a GT40 replica that
appeared briefly (in rolling chassis
form!) at the Exeter Show of
2005 and wasn't seen again. The
project came from Witney-based
Andy Bowl and was aimed at the
budget end of the market, with a
proposed £15,000 DIY-build cost,
although as it didn't stick around
no one ever found out if it could be done.
Ikon Car Craft 2005
Approx 1 made

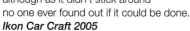

IMOLA

Very ambitious project from Peter Rawlinson (who had worked in
Jaguar's New Vehicle Concept department) and Nick Sampson,
featuring a stainless steel monocoque with BL Maestro/Montego
underpinnings. Company based in Evesham, Worcestershire.
Rawlinson would go on to work for several large car makers.
Imola Cars 1991
Approx 1 made

IMPALA BURRO

Came from a Dartmouth company run by boat designer and engineer
Alan Foulkes, who when he decided he wasn't earning enough royalties
from his boat designs decided to go into car production using his
favourite model – the Fiat 500 (its first use as a kit car donor, no less)
– as donor vehicle. Sold 12 kits in the first few months. A small utility
based on Fiat 500/126 mechanicals with a one-piece fibreglass body
fixed to a basic ladderframe chassis, it had a strange charm about it.
Kits cost just £626 in 1981. Early Impalas are distinguishable by their
square wheel arches, which soon became rounded.
Foulkes Developments 1981–85
Approx 30 made

IMPERIAL

Another superb traditional range
of vehicles from John Barlow, ex-
JBA and Royale Motor Company,
with input from David Chapman.
Launched at Stoneleigh Show in
2009. Featured a variety of vintage
body styles including a limousine
and even a hearse, all based on
FX4 London Taxi donor.
Imperial Motor Company 2009 to date
Approx 75 made

IMPERIAL ROYALE

Fully-built only traditional
1930s-style neo-classical
roadster running on Jaguar XJ12
mechanicals. Designer Terry
Marshall, who worked in California
for a time in the '80s, having
previously worked at Callington
Motors, had a penchant for

interesting vehicles and created the Royale while in America, basing
it on Lincoln Continental. When he returned to the UK in 1988 he
brought the idea with him and set up Imperial Trading Company in
Callington, Cornwall, although he went to the Sandown Show that
year with a Corsair from the Roaring Twenties Motor Company that
he'd brought home with him. This inspired him to come up with the
Royale, available in fully-built guise only at prices from £40,000. It's
included here only because it was advertised frequently in the kit car
press and appeared at shows for a time in the mid-'90s.
Imperial Motor Company 1996–97
Approx 1 made

INVADER

John Sprinzel, co-founder of
Speedwell, and synonymous with
go-faster parts for all manner of
vehicles such as the Austin Healey
'Frogeye' Sprite, designed the
Invader, commissioned by the
Daily Telegraph magazine to create
a beach buggy for their stand at
the British Motor Show of 1970.

Actually, Sprinzel imported a Scorpion LT buggy bodyshell from US
company Desert Fox Sand Buggies, putting a few of his touches to it.
The buggy required a 14½in chop to the Beetle floorpan.

John Cullen, who ran car sales operation, GB Motors, in Small
Heath, Birmingham, also at the time one of the many GP Buggy
agents, acquired the project soon after the show and put it into
production, calling it the Invader.

Sales were good until a big factory fire around Christmas 1971
put the brakes on. A Mk2 duly appeared, and was differentiated by
a 3in deeper tub, and a glassfibre windscreen surround. Cullen was
becoming more interested in his new furniture business and the
operation was passed to Bordesley Green, Birmingham, company
Croy Glassfibre Products in 1977, who produced it until 1979. Kits
were priced at £258.75 inc VAT.

Came to rest at bugu guru, James Hale's GT Mouldings operation.
GB Motors 1970-77
Croy Glassfibre Products 1977–79
GT Mouldings 1988–91
Approx 150 made

INVERTER

Indy 500 winner and ex-F1 designer Adrian Reynard entered the kit
car market with his Inverter trackday car in 2009. Power options are
Honda Fireblade and Suzuki Hayabusa. The car is called the Inverter
because Reynard and his partner Andre Brown say the downforce is
so high that it could be driven upside down. Available in kit or fully-
built form.
Reynard Racing Cars 2009 to date
Approx 5 made

INVICTA COBRA

Cobra replica based around Ford Cologne V6-power, made briefly by
Invicta Replicas of Heartenoak Road, Hawkhurst.
Invicta Replicas 1985
Approx 2 made

INVICTA TOURER

Jaguar XJ6-based roadster by
Invicta Cars, Plymouth. They also
acquired William Towns' Black
Prince (*qv*) recreation and revised
it into the Invicta Tourer.
Invicta Cars 1982–84
Approx 2 made

INVICTA TREDECIM

Jaguar XJ13-inspired, as the car
definitely wasn't a replica, being
longer and wider than the Jaguar
original. After Invicta went bust the
project went to Challenger makers
Triple C for a time. Incidentally,
Tredecim is Latin for 13.

Invicta Cars 1983–84
Car Care Clinic (Triple C) 1984–86
Approx 3 made

IPI FROGEYE

Came from an Isle of Wight
GRP company that also
made motorhomes under the
Romahome name. They had
been making the bodies for
Keith Brading's Supersprite 'frog'
replica, and when he started

producing his K-series-powered
SuperSprite version, IPI took over the original, powering it with a
Toyota engine.
Island Plastics 1999–2001
Approx 3 made

ISH 355

Radstock-based ISH was
founded by car enthusiast
Nathan Redfearn and ex-Triumph
employee John Bowness. The ISH
355 was a Ferrari F355 replica
based on Toyota MR2 Mk2, which
had originated from a half-finished
Pontiac Fiero-based one-off built
by a German architect.

ISH Car Company 1998–2000
Approx 25 made

ITALIA

Simpson Design of America created this Mazda MX-5-based
conversion kit, which was imported to the UK by Andy Benn of
Worthing, who sold around 12 before the project moved to a name
from the past – one Dave Perry, with his son Ross, who continue to
run the project as a hobby and have thus far sold around 50.
Retroforza 2005–6
Italia Sports Cars 2006 to date
Approx 42 made

A B C D E F G H I J K L M N O P Q R S T U V W X Y Z

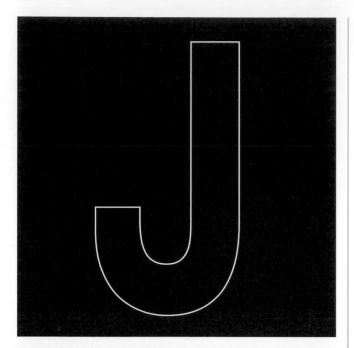

J15 – *see Sylva J15*

JACKAL (J3)

Viva-based traditional roadster in the style of the Mercedes Benz Mannheim, although not a replica. It was created by Bexhill-on-Sea school teacher and ex-art school graduate Peter Fairhurst, who traded under the Minion name in a premises next door to his school in Ashdown Road with day-to-day stuff handled by Colin Sayers and Andrew Carey. In 1985, Fairhurst teamed up with Eastbourne-based Peter Gowland, who ran a car sales business in the town, under the Imperial name.

As a result the company name changed to Imperial in 1985, while Ford-based versions of the Jackal were also created. Chassis contracted to Hastings-based Winstone Engineering (a rugged ladderframe fro 90mm x 50mm x 3mm steel), while bodies were made by Edenbridge-based Fi-Glass. Fairhurst would continue to design cars, including electric vehicles and a three-wheeler. He also won the prestigious 'BP Build a Car' competition in 1990.

Ended up at Eagle Cars where not much happened, until it was taken over by Hurstmonceaux-based Ken Wheatley, an industrial sign maker, who introduced a Ford Sierre donor option in 1997.

Final flourish, if that's the correct word, for the Jackal came from Cheltenham-based Cotswold Kit Cars, although they didn't last long.

Minion Motors 1983–85   *Imperial Special Vehicles 1985–87*
Eagle Cars 1988–95   *Jackal Cars 1995–98*
Cotswold Kit Cars 2001–2
Approx 42 made

JACKAL SPORTS

A convertible version of the standard Jackal with slightly revised styling. Created by Peter Gowland.
Minion Motors 1983–87
Imperial Special Vehicles 1985–87
Eagle Cars 1988–95
Jackal Cars 1995–98
Cotswold Kit Cars 2001–2
Approx 50 made

JACKDAW

A practical van-bodied version of the Jackal. Not many takers.
Minion Motors 1984–85   *Imperial Special Vehicles 1985–87*
Approx 7 made

JAGO GEEP – *see Jago Sandero*

JAGO MODEL B FIVE WINDOW COUPÉ

Coming after their Model T, this was Jago's second product, a Model B Ford replica that was available in Coupé, Sedan and Pickup body styles. Geoff had thought about adding to the Model T with a 'B', but his hand was forced when a customer told him where an old Model B body was languishing in a blackberry bush!
Geoff Jago's Custom Automotive 1976–84
Approx 600 made

JAGO MODEL B ROADSTER

Another well-known Jago model and natural sister to the existing Coupé and Delivery Wagon versions. Basic single-skinned GRP body that required the customer to cut out the door apertures, which although rudimentary did at least keep the price affordable, with the basic kit at just £100! If you wanted a chassis though, you couldn't get one from Jago and you had to make your own or butcher an old Ford Pilot item, and as such the 'B' Roadster was never really a serious production Jago model.
Geoff Jago's Custom Automotive 1969–84
Approx 5 made

JAGO AUTOMOTIVE

Geoff Jago was born in Portchester, Hampshire, and after school became a fitter at Portsmouth Naval Base, which he didn't enjoy very much as he was always into cars – a passion that was satiated when a friend of his father's got him an apprenticeship as a motor mechanic at a local garage.

During his spare time he built a stock car, using a pre-war American V8, with the rear half of a Humber Super Snipe grafted on to it, which raced on short ovals in the mid-fifties. One day, during a tea break, Geoff read a dog-eared copy of *Hot Rod* magazine, which really got his enthusiasm fired up and his creative juices flowing. So inspired in fact, that he took his dad's Ford Consul Mk1 and 'hot rodded' it with a mass of aerials, port-holes and the like. The sort of stuff he'd seen in the American magazine, in fact.

His boss took a bit of a dim view of Geoff's new interest and sacked him three weeks before his apprenticeship officially ended. Undeterred, Geoff went and found himself a scruffy 800sq ft unit in a Portchester farmyard, where he did general repair work. He did not actually get involved with building his own cars until 1963, when he paid £17 for an accident-damaged Ford Thames van, taking it and customising it to resemble the T-Buckets that had so attracted him in *Hot Rod* magazine. The resulting vehicle was soon christened 'Jago One' and is likely to have been the UK's first proper hot rod, certainly one of the first to feature Metalflake paint.

Geoff had also started sending off replies to adverts in American magazines, and regularly ordered bags of Metalflake, which he is credited as introducing to these shores. So much of it, that in the end the US company would make up pigments just for Geoff! See, I told you that Geoff was a pioneer…

Equally importantly, Geoff's rod made other car enthusiasts sit up and take notice of this young chap from a small town in Hampshire! Indeed, 'Jago One' took the best all-rounder prize at the important Rod & Custom show in 1964, organised by the fledgling British Hot Rod Association and held in the underground car park in London's Park Lane.

Geoff had well and truly arrived. At this time he started work on a more sophisticated Model T replica that he could sell in kit form, using a basic ladderframe chassis, a six-cylinder from a Ford Zephyr, gearbox, brakes and other components from a Triumph TR2. He produced a GRP tub, supported by a plywood base, scaling up drawings and photos he'd seen in *Hot Rod* magazine. He ran into a problem for the rear of the body, although he solved this by taking the back end of a knackered Singer Nine, turning it upside down and bonding it in, giving it the required 'C-Cab' look. He then took a mould from the finished body… He even placed his first advert (quarter page) in the BHRA's *Drag Racing* magazine, in spring 1965, offering his T-Bucket 'shells' for just £30. He told me once about his first test drive on the A27 in his new creation, during which he was stopped by plod six times in 12 miles. They, like most other motorists, had seen nothing like it before. It was through the adverts that he'd meet a man who would go on to become a great friend and also business partner, Richard Park. At the time, Park was also importing US go-faster goodies to the UK, albeit on a larger scale. Geoff purchased a period-looking replica 1923 Model T radiator shell in GRP. He also introduced a basic chassis kit to the catalogue of his company (known as Geoff Jago's Custom and Speed Shop), which cost just £35. He delivered every single order himself, travelling thousands of miles while doing so. What's more, he didn't charge for the privilege, seeing it as a good way to meet his customers and spread the 'Jago' word.

Suddenly the name Geoff Jago was everywhere within the motoring scene, while the first customer-built Jago Model T to be used on the drag strips was called 'Dragonfly' and owned/built by Pete Atkins. This period would regularly see future UK rodding royalty sitting on the grassy banks at Santa Pod, watching and getting ideas…Other notable Jago 'Ts' included 'Wild Cat' (Colin Mullen/Reuben Johnson), 'Zippety Zip' and that man

Atkins again, this time with 'Slo-Mo-Shun' that was named after a Jan & Dean song and campaigned by Richard Park's brother, Howard. Geoff could also supply the latest American gear, including Turtle Decks and Munster and Surfboard fenders (It's a custom car thing!).

A potential problem arose in September 1969 when Jago was served with a Compulsory Purchase Order, which would see his ramshackle premises pulled down to make way for what would become, Chichester Crematorium. He'd stayed in touch with Richard Park (who was running Custom City) and decided to join forces to form a new company called Rodding Scene, moving into a 3,000sq ft former brick and breeze-block works in Quarry Lane, Chichester, which Geoff told me was under 6in of water and had the roof missing. It would take a further three months to put right!

New magazine *Custom Car* was published in March 1970, and Geoff Jago, Richard Park and their Rodding Scene business were huge at this stage, and had started offering a part-to-fully built rod service, while a quartet of new Jago customer rods would bring more fame – all shared the distinction of being V8-powered. The first was built by accountant Micky Bray (a future great of the UK's hot-rodding scene), and featured a 2¼-litre Daimler V8. This was followed by Brighton Speed Shop's Chris Church's example, nicknamed 'ROD 5'. Next up was Malcolm Ockwell with 'The Octopus', complete with 6-litre Oldsmobile engine, followed by Irish potato farmer and future boss of Wolfrace Wheels (originally known as Wolferace after their founder, John Woolfe).

The arrival of the V8-powered Jago blew the market apart, as rivals such as Opus, Boler T-Bone and Eddie Wimble hadn't produced a V8 at that stage. Geoff's new found fame brought him the work to build Panther boss Robert Jankel's Westwind bodyshells. I always remember that my Uncle Tony sent off his 50p for Jago's 38-page catalogue, and was knocked out by the treasure contained within, if not the quality of the spelling!

By late 1969, Geoff reckoned that the time was right for a second model, and so he launched a Model-B Roadster replica that was moulded from an original car in return for a respray! This one was more basic with a rudimentary single-skin GRP shell, which relied on the customer to cut out the door and boot openings. If the customer wanted a chassis, they had to make their own or use an old Ford Pop item. Kits were cheap though, at just £100… The Model-B Roadster was nowhere as near as popular as the 'T', even with the introduction in 1971 of a £150 twin-rail chassis. The first customer-built example found its way to the strip in late 1976 (seven-year build!) and was powered by a Chevy 327ci V8. It was known as 'All Shook Up'.

Finding more favour in 1976 was the third Jago rod model, which came about after a customer gave Geoff the five-window roof section of an old stock car racer. Shells cost £300 when the new model was launched at Olympia in December 1976 for the National Custom Car show although, as was the Jago way, it had actually been in the catalogue since 1974. The roof gave the Five-Window Coupé real, all-weather practicality, which was reflected in its sales.

The company moved to their well-known Quarry Lane, Chichester, base in 1969, and their Jago Fabrications division made the chassis for several other manufacturers, including 164LM, CN Sprint and Stimson Trek. Park left due to illness in late 1970 and soon afterwards the company was renamed Jago Automotive.

To celebrate the company's 25th anniversary in 1985, Corgi produced a run of Escort vans with *Jago* script on them that cost £4.45 including P&P. How much are they worth today, I wonder? The marque celebrated its 50th anniversary in 2010.

Geoff Jago, a real legend.

JAGO MODEL B SEDAN DELIVERY WAGON

Similar layout to the Model B Coupé and could take V6 and V8 engines, but could also be underpinned by Jago's own Cortina-based chassis, using all the running gear from the Mk3 or Mk4 Cortina. In 1980 standard V6/V8 chassis cost £469 with the Cortina version at £504. Bodyshells cost £642. Customers could also choose a sedan saloon body.
Geoff Jago's Custom Automotive 1980–84
Approx 100 made

JAGO MODEL T

This Ford Model T 1923 replica was Jago's first product and the UK's first GRP-bodied version. A milestone car, bodies cost just £30 back in the day, and at one stage Jago was churning them out. Geoff's idea was to make an English version of the American 'T' using domestic mechanicals, including Dainler engine.

Geoff Jago's Custom Automotive 1965–84
Approx 900 made

JAGO SAMURI

Jago's take on the practical four-seater meets Dutton Sierra meets beach buggy theme. Individual styling with a beefy box-section chassis and Mk2 Escort donor parts.
Jago Automotive 1983–90
Approx 130 made

JAGO SANDERO

Launched in 1971 the Sandero was moulded from an original Willy's Jeep and based on a basic ladderframe chassis. Sales took off from the word go. One hiccup was the name. Originally called the Jago Jeep, Chrysler objected, as they also did to the alternative spelling 'Geep', hence the Sandero name in 1991.

The Mk1 was based on Ford Anglia 105E, Mk2 on Morris Minor from 1974, followed by an Escort Mk1/Mk2 in 1976. They also offered a Suzuki 4x4 option in 1984, although this didn't last long.
Jago Automotive 1971–97   Belfield Engineering 1999 to date
Approx 2,100 made

JAGO SANDERO

Not to be confused with the later Sandero renamed after Chrysler objected to the 'Geep' name. This was an intended new boxy utility that appeared in 1983, the same year as the Samuri.
Jago Automotive 1983
Approx 1 made

JAKABI JA8

Heavily inspired by the Audi R8, the JA8 was never intended as a replica. It was the brainchild of automotive clay modeller Paul Goldsmith, who based his car on Toyota MR2 Mk2.
Jakabi Design 2010 to date
Approx 1 made

JAMAICAN

American kit made by FiberFab imported to the UK by Sandbach Replica Cars.
Sandbach Replica Cars 1981–82
Approx 1 made (UK)

JAS BUGGY

A VW Beetle-based beach buggy available in short- or unmodified long-wheelbase form. Former GP employee of 30 years John Davies was the man behind the project, along with his wife Sharon.
JAS Speedkits 1998-2008
Approx 35 made

JAVAN R1

Javan Smith is one of the UK's foremost scale model makers and his work has included models right up ⅓ and to ¼ scale. In 2005 he acquired the rights to the Strathcarron project and spent three years modifying it to suit his purposes, introducing Renault power. Not available as a conventional kit but the customer could order it in 'turnkey minus' form, which is why it's included here.
Javan Sports Cars 2005–9
Approx 4 made

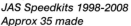

JBA ENGINEERING

Founded by Ken Jones, John Barlow and Dave Ashley, whose surname initials provided the JBA company name. The three were former design draughtsmen at Leyland Trucks and launched their first car in 1982. Barlow left quite soon after the launch, leaving Ken and Dave to continue the business. JBA was taken over by Tim Banwell in 2004, who only continued for a year before packing up.

JBA FALCON

Bill Willcock has long been a JBA Falcon (see following entries) enthusiast, and built several examples over the years, and his new Falcon has been under development since 2008, backed by his security shredding and recycling operation, Wilki Engineering. He was assisted by his son, Matt.

The new Falcon is based on BMW mechanicals (E36 or E46 generations) and is more akin in visual terms to the original JBA Roadster of the early eighties, using the windscreen mounting method (ie mounted to the top of the scuttle section) as per the Falcon Plus 2 of 1988.
JBA Motors 2011 to date
Approx 2 made

JBA FALCON PLUS 2

Replacing the Roadster (see next entry) in 1985 came the larger Plus 2, which featured a small bench seat in the rear that could accommodate children or jockey-sized adults. Had a steel body frame and a rear opening boot for the first time. Can be identified by a new windscreen that sat atop the scuttle, which was bolted directly to the top of it. Donor vehicle remained Ford Cortina.
JBA Engineering 1985–89
Approx 370 made

JBA FALCON ROADSTER

The first Falcon, launched in 1982. A competition on the Granada TV teatime news programme provided the model name. The original Roadster had an all-aluminium body, including doors, with fibreglass wings, and was based on Ford Cortina mechanicals. The original is identifiable by being smaller than later Falcons, and had a near-vertical windscreen. The rear bulkhead was a sloping affair that housed the fuel tank. Power options were Ford four-cylinder, as per the donor, or Ford V6, or even Rover V8.
JBA Engineering 1982–85
Approx 200 made

JBA FALCON SPORTS

Appearing in 1988, the Sports model was lower, smaller and sportier-looking but reverted to a non-opening boot, although an opening boot was later available. The first Falcon to feature a GRP body tub, what JBA called the Central Body Unit (CBU), which some felt diluted the purity created by the original version, although the new structure was definitely stiffer.
JBA Engineering 1988–2004
Approx 284 made

JBA FALCON SR/SRI

The first Falcon to be based on Ford Sierra. Similarly styled but actually had all-new CBU and chassis. The SRI (or SR MkII) arrived in 1995 with the 'I' suffix denoting a fuel-injected engine, but cosmetically differed slightly by having a more sloping grille, a lockable boot and revised interior.
JBA Engineering 1991–2005
Approx 270 made

JBA FALCON TOURER

The Tourer was a direct replacement for the Plus 2, and was introduced in response to the demand for a larger Falcon, being some 15in longer than the Sports model, with a 2+2 capability. Featured a distinctive, sloped windscreen, which is the visual giveaway for the *Top Trumps* spotter!

Remained available until the demise of the original JBA marque. Ken Jones and Dave Ashley retired and sold the project to a chap called Tim Banwell in 2004, who carried on until early 2006, although reportedly no kits or cars were sold after Ken and Dave retired. Project ended up with GTS Tuning where it was shelved.
JBA Engineering 1990–2005
GTS Tuning 2005–09
Approx 265 made

JBA FALCON TSR

A Tourer version of the SR and again based on Sierra, although could be ordered in strict two-seater or 2+2 guises.
JBA Engineering 1993–2004
Approx 310 made

JBA JAVELIN

Totally different in concept to the
Falcon, the Javelin was based on
Ford Capri MkII (or MkIII) with a
rugged ladderframe chassis and a
GRP body with targa front section
and a rear hood similar in style to
a Landaulet in execution.
JBA Engineering 1985–89
Approx 55 made

JBF BOXER

Just one of Atherton,
Manchester-based John B.
Fernley's highly rated Citroën
2CV-based barrelback trikes, the
Boxer was made in 1991/92.
John B. Fernley 1991–92
Approx 1 made

JEEPNI

Appeared once and once only at Stoneleigh in 1990.
Telstar 1990
Approx 1 made

JEFFREY J4

George Jeffrey set up his little
company in 1968 in the shower
block within old RAF Shilton in
Oxfordshire. He was a racing car
builder, with a 750 Motor Club
'750 Racer' their first product
before being followed by F1200,
Formula Vee and Midget racers.

    George never intended making road cars although his hand was
somewhat forced when some customers talked seriously about
converting their racers for road use, which he didn't agree with. So
to head off the idea he came up with the Lotus Seven-inspired J4,
which was based on a tube steel spaceframe chassis with aluminium
body panels and GRP wings, with power coming from a Ford Pre-
Crossflow 1500 GT engine.
Jeffrey Racing Cars 1971–72
Approx 30 made

JEFFREY J5

With the switch to a bigger
workshop in Little Clanfield,
Oxfordshire, came the launch of
the J5 (also known as the JS5)
in August 1972. By now Jeffrey
Racing Cars only made road cars.
The J5 was a more curvaceous
version of the J4, initially built

using an aluminium and fibreglass body, which was changed to all-
GRP from 1973. Featured a revised J4 tubular steel spaceframe.

    Like its predecessor, the J5 was one of the very best-handling kit
cars of all time. After making 26 kits George Jeffrey sold the project to
Emba Cars, run by Dave Cox, who sold a further six.
Jeffrey Cars 1972–74
Emba Cars 1974–75
Approx 32 made

JESTER – *see Sylva Jester*

JIFFY

Commissioned by Barry Badlands, the MD of leading trailer
manufacturers Indespension, via their Mechanical Services division,
he could see the potential for a small commercial-type Mini-based
vehicle to be added to his company's existing range, Richard Oakes
came up with a diminutive chassis/body unit for which customers
could specify a van or pickup-type rear body section. Badlands sadly
passed away and Indespension didn't continue with the project.
Mechanical Services (Indespension) 1982–85
Approx 11 made

JIMI JIMP

Classic car restorer Peter Kukla
of Sandbach, Cheshire, was the
man behind the Jimp, although
it had been designed by Steve
Kirk. A very angular utility vehicle
kit based on Reliant Kitten
mechanicals and chassis, to
which a steel body frame wrapped
in aluminium was bolted.

Kukla Restorations (PK Manufacturing) 1981–84
Approx 8 made

JIMINI

Created by a Dave Cameron. A metal-bodied Mk1 sold in good
numbers (around 200). Restyled with a fibreglass body with sloping
front in 1976, of which about 12 sold. Project then passed to RJB
Electronics of Shepperton, and later to JA Developments. Mini-based.
Van Spear Ltd 1973–76
RJB Electronics (Shepperton) 1976–77
JA Developments 1981–83
Approx 400 made

JIMINI 2

Jimini 2 replaced the original version in 1983 and had revised, more flowing styling and, most noticeably, a GRP monocoque. Also used a Mini windscreen. When creator Dave Cameron stepped aside from Jimini production for the second time in 1990 he went off to run a pub in Shepperton, Middlesex.

Jimini Automobiles came along in 1990 and was a general car repair business run by Ken and Carl Coombs, based in Botley, Hampshire. Main rivals Scamp acquired the project in 1993 with the sole intention of putting it out of production, but not before they had supplied a Trinidad company with 40 kits.

The Jimini's third gap in production ensued before current custodian Kerrion Marsh took control. He offered the project for sale in 2011.

Highlander Cars 1983–86
Jimini Cars 1986–90
Jimini Automobiles 1990–93
Scamp Motor Company 1993–2002
Jimini Automotive 2003 to date
Approx 60 made

JMA SEXO

An innovative bike-powered conversion for Citroën Saxo from Jack Marland of JMA Automotive, based in Oldham, a man with previous kit car experience as he'd built some rather special GP Spyders and also the demonstrator for a company called Speedsters back

in the '90s. JMA's conversion can be fitted to several other hot hatch vehicles, placing the engine (usually Suzuki Hayabusa) in the back.
JMA Automotive 2004 to date
Approx 25 made

JOHNARD DONINGTON

A Bentley *special* kit package made by John Guppy and Dudley Beck based in Dorset. A well-made and highly regarded product. A similar concept to the Bentley-based products from the likes of Mallalieu, Syd Lawrence and Halse Engineering, although

the Johnard was available in kit form, unlike most of the others which were usually fully-built .
Johnard Engineering 1974–78
Approx 16 made

JOU JOU

Short-lived replica of the Fiat Jolly based on Fiat 126, complete with wacky slatted wooden seats that would probably give an SVA IVA inspector a heart attack! Appeared briefly in 1999 at the Stafford Kit Car Show, marketed by a London-based company who described the car as 'a fashion statement.'
Ital Cars 1999
Approx 1 made

JOYRIDER SPORT

Revised version of the company's KR3 buggy (*qv*). Launched in 2010 with a new chassis, more rounded styling, and better suspension travel, although can be powered by the same range of engines from 900cc to 2.0 litres.
Blitzworld 2010 to date
Approx 25 made

JPC BUGGY

Made by Jeff Perry Conversions, and despite claims that it was a GP copy it wasn't. It was a GP. The company made and sold its own fully-built, well-appointed versions, while also supplying GP buggy kits.
Jeff Perry Conversions 1969–70
Approx 8 made

JPR SL

John Randall had worked at Dutton Cars for three years in the early 1970s before travelling the world, spending several years in Australia where he worked for a kit car company. When he returned to the UK he set up JPR Cars (the company name coming from his initials, John Paul Randall), based in the Super Shell building at Goodwood circuit formerly occupied by Alan Langridge's kit manufacturing operation.

This intended replica of the 1930s Mercedes SL (the convertible version of the legendary Gullwing) was his fourth creation, and was to have been based on a revised Wildcat (see below) chassis, altered to accept Ford Granada mechanicals and Mercedes Benz engines. However, it was never productionised.
JPR Cars 1993
Approx 1 made

JPR WILDCAT

John Randall was a fan of the E-type and so launched the Wildcat, not a replica of Jaguar's legendary car but a more than passable interpretation. Body mould was taken from an original Jaguar, although it was 8in wider at the rear to accommodate a Ford live axle. Initially based on Ford Cortina mechanicals, later options included Jaguar XJ6 (inevitably), Ford Sierra and a Mustang Pinto version for the American market. A chap called Terry Land assisted with the chassis development and worked for John for several years. The Wildcat is very well regarded.
JPR Cars 1985–96
Approx 122 made

JPR WILDCAT 2+2

A couple of years after the original Wildcat came the 2+2 version that enabled the carriage of small people on the rear bench or made passage easier for taller drivers, as the car was lengthened by 9in (4in of which was in the doors).
JPR Cars 1987–96
Approx 20 made

A B C D E F G H I J K L M N O P Q R S T U V W X Y Z

JPR WILDCAT LE MANS

John Randall was commissioned by an American customer to create a JPR version of the famous Lindner Nocker Lightweight E-type. Randall later offered the result for commercial kit sale, and made three standard-length cars and two extended by 9in.
JPR Cars 1991–96
Approx 5 made

JT7

Race-inspired kit from Formula Ford racer Graham Millar from Scotland.
RoTor Motive 1998–2001
Approx 2 made

JUVENTAS

Inspired by the Alfa Romeo-based version of Peter Pellandine's Pelland Sports (*qv*) that became known as the Kudos (*qv*), although not a replica. The company was based in Lincolnshire and run by Steve and Karen Gilchrist, and the car used Ford Escort Mk3 mechanicals, although they only built one. Juventas was the Greek god of boundaries! A proposed Jaguar XJ220 replica called Skylar was abandoned.
Alpha Centura Cars 2005
Approx 1 made

JZR

Created by classic car restorer and Morgan three-wheeler enthusiast John Ziemba of Wigan. Diminutive three-wheeler that features a steel box-section spaceframe chassis, steel side panels and GRP bonnet and tail. Available in either 'Beetle' or 'Barrelback' versions. Power comes from Honda CX or Moto Guzzi with rear drive coming via a driveshaft from the engine. Sold in Spain from 1995 as the Bandito.
JZR Vehicle Restorations 1987–98, 2000 to date
Approx 450 made

JZR DAYTONA

A very modern take on the JZR theme by John Ziemba, with power coming naturally enough from a Triumph Daytona bike engine. Commissioned by an existing JZR customer.
JZR Vehicle Restorations 2003 to date
Approx 2 made

K1 ATTACK

Slovakian product offered here in kit form for a time by former Jordan Formula One employee Mark Turner. Kit package was based on Honda mechanicals. Should have sold by the hundreds. Reborn as te Evillio, an electric car, in late 2011.
Dynamic Performance 2005–6
Approx 10 made (UK)

KAIG

Quirky utility-type low-budget offering from Richard Stewart, marketed under the Kaig banner that was actually intended for 'on-road' use! Taken over by Dave Hurst of Driffield, East Yorkshire, in 2002, although disappeared fairly quickly thereafter.
Robin Hood Engineering 1998–2002   Kaig Motors 2002–3
Approx 110 made

KAIG VAMP

Alternative convertible version of the Kaig made for a short while by Robin Hood Engineering.
Robin Hood Engineering 1999–2000
Approx 3 made

KAMALA

Project acquired from DJ Sportscars in 2001 by father and son team Tony and Mark Keen from Wymondham, Norfolk. They introduced a convertible version and also an alternative-styled front end with covered wings.
Kamala Cars 2001–2008
Approx 15 made

KAMALA FUTURO

Developed from the DAX Kamala *(qv)*, by Tony and Mark Keen when they acquired the project in 2001. Deserves its own entry here rather than being merely mentioned as derivative because its styling was very different, notably due to the 'closed-in' front wheel arches.
Kamala Cars 2004–2008
Approx 1 made

KARA 430/EVOLUTION 200/EVO200

A Southend-on-Sea-based company run by Richard Sellicks and Peter Baisden. Mid-1993 saw the project move down the road to Mercury Motorsports & Engineering, based in Shoeburyness. Sellicks had departed, but Baisden carried on with Richard Turner and Karl Seyfang joined him. One of the employees at Mercury was Paul Horner, who later went on to sell the car under the RS Automotive banner. Haulier Gary Campbell joined him in 1999, although the project moved to ex-RAF man Bill Watson of Kent-based RS Motorsport, who introduced an alternative donor to the Ford Cosworth, which by 2010 was becoming quite scarce. In 2011 they moved to a new premises at Manston Airport.
KaRa Sports Cars 1991-93 — *Mercury Motorsports 1993-98*
RS Automotive 1998-2004 — *RS Motorsport 2009 to date*
Approx 115 made

KARMA

Imported from the USA, where it was made by Custom Classics and known as the Kelmark GT. Marketed in the UK by Dave Perry, who sold 350 of them before it passed to egg-baron Roger Wooley of RW Kit Cars, who enjoyed even more success with it. The US original was VW-based, but Perry developed a Rover V8 mid-engined version along with a front-engined Ford Cortina-based variant, although the original Beetle underpinnings remained a constant option during its UK production life.

Perry, now involved with property management within the construction industry, remembers that the first one arrived in the UK in March 1980. He was originally a mechanical engineer in the oil industry and one evening while reading an American kit car magazine he'd been enamoured by the Karma and was prompted to phone the manufacturers. Within a few days he was sitting in their office in California doing a deal.

He sold around ten of the original versions before he commissioned a new set of moulds and made many improvements to the project. RW Kit Cars were initially agents for Perry's products before taking over completely as manufacturers.
Perry Automotive Developments 1980–83
RW Kit Cars 1983–2000
Approx 1,145 made

KAT MPV

Long before he launched the Ariel Atom, designer Simon Saunders had created the MPV via his North Perrott, Somerset-based KAT Designs operation. A multi-purpose vehicle in the truest sense of the word, it could be transformed into a variety of body-styles from saloon to jeep and all points in between. Based on Ford Escort Mk3 or 4. Intended for kit production, but project sold to a Midlands-based company and never heard of again.
KAT Designs 1988
Approx 1 made

KD 289

Came from a Wakefield, West Yorkshire, company run by Kevan Norbury, who had previously built a BRA 289 *(qv)*. For his own car he used Ford Cortina mechanicals. Resurrected by Melksham-based Jonathan Smith trading as Roman Kitcars in 2003, but although it was exhibited at Stoneleigh in 2004 nothing much more was heard of the company nor the project.
KD Kitcars 1991–96
Roman Kitcars 2003-5
Approx 11 made

KEITH ELAN S4

Lotus Elan S4 replica with a backbone chassis from SpyderSport and Mazda rotary power. Company were Mazda RX7 specialists based in Great Longstone, Derbyshire. Also made an RX7 body kit called the Roto Moto.
Keith Cars 1989–96
Approx 15 made

KELVEDON EUROPA

Kelvedon Motors were Lotus specialists from Spalding, Lincolnshire, run by Pat Thomas, who in 1987 could supply a Lotus 47/Europa GRP body for £2,100 and replica chassis for £1,500. A planned conventional kit package never materialised.
Kelvedon Motors 1987
Approx 1 made

KENLEY TT

Boxy traditional roadster based on Triumph Herald/Vitesse mechanicals.
Kenley Engineering 1986
Approx 1 made

KENMAR – *see Monkspath Shirley*

KESTREL

Protoflight was run by Peter Iredale and based in Gillingham, Dorset. As the name suggests, the company's main business was light aircraft. Their Kestrel project was based on VW Beetle floorpan and mechanicals, which didn't entirely endow it with stunning performance, although Iredale was a perfectionist so the car featured meticulously-made subframes, ultra-thick double-skinned fibreglass doors and one-piece body and a work-of-art chromed brass windscreen frame.

Dovetail Plastics of Lambourn, Berkshire, acquired the project in late 1985 before Scottish company FES took over in 1988, renaming the car the FES Briton (*qv*). Finally came to rest at Cartell, a Haydock-based operation run by design engineer Roger Relph and welder Alan McIlroy.
Protoflight (ISS Car Company) 1984–85
Dovetail Plastics 1985–88
FES 1988–89
Cartell 1989–90
Approx 15 made

KESTREL SCORPION

Was originally Tom Killeen's Scorpion (*qv*) before being revamped by Lambourn-based Dovetail Plastics in 1984. Run by Peter Sylvester, the company deleted the Scorpion's Imp donor and semi-monocoque, replacing them with a spaceframe chassis and suspension components that Sylvester said were co-developed with Lotus. An Alfa Romeo Alfasud engine provided the power. Kestrel Cars of Chesterfield, run by Victor Vaughan, took up the baton in late 1984 and reverted to a semi-monocoque structure built by Kevin Mason's Cheetah Cars, retaining the Alfa base.
Dovetail Plastics 1984
Kestrel Cars 1984-85
Approx 2 made

KF PREMIER

The original name for the AK 427 (*qv*) before Ken Freeman and Alan Frew became AK Sports Cars.

KHALEEJ SCARAB RUNABOUT

Khaleej of Lavant, West Sussex, run by Iain Falconer and Roger Whalley. The Scarab was a modern take on the Mini Moke based on Ford Ka mechanicals. Intended as a fully-built car for Arab markets, although they only made two prototypes and one production car. Two other models (Buddy, a commercial vehicle version, and a higher spec Surf) were stillborn.
Khaleej Cars Ltd 1998–2001
Approx 3 made

KILO SPORTS

Created by Bodmin car mechanic Dave Stiff. Quirky little traditional roadster based unusually on Morris Minor 1000 mechanicals. Featured a steel ladderframe chassis and angular one-piece fibreglass body and weighed in at just 595kg. Resurrected by Tintagel-based B&S Horton run by Brian Horton in 1986, but didn't last long.
The Thousand Workshop 1983–84
B&S Horton 1986
Approx 14 made

KING COBRA

Budget-orientated Cobra replica created by hot rod enthusiast David Jones. Was overshadowed by the Pilgrim Sumo (*qv*), which appeared at around the same time. The King Cobra was based on a beefy box-section chassis for Cortina MkIII/IV parts. A short-lived 289 version appeared in 1987. In 1982 Jones had designed a kit van but it was never marketed.
Libra Cars 1985–92
Approx 110 made

KING THING

Odd-looking single-seat hot rod from ex-Cooper Cars man Mike King, based in Liss, Hampshire, although he moved to East Dereham in spring 1971. £220 bought the customer a multi-tube chassis and GRP body that required an E93A transverse leaf front axle and a 100E Anglia engine to get you well on your way. King later developed the 'Thing' to accept 105E and Morris Minor mechanicals. No takers.
Mike King Racing 1970–71
Approx 1 made

KING TRIKE

Renault 4 supplied the power for the King Trike, with a GPR body with Lotus Seven front wings grafted to it. Revised Renault 5-based version was produced. No takers.
Mike King Racing 1970–71
Approx 2 made

KING TYPE 35

Bugatti Type 35 replica by car builder extraordinaire Mike King.
Mike King Racing 1970–71
Approx 2 made

KING TYPE 51

Mike King built two Bugatti Type 51 replicas complete with aluminium body. He also built MG K3 and 4½-litre Bentley replicas too. One of each.
Mike King Racing 1970–71
Approx 2 made

KINGFISHER COUNTESS

Created by later Prova boss Paul Lawrenson, who was also responsible for the Panache kit. Tapped into the growing eighties clamour for Italian exotica, and although only an approximation of the Lamborghini Countach, Lawrenson sold 10 kits before selling the project to boat builder, Dave Forsyth.

VW Beetle base was unusual fare, although a multi-tube spaceframe option for Austin Maxi was also available (from 1983) made by Preston engineering company, Specframe Engineering.

Forsyth had another attempt at Countach manufacture some years later under the GB banner.
Kingfisher Mouldings 1982–86
Approx 70 made

KINGFISHER KUSTOMS

Another very important name in kit car history is Dave Fisher. He'd been a design engineer for Birmingham company Archibald Kendrick for 11 years until he was made redundant in 1978. For many years he'd been mad on cars – customs and VW Beetles in particular. He built a GP LWB Buggy called 'Heart of Gold' in 1973 and was hooked. He'd also come up with a selecta drop arrangement for Beetle front suspension and been selling them in good numbers. After redundancy he teamed up with friends Alan Jones (ex-RAF) and John Gurney (ex-Jaguar) and put his £3,000 pay-off money into a new venture called Kingfisher Kustoms, derived from his surname and the fact that he was known as 'king of the buggies'.

The company still exists, and is still dispensing Veedub expertise to customers old and new. Over the years Dave and co have built some amazing vehicles, including a Reliant Robin with a Porsche 911 Turbo engine in the back that did wheelies!

KINGFISHER CHENOWTH

Once Dave Fisher got wind of how good the American Chenowth was he went to see the company's boss, Mike Thomas, and ended up competing in legendary dune races such as the Baja 500 and Parker 400, and was granted official UK and European sales rights. Made a jig from a production chassis.
Kingfisher Kustoms 1983 to date
Approx 180 made

KINGFISHER KAL

VW Beetle conversion. Californian-look styling.
Kingfisher Kustoms 1989–93
Approx 100 made

KINGFISHER KANGO

A South African kit imported to the UK by Dave Fisher and based on an unmodified VW Beetle floorpan. Despite being an angular design the Kango was very well made and was a versatile option in the mid-'80s. Fisher supplied the kits partially assembled, with windows, door catches and side panels pre-fitted.
Kingfisher Kustoms 1985–90
Approx 12 made

KINGFISHER KOMBAT

Originated from the 1970s Vulture buggy. A modified VW Beetle floorpan of 78½in formed the basis of the Kombat.
Kingfisher Kustoms 1983–91
Approx 100 made

KINGFISHER KOMMANDO

Off-road rail type vehicle that enjoyed great success and was generally regarded as superior (just) in competition to the rival UVA Fugitive (*qv*) but not quite as good as the Americana Chenowth that Dave also imported.
Kingfisher Kustoms 1983 to date
Approx 75 made

KINGFISHER KOMPETITOR

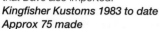

A road-going version of the Kingfisher Kommando that was devised by KK partners, Dave Fisher and Alan Jones. Well-made device as with all Kingfisher products and 40 hardy souls braved this hardcore sand-rail on the Queen's highway!
Kingfisher Kustoms 1984–90
Approx 40 made

KINGFISHER SPRINT

The brainchild of Luton craft teacher Roger King, who wanted to reinvent the Mini Jem (*qv*) as a much more serious proposition and intended to offer it as a Porsche 911 rival. In hindsight, this was perhaps a little overambitious but the Sprint was a good car based around a Mini Jem Mk2 that King had purchased.

The basic redesign saw it grow larger – 6in longer and 2in taller – while still retaining the Mini base. King also added large spoilers front and rear to give it a distinctive character. The windscreen came from a VW Beetle 1303, the rear screen from a Datsun 120Y, with Capri rear light lenses. The top model had a big bore 1,480cc Supersports engine with 125bhp and was equipped with a Rajay turbocharger.

The Sprint was launched at the British Motorshow of 1982 at the NEC and got a good reception.

The company moved to Rothbury, Northumberland, until it went bust in 1984. Briefly revived under Vortex Developments of Morpeth from 1985, although this was very short-lived.
Kingfisher Motors 1982–84
Vortex Developments 1985
Approx 35 made

KINGFISHER SHADOW

A Jaguar E-type replica – sort of! Legend has it that Derek Robinson of the Car Care Clinic (Triple C) was inspired to put the Challenger model into production after trying to build a Kingfisher Shadow. Rare adverts of 1984 vintage had the kit marketed under the Countess Cars banner. Underpinned by a spaceframe chassis with Ford Cortina running gear, with kit prices at £1,275.
Kingfisher Mouldings 1984–86
Approx 2 made

KINGFISHER VULCAN

A Bugatti Type 57 replica, based on Morris Marina mechanicals.
Kingfisher Mouldings 1984–86
Approx 1 made

KIRK P-TYPE

Quirky three-wheeler from Andrew Kirk of Chorley, Lancashire.
Kirk Sportscars 2005–7
Approx 2 made

KNIGHT MINI

A silhouette spaceframe chassis Mini from Wayne Nightingale of Holme-on-Spalding Moor, East Yorkshire. A nicely made, comprehensive kit package cost from £23,000 in 2008.
Knight Motorsport Engineering 2008 to date
Approx 1 made

KNW II

Created as a one-off by a chap called Keith Nigel Wilkinson-Hawley, the KNW was his second *special*. The response to the car was pretty good, but Wilkinson-Hawley didn't want to become a kit car manufacturer so he sold the project to Doug Pinchin of NCK.
Keith N. Wilkinson 1983
Approx 1 made

KÖMET – *see Banham 130 Spyder*

KOUGAR MONZA

Created by ex-Crosthwaite & Gardiner employee Rick Stevens at his Uckfield home. Initial versions were based on Ford Cortina before being switched to a combination of XJ6 and Rover V8-power. Ownership of the project followed the same sequence as the Kougar Sports model (see next entry).
Kougar Cars (Starcon & Wells Ltd) 1980–90
Kougar Cars (1990) Ltd 1990–94
Kougar Cars 1994–98
Kougar Car Company 1998–2001
Kougar Cars (Dunford Classic) 2001 to date
Approx 34 sold

KOUGAR SPORTS

Another genuine kit car icon, designed by Rick Stevens with input from Dick Crosthwaite and John Gardiner. He based it on Jaguar S-type mechanicals, although an XJ6 option came along later. A stylish vehicle with a distinctive grille and flowing front wings that first appeared in 1976 and sold in strong numbers.

A Mk2 appeared in 1986 with revised chassis and suspension, before the project passed to Phil Street in 1990, with Sam Cobley taking the reins in 1994. Ex-Jaguar engineer John Killick arrived in 1998, with former Lynx Cars and replica Jaguar maker Simon Dunford of Dunford Classic Cars buying the project in 2001. He spent three years revising the whole package, modifying the bonnet and wings, and relaunched it as the Mk4 at the Exeter Kit Car Show in 2004.
Kougar Cars (Starcon & Wells Ltd) 1976–90
Kougar Cars (1990) Ltd 1990–94
Kougar Cars 1994–98
Kougar Car Company 1998–2001
Kougar Cars (Dunford Classic) 2001-10
Fury Sports Cars 2011 to date
Approx 800 made

KR3

An off-road orientated vehicle hailing from Blitzworld of Stoke-on-Trent, run by Steve Malpass. Power comes from Fiat 900cc FIRE engine, Rover K-series or Ford Zetec.
Blitzworld 2006 to date
Approx 100 made

KÜBELWAGEN

A more than passable replica of the German Kübelwagen, made by Steve Smith of Robertsbridge, East Sussex, in the early '80s. Based unsurprisingly on VW Beetle mechanicals it featured an all-steel body from 18-gauge steel sheet that in 1981 cost £650 in basic form, or £1,350 for the deluxe package that included the all-important company palm tree logo! The kit was supplied in a package that resembled that of a garden shed.

Painstakingly created via over 100 drawings to ensure correct dimensions. Smith actually used his wife's Beetle as the guinea pig for his demonstrator. A business trip to Libya saw him return home with an authentic jerry can and spade. Smith got into car making when the air conditioning company he worked for lost a large contract and he was made redundant.
Steve Smith 1981–83
Approx 5 made

KUDOS

This one bore a definite resemblance to the Pelland Sports (*qv*) because it *was* the Pelland Sports, but with Alfa Romeo 33/Alfasud mechanicals. A corking thing to drive.
Square One Developments 1992–95
Approx 5 made

KUDOS ROADSTER

Swadlincote-based Square One Developments came up with this convertible version of the Kudos in 1993.
Square One Developments 1993–95
Approx 2 made

A B C D E F G H I J K L M N O P Q R S T U V W X Y Z

KUSTOM BUGGY

A fully-built, well-appointed beach buggy from mechanic and Formula Vee specialist, and EPC Hustler (qv) agent John Jackson of Acton Green, West London. Jackson would sell you a fully-built car from £499, or in complete kit form at £350 in March 1971.

Jackson's buggy was based on an 82½in floorpan, with several components supplied by Speedwell and engines from Cartune. Nicknamed the 'Nitty Buggy', the company's demonstrator was used in a Thames Television programme called *Jumbleland* in 1971.

Jackson's Kustom Buggies 1970–72
Approx 30 made

KVA COUNTACH REPLICA

Little known KVA replica of the Countach LP5000S, which had links to the replica briefly offered by GTD.
KVA 1987–88
Approx 3 made

KVA D-TYPE REPLICA

A Jaguar D-type replica from KVA that took a back seat to the GT40 clones for which they were best known.
KVA 1988–89
Approx 1 made

KVA GT40 MkI

After Kenneth Vincent Attwell's KVA GT40 MkIII (see next entry) had appeared, it very quickly became apparent that people wanted a Mk1 GT40 replica rather than the roadgoing Mk3 variant, and once Ken introduced his KVA GT40 MkI model in 1984 he didn't look back. This is the car that pretty much spawned the GT40 replica movement in the UK and beyond. As with his MkIII, he gained access to a genuine car for his take on the iconic MkI.

The designation 'B' type denoted Jaguar suspension, while a 'C' type for double wishbones appeared in 1987 and wasn't – as some thought – a KVA Jaguar C-type replica, although confusingly the company did offer a D-type clone for a time. The 'C' chassis was TUV-approved, could take up to 300bhp with ease and had more footwell space.

It's often been said that KVA had around ten sets of moulds for their cars, selling them to a variety of customers including a South African operation called KVA, which later ended up at Rudy Malan's KCC before inspiring the GT40 Developments and Africa40 projects. Others included GT40 Replication in Australia, ERA in America and DJ Sportscars in the UK.

Ken's son Paul Attwell took over the reins in 1988, although the operation was sold to a Florida company in 1994.
KVA 1984–94
Approx 400 sold

KVA GT40 MkIII

Ken Vincent Attwell was a senior production engineer at Ford Motor Company's Bridgend plant. He was responsible for the maintenance of Ford's historic car collection, making sure that they were ready for their many duties, including TV programme appearances, to carrying out repairs when the inevitable damage occurred.

Ken was particularly fond of the GT40s and had been producing his own replacement panels in glassfibre, so when he asked for, and received, permission from his bosses to produce a replica for his own use of Ford's MkIII he only needed to produce panels that he didn't already have.

Ken's GT40 was always intended to be used as his own daily transport; indeed it was registered as a 'KVA Special' on the V5. Attwell built his MkIII in four months, although he was no stranger to turning his hand to many tasks; he had refurbished a 13th century cottage, restored a selection of vintage motorbikes and built the KVA office.

The gifted Peter Jacobs, who had been responsible for the prototype shell of the Ford RS200, did the GRP work, while Ken used a box steel spaceframe rather than the original's thin wall monocoque.

Attwell claimed that his panels were better than the Ford, indeed they fitted a genuine '40 and the shutlines were good and very even. In all there were 19 separate glassfibre panels – the original chassis was a beefy item, with Attwell following a belt and braces approach and, unsurprisingly as he was a Ford-man through-and-through, he opted to use components he had easy access to. Even though the MkIII was nominally the road-going GT40, it was still underpinned by the racer's monocoque and could never be described as truly civilised. On the other hand, the KVA was designed for use on the road.

Ken used Cortina Mk3 or Mk4 suspension at the front end, although he attracted some criticism for eschewing the original's wishbone arrangement in favour of trailing arms made from box steel mounted on Transit van-spec metalastic bushes. Transaxle on Ken's car was from a Volkswagen Varient, which he claimed could cope with up to V6 engines with a Granada item used for V8 fitment. Talking of engines, although the original featured a turbocharged CVH four-cylinder, recommended fitments were Ford Cologne V6, Rover V8 or Ford 302 V8.

Attwell said the he'd originally considered wishbones at the rear but felt that suitable proprietary parts were too heavy, too wide, or both! With his later and upgraded C-type chassis variant he addressed this.

The KVA wasn't an easy car to build, but Attwell holds the distinction of creating the world's first GT40 replica. The customer was given an 18-page booklet listing extra parts required in the build, and tips on where to obtain them. The only original GT40 component was the windscreen, exclusively sold via Sebik Automotive Developments who had paid for the tooling that Triplex produced from. The customer had to fabricate things like the gearlinkage, and GTD set themselves up to help customers by successfully supplying the missing KVA parts.

In 1985, Attwell estimated that if a customer used entirely new components, a DIY build budget would be around £18,500, but using reconditioned parts would cost just £8,000. Kits cost from £3,000.

The first car was completed in June 1982 and Ken used it every day for all manner of trips and chores. After a few months, well-known journalist Howard Walker, who at the time was working for *Motor* magazine, gave the car a glowing review, which really set the KVA ball rolling.

Ford gave Ken permission to create further replicas, although for a time he continued to work at the Bridgend factory, so his wife Margaret ran the KVA operation, later assisted by their son Paul. For every order there were 60 enquiries requesting information. By September 1984 76 kits had been sold – people clearly loved the concept. More asked about an MkI version, so KVA created their own version of that car. A good move – they sold four times as many.

So impressed was Ford with Ken's efforts that they even displayed his replica in the Bridgend factory foyer, while Global Marketing Director, Bill Camplisson, was an early KVA customer. Ken famously didn't offer his customers a build manual, remarking that if they needed instructions they weren't competent to build one! This is how Autos International – later GTC – and MCR Phoenix, became agents for KVA.
KVA 1982–94
Approx 110 made

KVA XKSS REPLICA

Very low-key replica of the Jaguar XKSS from Ken Attwell that was completely overshadowed by his GT40 clone.
KVA 1988–89
Approx 1 made

KYOTE II

Created in America by buggy and rod guru Dean Jeffries, as the Kyote Bug, it even appeared in the *Batman* TV programme. Incidentally, Jeffries also designed the car for the opening credits of the Pink Panther cartoon series and the Moon Buggy on the James Bond film, *Diamonds Are Forever*.
A fellow American called Steve Remp owned two Kyotes, and when he moved to Germany with his father he took them with him. Then when they came to Britain, in 1971, he also acquired European production rights to the Mk2.

The Kyote II was based on an unmodified VW Beetle floorpan and, unusually for a beach buggy, featured doors (well, they were tiny, so I guess they should be called *doorlets!*). It featured in a TV advert for Falmers jeans, a brochure for the Raleigh Chopper and even a short documentary about popular singer of the day John Christie. Even Cliff Richard owned one for a while.

Remp quickly set himself up in business, initially calling his company Design Dynamics, based in an old warehouse by the River Thames in Vauxhall that he christened The Dune Buggy Centre. Here he was joined in November 1971 by enthusiast and Invader buggy owner Phil Ayres.

Adverts of the day proudly proclaimed that 'Britain is now Kyote country' although the fact that buggy sales were slowing down and that it was an expensive kit at £189 didn't help its cause, even if it was as Remp described it: 'A giant glass Lego set.' During the Remp period, 20 Kyote II kits were sold.

Although the Kyote II was generally regarded as one of the prettiest buggies of all time, by 1971 the UK buggy boom was waning and compared to others the Kyote was expensive. To help make ends meet Remp diversified into motorcycles, which proved a hit, and when he departed in 1973 to open a hotel in Aberdeen aimed at oil-rig workers, Ayres continued alone, although he changed the company name to Dune Buggy Constructors. To help the business, Ayres also propped up sales by selling Houndog Beetle conversion kits, and did general buggy repair work. In August 1974, after selling a further 15 kits, he dropped the Kyote II to concentrate fully on bikes. The moulds sat in the corner of the GRP laminators in Berkshire for a while (they did actually build one as a mobile advert for their fibreglass expertise).

After being out of production for a couple of years GP took the project on (they sold three) but soon quietly dropped it. And that was that, or so it seemed until beach buggy guru James Hale of GT Mouldings acquired it in 1995, marketing it for several years before it passed on to Martyn and Rob Falk of Birmingham-based KMR Buggies in 2003, along with the Manta Ray (*qv*) and Renegade (*qv*).

Always a highly regarded beach buggy, the Kyote II was well-made, with an opening tailgate and doors, and was probably among the first UK kit cars to make use of fire-retardant resin.
Design Dynamics (The Dune Buggy Centre) 1971–73
Dune Buggy Constructors 1973–74
GP Projects 1976–80
GT Mouldings 1995–2003
KMR Beach Buggies 2003-9
Approx 36 made (UK)

L&R 3

Pretty little Triumph TR3 replica from fibreglass specialists L&R Roadsters run by Les Hunt and Ray Beech, based at Bobbington Airfield near Stourbridge, known during WW2 as RAF Halfpenny Green. Project subsequently taken over by L&R's erstwhile chassis maker Tony Griffith, based in Kingswinford, West Midlands, who introduced some changes to the kit that made it easier to build, basing it completely on Ford Sierra parts. He wasn't around long.
L&R 1993–2002
Replicator Sports Cars 2008-10
Approx 3 made

LA GOLD

Emanating from Birmingham-based engineering company Procomp run by Ivan Gilmore, a motorsport enthusiast. Humble but highly capable Lotus Seven-inspired sports car that enjoyed a lot of success in the 750 Motor Club's Kit Car race series in the '90s and '00s.
Procomp Motorsport 1999 to date
Approx 25 made

LA LOCOST

Sister car to the LA Gold, the LA Locost is aimed at the 750 Motor Club's Locost Championship, although like the company's main model several have been made road-legal.
Procomp Motorsport 1999 to date
Approx 20 made

LALANDE

Based on the GP Centron II (*qv*) and offered for a time by GV Plastics Fibreglass Products of St Columb Major, Cornwall, run by Peter Gilbert. The company's main business was making motorcycle fairings and panniers. Made its debut at the Wheels & West Car & Hot Rod Show in 1983.

Fellow Cornish company Alternative Autos of Threemilestone took over briefly in 1985 but didn't last long, as the project was soon moved on to Mike Barton's MDB operation, where it became briefly known as the Sapphire (*qv*).
GV Plastics Fibreglass Products 1983–85
Alternative Autos 1985–86
MDB 1986–88
Approx 2 made

LAMBERT MOKETTE

The same company that acquired the Opus HRF (*qv*) in 1970 also offered this all-steel Mini Moke-type kit that was based on the Mini van.
Lambert 1970–72
Approx 3 made

LAMBERTI 3000

Bedfordshire-based Joe Lamberti came out with his take on the Austin Healey 3000 theme in 1998, basing his replica on Ford Granada running gear, with Ford 2.9-litre V6 power.

In 2008, Lamberti, along with former Sebring-importer Martyn Williamson, came up with a car called the Healy (*sic*) (*qv*), A modern take on the Austin Healey theme.

Lamberti also had involvement with the Minotaur and Mirage Countach replica during this period, acting as agents for those companies.
Lamberti Engineering 1998–2000
Approx 12 made

LAND RANGER 4x4

Conversion based on Range Rover Classic from a Gloucestershire-based operation.
Land Ranger 4x4 2006–7
Approx 15 made

LANDAR R6

30in high (or low?) Mini-based Can-Am style car made by Stafford company Radnall Brothers. After ten sales the project went to a Canadian firm.
Radnall Brothers 1968–70
Approx 10 made

LANTANA

French range of well-made and capable off-road buggies, which are also road-legal. Imported to the UK by Lincolnshire-based Phil Cowper of atv4x4 World, from spring 2011. The vehicles are made in the world's capital for microcars, France, by Route Buggy.

UK range consists of Nevada and Route M800i.
atv4x4 World 2011 to date
Approx 5 made (UK)

LARINI

Very tidy modern fixed-head two-seat sports car kit produced by brothers Simon and Jeremy Crowther, based in Ringwood, Hampshire, and definitely aimed at the Lotus Elise market. Based on VW Golf Mk2/Jetta mechanicals and a 16-gauge square tube spaceframe bolted to a GRP (or carbon fibre) tub. Weighed a claimed 550kg.

Purchased by a boat specialist from Lymington, Hampshire, who didn't really develop it, before ending up being advertised for sale on an Internet auction site. GTM Cars, under David Keene, purchased it in 2006 but after an initial launch at the Autosport Show in January 2007 didn't do very much with it.
Sculptural Engineering 1999–2001
MPR Engineering 2001–6
GTM Cars 2006
Approx 3 made

LATHAM F1

Paul and Julia Latham-Jackson ran a business called Specialist Cars in Bicester, Oxfordshire, which was a general kit car building company. Paul had previously spent several years working in the motorsport industry. The couple decided to put into practice what they'd learned building other people's kits. Their first model, the F1, featured a heavily modified Falcon bodyshell from the '50s that they based on Triumph TR4 chassis and running gear. They displayed it at Stoneleigh in 1982. It was always seen as a prototype for the later F2 Super Sports.

Specialist Cars 1983
Approx 1 made

LATHAM F2 SUPER SPORTS

Basing the F2 on their prototype F1, the Latham-Jacksons set about creating their first 'proper' model, settling on the Triumph Dolomite as donor vehicle and taking the time to create a perfect body outline. They moved to a unit near Penzance, Cornwall (Julia's home town), next door to a pilchard factory in Newlyn Coombe, and showed a quarter-scale model of the F2 to a receptive audience at the Stoneleigh Show of 1984. Another designer, Andrew Dawkes, joined the duo and contributed his ideas to the F2.

Summer 1986 saw the F2 officially unveiled and a steady flow of orders followed, coinciding with a move back to Bicester and the former Penske factory, where they had made Indycars. Sadly, however, despite the F2 being well received there just weren't enough orders coming in, so Paul Latham-Jackson took a job with Tom Walkinshaw at TWR in Kidlington, and Andrew Dawkes with Triumph Motorcycles in Hinckley, which left Julia Latham-Jackson and a couple of staff running the family business, although the operation didn't survive long thereafter.

The F2 Super Sports was a very well-engineered car and highly rated, albeit a tricky build. It featured a central fibreglass monocoque tub with front and rear subframes.

Latham Sports Cars 1983–90
Approx 26 made

LDD MONACO

Came from Roger Ludgate, who after he'd left Lynx Motors got involved in Mini conversions from a base in Staplehurst, Kent.

LDD Conversions 1981–86
Approx 7 made

LE CHAT

Not the best Lamborghini Countach replica ever. Seen at Newark in 1985 and not again. It was the work of civil engineer Bob Sutch, who had converted a TV remote control to operate controls on the dashboard and to work door locks! I'm not joking!

Sutch Automotive 1986
Approx 1 made

LE MANS

Gorgeous Aston Martin DBR1/ DBR2 replica conceived by Bob Egginton at ASD before passing to ARA Racing, who renamed it the ARA Le Mans Rogue (*qv*). Andy of AS Motorsport took over in 2007.

Automotive Systems Design Ltd 1999–2004
ARA Racing 2004–7; AS Motorsport 2007 to date
Approx 8 made

LE MANS D-TYPE

Stoke-on-Trent operation Le Mans Sportscars acquired Vic Minay's Stardust D-type (*qv*), which they marketed for several years (in addition to the C-type, D-type and XKSS fully-built replicas they already made) before they in turn sold the project to David Yoxall of Phoenix Automotive in 1997, who retained the Le Mans Sportscars trading name.

Yoxall subsequently modified the car to take Jaguar mechanicals and later sold it on to Tiger Racing. Acquired by Stag Owners' Club, trading as Lightning Motor Company, based in Headcorn, Kent, and run by Alan Marshall. They developed a Ford Sierra (and Mondeo) based version, although their demonstrator had Rover K-series power. Came to rest at the Leighton Motor Company run by Stuart Soutter, where it faded quietly away.

Le Mans Sportscars 1993–97
Le Mans Sportscars (Phoenix) 1997–2000
Tiger Racing 2000–1
Lightning Motor Company 2001–6
Leighton Motor Company 2006–9
Approx 30 made

LEADER – *see Sylva Leader*

LEAPING CATS C-TYPE

Quality of this faithful copy of Jaguar's C-type was very good.

Leaping Cats 1981–83
Approx 20 made

LEGEND

Lotus Seven-inspired sports car from Maidstone-based GKD Sports Cars and based on BMW 3-Series mechanicals. Known as the Legend 6 when using the straight-six Beemer engine.
GKD Sports Cars
2008 to date
Approx 40 made

LEGEND 550 SPYDER

Terry Sands was the man behind the Legend Motor Company. His 550 Spyder came from an American kit that he had procured, although he developed a multi-tubular chassis to underpin it.
Legend Motor Company 1997–2001
Approx 4 made

LEGEND CALIFORNIA

Terry Sands had created – and obtained the copyright on – this beefed-up bespoke take on the Speedster theme, many years before it appeared as a Legend Motor Company product. Indeed, DJ Sportscars had also sold it under licence for a time.
Legend Motor Company 1997–2001
Approx 20 made

LEGEND CONVERTIBLE D

A former Sheldonhurst product with similar power choices to the company's Speedster (see below).
Legend Motor Company 1997–2001
Approx 3 made

LEGEND GHIA

Originated from the Rudolph Sportwagen (*qv*) replica of the Karmann Ghia from Germany, although Sands revised the version that was imported into the UK by the Evergreen Motor Company.
Legend Motor Company 1999–2001
Approx 10 made

LEGEND SPEEDSTER

The Legend Speedster had its origins in the Sandwood and Sheldonhurst products with which Terry Sands was involved. Just one was made with VW Beetle power, the majority having VW Type 4, Subaru and Alfasud engines, mostly underpinned by a development of Sands' own Omegachassis.
Legend Motor Company 1997–2001
Approx 70 made

LEGENDARY 427

After building a well-known Cobra replica that cost a lot more than quoted and was also less than satisfactory, the Marsh brothers, Phil and Tim, who ran a well-established engineering company in Ashbourne, Derbyshire, set out to create their own Cobra replica. Launched in 1994, the car featured a STATUS-designed tubular steel chassis and wishbones, with power coming from Ford 302 5-litre V8 and independent suspension all-round.

Sold as a rolling chassis kit package from £13,660 in 1994 and fully-built from £25,635, the Legendary 427 was a well-engineered car. In 1998 it moved to Manchester-based Spring Vale Services, run by John Andrew.
Legendary Sports Cars 1994–98
Spring Vale Motor Services 1998–2001
Approx 5 made

LEIGHTON

Citroën 2CV-based three-wheeler devised by Hawke (*qv*) makers GCS Cars in 1997. Moved on to BRA Motor Works in 1999, who slightly revised the shape and made the cockpit larger. Featured a GRP body with a triangulated spaceframe. BRA fitted an A-series Metro arm instead of the horizontal Citroën 2CV springs and pattern dampers, which they dumped. Weighed in at just 350kg, and even with the 2CV's humble 30bhp performance was brisk.

Project acquired by Martyn Philpott of Maidstone-based Leighton Motor Company, then moved on to Stuart Soutter in 2004.
GCS Cars 1997–99
BRA Motor Works 1999–2002
Leighton Cars 2002–4
Leighton Motor Company 2004–7
Aero Cycle Cars 2007–10
Approx 55 made

LEMAZONE COMET

Lemazone was founded by Mike Parkington and based in Leigh, Lancashire. The Comet was a revamped version of Amplas' SN1 (*qv*) based on the VW Beetle. Lemazone also purchased

the rights to the Pulsar (*qv*) and also the old Beaujangle Can-Am (*qv*). The sharp, angular lines of the SN1 were smoothed over, although mechanically it was unaltered and retained its 2+2 seating configuration. Did they ever sell one?

Lemazone 1984–87
Approx 1 made

LENHAM GT

Lenham Motor Company was based in the leafy Kent village of the same name and was founded by Julian Kingsford-Booty and David Miall-Smith in 1962. Best known for their variety of GRP

panels, most notably for Sprite and Healey, and their motor-racing activities, Lenham also produced a couple of specialist cars. They designed the Lenham GT in 1969, a road version of their sports racer. They sold seven coupés and two convertibles. Project was inspired by racer Roger Hurst, who when he left in 1972 continued to produce race cars using the Lenham name.

Lenham Motor Company 1969–70
Approx 9 made

LENHAM HEALEY

Lenham Motor Company was founded by Julian Kinsford-Booty and David Miall-Smith in 1962 (February 9, to be precise!).

Best-known for their variety of GRP panels most notably for Sprite and Healey, and motor-racing activities, Lenham also produced a couple of specialist cars. The Lenham Healey being one of them.

Reminiscent of the Healey Silverstone produced briefly for a couple of years from 1949, the Lenham conversion was based on Healey 3000 or 100/6 and Lenham would convert a customer's car or present a fully-built one.

Lenham Sports Cars 1977–82
Approx 19 made

LENHAM LE MANS/GT COUPÉ/GTO ROADSTER

Based in a leafy part of Kent, Lenham Motor Company as founded by Julian Kingsford-Booty and David Miall-Smith in February 1962, when known as the Vintage Sports Cars Garage, located behind the Dog and Bear Hotel in The Square in Lenham.

An aluminium-bodied Mk1 Sprite *special*, with a distinctive hardtop, commissioned by a customer – was liked by all who saw it and the company received many requests to reproduce it. However, Booty reasoned that this would be uneconomical in time and cost.

But Julian was very interested in fibreglass and enrolled on a course, with the result that he launched a series of panels for the Spridget, firstly with the Lenham GT Coupé in 1963, which was designed for Mk1 'Frogeye', then Mk2 Sprite and also Mk1 MG Midget (basically, the pre-1964 cars).

Next came the Lenham Le Mans Coupé for Mk3 Sprite/Mk2 Midget, of which there were two versions, one having a 'scalloped' section behind the rear window, while the other was smoothed out. In 1966 Lenham launched the GTO Roadster, which was a convertible.

Other Spridget products included a Competition bonnet, the SLR (standard Lightweight replacement) bonnet, the Superfast and the 'John Britten Back' – a version of which was raced by the man himself. Lenham also made the 'Easyfit' and 'Torado Targa' hardtops for the Midget/Sprite.

It wasn't just Midgets and Sprites that came in for Lenham's attention, they also made fibreglass styling components for cars such as the Jaguar E-type, MGB and Triumph Spitfire, while in 1967 they launched the Healey Silverstone-inspired Lenham Healey with the sports-racer GT arriving in 1969. Meanwhile, the John Britten connection bore fruit again when Rix and Kingsford Booty helped deign the Arkley SS.

In 1968 they moved to larger premises in nearby Harrietsham in the old bakery and began trading as the Lenham Motor Company. Another very important name in the Lenham history, Peter Rix, joined the company in 1970 and still works there to this day.

Booty and Rix sold the company to Andrew Actman in 2005, who changed the name to Lenham Sports Cars, while they concentrated on restoration, general repairs and sales. Scott Reynolds bought the company in April 2011 and changed it back to Lenham Motor Company!

Meanwhile, after a gap of around 38 years, the Lenham Spridget glassfibre panel kits are available once more. A historic racer called David Coplowe purchased the moulds from Lenham in the late nineties and commissioned another historic racer, Shaun Rainford's Classic Cars of Kent & Sussex (CCK), to produce them under licence. CCK bought the moulds outright in 2010 as well as the Lenham GTO from David Matthews.

They offer the Lenham Le Mans for semi-elliptic cars and the Lenham GT for quarter-elliptic equipped vehicles, with the replacement rear ends costing around £714 and the front ends at £570, both inc VAT.

The convertible Lenham GTO rear ends cost £570 inc VAT, but for cosmetic reasons will require a hardtop. In addition, the company can also supply other Spridget-related products such as the sports-racer Rejo fronts and rears, their own GSR panels and the late Steve Everitt's Mojo Midget front.

Vintage & Sports Cars Garage 1963–68
Lenham Motor Company 1968–73; Classic Cars of Kent 2011 to date
Approx 220 made

LEOPARD CRAFT

Nice Brooklands-type '30s-inspired Bugatti-meets-Alfa-esque boat-tail created by Reg Croysdill of Salisbury, a friend of Mike Hawthorn in the late '50s. Based on Triumph Herald mechanicals with the company located in the wonderfully named Cheese House. A superb piece of kit that deserved to sell in much larger numbers, but ultimately was probably a little bit too expensive to produce.
Leopard Craft 1991
Approx 4 made

LIEGE

Company was founded by Peter Leigh-Davis, who had enjoyed much success rallying a Ginetta G4 he bought in 1967. Peter is also responsible for the Guild of Motor Endurance operation. Based on a frame chassis that was very clever in that it dispersed and directed torsional loads to a central pivot point on the swing

axle rear suspension. Tubular cross-members meant structure was very strong. Returned to production in 2010.
Liege Motor Company 1995-06; 2010 to date
Approx 80 made

LIGHTNING TS

The Lightning Targa Sport was a Ford Cortina Mk3/Mk4-based copy of the Corvette (sort of), created by Kim Terry Short from Stafford. Kits cost £1,575 plus VAT in 1985.
Lightning Sportscars 1984–85
Approx 4 made

LIMBO GALLARGO – *see Gallargo*

LIMITED EDITION BAJA BEETLE

After the Californian (see below), the second model from Limited Edition was a Baja Beetle, which aped the Baja desert racers. Based on Volkswagen Beetle.
Limited Edition Sportscars 1983–84
Approx 12 made

LIMITED EDITION CALIFORNIAN

Unlike the majority of beach buggies that had originated in the early seventies, the Californian was born in 1983.

The Warrington-based manufacturer, run by Terry Walsh, who had relocated from Manchester, was a general kit builder and sales agent for the GP range and Jago. The Californian was a distributed version of the long wheelbase GP Buggy and could be based on either a VW Beetle floorplan or a bespoke ladderframe, plus it had a few other touches exclusive to the Cheshire company, such as rectangular headlights and flared wheel arches,

Their brochure proclaimed: 'equally at home cruising the street or exploring the back roads.'

By the time it was launched, the beach buggy craze was well and truly over, and the Californian faded from view. The company concentrated on their Beetle parts business. Limited Edition was bought by Kingfisher Kustoms. Incidentally, the company was the first distributor for the Karma in 1983.
Limited Edition Sportscars 1983–87
Approx 30 made

LINCOLN

Period-style saloon from Fleur de Lys.
Fleur de Lys 1983–94
Approx 6 made

LINDY – *see HDS Warrior/Defender*

LIONHEART

BMW M1 replica. One prototype made, although it was never heard of again.
Lionheart Cars 1991
Approx 1 made

LISTAIR DASH

Listair Cars of Wrexham was set up by Mike Lister in 1985 to build and service two-seat GRP microlight aircraft. In mid-1986 Lister departed, leaving John Evans, Mike Davies and Colin Purcell in charge.

The Dash was originally the Pelland Sports (*qv*), although Listair purchased the project from Graham Autos and featured a semi-monocoque chassis. GM designer Mike Dickens revamped the bodyshell to give more interior space while he also lowered the cockpit sides. The rear suspension was an underslung transverse leaf spring set-up, although Listair replaced this with a subframe. Alfa Romeo option arrived in 1990, the same year that the project moved to Dash Sportscars.
Listair Cars 1985–90
Dash Sportscars 1990–93
Approx 22 made

LISTER BELL STR

A Lancia Stratos replica from Nottinghamshire-based Lister Bell Automotive run by ex-Gardner Douglas and Ultima man Craig White with John Davidson, who departed soon after launch, leaving Craig in sole control.
Lister Bell Automotive 2010 to date
Approx 16 made

LMC ROADSTER

Beautiful Reliant Scimitar roadster bearing a resemblance to the BMW 328. Created by master coachbuilder Roy Ashton, who initially christened it the Scimi.
Langley Motor Club 1999–2005
Approx 3 made

LOCO RANGE

Latching on to the boom for Locost models made popular by Ron Champion's book *Build Your Own Sports Car for as little as £250*, the Loco range came from Ian Gray of Stuart Taylor Motorsport, based in Ilkeston, Derbyshire. Proved to be extremely popular and could be had with a multitude of engines including Crossflow (LocoFlow) and Honda Fireblade (LocoBlade). Project was acquired by Aries Motorsport, run by Steve Huckerby, who developed other options including Zetec SE and Mazda MX-5.
Stuart Taylor Motorsport 1998–2007
Aries Motorsport 2007 to date
Approx 350 made

LOCOST

The Haynes book *Build Your Own Sports Car for as little as £250*, written by Oundle school teacher Ron Champion about his DIY Lotus Seven-inspired car, caused a phenomenon. To get anywhere near the £250 cost involved fabricating your own chassis and laminating fibreglass parts, but that didn't deter thousands of people from buying the book. In addition to inspiring home builders it also spawned several companies that could supply some or all of the parts needed to build a Champion-type car. Stuart Taylor Motorsport and MK Engineering were two high profile ones.

Not long after the publication of his book Ron Champion set up Locost Ltd, which did very well for a time opening up overseas agencies around the world, including America and Australia, although the company went into voluntary liquidation in January 2002. The project's erstwhile chassis makers carried on, trading as Luego Sportscars.
Ron Champion Locost Ltd 1998–2000
Luego Sportscars 2000–5
Approx 150 made

LOCOST 11

A lesser-known Ron Champion project that concentrated on building a homebrew Lotus 11 replica – on a budget, of course, and using the same principles as in his Haynes Locost book.
Ron Champion Locost Ltd 2000–1
Approx 14 made

A
B
C
D
E
F
G
H
I
J
K
L
M
N
O
P
Q
R
S
T
U
V
W
X
Y
Z

LOCUST S111

Created by Moss founder John Cowperthwaite, under the JC Auto Patterns banner from 1988. It followed the designer's penchant for plan-built kit cars, much like his Husky (qv) and Midge (qv) models. Main body tub was made from Medite/MDF skinned in aluminium sheet, with nosecone and wings in GRP. Slabby sides, due to wooden construction, but proved extremely popular due to potential low build costs.

Original was based on Triumph Herald running gear, with Ford Escort Mk2/Cortina Mk4 a later and more popular variant. A double wishbone and coil-over option was also introduced. Any engine that could be jammed between the chassis rails would do, although most popular choice was Ford Kent/Crossflow.

Rotherham-based T&J Sportscars, run by welder Trevor Barnes and wife Denise, along with trimmer Josef Horvath, took over the Locust in 1989 before announcing their own easier to build, similarly-styled and larger Hornet (qv) in 1991.

After they ceased trading in 1993, White Rose Vehicles, who had also acquired the Midge and Husky models, came on the scene. Their Locust IIIA was Ford Sierra-based, and designed to be SVA-compliant (from 1998). This version later passed to Richard Tilly of Roadtech Engineering, while the original and White Rose-developed 'ES' went to BWE Sportscars with the Hornet and Grasshopper.

JC Composites 1988–89
T&J Sportscars 1989–93
White Rose Vehicles 1993–2000
Roadtech Engineering 2001–6 (SIII & ES)
BWE Engineering 2000 to date (original Locust & ES version)
Approx 1,225 made

LOMAS VEE

Bonkers road-legal Formula Vee car from a Knutsford-based racing car manufacturer.
Lomas Motorsport 1971–73
Approx 2 made

LOMAX CARS

Company founded by Nigel Whall, with design input from Peter Bird. Initially based in Willoughton, Lincolnshire, before shifting to Bird's base in Snowhill, Birmingham, in 1984.

In 1984 Mumford Musketeer (qv) creator Brian Mumford took over the marketing of the kits from his operation in Nailsworth, Gloucestershire, before David Low came on board, initially managing the company for Whall before becoming a director.

Lomax traded from premises in Bewdley, Worcestershire, between 1986 and 1992 before settling in Halesowen – a base, incidentally, from where Vindicator Cars now trade.

In 2004 the Lomax projects briefly passed to Bob Turnock at RS Jigtec, also of Halesowen, and when this company ceased trading in spring 2005 they were acquired by Cradley Motor Works, run by Bob Bousell and based in St Leonards-on-Sea, East Sussex. A very important kitcar marque, the Lomax.

LOMAX 223

The second Lomax model was the iconic three-wheeled 223. It was modified by Brian Mumford, who devised a central location for the single rear wheel, adding a 6in tube to one of the donor Citroën 2CV rear arms. At the peak of its popularity the 223 was one of the fastest selling kits around, and although not the prettiest its low cost, buildability and charm were strong attractions. Incidentally, the name '223' came from it having two seats, two cylinders and three wheels.
Lomax Cars 1983–2003
RS Jigtec 2003
Cradley Motor Works 2003–8
Approx 3,500 made

LOMAX 224

Nigel Whall created one of the iconic kit cars when he launched his 224 in 1983. Donor was Citroën 2CV, Dyane or Ami, and it was an incredibly innovative package.
Lomax Cars 1983–2003
RS Jigtec 2003
Cradley Motor Works 2003 to date
Approx 550 made

LOMAX 423/424

Appearing in 1985 this was a real hot rod take on the Lomax theme and is easily recognisable by its enclosed, bulbous front end. Rather than 599cc twin-cylinder from the 2CV the 423/424 featured the 61bhp 1,015cc engine from the Citroën GS or GSA.
Lomax Cars 1985–2003
Approx 65 made

LOMAX FG SPECIAL

A trials-type Citroën 2CV-based car that debuted at the Donington Show in 1999. Drive supplied by an ingenious and patented chain-drive mechanism that aped the Fraser Nash 'chain-gang' style. 2CV engine was turned 180 degrees so that it was sited further back in the floorpan.
Lomax Cars 1999–2000
Approx 1 made

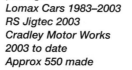

LOMAX LAMBDA 3

Based on a new ladderframe chassis rather than Citroën 2CV floorpan and didn't share much else with the standard 223/224 except a few obvious visual similarities.
Lomax Cars 1999–2002
Approx 50 made

LOMAX SUPA VEE

Possibly the ultimate Lomax, came with a spaceframe chassis and 1,543cc 100bhp air-cooled V-twin bike engine.
Lomax Cars 1995–96
Approx 1 made

LOMAX SUPER TOURER

This was the first non-223-derived Lomax model, with revised 'plush' interior and a steel tube ladderframe chassis rather than the 2CV floorpan. The four-wheeled equivalent of the Lambda 3.
Lomax Cars 1999–2002
Approx 20 made

LOTUS CARS (1957–73 CKD availability)

What hasn't been written about Lotus? Here we'll take a look only at the models that were available in self-build form.

LOTUS MkVI

Lotus founder Colin Chapman had been enjoying lots of racetrack success with his home-built cars and the MkVI was his first commercially available Lotus model. An effective little sports car with a delicate spaceframe underpinning an aluminium body with Ford beam axle and (usually) Ford 10 power.
Lotus Engineering 1952–56
Approx 110 made

LOTUS XI

An absolute classic. A beautiful lithe body with delicate spaceframe. Customers could choose from three versions – Le Mans, with 75, 83 or 100bhp Coventry Climax engines; Club, with 75bhp Coventry Climax engine, a live axle and coil springs; or Sport, with a Ford Sidevalve engine, live rear axle and independent front suspension.
Lotus Engineering 1956–60
Approx 426 made

LOTUS ELAN 26R

Produced in response to a demand for a racing version, the 26R was quite different to the road cars with a 145bhp twin-cam, lighter bodyshell, lowered and stiffened suspension and limited slip differential.
Lotus Engineering 1964–66
Approx 95 made

LOTUS ELAN SERIES 1

Designed by the late Ron Hickman (who later created the Black & Decker Workmate) and evolved from the prototype called the Métier. An absolute classic, and the car that is said to have inspired the Mazda MX-5. The overwhelming majority of Elans were sold in component form to avoid purchase tax, although, as with Gilberns, there really wasn't that much for the customer to do, as the factory did all the hard work. The first 22 cars had 1,498cc Ford Pre-Crossflow engines with a Lotus-designed twin-cam alloy cylinder head, before the iconic 1,558 Lotus twin-cam unit was introduced. Famed handling underpinned by a lightweight but very stiff steel backbone chassis with independent suspension and disc brakes all round.
Lotus Engineering 1962–64
Approx 900 made

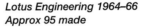

LOTUS ELAN SERIES 2

Just a few changes for the Elan S2 of 1964 with different tail lights, bigger brakes, polished wood dashboard and a lockable glovebox, setting it apart from the original.
Lotus Engineering 1964–66
Approx 1,250 made

LOTUS ELAN SERIES 3

The coupé version of the Elan S3 arrived first and incorporated a number of bodywork modifications. It was pretty well-appointed, with such niceties as electric windows and 105bhp engine as standard. An SE version had 115bhp.
Lotus Engineering 1965–68
Approx 2,650 made

LOTUS ELAN SERIES 4

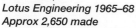

Instant giveaway for the S4 is the wide wheel arches and Jaguar E-type rear lights. The bonnet also gained a bulge to allow the fitting of Stromberg carburettors, although these were soon changed back to Webers. Biggest selling Elan model.
Lotus Engineering 1968–71
Approx 3,000 made

LOTUS ELAN SPRINT

Spotters' guide identification for the Elan Sprint is the two-tone paint scheme and 'Elan Sprint' side decals although a solid paint finish was an option. The Sprint also had a flat bonnet and the bumpers were painted gold. Tony Rudd redesigned the cylinder head with bigger valves and a higher compression ratio, which combined to produce 126bhp. The last cars had the option of a 5-speed gearbox.
Lotus Engineering 1970–73
Approx 1,353

LOTUS ELITE

Despite the initial success for Lotus on the racetrack, the Elite demonstrated beyond question that Colin Chapman could also build exquisite road cars. It was also the world's first monocoque. Featured independent front suspension with Chapman struts at the rear and Coventry Climax engines. Lotus apparently lost money on each one sold but it really was a great car.
Lotus Engineering 1957–63
Approx 998 made

LOTUS EUROPA SERIES 1A & 1B (LOTUS TYPE 46)

Inspired by the Ford GT40 and designed by the late Ron Hickman, the aptly named Europa (it was only available to overseas buyers until 1969) fulfilled Colin Chapman's desire for an affordable, yet revolutionary, mid-engined sportscar. The car was based on an Elan chassis turned through 180 degrees, with race-derived suspension and power coming from a modified Renault 16 engine giving 82bhp.

The backbone steel chassis was bonded within the GRP bodywork making the car very stiff, but a pig to repair or restore. Early cars had fixed side windows and seats, although the pedals and steering wheel were adjustable.

Series 1B cars featured removable side windows that could be stowed in the new integral door panels and also a wooden dashboard.
Lotus Engineering 1966–68
Approx 646 made (296 S1A, 350 S1B)

LOTUS EUROPA SERIES 2 (LOTUS TYPE 54)

Launched in April 1968, the S2 had several upgrades over the S1 Europa. Windows were now electric, seats were adjustable and the interior was all new, while bodies were now bolted to the chassis instead of bonded. Launched into the UK market in July 1969, the car still used the same Renault engine, although several tuners offered 'go-faster' upgrade packages.
Lotus Engineering 1968–71
Approx 3,615 made

LOTUS EUROPA TWIN CAM/SPECIAL (LOTUS TYPE 74)

Future Lotus MD Mike Kimberley was the chief engineer of the Europa Twin Cam project. Distinguished by its chopped rear buttresses – which improved the rear three-quarter blind spot – the main difference was the fitting of the 105bhp Lotus 1,558cc twin-cam engine, which significantly boosted performance. After around 1,580 Twin Cams were produced, the Special was launched in 1972 with the big valve 126bhp engine from the Elan Sprint and 5-speed Renault gearbox.
Lotus Engineering 1971–75
Approx 1,580 Twin Cams made
Approx 3,130 Specials made

LOTUS EUROPA TYPE 47

A pure racing version featuring a 165bhp Lotus 1,600cc twin-cam, vastly modified suspension and a 5-speed Hewland gearbox. The Type 47 made a winning debut at Brands Hatch on Boxing Day 1966, and went on to win many races. They are very valuable today.
Lotus Engineering 1966–68
Approx 65 made

LOTUS SEVEN SERIES ONE

Chapman always said he knocked the Seven off in a week! The Lotus Seven has since become a British institution. It had Lotus Eleven 'club' type suspension and a modified Lotus Twelve front end. Stressed alloy body panels. It can be identified by its 'droopy' nosecone and metal cycle wings.
Lotus Engineering 1957–60
Approx 245 made

LOTUS SEVEN SERIES TWO

The Series Two arrived in 1960 sporting flared GRP front and rear wings and a new GRP nosecone. The chassis was also much simplified over the S1. The Seven almost died in 1966 when Lotus moved premises, but demand persisted.
Lotus Engineering 1960–68
Approx 1,310 made

LOTUS SEVEN SERIES THREE

Appearing in September 1968, the Series Three was nearly 100kg heavier than the S2 it replaced, and the Seven received new impetus, as Lotus Components' chief executive Mike Warner was extremely enthusiastic about it.

Lotus had established a strong working relationship with Ford Motor Company, largely due to the huge success of Formula Ford, launched in 1968, within which Lotus excelled, particularly with the 51. As a result, a variety of Ford components appeared on the S3, including the live rear axle from the Escort Mexico (3.9:1 ratio) and, of course, the Ford Crossflow engine in 1300cc (68bhp) and 1600cc (84bhp) 225E guises.

Driven by Warner, 1969 saw Lotus develop relationships with the well-known engine builder Holbay, and a Lotus Seven S3 'S' version powered by a 120bhp Holbay-developed Crossflow was introduced in 1969, when fully-built entry level Sevens cost from £755.

The Series Three departed production in January 1970, although 1974 saw it reappear when Caterham Cars, who had taken over the rights to the Seven in 1973, ditched the S4 and returned to the classic Series Three shape, a model they still make today!
Lotus Engineering 1968–70
Caterham Cars 1974 to date
Approx 13,000 made (about 350 by Lotus)

LOTUS SEVEN SERIES FOUR

With the S4, Lotus hoped to capture the MG Midget and Spitfire market. To some extent it succeeded but it was not fully equipped to meet the MG buyers' expectations. It was a total departure from the previous Seven models. Alan Barrett styled the GRP body, which was bonded on to a new chassis, and it had a buggy-style look about it. Purists, however, think it's compromised and avoid it. Superb driver's machine.
Lotus Engineering 1970–72
Caterham Cars 1973
Approx 625 made (585 Lotus, 40 Caterham)

A B C D E F G H I J K L M N O P Q R S T U V W X Y Z

LOVEL F20

The brainchild of Belgian Gerhard ten Vegert, hatched from an idea he had while in the final year of a university technical degree in 1983, when he lusted after a Ferrari but couldn't afford one. He came up with the F20, of which there were several prototypes until he settled on an ultra-lightweight aluminium tubular frame. He ditched the initial ideas of BMW and Triumph engines, choosing the water-cooled Yamaha FZR 1000 unit that delivered 145bhp, providing the Lovel with a power-to-weight ratio on a par with a Ferrari F50! Things started to reach production readiness from 1995, when ten Vegert enlisted the help of twins Kees and Hans van der Starre of Star Twin Motorcycles, while he commissioned Sam Visser to design the modern, slightly bulbous GRP body.

By the late nineties ten Vegert had departed, and Karel Schoonbaert and Pierre Perraeke took over. Around this time the car was also available for a while in the UK, via a Grimsby-based company (kit prices listed at £7,000), until a nasty road accident involving one of the partners put a stop to things.

It was later marketed again in the Benelux countries under the Star Twin banner, but only in fully-built guise.
Lovel Cars UK 1999–2000
Approx 3 made (UK)

LR1

Created by well-known club and Mini racer Jon Lee and produced at his Milton Keynes base. Power came from a Yamaha R1 bike engine. Lee had previously been involved with the Global Lights GT project.
Lynx AE 2005–8
Approx 7 made

LR1300

Successor to the LR1 (see above), with revised bodywork, although it shared the same underpinnings and Yamaha R1 bike engine fitment.
Lynx AE 2008 to date
Approx 2 made

LUEGO BIKE-TO-TRIKE

A revised back-end conversion for a host of motorcycles that turned them into trikes.
Luego Sportscars 2004–5
Approx 5 made

LUEGO LOCOST

Basically the continuation of the Ron Champion Locost (*qv*) concept, which was taken over by the project's erstwhile chassis makers Luego (Spanish for 'then' or 'next'), run by Grant Lockhead and Matthew Wright from their base in Peterborough. It was the only kit officially allowed to be called 'Locost', incidentally. The company did well for several years and introduced new models such as the Velocity XT and Viento V8 (see below), as well as their Bike-to-Trike package.

Luego Sportscars ceased trading in 2005, when its projects, except the Bike-to-Trike, were acquired by Dean Roizer, who continued trading under the Luego banner from a base in Rutland. In 2007, however, the Luego brand moved to Aberdeenshire under the control of Ben Lord.

Luego Locost kit availability basically ceased with the demise of the Peterborough company, however.
Ron Champion Locost Ltd 1998–2000
Luego Sportscars (Peterborough) 2000–5
Approx 75 made

LUEGO VELOCITY XT

The Velocity XT was the second model launched by Luego Sportscars.
Luego Sportscars (Peterborough) 2001–6
Luego Sportscars (Newark) 2006–7
Luego Sportscars (Aberdeen) 2007–10
Approx 75 made

LUEGO VIENTO V8

Larger-dimensioned Lotus Seven-inspired sports car designed around a spaceframe chassis and V8 power.
Luego Sportscars (Peterborough) 2001–5
Luego Sportscars (Newark) 2005–7
Luego Sportscars (Aberdeen) 2007–10
Approx 70 made

LUNA BUG

A copy of the Stimson Mini Bug made in Portsmouth by the erstwhile chassis fabricator of said car! Undercut Stimson's version of the kit by £25, selling at £170. Like its inspiration, it was also based on Mini. Not around for long.
Self Fit Ltd 1970–71
Approx 1 made

LYNCAR

Originally commissioned as a one-off for the late US Baseball star Wilt 'The Stilt' Chamberlain in 1986, dubbed 'Searcher 1'. The bodywork was created by Peter Bohanna, while Martin Slater, formerly of Lola and McLaren – who had been involved with the design of cars for F1, Formula Atlantic, Formule Renault, Group C and Thundersaloons – was given the task of creating the chassis via his Lyncar Engineering operation based in Slough, Berkshire. He came up with a steel and aluminium monocoque, with steel-tube subframes at each end supplying the underpinnings. Power came from a mid-mounted Jaguar V12 engine. It also had to be spacious, as Wilt 'The Stilt' was 7ft 1in tall! Once the body and engineering parts were completed they were shipped to Richard Paul in California who did the final finishing and trimming out and also built the Chevy V8 engine.

Despite having all the makings of a veritable supercar, Chamberlain only drove around 400 miles in it, and plans for a limited run of 100 cars came to nought. Chamberlain died in 1999. Incidentally, the Lyncar project supplied the windscreen for Lee Noble's Ultima (qv).

Meanwhile, Slater had plans to put the car into production here in the UK and exhibited it at Stoneleigh in 1992, although again nothing came of it. The project then lay dormant for several years before the late Keith Kirk of Fiero Factory and Auto Speciali purchased it in 2006 (he had liked the car when he had first seen it back in 1990). He heavily revised the styling and pretty much everything else, renaming it the Veleno (qv), while fully-built versions were known as the Predator. Kirk based his version on the Toyota MR2, although he soon introduced a variant with a separate spaceframe chassis.
Lyncar Engineering 1990
Approx 1 made

LYNX

Mini-van-based plans-built utility kit. The Stoke-based company sold the plans for just £5 per set!
Home-Builts 1983–84
Approx 25 made

LYNX BOBTAIL

Another utility kit car, although this one was based on Ford Capri donor parts. The company was based in Westcliff-on-Sea and run by Jim Peters, Nick Rodgers and Steve Ahern.
Lynx Cars 1991–93
Approx 7 made

LYNX D-TYPE

Company founded in 1968 by Guy Black and architect Roger Ludgate, basing themselves initially in London W8, before moving to Staplehurst, Kent and then again to Northiam on the East Sussex/Kent border in 1976. Finally settled in St Leonard's, Hastings in 1980.

After concentrating on classic cars, particularly Jaguar, restoration and race preparation, they offered their first replica as early as 1973, based on Jaguar E-type and using the donor car's standard suspension (which meant IRS rather than live rear suspension), transmission and 4.2-litre XK engine, with modified subframes at each end. The Lynx model ended-up 5½in shorter than the E-type and 1in shorter in wheelbase than the original car. Triple Webers were used rather than the original's SU carbs, which wouldn't fit. The car was based on a square-section steel spaceframe and aluminium monocoque. Bodies were hand-rolled aluminium and were supplied by either Williams & Pritchard or RS Panels. Kits were offered from 1983, with the long-nose version standard and a short-nose variant as an (unpopular) option.

When the original (Black/Ludgate) Lynx operation went into liquidation in 1992, the marque was acquired by John Mayston-Taylor, who restructured the company from 55 employees to a more streamlined 19. The company remained in St Leonard's-on-Sea, although cars were only available fully-built, with the company renamed Lynx Motors International Ltd.

A Berkshire-based operation acquired Lynx Motors operation in 2009. We estimate that the original Lynx operation made 42 D-types, with another five or so produced by the Mayston-Taylor-era company.
Lynx Cars 1973 to 1992
Lynx Motors International 1992–2009
Approx 50 made

LYNX XKSS

Identical in every way except shape to the company's D-type (see previous entry), although was never as popular.
Lynx Cars 1975 to date
Approx 7 made

LYNX R1 MINI CONVERSION

Latest bike-engined Mini conversion hails from Jon Lee of Lynx AE, complete with Yamaha R1 bike engine mounted in the front, with very little mechanical modification required to the Classic Mini, even retaining the original subframes.

Based around the 1998–2007 R1 generation that produced around 150bhp. Lee had been responsible for the track-day-orientated LR1 and had previous involvement with the Global GT Lights.
Lynx AE 2011 to date
Approx 10 made

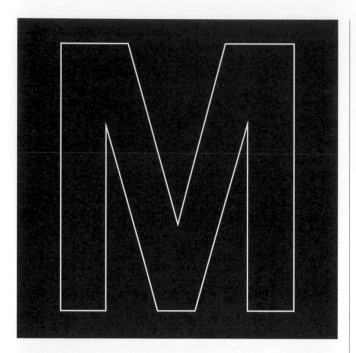

MAC#1 MOTORSPORTS TYPE 9R/ZR/WORX

MAC#1 were a Sheffield-based company founded in 2002 that produced a nicely-made and highly capable range of Lotus Seven-inspired sports cars. The Type 9R variant featured bike power, the ZR usually came with a Zetec, while the lightweight Worx also featured bike power, as did the even lighter Worx R, designed for Kawasaki ZX-10 engines, while its equivalent the Worx Z had a car engine. Company run by Mark Hinchcliffe and Colin Casterton, its name standing for 'Mark And Colin #1 For Motorsports'. They came back from a devastating factory fire in 2006.
MAC#1 Motorsports 2002 to date
Approx 220 made

MAC EM500R

'Eleanor' Mustang replica from Trevor Lewis' Preston-based Mill Auto Conversions.
Mill Auto Conversions 2006 to date
Approx 3 made

MACINI

A bike-powered Classic Mini conversion from MAC#1 Motorsports intended as a one-off, before passing to Nick Mossop of Long Eaton-based Red Line Minis. What set the Macini apart from rivals was that while it retained a front engine configuration (Kawasaki ZX-9 Ninja was preferred) it featured rear-wheel drive! Utilised a back end from one of MAC#1's Lotus Seven-inspired sports cars. A highly capable package.
MAC#1 Motorsports 2006–8
Red Line Minis 2008 to date
Approx 5 made

MACKINTOSH M1C

Created by Owen Mackintosh of Henfield, West Sussex, who was tragically killed while on a test drive in the demonstrator. Car was Mini-based with a steel tube spaceframe, with double wishbone front suspension and standard Mini fare at the rear.

Project passed to Automotive Design Technology for a short time in 1991, where it became known as the ADT Sprint (*qv*), before it finally came to rest at Colin Oberline-Harris' Mackintosh Design and was renamed the Mackintosh M3 (see next entry).
Mackintosh Design Ltd 1987–91
ADT Ltd 1991–97
Approx 3 made

MACKINTOSH M3

Evolved from the Mackintosh M1C (see above) created by the late Owen Mackintosh. The M3 was developed by Colin Oberline-Harris, based in Hampshire.
Mackintosh Design Ltd 1997–2003
Approx 1 made

MACO 10

Superb roadgoing historic Formula Ford-inspired car from expert of the discipline, Peter Alexander, of Kent. Name is derived from Formula Ford marque, Mahcon.
PA Engineering 2011 to date
Approx 1 made

MADGWICK ROADSTER

First model from Pagham-based Madgwick Cars, run by short-oval racing champion Dave Carruthers, assisted by his son Mike. Car was inspired by the Lotus Seven but with much larger dimensions, and was designed primarily around Vauxhall XE power, although other engines are options.
Madgwick Cars 1999-2004
Approx 8 made

MAELSTROM

Originally created by Mike Eydman, who marketed the car for a time before proper production got under way through PACE, who added a 'hammerhead' front option. Moved to Burnley company Evans Hunter Sports Cars, run by Dave Evans, for a couple of years, although nothing much happened with the project. Then moved to White Rose Vehicles of Gillingham, where again it lay dormant, before finally coming to rest with BWE Sportscars of Barnsley. A very capable and underrated kit car.
Maelstrom Cars 1986
PACE 1990–92
Evans Hunter Sports Cars 1993–94
White Rose Vehicles 1998–2002
BWE Sportscars 2002 to date
Approx 11 made

MAGENTA

Steve Johnson of Barnsley was the man behind the Magenta marque, and for several years he sold a lot of kits. A 1986 relocation to Cleveland saw the company name changed to Magna Sport, a division of his Fibre Glass Engineering Ltd operation, and the Magenta remained the last model standing when the company ceased trading in 1988. They also sold the Apal Speedster (*qv*) for a short time back in 1972.

The original model, launched in 1972, was Magenta's best-seller by a long way. It had a tube steel chassis with Austin 1100/Morris 1300 donor, using the unmodified Hydrolastic suspension. The Mk2 version from 1978 had a revised chassis. Quirky styling maybe, but it could seat four people, and Johnson sold 500 of them.
Lightspeed Panels 1972–86
Magna Sport 1986–88
Approx 500 made

MAGENTA LSR

The Light Speed Roadster arrived in 1979. It was a sleeker, two-seat version of the original Magenta with a completely revised front end, dispensing with the MG1100 grille. Donor switched to Ford Escort.
Lightspeed Panels 1979–86
Approx 40 made

MAGENTA SPRINT

The Sprint was still clearly a Magenta but more revisions and another donor change to Mini gave the car a distinct style all of its own (albeit still quirky).
Lightspeed Panels 1980–86
Approx 20 made

MAGENTA TARRAGON

The Tarragon was a departure for Lightspeed and was probably the first kit car to feature a hatchback. Described once as an Allegro with a droopsnoot! A genuinely practical car with Ford Escort donor parts.
Lightspeed Panels 1982–85
Approx 35 made

MAGENTA TXR

A racier replacement for the Tarragon (see above), based on Ford Capri parts and wider as a result. A big improvement but didn't sell in any real numbers and didn't last long.
Lightspeed Panels 1985–86
Approx 7 made

MAGIC

MFE were run by MGB expert Roger Mossop based in Tangmere, West Sussex, in Dutton Cars' old premises. Originally MGB-based, with a Ford Cortina MkIII version introduced from 1985. Clearly inspired in looks and price by close neighbours Dutton Cars, although it never sold in anything like the same numbers. GRP bodies of a high standard produced by Mike Rutherford's Mako Fibreglass.

Magic customer and buyer for a plastics company Robert Taylor, from Haslemere, ended up buying the project in 1988, and it became the first offering from his Scorhill Motors operation.
Metro Fibre Engineering (MFE) 1984–86
Motorspeed 1986–88
Scorhill Motors 1988–96
Approx 83 made

MAGNUM – *see AD 400*

MAGNUM 427

Maker Fieldbay was part of V8 engine specialist Mike Broad's company Auto Power Services. They were dab hands at sticking big V8s into unfamiliar situations, such as a Chevy 350 into a Ford Cortina! Their Magnum Cobra replica was aimed at the performance end of the market, with Kevlar®-reinforced areas on the fibreglass body. It sits lower and meaner than its rivals.

Fieldbay ceased trading in 1992, although Broad soon returned with his Magnum operation, in which he was joined by Robin Stewart in 2006, although by 2008 Broad had disappeared.
Fieldbay 1987–92
Magnum Engineering 1993–2009
Approx 85 made

MAHCON TF – *see Hutson TF*

MAHDEEN

A plans-built Lotus Seven-inspired sports car.
Mahdeen 1991–92
Approx 9 made

MALIBU

Ford-based utility designed by Steve Green, bearing a strong resemblance to the Mitsubishi Shogun/Pajero. Derek Robinson and John Wilkinson had great difficulty coming up with a name for the car and it was also briefly known as Marathon, Target and Tiger before they finally settled on Malibu.
Car Care Clinic 1991–93
Reiver Motor Car Company 1993
Avon Coachworks 1993–99
Approx 4 made

MALIBU RV4

Renault 4-based utility kit from E-Zee Automotive of St Anne's Well Mews, Exeter, run by Jim Daughtry. It was a take on the Plein Air.
E-Zee Automotive 1990–93
Approx 2 made

MALLALIEU

Mallalieu were not a kit car manufacturer per se, but they belong here as a true specialist operation. Derry Mallalieu was one of the first Bentley Mk6 *special* builders to go into 'production', alongside the likes of Johnard, Syd Lawrence, Harry Rose and Neville Trickett. He worked with the late William Towns in the mid-'70s and marketed his innovative Microdot city car for several years.

The easy availability of rusty Mk6 Bentleys and their separate chassis, proved ideal for building *specials*. Derry built his first Mallalieu in 1974, although he had already built a one-off in the '60s for an American customer. The first 'proper' one was called the Barchetta Open Tourer. He planned a two-seater called the Mercia (later Oxford).

Mallalieu died in 1975 and never saw the new Mercia/Oxford, which was completed in 1976. By this time demand was high, especially from the USA, making Mallalieu probably the biggest of the Mk6 converters. But they weren't cheap by any means, with the Barchetta at £9,950 and the Mercia at £15,000. A Barchetta took four months to build and a Mercia/Oxford six months.

By 1981 the company was experiencing financial difficulties and went bust. They left behind quite a few delightful Mk6 *specials*.
Mallalieu Engineering 1974–81
Approx 30 made

MALLOCK U2

There is some conjecture over the wonderful Mallock U2. Some say it wasn't a kit car per se, although I disagree, as although you could buy one fully built, some involved spanner-wielding by the customer, and adverts exist from the period mentioning component purchase that included a chassis.

Major Arthur Mallock originally built Austin 7-based *specials* as far back as 1936, and post WWII he and his contemporaries, such as Derek Buckler, were enthusiastic competitors and suppliers of a variety of go-faster components to eager customers. Mallock was based in a workshop in Roade, Northamptonshire. Mallock's *specials* building continued throughout the fifties, but by 1958 his first commercially available model, the U2, was advertised. The name was inspired by Charles Atlas's famous body-building adverts with the strap-line: 'You too can have a *body* like mine.' This appealed to Arthur's sense of humour, and he replaced the word *body* with *car* for his own ads.

The Mk2 was really the first 'proper' U2, and although many were supplied fully built, the customer could complete the build in their home garage if they preferred. The secret of the U2's success was a rigid spaceframe chassis, finely calculated suspension geometry and use of affordable parts from the likes of Ford, Triumph and BMC.

When the 750 Motor Club introduced their Clubman series in the mid-sixties, the Mallock U2 was ideally suited, and Arthur and his sons Richard and Ray were regular competitors. Ray went on to form Ray Mallock Ltd (RML) and enjoys a fine reputation for race and road car development. He was also a regular competitor in the Le Mans 24-Hour race. Meanwhile, Richard Mallock continued producing the U2 after Arthur's death in 1993, and still produces the car today, now in Mk36 form. The brothers collaborated on the RML Mallock P20 of 1999, while Richard produced the first mid-engined Mallock model in 1995 (designed by Mike McDermott), although he no longer offers U2s in kit form.
Mallock Sports 1958 to date
Approx 350 made

MAMBA C23

This pretty and capable little Lotus 23 replica originated from Shapecraft via Kitdeal and Auriga. Mamba's John Bridge made several alterations to the kit and added various engine options, and it remains a great car.

Kitdeal 1987–90
Auriga Developments aka Espero Ltd 1990–2000
Mamba Motorsport 1998–2008
Approx 110 made (includes Noble, Auriga and Mamba sales)

MAMBA PHOENIX – *see Moss Mamba*

MANTA RAY

Having previously made the Harrington & King's Sports Buggy (*qv*) under the Buggy Shop banner, Connaught Cars' forecourt manager Adrian Harrington came up with the Manta Ray in September 1969, based on the ubiquitous VW Beetle, with floorpan chopped by 16in. The company was based in an old air-raid shelter next door to Connaught Cars in Send, Surrey, who gave the operation their blessing.

Finance for their new venture, called Power on Wheels, came from Connaught director Alan Brown, and the Manta Ray did pretty well, with nearly 40 sold within eight months. It was inspired by the GP Buggy (*qv*) and also the Manx (*qv*), while its one-piece bodyshell made the car easier to build, but meant that it was tricky to access the engine and fuel tank. The company's demo car even had the honour of being on the front cover of the first issue of *Custom Car* magazine in March 1970. Of course, the company name allowed Harrington to use the 'POW' abbreviation!

A Mk2 arrived in August 1970 that had a deep lip under the longer nose, a line down the middle of the bonnet, and headlights moved forward by 6in. One complaint about the Mk1 had been its thin fibreglass, which was addressed by moving production from the Hastings laminator, more familiar with racing car bodies, to a company called C&D Automarine of Byfleet – who also made their own buggy called the Cobra (*qv*). The Mk2 also had lower headlights and a longer nose with a style-line down it. It truly hit the spot, and sold four times faster than the Mk1.

A company from Carshalton Beeches, Surrey, called CTR Enterprises, purchased a Manta Ray and promptly copied it, launching their own kit a few months later. Another Manta Ray copy was the Seaspray.

Brown's wife, Carol, a motoring journalist, raced a Manta Ray in the Boxing Day 1971 beach buggy race at Brands Hatch, while Dave Cameron, later of Jimini, successfully autocrossed a Manta Ray. 'Works' driver Brian Maynard drag-raced a Porsche-powered version.

The very enthusiastic Jeff Rosenbloom, an airline pilot, acted as Scottish agent for the Manta Ray in his spare time.

The company was closed down by Alan Brown in September 1971, when he stopped funding the operation. Adrian Harrington went to work for playboy industrialist, Gunther Sachs, in the south of France, running his car collection. Manta Ray then lay dormant for several months before it was taken over by JB Developments of Aldershot ('The Manta Ray still lives' proclaimed their adverts), moving to Volkscare & Custom of Horsham, run by Richard Cooke, in 1986, before buggy resting place GT Mouldings took over in 1987. They concentrated on the Manta Ray Mk2 before evolving it into the MkIII

with lower side panels, which ended up with Martyn and Rob Falk's Birmingham-based KMR Buggies operation in 2003 along with the Renegade (*qv*) and Kyote II (*qv*), from whom they remain available.

Power on Wheels 1969–72
JB Developments 1972–76
Volkscare & Custom 1986–1987
GT Mouldings 1987–2003
KMR Beach Buggies 2003–8
Approx 305 made (including approx 35 MkIs, 250 MkIIs and 30 MkIIIs)

MANTIS

Offered from 1965 this was a near identical copy of Dennis Adams' Probe (*qv*), on a Beetle chassis. This should not be confused with another Adams design, the Marcos Mantis (*qv*) that looked identical but was totally separate.

Mantis Cars 1965
Approx 2 made

MANX

Designed by Jim Clark who had a motorsport background with Chevron, Lola, Lotus and McLaren and had been responsible for such designs as the McLaren M6 and Chevron B16 plus the LDV (*qv*) for GP and the Griffin (*qv*), and had also worked at Specialised Mouldings in Huntingdon. His company was known as Plasticar Designs, although he marketed this quirky, angular and not unpleasant Citroën 2CV-based two-seater under the Manx Cars banner.

Kit car journalist Iain Ayre became involved for a while before the project passed to Ginetta and Onyx specialist Alan Fereday and was renamed the Vario (*qv*). In 2011 it was resurrected by Deauville Cars.

Manx Cars 1991–98   *Ayrspeed-Manx 1998–2000*
Fereday Cars 2000–2   *Deauville Cars 2011 to date*
Approx 12 made

MANX

Legendary and much imitated buggy created in America by Bruce Meyers, and the beach buggy that started it all back in 1964. Imported to the UK, officially, by Mel Hubbard's Manxbuggies operation from 1999, from a base in Dartford, Kent, before Hubbard moved to Wisbech in Cambridgeshire. In 2003 his projects all passed to Rob Kilham of East Coast Manx who was originally located in King's Lynn before moving to Rutland.

Manxbuggies 1999–2003
East Coast Manx 2003 to date
Approx 140 made (UK)

MANX II

Late '90s beach buggy from original Manx creator Bruce Meyers. Differs by having a restyled bonnet and a flat back seat. Imported to the UK by Mel Hubbard of Manxbuggies from 1999 and currently made by Rob Kilham's East Coast Manx.
Manxbuggies 1999–2003
East Coast Manx 2003 to date
Approx 100 made

MARCOS 3-LITRE FORD/2½-LITRE/2-LITRE/3-LITRE VOLVO

In 1969 Marcos owners at last got what they had wanted for ten years – more power, with the introduction of a Ford 3.0-litre engine. The first 119 cars had the traditional wooden chassis, replaced thereafter by an all-new visually identical steel affair. These were the Marcos models made at the new Engineer Road, Westbury HQ.

American-market cars used a Volvo 3.0-litre engine. A Triumph 2.5-litre PI engine lasted five minutes before a 2.0-litre Ford V4 option was introduced.
Marcos Cars Ltd 1969–72
3-litre Ford 1969–71 – approx 315 made
2½-litre 1971 – approx 12 made
2-litre 1970–71 – approx 78 made
3-litre Volvo 1969–72 – approx 172 made

MARCOS CARS

Born in 1930, Jeremy George Weston Marsh had a wonderfully varied and colourful early career after his nine-year stint with the Royal Navy had ended. His CV includes working as a technical representative for Firestone Tires, a short spell selling combine harvesters, and even as a performer for the Hollywood Motor Maniacs and European Motor Rodeo – so called because no one came from America and they never visited Europe! Marsh had also gained a great reputation as a successful 750 Formula racer, winning many prizes and building and driving his own *specials*. 'Jem' became properly involved with the automotive industry when he started Speedex Castings and Accessories Ltd in May 1957.

A chance encounter in a pub at a 750 Motor Club meeting in Luton was to change things dramatically for Jem Marsh. Enter one Frank Costin, a freelance designer of some note who had recently left the de Havilland Aircraft Company, where he worked on wooden-framed aircraft and aerodynamics. He was a notable designer even in those days, and had contributed to several racing cars for Vanwall and Lotus and had also been responsible for the highly acclaimed Lister-Jaguar (also known as the 'Knobbly'). It was a good meeting for both men as they each needed a new challenge and they got on well from the outset.

Costin put his aviation design skills to good use with a lightweight, wooden laminate monocoque body and chassis for a GT car, named the Xylon (Greek for wood), which although clearly not pretty and nicknamed 'the ugly duckling' (Costin was more interested in how a car worked than how it looked), it was extremely effective on British race circuits in the hands of Bill Moss, being both fast and streamlined and, for its day, very advanced.

In 1960, other men who became synonymous with the classic Marcos arrived in the shape of the Adams brothers Dennis and Peter. Dennis was working for Brian Lister Engineering with Frank Costin, who had been sufficiently impressed by this young designer to bring him on board. Frank, Dennis and Peter set up in Dolgellau in North Wales, while Jem carried on running Speedex in Luton. Frank Costin left the operation in 1961 to pursue other design interests after objecting to modifications that Dennis had made to his 'ugly duckling'.

In early 1962 financial constraints forced the closure of Speedex, with inevitable knock-on effects for Marsh and co. The Adams moved back to Audley End, Cambridgeshire, while Jem went

to work for Leslie Ballamy's respected LMB company in Guildford, another *specials* outfit who were selling go-faster parts (including a split beam front axle and their own brand of wheels) and a bodyshell called the Debonair (*qv*). After he'd sold a few 'shells the project was shelved at Jem's behest due to several factors, mainly that he deemed it too heavy and far too expensive.

With impeccable timing, a saviour appeared in the form of Lieutenant Commander Greville Cavendish, who had a passion for fast and interesting vehicles. He expressed an interest in resurrecting the 'ugly duckling' GT and funded new premises at Bradford-on-Avon in Wiltshire, which had formerly housed the Royal Enfield Motorcycle works.

Marcos Cars Limited (the name came from Marsh and Costin's surnames) now officially existed. Cavendish remained involved until 1965, when he retired. However, he is a key, if understated, cog in the company's history, providing funding and convincing Jem to carry on with the 'Marcos way'.

In 1964 the shape that has since remained synonymous with Marcos was launched, the Volvo-engined 1800, which met with much critical acclaim although sales were quite slow to begin with. Initially Jem veered away from the logical Ford powerplants due to the Essex marque's 'boy racer' image but eventually succumbed and used the 1500GT Pre-Crossflow engine and then the new 1,600cc Crossflow unit in 1967, resulting in possibly the best-balanced Marcos ever.

Any history of Marcos would not be complete without mention of the Mini Marcos, which came on to the price lists in 1965 and was inspired by the 1963 DART Mini *special* designed by Dizzy Addicott. Jem liked the concept very much but disagreed with the plan to make it an expensive model. Instead he believed that if the body was made from GRP and was at the budget end of the market, utilising all-Mini components, fitted unmodified, it would sell in good numbers. He was proved right as it turned out. He commissioned another maverick, designer friend Malcolm Newell (who was responsible for the Quasar 'two-wheeled car', a bicycle design, years ahead of its time), to do the work, and the rest, as they say, is history.

In 1969 Marcos finally stopped making wooden chassis and came

MANXTER 2+2

Bruce Meyers' second update on his legendary Manx theme was the Manxter 2+2, a modern and pleasing body style but still based on VW Beetle floorpan. Sold in the UK by Mark Dryden of Flatlands Engineering in King's Lynn. Subaru Impreza engine could be used, too.
Flatlands Engineering
2004 to date
Approx 25 made

up with an Adams-designed square-section, steel-tube lightweight replacement. Originally wood had been a cheaper alternative to steel, but was also very labour-intensive, but that had now changed so metal would save money and labour.

By the end of 1969 there were 120 people at the factory turning out ten cars a week, helped considerably by North American sales, which were booming. The US cars were equipped with the straight-six engine from the Volvo 164. Jem didn't use the obvious choice, the British-specification Ford 3.0-litre V6, as it was, in his opinion, too heavy and oily, for the American market.

The company moved from their outgrown premises in Bradford-on-Avon to a new site in Westbury in 1970. Things rolled along quite merrily until, one day in 1971, Marcos suffered severe problems when a bulk consignment of 27 cars were impounded at the docks by US customs. It was not, contrary to popular belief, due to failure to meet emissions requirements (as any specialist car manufacturer producing less than 500 units per year was exempt), it was entirely due to officials not believing that a tiny British car maker could have the resources to ship this number of vehicles in one consignment. As it happens, Marcos could, but at the expense of tying up crucial capital.

The US operation subsequently collapsed, leaving Marcos £30,000 worse off. If you add this to that year's introduction of VAT it was inevitable that Marcos, like all specialist car manufacturers of the day, were going to suffer. So Jem sold out to Hebron & Medlock Bath Engineering Ltd, who within six months had also gone into receivership. The Rob Walker Group subsequently purchased all the remaining stock and assets.

In 1972, with just a couple of hundred pounds to his name and a lot of determination, Jem set up a spares and restoration company for Marcos owners in a unit he rented from Rob Walker. This was successful enough by 1976 for him to have reacquired the Marcos name and moulds from the Rob Walker Group and in 1981 had also secured the capital to start manufacturing his beloved Marcoses again. Clearly there was still a demand for his vehicles, and in 1984 the move was made that turned Marcos into an exotic vehicle manufacturer – the launch of the Rover V8-powered Mantula, an inspired step that paid significant dividends. The open-topped Spyder version followed in 1985.

The fully-built Mantara superseded the Mantula in 1992, which although looking very similar had been subject to intensive detail development during the intervening years. Almost every part had been

replaced, including the powerplant, which was now the uprated 3.9-litre Rover V8, upping maximum power to 198bhp or, in sports guise, 240bhp with the addition of an NCK Sports Pack.

Philip Hulme realised a lifelong ambition in 1990 to own a Marcos and to coin the cliché 'he liked the company so much he bought into it'! He was the proprietor of the Computacenter chain, and with his continued support Marcos was able to develop its GT Racers, the LM 500 and LM 600, which competed successfully at Le Mans.

The Mini Marcos was reintroduced in 1991 as a recession-beater and also the Martina (in Coupé and Spyder forms), which was a Cortina-based budget version of the Mantula, meaning that Marcos now had a model to suit all budgets. The company dropped kit production in 1993, preferring to concentrate on fully-built cars.

Their later day history is well documented elsewhere. Suffice it to say that the Marcos marque remains an extremely well-respected one, and former Marcos employee Rory MacMath can supply all parts and servicing for owners via his Marcos Heritage operation.

For completeness' sake, here are the Marcos models that were not available in kit-form:

Marcos XP 1968 – 1 made
Marcos Mantara 1992–98 – Approx 137 made
Marcos LM 500 Racer 1994 – Approx 7 made
Marcos LM 600 Racer 1995 – Approx 4 made
Marcos LM 200 1995 – Approx 1 made
Marcos LM 400/LM 500 1995–98 – Approx 34 made
Marcos Manta Ray 1997–99 – Approx 26 made
Marcos Mantis 1997–2000 – Approx 51 made
Marcos Challenge 1999 – Approx 38 made

Marcos went into administration in 2000, with assets purchased by Rory MacMath of Marcos Heritage. However, Jem Marsh made another comeback in 2002, from the Westbury factory, although the company was owned by Californian Tony Stelliga. By early 2004 they'd moved to a new site in Kenilworth, Warwickshire, trading as Marcos Engineering although they closed the doors for the final time in 2008:

Marcos TS 250/Marcasite 2002 – Approx 7 made
Marcos TS 500 2003 – Approx 4 made
Marcos TSO GT 2003-4 – Approx 2 made

MARCOS 1600 METAL CHASSIS

An economy model with no bumpers, brightwork or headlight covers.

Marcos Cars Ltd 1969–72
Approx 6 made

MARCOS 1800/1500/1600/1650

Featured a laminated plywood chassis that was amazingly strong, topped by a fibreglass body. Designed by Dennis and Peter Adams, while the engine came from a Volvo P1800, which replaced the 1500 powered by Ford Pre-Crossflow in 1964,

changing to 1,600cc Crossflow from 1967. A Chris Lawrence-prepared 1,650cc engine powered the 1650 of 1967, of which 20 were made.

Underpinnings remained unchanged with Triumph suspension and Ford live axle throughout its life.

Marcos Cars Ltd 1964–67
1800 1964–66 – approx 100 made
1500 1966–67 – approx 98 made
1600 1967–69 – approx 200 made
1650 1967 – approx 20 made

MARCOS FASTBACK – *see Marcos Spyder*

MARCOS GULLWING/XYLON

Nicknamed 'the ugly duckling', this was designed by Jem Marsh and Frank Costin and was known as the 'wooden wonder', due to the fact that it was largely constructed from wood, including the monocoque. However, the nosecone, available in a variety

of styles, was made from fibreglass. Mechanical components were a mixture of Triumph and Ford. Very successful on the racetrack with several notable racing drivers doing well in it, including Sir Jackie Stewart and Jackie Oliver.

The first seven had a split windscreen and cycle-type front wings, while an 'intermediate' version (two sold), featuring an all-enveloping body, appeared later in 1960.

Speedex 1959–60
Approx 9 made

MARCOS GT

The 'new' Marcos GT breathed its first in 1981. Clearly a Marcos, it was actually a revised Marcos 3-litre/2½-litre featuring a square tube spaceframe chassis and Ford engines.

Marcos Sales 1982–91
Approx 220 made

MARCOS 'LUTON' GULLWING

Complete restyle of the original Gullwing/Xylon (see above) by Dennis and Peter Adams, much to the chagrin of Frank Costin, who felt so strongly about it he promptly left the company as a result. More fibreglass used in its construction. Derek Bell raced one of these.

Marcos Cars Ltd 1961–63
Approx 13 made

MARCOS MANTIS M70

The first four-seat Marcos with controversial Dennis Adams styling, which although very modern for the time did not capture people's imaginations. An executive 2+2 saloon with plenty of luxury to satisfy fat businessmen. Had a semi-

spaceframe chassis and Triumph 2.5-litre six-cylinder engine from the TR6. With just 32 sold, it's often been accused of being the cause of Marcos' 1971 crash, which is a bit unfair. Resurrected briefly, albeit revised, by Autotune as the Autotune Mirage (*qv*) in 1985.

Marcos Cars Ltd 1970–71
Approx 32 made

MARCOS MANTULA COUPÉ

Quite simply a classic Marcos. A revised 3.0-litre GT with chest-beating Rover V8 power. Got the performance it deserved. Its name was a combination of 'Mantis' and 'Tarantula'. Independent rear suspension introduced from 1986.

Marcos Sales 1983–94
Approx 170 made

HIT KIT

MARCOS MANTULA SPYDER

A beautifully styled convertible version of the Mantula, again with V8 power. These were the last Marcos products to be available in component form, as from 1994 they made only fully-built cars.
Marcos Sales 1985–92
Approx 119 made

MARCOS MARTINA SPYDER & COUPÉ

Marcos' answer to the recession of the early 1990s. A budget Ford Cortina-based version of the GT with four-cylinder engine, available in both Spyder and Coupé guises. Christened by Jem's wife Lyn.
Marcos Sales 1991–94
Approx 80 made

MARCOS SPYDER/FASTBACK

Created by Dennis Adams and his brother Peter. Originally a convertible (three sold), but soon changed to a fixed-head configuration. Although it still used a lot of wood in its construction, this was the pioneer of the traditional Marcos shape.
Marcos Cars Ltd 1963–64
Approx 18 made

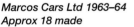

MARCOS XYLON – *see Marcos Gullwing*

MARKHAM-PEASEY SABRE

The Sabre appeared in 1958 and was based on Ford 10 90in wheelbase in two- or four-seat configurations.

Although a child of its time complete with spats covering the rear wheels, the Sabre was actually a very stylish motorcar of the day. Company originally based in Gleneldon Mews, Streatham.
Markham-Peasey Laminated Plastics Ltd 1958–61
Super Accessories 1961–63
Approx 200 made

MARKHAM-PEASEY CELESTE

Croydon High Street based company with Roy Markham and Wally Peasey the men behind the operation. Very ambitious American-styled bodyshell launched at the Racing Car Show of January 1961. Company sold to rivals Super Accessories in February the same year.
Markham-Peasey Laminates Ltd 1961
Approx 5 sold

MARKHAM-PEASEY SUPER SABRE

Pretty much the same as the standard Sabre but designed for Austin 7 mechanicals. If the customer was using a post-war donor then the bodies could be had with bonded floors.
Markham-Peasey Laminates Ltd 1959–61
Super Accessories 1961–63
Approx 100 made

MARLBOROUGH SR

Verwood, Dorset, company run by Derek Smith, who produced this traditional little roadster based on Morris Marina donor parts. Used the motto 'the car with space, pace and grace'.
Marlborough Cars 1985–86
Approx 1 made

MARLIN 5EXI

Marlin's 5EXI, inevitably nicknamed 'the Sexy', is a pretty little modern, mid-engined two-seater, and a complete departure for Marlin, best-known for their traditional roadster models. Rover 200 donor parts, with an 5EXI-R ('Sexier') Honda Civic option from 2005.
Marlin Cars 2003 to date
Approx 60 made

MARLIN BERLINETTA 2+2

Shared similar styling to the company's Roadster, but didn't share any panels, being bigger with a 2+2 configuration. Based on Ford Cortina, it featured an aluminium and fibreglass body, doors and wind-up windows (an unusual kit car attribute in 1984) and perhaps one of the prettiest hardtops yet seen on a specialist car. A Ford Sierra-based donor option was introduced in 1990. Taken over by agents YKC in 1993.
Marlin Engineering 1984–93
YKC Sports Cars 1993–98
Approx 500 made

MARLIN CABRIO

Paul Moorhouse had been working on his updated Cabrio model for a couple of years and had cleared the decks, selling the Roadster and Berlinetta projects to YKC in 1992, enabling him to concentrate fully on the new model.

Clearly still a Marlin, it was heavily revised and updates began based on Ford Sierra. Developed further by new Marlin owners Mark Matthews and Rodney Rushton (based in Crediton), who acquired the company in 1993, initially trading as Cabrio Sportscar Company, Ruston soon went off to do this own thing. This involved marketing the Kennedy Squire (briefly), the former BRA P-Type project, supplying vintage cars to film and TV companies and breeding a supply of rabbits to pet shop chains in the UK. Mark was joined at Marlin by his wife Terry. A Mk2 version of the Cabrio appeared in 2000. Mark came up with a superb BMW-based version from 2004 and when sold in fully built guise the car was called Hunter. Project taken over by Bradford-based Dave Kitson of Javelin Sports Cars in 2007.
Marlin Engineering 1992-93 *Cabrio Sportscar Company/*
Javelin Sports Cars 2007-8 *Marlin Cars 1993-2007*
Approx 50 made

MARLIN ROADSTER

Launched by Paul Moorhouse in 1979. A very fast seller. By 1989 he'd sold 1,111 kits! Not a replica, but definitely had a hint of classic Alfa Romeo about it. Early ones were based on Triumph Herald mechanicals on a tube steel chassis with a body made from aluminium and fibreglass. A new Morris Marina donor option arrived in 1983. Ford-based versions were developed by erstwhile Marlin agents YKC, who acquired the project in 1992, leaving Moorhouse to work on his all-new Cabrio model, before he became submerged in his new underwater projects!
Marlin Engineering 1979–92 *YKC Sports Cars 1992–2005*
Aquila Sports Cars 2005–7
Approx 1,575 made

MARLIN SPORTSTER

The first Matthews-era Marlin product was the Sportster from 1998. Combining traditional styling with hints of Lotus Seven (certainly in the handling department), this Ford Sierra-based car was highly capable. A BMW donor option with fire-breathing 343bhp E46 M3 option became available in 2002.
Marlin Cars 1998 to date
Approx 75 made

MARTIN GTA 40

Martin were a French company, based in Olonne-sur-Mer, which set up a UK operation in Clacton in the 1990s run by Dave Bennett. The GTA 40 was a budget-orientated GT40 replica with power from Ford V6.
Martin Automobiles UK 1994–96
Approx 5 made (UK)

MARTIN MATOU

Cobra replica very similar to the Pilgrim Sumo (*qv*). Based on Ford Sierra and normally powered by Ford V6.
Martin Automobiles UK 1990–96
Approx 7 made (UK)

MARTIN TILBURY

Traditional roadster kit with Morgan influences, based on Renault 4 donor, which was originally made by Stylisme et Mécanique Sportive from 1986 and acquired by the French Martin operation from Vibraction of Roanne in 1990. A Mk2 based on Renault 5 came along in 1993.
Martin Automobiles UK 1990–96
Approx 3 made (UK)

MARTIN TTM/GMO

The TTM was a Lotus Seven-inspired sports car that had a tubular steel spaceframe, with Ford mechanicals and a body of bonded and riveted aluminium with fibreglass wings.
Martin Automobiles UK 1986–96
Approx 5 made (UK)

MARTLET

A classic car restoration company who produced a lovely little sports car that was raced with great success in the 750 Motor Club by the young and then unknown Martin Short, who finished fourth in his first season in the Kit Car Championship in 1987 and later went on to compete in top-level GT racing and found leading rollcage company Rollcentre.
Martlet Restorations 1984–87
Approx 3 made

MARTLET

Citroën 2CV-based van kit from Deauville Cars, with a back end designed by Jago Developments that gives it a period '20s style.
Deauville Cars 2010 to date
Approx 2 made

MARTYNI C23

Lotus 23 replica made by Martyn Perks with assistance from his father, Malcolm. Company based in Bilston, West Midlands. Car featured a Zintec steel monocoque rather than a more conventional spaceframe. Perks made parts such as double wishbones and hub carriers in-house, with Ford Sierra hubs at the rear and Alfa Romeo 33 power. The glassfibre body kit was supplied in three sections. A well-made and well-regarded replica.
Martyni Sportscars 1999–2008
Approx 30 made

MARU KATSU NOBLE SPYDER

Visitors to Lee Noble's Kitdeal operation in late 1989 would have seen a 550 Spyder replica in his workshop, since he briefly marketed the Brazilian Chamonix project in the UK. Featured a round-tube chassis fitted with standard VW Beetle parts and was part of a deal involving his Japanese agent that amounted to nought.
Kitdeal 1989
Approx 1 made

MASTERCO COUNTACH

From a company based in Bolton, this car was a revised version of the Panache LP400 (*qv*). In 1991 Masterco sold the kits at £2,500, and claimed that a DIY-build could be completed for under £9,000. It isn't known if that figure was achieved by customers.
Masterco Engineering 1991–93
Approx 5 made

MAY CORP

Designed by ex-Vauxhall man Chris Field (based in Totnes, Devon), who also designed the Mirach (*qv*). Launched at the Frankfurt Motor Show in 1991, the May Corp was a mid-engined sports car with a retracting rear screen and targa top arrangement that could be powered by most front-wheel-drive engines from 1.6-2-litre used in rear-wheel-drive format. Shelved after investment wasn't forthcoming.

After a long time away, it was last heard of as the ECU, sold by RJH Sportscars.

May Corp 1991
RJH Sportscars 2004–5
Approx 2 made

MAYA GT

After his split with Checkpoint Ltd, George Holmes revised the Camber GT (*qv*) himself and carried on under the Maya banner. He restyled the front end, sorted out the illegal headlight issue and named the revised car Maya after his wife's horse! Tragically Holmes was killed when out driving the Maya demonstrator after he stopped to attend to an injured bird and was run over.

W. West (Engineers) Ltd 1967–69
Approx 6 made

MB 750

Plans-built, plywood-bodied Austin 7-based Roadster that used a Reliant 700/750/850cc engine, although the customer could opt for Vauxhall Viva mechanicals as an option. The company was based in Preston, Lancashire.

Ribble Publishers 1984–86
Approx 10 made

MC ACER

What a lovely little car the Acer was. A tip of the hat to the classic '60s Turner Sports (*qv*), re-engineered to accept more modern Vauxhall Viva or Ford Escort mechanicals. The men behind the project were Sheffield-based Mark (and wife Joy) Clarkson (whence 'MC') and business partner Phil Booth.

A Mk2 version added 5in to the length of the original Turner. Project taken over by Carlton Automotive (big kit car players of the 1980s) in 1989, although they fared no better than MC Cars, with the Acer briefly ending up under the control of Ian Birks back in Sheffield in 1995. Should have sold in bigger numbers.

MC Cars 1984–89
Carlton Automotive 1989–95
Ian Birks Car Care 1995
Approx 8 made

MCA SPORTS COUPÉ

Created by Italian ex-racing driver Aurelio Bezzi, based in Bognor Regis. A really sweet little car based on Fiat 126 donor parts including buzzy 594cc engine, pretty fibreglass body panels and a simple twin-rail Jago Fabrications ladderframe chassis.

Bezzi emigrated to Italy in 1988 and the project moved to fledgling Minari Engineering for a couple of years and was their first attempt at car manufacture before their own critically acclaimed model.

In 1990 it moved on again, to Dash Sportscars (who created a convertible version) and then Hadleigh Sprint makers IPS Developments for a couple of years in 1994 before it sadly faded away.

Bezzi Cars 1983–88
Dash Sportscars 1990–94
Approx 26 made

Minari Engineering 1988–90
IPS Developments 1994–96

McCOY

Former Lotus employee Arthur Birchall (he ran the works race team and had been Jim Clark's mechanic for a time), based in Barnham Broom, had also been involved with the Clan Crusader (*qv*), which inspired the McCoy, launched ten years after the Crusader departed the scene.

Birchall utilised a Crusader body that he revised to form his prototype McCoy, which was Mini-based with front engine, the screen being the only thing that remained the same after he'd finished. Another ex-Lotus man, Brian Luff, founder of the Status Car Company, designed the chassis. The car was crash-tested, which was unusual for a kit car, at a Scottish university.

Due to Birchall's illness the project was taken over by employee Neville Wynes, who sold a further 15 examples, initially from North Buddenham before moving to Fakenham in 1990.

Birchall Automotive 1984–88
N.G. Wynes Fibreglass (McCoy Cars) 1988–90
Neville Wynes Fibreglass Products 1990–2001
Approx 100 made

McCOY TR REPLICA

Sweet little Triumph replica that Neville Wynes added to the McCoy range for a time, which could be had in TR2, TR3 or TR3A guises.

N.G. Wynes Fibreglass (McCoy Cars) 1988–90
Neville Wynes Fibreglass Products 1990–98
Approx 12 made

McIVOY

A four-seat estate-bodied version of the McCoy.

Birchall Automotive 1986–88
N.G. Wynes Fibreglass (McCoy Cars) 1988–90
Neville Wynes Fibreglass Products 1990–98
Approx 5 made

MCR PHOENIX

MCR Phoenix Automotive, based in Tenbury Wells, was an agent for KVA and could supply their own take on Ken Attwell's GT40 replica

in kit and complete car forms. Described by *Motor* magazine as the 'ultimate replica' after they tested the company's demonstrator. in 1985
MCR Phoenix Automotive Ltd 1984–87
Approx 7 made

MCR S2000

Designed by Brazilian Luis Fernando Cruz, the S2000 is aimed very much at the race and trackday markets. The company is based in St David's, Pembrokeshire, and run by former Gilbern Cars test driver Clive Hayes. Successful in sports car racing as the name implies.
MCR Race Cars 2008 to date
Approx 5 made

MDA GT40 REPLICA

Former GTD employee Mark Sibley was the man behind this GT40 replica. Based in Honiton, Devon.
MDA GT40 UK Ltd 2000–8
Approx 30 made

MDB SAPPHIRE

Bbased on the GT Centron (*qv*) and a real mix-and-match affair with front end of Saturn and rear of Saratoga. It remained based on VW Beetle but Barton did create a Ford Cortina donor option. Did they make any?
MDB Sportscars 1986–87
Approx 1 made

MDB SARATOGA

MDB was run by Tredegar-based Mike Barton, and the Saratoga was originally known as the Charger (*qv*), one of the top 50 best-selling kits of all time. Subsequently became the Viking Dragon Fire. Barton had devised a Ford Cortina-based version, although were any sold?
MDB Sportscars 1986–87
Approx 1 made

MDB SATURN

Known originally as the Charger 2 (*qv*). Subsequently became the Viking Dragon Fly (*qv*).
MDB Sportscars 1986–87
Approx 1 made

MDV RR

A rally-orientated device with links to Ford, before being developed by Peter Bennett's MDV operation and offered in kit form from their base on disused Bradwell Airfield in Essex.
MDV Specialist Engineering Ltd 2004–6
Approx 15 made

ME4

Scorhill was the retirement home for old kit cars but in 1996 they announced their first original design called the ME4, a two-seater coupé.
Scorhill Motors 1996–97
Approx 1 made

MERCEDES 320 REPLICA

Replica of a German WW2 staff car. Donor vehicle was a Jaguar MkIX of all things. The same company was also responsible for the SS100-style Viking 380 SSR (*qv*).
Classic Cars of Coventry 1982
Approx 2 made

MERLIN MONRO/PLUS TWO

Was it named after popular '60s crooner and former bus driver Matt Monro? Car was to have been sold in the UK by Thoroughbred Car's agent, who went bust almost immediately. Peter Gowing's company finished off the first demonstrator before they too ceased trading in 1984 and the project was taken over by agents CVC of Redditch, run by Terry Sands.

Gowing bounced back as Paris Cars and renamed the car Plus Two in April 1985. Revised chassis and rear suspension gave more space and an extra row of seats for small people. Very popular.
Thoroughbred Cars 1983–84
Paris Cars 1985–2003
Approx 700 made

A B C D E F G H I J K L **M** N O P Q R S T U V W X Y Z

MERLIN TF

Imported from the US, where it was known as the Witton Tiger, based on VW Beetle. Designed by American Leonard Witton while he was living in London. On returning home he took the idea with him and put it into kit production.

Peter Gowing of Essex-based Thoroughbred Cars marketed it in the UK, initially retaining the rear-mounted VW Beetle engine and mechanicals, resulting in just one sale before he swiftly amended the car to a ladderframe chassis with Cortina donor, trailing arm rear suspension, Panhard rod and a front-mounted engine. When Gowing went into liquidation in 1984 the rights to the car were taken over by agents CVC of Redditch. Resumed by Gowing under Paris Cars banner in 1985.

The traditional styling was actually very attractive and the two-seater sold well, although not as well as its 2+2 brother (see previous entry). In the late '80s and early '90s Jack Langford and Bill Herrett were responsible for marketing the cars. A Ford Sierra donor option was available from 1992.

Garry Wilson quietly resurrected the TF in 2009, developing a Vauxhall Omega-based option.

Merlin Cars 1980
Paris Cars 1985–2003
Approx 300 made

Thoroughbred Cars 1980–84
Merlin Sports Cars 2009 to date

METALINE 690

Originally based in Ascot, Berkshire, before moving to Wisbech, the 690 was created by piano tuner Howard Brooker. The Metaline was one of the better Cobra replicas, although never a volume seller, and each one was tailored to the customer's needs. Featured a semi-monocoque tub-type bodyshell mated to a semi-spaceframe chassis. Known as the Brooker 690 when sold in fully-built guise. Prior to launching his Cobra replica, Brooker was an agent for Caterham Cars, selling fully built sevens.

Arguably the first of the UK's Cobra replicas, Brooker announcing his 'replica Cobra kit' for £1,017.75 inc VAT in an advert in the Autumn 1981 issue of Peter Filby's *Kitcars & Specials* magazine, although Unique Autocraft (Pete & Mart's Rod & Custom Centre, at the time), DJ Sportscars and Beribo Replica Automobiles might also lay claim to being numero uno.

Metaline 1981–2006
Approx 25 made

MÉTISSE

The relaunched Rickman operation reused one of their famous 1960s motorcycle names for this pretty four-seater. Project acquired in 1995 by a Bridgend-based hot rod and GRP operation run by Brian Cull, Terry Coles and Jack Sayward.

A revamped Métisse II with restyled front end appeared in 2001, though the original version remained available. Coles was left on his own when first Cull and then Sayward departed.

Rickman Bros Engineering 1993–95
Métisse Cars 1995–2007
Approx 20 made

MÉTISSE PICKUP

Based on the established four-seater Métisse theme with pickup rear section created by Terry Davies.
Métisse Cars 2005–7
Approx 2 made

MEV 4x4

Beefy off-road kit based on Range Rover.
Mills Extreme Vehicles 2006–7
Approx 2 made

MEV TREK

Development of Stuart Mills' original MEV 4x4 project.
Mills Extreme Vehicles 2007
Approx 1 made

MICHALAK C7

A diminutive and superb Smart ForTwo-based roadster from well-known German tuner, Bernd Michalak. All Smart components simply fitted to the C7, which was some 170kg lighter than the donor, thus giving decent performance.

Originally marketed in the UK by Smarts R Us (who later became Road Track Race) before Bernd and wife Uther handled UK sales direct from Germany.
Smarts R Us 2006–2007
Michalak 2008-2009
Approx 3 made (UK)

MICRON GT

Brian Bray was the man behind the Micron GT, which he built with his brother, Rex. A really promising little two-seater that featured a mid-mounted Mini engine with gullwing doors and a wooden monocoque à la Marcos, clothed in a fibreglass body.
Micron Cars 1968–73
Approx 2 made

MICROPLAS

Microplas was the trading name of Micron Plastics, based in Rickmansworth with a second base in Mitcham, Surrey. They were a main protagonist in the supply of fibreglass and resin products and bodyshells during the 'specials' era. The company was run by Bill Ashton, Roger Everett, Mike Eyre and brothers, Sandy and Tony Wemyss.

MICROPLAS MISTRAL

Spring 1955 saw the introduction of Micron's second product, the Ford 10-based Mistral bodyshell. Used for the prototype Fairthorpe Electron (*qv*) in 1958.
Micron Plastics 1955–59
Approx 500 made

MICROPLAS SCIMITAR

Summer 1955 saw the arrival of the Austin 7-based Scimitar.
Micron Plastics 1955–59
Approx 40 made

MICROPLAS STILETTO

Micron's first shell was the Austin 7-based Stiletto. Many years later this shell inspired the Pilgrim Hawthorn (*qv*).
Micron Plastics 1955–59
Approx 500 made

MICROPLAS TOLEDO

Final bodyshell from Microplas, for 80–84in wheelbases, designed by Bill Ashton.
Micron Plastics 1955–59
Approx 50 made

MIDAS CARS

Harold Dermott gained a degree in mechanical engineering from Southampton University and worked at Leyland for a time, but by the late 1970s he was running D&H Fibreglass Techniques Ltd in Oldham, Lancashire. After acquiring the Mini Marcos project in 1975 he commissioned Richard Oakes to come up with a revised and revamped version to be known as the Midas.

A devastating factory fire led to the liquidation of the company in November 1989. Rights to the Midas range were bought by Pastiche Cars (who had also bought the NG marque), who relaunched the Midas Gold Convertible, albeit with a reduced specification, in February 1990. Pastiche took ten orders for the kit, but didn't supply any before they went bust in 1991.

GTM Cars of Sutton Bonington, Nottinghamshire, then picked up the NG and Midas ranges previously offered by Pastiche and relaunched them at Sandown Park Kit Car Show in August 1991. At this time GTM sold the Midas Gold to a Berlin-based college and nothing more was heard of it until the owners' club rescued it from a German warehouse in 2007, while Terry Mulloy of Midtec Sports Cars bought the Bronze project, selling it alongside the Midtec Spyder model from 1992.

GTM did much to re-establish the Midas marque during their tenure, developing new models including the 2+2 in Coupé and Convertible guises. Their custodianship ended after ten years when they sold the Midas operation to a new company based in Redditch run by Mark Bailey, who renamed the 2+2 Coupé the Cortez, while officially launching the 2+2 Convertible, rechristened Excelsior, at Donington Kit Car Show in September 2001 and continuing to offer the Gold Convertible. Bailey's operation didn't last very long and ceased trading in 2003.

Early 2004 saw the Midas marque rescued by Alistair Courtney of Alternative Cars Ltd, who has done much to re-establish the brand.

MIDAS 2+2 CONVERTIBLE

GTM Cars devised the 2+2 Convertible, although they didn't do much with it before selling the Midas range to Mark Bailey in 2001.

Bailey officially launched a lurid lime green example at the Donington Show of September 2001. Featured a cunning integral soft-top that when down was stowed away under a panel in the rear bulkhead.

When current Midas custodian Alistair Courtney took control of the project he reverted to the 2+2 Convertible moniker.
GTM Cars 2001
Midas Cars 2001–3
Alternative Cars 2004 to date
Approx 18 made

MIDAS 2+2 COUPÉ

Designed by Richard Oakes for GTM Cars in 1995. A longer and wider car but still definitely a Midas product. Could be based on Austin Metro or Rover 100 mechanicals, the latter featuring K-series power. Renamed the Cortez by Mark Bailey's Midas Cars in 2001, but his Redditch-based operation didn't last long before it ceased trading. Alistair Courtney of Alternative Cars then acquired the Midas range in spring 2004 and reverted to the 2+2 Coupé name.

GTM Cars 1995–2001
Midas Cars 2001–3
Alternative Cars 2004 to date
Approx 20 made

MIDAS COUPÉ/BRONZE/MK1/MK2

Designed by Richard Oakes and launched at the 1978 Performance Car Show. Based on Mini mechanicals, it was 20kg lighter than the donor Mini but had nearly 20 times the structural rigidity. Used Fiat 126 windscreen and Triumph TR7 rear light lenses, and is distinguishable by the Mini indicators below the separate one-piece front bumper. Often advertised as the kit car for people who didn't want a kit car!

Brabham F1 designer Gordon Murray bought one of the 57 sold. Suspension input came from ex-Lotus man Arthur Birchall, who created the McCoy (*qv*), for which Dermott made the bodies.

Murray suggested some aerodynamic alterations for what became the Mk2 version designed by Oakes in 1981, at which point the Bronze suffix was introduced along with Silver and Gold options that were dependent on what spec the car came with. The Mk2 came with a new dashboard with Austin Metro pod and bumper-mounted indicators.

Some 285 kits sold by 1992, when Midtec took over. They sold a further 20 or so.

D&H Fibreglass Techniques Ltd 1978–79
Midas Cars 1979–89
Pastiche Cars 1990–91
GTM Cars 1991
Midtec Cars 1992–97
Approx 305 made

MIDAS CORTEZ – *see Midas 2+2 Coupé*

MIDAS EXCELSIOR – *see Midas 2+2 Convertible*

MIDAS GOLD CONVERTIBLE

This one was launched at the British Motor Show in 1988 and the revisions from the Coupé were done by Steve Pearce, allegedly with a chainsaw! A very practical Midas, particularly due to the large boot, while many have been fitted with the stylish, optional hard-top.

Model was offered by Pastiche Cars when they took over the Midas marque in February 1990, although they reduced the specification offered and also left the customer with more work to do in the build, although this was all

irrelevant because although they took ten orders for the car they went bust before they could supply one!

GTM Cars rescued the Midas name and relaunched its products at the Sandown Park Kit Car Show in August 1991. The Gold Convertible model has survived to this day and remains in production.

Midas Cars 1988–89
Pastiche Cars 1990–91
GTM Cars 1991–2001
Midas Cars 2001–3
Alternative Cars 2003 to date
Approx 140 made

MIDAS GOLD COUPÉ

Designed by Richard Oakes and launched at Motorfair in London in 1985, the Mk3 Midas was now known as the Gold model and was based on a Metro donor. A modern-looking car with fresh styling it also looked bigger than its predecessors.

When GTM Cars acquired the Midas models in 1991 they sold this project to a college in Berlin. Although nothing much further was heard about it, the moulds turned up out of the blue in 2007, and the owners' club dispatched a truck to Germany to collect them and bring them home. The club now supplies bodyshells and parts for the Gold Coupé.

Midas Cars 1985–89
Approx 171 made

MIDGE

Created by Moss founder John Cowperthwaite, and constructed from plans using Medite panels. Only GRP part was the dashboard. Used Triumph Herald or Ford Escort MkII donor and was the first of his 'plan and pattern' cars.

Jim Day's Hampshire Classics bought the whole range of Moss models but didn't really do anything with them, although this changed when several members of the owners' club formed Moss Cars (Bath). When they stopped trading, T&J – run by fabricator Trevor Barnes and trimmer Josef Horvath, overseen by Trevor's wife Denise – took over, before they too ceased trading in 1993.

At this stage the project returned to John Cowperthwaite and his Real Life Toys operation, which concentrated on plan-built cars for children, such as the Mayfair Mini Land Rover. Next on the scene came White Rose Vehicles of Kent, who did a lot of marketing and show exhibiting. The company was run by John Richards. White Rose Vehicles evolved from Medway Itec Training Services (MITS), a business creation institute based in Gillingham, Kent, which was basically a job-creation scheme.

When they packed up in 2000 the Midge Owners' and Builders' Club purchased the rights to the model, and it remains available to this day albeit in a low-key way.

JC Composites 1985–87
Hampshire Classics 1987
Moss Cars (Bath) 1987–91
Real Life Toys 1991–92
T&J Sportscars 1992–93
White Rose Vehicles 1993–2000
Midge Owners' & Builders' Club 2000 to date
Approx 100 made

MIDI

A mid-engined Lotus Seven-inspired replica from MK founder Martin Keenan, based in Rotherham.
MK Engineering 2009 to date
Approx 10 made

MIDI MOKO

Another Mini Moke-type kit, this time based on Austin 1100/Morris 1300 (Allegro option), offered briefly by a company located in Camborne, Cornwall, run by Clive Dale. Looked quite convincing.
Moko Component Cars 1984–85
Approx 1 made

MIDLAND CLASSIC SEBRING SPRITE CONVERSION

A body conversion for the MG Midget that turned the donor into a more than passable evocation of the Sebring Sprite.
Midland Classic Restorations 2010 to date
Approx 5 made

MIDTEC CALICO

A modern two-seat sports car from Midtec that appeared for a time in 1993. Based on Ford Sierra, with Vauxhall Corsa lights front and rear and a backbone chassis with unequal-length double wishbones.
Midtec Sports Cars 1994–96
Approx 4 made

MIDTEC SPYDER

Never one to shy away from brave designs, Lee Noble came up with his revolutionary looking Midtec Spyder in early 1988 and based it around Ford mechanicals, although a whole host of other engines, including Renault V6, could be used. Naturally, being a Noble product, the car worked really well, although the styling wasn't to everyone's liking.

Midtec Sports Cars was the name of a new company selling Lee Noble's innovative two-seater from 1989, run by Terry Mulloy, who also ran a company in Leicester Forest East called Modern Motors Ltd. He marketed the car under the Midtec Sports Cars banner for several years before he moved on to general car sales and the manufacture of security grilles.

Ian Gray of Stuart Taylor Motorsport dusted the project down in 2001 and relaunched it with a new round-tube chassis and V-Twin bike power – either Firestorm or Honda SP1/2. In 2005 STM sold the project to Terry Francis of Midway Sports Cars in Hextable, Kent, where it resided for several years before being sold to a chap in Ireland in 2009. Its fate remains uncertain at the time of writing.
Kitdeal 1988–89
Midtec Sports Cars 1989–97
Stuart Taylor Motorsport 2001–5
Midway Sports Cars 2005–6
Approx 32 made

MILANO

Simon Hilton was born in England but emigrated to Australia with his parents in 1950. He returned to the UK with wife Joan in 1972 and started a business making four-poster beds. As a car enthusiast, he also began offering kits of his Alfa GTV-based conversion,  allegedly inspired by Pininfarina's XJS concept. Initially this was only intended to be a sideline but he went on to do quite well. His kit company S&J Motors was based in Victoria Road, Bexhill, but by the late '90s it was all over and the Hiltons had returned to Australia.
S&J Motors 1984–86
Approx 43 made

MILLE MIGLIA

Revision of YKC's Romero (*qv*), which itself was inspired by the Marlin Roadster (*qv*) that YKC had taken over in 1992. Designed by Clive Gamble. Semi-monocoque perimeter frame chassis with sealed box-section main rails. Ford Sierra running gear, with de Dion rear end with four trailing arms.
YKC Sportscars 1999–2005
Aquila Sports Cars 2005–7
Approx 25 made

MINARI CLUBSPORT

Minari Engineering were run by Sean Prendergast and Andrew Borrowman, who had graduated from Hatfield Polytechnic in 1988 and set up base in Sleighford, Staffordshire. Their first project was the ex-Aurelio Bezzi MCA Sports Coupé (qv) before they came up with their own design, the Alfa Romeo Alfasud-based Minari ClubSport (Mk1), an achingly pretty two-seater, with flip front section and a stiff GRP monocoque with steel subframe.

Borrowman and Prendergast went on to become part of the team behind the Delfino Feroce sports car with Allard Marx.
Minari Engineering Ltd 1990–2000
Minari International 2000 to date
Approx 12 made

MINARI ROADSPORT

The Mk2 or RoadSport version of the ClubSport came along in 1993 and featured a sleeker body-styling with shallower sills and wind-up windows. Retail sales were via Chameleon Sports Cars, run by John Anthistle and David Rutherford (who went on to work for Phantom Automotive). In addition to the Alfasud, customers could now also use the Alfa 33 range as donors. The car used a Mazda MX-5 windscreen wiper mechanism, while a Mazda MX-6 headlight arrangement was optional.

The Mk2 project ended up with Adrenaline Motorsport in 2006, who used it as the basis for the Subaru Impreza-based Murtaya (qv) before they passed the project on in 2008 to Paul Featherstone-Harvey's Peninsula Sportcars operation, who later also acquired Richard Stewart's post-Robin Hood Engineering Super-Snake project (qv).
Minari Engineering Ltd 1993–2000
Adrenaline Motorsport 2006–8
Peninsula Sportscars 2008 to date
Approx 130 made

MINARI RSR

Based on the Mk2 RoadSport, the RSR was a windscreen-less, stripped-out racing version of the Minari.
Minari Engineering 1997–2000
Adrenaline Motorsport 2006–8
Peninsula Sportscars 2008 to date
Approx 4 made

MINETTE

Stillborn six-seater micro city car based on Mini mechanics.
Minette Cars 1974
Approx 1 made

MINI JEM Mk1

Named after Jeremy Delmar-Morgan and sired by Dizzy Addicott's DART prototype, as was the Mini Marcos. Delmar-Morgan produced the project to become the Mini Jem in 1967 (Jem was short for Jeremy). Unlike the aluminium prototype, the body was GRP with wood and steel reinforcements in areas of stress, with a very upright windscreen. On launch it cost £10 less than the Mini Marcos, although it shared that car's Mini donor. Robin Statham took over the project in late 1967 and traded as Jem Cars.
Delmar-Morgan 1967
Jem Cars 1967–69
Approx 35 made

MINI JEM Mk2

Robin Statham's Mk2 version was launched at the Racing Car Show in January 1969. It was radically modified featuring a windscreen raked back 9in, a higher roof and no door handles. High Performance Mouldings of Cricklade took over in 1972.
Jem Cars 1969–72
High Performance Mouldings 1972–75
Approx 160 made

MINI JEM Mk3

Fourth Mini Jem custodians, Fellpoint of Salthouses, near Barrow-in-Furness, launched the Mk3 in 1975, which now featured an opening rear hatch. They also made one estate version.
Fellpoint 1975–77
Approx 150 made

MINI MALIBU

A very popular Mini conversion body kit.
Custom Cabrios 1994–99
Approx 150 made

MINI MARCOS MkI

Born, like its cousin the Mini Jem, out of ex-RAF and BOAC pilot Dizzy Addicott's DART prototype, designed with Jem Marsh's input. Launched at the 1966 Racing Car Show, the Mini Marcos featured revised styling from Brian Moulton and Quasar bicycle designer Malcolm Newell. The MkI had a GRP monocoque, Mini subframes bolted to the chassis through metal plates, and solid fixed side windows with sliding vents. Kit prices started low, so it was no surprise that it was a fairly basic machine. Its biggest claim to fame was that it was the only GB finisher at Le Mans in 1966.
Marcos Sales 1965–66
Approx 143 made

MINI MARCOS MkII

Only available very briefly in late 1966. Differed from MkI only in having aluminium window frames.
Marcos Sales 1966
Approx 4 made

MINI MARCOS MkIII

1967's MkIII was a real progression and made the already popular little car more attractive by sharpening up its looks. Came with semi-circular wheel arches, a deeper front panel, recessed fuel filler cap and an option of opening rear hatch.

Marcos went into liquidation in 1971, with the rights purchased by Fraternal Estates, owned by actor and director Richard Attenborough. One of the other companies under their umbrella was Rob Walker Garages, who ticked along until the Mini Marcos was bought by Harold Dermott's D&H Fibreglass Techniques Ltd operation.
Marcos Sales 1967–71
Approx 718 made

MINI MARCOS MkIV

The MkIV of 1974 was taller, with a longer wheelbase and a floorpan from the Mini Traveller, while the opening hatchback now came as standard.
D&H Fibreglass (became Midas Cars) 1974–81
Approx 335 made

MINI MARCOS MkV

After the disastrous fire at D&H Fibreglass, by now named Midas Cars, in November 1990 the company went into liquidation and the canny Jem Marsh regained control of the Mini Marcos, as he had inserted a clause into D&H's contract that he would get the Mini Marcos back if they ever ceased trading!

The MkV of 1991 celebrated the car's 25th anniversary and was distinguishable by wider arches that could now accept 13in wheels, a deeper front splitter, rubber-mounted subframe, push-button door handles and wind-up windows. Remained in production until Marcos Sales ceased trading in 1996.
Marcos Sales 1991–96
Approx 65 made

MINI MARCOS MkVI

A resurrection of the Mini Marcos took place under former Marcos sales manager and marque expert Rory MacMath, who under his Marcos Heritage banner launched a MkVI version in 2004. Featured new rear lights and Perspex headlight covers.
Marcos Heritage Spares 2004 to date
Approx 5 made

MINICOS

Norfolk-based styling company Auto Fashion, founded in 1993 by Phil Chapman, made over 50 different GRP conversions for the Mini including the Minicos, Magic and Animal.
Auto Fashion 1993 to date
Approx 8,000 made

MINIEXVO

Yamaha R1-powered Mini conversion from Mark Wills of Seavington St Michael, Somerset.
MINIeXvo 2007 to date
Approx 20 made

MINOS – *see Hacker Maroc*

MINOTAUR

John Forakis developed this exotic-looking original design at his Isle of Sheppey base and launched the prototype memorably at the Chatham Show of 1993, though nothing much was heard of it until its relaunch in 1998 at Donington.

Used in a Barclays TV advert and licensed to the EIG Group in 2002 with Forakis still making them, until he regained full control in 2004. In 2006 he licensed the Mk2 to Tony Holmes' Pilgrim Cars UK Ltd, before they too went into liquidation in 2009. Holmes later relaunched the car under the Vision Sportscars banner, albeit briefly.

Minotaur Cars 1993, 1998–2006
Pilgrim Cars 2006–9
Vision Sportscars 2009 to date
Approx 8 made

MINUS

Created by former Lotus engineer and Status Motor Company founder Brian Luff, but was productionised by his friend and fellow ex-Lotus employee Keith Lain. Inspired by the concept of Neville Trickett's MiniSprint, the Minus was a de-seamed, fibreglass-bodied Mini bodyshell that sat 4in lower and thus performed much better than the steel original. A Mk2 version appeared in 1987 featuring internal door hinges and a revised rear window. Project bought by 224 Engineering boss Shaun Dyson in 2005.

Minus Cars 1982–2005   Minus Cars (224) 2005 to date
Approx 230 made

MINUS MAXI

Best described as a kit version of the Talbot Rancho in concept, although definitely not a replica. It used all-Mini running gear and a GRP monocoque with steel doors. Body kits cost £995, with a £60 premium for coloured gelcoat. Taken over by Wymondham-based PSR in 1990.

Minus Cars 1985–90
PSR Fabrications 1990–93
Approx 25 made

MINUS PICKUP

A pickup version of the Minus came from Shaun Dyson in 2010. Bodies cost £3,000 and the customer just needs a Classic Mini donor vehicle.

Minus Cars 2010 to date
Approx 12 made

MIRACH

Designed as a mobile advert for his skills by former GM designer Chris Field of Totnes, Devon, and intended as a stripped-out no-frills sports car when launched at the Racing Car Show of 1989. Priorities changed when a Japanese company wanted the car for their domestic market in fully-loaded form, with full leather trim and other luxuries. Fully-built price was around £52,000.

Original version had a backbone spaceframe, Cortina uprights, Rover V8 power (250bhp) and a five-link rear axle that was quickly replaced by a double wishbone arrangement with coil-over dampers. Les Hindley, later of Stimulator Cars, welded original Mirach chassis.

Sadly, promised investment never materialised and the company ceased trading in 1991 after around ten had been sold.

One of Field's suppliers, South West Engineering, run by Jon Fallows, put together a consortium that included historic race car engineer (Lola T70s in particular) Clive Robinson, which took the project over. Indeed, it was Robinson, in his role as technical director, who suggested making it available in kit form. They also came up with a modified and stronger chassis and amended the car to run on Ford Sierra mechanicals.

Despite various efforts and pushes, the Mirach Roadster, as it ultimately became known, didn't really take off for South West Engineering, and in 2000 it was taken over by short-oval fan Rob Hancock, who worked for Fallows as a laminator. He set up base in a workshop in Wrangaton as RJH Panels & Sportscars, he ceaesd trading in 2007.

As we closed for press, Rob Hancock announced a re-birth of the Mirach under the Phoenix Automotive Developments banner, from a unit in South Brent, Devon. Maybe, this time?

Mirach Sportscars 1989–91
South West Engineering 1991–2000
RJH Panels & Sportscars 2000–7
Phoenix Automotive 2011 to date
Approx 21 made

MIRACH SC/ECU

Another Chris Field design, a futuristic two-seater christened the ECU by the ex-GM designer. Used Ford Sierra donor components. Like the Mirach (above) the ECU (intended as a *EUROPA* car) ended up under the control of Rob Hancock of RJH Panels & Sportscars, who renamed the car the SC and amended the donor to Ford Mondeo Mk2.

Utilised the donor engine, be it four or six-cylinder, which was mid-mounted transversely. Offered in kit form by Hancock.

Mirach Sportscars 1991
South West Engineering 1991–2000
RJH Panels & Sportscars 2000–2007
Approx 3 made

MIRACH eMVii

A Lotus Seven-inspired sportscar from Rob Hancock's RJH Sportscars & Panels, that was ultra lightweight at sub-500kg and based on Ford Sierra. The car shared the Mirach Roadster's inboard front suspension and independent rear suspension system, so handled very well. Power came from any bike engine, including twins, triples and in-line fours.
RJH Sportscars & Panels 2006–2007
Approx 4 made

MIRAGE COUNTACH REPLICA

Mirage Replicas based in Wellingborough was founded by former Venom boss Gary Thompson and Phil Cheetham. The latter was in sole control from 1991. They were one of the last Countach replica suppliers in the UK when they ceased trading in 2002, although the kit was kept in production by DH Supercars, run by ex-Hand Crafted Cars partner Dave Harrison and Clive Dingwall.
Mirage Replicas 1988–2002
DH Supercars 2004–7
Approx 70 made

MIRAGE M12B REPLICA

Cheshire-based Paul O'Connor announced a replica of the Mirage M12B racer in 2005, although only a prototype was made and it never went into production.
POR Fabrication 2005
Approx 1 made

MISSILE

Another stylish design from the prolific and innovative Stuart Mills. A modern take on the Lotus Seven theme underpinned by a spaceframe chassis with built-in rollbar. Donor vehicle was the Ford Focus Mk1.
Mills Extreme Vehicles 2008–10
Approx 30 made

MISSION

Fully triangulated spaceframe chassis from round and square tube. A finely-honed trackday warrior cum racer that usually featured bike power, although many other choices could be used from humble Pinto to Jaguar V8. Tom Sadler of Burnham-on-Crouch was the man behind the project, although he'd revised a former Nemesis racing project for the Mission.
T5 Developments 2002–7
Approx 12 made

MISTRAL

Ben Sparham was the man behind the exotic-looking Mistral.
BJS Motors 1985
Approx 1 made

MK1

This Austin Healey 'Frogeye' Sprite replica was STM's first model. Backbone tube spaceframe chassis developed by Ivan Gilmore of Procomp. Used a variety of proprietary parts including from a Bedford Rascal.
Stuart Taylor Motorsport 1998–99
Approx 1 made

MK BEAM-R

BMW E36-based Lotus Seven-inspired sportscar designed around 318i model, from Martin Keenan, announced just as this book went to press. Typical Keenan-innovation. One of the sharpest minds ever to grace the UK kit-car industry.
MK Engineering 2011 to date
Approx 1 made

MK CALIFORNIAN

Moke-style kit emanating from Hong Kong, imported to the UK by well-known Mini accessories company Minisport of Oldham for a time.
Minisport 2008
Approx 20 made

MK GT1

Taken over from MK Engineering by Robert Lewis of Cheshire-based Evolution Sportscars in 2003.
MK Engineering 2002–3
Evolution Sportscars 2003–4
Approx 14 made

MK GT2

Originally known as the Banshee before name changed to MK GT2. Project bought by Paul Nightingale of Spire Sportscars, who developed the car further and came up with several additional engine options including Renault and Kawasaki. He also renamed the car the Spire GTR (*qv*).

MK Engineering 2004–5
Spire Sportscars 2005 to date
Approx 70 made

MK HSR

Developed from the stillborn Sterling Roadster produced by Formula 27 Sports Cars under Steve Porter back in the late nineties. It was an Austin Healey replica. Acquired by all-round good bloke, Pat Jackson, under his DriveAction banner and developed into a doorless trackday alternative, clearly still Healey-inspired but powered by a bike engine and underpinned by an MK Indy chassis with outriggers. Marketed from 2009 as an MK product.

MK Sportscars 2009 to date
Approx 2 made

MK INDY

Created by Martin Keenan and inspired by the Ron Champion Locost book for which Martin was an official supplier of parts. First shown as a selection of parts (MK Locost) displayed on a blanket at Stoneleigh Show in 1998. Martin though, ever the innovator, enhanced the product, making it his own, based on Ford Sierra.

Project taken over by brothers Phil and Barry 'Bas' Lunn who traded as MK Sportscars in 2002, leaving Martin Keenan to concentrate on his GT1 project and a steady stream of models ever since.

The Indy has grown to become one of the foremost kit cars in the UK and MK as a company are national treasures. A multitude of engines have been used from Pinto to supercharged Suzuki Hayabusa.

MK Engineering 1998–2002
MK Sportscars 2002 to date
Approx 1,000 made

MK LOCOST

This was Martin Keenan's initial attempt at kit production, inspired by the Ron Champion *Build Your Own Sports Car for £250* book from Haynes Publishing, although soon superseded by the more sophisticated Indy (*qv*) model.

MK Engineering 1998–2007
Approx 250 made

MK TRIKE

Superb trike conversion from MK Sportscars that could give most motorcycles a three-wheel facility. The conversion was reversible and similar in style to the Grinnall and Luego bike-to-trikes.

MK Sportscars 2006 to date
Approx 100 made

ML 11

Beautiful Lotus X1 replica from aluminium body specialist Malcolm Linder of Sturminster Newton, who created a superb alloy-bodied prototype that he debuted at the Stafford kit car show in March 1999. There were plans to offer it in kit form with a

GRP body, Ford CVH power and MG Midget gearbox. He was also going to offer Ford Zetec E and bike engine versions. Proposed prices were competitive – body kit from £1,000 and chassis package from £1,400. However, after Stoneleigh 1999 nothing much more was heard from the car. One that got away, I'd say.

Zero Racing 1999–2000
Approx 1 made

MNR LMP

An enveloping-bodied version of the MNR VortX (see below), with revised chassis and bike power.

MNR Ltd 2010 to date
Approx 5 made

MNR VORTX

Father and son team Chris and Marc Nordon were behind the MNR VortX range. Marc had previously competed in the British Touring Car Championship. The VortX is available with outboard or inboard dampers and car and

bike engines, with a Mazda MX-5 option introduced in 2009 and a BMW 3-Series version from 2010.

MNR Ltd 2004 to date
Approx 160 made

MODEL A

A Ford Model A rod-style kit from Rodbodys of Three Holes, Cambridgeshire, run by Glen Whetrans. Products also sold through Mark Hempson's Fenland Rod & Custom operation.
Rodbodys 2005-7
Approx 5 made

MODEL B JALOPEE PICKUP

Hailing from Gary Janes' Bay Area Rods of Poole, the Jalopee is an innovative blend of traditional Model B and practical pickup.
Bay Area Rods 2008-9
Approx 10 made

MODULO RS1100

Wacky yet fierce three-wheeler made in Italy, and designed by Carlo Lammattina. Launched at the Geneva Motor Show of 1994. Its claim to fame is that ex-F1 world champion Nigel Mansell once owned one. The car was offered in the UK for a short while. Imported by Tarox Brakes' UK operation.
Frenitalia 1998–99
Approx 1 made (UK)

MOHAWK

Devised by Dennis Webb (short oval hot rodder) and Ian Cross (an early Dutton employee) in Bognor Regis, and was originally intended as a Lotus Elite replica. The duo wrote to Lotus, telling them what they were planning! Understandably, Lotus weren't that happy, especially as the Elite was at the time a current model, so the car was revised to distance itself, although the Elite outline could still be seen. Mike Rutherford of Mako Fibreglass did the design and GRP work. It became the RAM 4S.
Bruce Dixon (1986) Ltd 1989–92
Regis Automotive 1992–94
Approx 9 made

MOJO – *see Sylva Mojo*

MONACO

Created by aeronautical engineer Paul Bailey, who had been building special vehicles for many years including six-door Rolls-Royces, Lotus Esprit convertibles and luxurious coaches. The Monaco was a body conversion for the Jaguar XJS and similar in concept to the Banham XJSS (qv).
Paul Bailey Design 1996–2002
Approx 10 made

MONACO TS-10

Created by Peter Allen of Image Sports Cars. A bike-powered (Honda Fireblade CBR1000) two-seater very much in the style of a 1960s Formula Junior.
Image Sports Cars 2007 to date
Approx 8 made

MONGOOSE

Inspired by a 1927 Model T-type racer. Based on Ford Cortina and marketed by Terry Sands via his Muscle City company that morphed into Sandwood Automotive before merging with Terry Cook's Sheldonhurst operation. When that went pop, Sands took the Mongoose with him to his then new Alternative Vehicle Centre in Redditch. Terry says he sold 100 under the Mongoose banner, 20 at Sheldonhurst and another 50 at AVC.
Muscle City 1977–80
Sandwood Automotive 1984
Classic Reproductions 1984
Sheldonhurst 1984–85
Alternative Vehicle Centre 1985–90
Approx 170 made

MONKEYLAGO

A short-lived Murciélago replica from David Adlard of Abingdon.
Rapid Productions 2003
Approx 1 made

MONKSPATH SHIRLEY

A revised Kenmar shell taken over by Monkspath Garage Ltd of Solihull in late 1958. Based around Ford 8/10 mechanicals. The Kenmar had been built by Ken Muggleton in 1958.
Monkspath Garage Ltd 1958–61
Approx 200 made

MOONS MOKE

An, er, Moke-inspired package from a Birmingham-based company featuring an all-steel body.
GL Enterprises 1992
Approx 4 made

MORFORD FLYER

Angular and quirky three-wheeler that handled like a deity. A partnership between school teacher Peter Morley and engineer Pete Crawford, based in Whaddon, Cambridgeshire, with the company name a conflation of their surnames. Renault 5-based, with the Gordini version a favourite engine, equipped with a Jaguar spring and damper at the rear. They produced three cars in total, one of which was a Mk2 in 1995, which featured a few more curves in its aluminium body. Ugly but brilliant.

Morford Motor Company 1993–99
Approx 3 made

MOSQUITO

Created by Kidlington-based Robert Moss in 1974, the Mosquito was inspired by a fiendishly successful trials and hillclimb car built by Tony Greenwood. It was a three-wheeler based on Mini engine, gearbox and suspension with a single trailing arm and GRP body. Moss sold around six before shelving the project for several years.

The Mosquito buzzed again in 1984 after the project was sold to a motorcycle shop in Hereford run by two chaps called Mead and Tomkins, friends of Moss. They made new moulds and offered the original version of the cae, plus one with alternative rear lights and even a variant with the rear screen from a Mini acting as a windscreen (one made). Production ceased after Mr Tomkins was tragically killed in a car crash while on holiday abroad. Mead & Tomkins sold three kits during their tenure.

Once again the Mosquito project lay dormant for a time, until it came under the control of Rick Jones and Ian Bowse, trading as Malvern Autocraft, who changed its name to Triad (*qv*). The car now featured a one-piece GRP body, revised rear suspension and an exterior mounted spare wheel. They offered the Triad Sport and slightly altered Triad Warrior. By the time production ceased for the final time in 1993 a further 12 kits had been sold (nine Sports and three Warriors).

Mosquito Cars 1974–77
Mead & Tomkins 1984–87
Malvern Autocraft 1991–93
Approx 9 made (plus 12 Triads)

MOSQUITO

Mini-based utility kit produced by Chris Hollier of Ruislip, Middlesex, using a Mini front subframe at either end. Hollier, a skilled mechanic, had previously spent four years with Vulcan Engineering. He moved to Stoke Ferry, Norfolk, in the late '80s, and later co-designed the Sebring Exalt (*qv*).

C.L. Hollier Services 1989–93
Approx 3 made

MOSS CARS

John Cowperthwaite is a name that belongs right up there in the annals of UK kit car history. His car-building bug started when he turned an Austin 7 into a Midget-style *special* when he was 18. Then he moved on to MG restoration and in 1975, after getting married, turned a BMC LD30 van into a Mercedes Benz SSL. He followed this up with a special commission from a female restaurateur. Inevitably, when others saw it they wanted one, plus his beloved MG marque was dying, so he came up with the name Moss (evolved from his original Mosquito selection), under which he sold his kits commercially, as he reckoned it had the right sound to it.

Went on to sell a lot of kits over the years to a very appreciative audience. A devastating fire at the Liversedge factory in 1985 stopped production and destroyed all the moulds, although the company managed to carry on by relocating to another site. Recovery from the fire was a hard slog, but recover Cowperthwaite did, and renamed his company JC Autopatterns. John later came up with several other notable kit cars such as the Husky (*qv*) and Midge (*qv*), as well as the Real Life Toys operation.

After being briefly owned by CSA Character Cars of Radstock in 1987, Hampshire Classics of Basingstoke, run by Jim Day, took over, but didn't really do much with the projects, selling just seven kits in total.

Final custodians, from 1987 until 2000, were Moss Cars (Bath) Ltd, consisting of owners' club members David Pegler, Peter Barfield, Jenny Tarbutt and Steve Tarbutt.

Incidentally, John Cowperthwaite subsequently enjoyed a decent career performing as one half of a Country & Western duo after he sold Real Life Toys in the '90s, but Newark 2010 saw him return with a rather innovative child's race car made from MDF, a washing basket and flip-top kitchen bin, with power coming from a household drill! Plan sets cost just £15, with a DIY build cost of around £70. You can't keep a good (kit car) man down!

MOSS MALVERN

First seeing the light of day in 1983, the Malvern was a 2+2 version of the Roadster model and over the years received the same chassis updates and revisions as the two-seater.

Moss Motor Company 1983–85
Moss Sportscars 1985
JC Autopatterns 1985–87
CSA Character Cars 1987
Hampshire Classics 1987
Moss Cars (Bath) Ltd 1987–2000
Approx 500 made

MOSS MAMBA

The Mamba was inspired by the *specials*-era AKS Continental (*qv*). Based on similar underpinnings to the Moss Roadster and Malvern models, although unlike them it didn't sell like the proverbial hot cakes. Originally based around Triumph Herald/Vitesse mechanicals, with a Ford Escort-based version arriving in 1984. Moss quietly dropped the Mamba after the factory fire of 1985, but it was surprisingly resurrected by CSA Character Cars of Radstock as the Mamba Phoenix (out of the ashes?), but again didn't last long.

Moss Motor Company 1981–85
CSA Character Cars 1987
Approx 10 made

MOSS MONACO

It might have looked like a cigar and/or loose interpretation of a 1950s racing car, but you poked fun at the Moss Monaco at your peril, as a lot of kits were sold and a well-built one was a very capable device. Donor was Moss favourite Triumph Herald/Vitesse

or a separate box-section chassis for Ford Cortina mechanicals to which a simple one-piece fibreglass body (sans weathergear of any description) was bonded. Hardcore kit car motoring of the old school variety, but I guarantee there aren't many others that can provide

more fun. The author once drove a Monaco equipped with a Chevy 350 small block engine!

Moss Motor Company 1981–85
Moss Sportscars 1985
JC Autopatterns 1985–87
CSA Character Cars 1987
Hampshire Classics 1987
Moss Cars (Bath) Ltd 1987–2000
Approx 300 made

MOSS ROADSTER

The early '80s was a good time to be selling traditional 1930s roadster kits, although the established ones weren't exactly budget-orientated and John Cowperthwaite recognised the potential for such an offering. Sales of the Roadster were

good from its launch in 1981. Based on a slightly revised Triumph Herald chassis (Vitesse could be used too), although both a bespoke ladderframe and a Ford Cortina donor option were offered from 1983.

Final custodians Moss Cars (Bath) Ltd introduced an all-new Ford Sierra-based option from 1992 that was also able to accept Rover V8 engines.

Moss Motor Company 1981–85
Moss Sportscars 1985
JC Autopatterns 1985–87
CSA Character Cars 1987
Hampshire Classics 1987
Moss Cars (Bath) Ltd 1987–2000
Approx 500 made

MOTORVILLE

After Air Vice Marshal Don 'Pathfinder' Bennett, founder of Fairthorpe, died in September 1986. Father and son team Frank and Martin Collins bought the rights to the company's models from Bennett's son Torix. Indeed, Frank – who based himself in the old Fairthorpe factory in Denham – had been one of the three 'works' Fairthorpe racing drivers.

The Motorville was a resurrection of the Fairthorpe Electron Minor (*qv*) with revised styling, a semi-spaceframe chassis and a longer wheelbase. Donor was a Ford Cortina MkIII or MkIV. The standard model could accept Rover V8 power while the 'S' model was based on Ford Escort Mk2.

Motorville Watford 1987–93
Approx 12 made

MOUNTAINEER

An even more off-road-orientated version of the Mosquito (qv).
C.L. Hollier Services 1991–93
Approx 2 made

MR ED's MODEL A

It's often been claimed that Eddie Wimble was a born hot rodder. His Model A, a loose replica of a Ford 28/29 Model A Roadster, was moulded from a genuine car, one of only three in the UK at the time, although it wasn't as successful as his Model T offering. Body/chassis units cost £617 in 1979. His company was based in Streatham, South London, before moving to Brixton, West Croydon and then back to Streatham again.
Mr Ed's Specialised Auto Design 1970–82
Approx 25 made

MR ED's MODEL T

One of the pioneers of the UK kit rod movement in the seventies was Eddie Wimble, who was almost born with a copy of *Hot Rod* magazine in his hands and started playing with cars from just eight years old. From the age of 15, he was rebuilding old Ford Pops and Anglias, while preparing his own Model T rod kit, and became  known for doing a good job to a very high standard. His creation, 'The Outlaw', became a bit of a legend on the rod scene after making its debut at the Crystal Palace Hot Rod Show of February 1974.

Wimble was an engineering apprentice by day, although during his spare time he worked from a shed behind a Tulse Hill launderette. He introduced his own twin-rail chassis made from 1½in x 3in box section pig-iron. The initial idea was to produce a modified Jago body, but this didn't work out, while a Wimble-made scratch-built shell wasn't suitable either. Third time lucky saw him 'splash' a genuine 1923 Model T body, of which he offered replicas for just £30.

In late 1971 he moved to a new workshop in Brixton Hill, and again to a larger one in Streatham Hill in 1972. He moved around a lot actually, and after a spell in West Croydon he moved back to Streatham, which is where he stayed. In late 1974, Wimble took his first trip to America and did a deal to buy a new 'Fad-T' 'shell from CAL Automotive in Florida. He subsequently sold copies of it in the UK.

When things were quiet, Ed would turn his hand to glass embossing or signwriting. His attention to detail became legendary,

while he became a walking expert on the American rod scene and knew everything about Model As and Model Ts. He'd also pick up the phone and speak to famous US rod builders, such as Dan Woods and painter Art Himsl.

Basic chassis cost just £90 in 1979, with a bare body from £108. Wimble also offered a more authentic 'sectioned' version. Both were underpinned by Jaguar S-type suspension. In 1977, Mr Ed introduced a 1923–25 Model T Tudor bodyshell of which around 15 were sold.
Mr Ed's Specialised Auto Design 1970–82
Approx 75 made (including 15 Tudor bodies)

MR Z

Nissan 240/260Z-based Ferrari 250 GTO replica from Andy Turner of Billingshurst, West Sussex. Turner was a Datsun 240/260Z specialist, although his company, ACT, had originally been set up as a mechanical design office in 1969. His short-lived take on the theme could feature a revised fastback rear treatment, as an option.
ACT Engineering 1994
Approx 4 made

MR2 KITS GTA

A Ferrari F360 based on Toyota MR2. Project passed to erstwhile MR2 Kits customer and petrolhead, Steve Bicker, of Ferndown, Dorset, in April 2011, who retained the company name.
MR2 Kits 2002 to date
Approx 60 made

MR2 KITS GTB

A Ferrari F355 replica made previously by Roy Kelly Classics that was taken over by Gloucestershire-based Dave Jones of MR2 Kits in 2002. Body conversion based on Toyota MR2 Mk2.

Project passed in April 2011 to former MR2 Kits customer Steve Bicker of Ferndown, Dorset, who retained the company name.
Roy Kelly Classics 1999–2002
MR2 Kits 2002 to date
Approx 75 made

MR2 KITS GTC

A body conversion based on Toyota Celica Convertible (1994–99) and inspired by the Aston Martin Vantage. Although it was displayed on the company's stand at Stoneleigh 2010 it wasn't offered for commercial sale thereafter.
MR2 Kits 2010–11
Approx 1 made

MR2 KITS GTD

Another body conversion kit, based on Toyota Celica like the stillborn GTC but this time an all-original design.
MR2 Kits 2010–11
Approx 1 made

MR2 KITS GTF

F430-replica from David Jones' Gloucestershire operation. Again a body conversion on Toyota MR2.

Project passed to erstwhile MR2 Kits customer Steve Bicker of Ferndown, Dorset, in April 2011, who retained the company name.
MR2 Kits 2008 to date
Approx 35 made

MRF360

Originating in Germany, this F360 replica was based on Toyota MR2. Operation was an offshoot of the Dynamic Performance operation run by Mark and Robert Turner.
MR2 Tuning 2004–8
Approx 12 made

MUMFORD MUSKETEER

Three-wheeler created by trailer specialist Brian Mumford and based on Vauxhall Chevette or Viva mechanicals. An initial five-year production run didn't yield many sales but a slightly revised version was launched in 1983 and remained in production right through to 1999.
Mumford Engineering 1973–78, 1983–99
Approx 11 made

MURTAYA

Created by ex-Lotus engineer Dan Muir with Tom Taylor and Neil Yates, who formed Adrenaline Motorsport, the Murtaya (a conflation of their surnames) is a Subaru Impreza-based two-seater that used the Minari RoadSport (*qv*) as the basis of the project. Company ceased trading in 2009 after some 45 had been sold. Most were built for road use but others ended up rallying, and Adrenaline also offered a lightweight version.

Relaunched in 2010 by a new company called Murtaya Sportscars, run by Andy White and Graham Codling, and based near Exeter, Devon.
Adrenaline Motorsport 2007–9
Murtaya Sportscars 2010 to date
Approx 55 made

MUSCLE CITY COBRA

Terry Sands was behind this early UK Cobra replica dating from 1978. Body taken from the Steve Arntz US car, mated to a chassis that Sands had already designed and MGB running gear.
Muscle City 1978–79
Approx 82 made

MUTANT 4x4

Kevin Dempsey, located in Ashford, Middlesex, created the rugged and funky Mutant 4x4, derived from a Dakar and based on Land Rover Discovery.
Mutant 4x4 2009 to date
Approx 2 made

MYSTIQUE

Alex Thompson built this BMW M1 replica powered by Rover V8. Stillborn.
Mystique Cars 1985
Approx 1 made

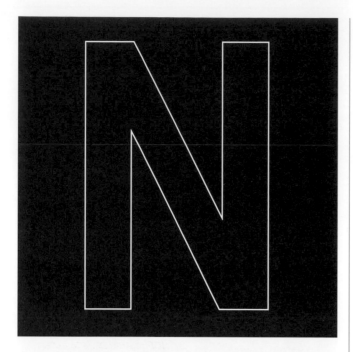

NAVAJO

An Austin 1100/Morris 1300-based utility made from a sheet steel 18-gauge Zintec monocoque rather than a tubular steel chassis. It featured an 1100/1300 subframe at the front, with modified trailing arms and coil-overs replacing the Hydrolastic suspension. The bonnet was the only GRP item. Kits cost £995 including VAT. Maker Alan Langridge's company was based in the Super Shell Building at Goodwood motor racing circuit that was later occupied by JPR Cars. Langridge had previously run well-known Formula Ford 1600 manufacturer, Image Race Cars (1969–82) and had also built a replica of Bertone's Carabo sportscar concept, complete with rear-mounted BL Mini engine.
Langridge Developments 1982–86
Approx 20 made

NAYLOR 1700 TF

Well-known MG restoration company Naylor Brothers (founded by Alistair and David in 1966) launched their own MG TF replica in the summer of 1984. The Naylor version was a top quality, hand-built, type-approved car (from March 1985) based on the Morris Ital, and cost from £13,000. It

was well received but ultimately proved to be too expensive and the company went into liquidation in July 1986 after around 100 were sold.

The project was rescued by chartered engineer Maurice A. Hutson, chairman of heavy engineering company Mahcon Group, who specialised in dock plant and quarry equipment. He installed his son Mark as MD of the newly formed Hutson Motor Company and renamed the car the 1700 TF.

They kept the fully-built version, now priced from £15,000, retaining its hand-built nature and the ash-over-steel tub, but also introduced a kit package that could be based on Marina instead of Ital if the customer preferred. This was launched at the Newark Show of 1986 and was slightly simplified by using the Marina's semi-elliptic springs and Armstrong dampers, although the fully-built version's set-up of Ital live axle, located by four trailing links and Panhard rod tweaked by none other than Lotus, was an option. They sold a further 61 examples.
Naylor Brothers plc 1985–86
Hutsons Motor Company 1986
Approx 161 made

NC1000 COUPÉ

A superb 'continuation' model of the Ogle SX1000 from Nostalgia Cars (UK) Ltd, and based on Classic Mini.
Nostalgia Cars UK Ltd 2006 to date
Approx 10 made

NCF BLITZ

Fiat 126-based single-seater styled around the off-road rail theme, from NCF Motors' Nick Findeisen, who utilised a scrap Fiat 126 for donor duties. Although a single-seater, the Blitz captured people's imagination very quickly and sold in good numbers. One of the reasons for the switch to a Mini-base for the Blitz 2 (see below) was because it was becoming easier to find a mini than a Fiat donor!
NCF Motors 1996–98
Approx 400 made

NCF BLITZ 2

Mini-based version of original Fiat-based Blitz with two seats and Mini subframe for mid-mounted engine configuration. Sold well, but although still available sensibly-priced Mini donors are getting harder to find.
NCF Motors 1998 to date
Approx 200 made

NCF BLITZ 4x4

A Blitz with four-wheel drive, meaning this one really can go anywhere. Based on Suzuki SJ.
NCF Motors 2001 to date
Approx 50 made

NCF DIAMOND Mk1

Nick Findeisen's first model and a mightily popular one. A kit car enthusiast, he'd originally intended to build a two-seater sports car but he saw that the '80s market was flooded with them so he fortuitously settled on the rugged, hugely practical Diamond, which was a rarity in that it was a kit car with a metal body and was Ford Cortina-based. All the hard work was done for the customer, as doors, bonnet and tailgate were all gapped and pre-hung. One of the milestone kit cars. Also offered a 4x4 version based on Toyota Hi-Lux but only a handful were made, while a Sierra 4x4-based Diamond remained a one-off.
NCF Motors 1985–90
Approx 300 made

NCF DIAMOND Mk2

With Cortinas beginning to get scarce, Nick Findeisen shifted to Ford Granada Mk2 for the second generation Diamond. At the same time he introduced a bigger, squarer body.
NCF Motors 1990–93
Approx 250 made

NCF DIAMOND Mk3

The Mk3 Diamond remained Ford Granada Mk2-based but now featured the donor's curved windscreen and shorter tail, giving a smoother appearance. The burgeoning success of the newly introduced Blitz put paid to Diamond production before a planned Mk3 Granada Scorpio version could be unveiled.
NCF Motors 1993–96
Approx 150 made

NCF OUTBAK

A rugged, typically beefy product from Nick Findeisen, the Outbak is based on Suzuki Vitara.
NCF Motors 2005 to date
Approx 110 made

NCF ROAD RAT

The least popular of NCF's models, the Road Rat was based on Fiat Panda mechanicals.
NCF Motors 1994–95
Approx 5 made

NCF TORINO

Coming on like a scaled-down Diamond, the Torino used a modified Road Rat chassis. Fiat Panda-based.
NCF Motors 1995–97
Approx 30 made

NCF TRAKA

A large, rugged, go-anywhere kit from NCF Motors based on Range Rover Classic.
NCF Motors 2004 to date
Approx 75 made

NCF SAHARA

Taking advantage of the huge amount of forlorn Land Rover Discovery Mk1s around that were scruffy visually, yet bombproof under the skin, the Sahara is the latest model from NCF and a natural successor to the Diamond.
NCF Motors 2008 to date
Approx 75 made

NCK HORNET

Production version of Keith Wilkinson-Hawley's KNW II (*qv*) special taken over by Doug Pinchin of North Shields-based Northern Car Kits, who later moved to Ponterwyd, Wales.
Northern Car Kits 1985–87
Approx 1 made

NELSON 350F

Created by Bryce Nelson in Shepperton, Middlesex, the 350F was a nicely made big old '50s-inspired sports-racer type hindered by the need for two donors – a Rover SD1 and Jaguar XJ6.
Nelson Motors 1989–94
Approx 12 made

NEMESIS

Heavily Italian-inspired supercar from RV Dynamics, run by Essex-based Roy Sellwood and Vince Wright. Sellwood departed after a couple of years.
RV Dynamics 1995–2005
Approx 7 made

NEWARK LANDAULET

Traditionally styled saloon.
Fleur de Lys 1992–93
Approx 8 made

NEWARK VAN

Traditionally styled van range.
Fleur de Lys 1983–94
Approx 7 made

NG CARS

Founded in 1979 by Nick Green, who had a degree in Mechanical & Aeronautical Engineering and Design from Hatfield Polytechnic. He was a real car enthusiast, especially for MGs, and was pretty taken with the Arkley SS, of which he built quite a few examples, several of which were used by John Britten Garages as demonstrators. He was an MGB fan in particular, and used one as his daily driver, so it was logical that he'd build his car business around that donor. His company was initially called NCG Design (Nick's initials) before changing to NG Cars.

NG owner and club member Peter Fellowes, who had bought a TA kit in 1986, liked the product so much that he ended up buying the company. His day-job was as a training manager for a big retailer. He initially acquired the TA – setting up the TA Motor Company in the process – before taking over the whole range, trading as Pastiche Cars, when Nick Green wanted to relinquish control to return to Southampton University to do a postgraduate degree.

At the time MGBs were quite hard to source and in Fellowes' view too expensive, so he set about revising the range to accept Ford Sierra mechanicals (Cortina could also be used), renaming the models at the same time.

Pastiche crashed in 1991 and the range went to GTM Cars, who re-engineered the models and restored the marque's reputation.

In 1993 another enthusiastic NG owner, John Hoyle, based in Epsom, Surrey, took over the reins and immediately reverted to MGB mechanicals, dropped the TA model, and set about passionately putting the NG marque back on track. However, since he wanted to concentrate on his excellent MGB suspension conversion kits that he had developed in association with Gerry Hawkridge, he sold NG in 2000 to Derek Smith of IGI, who ceased trading in 2002. Current custodian Nigel Brooks of Findhorn Cars, a patent attorney, acquired the marque in the same year.

NG SEDAN

Once Nick Green had sold the main NG product range to Peter Fellowes, he turned his attention to developing the Sedan model. Green was going to offer the first 20 in kit form before offering it as a fully-built, type-approved vehicle.

The Sedan was based on Rover SD1, as NG's traditional and beloved MG donor was beginning to increase in value at the time. The flowing, fixed-head body was underpinned by a cruciform-type chassis in 100mm x 50mm steel. The prototype had a hand-rolled aluminium body, although the intention was to offer GRP as an option on production versions. Rover SD1 supplied a variety of components, including the live rear axle that also featured trailing arms and a Watts linkage for lateral location. Fully-built car prices were announced as £24,150 for the straight-six 2.6-litre version and £29,900 for the full-hit 3.5-litre V8.

An eagerly awaited car at the time, although sadly, despite several attempts, the Sedan didn't reach production.
NG Cars 1988–89
Approx 1 made

NG SPEEDWELL SPECTRA

Not really an NG product at all, preceding that company's formation by a couple of years. Nick Green was originally an agent for John Britten Garages' Arkley SS and initially traded as the Speedwell Motor Company from his New Milton base in Hampshire.

The MG Midget enthusiast described his Spectra model as a 'customisation' job on a standard car that saw the front bodywork ditched and replaced by a beefier, GRP flip-front. A nice conversion, but at £1,200 it was expensive compared to the Arkley's new front-end price of £360! Nick soon moved on to the MGB-based NG Cars range. Briefly reappeared under the Spectra Cars banner in May 1985 from a London-based company.
NG Cars 1979–83   *Spectra Cars 1985*
Approx 10 made

NG TA

Inspired by the Aston Martin International, although not a replica, and along with the Marlin Roadster (*qv*) was the first period-correct traditional roadster kit. Sold 50 in 11 months in 1980. A revised Mk2 version appeared in 1985.

Project was sold in 1987 to erstwhile NG customer Peter Fellowes, who named his new venture TA Motor Company, moving from the home counties to Rotherham, South Yorkshire. Became the Pastiche Motor Company in 1989, who renamed it the Pastiche International (*qv*). Reverted to NG TA name under GTM Cars' ownership.
NG Cars 1979–87   *TA Motor Company 1987–89*
Pastiche Motor Company 1989–91 *GTM Cars 1991–93*
Approx 410 made

NG TC

Aston Martin Ulster-inspired traditional roadster with pretty 'boat-tail'. Quite a milestone kit car, the TC. A lithe roadster with sexy styling and a pitch-perfect build quality. Where the TA was inspired by the Aston Martin International, the TC lightly echoed the same manufacturer's Ulster model. Under Pastiche ownership it briefly became the Pastiche Gladiator (*qv*).

When GTM took over the bulk of the NG range, after the demise of Pastiche in 1991, they retained/reinstated the MGB mechanics but also introduced a Morris Marina donor option for the TC.

NG Cars 1982–89
Pastiche Motor Company 1990–91
GTM Cars 1991–93
NG Cars 1993–2000
NG Cars (IGI Group) 2000–2
Findhorn Cars 2002 to date
Approx 400 made

NG TC V8

Also known as the TCR. When it first appeared, the Rover V8-powered TC V8 set the kit car world alight. Lower, shorter and chest-beating, it enjoyed decent success in the 750 Motor Club's Kit Car Challenge series in the '80s.

NG Cars 1981–89
Approx 10 made

NG TD

The least successful mainstream NG model, the TD was effectively a 2+2 version of the popular TC, though as a result of the extra seating capability it lost the distinctive and pretty boat-tail rear end.

NG Cars 1983–89
Pastiche Motor Company 1989–91
GTM Cars 1991–93
NG Cars 1993–2000
NG Cars (IGI Group) 2000–2
Findhorn Cars 2002 to date
Approx 100 made

NG TF

The graceful flowing wings of the TF caught the public's imagination and it went on to become the biggest-selling NG model by a large margin. Just prior to selling the range to Pastiche Cars, Nick Green came up with a Ford Cortina/Sierra-based version of the TF that he named the (Pastiche) Henley (*qv*), while the original MGB-based car became the Pastiche Ascot (*qv*). They also introduced a Marina donor option. When John Hoyle took over the marque in 1993 he introduced a Rover V8-powered option and reverted to the TF model name.

NG Cars 1983–89
Pastiche Motor Company 1989–91
GTM Cars 1991–93
NG Cars 1993–2000
NG Cars (IGI Group) 2000–2002
Findhorn Cars 2002 to date
Approx 1,200 made

NG TS

When patent-attorney and MG enthusiast Nigel Brooks took over the NG marque he was aware that he needed to address the relative lack of cockpit width in the NG range, so he came up with the TS, a TC with an extra 4in of room across the car.

Findhorn Cars 2004 to date
Approx 2 made

NG TOURER

While the industry was keenly awaiting the trumpeted NG Sedan (*qv*), Nick Green surprised everyone with the announcement of his four-seat Tourer model, which came after he had sold the previous range of NG models to Peter Fellowes of Pastiche.

The Tourer was very much in the style of a traditional-type NG, although had an extra row of seats and thus was more practical. It was also notable for being based on Ford Sierra, as Nick's usual choice of MG donor had seen rising prices in the late eighties.

The Tourer was underpinned by an all-new MIG-welded cruciform chassis, with independent suspension all round, including the Sierra's solid-mounted differential, with double-jointed half-shafts and twin semi-trailing arms. The front suspension was a combination of upper rocker arm and wishbones. For whatever reason, the Tourer didn't really catch on.

In 2004, Nigel Brooks' Findhorn Cars would revisit the concept of a four-seat, larger NG model with their TS.

NG Cars 1988
Approx 1 made

NG TYCOON

Although this was actually Nick Green's project at university he did put the mid-mounted Rover V8 coupé into production briefly prior to the Speedwell Spectra and TA.
NG Cars 1979
Approx 1 made

NICKRI ALPINE

Launched in spring 1960, the Alpine had the added sophistication of a reinforcing frame structure for the bodyshell, which added extra strength and rigidity. Looked quite similar to the TWM 'shell. Makers Nickri Laminates were based in Romford, Kent.
Nickri Laminates 1960–61
Approx 50 made

NICKRI CHALLENGER

By now, in addition to the standard fare bodyshell for Ford 8 and 10, Nickri could offer a bespoke Belford ladderframe chassis that was designed to accept Ford E93A components.
Nickri Laminates 1961–62
Approx 50 made

NICKRI CHAMPION

A four-seater launched in 1962 that had a similar specification to the Alpine.
Nickri Laminates 1962–63
Approx 25 made

NICKRI EXCELL

The first model from Nickri Laminates, and if you were a reader of *Car Mechanics* magazine in its inaugural year of 1958 you might remember seeing a build series feature. Based around the Ford 8 and 10 it was quite a sophisticated shell for its time, complete with (almost unheard of for 1958) returned edges on the fibreglass. Nickri claimed that it could be fitted to your ratty Ford chassis in less than a minute! Quite a claim.
Nickri Laminates 1958–59
Approx 100 made

NICKRI SPYDER

Nickri Laminates followed up the Excell with the Spyder, which was effectively a Mk2 Excell. Included several amendments.
Nickri Laminates 1959–60
Approx 250 made

NIFTY

Unveiled at the Stoneleigh Show of 1984, the Nifty was an obscure Mini-based estate-style kit.
Nifty Cars 1984
Approx 1 made

NIMBUS COUPÉ

Imp-based two-seater designed by Ian Shearer and financed by Ian McClean. The Nimbus was actually quite advanced for its time, with a GRP monocoque with a balsa/Kevlar® sandwich in places of stress. Used Ford Escort Mk2 windscreen and VW Scirocco headlights. Reputedly quite difficult to build. Niall Johansson, future MD of Swindon Sportscars, raced one in the mid-'80s.

Ian Shearer departed in 1986 to work on his Boxer Sprint (*qv*) project, and Anthony Coleman of body-makers Custom Moulds took over. Tragedy struck later in 1986 when Ian McLean sadly died, and a proposed McLean Convertible was stillborn. Nimbus faded away in early 1987.
Nimbus Projects Ltd 1984–86
Custom Moulds 1986–87
Approx 24 made

NIMROD

Illustrator Mike Jupp was commissioned to design a car in 1969 by Ray Jay, who built the prototype and funded the project. The result was a wild-looking creation called the Nimrod that featured a Mini front subframe and trailing arm rear suspension underpinned by a spaceframe chassis. The rollbar was made from bent scaffold tubing, and the chassis featured a plywood floor with Hillman Hunter headlights.

Just before its intended launch in 1972 Jay pulled out, so it was produced by Mike Jupp alone, trading as Nimrod Engineering. He sold five kits before laying the project to rest pretty quickly.

It rose from the ashes in 1979 revived (albeit very briefly) by Vic Elam, also marketing the Nova (*qv*) at that time. Nigel Talbott of TACCO (Talbott Alternative Car Company) resurrected it again in 1981, selling a further ten kits over the next six years.

Westbury-based Marcos GRP maker Fibreglass Applications, run by Pat Cuss, had been making the Nimrod bodies for TACCO, and they took over production in 1986.
Nimrod Engineering 1972–73
Nova Cars 1979
TACCO 1981–86
Fibreglass Applications 1986–88
Approx 15 made

NOBLE 23

Originally marketed by Shapecraft, Lee Noble acquired the project in 1988. Noble himself raced a 325bhp V6-powered version with some success. Project passed to Colin Strauss' Auriga Developments and subsequently became the Mamba C23 (*qv*).
Kitdeal 1987–90
Auriga Developments aka Espero Ltd 1990–2000
Mamba Motorsport 2000 to date
Approx 100 made (includes Noble and Mamba sales)

NOBLE Mk4

Lee Noble replica with superb aluminium bodies available from Clive Smart of Shapecraft. Moved on to Deon briefly before ending up at NF Autos, where Neil Foreman further developed the car and made another 55.

Noble Motorsport 1987–92   Deon Cars 1992–95
AJ Performance Cars 1995   NF Auto Developments 1995–2008
Dunlop Systems & Components 2008 to date
Approx 250 made

NOBLE M10

Lee Noble's tenth design and thus M10. Also his last project available in kit form. Superb two-seater powered by mid-mounted Ford Zetec E. Later reworked as the fully-built only M12 GTC.
Noble Moy Automotive 1997–99
Approx 32 made

NOBLE MOTORSPORT – *see Ultima Sports*

NODDI – *see Sun Roadster*

NORDEC

Nordec (a conflation of North Downs Engineering Company) was set up by former Convair co-founder Clive Wrenn (based in Cathall Street, Leytonstone) from a Surrey base in Whyteleafe. Same shell as brother Terry's TWM operation but also offered in kit form with LMB split beam axles and a supercharged Ford engine.

In the late 1940s Nordec had also produced a trials car that didn't sell more than a handful (bettered by the Dellow in every way, including price). They also made Leslie Ballamy's (LMB) IFS split front axle, so beloved by many *specials* builders of the day, and also a supercharger kit.
North Downs Engineering Company 1959–61
Approx 2 made

NORTHLIGHT K4

Justin Gudgeon bought the GTM Rossa K3 project (*qv*) in 2003, heavily revised it and renamed it the K4. It featured twin headlights, a deeper front splitter, a new dash and MGF componentry. Wasn't around for long. Gudgeon was located in Cornhill-on-Tweed, Northumberland. He had formerly worked for Perkins and also fibreglass company Specialised Mouldings.
Northlight Sportscars 2003–4
Approx 1 made

NOSTALGIA C-TYPE REPLICA

After the success of their XK120 and XK140 replica, Nostalgia Cars UK Ltd launched their take on the Jaguar C-type, based on big cat mechanicals from the XJS or XJ6. Featured a GRP body as standard, but an aluminium option was available. Company acquired by mother and son team Heather and Matt.
Nostalgia Cars UK Ltd 2004 to date
Approx 25 made

NOTA FANG

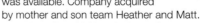

Should really be appearing in an A–Z of Australian kit cars book (now there's a spin-off idea!), *but* the Nota Fang was designed by an English ex-pat named Guy Buckingham, who sold two kits in the UK when he briefly returned to his homeland in 1972. He had emigrated to Australia in the early '50s and had set up Nota Cars, enjoying much success on the race track with a succession of models. The Fang was launched in Australia in 1969 and continues in production there today.
Nota Cars 1972
Approx 2 made (UK)

NOVA

An incredibly swoopy design from ex-Davrian Cars employee and Tramp beach buggy designer Richard Oakes, in association with Phil Sayers. Despite the exotic styling the Nova was based on VW Beetle floorpan and mechanicals with entry/exit via a clamshell canopy-type affair.

Prior to production, Oakes' as then unnamed prototype had received rave reviews from *Hot Car* magazine, while it was later described by *Autocar* as 'the most beautiful car in the world'. A legendary kit car, for sure.

Automotive Design & Development Ltd was based at John Willment's shipyard in Woolston, and in an area where boat-building was such a big business it wasn't hard to find quality laminators. The first Nova bodies were made by perhaps the greatest UK fibreglass artisan of all time, the late John Ingram, who went on to form Domino Cars with John Chapman.

Oakes and Sayers had sold 130 kits by the time they moved to Accrington in January 1974. Sadly, the company went into liquidation in 1975.

The project then ended up with a Bradford chap called Neil McManus (also known as Noel Redding – no, not the bass player with the Jimi Hendrix Experience!), who had acquired the moulds, but they remained unused until 1979 when haulage contractor Vic Elam took them over and put the car back into production.

Elam introduced the 'Nova Bermuda' version in 1984, which had a removable roof section and a variety of body modifications. It became known as the Nova S2. Elam initially traded from a garage in Queensbury using the existing moulds, before he outgrew that and moved to bigger premises in Ravensthorpe, before finally relocating to a former Datsun dealership in Mirfield.

After Elam's tenure, the Nova headed south to Leigh-on-Sea-based Graham Slayford, although he ceased production in 1991, leaving the Nova unavailable until it came under the control of Cornishman Sam Cobley of Newquay and his wife Lynne, who purchased the project from Slayford's GRP laminators Vanguard. The Cobleys did a lot to put the Nova back on the map, develop the kit, and help with parts supply. Sam Cobley had previously worked at American kit car manufacturer Exotic Coachcraft in San Diego, incidentally.

Cobley advertised the project for sale in late 1996 and it was purchased by a Brentford company called Aerotec, run by Shashi Vyas, who relaunched the car as the Nova 3000, with Ford underpinnings, at Stoneleigh in May 1997. Proposed kit price was £3,300. Nothing more was heard from them. Thankfully the owners' club is very enthusiastic and can supply most of the tricky parts specific to the car, such as the roof system.

The Nova is the most licensed kit car of all time, known by a variety of names around the world, including Sterling and Sovran (USA), Defi (France), Totem and Puma (Italy), Tarantula (Zimbabwe), Purvis Eureka (Australia), Ledl (Austria) and Gryff (Switzerland).

Automotive Design & Development Ltd 1971–75
Nova Cars Ltd 1977–79 (Bradford)
Nova Cars Ltd 1979–82 (Dewsbury)
Nova Sports Cars Ltd 1982–90
Nova Kit Cars 1990–91
Nova Developments 1994–97
Aerotech Engineering Ltd 1997
Approx 503 made (UK)

NU-SNAKE/SUPERSNAKE

Created by Robin Hood Engineering founder Richard Stewart in 2007. After he had sold the RHE marque, the Nu-Snake was his take on a modern-day interpretation of the Cobra that also had elements of 'Big' Healey in the mix. Based on floorpan of Ford Mondeo Mk2 and utilised much of the donor. Sold to Cornwall-based Peninsula Sports Cars run by Paul Featherstone-Harvey in 2008 who changed the name to Supersnake.

Richard Stewart 2007–8
Peninsula Sports Cars 2008 to date
Approx 2 made

NYMPH

Clever little concept created by Peter Bohanna and Robin Stables, who had previously designed the car that became the AC ME3000 and also the Austin Maxi-powered Diablo. This Hillman Imp-based utility appeared in kit form in 1976 after a proposed deal for 5,000 units with Chrysler fell through.

Stables worked from a barn next to his house in Cadmore End, Buckinghamshire, and created the styling for the Nymph in September 1975, using a £35 MoT failure Hillman Imp as the donor, while also moulding its floorpan. The first demo car was finished in a lurid light green.

The Nymph was underpinned by a GRP monocoque, and Bohanna Stables took the plunge after the Chrysler deal went south and marketed the car themselves, commissioning an Essex boat-building company to produce their bodies, which actually turned out to be of poor quality, so production was switched to Specialised Mouldings, although these were deemed too heavy! Stables was able to do his party trick at shows, however, of jumping up and down on the body to prove its strength. This was a gimmick pioneered earlier by Giles Smith of Gilbern.

A move to larger premises didn't last long, especially after several customers complained that their bodies were either too thin or too hefty, so they moved back to Stables' barn, although within eight weeks they had upped sticks again and moved into a 5,000sq ft premises in Checkendon. As a result, kit prices rose from £378 to £632.50.

Things were looking good until Bohanna left, so it was back to Cadmore End, AGAIN!

You probably won't be surprised to find out that Stables moved to Beaconsfield in December 1976, at which point orders had dried up, despite a high profile appearance at the National Custom Car Show at Olympia in January 1977, although this didn't run at all smoothly because the new demo was two days late turning up!

The Nymph story, as far as Robin Stables was concerned, ended in April 1977, although a potentially life-saving order of 25 Nymphs for a Barbadian hire car operator arrived two weeks after Stables shut the doors! A cruel twist of fate…

A capable little car all the same.

Bohanna Stables 1976–77
Approx 34 made (plus 25 not delivered)

NYVREM NIRVANA

Created by a bloke called Mervyn Edwards, who spelt his first name backwards to get Nyvrem! Featured Cortina running gear and was the culmination of a lifelong ambition by Edwards to build his own dream car, fuelled by his dissatisfaction with proprietary kits on the market at the time. Ian and Michael Hayles helped Edwards build the prototype and the first production car.

Nyvrem Cars 1987
Approx 2 made

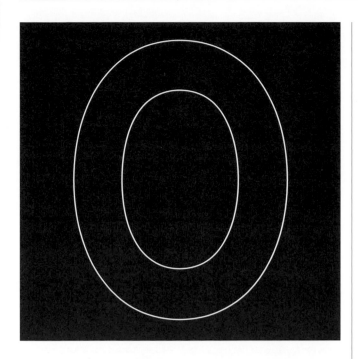

O&C SERAC

Adventurous model from Ruth Oldham and Martin Crowther, formerly known as WV Engineering.
Oldham & Crowther Engineering 1988
Approx 1 made

O&C SERAC SS

Ambitious project from O&C based around Toyota twin-cam, this coupé never reached production.
Oldham & Crowther Engineering 1989
Approx 1 made

O&C SONNET

A revision of the Sport theme (see next entry). More aggressive styling.
Oldham & Crowther Engineering 1985–88
Approx 5 made

O&C SPORT

The first model from Oldham & Crowther and one of the first replica Lotus Seven-inspired kits available in the UK. Not the prettiest car maybe, but O&C's products were fiendishly capable on the track and did well in the 750 Motor Club's Kit Car Challenge series during the '80s. Especially potent in the hands of Heather MacAlpine née Baillie. Customers could choose from one of four donor packages – Morris Marina, Morris Minor, Toyota Carina or Toyota Corolla.
Oldham & Crowther Engineering 1984–88
Approx 17 made

O&C SPRINT

The Sprint was a mix of Lotus Seven-inspired sports car and traditional roadster. Donor choice was the same as the Sport, and customers could have either cycle or clamshell-type wings. Eschewed with fibreglass as the body was a steel monocoque affair.
Oldham & Crowther Engineering 1984–88
Approx 110 made

O&C SUPER SPORT

Very similar to Sport model (see above), despite O&C making some wildly grand claims in their publicity blurb that it belonged in the exotic car category. Featured revised front wings and Rover V8 power, and actually worked pretty well.
Oldham & Crowther Engineering 1985–88
Approx 8 made

O&C THRUXTON

Out and out racer, although could also be used on public roads, as with all O&C products. No donor vehicle for this one and any engine could be fitted up to Rover V8, while it had a pressed steel body/chassis monocoque. Were any sold?
Oldham & Crowther Engineering 1985–88
Approx 1 made

OASIS SCORPION – see El Cid

ODYSSIS F328

American-made Ferrari 328 body conversion on Pontiac Fiero that was imported to the UK very briefly by Alan Currall of Odyssis Designs.
Odyssis Designs 1997-98
Approx 1 made

ODYSSIS F512

Ferrari 512 replica imported from America by Kettering-based Odyssis Designs.
Odyssis designs
Approx 1 made

ODYSSIS FF110

A Bugatti EB110 approximation imported to the UK by Odyssis Designs.
Odyssis Designs 1997-98
Approx 1 made

ODYSSIS F-GT

A Ferrari F355 replica from the mile-long catalogue of Kettering-based Odyssis Designs. Sold in the late nineties.
Odyssis Designs 1997-98
Approx 1 made

ODYSSIS HURRICANE

American Dodge kit imported to the UK briefly by Odyssis Designs of Kettering, run by Alan Currall.
Odyssis Designs 1997-98
Approx 1 made (UK)

ODYSSIS McLELA

American VW Beetle-based McLaren F1 replica imported to the UK briefly in the late '90s.
Odyssis Designs 1997-98
Approx 1 made (UK)

ODYSSIS PHANTOM

Dutch-made Diablo replica that was imported here briefly by Odyssis Designs.
Odyssis Designs 1997-98
Approx 1 made (UK)

OMATIC AMARILLO

Appearing in 2001, the Omatic was a mysterious product with Spanish origins from an Ely, Cambridgeshire, operation backed by a group of trackday enthusiasts, but rumoured to have been designed by a famous racing car designer. Wasn't around very long but the Amarillo claimed to bring a new dimension to the Lotus Seven-inspired concept. Featured an aluminium chassis and a Daewoo engine. Build costs were claimed to be low budget, but high quality. Big plans claimed that servicing would be available at Honda and Vauxhall dealers. Nothing came of it, despite the pre-launch fanfare.
Omatic 2001
Approx 1 made

OMATIC ANARANJADO

Similar to the other models in the range but featured a Honda VTEC engine producing 240bhp sourced from an S2000.
Omatic 2001
Approx 1 made

OMATIC AZUL

Revised body styling but sharing the same engine and power output as the Omatic Verde.
Omatic 2001
Approx 1 made

OMATIC ROJO

Honda VTEC power for the race-orientated model of the Omatic range. Fully-built prices around £30,000 in 2001.
Omatic 2001
Approx 1 made

OMATIC VERDE

Entry-level Omatic product with 110bhp Vauxhall XE unit and a sub-£9,000 price tag.
Omatic 2001
Approx 1 made

ONYX SPORTSCARS

Onyx founder David Golightly did an engineering apprenticeship with the electricity board, which regularly involved scratch-making all sorts of obsolete parts, including ad hoc specialist vehicles to enable access to remote pylons and other equipment.

He also started a bit of rallying and auto-testing with a fellow apprentice. He then opened his own garage repair business with a definite leaning towards motorsport. He competed in the British National Rally Championship in 1977 in Group A and was runner-up in a self-prepared Hillman Avenger. As part of his prize, the following season saw him running a then new Sunbeam donated by Chrysler's Competition Department.

A passion for auto-testing led to an association with dentist David Rivet, who knew Bill Last, founder of Viking Minisport and a TVR specialist. The pair were twice runners-up in the national championship. This led to David coming up with his own car and his own company, Onyx Sportscars, based in his home town of Grimsby. The company name was chosen by David Rivet's daughter Pamela.

A move to new premises in Scunthorpe in 1995 boded well, although a devastating fire soon after tested David's resolve to the limits. Undaunted, he shifted production temporarily to southern agent Alan Fereday's base in Hartley Wintney, Hampshire, until a new HQ back in Grimsby was ready. In recent years David, an affable and talented chap, has teamed up with Carla Smith.

ONYX BOBCAT

Based on the concept of one of David Golightly's auto-test cars, the Bobcat replaced the Onyx Tomcat (*qv*) in 1998. Like the Tomcat it used Mini mechanicals, although instead of using the subframes David created a spaceframe chassis from 25mm square 16-gauge ERW steel tube. Had a narrow-track rear end, which meant that the car could be a four- or three-wheeler.
Onyx Sportscars 1998–2001
Approx 60 made

ONYX FASTCAT

Similar to the Onyx Firefox (*qv*), again using Metro/Rover 100 mechanicals, but featured more bodywork and thus more practicality.

Onyx Sportscars 2004–6
Approx 4 made

ONYX FIRECAT

Joining the Firefly (see next entry) in 1993 was the bigger yet similarly styled Firecat, which retained the Fiat donor, but this time used Uno parts. It is one of the most capable kit cars that this author has ever driven.

Came under the control of Steve Rose of RPM Sportscars from Ringwood, Dorset, who created a revised version based on Fiat Seicento donor, although illness forced the sale of the project. Purchased by Wojcech Pajer from Poland, who intends to finish off RPM's upgrades and to return the car to the market.
Onyx Sportscars 1993–2000
RPM Sportscars 2008–9
Pajer Engineering & Media 2010 to date
Approx 51 made

ONYX FIREFLY

David Golightly's first car, based on Fiat Panda mechanicals that he reasoned were affordable, robust and capable, this stylish two-seater was launched in 1990. Onyx sold 54 examples. The project was then acquired by erstwhile Firecat customer John

Laking, who set up Formby Kit Cars to market them and sold a further three before he moved to Spain.

After several years, the project was picked up by kit car enthusiast Trevor Rolph of Dart Cars, who made one before selling it on to Dutch company Alphax Kit Cars, run by Geert Swan, who lasted a couple of years before moving to pastures new.

Onyx Sportscars 1990–98　　*Formby Kit Cars 1998–2000*
Dart Cars 2005–6　　*Alphax Kit Cars 2006–8*
Approx 58 made

ONYX FIREFOX

Essentially a Bobcat (*qv*), but based on Rover Metro/100 mechanicals rather than Mini, which at the time were becoming quite scarce and thus more expensive. The company's demo car was equipped with a 1.8 VVC K-series, which delivered 160bhp. With an all-up weight of 400kg, this meant a power-to-weight ratio of around 350bhp per tonne. Early versions featured a rear subframe before this was replaced by Onyx's own arrangement. Clubsport was a competition version, Roadsport aimed at the Queen's highway.
Onyx Sportscars 2001–9
Approx 15 made

ONYX MONGOOSE

Mid-engined lightweight two-seater that featured a spaceframe chassis, with the K-series engine mounted low and canted forward for perfect balance.
Onyx Sportscars 2006–9
Approx 8 made

ONYX ROADCAT

A utility-type kit from Onyx that belonged in the style box marked Moke and Scamp. Metro-based and used that car's A-series engine with a rugged ladderframe chassis.
Onyx Sportscars 2003–2004
Approx 5 made

ONYX TOMCAT

A complete change of direction for Onyx came in 1997 with the launch of the Tomcat, a search for a more affordable basic kit car, while retaining the Onyx values of fine handling. The idea was hatched by Dave Sewell of chassis makers Fibreform, and created by David Golightly, using the basic idea of one of his successful auto-test cars and was based on Mini mechanicals.
Onyx Sportscars 1997–98
Approx 50 made

ONYX TYPE EB37

Never afraid to push the boundaries, Onyx's next project was built initially as a one-off for David's partner Carla Smith's father, Tim Glennie, who wanted a Bugatti replica but couldn't find a suitable one. He asked David to build him a Bugatti Type 37, which featured Midget mechanicals and K-series 1.4 MPI power. Inevitably, once it was built others saw it and wanted one. Hence a new Onyx model was born.

Marque expert Ivan Dutton helped with the manufacture of the aluminium bodies and Onyx set out to create a replica that was as close to the original as it could be, complete with solidly mounted engine.
Onyx Sportscars 2007 to date
Approx 18 made

OPPERMAN STIRLING 2+2 COUPÉ

S.E. Opperman was a tractor manufacturer based in Elstree, Hertfordshire. The Stirling was a 2+2 version of their Unicar (see below), although it had a wider track and a slightly larger 424cc Excelsior engine.
S.E. Opperman 1958–59
Approx 2 made

OPPERMAN UNICAR

Opperman commissioned Lawrie Bond to design them a three-wheeled microcar powered by a 328cc Excelsior engine with 18bhp. Launched in 1956, with kit availability from 1958.
S.E. Opperman 1958–59
Approx 200 made

OPUS HRF

The HRF (Hot Rod Ford) was a Neville Trickett design for Geoff Thomas, with whom he had collaborated on the classic MiniSprint. Chassis/body kits cost under £100 and the tiny device had quirky looks. It was aimed at the hot rod element, being based on

Ford Anglia and Popular parts with a Crossflow/Kent engine providing the power and bodies by Pat Cuss of Marcos. Handling was variously described as roller-skate or scary, depending on who you spoke to.

When Trickett left in search of a new challenge with Siva Cars, Thomas (a qualified chemist) ran the operation with his secretary Jill Barwood, and although things went well initially they didn't pick up until his personal assistant Sue Preece-Murray breathed enthusiastic new life into the project. The company was based at Knowle in Bristol.

The Opus sold in decent numbers but was never taken completely seriously by hardcore rodders, or indeed the police, with one customer getting stopped 14 times in one day. A planned hardtop version called the Opus 2, or indeed a revised Opus 3, never materialised.

Project was taken over by VW dealer and Formula Vee racer Roy Dickinson of Bristol-based HSP Motors in 1970, who sold a further 20 examples, before calling time on this quaint little kit car.
Opus Cars 1966–70
HSP Motor Company 1970–72
Approx 224 made

OPUS SPRINT

Sister model to the Larini (*qv*), although this one was a Lotus Seven-inspired sports car powered by Honda Fireblade. Not around long.
Sculptural Engineering 1998–99
Approx 2 made

OSPREY

Cornishman Jack Evans was a boat builder by trade who went off to run operations in Majorca, Greece and California before returning home to Redruth, Cornwall, in 1981. A shift in business to car making commenced with the building of a MkVI Bentley *special* for Trago Mills owner Mike Robertson, followed by the Osprey, which although looking very similar to the American Classic Motor Carriages Mercedes SSK replica was designed by Evans and based on Ford Cortina Mk3. In 1984 Evans added to his range by taking over the former Siva Parisienne (*qv*).

In 1987 the company ceased automotive operations, although the Osprey turned up again with Bob Lewis' Projects of Distinction for a short time.
Cornish Classic Cars 1985–87
Projects of Distinction 1987–88
Approx 8 made

OVERLANDER

A quirky but effective off-road-style conversion for Citroën Dyane from Liskeard-based Trevor Gash.
TJ Overlanders 1985–92
Approx 60 made

OWSTON

A period van in Model A style from Vintage Motor Company.
Vintage Motor Company 1994–2003
Approx 20 made

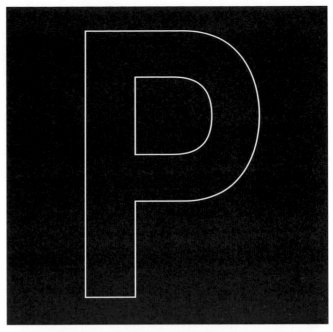

PANACHE

Originally built as a one-off by Paul Lawrenson, later of Venom and Prova, in 1978. Subsequently created a second set of moulds and produced commercially with business partner Peter Robinson. Used a standard VW floorpan.
Panache Kit Cars 1981–85
Approx 71 made

PANACHE LP400

The LP400 version of the Panache was a big improvement on the original. It was devised by Paul Lawrenson and Peter Robinson before they sold the company to Bob Davies. It featured a front end inspired by a Japanese Dome supercar. Memorably described by the manufacturers as 'The most exotic and futuristic component car available'. To be honest, Davies did improve the kit and came up with a box section ladderframe chassis to accept Rover V8 power, that used Triumph Herald front suspension, Citroën Gd instruments and a UV4-supplied adaptor plate for mating VW transaxle to Rover engine.
Panache Cars Ltd 1985-87
Approx 60 made

PANIC GT

Created by Sports 2000 enthusiast Gary Schoultz, who ran a spray shop in Dartford, Kent. Powered by bike engine. Not around very long.
Panache Cars Ltd 1981–85
Panic Motorsport 2004–6
Approx 2 made

PANTHER

Ford-Sierra or BMW-based, Locost-inspired, Lotus Seven-inspired sports car from former John Barnard employee Darren George. The R-Max version used all-new components.
GTS Tuning 2001-9
Approx 50 made

PARABUG

One of the few kit cars built in Scotland made by a boat-building outfit from Tullos, Aberdeenshire.

The Parabug required the VW Beetle floorplan to be shortened by 13in, while it was designed by a Glasgow design studio, called Anderson Bonar Industrial Design.

Utility kit based on VW Beetle mechanicals, and although more than a little angular in styling, was of good overall quality. The brochure described the available colour choices as 'Combat Colours', which were Jungle Green, Panzer Grey, Desert Yellow, Marine Blue and, er, Scorched Earth. Someone had an interest in militia, then!
North East Fibreglass Ltd 1971–78
Approx 19 made

PARALLEL COBRA

A departure for Parallel Designs from their usual Lamborghini-isnpired fare is a BMW-based Cobra replica, derived from the Python.
Parallel Designs 2008-10
Approx 12 made

PARALLEL MIURA

Sister model to the company's Lamborghini Diablo replica, this one was a modified version of the Prova ZL, although much updated, which used Audi power, including the potent RS4 unit.
Parallel Designs 2006-10
Approx 6 made

PARISIENNE

This was the former Edwardian series Siva Parisienne (*qv*) acquired by Jack Evans of Cornish Classic Cars, who also made the Osprey (*qv*). It had for a time been with a Devon company called Edwardian Cars although they did very little with it.
Cornish Classic Cars 1984–87
Approx 3 made

PASTICHE ASCOT

This was Pastiche Cars' Marina-based NG TF (*qv*) that sat alongside the MG-based original.
Pastiche Cars 1989–91
Approx 200 made

PASTICHE GLADIATOR

Ford-based version of the NG TC (*qv*) offered for a time by Pastiche Cars.
Pastiche Cars 1990–91
Approx 2 made

PASTICHE HENLEY

Ex-NG TF (*qv*) renamed and redeveloped to accept Ford Sierra mechanicals. Later went to Challenger (*qv*) makers Challenger Cars briefly.
Pastiche Cars 1990–91
Challenger Cars 1991–93
Approx 100 made

PASTICHE INTERNATIONAL

Ex-NG TA (*qv*) bought by Peter Fellowes of Pastiche and renamed International.
Pastiche Cars 1987–91
Approx 50 made

PEEL ENGINEERING COMPANY

The Isle of Man's only car manufacturer, founded in 1953 by ex-Wellington bomber pilot Cyril Cannel and based in Peel Harbour on the River Neb. Cyril also owned West Marine, who made a range of boats (from a base in Jurby) for Peel Engineering Company. They offered the 18ft Peel Inshoreman aka Peel Pig, the 25ft Midshoreman and the 33ft (or 35ft) Offshoreman. Indeed, Peel were one of the early pioneers of fibreglass and also made motorcycle race fairings among other things.

The company was relaunched by Gary Hillman and Faizul Khan in 2008, trading as Peel Engineering, who offer 'replicas' of the Peel P50 and Peel Trident. They appeared on the BBC TV programme *Dragons' Den* in August 2010, securing investment from James Caan, and have plans to develop the brand.

PEEL MANXCAR

The Manxcar was originally known as the Manxman, but name was changed due to objections from the Excelsior motorcycle company. Power came from an Anzani 250cc.

Peel Engineering Company 1955
Approx 1 made

PEEL P50

Described in promotional literature as 'a chair-in-a-box on three wheels', and still resides in the *Guinness Book of Records* as the smallest production car ever made, at just 54in long!

Featured a 49cc 4bhp Zweirad Union (DKW) engine good for a 38mph top speed, which was plenty enough for a little road-legal car weighing just 59kg! Had one door (on the left-hand side) and one headlight. Peel described the car as being big enough for 'one adult and a shopping bag'. Three colours were available – Daytona White, Dragon Red and Dark Blue – and P50s cost £199 in 1963. If you ordered a kit, the package came in a big wooden crate.

Peel also made one prototype of a version called the P55 Saloon Scooter, which had a single wheel at the front and two at the rear. This wasn't proceeded with.

Resurrected in 2008 by businessmen Gary Hillman and Faizul Khan.

Peel Engineering Company 1963–65
Peel Engineering 2008 to date
Approx 65 made (47 in the 1960s)

PEEL P1000

Much more sophisticated Ford-based shell with pre-bonded bulkheads and dashboard.
Peel Engineering Company 1956–58
Approx 150 made

PEEL TRIDENT

Peel's 'shopping car' successor to the P50, the Trident was described as a 'terrestrial flying saucer'. Slightly larger than the P50, at 72in long (or short...), and heavier at a still featherweight 90kg, it retained the same 49cc Zweirad Union (DKW) engine and three-speed manual gearbox. At just £190 Peel described the Trident as being 'Almost cheaper than walking'. Could be ordered with one or two seats and came with a detachable shopping basket. Really!

Offered again from 2008 by resurrected Peel Engineering, run by Gary Hillman and Faizul Khan.
Peel Engineering Company 1965–66
Peel Engineering 2008 to date
Approx 60 made (45 in the 1960s)

PEEL TRIDENT MINI

Launched at the 1966 Racing Car Show, this was designed by Peel founder Cyril Cannel. It soon became the Viking Minisport (*qv*) under Bill Last of Viking Performance.

Peel Engineering Company 1966
Approx 2 made

PEEL TYPE 1

Quite rudimentary shell available in similar 1a and 1b forms designed for a Buckler spaceframe chassis.
Peel Engineering Company 1953
Approx 40 made

PELL GENESIS

Developed by Tim Pell from his Bradford, West Yorkshire, base this was the first of the modern generation of bike-engined kit cars, being powered by Kawasaki ZZR-1100. Tim later developed a Peugeot 205 GTI-powered version and also an Evo model that was later taken over by Aeon Sportscars (see Blaze RR). The suspension was set up by late suspension guru Allan Staniforth, so it handled beautifully.

Incidentally, prior to the Genesis Tim Pell had made a hardtop for the SR V8 Cobra replica from 1993 that he offered commercially.
Pell Engineering Co 1995–2004
Approx 8 made

PELLAND COUPÉ

When Peter Pellandine returned again from Australia in the late eighties he launched his coupé model from his base in Harleston, Norfolk. Later sold to Square One Developments who created a convertible version of the renamed Kudos and didn't help its styling by chopping off the distinctive 'nose-edge', the roof, and fitting angular quarter-lights.

Pelland Engineering 1989–92
Approx 2 made

PELLAND SPORTS

When Peter Pellandine returned from Australia for the first time in 1978 he brought with him the idea for the Pelland Sports, which he duly created and marketed himself in the UK. The car had actually been available since 1973 in Australia. It was based on VW Beetle mechanicals, with the air-cooled engine installed 'back-to-front' to give a mid-mounted configuration. Giving strength to the structure was a GRP monocoque. Its mechanical layout was akin to a Formula Vee racecar.

Taken over by Jerry Grolin of Ryder Designs in 1980, who renamed it the Ryder Rembrandt (*qv*), it was a very capable car that sadly passed through a lot of hands without ever really achieving the success it deserved.

Moved to North Shields-based Graham Autos, who didn't do much with it and possibly didn't sell one, then moved to Listair Cars who renamed the car the Dash, before finally ending up with Simon Parker at Dash Cars in 1990.

Incidentally, in 1990 Pellandine produced a Mk2 Alfa-based version of the Sports called the Kudos (*qv*) before he sold that project and returned to Australia and concentrated on his steam-powered car, the Steamer. A remarkable man and iconic kit car designer.

Pellandine 1978–80
Ryder Designs & Engineering 1980–82
Graham Autos (Glassfibre) Ltd 1982–85
Listair Cars 1986–90
Dash Sportscars 1990–93
Approx 31 made

PEMBLETON BROOKLANDS

Phil Gregory, formerly of Gregori Sportscars, was the man behind the Brooklands, a four-wheeled version of the SuperSports (see next entry). Incidentally, Phil had held the motorcycle record at Shelsley Walsh hillclimb for some 15 years.

Pembleton Motor Company 2002 to date
Approx 280 made

PEMBLETON SUPERSPORTS

Superb little three-wheeler that was conceived as a one-off 'holiday-in-Ireland' car (built because three-wheelers got a discount on the ferry) that ended up going into production. Was initially christened the Grasshopper, but creator Phil Gregory thought that SuperSports was more serious. The Pembleton company name was inspired by a make of caravan (Pemberton) that donated its aluminium body for the prototype and got revised a bit!

The SuperSports was based on Citroën 2CV and a 2+2 layout was an option with a spaceframe chassis and stressed aluminium panels. First shown under the Gregori banner that Phil was part of with his brother, Roger.

Pembleton Motor Company 2003 to date
Approx 100 made

PENNON TYPE 35

Another mayfly kit car, this time a VW Beetle-based Bugatti Type 35 replica. Did anyone every see, let along buy, one?

Pennon Cars 1985
Approx 1 made

PEREGRINE

Designed by Paul Banham, the Peregrine was the first kit car to use the ubiquitous FX4 taxi as a donor vehicle. Although not a replica its lines were reminiscent of a Derby Bentley from the '30s. Marketed by Watford printer Colin Gontier, the Peregrine kit cost £6,456 when launched in 2005 and £13,000 would see a very nice example completed by a customer. Sadly, 356 Sports closed before they got the model established.

356 Sports 2005–6
Approx 1 made

PETERWORTH

Three-quarter-scale evocation of a bonneted American 'Semi' truck as made by Peterbilt and Kenworth, which was based on Ford Sierra. Superb concept by Peter Funnell but only made one before selling the project to a promotional company called Lil Big Truck. Got lots of publicity and was received well by the truck fraternity. Was special guest at Truckfest, South West, in 1999, all sadly to no avail.

Peterworth Trucks 1998–2000
Approx 1 made

PHANTOM/VORTEX GTR

Company named after the series of race cars designed by Chris Greville-Smith, whose race models included P80, P90 and P92 Supersports cars. The GTR (the Vortex prefix came later) was a two-seat coupé from Greville-Smith and ex-Rover production feasibility engineer Norman Morris based on Rover Sterling/827 mechanicals.

Greville-Smith was a designer of real note, working at various times for Ford, Jaguar, Land Rover and Rover, and responsible for, and working on, a variety of top cars such as the Jaguar XJ6 and Freelander 2, to name but two. He has

designed over 100 alloy wheel styles that reached production, such as the standard rims found on the MGF. He also produced a string of successful racecars under the Phantom name from the early '70s.

The Phantom made its debut at the Stoneleigh Show in 1997 and caused a sensation. It was another year before it was production-ready. Based on a spaceframe chassis with bespoke suspension components, double wishbones and aluminium uprights, and a de Dion rear end with four trailing arms.

Renamed Virago in 2007 (a Greco-Roman term meaning Amazonian-

style, feisty warrior woman) and offered in fully-built only guise.

Reappeared in kit form as the GT3 under the Vortex Automotive banner at the Stoneleigh Show in 2010, with Ford ST-spec Duratec V6 power or GTV with Volvo i5 turbopower delivering 300bhp.

Phantom Automotive 1997–2007
Virago Cars 2007–9
Vortex Automotive 2010 to date
Approx 30 made

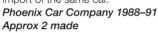

PHAROS

Four-wheeled version of the equally short-lived Triune (*qv*). Never reached production.
CDM 1983
Approx 1 made

PHOENIX

After the sad collapse of the Clan Crusader, the driving force behind that project, Paul Hassauer, concentrated on general fibreglass work from his base in Gloucestershire. But he couldn't keep away from car manufacturing and in 1983 unveiled his Phoenix, a

GRP-bodied Mini Clubman estate that benefited from light weight, no rust and a proper opening tailgate. Body styling was by Richard Oakes with GRP mouldings by Peter Hilken. Taller than a standard Mini Estate, by 2½in at the front of the roof rising to 4½in at the rear.
Phoenix Automotive 1983–86
Approx 50 made

PHOENIX

Originated from the American CMC Mercedes SSK replica and available here in various guises since 1975. Nothing to do with Dave Perry's Adam SSK official import of the same car.
Phoenix Car Company 1988–91
Approx 2 made

PHOENIX

Originally known as the Sylva Striker Mk4 (*qv*), denoting the fact that it was basically a Striker with a fully enveloping body. It became the Phoenix in 1999 when it received a restyle. Andy Waters, now of GT40 Supercars, had much success driving one during the '90s in the 750 Motor Club's Supersports championship.

The original Phoenix, the Striker Mk4, was picked up by Cyana Cars of Runcorn run by Ian Boulton, while Stuart Taylor Motorsport marketed the revised version from 2003 before selling it on to Rainbird Racing in 2008. Meanwhile, Cyana also created a Mazda MX-5-based version of the Phoenix, which was sold to Phil Squance's Rainbird Racing operation. Did you keep up?
Sylva Autokits 1986–2003
Stuart Taylor Motorsport 2003–5
Cyana Cars 2005–8
Rob Johnston Chassis Fabrication 2008 to date
Approx 30 made

PHOENIX Mk2

Evolved from the superb Sylva Striker Mk4 (*qv*), later known as the Phoenix, and designed by Jeremy Phillips of Sylva Autokits.

The Mk2, with revised bodywork, appeared in 1999, and this project was taken over by Ian Gray of Stuart Taylor Motorsport in 2003. Within a couple of years he sold the Mk1 Phoenix to Ian Boulton of Cyana Cars, enjoying much success with his revised version (new Caged-designed chassis), with Tim Gray (no relation) and Martin Brooks dominating the 750 Motor Club's RGB Championship in the mid-2000s.

Ian sold the Phoenix Mk2 project to Caged boss, Phil Squance, who set up a new company called Rainbird Racing in 2008 to market the car. Due to pressures of making rollcages and the like, he didn't do anything with the project, selling it to Callum and Jeremy Bulmer who also took over the Striker project in September 2010. Biggest visual differences were a revised front and altered rear.

Sylva Autokits 1999–2003
Stuart Taylor Motorsport 2003–8
Rainbird Racing 2008–2010
Raw Engineering 2010 to date
Approx 100 made

PHOENIX 037

A Lancia 037 replica marketed by Martin Kift of New Addington, Surrey.
Phoenix Cars 1997–99
Approx 2 made

PIKE PREDATOR

Originally known as the PYK Whirlwind. Project started by nuclear engineer Arnold Pearce and his son, who imported a pair of VW Beetle-based Witton Tigers (the inspiration behind the Merlin) to build for themselves. An engineer called Steve Keele got involved, as did a chap called Yann Yardley. The impromptu company set themselves up in a workshop at Bruntingthorpe Proving Ground near Lutterworth, with the PYK name coming from Pearce, Yardley and Keele. A man called Micky Finn was also involved.

Things didn't work out and Arnold Pearce and his friend Tony Brown bought the rights and moved the operation to a workshop in Melton Mowbray in 1986, renaming the business Pike Automotive. Car was revised for Ford Sierra mechanicals although still bore a strong visual resemblance to the Merlin. The four-cylinder version was known as the Predator with the V6-powered car being the Invader, until the Gilbern Owners' Club objected. Both were subsequently known as the Predator.
Pike Automotive 1987–89
Approx 16 made

PILGRIM BULLDOG

Truly a milestone kit car. Its designer Den Tanner had studied at Brighton University and obtained a degree in electrical and electronic engineering in 1981. He went to work at a company called Eurotherm (manufacturers of electronic temperature and systems controllers), and moved on Marconi Underwater Systems and then moving to Plessey. He designed the Bulldog in his spare time from 1982 until 1984 and, needing a fibreglass laminator, he found local artisan Bill Harling in Yellow Pages and the rest, as they say, is history.

They set up a fledgling business called Pilgrim (the name came from the 'To be a Pilgrim' hymn that Den and Bill were humming one morning!), with their first base in Sillwood Street, Brighton, where they made around 50 Bulldogs before the fibreglass smell led to complaints from neighbours. They transferred to Lady Bee Marina right on the seafront, next to the docks in Hove, before moving slightly inland to the current base in Small Dole where they've been since 1987.

The humble Bulldog really caught the public's imagination and followed the Dutton philosophy of amazing value for money, although it was based around the traditional roadster concept, featuring (initially) a Morris Marina donor. Its first incarnation sold about 50 examples. The Mk2 had a revised grille and small doors, the Mk3 was purpose-made for (larger) doors, the Mk4 was based around Ford Cortina mechanicals, while a more detailed styling revision and an improved chassis came with the MkV of 1992.
Pilgrim Cars 1985–97
Approx 2,000 made

PILGRIM FAMILY TOURER (FT)

With a young family Den Tanner found it difficult to get a carrycot and toddler in the back of a Bulldog, so he set out to address that with a 2+2 seating configuration while also improving on the original Pilgrim model.
Pilgrim Cars 1989–2000
Approx 250 made

PILGRIM HAWTHORN

This was Pilgrim's second model, intended to be called the Rapier before a last-minute change to Hawthorn. Shell originated from a 1950s Microplas Stiletto *special*. It was a pleasing retro-styled sports car that was replaced by the Sumo (*qv*).
Pilgrim Cars 1986–87
Approx 105 made

PILGRIM MARTINI

A Ford Capri-based (Mk2 or 3) body conversion that gave the donor the look of an Aston Martin Vantage Volante.
Pilgrim Cars 1992–94
Approx 5 made

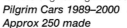

PILGRIM MX2

Pilgrim's take on the Lancia Stratos theme; created as they had the Allora moulds when Handmade Cars went bust.

Pilgrim's Den Tanner revised the mould to accept Ford Mk3 or Mk4 Escort components including hubs, struts, braking systems, a 1600CVH engine mid-mounted, and Cortina uprights at the front.

A prototype was produced but then the idea was shelved due to the sales success of their Sumo Cobra replica.

Pilgrim Cars 1989-90
Approx 1 made

PILGRIM SPEEDSTER

Evolved from the model developed by Pilgrim agent Willy Lambrechts of LB Cars, Zandhoven, Belgium.

Tony Holmes, a well-known kit car builder of note, worked at Pilgrim Cars as works manager for several years before taking over the company in 2002, slightly revising the name to Pilgrim Cars (UK) Ltd, although still trading from the same Small Dole, West Sussex, base.

Based on VW Beetle mechanicals and floorpan, Tony Holmes even developed a four-seat version. In all, he sold around 300 kits before he ceased trading in 2008. When Pilgrim co-founder Den Tanner subsequently returned he kept the Speedster on the price-list.

Pilgrim Cars (UK) Ltd 2002–8   *Pilgrim Cars 2008 to date*
Approx 310 made

PILGRIM SUMO

The biggest-selling Cobra replica in UK kit history. Its Sumo moniker came from a 'Name That Car' competition in *Kit Cars & Specials* magazine in 1987, won by a lady called Angela Bromfield, who also won a Bulldog kit as her prize. The intention was to offer a budget Cobra replica kit, and Den Tanner achieved his aim. It was based on a modified Bulldog chassis and sales simply took off.

Much-improved Mk2 featured a semi-monocoque, while Mk3 – the best-selling Sumo – saw the introduction of Sierra donor with Jaguar XJ6 option. A milestone in UK kit car history.

Pilgrim Cars 1987 to date
Approx 3,500 made

PILGRIM SPEEDSTER FOUR-SEATER

This one certainly divided opinion, with the purists not liking the idea of a four-seat Speedster, while it definitely appealed to those with a family.

Based like the standard car on VW Beetle, it was provided with a subframe to add the required extra length to the floorpan, enabling fitment of a second row of seats. Always a niche product.

Pilgrim Cars (UK) Ltd 2002–8
Approx 8 made

PIPER GTR

Hailing from the innovative mind of serial kit car designer, Tony Claydon (Tara 2, Candy Apple Finale, CHAD among others), from Maldon, Essex, the Piper GTR was a recreaton of the glorious sixties Piper GTR sports racer, of which just three were built. Track-orientated, with no roadgoing version available, the modern Piper featured a Ford Duratec engine and was fully built from £28,000, with a rolling-chassis version also available, hence its inclusion here.

Piper Racing Cars 2006 to date
Approx 3 made

PIPER GTT

Company founder George Henrotte ran the Gemini race team in 1963 and moved to the former Campbell's Garage in Hayes, Kent, in 1965. General repair work led to the formation of Piper Cams and engineer Bob Gayler joined the company, to design some racing cars. Work started on the production of a convertible sports racer after Sprite owner Keith Grant appeared one day wanting a new rakish body to be put on his chassis and promptly placed an order for four cars. This order and a design brought to Piper by racing car designer Tony Hilder (ex-Brabham, Lola and McLaren) convinced Henrotte and Gayler that they should go ahead, although their resolve was tested when Grant cancelled his order in November 1966.

The subsequent car became the GTT. It was launched at the Racing Car Show of 1967, where it received 18 orders! After a few were built work at the factory stopped to sort out some teething problems, although Brian Sherwood's appearance one day – he had bought one of the very early convertible GT cars – would see him become a director and take production of the GTT to his factory in Wokingham.

Incidentally, it was Sherwood, who was obsessed by racing, who was behind the futuristic-looking GTR, a Group Six racer with plywood and fibreglass monocoque, of which four were built.

Sadly Sherwood was killed in a road accident in his GTT in December 1969, but Piper Cars carried on for a while under the control of his employees Bill Atkinson and Tony Waller, who pressed ahead with a new Piper model, the P2 (see next entry).
Piper Cars 1967–71
Approx 38 made

PIPER P2

Launched in February 1971 the P2 had twin round rather than faired-in rectangular headlights, a beefier chassis and a better ride, plus it was some 12in longer and came with flared wheel arches. However, despite it being well-received the company was hit by Ford factory strikes and couldn't get parts, which led directly to the company going into liquidation in June 1971.

Undeterred, makers Bill Atkinson and Tony Waller recommenced work in the same factory as Emmbrook Engineering and introduced pop-up lights for the P2 from early 1972, while June 1973 saw them move to a new factory in South Willingham, Lincolnshire. They even had ambitious plans to resurrect the GTR Group Six racer, based on a Volkswagen chassis.
Piper Cars 1971
Emmbrook Engineering 1971–75
Approx 41 made

PIZAZZ

Not a kit car as such, but created by William Towns of Hustler fame (like many others in this book) and was a styling exercise on the Peugeot 205 hatchback.
Interstyl 1986–87
Approx 3 made

PKA V12 – *see EG Arrow*

PLUS TWO – *see Merlin Monro*

POWERBUG

Mervyn Aldridge was the man behind this Kent-based company. The Powerbug's styling was influenced by another Bromley-based kit, called the Vulture. It seems that the various beach buggy manufacturers of the early seventies were set on trying to outdo each other with their advertising spiel, in Powerspeed's case: 'The new dimension in dune buggies.' Apparently, Powerspeed's in-house glassfibre skills often let them down, although they could offer lots of other useful services to their customers including converting Beetle electrics to 12V and supplying wheel adaptors so that customers could choose alternative, and bigger, 13in wheels.

Powerbug based on either un-modified or shortened (77¾in) VW Beetle floorpan. Scary Convair V8 example featured in *Hot Car* magazine in 1970, although they happily offered V8 and even Porsche-powered versions. Yikes!
Powerspeed 1970–71
Approx 148 made

PREDATOR

VW Beetle-based beach buggy from the wonderfully named BuzzBugs, run by David Waspe. Later changed their name to Autobuzzi before the project moved to Rob Kilham's East Coast Manx of King's Lynn and later Rutland.
BuzzBugs 1998–2003
East Coast Manx 2003 to date
Approx 25 made

PREDATOR 250

This short-lived Countach replica from a Birmingham company was an anniversary version based on Ford Scorpio donor.
Cybertech Cars 1992–93
Approx 2 made

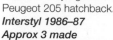

PRO-MOTIVE MINI

Superb bike-engined conversion kit for Classic Mini from Land Rover employees Darren Grasby and Philip Jennings, based in Bromsgrove, Worcestershire. Very nicely made and thought-out package. Usual power choice is Yamaha R1, although others can be used.
Pro-Motive 2006 to date
Approx 100 made

PROBE 15

Officially known as Design Probe Number 15. An amazingly low-slung exotic that was just 29in high (or low?), from Marcos designers Dennis and Peter Adams. Comprised, unsurprisingly, a wooden monocoque clothed in a fibreglass body, and had a mid-mounted BMC 1800 engine, with a Perspex canopy for entry/exit. The prototype was tested at Keevil airfield, but the project was intended as a design concept and never made it into production. However, when customers arrived waving cheques for Design Probe Number 15 they decided to come up with a production version, which became the Probe 16 (see next entry).
Adams Brothers 1968
Approx 1 made

PROBE 16

The Adams brothers modified Probe 15, making it slightly longer to accommodate a Maxi 1,500cc engine rather than Hillman Imp unit. They made the seats more upright, although the steering wheel was still near vertical, and fitting a curved windscreen. When the key was turned in the door lock the roof and seats moved back electrically on runners, which enabled entry. All trick stuff, especially for 1969.

The Probe 16 was 34in high – slightly taller than Probe 15 – and the prototype was shown on the Institute of British Carriage & Automotive Manufacturers stand in association with the *Daily Telegraph Magazine* at the 1969 Motor Show, where it met with a great response. Jack Bruce, bassist from the rock band Cream, ordered one. The engine was a BMC 1,800cc unit, tuned and bored out by Janspeed Engineering, while the car also appeared in the Stanley Kubrick film, *A Clockwork Orange*.

A Solihull-based company called Concept Developments later produced the Probe 16, calling it the Concept Centaur (*qv*), although in 1978 the nettle was grasped by Mirage Developments of Melody Road, Biggin Hill, who renamed the car the Pulsar 2 (*qv*).
Adams Brothers 1969–70
Concept Developments 1974–77
Approx 5 made

PROBE 2001

When a businessman suggested to Dennis and Peter Adams that they should come up with a more practical Probe and offered to provide finance they took notice. They modified a Probe 16, gave it gullwing doorlets (though the clever sliding canopy roof remained) and sharpened up the styling, resulting in a larger boot space. The resultant Probe 2001 was 37in high and 4in longer than the Probe 16. Things gathered speed when they moved out of Bradford-on-Avon's Old Forge and into Marcos' former riverside wharf building, and the first model was completed in spring 1970. Despite continuing in production after finance was withdrawn, only four were built before the company was liquidated later the same year.

The production rights were acquired by Scottish company W.T. Nugent (Engineering) Ltd of Ayr, who, for a while, continued making them in Bradford-on-Avon (in a different factory, but with the old staff) and completed another six before moving everything back to their Scottish base, where six more were constructed before they sold the rights to an Edinburgh operation called Caledonian Probe Motor Company, who didn't produce it.
Adams Brothers 1970–71
W.T. Nugent (Engineering) Ltd 1971–72
Caledonian Probe Motor Company 1972
Approx 16 made

PROSPORT

Although they didn't offer their top-notch range of track-orientated cars as kits, Radical did offer the last batch of their Prosport model as a kit package in late 2005.
Radical Sportscars 2005
Approx 25 made

PROTEUS 300 SLR

Superb Mercedes 300 SLR
'Gullwing' replica created by Jim
Marland. Model took a bit of a
backseat in the John Gregson
and Enduro Cars Proteus years,
but when Tony Gott acquired the
marque and also the Lynx brand,
he once again offered it for sale,
although kit versions weren't available.

Proteus Cars 1993–99
Classic ERA 1999–2005
Enduro Cars (renamed Proteus Cars 2006) 2005–08
Proteus Sports & Racing Cars 2010 to date
Approx 7 made

PROTEUS C-TYPE

Jim Marland's Proteus, originally
trading as Copycats, appeared
in 1982. Jim's version has a very
fine reputation. His first models
came with aluminium bodies and
were based on Jaguar Mk2 and
therefore had the correct rear
track width.

A glassfibre body option was introduced in 1987 and was 2½in
(50mm) wider, as it featured independent rear suspension and
Jaguar XJ6 running gear. It was this Proteus model that begat a large
percentage of other C-type replicas.

Jim Marland sold his company in 1999 to Classic English Racing
before it passed to Enduro Cars. It is now under the same ownership
as Lynx Motors.

New versions are not available in kit form, and have a Superform
aluminium body with fuel-injected XK 3.8-litre engine, that interestingly
use the later 50mm wider Proteus body. Prices from £87,000 at the
time of writing. Superb.
Copycats 1982–85
Proteus Reproductions 1985–99
Proteus Cars 1991–99
Classic ERA 1999–2005
Enduro Cars (renamed Proteus Cars 2006) 2005–2007
Approx 220 made

PROTEUS D-TYPE

Another glorious Jaguar replica
from Jim Marland's Bolton-based
Copycats operation, appearing
in 1982. The company amended
their name to Proteus Cars
(probably named after Donald
Campbell's Bluebird-Proteus).

At first the car was only offered
in fully-built guise with aluminium bodies, until a glassfibre option
arrived with component availability in 1991. Its life as a kit ended when
Marland sold his company in 1999. The Proteus marque does still
exist, although at the time of writing they only make the C-type. Also
offers an XKSS variant.
Copycats 1982–85
Proteus Reproductions 1985–99
Classic ERA 1999–2005
Enduro Cars 2005–7
Proteus Sports & Racing Cars 2008 to date
Approx 40 made

PROTEUS NORSEMAN VAN

A big departure for Proteus. A van...based around a 1931 Ford
commercial vehicle. Donor was Sherpa van.
Classic Commercials (part of Proteus Cars) 1992–94
Approx 3 made

PROTEUS P90

Stunning Jaguar XJ13 replica from
Jim Marland's Proteus operation,
created from photographs. Car
featured a semi-monocoque with
separate spaceframe structure
and bodies could be in fibreglass
or aluminium. Donor vehicle was
Jaguar XJ12.

Proteus Cars 1992–99
Approx 2 made

PROVA COUNTACH

Lee Noble created the chassis for this Prova model, which was one
of the top Countach replicas and certainly one of the biggest sellers.
Prova and former Panache Cars founder Paul Lawrenson supplied
six cars for the film *It Takes Two*, which gave it instant charisma. The
Prova model was endorsed by Ferrucio Lamborghini after he'd sold
his eponymous supercar maker, allegedly commenting that it was
better than his own Countach!
Prova Designs 1986–99
Approx 1,200 made

PROVA ZL

Miura replica that featured a
steel tube chassis as per the
company's Countach replica,
Ford Granada running gear and
Renault V6 engine. Joe Lamberti
marketed the car for a time before
he emigrated to Italy. It then
reappeared under the Parallel

Designs banner, who modified it to comply with SVA (and later IVA).
Prova Designs 1989–2002
Lamberti Classic Cars 2003–4
Approx 55 made

PROWLER

VW Beetle-based beach buggy created by Mel Hubbard. Passed to Rob Kilham's East Coast Manx operation, initially based in King's Lynn before moving to Rutland. With its Beetle floorpan chopped by 15½in, the Prowler features quite similar styling to the Manx but with more modern styling and an open rear end. Also wider than the Manx.

Manxbuggies 1999–2003
East Coast Manx 2003 to date
Approx 10 made

PULSAR

Trackday car created in 1983 by Rob Bicknell of RBM Motorsport, based in Little Staughton, Bedfordshire. Featured a steel tube spaceframe panelled in NS4 aluminium, with double wishbone front suspension, Ford RS200 live axle and Vauxhall XE power. The track version was called '931' and the roadgoing option '942'. Production version was sold under Bicknell's Midas Racing Services banner.

Moved on to Hampshire-based Matt Brace, who modified the car to accept bike power. Project then acquired by Richard Cox of West Sussex, who ran it on a part-time basis before pressures of his main business meant he couldn't devote sufficient time to it. Ended up with 750MC racer Phil Alcock and marketed through Stuart Taylor Motorsport, who re-engineered the car to accept the Caged developed chassis that had originally been created for the Phoenix Mk2 (*qv*, ex-Sylva Autokits car that he manufactured at the time), and was then raced successfully in the 750 Motor Club's Road-Going Bike Championship for a couple of seasons.

RNM Motorsport 1993
Midas Racing Services 1993–96
Brace Engineering 1998–2000
Pulsar Sportscars 2004–5
STM/Phil Alcock 2005 to date
Approx 15 made

PULSAR

The first kit car industry Porsche 911 replica, just beating the Covin Turbo (*qv*) to the market. Unlike the latter the Pulsar didn't use a shortened VW Beetle floorpan but a box-section ladderframe instead, although the Veedub

parts bin was plundered for items such as front axle, steering and air-cooled engine. For the record, the windscreen came from Citroën GS.

Amplas of Chalgrove, Oxfordshire, were behind the project, although they sold it to Lancaster-based Lemazone after a couple of years, run by Mike Parkington, who had previously built probably the only Kingfisher Countess to hit the public highway.

Amplas 1984–85
Lemazone 1985–87
Approx 16 made

PULSAR 2

The Pulsar 2's ancestry can be traced back to Dennis and Peter Adams's Probe 16 (*qv*) that had been productionised by Solihull company Concept Developments, and the Pulsar 2 was basically a Probe 16 Mk2. Mirage Developments of Melody Road, Biggin Hill, was the manufacturer.

By now the car had gained doors, rather than the original Perspex canopy, and a windscreen from a Vauxhall Ventora. Concept Developments had switched the engine to Hillman Imp, which Mirage retained, although they soon offered Ford and Mini options too. Their version was called the Concept Centaur (*qv*).

For the last two years of its life the Pulsar 2 was produced by Trowbridge-based company MR Developments.

Mirage Developments 1978–80
MR Developments 1980–82
Approx 26 made

PULSAR 3

The Pulsar 3 was effectively a two-seat rather than 2+2 and was as mad-looking as the original Probe. Same running gear and power options as Pulsar 2 (see above).

Mirage Developments 1978–80
MR Developments 1980–82
Approx 4 made

PYTHON

Well-known UK hot rodders Pete Gottlieb and Martin De'Ath had been trading as Pete & Mart's Rod Shop in Finchley since 1980 and had been responsible for some of the UK rodding scene's most notable cars, such as a Daimler-powered C-Cab and a V6 Fordson. They and former Jago

chassis-man Kris Brown, trading as Pop Brown's, joined forces as Unique Autocraft in 1981.

Their Python was Jaguar-based and featured a 92in wheelbase (2in longer than standard). Unique Autocraft was based just a short way from DJ Sportscars in Harlow.

Unique Autocraft 1981–93
Approx 99 made

PYTHON

Although this version of the Python evolved from the Unique Autocraft kit (see previous entry) it was a very different car, being based on BMW 5 Series (E34 variant), and was acquired by Vince Wright of RV Dynamics who at the time was based in Sri Lanka

and he left marketing in the UK to Peter Filby and Sally Mitchell, then of *Which Kit?* magazine, who co-owned the project for a time.

RV Dynamics 2001–8
Approx 27 made

QUADRIGA

Makers PACE (Performance Automobile Construction Engineers), founded by Robert Scott, Steve Elvy and Alec Wilson in 1989, marketed the Quadriga, which although not a replica was heavily influenced by Italian supercars of the day. The company also offered general kit building services.

The Quadriga was based on a rugged spaceframe chassis with Lancia subframe housing a 2.0-litre Lancia turbo unit and most of the Beta bolted to the chassis. Could be ordered in Coupé or GTS (targa) versions, while other engines that could be used included Lancia Thema, MG Maestro and Rover 800.

Scott left in 1990, replaced by Bob Whiteside, but regained control of the operation in 1991. The Quadriga passed to Vic Minay and his Auto Milan operation in 1993.

PACE 1989–93
Approx 2 made

QUANTUM H4

The Quantum Sports Cars company of Stourbridge was founded by ex-Shell UK employees Harvey and Mark Wooldridge, who between them had 22 'O' levels, six 'A' levels and two engineering degrees! Appearing in 1998, their H4 ('H' for Harvey and '4' denoting his fourth design) built on the success of the Saloon and 2+2 models, while raising the bar yet further. Based on Fiesta Mk3 mechanicals, the H4 was one of the most sophisticated kit cars ever launched, featuring

thoroughly modern styling and a class-leading roof system that converted the hardtop into a convertible in a flash.

Company sold to John and Rosemary Sampson of Kingsbridge in 2001. Quantum H4 model was subsequently sold to an Iranian fire engine manufacturer, although could still be supplied under license by Quantum Sports Cars.

Quantum Sports Cars 1998–2001 (Wooldridges)
Quantum Sports Cars 2001–3 (Sampsons)
Approx 164 made

QUANTUM HATCHBACK

The first product from Harvey and Mark Wooldridge. Mk1 Fiesta-based kit with hatchback and clear polycarbonate headlight covers.
Quantum Sports Cars 1985–93
Approx 25 made

QUANTUM NAPIERSPORT

An LMP-type kit car from the drawing board of Richard Ashby that could be powered by bike or car engine. Fully built versions marketed by Lionel Gooch's Napiersport concern.
Quantum Sports Cars 2002 to date
Approx 2 made

QUANTUM OF SOLACE

Intriguing Aston Martin-inspired body conversion based on Toyota Supra Mk4 (produced between 1993 and 2002), named after the star car in the James Bond film, *Quantum of Solace*. The company name was also a bit cheeky. The man behind the project was Lincoln-based Mark Palmer.
MI6 Cars 2010
Approx 1 made

QUANTUM SALOON

Essentially a Mk2 version of the Hatchback with opening boot, pop-up headlights and smoother styling. Featured some 25 amendments and was the model that really put the Wooldridge brothers on the map. Practicality was high, it was affordable, and the choice of Fiesta as a donor car was inspired. Switched to Fiesta Mk2 donor in 1991. Underpinned by a sturdy GRP monocoque tub.

Quantum Sports Cars 1989–99
Approx 216 made

QUANTUM SUNRUNNER

A Richard Ashby creation that melds Mini Moke and beach buggy into a fun, capable little package using Ford mechanicals. When Mark Burley acquired the Quantum Xtreme project (see below) in March 2010 the Sunrunner went to the Sampsons under the Quantum Heritage banner.

Quantum Sports Cars 2004–10
Quantum Heritage 2010 to date
Approx 10 made

QUANTUM 2+2

If Quantum thought the Saloon was a success then they weren't prepared for the buzz that accompanied Harvey Wooldridge's 2+2 of 1993, again based on Fiesta Mk2. A crisp design that sold strongly from the off. Slight revision in 1998 freshened up the styling further. One of the industry's iconic cars.

When John and Rosemary Sampson purchased the Quantum marque in 2001 they also acquired the 2+2; and likewise, when they sold the Xtreme model to Mark Burley in 2010 they retained the 2+2 under the Quantum Heritage banner.

It was announced in December 2010 that Quantum Heritage had sold the rights to the 2+2 to fanatical Quantum owner, Eddie Ruskin of Bristol-based Dynamic Mouldings.

Quantum Sports Cars 1993–2001 (Wooldridges)
Quantum Sports Cars 2001–10 (Sampsons)
Quantum Heritage 2010 (Sampsons)
Quantum Kit Cars Ltd 2010 to date
Approx 470 made

QUANTUM XTREME

When looking for a Lotus Seven-inspired car for his son to build, steel company owner Ian Pettinger, based in Sheffield, became disillusioned and so created his own, commissioning talented engineer Steve Greenwood – a name well known in the industry for several cars, including the Litton Corse (*qv*) – and designer Richard Ashby to make him one. Together they created a company called Sector Three to market it, and it made its debut at Stoneleigh in 1998.

A modern take on the Lotus Seven theme, being based on a massively strong stainless steel monocoque using Ford Sierra mechanicals.

Snapped up pretty soon after its debut appearance by Quantum boss Mark Wooldridge, who christened it the Xtreme and sold around 44 examples. Multiple British Sprint Class Champion and Devon farmer John Sampson bought an Xtreme from Mark Wooldridge and found it competitive, so in finest Victor Kiam fashion he and wife Rosemary bought the company in July 2001. They concentrated on refining the Xtreme further, developing it from a budget contender into the equal of anything else on the market.

Sold to Mark Burley of MB Motorsport in 2010, who operated under the Quantum brand name from the Sampsons' old premises in Kingsbridge.

Sector Three Sports Cars 1998–99
Quantum Sports Cars 1999–2001 (Wooldridges)
Quantum Sports Cars 2001–10 (Sampsons)
Quantum Sports Cars 2010 Ltd 2010 to date (Mark Burley)
Approx 225 made

QUANTUM XT

Launched in early 2011, the XT is a development of the Xtreme, with slightly revised body, but the same excellent underpinnings.

Quantum Sports Cars 2011 to date
Approx 2 made

QUDOS VIPER

Scottish Cobra replica that wasn't around for long.

Qudos Cars 1981–82
Approx 1 made

R2

Interesting two-seater that featured a staggered seating position, with the passenger located alongside, but just behind the driver.
Mills Extreme Vehicles 2006–7
Approx 2 made

R3

Diminutive three-seater with central driving position, designed by Stuart Mills. Ford Mondeo Mk2 donor with V6 Duratec the suggested powerplant.
Mills Extreme Vehicles 2007–8
Approx 2 made

R40

Modern sports car styling for this pretty two-seater from transmission specialists RT Quaife that appeared briefly in 2005. Mooted turnkey-minus price of circa £35,000.
RT Quaife Ltd 2005
Approx 1 made

RACECORP LA/LAi

Chinnor-based company run by Australians Jeff and Bev Amos along with son Steve. Back in Australia, the Amoses were boat and race car builders (a very successful Racecorp model was the T199 V6 of 1989). When they relocated to Oxfordshire Steve became composites manager for Arrows F1 before rejoining the family business and continuing to supply all sorts of carbon fibre products to race teams. The Light Auto (LA) roadster was created as a winter project to keep the staff busy during the off-season, but press response was so good that it was put into kit production, with an IRS-equipped LAi appearing soon after. Highly acclaimed chassis was developed by Roger Rimmer. Subsequently became Eldon Roadster (*qv*), Razer (*qv*) and then Razor.
Racecorp Ltd 1991–93
Approx 12 made

RADBOURNE ABARTH

Not really a kit car – well, it kind of was...sort of. Well known for Fiat sales and tuning, Radbourne Racing's managing director spotted around 30 unused Abarth-Simca bodyshells languishing in the corner of the Fiat factory while on holiday in Turin in 1968, which he quickly snapped up. He then set about marrying them – fully trimmed – with a Simca 1000 chassis, Fiat 124 engine and suspension components, and offering the whole lot as a comprehensive kit package. Demand was good, although after just 12 were sold the remaining 18 shells were found to have Italian tin-worm and couldn't be used.
Radbourne Racing 1968–71
Approx 12 made

RAFFO TIPO 11

First road-going car from Formula Vee builder and top pasta maker John Raffo, from Southport. Angular styling, although extremely capable, with spaceframe chassis, fibreglass body and a canopy similar to that of a Bond Bug. Powered by a lusty Alfasud flat four engine with right-hand gearchange.
Raffo Cars 1986–88
Approx 11 made

RAFFO TIPO 12

Following the Tipo 11 was the less angular Tipo 12, a wonderfully capable car typical of Mr Raffo. Underpinned by a spaceframe chassis, it featured independent rear suspension, with double wishbone front suspension, and could be ordered in open or closed body styles. Power came from Alfa Romeo flat-four and body/chassis kits cost £1,950 when launched in 1988.
Raffo Cars 1988–91
Approx 14 made

RALLY KART

An off-road kart from Blitzworld of Stoke-on-Trent. Powered by 390cc or 620cc Honda engine.
Blitzworld 2007 to date
Approx 50 made

RALLY REPLICAS 200

Highly innovative Ford RS200 replica based on Toyota MR2 Mk2 from Ramsgate-based engineer Mike Noy. Not productionised.
Rally Replicas 2009-10
Approx 1 made

RALLYE 037

Lancia 037 replica based on Monte Carlo. Appeared briefly in 2007. Hailed from a Blackpool company run by John Lambert, and probably originated from the remains of the Rallye Junior (*qv.*) project of 1990.
Race & Rally Replicas 2007
Approx 1 made

RALLYE JUNIOR

Another Lancia 037 replica from Jim Kerr and Bob Russell of Livingstone, Scotland, that appeared at Stoneleigh in 1990 but wasn't seen again until (probably) turned up 17 years later as the Rallye 037.
Rallye Cars 1990
Approx 1 made

RAM 4S

A Ford Cortina-based version of the 1970s Lotus Elite that Lotus objected to. It was revised and went on to become the Mohawk (*qv*). Offered by Bognor Regis car dealer Bruce Dixon.
Bruce Dixon (1949) Ltd 1985–88
Approx 9 made

RAM LM

LR Roadsters was founded by Adrian Cocking of Chingford. He had set up his own business making fibreglass fairings for motorcycles, which brought him in contact with Derek Johns, then DJ Sportscars boss, who was also into bikes. In 1982 he went to work for DJ as sales manager, being the instigator of that company's Cobra replica, and is also credited with coming up with the DAX name after a hero in a Harold Robbins novel he was reading. Set up LR Roadsters in 1984, the company name coming from resin suppliers Llewellyn Ryland!

The Ram LM was a Jaguar D-type replica famously described in the company's advert as 'the nicest way to have the hump'. Adrian Cocking could offer you every type of D-type style from long-nose to fixed rear fin, all in fibreglass. A well-regarded replica, almost always fitted with a straight-six Jaguar XK engine.

Still available when LR Roadsters became Realm Engineering, although after 2003 the latter concentrated on their newly acquired Heritage C-type (*qv*). Made 12 cars for the John Arnold's Everyman Racing concern as part of a one-make race series in 2001.
LR Roadsters 1985–2000
Realm Engineering 2000 to date
Approx 200 made

RAM RT

Ferrari Daytona replica from Adrian Cocking.
LR Roadsters 1987–90
Approx 30 made

RAM SC

The Ram SC is one of the most highly regarded Cobra replicas of all time, with even Carroll Shelby himself authorising the product in the early '90s. Even had a one-make European race series called the Bardahl Trophy.
LR Roadsters 1984–86 (Chingford)
LR Roadsters 1986–93 (Newmarket)
Ram Automotive 1994 (Cardiff)
Ram Automotive 1994–98 (Witham)
Realm Engineering 2000 to date
Approx 1,500 made

RAM SS

Made its debut at the Stoneleigh
Show of 1988 and was a replica
of the roadgoing version of the
Jaguar D-type known as the
XKSS.
LR Roadsters 1988 to date
Approx 80 made

RANA

Restoration/conversion kit for Spridget; an original Sprite Mk1
'Frogeye' can be used, or indeed the other versions, as can MG's
Midget. Comes from accessories supplier Tifosi's Star Motor
Company division based in Chulmleigh, Devon. Became part of Mark
Burley's Quantum Sports Cars in 2011.
Star Motor Company 2006-11
Quantam Sports Cars 2011 to date
Approx 50 made

RANA RS

A wider and longer version of the
Rana than the standard model.
Based on a separate spaceframe
chassis.
Star Motor Company 2009
Approx 1 made

RANA TS

A Mazda MX-5 based version of
the standard Rana.
Star Motor Company
2010
Approx 2 made

RANGE OVER

A fiendish conversion kit that
turned a P38 (Mk2) Range Rover
into a Mk3 L322 lookalike.
Range Over Kits 2007 to date
Approx 200 made

RANGER – *see Bedouin*

RANGER 80

A Moke-inspired kit. Nothing
unusual in that, but the choice
of donor was – not Mini, rather
Austin 1100/Morris 1300.
    Ranger Automotive was run
by Eric Salmons, originally based

at his old used car lot before moving to the (allegedly haunted!) former
Corona Cinema in Leigh-on-Sea, Essex. The same company was later
responsible for the Ranger Cub series (see below). The Ranger was
subsequently resurrected by Ranger Ltd, based in Glenhufa Road,
Llangefni, on the Isle of Anglesey.
EJS Products 1971–72   *Ranger Automotive 1972–76*
Ranger Ltd 1984–85
Approx 303 made

RANGER CUB

Designed by Alan White. Series
1 appeared in 1974 and around
20 were sold, with a revised and
more pleasing Mk2 coming along
in 1975, of which 180 were sold.
Ranger Automotive 1974–76
Approx 200 made

RANGER CUB 4

Latching on to the success of the
three-wheeled Cub, Ranger boss
Eric Salmons reckoned that a four-
wheeled pickup version couldn't
fail. It did. Only four made.
Ranger Automotive 1975–76
Approx 4 made

RANGER CUB 6

Innovative one-off six-wheeler created by Ranger's Midland agent
John Thomas, who had formerly worked at Broadspeed.
Ranger Automotive 1975
Approx 1 made

RANGER JEEP

A one-off Austin 1100-based utility
from the Ranger Cub makers.
Ranger Automotive 1976
Approx 1 made

RAT

The Rat was another beach buggy inspired by the GP Buggy (*qv*). It came from FibreFab of Wokingham and its main identifying feature was its nose area. Its RAT name came from the first-name initials of the three men responsible for it – Robert Taylor, Anthony Hill and Trevor Pym. The standard Rat was based on a VW Beetle floorpan of 78¾in, with a long-wheelbase version using an unmodified 94½in floorpan introduced in 1974. Meanwhile, the poor old short-wheelbase moulds had so many 'pulls' taken from them that they were discovered to be warped in 1979 and a new set had to be produced.

The three protagonists fell out in 1972, leaving Hill to run the company on his own until he emigrated to Australia in 1981, when the project was taken over by Tim Cooksey, who changed the company name to FF Kitcars & Conversions and also introduced a body styling kit for Alfasud. Cooksey in turn sold the operation in 1985, returning to his previous exhibition company before moving on to property renovation. Meanwhile, the FF operation was acquired by Stephen Wilson of Basingstoke-based Country Volks, who traded until 1992, chopping up the moulds when he ceased trading.
FibreFab 1970–81
FF Kit Cars & Conversions 1981–85
Country Volks 1987–93
Approx 420 made

RAWLSON 250 LM/164 LM

Interesting one this. Clearly inspired by the 250 LM although not a replica. Don Rawlson, boss of well-known Dover-based fibreglass company Rawlson Ltd, was the man behind it, and his employee Barry Sheppard came up with a four-seat VW Beetle-based version. First prototype was ready as far back as 1976, but didn't reach production readiness until 1982. Customers had to visit Alan Hatswell's Replicar operation to buy one.

Rawlson agreed that the VW basis had to go so commissioned a ladderframe chassis from Jago Automotive and used Ford CVH engines instead of the air-cooled Beetle from 1983.

In 1984 the project was briefly with Ken Sharman, before moving to Classic Replicars run by Mike Lemon and Bruce Swales, based in the New Forest. After their tenure, Alan Frener of Western Classics took over. It was he who created a new chassis to accept mid-mounted Alfasud engines and renamed it the 164 LM.

The project ended its days with Tiger Racing, where it was one of Jim Dudley's first products, based around VW Golf engines.
Rawlson 1982–84
K. Sharman & Co 1984–86
Classic Replicars 1986–87
Western Classics 1987–89
Tiger Racing 1989–98
Approx 15 made

RAWLSON CR8

Prior to the 164LM (see previous entry), Don Rawlson collaborated with Belgian maker Liberta on this Renault 4-based coupé.
Rawlson 1972
Approx 1 made (UK)

RAY'S RODS

Born in 1940, Ray Christopher grew up playing around a dumped collection of old Ford C-Cab vans near where he lived in Dorset. He was also heavily inspired by watching grainy newsreel film clips of Grand Prix racing. He built his first car, the Kookie T, in 1959 while at college to studying heating engineering. Its inspiration came from American TV series *77 Sunset Strip* in which a character called Kookie Byrnes drove a heavily customised 1922 Model T Ford. Later on Ray would meet the builder of that car, Norm Karoski, along with others of his ilk such as George Barris and Daryl Starbird.

Ray became a professional wrestler in 1960 and went on to become Southern Area Welterweight Champion, with a special move called the 'Nagasaki Chufflock', of which he was the world's only exponent. However, his wrestling career meant he had no time to devote to cars until he read the Opus HRF feature in the second issue of *Hot Car* magazine, which prompted him to travel to Warminster and place an order for one. After the Opus came (ironically, given his future career) a Ford GT40 modified with a Jaguar E-type bonnet, followed in turn by a Jago T-Bucket in 1969.

Ray crafted his own 1923-inspired C-Cab from the Jago in 1973, and decided that he'd take it to the Crystal Palace Custom Car Show and if he received two or more orders he'd go into business supplying kit replicas and give up wrestling. He ended up taking four orders, and so Ray's Rods was born (albeit known at that time as the Dorset Rodding Centre), Dorset's first hot rod business. He based himself in a disused grocer's shop that came complete with stock, including hundreds of tins of beetroot.

Well-known creations from Ray included 'Beerwagon', 'LA Fire Dept', 'Paddy Wagon', 'Heavy Breathing' and 'Moonshine Madness'. One notable commission came from the *Daily Mirror* and was to be a competition prize. A certain Robert Maxwell came to pay for it!

In 1976, after selling around 60 C-Cab kits, Ray sold his operation to marine fibreglass specialist Tom Pawley of Exe Marine Ltd based in Newton Abbot. Within a year or so Pawley's firm was struggling, but as he'd purchased the Ray's Rods mould personally he set up a new company called Termtrend Ltd to carry on marketing them.

In 1978 Termtrend merged with Topsham-based Devon Moulding Company Ltd, who moved to Okehampton in 1979 before ceasing operations completely.

Meanwhile, Ray Christopher took a job as a contract welder, but in his 'spare' time continued to build cars, some for TV series such as *The Duchess of Duke Street* and *Doctor Who*, one for the *Bladerunner* film, one for Paul McCartney and another for comedian Mike Reid, while 1977 saw the arrival of the 'Past-yer-eyes Express', a V8-propelled milk float. Ray became known as 'The Rodfather' and went on to form GTD, who initially became agents for Ken Attwell's range of KVA GT40 replicas before creating their own highly regarded GT40 replica.

RAY'S RODS C-CAB MODEL T

Replica of Ray Christopher's Model T-inspired C-Cab of 1973, with Chevy 238 V8 engine, Triumph suspension and chromed Ford Zephyr rear axle. Kit prices started at £85.

Ray's Rods 1973–76
Exe Marine Ltd 1976–78
Devon Moulding Company 1978–79
Approx 85 made

RAY'S RODS MODEL-T

Shortly after he'd started his Ray's Rods operation in 1973, Ray Christopher was filling up with fuel at a Poole petrol station when he saw a Model T being restored in the garage on site. Further enquiries resulted in him buying the car and soon afterwards offering replica bodies at £30.

Ray's Rods 1973–76
Exe Marine Ltd 1976–78
Devon Moulding Company 1978–79
Approx 35 made

RAY'S RODS PLYMOUTH FIVE WINDOW

Third model from Ray Christopher's Ray's Rods operation was a Plymouth Five-Window.

Ray's Rods 1973–76
Exe Marine Ltd 1976–78
Devon Moulding Company 1978–79
Approx 28 made

RAZER/RAZOR

Developed from the Racecorp LA (*qv*) and Eldon Roadster (*qv*), known as the Razer when owned by Peter Filby and marketed by Richard Tilly of Roadtech under the Razer Sports Cars banner. Was taken over by Andrew Bause and renamed the Razor in 2007.

He modified the car quite extensively and also introduced a wide-bodied version. Operation based in Crawley, West Sussex.

Razer Sports Cars 2003–7
Razor Sports Cars 2007-10
Approx 6 made

RCR 40

Superb American GT40 replica made in Detroit by ex-pat Englishman (Isle or Man native) Fran Hall. Initially imported to the UK by GT40 authority Chris Melia, before Terry Hennebery of Maidstone took over. Cars arrived in the UK almost fully built, just requiring fitment of engine and a few sundry items. Featured a stainless steel monocoque.

Chris Melia 2006
Speedwell Replica Cars 2008–9
Arden Automotive 2011 to date
Approx 10 made (UK)

RD1

Lamborghini Diablo replica based around Ford Granada components and V8 power, from Croydon-based Hand Crafted Cars, run by Ron Spearink and Dave Harrison. After Ron departed the scene Dave teamed up with Clive Dingwall to create DC Supercars, based in Lincolnshire.

Hand Crafted Cars 1998–2003
DC Supercars 2003 to date
Approx 40 made

RD1 ROADSTER

A convertible roadster version of the Lamborghini Diablo.
Hand Crafted Cars 2002–3
DC Supercars 2003 to date
Approx 16 made

REALM C-TYPE

Formerly the Heritage C-type (*qv*). A superb recreation of one of Jaguar's all-time greats.
Realm Engineering 2003 to date
Approx 110 made

REEVES MATRIX

Three-wheeler from Newark-based Reeves Developments run by Paul Reeves, shown at Stoneleigh and Newark in 1985. Often compared in style to a bumper car.
Reeves Developments 1985–88
Approx 1 made

REEVES REVERA

First appeared at the Stoneleigh Show in 1988 in very much unfinished form. Not seen for next eight years, but reappeared – briefly – in 1996. Based on the unusual donor choice of Austin Princess/Ambassador. Reappeared – once more briefly – in 2000 as the Zyntech, but again not much happened.
Reeves Developments 1988, 1996
Zyntech Engineering 2000
Approx 1 made

REFLEX

Created by Gareth Atkinson, former designer at Davrian Cars in Lampeter (workshop was a former Italian prisoner of war camp). He gained an engineering diploma at the Royal Aircraft Establishment before moving to Ford at Dunton Green and then the Royal Navy. Based on Lancia mechanicals, his Reflex project was massively underrated. A later development saw a Ford version offered. The original Reflex featured a monocoque although this was later revised to a spaceframe chassis.

BP used a Reflex – well, half of a Reflex bodyshell anyway – for an advert for unleaded petrol in 1989.

A Preston company run by Rob Beardshaw and Graham Seed took over and sold a further handful before the project sadly disappeared until Gareth came back in 1992 for a brief time. He later moved back to mainstream motor design with the likes of Audi and BMW, and appeared on the seventh series of BBC TV programme *Dragons' Den* looking for funding for a typically innovative folding car trailer. One of the industry's good guys.
Reflex Cars 1986–89, 1992
Approx 18 made

REGENT TOURER

Created by Royale Motor Company founder John Barlow. Beautifully-built and highly innovative period tourer, based on London Taxi FX-4 chassis. Taken over by Francis Richards and David Cleaton of Caremore Cars in 2008, who continue to offer kits and fully-built cars under the Regent Motor Company name.
Regent Motor Company 2006–8
Regent Motor Company (Caremore Cars) 2008 to date
Approx 50 made

REMBRANDT

This capable two-seater was originally created by legendary kit car designer Peter Pellandine and known over the years as the Listair Dash among other names.
Ryder Designs & Engineering 1980–82
Approx 8 made

A B C D E F G H I J K L M N O P Q R S T U V W X Y Z

RENEGADE

A rather grandly named operation, with a background in pirate radio, run by Philip Pell and John Abrahams. Attracted, like many others, by the buoyant late sixties beach buggy scene in America, Pell Abrahams Broadcasting Corporation Ltd (PABC) of London was soon importing the buggy made by Glassco Inc, known as the Renegade. It was refreshing that it wasn't merely a clone of a Meyers Manx/Lolette/GP – it had its own identity. Pell's father, a successful handbag mogul, financed the UK operation, and although they intended to produce the Glassco Renegade under licence, they ended up making several changes for the UK market.

VW Beetle floorplan was chopped by 14½in. Kits sold at £145, which included the curved windscreen from a Ford Anglia. The early adverts proclaimed; 'California Dreamin' has become a reality!' Initial colour options were as extrovert as Pell and Abrahams – Randy Red, Itchy Indigo, Lousy Lavender, Banal Blue and Monstrous Marigold were the options.

Early quality issues, particularly with the thickness (or lack of it) of the fibreglass meant that most customers headed to agent Bob Ridgard at Four Seasons Buggy Company (a sideline to his main business; a motor accessory shop called 'Little Big End' in Fulham), for their Renegade buggies. Ridgard built top-notch fully built examples from a lock-up under the railway arches at London Bridge. The nifty special gelcoat finish called 'Fireflake', made by the Metalflake company, eased quality issues as customers really liked it.

Ridgard eventually acquired the rights to the project in late 1972 when the UK buggy boom was on the wane, although his location close to US air bases provided a sales boost. A huge one, actually, as most of his customers were US servicemen.

Always ambitious, his company placed expensive Anglia TV adverts in their locale, while the car also appeared in numerous magazine advertisements, a promotion for Harrods, a 10-minute documentary and the BBC programme *Wheelbase*, the forerunner to *Top Gear*.

Two Renegades took part in the legendary (infamous?) beach buggy race at Brands Hatch on Boxing Day 1971, driven by Tony Lanfranchi and Bob Ridgard, in 1,700cc and 1,600cc SuperVee-spec engines, respectively, even though the race was for 'up to and including 1500cc standard engines'. A long wheelbase version was introduced in 1973.

Once Ridgard had packed up in 1975, GP took the project over for no other reason than because they could, although they shelved it after about 18 months. It ended up with buggy guru James Hale's GT Mouldings operation, where it stayed until Martyn and Rob Falk of Birmingham-based KMR Beach Buggies acquired the rights to the Renegade, along with the Kyote II and Manta Ray in 2003.

Pell Abrahams Broadcasting Corporation Ltd 1970-71
Four Seasons Buggy Co 1971-75
GP Projects 1975-76
GT Mouldings 1995-2003
KMR Beach Buggies 2003 to date
Approx 310 made

RENEGADE SPEEDSTER

Porsche 356 Speedster replica from Dave Stannett of Buxton, Norfolk. Aimed at the budget end of the market.
Renegade Speedsters 2008 to date
Approx 2 made

RENEGADE T

A Belgian-British hybrid! Originally known as the Apal Au-ki. Four Seasons swapped a long-wheelbase Renegade buggy mould for a set of Apal moulds and called it the Renegade T. Meanwhile, Apal called their new acquisition the Jet. The Renegade T was based on an unmodified VW Beetle floorpan.

The 'T' would later be taken back to America, with a returning US serviceman, to become the Tuff Tub buggy produced by Perfect Plastics of Philadelphia.
Four Seasons Buggy Co 1973–74
Approx 10 made

REPLICAR SS100

Alan Hatswell owned and ran the well-known car sales operation Motorway Sports Cars on the A2, near Faversham, Kent, which he sold in 1978. He then took a three-year break from cars before founding Replicar Imports in 1981, which he set up to import American kits to the UK.

The Replicar SS100 originated with Antique & Classic Automotive of Buffalo, and was imported by Replicar from 1981. As with his Type 35 kit (see next entry), Hatswell didn't care about convention or what the purists would say about a rear-engined VW Beetle-based Jaguar SS100 with the floorpan lengthened to give the same wheelbase as the original.

As with the company's Type 55 Bugatti replica (*qv.*) the quality was very high – as was the kit price of £4,000, which helped put people off.

The Replicar SS100 would form the basis from which the Carisma Century was created.
Replicar Imports 1981–84
Approx 13 made (UK)

REPLICAR TYPE 35

Replicar's first product was a Beetle-based Bugatti Type 35 replica that used a modified Beetle floorpan and mechanicals with engine mounted in the rear, which sent the purists mad, as you'd expect. Quite a tricky build, apparently, but the quality must have been fairly high as there are a fair few survivors around. If you wanted a folding aero-screen then Hatswell sold you his Type 35C variant.

Project was bought by Chiltern Motors in 1985, before moving to PB Motors of Carshalton, Surrey, run by Paul Mallinson. Ended its days in South Norwood under the control of Lurastore.

Replicar Imports 1981–86   *Chiltern Motors 1985–88*
PB Motors 1988–93   *Lurastore 1993–95*
Approx 95 made

REPLICAR TYPE 43

When customers with children complained about the two-seats in the Replicar Type 35, Alan Hatswell came up with the Type 43 version, which thanks to some bodywork revisions had an extra row of seats. Obviously the potential customer demand wasn't there because Replicar only made one.

Replicar Imports 1983
Approx 1 made

REPLICAR TYPE 55

After several years away, Alan Hatswell, by now located in Whitstable, Kent, returned to the kit car marketplace with a Sherpa-based Bugatti Type 55 replica, powered by a BL O-series 1.7-litre engine.

Replicar Imports 1991–92
Approx 5 made

REPLICATOR RT3

Superb Triumph TR3 replica formerly made by L&R. Resurrected by Tony Griffiths of Replicator Sportscars in 2008, who, ironically, had formerly made the chassis for L&R. He revamped the kit, making it easier to build based on Ford Sierra mechanicals.

Replicator Sportscars 2008-9
Approx 3 made

RETOGA

Gary Gunn, well-known race car designer, created the underpinnings for this pretty closed two-seat track-orientated two-seater. 'Retoga' was an anagram of Kellforms' Kevin and dad Alan Goater's surname.

Kellforms Woodmasters
2004 to date
Approx 3 made

RETOGA RT

Ford Focus-based Gary Gunn-designed sports car with road orientation. Originally scheduled to have an 'exo-car' outline, although later amended to a more conventional body style.

Kellforms Woodmasters
2007-9
Approx 2 made

REVELATION

Tim Harmer, based in Bradford, is the man behind the Revelation single-seater. Has a spaceframe chassis and a Kawasaki ZX7R bike engine.

Revelation Motorsport 2007 to date
Approx 10 made

RGS ATALANTA

The importance of one Richard G. Shattocks to the British specialist car industry shouldn't be underestimated. Dick was probably the first person to sell a GRP car body in the UK from his Windsor base. He'd bought the remains of the JAG marque in 1949 and could see untapped potential in their Atalanta, that first appeared in 1937. The JAG company had sold around 20 of the so-called 'Goddess of Speed' from their Staines base before the outbreak of war in 1939 caused production to cease.

Shattocks, located in Winkworth, decided to offer a kit version of the Atalanta, with chassis appearing in 1953. He sold 12 very quickly, even before the John Griffith-created ladderframe chassis was launched the same year. Bodies were initially made by North East Coast Yacht Building & Engineering Company Ltd and from 1958 by Precision Reinforced Mouldings Ltd and then Microplas. Around 100 shells were sold before the demise of Shattocks' company in 1962.

RGS Automobile Components Ltd 1953–62
Approx 100 made

RHINO

The Rhino, from brothers Don and Terry Mackenzie, was VW Beetle-based complete with engine in the rear. Eagle Cars bought the project in 1983, converted it to Ford running gear and called it the Eagle RV (qv).
Eland Meres 1981–83
Approx 10 made

RHINO BLIZZARD

Australian Hummer replica from Rhino Buggies, briefly imported to the UK in 2004 by Karen Garrity of Leeds. Also intended selling the same company's Hammer and Jammer models, although this ultimately didn't happen.
Rhino Buggies UK 2004
Approx 1 made (UK)

RHINO INTRUDER

A trike from Nick Boyland of Winsham, Somerset.
Rhino Trikes 2003 to date
Approx 20 made

RHINO RALLY KART

Off-road-type vehicle based on Fiat Uno parts from Kilmarnock engineering company McLelland & Co, run by Iain McLelland.
McLelland & Co 1997–2001
Approx 12 made

RICKETTS GILCOLT

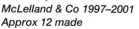

Arguably one of *the* most amusing kits ever. Ricketts was a Streatham-based Reliant dealer who briefly offered a body conversion kit complete with gullwing doors for the Regal. It used the donor's chassis and running gear. Looked like a slip-on shoe!
Ricketts of Streatham 1972
Approx 4 made

RICKMAN RANCHER

If the Rickman name was familiar it was because they were the same company that formerly made bikes, and were one of the great names of the British industry. Back in the day, Rickman brothers Derek and Don had been successful in motocross, Derek even winning the European Championship in 1966, while Don came third in the 500cc motorcycle World Championship in 1968. In all the company made some 12,000 motorbikes, of which 85% were exported.

Derek and Don's love of motorcycles came from their dad, Ernie, a successful speedway rider for Southampton before WWII, and later opened up a motorbike dealership in New Milton, acting as agents for the likes of Francis Barnett, James, Triumph and Lambretta.

Their own bikes were sold under the MƩétisse model name, which means 'mongrel' in French. The Rickman brothers used this because their bikes featured a frame from one manufacturer (usually Norton) and an engine from another (normally Triumph). They initially built bikes for themselves before others asked for 'replicas' and they became production models, while also becoming lighter and more sophisticated. The best-seller was the Metisse 125cc Enduro, with a Zundapp engine, of which around 8,000 were sold. Before putting their bikes into production, they offered the project to other manufacturers for free if they would put it into production. No one stepped forward so they did it themselves.

After they ceased making bikes in their 36,000sq ft factory in New Milton their 75 staff concentrated on making stuff such as fairings, BMX frames and even hospital beds and, of course, cars.

They were already making fibreglass bodies for several kit-car manufacturers such as Eagle Cars (Rob Budd was a friend of the Rickmans) and at the time Derek's daughter lived next door to one Nick Green, so it seemed a natural progression to move into vehicle manufacture.

Another successful motorcycle rider, Adrian Moss, joined the company and was heavily involved in the decision making process.

Derek and Don sold the operation in late 1990 to a company called FSV International Ltd, although this would lead to liquidation in 1991. The Rickman brothers bought back the rights, restarted production on a smaller scale and proceeded with development of their Métisse (qv) four-seat sports car, named after the early Rickman motorcycles. In 1993 the whole caboodle went to Lomax, for whom Andy Blakemore looked after the Rickman operation.

Lomax stopped selling the Rickman products in 1999, at which time the rights and assets were purchased by the Rickman Owners' Club.

The Rancher was a motorhome version of the company's Ranger (see next entry). Picked up on the sales success of the Starcraft (qv).
Rickman Bros Engineering 1987–90
FSV International Ltd 1990–91
Rickman Developments 1991–93
Lomax Motor Company 1993–99
Approx 250 made

RICKMAN RANGER

Rickman's first motor vehicle, an SUV-style kit that appealed to many people from launch in April 1987. It was based on Ford Escort mechanicals.
Rickman Bros Engineering 1987–90
FSV International Ltd 1990–91
Rickman Developments 1991–93
Lomax Motor Company 1993–99
Approx 900 made

RICKMAN SPACE RANGER

Elongated version of the Ranger (see above) launched in March 1989.
Rickman Bros Engineering 1987–90
FSV International Ltd 1990–91
Rickman Developments 1991–93
Lomax Motor Company 1993–99
Approx 90 made

RICO

Before Deauville Cars, Mike Richards ran Rico Cars. The Rico van was based on 2CV running gear.
Rico Cars 1996–2000
Approx 11 made

RIDGWAY SPORTS CONVERSION

A front-end restyle kit for Mini that cost the princely sum of £24 in 1965 from Farnham-based BL dealers.
Ridgway Road Garage 1965–67
Approx 12 made

RIOT

American kit made by Thunder Ranch, briefly imported to the UK by well-known VW and hot rod company Paintbox of Maldon, run by Simon Emery (ex-Karmann Konnection and trained by leading UK customiser Ritchie King) and Shane Whitworth, based in Maldon, Essex.
PB2 (Paintbox) 1998
Approx 1 made (UK)

RIOT – see *Sylva Riot*

RKC PORSCHE GTO

Roy Kelly is a leading light in the Italian Replica Owners' Club and previously made the F355 replica now made by MR2 Kits. His current offering is a 250 GTO replica based on Porsche 924/944/968 and is a ten-piece GRP body conversion. Quality is high and the use of Porsche mechanicals is innovative. Based in Ossett, West Yorkshire.
Roy Kelly Kits & Classics 2008 to date
Approx 5 made

RMB HEALEY

Came from former Triumph engineer Roger Blockley, and was sister model to the very successful Gentry (*qv*).
RMB 1985–88
Approx 12 made

ROADHOG

Created by Basildon-based Stephen Foster, one of the main suppliers of fibreglass parts for a multitude of production cars. In later years Foster made a whole raft of GRP stage sets for an array of Hollywood blockbuster films.
Fibresports 1969 to date
Approx 1,000 made

ROADSTER SPORTS

A low-cost Model B Ford rod kit from Mark Plant of High Wycombe-based Chassis Works. Underpinned by a boxed ladderframe traditional hot-rod chassis, and based on Ford Cortina MkIII, IV or V running gear. Featured a GRP body. Power could be a four-cylinder from the donor, V6 or V8. The Roadster Sports could be chosen in several body styles.
Chassis Works 1989–2007
Approx 30 made

ROAMER

Hailed from a Birmingham company and was an Austin Metro-based Moke-inspired utility vehicle underpinned by a square-section chassis, with a body from mild steel. Connections with the short-lived Moon's Moke project.
GB Restorations 1992–96
Approx 3 made

A
B
C
D
E
F
G
H
I
J
K
L
M
N
O
P
Q
R
S
T
U
V
W
X
Y
Z

ROBIN HOOD ENGINEERING

Founded in 1979 by Richard Stewart, who had from an early age learnt to innovate and create things. By 19 he was a skilled panel-beater, specialising in monocoque repair, an area that would be beneficial to him in later years. He went on to become one of the most important people ever in the UK kit car industry – an innovator, definitely; a maverick, maybe; but someone who knew what the public wanted when it came to selling kit cars.

He graduated into classic car repair and restoration and created a succession of hot-rodded cars, from a pickup with six wheels to a monster Ford Anglia with Jaguar XK 3.8-litre engine and running gear that was christened 'The Janglia'. He also ran around in a variety of classic cars from Jaguar E-type to Corvette Stingray, and the sale of a Bentley S3 enabled him to fund the acquisition of a factory in Sherwood, Nottinghamshire, that had formerly been a Wesleyan chapel.

Richard always said that he'd got in to kit car manufacturing almost by accident, as he'd badly wanted a Ferrari Daytona but couldn't afford a real one, so decided to make his own! This led to the RS Daytona replica, the first one based on Rover SD1, followed by Jaguar XJ and finally Triumph TR7. They fetch good money nowadays.

In 1989 he decided to change direction entirely and offer a low-cost, highly affordable Lotus Seven-inspired sports car based on the Triumph TR7, using leftover unused donors from the RS Daytona. With kit prices at just £995, he further developed Dutton's 'pile 'em high, sell 'em cheap' philosophy. There wasn't a shortage of customers, although one complaint was the lack of engine choice.

To solve this, Richard replaced the TR7-based kit with another Triumph donor, the Dolomite, and in doing so allowed engine choices of 1,300cc, 1,500cc, 1,850cc and the 2.0-litre from the Dolomite Sprint. As a result more and more customers continued

to flock to the company's doors. One problem, though: Richard, a genuine character, didn't allow customers to just turn up on spec, and only opened the showroom doors on Saturday mornings, a policy that was strictly adhered to.

High Court action from Caterham Cars over alleged copyright infringement almost ended production in the early '90s but ultimately resulted in Robin Hood Engineering agreeing to follow certain guidelines with their subsequent models. The most notable change was a sheet steel monocoque in lieu of a spaceframe chassis. Richard soon coined the phrase: 'one kit + one donor vehicle = car-on-the-road', and this became a massively attractive selling point for the raft of Lotus Seven-inspired models that would appear, using Ford Cortina and then Ford Sierra as donor vehicles.

Robin Hood regularly sold over 600 kits per year, their no-frills way of doing business proving ever more appealing, and the company moved to a 30,000sq ft factory in Mansfield Woodhouse, where large-scale kit production took place. Other Richard Stewart policies included not supplying kits to overseas customers and not supplying fully-built cars.

A new introduction in the late '90s saw Robin Hood Engineering come up with their bulk collection days on specific Saturdays, when customers would turn up en masse and collect their kit packages. Numbers approaching 150 kit collections were regular occurrences.

After a period of reappraisal, Richard invested in some serious state-of-the-art machinery, including CNC machines, plasma cutters and all manner of other equipment. Ably assisted by Gina Crampton, who'd been with the company since the beginning, Richard came up with another innovative new model that had a tubular chassis that his machinery could produce in ten minutes. His staff nicknamed it the 'tubey', which kind of stuck, and the '2b' was born. It would go on to become a big seller for Robin Hood.

Other models were toyed with over the years including the Rager, Kaig and Go, but it was always his hardcore Lotus Seven-inspired kits that sold in biggest numbers.

A man never afraid to stand his ground and do things his way, Richard Stewart a man would really deserve his place in the UK kit car hall of fame, if there was one. Like Tim Dutton before him he had his critics, but as with Tim, anyone who can sell kit cars in the kind of volume that he could demands respect.

In 2006 Richard decided to retire and sold the company to some businessmen, who retained the Mansfield Woodhouse premises, with Gina Crampton staying on for a while. Unfortunately the operation lasted only around 18 months before they ceased trading. However, erstwhile manager Ian Rowley and employee Richard Hall quickly resurrected the marque under the Great British Sportscars banner, although Rowley departed in 2009 leaving Hall in sole charge.

ROBIN HOOD 200

Mid-mounted Rover 200-spec powered model based on a Rover donor.
Robin Hood Engineering 1998

ROBIN HOOD 2B DOHC

A 2B model based around the Ford DOHC engine from the Sierra.
Robin Hood Engineering 2003–6

ROBIN HOOD BARRELBACK SERIES 6

A curious rolled back-end styling for this Robin Hood model, known as the Barrelback.
Robin Hood Engineering 1991

ROBIN HOOD BOLTEON –
see Robin Hood Lightweight

ROBIN HOOD RS DAYTONA (JAGUAR XJ CONVERSION)

A development of Robin Hood's original Rover SD1-based RS Daytona (see next entry), this one was based on XJ6 or XJ12.
Robin Hood Engineering 1987–89
Approx 18 made

ROBIN HOOD RS DAYTONA (SD1 CONVERSION)

The UK's first Daytona replica actually came from Robin Hood Engineering in 1985, when boss Richard Stewart decided to prove the theory that the Rover SD1 looked like the Ferrari Daytona by using one as the basis for his first model. He also badly wanted a real one, but couldn't afford the £50,000 price tag they commanded in the late 1970s, so he built his own.

With a shortened wheelbase and revised Rover body it worked very well, and today these change hands for a lot of money.

Stewart made seven steel conversions and a further 28 Jaguar XJ6 fibreglass-bodied true kit examples from 1987 before he created a Triumph TR7-based Daytona replica the same year.
Robin Hood Engineering 1979–84
Approx 70 made

ROBIN HOOD RS DAYTONA (TRIUMPH TR7 CONVERSION)

With a desire to create a more affordable Ferrari Daytona replica, Richard Stewart reasoned that with some 52,000 TR7s sold in the UK there was no shortage of donor vehicles suitable for plundering for the purpose.

Sadly, this model didn't catch on like its predecessors, and the large number of Triumph TR7 donors that Richard had purchased in expectation of needing them for his RS Daytona model weren't required. At this point he hit upon the idea of a Lotus Seven-inspired sports car, using – surprise, surprise! – a TR7 donor.
Robin Hood Engineering 1989
Approx 7 made

ROBIN HOOD DONINGTON

Interesting rear-end treatment on this one, using a chopped Sierra tailgate.
Robin Hood Engineering 1993

ROBIN HOOD EXMO

Sliding pillar front suspension (à la Morgans of yesteryear) and an alligator-style bonnet.
Robin Hood Engineering 1997–98

ROBIN HOOD FERRENZO

Ferrari F360 replica based on Toyota MR2 Mk2 donor created by the 'new' Robin Hood Sportscars post-Richard Stewart.
Robin Hood Sportscars 2005–7

ROBIN HOOD FORD SIERRA-BASED

After the Cortina-based S7 had sold in huge numbers, Richard Stewart moved on to the Sierra, which once more accelerated sales.
Robin Hood Engineering 1994–95

ROBIN HOOD GO

A short-lived Metro-based mid-engined sports car from Robin Hood. Made its debut at the Sandown Show of 1997 and was ditched after just two sales.
Robin Hood Engineering 1997
Approx 2 made

ROBIN HOOD LIGHTWEIGHT

Originally known as the Bolteon. A Robin Hood model based on Ford Sierra that was, er, lightweight.
Robin Hood Engineering 2002–7

ROBIN HOOD MID-ENGINED

Metro-power mounted amidships using Rover Tomcat engines. Intention was to use the leftover Rover engines and running gear that didn't get used on the ill-fated Go model. Not around for long.
Robin Hood Engineering 1997

ROBIN HOOD NEW SERIES 3

New chassis for the S3, with several other amendments and upgrades.
Robin Hood Engineering 1998–99

ROBIN HOOD ONE-O-SAX

The One-O-Sax was a detour back to Richard Stewart's body conversion days, which tarted up the styling of the boy racer's favourites, Citroën Saxo or Peugeot 106. Didn't catch on.
Robin Hood Engineering 2000–1

ROBIN HOOD PROJECT 2B

This was an all-new Robin Hood with a tubular chassis made on Richard's amazing machinery in just ten minutes. Back to a spaceframe chassis for this one. Staff nicknamed it 'tubey' during development, hence its '2b' designation. Big seller.
Robin Hood Engineering 1999–2001

ROBIN HOOD PROJECT 2B/4

Originally known as the Sub-K, because it cost £995, this kit was supplied with stainless-steel panels.
Robin Hood Engineering 2003–6

ROBIN HOOD PROJECT 2B PLUS

A 2b with enhanced specification.
Robin Hood Engineering 2003–7
Great British Sportscars 2007–9

ROBIN HOOD RAGER

Richard Stewart's attempt at a rugged off-road-style kit car based on Ford Sierra donor. Unveiled at the Donington show in 2003 to gauge reaction but never launched. Just the one prototype made.
Robin Hood Engineering 2003
Approx 1 made

ROBIN HOOD S5

Launched at the same time as the S6, and was identical except the S5 used Ford Cortina (Mk4 or 5) suspension all round.
Robin Hood Engineering 1990–91

ROBIN HOOD S6

Visually identical to the S5 but used Ford Cortina (Mk 4 or 5) suspension only at the rear, featuring a bespoke wishbone arrangement at the front.
Robin Hood Engineering 1990–91

ROBIN HOOD S7

One complaint levelled at the S7 TR7 was that there was only one engine choice – the 2.0-litre from the donor, delivering 92bhp, so Richard Stewart set about coming up with a replacement. He remained with Triumph, but changed the donor to Dolomite, which offered four engine options – 1,300cc, 1,500cc, 1,850cc and the feisty 2.0-litre from the Dolomite Sprint. Something for everybody, in fact.

Initially came with a slightly modified chassis from the TR7-based S7, but, harking back to his experience of repairing monocoques for a living as a young man, Richard launched a version of the S7 based on one that he called The Unique.
Robin Hood Engineering 1990–94

ROBIN HOOD S7 FORD CORTINA-BASED

This one used the donor Cortina's engine. To satisfy the volume sales that Richard Stewart foresaw he needed a mass-produced donor vehicle, and Ford's best-seller fitted the bill perfectly.
Robin Hood Engineering 1991–94

ROBIN HOOD S7 JAGUAR-BASED

Powered by a V12 Jaguar engine squeezed into the Robin Hood spaceframe. Effortless power, backed up by a massive twist of torque. Only one example made.
Robin Hood Engineering 1990–91

ROBIN HOOD S7 THE UNIQUE

Hailed as being 'unique' when launched, the monocoque underpinned S7 was claimed to be the only specialist car of its type. This particular version was a one-off and featured a walnut-clad dash and Bentley grille. More expensive at £2,702 including VAT, the kit was pretty comprehensive, requiring just a Dolomite donor to build a car. Like the standard spaceframe version, it proved popular.
Robin Hood Engineering 1990

ROBIN HOOD S7 TR7

TR7-based LSIS with a spaceframe chassis from square-section steel tube, with pre-cut, pre-folded stainless steel panels. Launched at Stoneleigh Show in May 1989 and immediately 'hit the spot' for lots of

people, with a kit price of £1,169 including VAT and a promised DIY self-build price of around £2,000. Launched with the marketing line of 'The latest chapter in the evolution of the Super Seven', which, as one might imagine, didn't please Caterham Cars very much.
Robin Hood Engineering 1989–90

ROBIN HOOD S1 CHEVEN

The Cheven was another example of Richard Stewart's innovation and ability to spot a donor. For the Cheven he used the Vauxhall Chevette, which was a pretty unremarkable car except for the fact that there were lots of them around.
Robin Hood Engineering 1993

ROBIN HOOD SERIES 2

Development of the Ford Sierra-based LSIS delivering typical Robin Hood value for money.
Robin Hood Engineering 1995–96

ROBIN HOOD SERIES 3

A raft of upgrades over the Series 2 it replaced. Still used Ford Sierra as donor but you got more in the kit. Lots sold.
Robin Hood Engineering 1997–98

ROBIN HOOD SERIES 3A

Final development of the very popular Ford Sierra-based Robin Hood model.
Robin Hood Engineering 1998

ROBIN HOOD SUB-K

So-called because the kit cost just £995. A real back-to-basics Robin Hood model.
Robin Hood Engineering 2002

SPEC

Ford Sierra-based Robin Hood that came with every last nut and bolt required to build a car.
Robin Hood Engineering 2002–7
Great British Sportscars 2007
to date

ROBIN HOOD THE BULLET

A quirky three-wheeler that arrived in 2008, in the final months of the post-Richard Stewart Robin Hood Engineering operation. The Bullet was powered by a 125cc scooter engine.
Robin Hood Engineering 2008

ROBIN HOOD THE HOOD

A 'new' Robin Hood Sportscars project developed in association with former Tyrrell engineer Colin Denyer. Notable for its restyled and distinctive nosecone.
Robin Hood Sportscars 2007

ROBIN HOOD TRADITIONAL

A traditionally styled, stainless steel-panelled Robin Hood based on Ford Sierra.
Robin Hood Engineering 1998–99

Grand total of all Robin Hood Sportscars kits made is hard to calculate but must be around 10,000

ROCA ALPHA

One of the few kit car makers to hail from the Isle of Wight, Cowes-based Roca Engineering revised a US kit for the UK market. It was run by Australian aviation engineer Rod Ogilvie. Made a low-key debut at the Stoneleigh Show in 1989. Several options available – Sierra or Granada-based, therefore front or mid-engined, or even VW Beetle-based with conventional rear-mounted engine – and could be had in Turbo or Panamericana body styles. A planned 'Beta' version, which replicated the Strosek Porsche, was stillborn.
Roca Engineering 1988–1989
Approx 1 made

ROCHDALE MOTOR PANELS AND ENGINEERING LTD

Founded by Harry Smith and Frank Butterworth in, er, Rochdale in 1948, and set up in an old mill in Hudson Street. A very important name in the annals of the kit car and *specials* market, albeit an underrated one. Rochdale was easily the most successful of the companies that supplied bodies for British *specials* builders in the '50s.

Though the factory was destroyed by fire in 1961, the company managed to recover from the ashes and set up again in Littledale Mill, where they managed to launch the Olympic Phase II, which unofficially went out of production in 1966 but was theoretically available into the early 1970s.

Having sold hundreds of bodyshells, Rochdale decided that there was more money in industrial GRP and ended its automotive activities.

ROCHDALE Mk1 ALLOY BODY

Aluminium bodyshell for Austin 7 mechanicals.
Rochdale Motor Panels & Engineering Ltd 1948–54
Approx 10 made

ROCHDALE Mk2

A revised Mk1 body.
Rochdale Motor Panels & Engineering Ltd 1952–54
Approx 6 made

ROCHDALE MkVI

Rochdale's first fibreglass bodyshell and one of the first commercially available in the UK, highlighting the potential of this exciting new material, although initially as expensive as their aluminium bodies. Very basic model, leaving the customer with a lot of work to do. Intended for Ford 7ft 6in chassis.
Rochdale Motor Panels & Engineering Ltd 1954–61
Approx 150 made

ROCHDALE C-TYPE

Inspired by the Connaught ALSR, designed for Ford 10 mechanicals.
Rochdale Motor Panels & Engineering Ltd 1955–61
Approx 30 made

ROCHDALE F-TYPE

One-piece GRP moulding inspired by Ferraris of the day. Very rakish and low-slung.
Rochdale Motor Panels & Engineering Ltd 1955–61
Approx 50 made

ROCHDALE GT

Allegedly created because co-founder Harry Smith's wife wanted a 'proper' car with a roof and room for children in the back! Most adventurous Rochdale yet, with pre-hung doors and bonnet. Most popular model by a long way.
Rochdale Motor Panels & Engineering Ltd 1956–63
Approx 1,350 made

ROCHDALE OLYMPIC PHASE 1

The world's second GRP prototype (after the Lotus Elite). It was a smart and well-engineered car, described by the press as a 'British Porsche 911'. Used Riley 1.5 or Ford Sidevalve engines, Riley IFS and coil sprung rear suspension. Designed by Richard Parker.
Rochdale Motor Panels & Engineering Ltd 1960–61
Approx 250 made

ROCHDALE OLYMPIC PHASE II

Following the factory fire in 1961, Rochdale set about restarting Olympic production and came up with the Phase II, which moved the car into more sophisticated territory. Kits were offered until 1966.
Rochdale Motor Panels & Engineering Ltd 1963–66 (bare shells until 1973)
Approx 150 made

ROCHDALE RIVIERA

Essentially a GT with the roof cut off and a few body revisions.
Rochdale Motor Panels & Engineering Ltd 1959–61
Approx 50 made

ROCHDALE ST (SPORTS TOURER)

First out-and-out Rochdale road car, much more sophisticated than the company's other 'shells.
Rochdale Motor Panels & Engineering Ltd 1955–59
Approx 100 made

ROCHE

A short-lived Le Mans-spec BMW M1 replica from a Blackburn company run by Peter Jackson, who also had involvement with Paul Lawrenson's Prova operation.
Sports Cars & Specials 1987
Approx 1 made

ROCKET

Ford Focus-based exo-skeletal-type kit that spawned the Smart ForTwo-based Zonta (*qv*). Approved for Australian ADR regulations in early 2011. Designed by the innovative Stuart Mills of MEV Ltd, the Rocket seems to have hit the perfect balance between fun, affordability and performance.
Mills Extreme Vehicles 2007–9
Road Track Race Ltd 2009 to date
Approx 300 made

RODLEY '32 CHEVROLET/'32 MODEL B FORD

Bradford-based Rodley Motors imported steel-bodied replicas of the Experi-Metal Inc '32 Chevy and '32 Model B Ford from late 1991 that were said to be exact copies. The chassis was a diagonally cross-braced steel ladderframe with power coming from a V8. Experi-Metal Inc was based in Sterling Heights, Michigan, close to the 'Motor City' of Detroit, and regularly did test pressings of prototypes for GM and Ford Motor Co, using its in-house foundry. Not available in the UK as kits per se, fully built examples cost from £25,000 in late 1991.
Rodley Motors 1991–94
Approx 8 made

RODSHOP 29 FORD

A '29 Ford available in a choice of three bodystyles – Sedan, Delivery Van and Pick Up, with two chassis options available. The first was a very basic frame from which the diehard rodder could do their own *thang,* while a more complete chassis package was set up to accept Ford Cortina Mk3, 4 or 5 running gear. Tarrant Road, Bournemouth-based outfit run by street rod enthusiast, David Palmer. In 1984, body kits started at £950 with chassis packages from £275.
Rodshop 1982–87
Approx 24 made

RODSHOP MODEL B

Another offering from rodder David Palmer, who offered what he claimed was the only one-piece Model B chassis in Europe, while the body could be in 'Highboy' or 'Fendered' (with wings) styles. Body kits cost £650 in 1984, with chassis at £950.
Rodshop 1982–87
Approx 14 made

ROMERO

Designed by Steve Himsworth and Clive Gamble and was a nice update on the old Marlin Roadster (*qv*) model the company had acquired in 1992. It was based on Ford Sierra, featured a kind of three-dimensional semi-monocoque with a perimeter frame, with sealed box section incorporating a steel windscreen frame. Contrary to belief it wasn't named after actor Cesar Romero who played *The Joker* in the 1960s *Batman* TV series!

The Romero was unusual in that it retained unmodified Ford Sierra front suspension with a de Dion rear end with Sierra differential and shortened driveshafts.
YKC Sportscars 1997–2004
Aquila Sportscars 2004–7
Approx 40 made

RONART GP RACER

Company founded by Rona and Arthur Wolstenholme, who were inspired by a visit to the Daimler-Benz Museum in Stuttgart. Arthur had previously restored several classic motorbikes. The GP Racer appeared in 1999 and was clearly heavily influenced by '50s single-seaters with a tandem two-seat arrangement, designed for children and jockey-sized adults.
Ronart Cars 1999–2003
Approx 4 made

RONART VANWALL GPR 12

Rebirth of the famous Vanwall name from Arthur Wolstenholme of Ronart Cars, with Jaguar V12 power and a beautiful level of build.
Vanwall Cars 2006 to date
Approx 3 made

RONART W152

Featured a chassis by Spyder Engineering. Originally called the Alicat due to its body being made of aluminium and having Jaguar XJ underpinnings. The prototype made its debut at the National Classic Car Show of 1984. Wolstenholme was inspired by post-war GP racers and had restored a number of vintage motorcycles. A Mk2 arrived in 1997 with revised SpyderSport chassis, Rose-jointed rear radius arms and wider footwells.

When Wolstenholme relaunched the Vanwall marque in 2006 he placed the Ronart models under that banner for a time.
Arthur Wolstenholme 1984–7
Ronart Cars 1987–2006
Vanwall Cars 2006-8
Ronart Cars 2008 to date
Approx 110 made

ROTRAX

Created by former Marcos man Dennis Adams. Had sold 60 kits by mid-1990. The Rotrax Sport was a two-seater and the Safari was a four-seater. Project sold to Mike Kenyon of Rotrax Sales in 1991 just after Adams had announced the four-seat version, and passed to Paul Jelf in 1994, although after the initial burst of interest, sales dwindled.

Adams Rotrax 1988–91
JS Rotrax Sales 1991–94
Rotrax Sales 1994–97
Approx 75 made

ROWFANT ROADSTER

Traditional-type styling created by Peter Simpson, a friend of Scamp boss Andrew McLean. Based on Suzuki SJ410, 413, Samurai or Santana and featured an aluminium body.
Scamp Motor Company 2001–3
Approx 1 made

ROYALE DROPHEAD

John Barlow's first independent design post-JBA. The wondrous Drophead arrived in 1991 and gave limo-type vintage grand touring a new lease of life. Based on Ford Granada underpinnings. Not feasible to make it SVA-compliant so it was replaced by the even grander Windsor.

Royale Motor Company 1991–98
Approx 50 made

ROYALE SABRE

Glorious '30s-style tourer from the pen of the master of such vehicles, John Barlow. Featured a twin-rail ladderframe and Granada mechanicals. Launched at the Stafford Kit Car Show of March 1994.

Project was bought by Dutch operation Empire Car Company in 2001, and when they ceased trading in 2002 it moved to Alan Beillby at VMC, where it gradually faded away. Resurrected in 2009 by Wimbledon-based Sabre Sportscars, part of Asquith Motors, run by Simon Rhodes, later passing to Malcolm Badger.
Royale Motor Company 1994–2001
Empire Motor Company (Netherlands) 2001–2
Vintage Motor Company 2002–6   Sabre Sportscars 2009 to date
Approx 260 made

ROYALE WINDSOR

Launched at the Newark Show in summer 1998, intended as a replacement for the Drophead model. Underpinned by a substantial ladderframe with a central cruciform section, donor parts from Ford Granada.

Royale Motor Company 1998–2001   Vintage Motor Company 2001–6
Approx 75 made

RSK SPYDER

Cheltenham-based Rob Lindsay keeps a low profile but makes a nice job of his Porsche RSK replica and does a lot to help builders of GP Spyder kits finish their builds and/or obtain parts. Usual VW Beetle underpinnings and a part-stressed GRP body complete his own ensemble.

Spyders Inc 2004 to date
Approx 50 made

RT1/RT BLAZE

Before acquiring the Razer project, Roadtech, run by ace general kit builder Richard Tilly, made this budget-orientated Lotus Seven-inspired sports car that had its origins in the Locust. First car had MDF cockpit side-panels, later changed to aluminium, with GRP wings and nosecone.

Roadtech 1999-2003
Approx 5 made

RUDOLPH SPORTWAGEN

German kit inspired by the legendary Karmann Ghia that was imported to the UK by Pete Murphy of the Evergreen Motor Company, based in Cornwall.

Evergreen Car Company 1995–2001
Approx 15 made (UK)

RUGGER

American import utility kit based on VW Beetle, imported to Europe by Jersey-based Replica Car Imports, who also marketed the Allison MG replica (*qv*) for a time. Featured a rugged box-section steel chassis and all-steel, rather than GRP, body. Based on VW Beetle, which meant engine in the back. Later became the Willeep Rugger under the control of Rugger Agency of London, NW8. Neither venture lasted long.
Replica Car Imports 1980–81
Rugger Agency 1981–83
Approx 1 made (UK)

RUSKA REGINA

Ruska was a Dutch company whose Regina was a bit like a Mercedes SSK (if you closed one eye!). Imported to the UK by Dovercourt of Stratford, East London. Only available in fully-built guise, the Regina cost from £7,000 in 1980.
Dovercourt Plaistow 1980–83
Approx 1 made (UK)

RUSKA SPRINTER/CLASSICA

This was basically Ruska's version of the well-known UK kit the Renegade T (*qv*) based on a shortened VW Beetle floorpan. Available in the UK in fully-built guise only from £6,000 in 1980.
Dovercourt Plaistow 1981–83
Approx 1 made (UK)

RUSKA TYPE 35

Dutch attempt at a Bugatti Type 35, although like the same company's Regina and Sprinter (see above) it was too expensive for UK tastes, being £7,500 in 1980.
Dovercourt Plaistow 1980–83
Approx 1 made (UK)

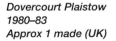

RW 427

Came from Roger Woolley's Melton Mowbray-based RW Kit Cars operation. Related to the AD 427 (*qv*), from which it evolved. Ten kits supplied to a French customer that were based on VW Beetle mechanicals.
RW Kit Cars 1988–90
Approx 28 made

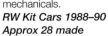

RW CHOPPER

VW Beetle power for this trike from Roger Woolley.
RW Kit Cars 1983–84
Approx 5 made

RW TAURUS

Countach replica based on VW Beetle that had been started, but never productionised, by Dave Perry of Automotive Design. Around 30 of the cars produced went to Germany.
RW Kit Cars 1985–86
Approx 32 made

RYCAM MIRAGE

Tom Killeen-penned Imp-powered sports car that predated the same designer's Scorpion creation (see Kestrel Scorpion). Revised by Sutton Coldfield-based Rycam Engineering complete with a tuned Imp Sport 998cc engine. Didn't make production. Resurrected as the Kestrel Scorpion (*qv*) by Dovetail Plastics in 1984.
Rycam Engineering 1973
Approx 1 made

RYDER REMBRANDT

Coventry-based Ryder Automotive was run by Rob Ryder and Jerry Grolin. The car was originally known as the Pelland Sports (*qv*), created by Peter Pellandine. Later passed to Graham Autos of Carlisle.
Ryder Automotive 1980–82
Approx 15 made

RYDER ROYALE

VW Beetle-based Morgan replica from the same company that had acquired the Pelland Sports. Nothing wrong with the Royale, but not really outstanding. Later offered by Graham Autos of Carlisle, Cumbria and then Sabre Card of Wallsend. Briefly reappeared as the Montreaux, in 1990, offered by Newcastle upon Tyne-based Fabrication Design, and based on Vauxhall Viva mechanicals. Wasn't around for long.

Ryder Automotive 1981–82   *Graham Autos (Glassfibre) Ltd 1982–84*
Sabre Cars 1984–87   *Fabrication Design 1990*
Approx 12 made

RYECROFT

Period vehicle kit from Bramwith Motor Company, originally devised by Alan Beillby of Vintage Motor Company. After Bramwith's demise, the product was taken over by John and Gill Ford of Wirral-based AWS Ltd.
Vintage Motor Company 1997–2007
Bramwith Motor Company 2007–2010; AWS Ltd 2011 to date
Approx 10 made

SABRE

Trackday/racer style car from well-known bike engine tuner and engineer, Andy Bates of Buxhall, Suffolk. Sabre based around bike engines such CBR1000 Fireblade, with an example raced by Richard Wise in the 750 Motor Club's RGB Championship in 2010. Bates appeared on BBC TV's Dragons' Den programme in 2011 and was successful in gaining investment from Peter Jones.
AB Performance 2010 to date
Approx 6 made

SABRE SPRINT

Sabre Cars was founded in 1984 by Steve Crabtree of Wallsend. The company's main business was fibreglass mouldings, making such diverse stuff as sunbeds, canoes and garden ponds.

The Sabre Sprint was Mini-based and featured a GRP monocoque. A revised Mk2 with new grille and twin headlights appeared in 1985. An intended range of Sabre camper vans came to nothing after just one was made.

Erstwhile agents DC Kit Cars, run by David Cawston, took over the Sabre Sprint project in late 1986 but only lasted a couple of years.
Sabre Cars 1984–86
DC Kit Cars 1986–87
Approx 14 made

SABRE VARIO

Had an interchangeable roof and was basically a Mk2 version of the Sabre Sprint.
Sabre Cars 1985–86
Approx 5 made

SAFIR Mk5

A superb vehicle and definitely not a kit car, but of the 41 made ten were supplied in rolling chassis form and as a completist I felt it only right to include them here.

Created by Peter Thorp, who had been looking for a genuine GT40 but failed to find one to meet his requirements. His company had built some very decent Formula 3 cars in the 1970s and for a time was even a privateer Formula 1 team. Thorp decided to build his own GT40 and John Willment became part of his operation.

Initially a replica was intended but they went to Ford and got permission to build a batch of 25 officially blessed cars that came complete with continuation chassis numbers, the first Safir chassis number being 1090.

In addition to Willment, Len Bailey was also involved and from the early '90s bodies were changed to carbon fibre and chassis plates bore the legend 'JW Automotive Engineering Ltd'.

Quality was extremely high and the turnkey versions featured Mathwall-built engines, while the chassis were built by Adam-McCall Engineering.
Safir Engineering 1980–91
Approx 10 made

SAHARA BUGGY

When beach buggy guru James Hale acquired the Baja GT project (*qv*) he set about creating a long-wheelbase version, which he called the Sahara.
GT Mouldings 1985–87
Approx 5 made

SAIGA

Launched at the Stoneleigh Kit Car Show in 1989 by SEM Cars, run by former TVR duo Tony Edwards and Terry Steptoe. Basically a revised '60s TVR 3000M.
SEM Cars 1989–91
Approx 4 made

SALT FLATS RACER

Penrith-based Cygnus Custom & Classic was the company behind this take on a 1940 salt-flats racer, which was based on a fenderless 1930 Ford Coupé body that was chopped and channelled and sat on a Model A-style twin-rail chassis. The company also acquired the Markham Street Rods range of hot-rod bodies.
Cygnus Custom & Classic 2011 to date
Approx 2 made

SAMMIO SPYDER

Created by well-known hot-rodder and original member of the famed UK Low Riders Club, Gary Janes, who had also founded the Dooster operation. He sold the projects on and came up with the Bay Area Rods idea. He then created the delightful little Triumph Herald or Vitesse-based Sammio Spyder, inspired by a fifties bodyshell, which Gary estimated could be built for sub-£2,000. In early 2011 he was getting a lot of interest in the car, which he supplied from his Bournemouth workshop.
Sammio Motor Company 2010 to date
Approx 90 made

SANDBACH DUKE

American Beetle-based SS100 import. Sandbach later developed their own Vauxhall Chevette-based chassis.
Sandbach Replica Cars 1983–84
Approx 3 made

SANDBACH SAXON

American import based on Austin Healey 3000 and a pleasant-looking fixed head two-seater. Sandbach developed a Vauxhall Chevette-based chassis of their own. Known in America as the Fiberfab Jamaican.
Sandbach Replica Cars 1983-84
Approx 2 made

SANDBACH TD

American import (FiberFab Migi) Beetle-based MG TD replica that Sandbach imported to the UK before they started production themselves, converting it to Vauxhall Chevette running gear while doing so.
Sandbach Replica Cars 1983–84
Approx 2 made

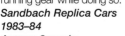

SANDWOOD BUGATTI TYPE 49 REPLICA

'Splashed' from a genuine Bugatti Type 49 and eventually sold to Wayne Roper of Europa Specialist Spares. Only one made.
Sandwood 1983–84
Classic Reproductions 1984
Sheldonhurst 1984–88
Approx 1 made

SANDWOOD/SHELDONHURST CALIFORNIAN

Terry Sands is a name entwined with the UK kit car industry from the early '80s, having an involvement with many well-known kits. He had his origins at Ford Motor Company's SVO as a design draughtsman. His Muscle City operation evolved into Sandwood, and Sands satisfied a growing UK demand for a Porsche Speedster replica, which at that time could only be filled by the more expensive Apal Speedster (*qv*). His solution was an affordable package based initially on his 'Alfachassis' for Alfa Romeo parts as he didn't like the VW Beetle, although he soon gave in and made one of them based on a chopped Beetle floorpan. Quality rated as being pretty good. Also offered a Californian big arch, de-chromed version, later sold by DJ Sportscars for a time.

Meanwhile, after a brief company name change to Classic Reproductions, Sands merged with Bill Cook's Sheldonhurst operation, which lasted a few years. Sands took the Californian and Speedster with him to AVC Ltd from 1985 and the kits formed the basis of his Legend Motor Company operation from the mid-'90s.
Sandwood 1983–84
Classic Reproductions 1984
Sheldonhurst 1984–85
Alternative Vehicle Centre 1985–90
Approx 150 made

SANDWOOD/SHELDONHURST COBRA

Developing his Cobra replica from the original Muscle City car that used MGB running gear which was a copy of the American Steve Arntz bodyshell, Terry Sands made revisions to it under the Sandwood name.

One day Terry placed an advert in the *Birmingham Post* for an investor with 'more money than sense' to get involved in a car business. This is exactly what the advert said! One Bill Cook noticed it and, abandoning his intention to buy a carpet warehouse, contacted Terry, and before very long they had set themselves up in a factory in Tyseley, trading as Sheldonhurst, from 1984.

Bill Cook underpinned the car with a backbone chassis and Ford Granada mechanicals and it can lay claim to being the UK's first budget Cobra kit. After Sheldonhurst ceased trading, erstwhile agents Brightwheel and Cobreth took the project on as manufacturers, developed it further and sold a lot more kits.
Sandwood 1984
Classic Reproductions 1984
Sheldonhurst 1984–88
Approx 300 made

SANDWOOD GOPHER

Sandrail that was developed in response to the UVA Fugitive (*qv*) and Kingfisher Chenowth (*qv*), both very popular at the time. Based like them on VW Beetle mechanicals.
Sandwood Automotive 1983–84
Approx 150 made

SANDWOOD SCORPIONE GT

Very similar visually to an Avante (*qv*), for which Sands had developed his 'Alpha-chassis'.
Sandwood Automotive 1983
Approx 20 made

SPEEDSTER

Developed along the same lines as the alternative-bodied Californian model, sharing the same running gear. Morphed into the Legend Speedster (*qv*).
Sandwood 1984
Classic Reproductions 1984
Sheldonhurst 1984–85
Alternative Vehicle Centre 1985–90
Approx 500 made

SANDWOOD/SHELDONHURST XK120

American import from the East Coast Carriage Company that came based on Ford Pinto donor. Terry Sands kept this option available but could see that this would never be accepted in numbers by UK customers, so came up with a new box-section

ladderframe chassis for the inevitable Jag XJ6 components, which added 2in to the width of the American original.
Sandwood 1983–84
Classic Reproductions 1984
Sheldonhurst 1984–86
Approx 20 made

SANTOR

Weird amalgamation of Sapphire and Saturn offered briefly by Mike Barton's Slough-based MDB operation in 1986.
MDB Cars 1986
Approx 1 made

SAPPHIRE

A two-seater from Mike Barton, originating from the GP Centron II (*qv*).
MDB Cars 1986–88
Approx 1 made

SATURN ROADSTER/ROADSTER RW460

Appeared in late 2009 and was based around Chris Gibbs' successful Haynes book *Build Your Own Sports Car on a Budget*, which spawned the Haynes Roadster, of which around 350 are thought to be building.

Hartlepool-based Saturn Sports Cars, run by Andy Hugill (helped by Andy Smales), set up to supply everything from complete kits to individual parts for this Ford Sierra underpinned two-seater.

A Mazda RX-8 donor option was developed for 2011, when the car was known as the Roadster RW460.
Saturn Sports Cars 2009 to date
Approx 10 made

SAVANT 175

Huddersfield-based Ian Pettinger ran a steel company and was intending to buy a Lotus Seven-inspired sports car for his son, but after researching the market wasn't impressed with what was available, so he commissioned former Corse (*qv*) manufacturer Steve Greenwood and Richard Ashby, to design a modern take on this traditional theme, which he did, coming up with a choice of three slightly different body styles. Launched at Stoneleigh in 1999, the project was soon purchased by Wooldridge-era Quantum Sports Cars, where its name was changed to Quantum Xtreme.
Sector Three Engineering 1999–2000
Approx 2 made

SAXAN CRUSADER

An updated version of the Warrior (see next entry) with bigger windscreen, wider doors with sliding windows, and more room in the rear. Also, the flat panels of the Warrior now had curves. Based on Daihatsu Fourtrak.
IJF Developments 1993–2000
Approx 4 made

SAXAN WARRIOR

Ian Ferrier was the man behind this one. Based on Daihatsu Fourtrak.
IJF Developments 1992–2000
Approx 8 made

SCARAB

Dragsport of Rawdon, Yorkshire, intended to produce this mid-engined coupé designed by Allan Staniforth (with input from Bob Coats and Murray Rose) and based on his Terrapin project made famous by his *High Speed Low Cost* book. Indeed, Staniforth raced one in 1971 when it was known by the wonderful name of 'Whippingham Wrogue'. Dragsport was the trading name of Sarcon Ltd, who went into liquidation in late 1972.
Dragsport 1972
Approx 1 made

SCAMP Mk1

Farmer Robert Mandry of Whitchurch Hill, near Reading, was the man behind this very successful kit car. He had also been a successful club racer in Minis. Clearly inspired by the Mini Moke, Mandry came up with a rugged multi-tube semi-spaceframe chassis with Mini

subframes and a body made from aluminium panels. Ever versatile, you could choose between four and six wheels (an additional Mini subframe was used) in a multitude of body styles and wheelbases. Company name changed in 1974 when Mandry went solo.
Miller Mandry 1969–74
Robert Mandry Scamps 1974–77
Approx 700 made

SCAMP Mk2

If the Mk1 had been successful then the Mk2 from 1978 went ballistic. Using similar mechanicals and construction methods, the second iteration of the Scamp had a squarer, more Moke-like appearance, but could still be ordered in all sorts of

configurations, including van, pickup or estate bodies or even with six wheels.

Part-time fireman Andrew MacLean, based in Rowfant on the Surrey/West Sussex border, acquired the project in 1987.
Robert Mandry Scamps 1977–87
Scamp Motor Company 1987–2000
Approx 2,000 made

SCAMP Mk3

Had a tubular steel perimeter frame with internal cockpit cage, with A-series or A+ engine.
Scamp Motor Company 1990–98
Approx 275 made

SCAMP Mk4x4

Suzuki SJ-based version.
Scamp Motor Company 1995-2005
Approx 25 made

SCAMP GRASS TRACKER

Not really a grasstracker, but more of a Scamp that ran on grasstrack-style beefy tyres! Particularly good off-road though.
Scamp Motor Company 1993–98
Approx 3 made

SCHMITT

Came from Preston-based bubble car restorers run by Rick Edwards and Dave Chapman, sister product to their Zetta 300 (*qv*) Isetta replica.

This one was a copy of the Messerschmitt KR200 featuring a GRP monocoque with integral steel chassis structure, and weighed in at just 270kg. Also available with a Tiger-style front.
Tri-Tech Automotive 1998–2002
Approx 15 made

SCIMI – *see LMC Roadster*

SCOOBY 200

Subaru Impreza-based RS200 replica from Mill Auto Conversions of Preston, Lancashire devised by Trevor Lewis.
Mill Auto Conversions 2006-8
Approx 6 made

SCORPION K19

Tom Killeen created several *specials* as well as claiming to have come up with the world's first monocoque in 1950. The Scorpion was inspired (funnily enough) by his K18. It featured gullwing-type doors and was powered by a Hillman Imp engine

hanging out back, with a fibreglass semi-monocoque arrangement. Its main rival, the similarly powered Clan Crusader (*qv*) was more popular and the Scorpion faded away. Dovetail Plastics later decided to resurrect it as the Kestrel Scorpion (*qv*) in 1984.
Tom Killeen 1972
Approx 11 made

A
B
C
D
E
F
G
H
I
J
K
L
M
N
O
P
Q
R
S
T
U
V
W
X
Y
Z

SCORPION

Alf Evans had been responsible for the '50s Delta (*qv*) bodyshell and returned some 20 years later with a Triumph Spitfire-based MG TF replica. His Stourbridge company lasted just a couple of years.

A. Evans Mouldings 1979–81
Approx 3 made

SCORPION

Formula-inspired three-wheeler designed by Dennis Aldred and Neil Edwards, who ran a company called Motorsport Components, based in Bolton, that supplied all manner of parts to a variety of Formula 1 teams of the day including Arrows, Lola and Zakspeed. It was a Yamaha ZFR 1,000cc Genesis bike engine with a spaceframe chassis, pushrod front suspension and Watts linkage.

Project was almost immediately put up for sale due to the pressures of the creators' main business, and nothing more was heard of it.

TriSport 1990
Approx 1 made

SCORPION GTZ

Originally an American kit, this Nissan 240/260Z-based 250 GTO conversion was purchased in 2007 by German Oliver Meulbrouck, who runs the company from bases in Germany and Tirley, Gloucestershire.

OM Sportscars 2007 to date
Approx 5 made (UK)

SCOUT

Over the years the kit car industry has had more than its fair share of Moke-type alternatives, some very good, many best forgotten. The Scout was actually one of the best of them, with an all-steel monocoque with Zintec panels, and could be had in four- or six-wheel guises.

Initially known as the TMC Scout, it was launched in 1983 by a Spalding, Lincolnshire, company called Import Export. After being unavailable for a couple of years after Import Export packed up, Automotive Engineering & Manufacturing – founded by Bob Wareham, Kent Davies, Richard Barwick and Ian Bishop, and based in Merthyr Tydfil – took up the baton and spent a lot of money heavily promoting the product.

After they failed it was out of production for another two years until Solihull-based Sun Motor Company thought it might be third time lucky. It wasn't.

Import Export 1983–85
Automotive Engineering & Manufacturing 1987–88
The Sun Motor Company 1990–91
Approx 150 made

SCS MAKO

A Jaguar XJ6-based replica of the Corvette Stingray that used a revised version of the same company's Cobra replica chassis. Project sold to a German company and not heard of again.

Sports Cars Services 1986–88
Approx 3 made

SCS ROADSTER

SCS was run by Stuart Titman and based in Peterborough. A budget Cobra offering that didn't set the world alight. One of the first SCS customers, incidentally, was Ken Freeman, later co-founder of AK Sportscars.

Sports Cars Services 1986–88
Approx 12 made

SD500

Ferrari 1954 Mondial 500 replica originally intended as a one-off, produced by Stan Daniels, who created the glorious body from photographs! Lightweight spaceframe with Alfa Romeo mid-mounted power. Subsequently built by Gerry Hawkridge of Hawk

Cars for a couple of years before Daniels took over again under the Elmsett banner.

Stan Daniels 1986–87
Transformer Cars 1987–89
Elmsett Road Racing 1989–98
Approx 5 made

SEAGULL

The handiwork of Aldershot-based ex-school teacher David Calvert. Based on Mini mechanicals with a rear-mounted A-series engine, an aluminium centre section and fibreglass front and rear ends.

Seagull Cars 1984
Approx 3 made

SEARCHER 1 – *see Lyncar*

SEAROADER

Amphibious project in four- or six-wheel guise created by Formula 27 and Evolution 1 founder Mike Ryan. In 2004 the project moved to Bideford-based Rob Andrews, although within 18 months it was back with Mike Ryan.
SeaRoader Cars 2003 to date
Approx 10 made

SEASPRAY

Heavily inspired by the Manta Ray (*qv*) and could possibly be described as a copy of same. Company was based in Iver Heath, Buckinghamshire.
Seaspray Buggies 1971
Approx 5 made

SEBRING

Originating from American manufacturer Classic Roadsters, these Healey replicas were first marketed in the UK under that name from 1991 by a company set up by Martin Williamson, Rodney Rushton and John Batchelor, who soon adopted the Sebring Cars company name. They based themselves in Sunbury-on-Thames. Intentions to import the same company's Duke and Duke SS100 replicas came to nothing. At the company's Stafford Show stand in 1992, the legendary late rally driver Roger Clark was on duty promoting the products.

A chap called John Butcher took over from Williamson and operated from Three Holes, before Rob and Paul McMillan took the reins in 1995, based near Wisbech, Cambridgeshire. Rob's son Liam later became a top saloon car racer in the BTCC and was one of the youngest-ever competitors in that championship.
Classic Roadsters 1991
Sebring Cars 1991–94
Sebring International 1995 to date

SEBRING EXALT

Martin Reynolds took over Sebring in 2003 and was responsible for the track-orientated ZX and all-new Exalt, designed by Mark van Driel and Chris Hollier. A modern take on the Healey theme by Sebring with a tasteful update on the original's classic lines. Sebring product quality is first class.
Sebring International 2007 to date
Approx 10 made

SEBRING MX

A wide-bodied version of the SX.
Sebring Cars 1992–2003
Sebring International 2003 to date
Approx 150 made

SEBRING MXR

Effectively a de-chromed TMX/MX.
Sebring Cars 1993–2003
Sebring International 2003 to date
Approx 25 made

SEBRING SPRITE

Superb little Sprinzel replica created by Brian Archer, from his Birmingham base. When Brian sadly passed away in 2008, the company was taken over by Andrew Forster, who had worked closely with Archer for many years. Brian had wanted to reproduce John Sprinzel's very pretty streamlined-bodied Sebring Sprite for some years, and was finally able to do so in the early nineties. The hardtop from the original 'WJB 707' and a 'good' Sebring bonnet were the basis for the creation of moulds, and from these fibreglass replica parts were produced. They have since sold over 70 kits to date.

In addition to the standard Coupé, a Fastback version, originating from a Peel Coachworks hardtop-equipped car (about three made in the sixties) as well as Speedwell Monza bonnets, were all available at the time of writing. Andrew also works closely with Bryan Wheeler of Wheeler & Davies, makers of Sprite 'Frogeye' bodyshells, while the glorious aluminium CC Coachworks panels can also be supplied. Any Sprite or Midget can be used.
Archer's Garage 1993 to date
Approx 73 made

SEBRING SX

Truest model to the original Big Healey in style. Based on a ladderframe chassis and Ford Granada Mk3 donor. Nissan straight six a popular choice for the SX.
Sebring Cars 1991–2003
Sebring International 2003 to date
Approx 200 made

SEBRING TMX

Wide-bodied and more chrome-laden Sebring model with beefy wheel arches.
Sebring Cars 1995–2003
Sebring International 2003 to date
Approx 25 made

SEBRING ZX

A very track-orientated take on the Healey theme. Created around Sebring boss Martin Reynolds' desire for a serious trackday weapon. Weighed in at just 520kg with power coming from a Ford 347 Stroker V8.
Sebring International 2006 to date
Approx 4 made

SERAPH 115 & 215

Developed from the Bonito (*qv*) by John Grossart, who had spent 12 years in the RAF followed by three years designing several of Mickey Thompson's Indy challengers in the 1960s, and then a spell as a senior project engineer at Lucas Girling. It was also related to the Excalibur Crusader (*qv*) project. The Seraph 115 version was powered by a 2.0-litre Ford engine, while the '215' featured the Rover V8, the names referring to the engines' cubic capacity. A Seraph, incidentally, is a six-winged angel.

Resurrected briefly in 1991 as the Whitfield Seraph by Gary Whitfield and revised for Ford Capri running gear.
Seraph Cars 1985–87
Whitfield Specialist Cars 1991
Approx 35 made

SERAPH SPORTS RACER

Prior to Seraph Cars taking over the Bonito (*qv*) they made a purposeful wedge-shaped mid-engined coupé with Ford Crossflow power. Many people lusted after it although for some reason no one parted with any money to buy one.
Seraph Cars 1984–85
Approx 1 made

SETA

A chap called Malcolm Wilson was the creator of the SETA. A gullwinged sports car based on VW Beetle mechanicals and unmodified floorpan. Kits were actually very comprehensive. Renamed the ZETA in 1979 when the project was unsuccessfully offered for sale.
Seta Cars 1976–78
Approx 6 made

SETHERA

Swede Sven-Harry Akesson of SH Design developed this GT40-inspired car. Initially available for VW Beetle mechanicals, although a long-wheelbase, mid-engined version with spaceframe chassis soon followed. Marmite styling. UK operation run by Andrew Moss based in Caerphilly.
Sethera Cars 1989
Approx 1 made

SEVERN

Mayfly set of Lotus Seven-inspired plans based on Ford mechanicals. Caterham Cars didn't much like the name.
Severn Automotive 1990–91
Approx 10 plan sold

SHADO SORENTO

Cizeta-inspired exotic from Workington, Cumbria-based Shado Design run by Steven McClure that wasn't around very long. It had a tube steel semi-monocoque construction with an inline Jaguar V12 engine that was solid-mounted with no propshaft.
Shado Designs 1996
Approx 1 made

SHADOW LE MANS

Replica of the Toyota MC8R, basically a race version of the MR2 and based on, er, Toyota MR2. Came from a Cambridgeshire fibreglass company run by Stuart Elliott, who later went on to make the X-BOW-esque Typhoon Valdris (*qv*).
Shadow Auto Styling 2005–6
Approx 1 made

SHAPECRAFT ELAN

The manufacturers of the Birchfield Sports (*qv*) had previously made the Shapecraft Elan, which came about when Elan racing driver Barry Wood commissioned them to make an alternative rear body section out of aluminium for his crash-damaged Lotus. Shapecraft boss Clive Smart was an ex-Panther employee.
Shapecraft 1983–85
Approx 20 made

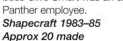

SHAPECRAFT SR

Sister model to the Birchfield Sports (qv) that bore a similarity to the Lotus 15, although it was aimed at the racetrack. One was very successfully raced by Bob Light in the 1990s.
Shapecraft 1984–88
Approx 11 made

SHARK

Came from Plymouth-based Morris Minor specialist Steve Hawes. Based on Reliant Scimitar. It wasn't a replica but had a definite exotic influence.
Classic Motors 2004–6
Approx 1 made

SHARK

Woolferace Wheels boss and 'potato baron' Barry Treacy's brother Derry was behind the Shark, which like many rivals of the day had been inspired by the GP Buggy (qv), with the addition of a sleek new nose. The Shark Buggy Shop was located in Wembley until 1971, when they moved down the road to Staples Corner, with turnkey examples produced in a workshop in Cricklewood. Based on VW Beetle, with the donor floorpan chopped by 16¼in. Unlike some, Treacy's revisions were attractive and the Shark sold in strong numbers over an 18-month 'buggy-boom' period, possibly due to the fact it was cheap, at just £112!

It actually remains one of the most stylish beach buggies. The operation was absorbed into Woolferace Wheels, and Derry worked there for a time before moving to Ireland to become a restaurateur. The company's publicity blurb of the day was quite memorable, claiming: 'This is not just another buggy, but something really new in style.'
The Shark Buggy Shop (Treacy Ltd) 1970–72
Woolferace Wheels 1972
Approx 300 made

SHARK T

Another Derry Treacy project. Based on a Jago T-Bucket shell and didn't prove very popular.
The Shark Buggy Shop (Treacy Ltd) 1971–72
Approx 2 made

SHAWSPEED SK1.6/2.0/SBK

Lindsey Shaw and Jon Sharples were the men behind this Lotus Seven-inspired sports car powered by Ford Sigma (1.6) or Duratec (2.0) engines. Their SBK model was powered by a variety of superbike engines.

Based in North Wales, the company also specialised in the supply of Ford four-cylinder engines and tuning parts. Shaw was a former WRC mechanic wielding the spanners for the likes of Carlos Sainz and François Delacour. In 2006 he moved to Spain, after which the company concentrated on engines with Sharples in sole control.
ShawSpeed 2003–6
Approx 15 made

SHEEN IMPERATOR GTS

An interesting one. It was the brainchild of a wine merchant called Peter Sheen. Incidentally, *Imperator* is a Latin word that roughly translates to 'Emperor'.

Sheen had identified the need for an affordable sports car, so came up with a fairly sexy styling concept, realised in aluminium by The Robert Peel Company of Kingston upon Thames, who marketed the kits. The car was launched to the Press in a blaze of glory at Brands Hatch in September 1964.

Donor parts were Hillman Imp with a Nathan, or Willy Griffith-tuned variant was the entry-level engine with a Paul Emery-prepared 1,147cc, 105bhp unit also an option.

Sheen did a deal with Chrysler for factory supply of components while at the same time he also planned a less expensive fibreglass body option, but at the last minute, parts weren't supplied and the project was shelved after just two were sold. Another member of 'the ones that got away' club.
The Robert Peel Company 1964–65
Approx 2 made

SHEFFIELD BEACH BUGGY

A GP-inspired beach buggy from, er, Sheffield, based in the Norton district of the city. They sold their kits at £140, and fully-built buggies from £440.
Sheffield Beach Buggy Co 1970–71
Approx 2 made

SHEPHERD

An angular utility vehicle from Colne-based boat-builder Jim Graham. Used Ford Cortina mechanicals, with plywood body panels cut out from cardboard plans.
Shepherd Developments 1985–86
Approx 1 made

SHELSLEY SPYDER

Nice car, the Shelsley Spyder, made by Burton-on-Trent company AG Thorpe Developments, who were always kept busy with their Custom Spridget (*qv*) body conversion, which left little time for the Spyder. Could be based on a Triumph Vitesse or bespoke spaceframe if using a Lotus Twin-Cam or Ford Crossflow engine.

AG Thorpe Developments 1983–84
Approx 5 made

SHELSLEY T2

Peter Needham Engineering developed this pretty Rover-based sports car. Initial versions were doorless although doors later became an option. Capable car.

Shelsley Cars 2000–5
Approx 20 made

SHERBORN

A period (Sherpa-based) van from Redditch-based Projects of Distinction. Steel frame was added to Sherpa and then panelled in aluminium.

Projects of Distinction
1993–95
Approx 17 made

SHERPLEY SPEED FOUR

A simplified, if not any less impactful, version of the Sherpley Speed Six (see next entry) that was SVA-exempt because it was based on an unmodified Sherpa 200 Cab chassis, with engine and radiator moved back 36in. DIY build cost worked out about £2,000 cheaper but it was the build itself that was made so much easier than the Speed Six.
Sherpley Car Company 2000–4
Sherpley Motor Company 2004–7
Approx 15 made

SHERPLEY SPEED SIX

Blower Bentley replica based on a combination of Sherpa and Ford Granada (1977–85). The Sherpley name was an amalgamation of Sherpa and Bentley. The company was based in Lancashire and run by Bryan Pickup, a mechanical engineer who previously built horse-drawn landaulets and coaches. Options included replica André Hartford dampers for extra authenticity.

Taken over by Pembrokeshire-based Glen Elliott in 2004, but the pressures of his main business meant he didn't do much with the project, sadly.
Sherpley Car Company 1997–2004
Sherpley Motor Company 2004–7
Approx 12 made

SHERWOOD

Operation was part of the Spartan empire, with the Sherwood part run by Steven Beardsall. Much like the same company's Starcraft (*qv*) motorhome kit, the car used a complete central section of Ford Cortina MkIV, which fitted to the Sherwood ladderframe.

Sounds easy but the build was apparently very difficult to crack, with 14 separate GRP body panels, which is why you used to see a lot of unfinished Sherwood projects for sale. Customers could choose from three- or five-door configurations.
Sherwood Vehicles 1984–92
Approx 110 made

SHIKARI

Originally the Stimson Safari Six (*qv*), bought by Automotive Services. The Welsh company planned a relaunch but it was ultimately stillborn.

Shikari Cars 1973
Approx 1 made

SHP ENGINEERING ESCORT MK1

This Ford Escort Mk1 replica came from well-known hot-rodder and short-oval expert, Sonny Howard, via his Littleport-based SHP Engineering operation. Of course, UK interest in all things Mk1 and Mk2 Escort became massive in the new millennium, although the SHP package was the first genuine kit offering,

available in a rolling chassis package that cost £13,056 inc VAT in March 2011. Power could be humble Ford Pinto, to Cosworth YB, or Duratec HE, with a Watts linkage rear end and a perfect blend of originality and modern componentry. A DIY build would be expected to cost around £50,000.
SHP Engineering 2010 to date
Approx 25 made

SIDEWINDER

Lifelong beach buggy enthusiast Mel Hubbard was the man behind the Sidewinder. He bought his first buggy in 1974. A subsequent meeting with Bruce Meyers, creator of the legendary Manx (*qv*), saw Hubbard importing the Manx and the then new Manx II (*qv*) to the UK in 1999, as well as

creating the Predator (*qv*), Bounty Hunter (*qv*) and Prowler (*qv*), which in 2003 passed to East Coast Manx. After a year 'off' Mel Hubbard came up with the Sidewinder, a short-wheelbase buggy based on VW Beetle floorpan.
Manxbuggies 2004–6
Approx 10 made

SIENNA COUNTACH

Sienna Cars, run by Kiwi sheep farmer Alan Booth, were based on the same estate in Dorking as well-known custom car builder Nick Butler's Auto Imagination, and were originally agents for Prova Designs. Launched their own version of the Countach in

1988. Arguably one of the best of the many Countach replica kits. Body was by Pat Cuss' Fibreglass Applications (who also produced Marcos bodies), with Lee Noble's Kitdeal supplying chassis.

Moved to Wiltshire in 1989 where production started again in 1991. Booth then took a break for a couple of years, shifting production to the Czech Republic, before starting again in 1993. The company closed for good in 1994.
Sienna Cars 1987–92, 1993–94
Approx 24 made

SILHOUETTE GS70

A VW Beetle-based coupé from a Lewisham company run by Peter Zagaroff. You could order a 'Grand Sport' GS70 with conventional or gullwing doors at £450 in 1971. They sold five of the latter, which they called the Zagaroff. Production ceased in 1973,

although that's not the end of the story, as Adrian Wood of Lichfield, Staffordshire, briefly brought the GS70 back to life in 1978. His short-lived resurrection featured a chassis designed by Terry Sands.
Grand Prix Metalcraft t/a Silhouette Cars 1971–73
Adrian Wood Automotive 1978
Approx 18 made

SILHOUETTE SC5000S

One of the better-rated Countach replicas and eagerly awaited when it broke cover in 1988. Corby-based Silhouette Cars were run by Sue and Colin Winter, a former Jaguar engineer and one of the country's leading V12 engine exponents.
Silhouette Cars 1987–88
Approx 23 made

SILURIAN

Possibly the largest kit car ever made, bigger even than the Durow Deluge VS (*qv*) and Atlantis (*qv*). Hailed from a Welsh company, and was a running-board-equipped twenties-style roadster with four doors and five seats. Based on Jaguar XJ components.

The men behind the project were Mike Phillips and his partner Jack Orwin, who ran a classic car restoration business from a wonderfully-named place called 'Brassknocker Street' in Magor, Gwent. The Silurian was influenced by models from Bentley, the Vandenplas Tourer and Lagonda (Phillips owned a Lagonda T7 3-litre from 1933). Underpinned by a twin-rail ladderframe with a beautifully made aluminium-over-plywood body, including bonnet and wings, with Jaguar XJ6 acting as the donor. Had four doors and five seats. The Silurian name came from a particularly feisty Welsh tribe who often gave the Romans a kicking circa AD70, who were based around the Monmouthshire area.
MGP Restorations 1992–96
Approx 2 made

SIMOD 595

Designed by Chippenham-based Simon Head, inspired by the Barchetta 595 (*qv*) and based on the Fiat 500/126.
Simod Design 1998 to date
Approx 3 made

SIVA

After GT Equipment, MiniSprint and Opus HRF designer Neville Trickett moved to Blandford Forum in the late 1960s to work with Michael Saunders of Siva Engineering, who, as a fan of Edwardian vehicles, commissioned him to come up with a range of quirky homages to that period. The fast-working Trickett tore into a succession of models for Saunders before he teamed up with Robert Paterson to form Siva Motor Company, with the S160 their first offering.

SIVA LLAMA

Developed from the Siva Mule but ditched that car's Mini running gear in favour of Hillman Imp mechanicals with the engine mounted in the rear. Neville Trickett came to an agreement with Imp makers Chrysler, who assured him that they would supply him with mechanicals and could guarantee supply. Within a few months they'd stopped production of the Imp!
Siva Motor Company 1974–76
Approx 50 made

A B C D E F G H I J K L M N O P Q R S T U V W X Y Z

SIVA MEHARI

A Citroën 2CV-based Mehari replica that wasn't around very long at all. Trickett had his eye on new challenges by this time.
Siva Motor Company 1976
Approx 1 made

SIVA MINIBUGGY

Biggest-selling Siva model. Unlike most beach buggies this was based on Mini donor rather than VW Beetle. A lot were sold by Phil Alleston's Bespoke Buggy Company, based in Wimbledon. Body/chassis units cost a princely £195 in 1970.
Siva Motor Company 1970–76
Approx 95 made

SIVA MULE

Another take on the Mini Moke theme, but an original design by Neville Trickett based on a steel-tube chassis with Mini subframes. The Mule was later revised to become the Llama.
Siva Motor Company 1970–75
Approx 12 made

SIVA PARISIENNE (EDWARDIAN SERIES)

Neville Trickett loved the Citroën 2CV and probably pioneered its use as a donor in the kit car industry, starting with his Raceabout (see next entry). The two-seater Parisienne was similar in looks to the Ford-based Siva Tourer (*qv*), but serial Siva fans knew that apart from the running gear, it could be distinguished by the three little horizontal slats in the bonnet. The Parisienne was launched at the Paris Motor Show of 1970 as Trickett had vainly hoped to sell them in France.

It was briefly resurrected by a Devon company called Edwardian Cars before ending its days with Jack Evans' Cornish Classic Cars of Redruth in 1984.
Siva Engineering Sales Company 1970–76
Approx 7 made

SIVA RACEABOUT (EDWARDIAN SERIES)

The third of the Siva Edwardian series was a tribute to one of the Régie's early Renault models, although it was actually based on VW Beetle mechanicals, and was an easy build and an affordable one too. One quirk involved lengthening the steering column by nearly a yard (36in)! This one was almost too mad even for dear old Neville.
Siva Engineering Sales Company 1970–76
Approx 6 made

SIVA ROADSTER (EDWARDIAN SERIES)

Neville Trickett's first design within the Siva Edwardian range was the two-seat Roadster, based on Ford 8 or 10 or later 103E Popular chassis. Kits cost £145 in 1970. Siva's sales office was located in Weymouth, Dorset, and kits were produced at Neville Trickett Design premises in Blandford forum.
Siva Engineering Sales Company 1969-74
Approx 25 made

SIVA S160

Jem Marsh commissioned Neville Trickett to design a coupé for Marcos but rejected the bright orange Hillman Imp-based end product. However, Jan Odor, boss of Janspeed, saw it and put it on his company's stand at the Racing Car Show of 1969. In a roundabout sort of way this prototype ended up as the Siva S160, which Trickett modified to accept VW Beetle components. This almost struck gold, because when Volkswagen UK saw it at the 1971 Racing Car Show they were interested in selling it in volume, although ultimately a deal never happened. The switchgear was mounted in the driver's door panel, which was a novel arrangement.

Trickett also came up with an S530 derivative that featured a Ford V6 engine, which was 11in wider and 8in longer, with a monocoque built by Maxperenco Products of Didcot. The car was sponsored by the *Daily Telegraph* for the 1971 Motor Show and was actually a very sophisticated design. Aston Martin apparently hinted at volume production.

A Siva V8 prototype was also created with a shorter nose and longer tail. One made.
Siva Motor Company 1971–72
Approx 12 made

SIVA SALUKI

The Saluki was developed from the Siva S160 (see previous entry). It was launched at the Racing Car Show of 1973, retaining its VW Beetle base although by now the complete switchgear panel was moved from the driver's door panel to a 'coffee table'-type arrangement, centrally-mounted. Later taken over by Mike Carlton of MBC Cars to become the Chepeko (*qv*).
Siva Motor Company 1973–76
Approx 12 made

SIVA SAN REMO (EDWARDIAN SERIES)

The Parisienne was a two-seater, and when several people asked about a four-seater, Trickett – ever willing to give the customer what they wanted – came up with the San Remo, based on unmodified VW Beetle floorpan.
Siva Engineering Sales Company 1970–76
Approx 8 made

SIVA SIERRA

This Willys Jeep clone based on Mk2 Escort mechanicals came right at the end of Neville Trickett's Siva Cars involvement.
Siva Motor Company 1976
Approx 3 made

SIVA TOURER (EDWARDIAN SERIES)

The Tourer was the four-seat sister model to the Siva Roadster, based, like the Roadster, on Ford 8, 10 or 103E Popular components.

The BBC purchased a kit, built by Siva for £160 in 1969 (£182 with 'extras') spending £500 in total having it built. The late John Pertwee and Tom Baker used the car, known as 'Bessie', in the TV series *Dr Who*. The first episode was Pertwee's second; 'The Silurians', and the last was 'The Robots' with Baker.
Siva Engineering Sales Company 1969-74
Approx 80 made

SK ROADSTER

MGB-based hybrid sort of design with an Allard-inspired front and Morgan-esque rear. Created by two Ford employees, Steve Blakey and Kim Ford (who worked at the Dunton plant), who wanted a Morgan but didn't like the waiting list, they set about building the SK Roadster. Launched at Stoneleigh Show in 1985 but it never really caught on, although it was only a part-time project for the two protagonists. Built a car each that cost just £1,100 apiece!
SK Automotive 1985–86
Approx 2 made

SKIP 1000

Created by ex-Milk Marketing Board employee Jeff Calver of Crossgate Moor, Durham. It was a Mini-based three-wheeler, designed to go trialling.
J.J. Calver Industrial Engineers 1991
Approx 2 made

SKUNK S1 & SS1

Jon Malone created a three-wheeled go-kart for his son Jerome, who liked it so much that as he got older he saved £1,000 of his pocket money and asked his dad to build him a full-sized one! Malone senior developed it with classic car restorer Tim Boswell, who had the first test drive. He returned pleased but covered in smelly cow shite. When asked how it had gone he said it 'went like stink'. Hence the Skunk was christened!

Main body tub bolted and bonded to aluminium panels and square tube chassis. Front suspension utilised oval tube wishbones, with Malone's own single-sided swing arm. Usual engine fitments are Suzuki GSX-1100 and Yamaha XJ900 with a bespoke propshaft feeding drive. Weighing in at just 300kg, Malone describes it not as a three-wheeler car but a three-wheeled motorbike!
Malone Car Company 1998 to date
Approx 25 made

SKYSPEED BUGGY

A GP agent supplied this fully-built luxury version of the GP Buggy (*qv*). The company was based in Heston, Middlesex, just down the road from GP, and also marketed the Humbug (*qv*) Beetle conversion too.
Skyspeed 1969–72
Approx 5 made

SM1

Created by 750 Motor Club racers Paul Boyd and Clive Hudson and powered by chain-driven Ford Duratec. Suited to race, trackday and even road use.
Eclipse Sportscars 2009 to date
Approx 3 made

SMS BEETLE

SMS specialised in body conversions for Beetle and Mini.
SMS Conversions 1989–92
Approx 10 made

SN1

Princes Risborough-based operation run by partners Steve Collins, a skilled fibreglass laminator who worked at Porsche specialist Autofarm, and local hairdresser Neil Morgan. The SN1 originated from of Mike Carlton's (MBC/Embeesea) Eurocco (qv) prototype, which was intended as a sister model to the company's Charger (qv), although the success of that meant the Eurocco was shelved. Came from an idea by journalist Peter Filby, who suggested to Carlton that a new 2+2 model might be a good idea, and proposed Richard Oakes as designer of the new car. The result didn't excite Carlton sufficiently, as he reckoned that it would be too hard to produce bodies from the new moulds. So, he set about altering the Oakes design and creating a new Eurocco of his own, although he did sell a couple of bodies before dumping said moulds into a hedge in his yard.

Collins and Morgan went to MBC as potential Charger customers, had a general look around at how a kit car manufacturer operated and spotted Oakes' Eurocco moulds with grass and lichen growing on them. One and one made two, and they were soon putting kits into production.

There were various reasons for its failure. It had an incredible amount of fibreglass in its body and parts came from all over the place – Escort Mk2 windscreen, door windows from Cortina Mk3 two-door, rear window from Cortina Mk3 Estate, Fiat 126 quarter lights, door hinges from Bedford CF van etc etc.

The SN1 – ie, the Oakes-designed Eurocco – was a 2+2 notchback, but Carlton's revised version, also later known as the Eurocco was a fastback. Confused? You should be!
Steaney Developments 1982–84
Amplas 1984-86
Lemazone 1986
Approx 8 made

SNAKE

A half Cobra, half Lotus Seven-style car based on Ford mechanicals. Created by Sports Power Drive, who sold three kits before it went to RS Jigtec (briefly) and then to Cradley Motor Works in St Leonards-on-Sea, run by Bob Bousell.

Sports Power Drive 1999–2001
RS Jigtec 2001–3
Cradley Motor Works 2003–8
Approx 8 made

SNOWDONIA – *see Bedouin*

SOMERSET

Made by Classic Car Panels of Frome. Basically a four-wheel version of the Tri-Pacer (qv), complete with close-coupled rear wheels, a beautiful hand-made aluminium body, and Citroën 2CV mechanicals and floorpan.
Classic Car Panels 1998–2001
Approx 5 made

SON OF A BEACH – *see Hoppa*

SONIC

Modern take on the Lotus Seven-inspired sports car theme from the prolific Stuart Mills of MEV. Based on Ford Focus mechanicals.
Mills Extreme Vehicles 2008 to date
Approx 35 made

SOUTHERN GT

A high-quality GT40 replica from Mick Sollis of Botley, Hampshire.
Southern GT 2005 to date
Approx 7 made

SP1 – *see Helios*

SP 24/7

Sports car designed around 750 Motor Club Sports 1000 regulations by classic car restorer and historic racer Trevor Farrington, who was later involved with the Roy Ashton-designed BMW Mille Miglia replica.
Trevor Farrington Ltd 2002–4
Approx 5 made

SP350 REPLICA

Daimler Dart replica emanating from boat builders Tyler Industrial Mouldings, run by Sheridan Bowie, who acquired the BRA 289 (qv) project in 1994. Used a slightly revised BRA 289 (a couple of inches added to the wheelbase) chassis and MGB mechanicals. Tyler had been Daimler Dart (and Reliant Scimitar) specialists since 1976 and thus had the know-how to produce a replica. Kits were advertised at £4,000 in 1998.
Tyler Industrial Mouldings 1994–98
David Manners Ltd 2001-04
Approx 5 made

SP ESTATE

Estate version of the Highwayman (see next entry).
Hooe Garage (East Sussex) Ltd 1972
Approx 1 made

SP HIGHWAYMAN

A convertible from East Sussex-based Bugatti restorers Derek Skilton and Jack Perkins. Possibly one of the first Rover V8-powered kit cars?
Hooe Garage (East Sussex) Ltd 1972–74
Approx 2 made

SPARTAN

One of the biggest-selling kits of all time in the UK, the Spartan was the first of the so-called traditional '30s roadster-style kits and as a result scored big. The Pinxton, Nottinghamshire-based company was run by Jim McIntyre.

Loosely inspired by the MG TF and other old British cars of that period, it was in no way a replica and featured aluminium body with fibreglass wings. Very early ones had two seats and 'suicide' doors with original basis being Triumph Herald/Vitesse/Spitfire, although a 2+2 configuration was soon settled on.

From the mid-'70s a bespoke ladderframe chassis was available. A Ford Cortina donor option arrived in 1981, with most customers thereafter generally choosing the engine from the donor vehicle. Steven Beardsall, who had been the works manager for many years, took the company over from McIntyre in 1993.
Spartan Cars 1973–95
Approx 4,000 made

SPARTAN BANDIT

Hot rod-style '27 Ford Model T with twin-rail ladderframe and Cortina suspension. A budget offering with kit costing just £995.
Spartan Cars 1994–95
Approx 3 made

SPARTAN TREK

Ford Fiesta Mk1 or Mk2-based utility created by Steve Beardsall.
Spartan Cars 1993–95
Approx 40 made

SPD 7

West Midlands-based Steve 'Sport' Griffith's first model was the Locost-inspired SPD 7, based on Ford Sierra.
Sports Power Drive 1999–2000
Approx 20 made

SPD 200

Sierra-based Ford RS200 replica from Steve 'Sport' Griffiths, who made six examples. Project taken over very briefly by RS Jigtec before coming under the control of Cradley Motor Works run by Bob Bousell after the former ceased trading.
Sports Power Drive 2000–1
RS Jigtec 2001–3
Cradley Motor Works 2003–8
Approx 15 made

SPECFRAME SPECTRE

Preston-based Specframe were run by an ex-TVR engineer, who offered this Cortina-based sports car kit for a couple of years in the mid-1980s. The car's chassis and engineering prowess were always highly rated, but the styling less so.
Specframe Vehicle Company 1983–85
Approx 4 made

SPECTRE

Originally a 1961 trials car that was relaunched, albeit briefly, in kit form in 1994. The Bristol-based company had a background in midget racers.
Spectre Designs 1994
Approx 2 made

SPEEDEX 750

After his spell at Robin Read's Dante operation, Jem Marsh – prior to Marcos – set out on his own as Speedex Castings & Accessories Ltd, still based in Luton. Among his range of go-faster parts were wheels and a nice range of tuning equipment. The Speedex 750, an aluminium-bodied shell based around Austin 7, was his first car in October 1958.
Speedex Castings & Accessories Ltd 1958–62
Cambridge Engineering 1962–63
Approx 150 made

SPEEDEX SILVERSTONE

The Silverstone appeared in 1959 and was Austin 7-based just like its sister 750 (see previous entry).
Speedex Castings & Accessories Ltd 1959–62
Cambridge Engineering 1962–63
Approx 50 made

SPEEDEX SIROCCO

1960 saw the introduction of the Ford 10-based Sirocco, which was a creation of future Vauxhall designer Peter Hammond.

Speedex Castings & Accessories Ltd 1960–62
Cambridge Engineering 1962–63
Approx 11 made

SPIRE GT3

Appearing in spring 2011, the all-new car from Spire – sharing no panels with the GT-R version – is a dedicated trackday/circuit racer. Featuring revised body panels and a Honda CBR1000RR (Fireblade) engine, with fully Rose-jointed suspension, Quaife chain-driven differential with electric reverse, inboard pushrod-operated suspension, and sidepods now featuring radiators.

Won, first time out, in the hands of Spire 'works' driver, John Cutmore at Mallory Park in April 2011. Superbly capable.

Spire Sportscars 2011 to date
Approx 3 made

SPIRE GT-R

The former MK GT2 (*qv*) and a highly capable LMP-style car that could be powered by bike and car engines, with much success coming on track in the hands of well-known 750 Motor Club RGB racer John Cutmore, who won class B of the RGB Championship in 2009 in a Spire GT-R.

Spire Sportscars 2005 to date
Approx 80 made

SPIRIT SS

American VW-based Mercedes SSK-type kit made by Classic Motor Carriages and known as the Gazelle, imported to the UK by Dave Perry, a man who has been very influential in UK kit car history. The Gazelle was a VW Beetle-based Mercedes SSK replica that

Dave arranged to market in the UK. He sold two of the original US version before adding 6in to the width, making the doors longer and converting the donor to Ford Cortina and thus front-engined. The majority sold by Perry were given Rover V8 engines.

Subsequently passed to London-based Spirit Cars, Bridlington-based Classic Automotive Reproductions, Daytona Classics (aka Gatsby Cars) and then Roger Woolley of RW Kit Cars, before it faded very quietly away as the *Phoenix* under D&S Engineering.

Several other companies did deals with Classic Motor Carriages over the years and had a go at importing the VW-based Gazelle to the UK, and it's consequently been known at various times as the Amica (*qv*), Delta (*qv*), Osprey (*qv*), Gatsby (*qv*) and Phoenix (*qv*).

(Perry) Automotive Design 1979–83
Spirit Cars of London 1983–84
Classic Automotive Reproductions 1984
Gatsby Cars (Daytona Classics) 1984–86
RW Kit Cars 1986–87
D&S Engineering 1987–88
Approx 16 made (2 VW/14 Ford)

SPM 286

Specialist Performance Mouldings (SPM) was based in Whitminster, Gloucestershire, and run by John Martin and Paul Ashworth, who ran the Fromebridge Garage. Their body conversion was initially imported from an American operation and was a Ferrari 308 lookalike based on Pontiac Fiero.

Later passed to Steve Bridden, Roy Morris and Terry Sands, of Fiero Factory, before moving to Dave Fuell's Lakeside Carriage Company.

Specialist Performance Mouldings 1991–2002
Fiero Factory 1992–94
Lakeside Carriage Company/SPM 1994–2002
Approx 50 made

SPORTCYCLE

Wacky Formula 1/Indycar-style three-wheeler with superbike back end, usually a Kawasaki ZRX1100 although any could be used. Designed by American Jim Musser and briefly imported here by Simon MacKenzie of Corsham, Wiltshire.

After a couple of years lying dormant, SoloSport acquired the project and offered kits for sale once more. However, as we closed for press, the operation was for sale once more.

SportCycle 2002–3
SoloSport 2005-9
Approx 6 made (UK)

SPORTIVA

Second model from Battle-based S&J Motors and like its Milano (*qv*) sister was Alfa-based. After being mothballed for many years the project was bought by Lee Smith of Birmingham company Smith Auto Blast, although nothing more was heard.

S&J Motors 1985–88
Smith Auto Blast 1999
Approx 5 made

SPORTS BUGGY

Prior to the Manta Ray (qv), Connaught Cars' forecourt manager Adrian Harrington and his friend Roy King made the Sports Buggy from their base in a former air-raid shelter. It was heavily inspired by the GP Buggy (qv), which isn't surprising, as many buggies of the period were – and Harrington owned one. Later resurrected by C&D Automarine of West Molesey, who made the Manta Ray bodies for Power on Wheels.
Power on Wheels 1969–70
Approx 15 made

SPORTS CARS & SPECIALS 959

This was a body conversion based on Porsche 911 that turned it into a 959 replica. It appeared in summer 1988. The kit originated in America and was made by Getty Design. The men behind Sports Cars & Specials were Peter Jackson and Ged Dunbar (who had previously worked with Garry Thompson at Venom Cars), based their company in Blackburn, Lancashire. They didn't sell many.
Sports Cars & Specials 1988–90
Approx 2 made

SPRINT-R/SR1

A cracking single-seater with Yamaha R1 power from Martin Keenan. Passed to RoadRunner Racing run by Kevin Hickling, who moved from Worksop to Rotherham in spring 2010. Sold to a company in spain.
MK Engineering 2007
RoadRunner Racing 2007-9
Approx 20 made

SPYDER DONINGTON CONVERSION

Available for a time from chassis-makers par excellence Spyder Engineering, run by Vic Moore and CG Price. A conversion for the Lotus Elite and Eclat. Visually identical to the Lotus originals, it was under the skin that Spyder weaved its considerable magic, fitting its own chassis and suspension, a Rover V8 and Jaguar differential.
Spyder Engineering 1991–92
Approx 12 made

SPYDER ELAN/ELAN +2 CONVERSION

Not really a kit in the conventional sense, but famed chassis experts Spyder Engineering will sell you a new chassis kit that you can DIY fit to your Lotus Elan or Elan +2, so it is (tenuously) included here.
Spyder Engineering 1991 to date
Approx 600 made

SPYDER SILVERSTONE

Lotus Seven-inspired sports car from Spyder Engineering. From the mid-seventies, Spyder had been building replacement chassis for a variety of cars, with Lotus a particular specialisation, and had gained a formidable reputation for their engineering excellence.

The Silverstone was built around a multi-tubular (18-gauge steel), stressed-skin composite MIG-welded chassis (basically a semi-monocoque), with double-wishbone (flat tube) suspension. It had similarities to Spyder's successful Elan and Europa conversions. A very intricate arrangement for which Spyder even gave a six-year anti-corrosion warranty, and so time consuming and expensive that it led to the car being withdrawn – it was simply too expensive to produce. Fibreglass was used for wings, nosecone and scuttle. There were two main engine options – Ford 'Kent' Crossflow, including highly-strung Lotus twin-cam and BDR derivatives, or the spiteful Toyota 2TG Twin Cam, the same engine that formed the basis of the Formula Three Novamotor.

Well-known broadcaster and investigative journalist, Roger Cook, was an enthusiastic Silverstone owner.

One of the greatest kit cars ever produced. Brilliant.
Spyder Engineering 1985–89
Approx 23 made

SQUIRE

The original Squire was a grand old tourer produced for a couple of years in the mid-'30s that promised a lot but sold just a handful. Hartlebury-based Phil Kennedy revealed his (pretty accurate) replica in 1984 that came with a Ford Cortina donor and steel ladderframe chassis. No fibreglass was used for the Squire recreation, well, except on the wings. Kennedy followed the traditional method of hand-beaten aluminium body over an ash frame.

Merged with Vicarage Classic Car Company of Walsall (Bridgnorth from 1988) in 1987 run by Nick Goldthorp, and introduced a less expensive scaled-down GRP version that was known as the Squire Sports, with the original replica renamed the Squire S.

Project bought by Rodney Rushton in 1993, who also made the BRA P-Type (qv), although it soon passed to Marlin Cars. However, they quickly shelved it due to healthy sales of their mainstay products.
Kennedy Design 1984–86
Squire Sports Car Company 1986–93
Squire Motors 1993
Marlin Cars 1993
Approx 20 made

SR1/SR2

S&R Sports Cars boss Roy Coates had purchased a Eurocco (qv), and although a bit forlorn he liked it so much he bought the rights to the project in 1982. He then spent three years revising it and getting it how he wanted it before showing it for the first time as the SR1 in 1985. It was a big improvement and well-made, although it didn't attract many takers. VW Beetle-based.

He soon followed it up with an SR2 (2+2) version that was based on an unmodified Beetle floorpan, again well built and again using Audi UR Quattro headlights.

S&R Sports Cars 1985–86
Approx 3 made

SR V8

Founded by brothers Ian and Brian Nicholls in 1985, Southern Roadcraft were based in Brighton, West Sussex, and came up with one of the most well-respected Cobra replicas around. Chassis originally by Kiwi Pat Hansen with power coming from V8 engines. In 1997 Brian concentrated on his Repower V8 engine and performance parts business while Ian pursued other career paths including film stunt work.

Project taken over by Geoff Mills, erstwhile of Direct Specialist Supplies, who changed the company name to Roadcraft. In 1998 he teamed up with Sheridan Bowie's Tyler Industrial Mouldings operation to sell the SR V8 and BRA 289 (qv).

In 2001 it was acquired by Pagham-based Dave Carruthers, who along with son Mike put the car back on the map, servicing and supplying parts for the original cars while also revising the kit, making improvements and selling new ones.

Southern Roadcraft 1985–97
Roadcraft 1997–99
Madgwick Cars 2001 to date
Approx 600 made

SR2

Mazda MX-5-based, Lotus Seven-inspired sportscar from RoadRunner Racing, launched in 2010 from a new base in Rotherham, South Yorkshire. Erstwhile boss Kevin Hickling was joined by his brother-in-law, Steve Holland, who became the MD.

After several kit sales, Kevin left for pastures new, and in October 2010 the project was sold to MX-5 specialist Mike Longstaff, who retained the company name, but moved the project to a new unit in Hull, East Yorkshire.

RoadRunner Racing 2010 to date
Approx 16 made

SR V12

Having seen the *Miami Vice* TV series that featured a Corvette-based McBurnie Coachworks Daytona replica, Southern Roadcraft's Ian and Brian Nicholls initially acted as agents for the car in the UK. However, it wasn't correct dimensionally so they revised it for the UK market, basing their SR V12 on Jaguar XJ12 with a revised chassis as used on their SR V8 Cobra replica. Briefly revived by Jay Leonard of Racetec in 1999, although it's not known if he made any further examples.
Southern Roadcraft 1988–93
Approx 120 made

SRC MG TD REPLICA

A low-key Scottish-made MG TD replica from a classic car restorer.
Scottish Replicars & Classics 1984
Approx 1 made

SRC MG TF

Obscure Scottish MG TF replica that wasn't around for long.
Scottish Replicars & Classics 1984–85
Approx 2 made

SRC SPEEDSTER

A very obscure Speedster replica.
Scottish Replicars & Classics 1984–85
Approx 3 made

SRC TURBO

Porsche 911 Turbo replica inspired by the Covin Turbo (*qv*).
Scottish Replicars & Classics 1984
Approx 2 made

STAFFORD RENATO

Another of the long line of Bentley MkVI specials (the Bentley version of the Rolls-Royce Silver Dawn), such as those made by Johnard, Syd Lawrence, Mallalieu, Rose, Shrive and Westminster. Unlike some of the others this one was offered in kit form by Harry Sibley's Stafford Coachworks, based in Bude, Cornwall.
Stafford Coachworks 1981–90
Approx 11 made

STALLION

A vintage military staff car-style Jaguar XJ6-based four-seater from Steven Povey of Redditch. Didn't find any takers and so wasn't around for long.
SP Engineering 1985
Approx 1 made

STANBURY TT

Designed by David Quick of Weston-super-Mare (Worle, Avon, from 1985). A basic little roadster based on a Triumph Herald chassis that was actually a nice performer. Had a wooden body skinned in aluminium. The company was fronted by Dave's wife, Jan.
Stanbury Design Services 1983–86
Approx 12 made

STANZANI – *see Gandini*

STAR – *see Sylva Star*

STARBORNE SPEEDSTER

Apal imported to the UK by one Tim Dutton. UK's first Speedster replica, imported by several other companies over the years without much success.
Dutton Cars 1978
Approx 3 made

STARCRAFT

One of the first kit-built motorhomes hailing from the prolific Spartan operation, of which Starcraft was part. Based on Ford Cortina – everything behind the front doors was cut off and a motorhome-style 'pod' was added in its stead. Very successful.
Starcraft 1986–93
Approx 200 made

STARDUST/MILAN D-TYPE

Vic Minay of Twickenham, Middlesex, was the man behind this Ford-based affordable Jaguar D-type replica. Minay had previously earned his living in the film industry as an animator, and had worked on films such as *Star Wars* and *Roger the Rabbit*.

His D-type replica had a MIG-welded spaceframe, Cortina uprights, live Escort rear axle and 2-litre Pinto. As a humorous aside, I recall that Minay's mechanic was called Lee Walsh, but was better known as 'Clive the Model' thanks to all the advert and catalogue work he had done.

Renamed Le Mans Sportscars in 1993, which coincided with a Mk2 version with revised chassis made by DFE Engineering that was a spaceframe with a central backbone section that could accept Jaguar components. This was known as the Milan.

The Jaguar Milan version was sold to David Yoxall, who retained the Le Mans Sportscars name, while the original Ford-based project was sold to Tiger Racing, before subsequently moving to Lightning and Leighton. Minay, meanwhile, acquired the PACE project, renaming it Auto Milan, which he marketed for several years.
Stardust Sports Cars/Le Mans Sportscars 1990-94
Approx 11 made

STATUS MOTOR COMPANY

Founded by Brian Luff, former Vehicle Engineering Manager at Lotus Cars, who set up as a freelance engineering company. Name came from Luff's favourite band, Status Quo. He went on to create some pretty cool cars under the Status name. Over the years the company was known by various names and based in myriad locations:
Status Company 1971 (Norwich)
Status Motors 1971–73 (New Buckenham)
Motors Marianne 1973–74 (New Buckenham)
Status Company 1974–75 (New Buckenham)
Brian Luff Ltd 1976–77 (New Buckenham)
Brian Luff Ltd 1980–81 (Jersey)
Brian Luff Ltd 1985–86 (Norwich)

STATUS 365

Called the 365 because designer Brian Luff reckoned it could be used every day of the year. Followed the company's Minipower concept, retaining the Mini donor mechanicals and utilising a GRP monocoque with styling by another ex-Lotus man, John Frayling (Lotus Elite, Clan Crusader and Birchall McCoy). Excellent handling and performance, complete with four seats and a big boot.
Status Cars 1974–81
Approx 40 made

STATUS ABACUS

Brian Luff creation, with modern styling that was typically innovative.
Status Cars 1985
Approx 1 made

STATUS MINIPOWER

This was originally the Symbol (see below) with the name changed to give it a more serious image. Although Luff sold 20 chassis only eight bodies were among them. Colin Chapman reputedly liked it, as did the motoring press. Apparently it was very costly to produce.
Status Cars 1972–73
Approx 20 made

STATUS SABOT

Mini-based utility that was a very modern take on the Moke.
Status Cars 1985
Approx 1 made

STATUS STREAKER

Another Brian Luff-penned sports car. Stillborn.
Status Cars 1985
Approx 1 made

STATUS SYMBOL

The first Status model was the Symbol, based on Mini mechanicals with double wishbones all round, Austin 1,100cc driveshafts and A-series power. Light (450kg) and very agile. Name changed to Minipower in 1972.
Status Cars 1971–72
Approx 8 made

STEADMAN TS

Beautifully made aluminium-bodied Jaguar SS100 replica from Ottercraft, run by Bill Steadman, a division of parent company Traditional Car Panels based in Hayle, Cornwall. Bill had worked in America for 20 years and created the TS when he returned to the UK. Spent a reported £300,000 on factory machinery alone and at one point employed 30 staff.

Available in fully-built form only (at first), with a high profile order from Peter de Savary, although an expected overseas order worth £2 million didn't materialise. Turnkey prices started at £21,995 on launch in 1987 but soon rose to a hefty £49,500! Steadman offered the car in kit form from 1990, with prices starting at £14,000 with fibreglass body, although an aluminium option was available.
Ottercraft 1987–93
Approx 18 made

STEALTH B6

Created by Terry Pudwell, the GpC-inspired Stealth wasn't a kit car in the true sense of the word but was available in pretty complete component form. The Oxfordshire-based makers were helped by well-known club racer Bob Light, who dominated the Castle Combe Special GT championship in one for several years.
Stealth Cars Ltd
Approx 8 made

STERLING ROADSTER

Healey 3000 replica that was originally announced by Steve Porter as far back as 1995. Revived by Pat Jackson in 2010 and sold under the MK HSR *(qv)* banner.
Formula 27 Sportscars 1996–98
Approx 3 made

STIMSON BUGGY

Could well be the most production-car-like of any Stimson creation. The Buggy was on a par with the buggy-inspired concepts produced by the likes of Mercedes Benz and Peugeot, mixed with retro beach buggy styling and was based on Ford Fiesta (1997–

2002), with a high-specification including ABS brakes, airbags and side-impact protection. The Minibug revisited.

The customer supplied Stimson Designs build operation, Design Developments, with the donor, and much of the build was done for them, leaving just the finishing touches to be completed. No takers.
Stimson Designs 2004–2007
Approx 1 made

STIMSON CS+1

Stimson's Barrian Cars was based in London when this model was introduced. Subsequently offered through Lainston of Sparsholt, Hampshire. Basically a revamped Mini Bug 2.
Barrian Cars 1973
Lainston Investment Services Ltd 1973
Approx 4 made

STIMSON CS+II (aka CS2 aka CS+2)

A typically innovative design from Barry Stimson (trading as Noovoh Developments at the time), who sold a couple before project passed to Evans Developments (Portsmouth) Ltd of Gosnall Avenue in 1977 for a very brief period. It moved north

to Rochdale that same year, to a company called Mini Motors, who for some reason renamed it the CS2 in 1979. This company sold about 40 kits.

In 1982 the project moved again, to Automotive Services, who tweaked the name again, this time to CS+2. They even made an electric version in 1984.
Noovoh Developments 1975–77
Evans Developments (Portsmouth) Ltd 1977
Mini Motors CS+2 1977–82
Automotive Services 1982–86
Approx 50 made

STIMSON MINI BUG 1

First effort from then Chichester-based designer Barry Stimson. First prototype cost Barry just £25 to make, with a radiator surround borrowed from a local brasserie.
Design Developments 1970–71
Approx 20 made

STIMSON MINI BUG 2

After 20 sales, Barry gave the Mini Bug a revamp with a more rounded and customer-pleasing shape. Stimson's Barrian Cars Ltd was based in Westbourne, Hampshire, before moving to Goswell Road, London in 1973.
Barrian Cars Ltd 1971–73
Approx 160 made

STIMSON SAFARI SIX

Yet another Mini Moke-style kit, but as it came from the innovative pen of Barry Stimson it was guaranteed to be a bit out of the ordinary. For a start, a clue came in the form of the name, Safari Six, which meant it had six wheels. Based on the ubiquitous Mini

mechanicals and could seat four people.

Barry planned a more conventional four-wheeler, but this never appeared, and in 1973 the project was taken over by Shikari Cars, who spent a ton of money on it and renamed it the Shikari (*qv*), but again it didn't last long.
Barrian Cars 1972–73
Lainston Investment Services Ltd 1973
Fauchen Plastics 1973
Approx 12 made

STIMSON SCORCHER

One of *the* most bonkers kit cars ever made and it just had to come from Barry Stimson. Whereas some similarly mad creations of the era were laughed at because they were horrible, there was a strange charm and highly serious performance edge to the Scorcher. The rider/driver sat astride the device with a centrally-mounted gearlever, and there

was room for two passengers in a tandem arrangement. Project was bought by Gerald Pickford, of Clanfield, Oxfordshire, who planned a relaunch with a batch of three kits featuring slightly revised bodywork such as a lower front panel and addition of an air dam. Ultimately, this didn't happen.
Noovoh Developments 1976–81
Approx 30 made

STIMSON STING

A typical Barry Stimson design full of ingenuity and innovation. Of all his creations, I got the distinct impression that the Sting was perhaps *the* one that pleased him most. A three-wheeler, powered by Suzuki Bandit motorbike engine, the wheelbase was extremely long

to help with stability, while the GRP body was a two-seater. All-new parts, with no donor components, the Sting was capable of 0–60 in under four seconds! A truly fun kit car. A modern Scorcher? Probably.
Stimson Designs 2002–2007
Approx 1 made

STIMSON STORM

Another bonkers three-wheeler from Barry Stimson. Aimed at born-again bikers and people who really wanted to be different. Could seat four people. The Storm used the complete front section of the bike, with a two-wheel rear, and was reminiscent of a more

traditional biker's trike, albeit with plenty of Barry Stimson flair thrown in for good measure. None sold, sadly.
Stimson Designs 2002–2007
Approx 1 made

STIMSON TREK

Another Mini-based kit, styled like a golf buggy meets off-road rail, with three seats – one centrally mounted at the front for the driver and the other two in the rear for two passengers. Underpinned by a backbone spaceframe chassis, with a Mini subframe at the front and trailing arms at the rear, with motorcycle coil-over-damper units. The driver sat astride the chassis, like a motorcycle, or indeed Stimson's earlier Scorcher *(qv)* creation. Quite an adventure for the two rear-seat passengers though! Chassis was made by Jago Automotive. A Birkenhead-based company, called Sarronset, marketed the car for a couple of years before disappearing.

Stimson's company name was revised from Noovoh to Nouveau Developments and relocated from Brighton to Southsea, although this was the period just before he emigrated to Australia.
Nouveau Developments 1981–83
Sarronset 1983–85
Approx 38 made

STIMULATOR

Big-dimensioned Lotus Seven-inspired sports car that started out as a one-off for creator Les Hindley, from Paignton, Devon. Other people were sufficiently impressed to want one of these fierce V8-powered cars of their own. Some 25 were made in total.

Stimulator Cars 1988–97
Approx 25 made

STINGER

A curious three-wheeler that mated a BMW K1100 motorcycle rear end with the front section of a Sylva Striker *(qv)* complete with a spaceframe structure. Brainchild of Tony Bradwell, based in Stratford-upon-Avon.
Stinger Cars 1994–96
Approx 1 made

STINGER

Off-road type rail kit that came from a Colchester-based operation. Used Mini A-series engine.
Stinger Automotive 1998–2000
Approx 8 made

STOHR WF1

Hailing from Portland, Oregon-based Stohr Cars & Parts, the WF1 is a highly impressive track-orientated car that features a carbon-fibre monocoque, with power provided by any in-line four-cylinder bike engine.

Available in the UK from John Hewat's Blaze Motorsport operation and available in rolling-chassis form.
Blaze Motorsport 2010 to date
Approx 2 made (UK)

STORM WARRIOR

Huge Hummer H1 replica based on Range Rover Classic from stuntman and ex-Speedway rider Lex Milloy. A very large, effective and imposing vehicle that could be built very inexpensively.

Action Automotive 2003 to date
Approx 10 made

STREET BEETLE

Beetle-tuning guru Chris Boyle came up with his take on the Porsche 356.
Street Beetle 1990–91
Chesil 1991 to date
Approx 5 made

STREET HOPPA

Originally known as the 'Hoppa–son of a beach' from the memorably named Fubar Factory, it was designed by John 'Village' Warner before his automotive clay model-maker father Barry took over. Cracking modern take on the beach buggy theme with VW Beetle underpinnings.

Street Hoppa 2008-10
Approx 5 made

STREET RAT

Richard Ashby (of TW Design) designed two-seater, marketed by Martin Griffin's Margin Sports Cars operation, with a chassis devised by Dave Sewell of Fibreform. Based on Ford Fiesta mechanicals. Resurfaced for a time at YKC Sportscars, where Griffin worked for a while.
Margin Sports Cars 1999–2001
Approx 4 made

STRIKER

Along with the Caterham Seven the most successful kit car ever in competition, although this diminutive Lotus Seven-inspired roadster is a serious challenger on the Queen's highway too.

The first version was a one-off, the Mk2 was a stripped-out budget version, and the Mk3 – depicted here – was the definitive Striker. Incidentally, the Sylva Phoenix (*qv*) was initially known as the Striker Mk4.

Taken over in 2002 by ex-chicken farmer and motorsport fan Mel Coppock, who made several revisions over the years including offering bike engines and the Toyota 4A-GE unit, in which his company specialised. In September 2010 it was announced that Mel had sold the project to brothers Callum and Jeremy Bulmer (part of the cider dynasty), who continued trading in Mel's erstwhile base in central Hereford but revised the company name slightly.
Sylva Autokits 1985–2002
Raw Striker 2002–10
Raw Engineering 2010 to date
Approx 650 made

STYLUS – *see Sylva Stylus*

SUFFOLK C-TYPE

Exact dimensions and a perfect match for the company's SS100 replica (see next entry). Suffolk Sportscars is run by ex-Wilhire founder Roger Williams.
Suffolk Sportscars 2008 to date
Approx 12 made

SUFFOLK SS100

Originally conceived by well-known Jaguar restorer Terry Rowan of TRAC Engineering, who specialised in SS100s. It came under the control of Suffolk Sportscars from 1995. Visually identical to a 1937–39 Jaguar SS100. Beautiful.
TRAC Engineering 1991–95
Suffolk Sportscars 1995 to date
Approx 125 made

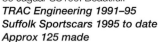

SULTAN

A Dagenham-based company who owned the international sales rights to the Rickman Ranger and revised it in 1996 to accept Renault Clio parts. The Sultan was their other vehicle of similar, albeit more rounded, styling, also based on the Renault Clio that had undergone crash testing at MIRA and was aimed at Australian, Japanese and European markets. Kamran Naghdi ran the company – not sure if they sold any in the UK.
BMS Automotives 2000
Approx 1 made

SUMMERFIELD SOLAR

Beautiful replica of the Lola Mk1 of 1958–62, created by Tim Summerfield aided by Baz Cope based in Craven Arms. Had a delicate spaceframe chassis with aluminium inner panels. Power came from an Alfa Romeo GTV, as did much of the running gear.
Summerfield Car Company 1992–94
Approx 12 made

SUN ROADSTER

North London TVR specialists Coupés of London had an original Vignale-Fiat Gamine and decided to offer replicas. Originally called the Noddi before being rechristened the Sun Roadster. Based on Fiat 126 mechanicals and underpinned by a ladderframe chassis. Kits cost £2,495 in 1997.
Coupés of London 1993–96
Sun Carriage Company 1996–2001
Approx 22 made

SUNLIT

Designed in Italy, the Sunlit was a two-seater coupé based around Fiat 126/500 mechanicals. No sales.
Sunlit Cars 1983–84
Approx 1 made

SUPACORSE

F355 replica from a Birmingham company whose BAD moniker was an acronym of the three protagonists' first names – Brian, Andy and Darren. Project acquired in 2010 by a chap called Bob Atkinson, based in the North-East, who intended a relaunch with several revisions.

BAD Design 2001–4
Bob Atkinson Design 2010 to date
Approx 250 made

SUPER 750

Bromley furniture shop owner Les Montgomery's first car was the aluminium-over-ash-frame Super 750. His newly created Super Accessories operation would rise to be perhaps *the* emporium for early '60s *specials* builders. In addition to all the tuning equipment they were also agents for Hamblin and acquired the Markham-Peasey operation in 1962. They also organised what was probably the first kit car show at Biggin Hill in May 1961, called the 'Super Accessories Concourse d'Elegance'.

Super Accessories 1957–63
Approx 20 made

SUPER COUPÉ

A pretty convincing and funky take on the forties Willys Coupé from well-known Bournemouth-based rodder, Chris Boyle, assisted by Ian Coombes, before it passed to David Palmer of the Rodshop, also based in Bournemouth.

Boyle, part of the UK's rodding royalty, had originally imported the kit from American company BGW, before revamping and improving it to suit the British marketplace. Boyle had previously been responsible for several well-known hot rods, including 'Moulin Rouge', which had been used by John Brown Wheels as their publicity vehicle.

The car ended its days at Pete Cheeseman's Wizard of Rods (*qv*) operation in Slough, Berkshire.

Everyday Vehicles 1981–85
Rodshop 1985–87
Approx 15 made

SUPER SPORTSMAN

An Austin 7-based bodyshell designed for Super Accessories boss Les Montgomery by Jim Shaw.

Super Accessories 1957–63
Approx 15 made

SUPERLITE® COUPÉ SL-C

Hailing from the well-regarded American manufacturer Race Car Replicas, under the Superlite® banner. The company is based in Clinton Township, Michigan, and run by ex-pat Englishman, Fran Hall. Fran offers the original Superlite® brand in addition to the RCR range of replicas.

The Coupé SL-C is a Le Mans-style sportscar with an aluminium TIG-welded semi-monocoque tub, and double wishbones and billet uprights allround. Power comes from GM LS range of V8 engines. The range was imported to the UK by Arden Automotive of Didcot from April 2011.

Arden Automotive 2011 to date (UK)
Approx 1 made (UK)

SUPERLITE® NEMESIS SL-N

Latest model to join the Superlite® range is the Nemesis, which like the SL-R, features an exo-skeletal body style, with a CNC-bent spaceframe and Suzuki Hayabusa power.

The range was imported to the UK by Arden Automotive of Didcot from April 2011.

Arden Automotive 2011 to date (UK)
Approx 1 made (UK)

SUPERLITE® ROADSTER SL-R

Superb Superlite® Roadster follows the exo-skeletal theme with state-of-the-art mechanicals and suspension.

The range was imported to the UK by Arden Automotive of Didcot from April 2011.

Arden Automotive 2011 to date (UK)
Approx 1 made (UK)

SUPERSTRATOS

Basically a silhouette 1976 Group 5 Stratos Evoluzione racer with spaceframe chassis.
Hennessey Racing 1996 to date
Approx 2 made

SUPER THREE

This was a Ford Popular-based version of the Super Two (see next entry).
Super Accessories 1961–65
Approx 30 made

SUPER TWO

Les Montgomery's most successful model, which was actually made for him by Sid Hamblin in Dorset and was an enlarged Hamblin Cadet for Ford 90in wheelbase. It might have been cheap at £99 and a bit basic, but 200 found homes. It came with a tube chassis, rudimentary fibreglass cycle-winged body and the addition of a Spartan interior and engine from Ford E93A. The chassis was made by Bowden.

After some 48 years out of production, Leighton Motor Company of Biddenden, Kent, run by Stuart Souter, put a revised version back into production in 2008 briefly.
Super Accessories 1960–65
Leighton Motor Company 2008-9
Approx 201 made

SUPERFORMANCE Mk3

Cobra replica made in South Africa by Hi Tech Automotive based in Port Elizabeth. Very popular in North America and imported to the UK by Le Mans Coupés. Sold in fully-built and turnkey minus form, which means they fall within the remit of this book.
Le Mans Coupés Ltd 2009 to date
Approx 5 made (UK)

SUPERFORMANCE CONTINUATION GT40

A superb car made in South Africa by Hi Tech Automotive and given continuation chassis numbers licensed by Safir Spares. Underpinned by a monocoque, just like the genuine GT40s, and 90% of its parts could fit on to a real '40. Power came from Roush-prepared V8 engines. Primarily sold as fully-built cars but can be purchased in turnkey minus form. Sold in the UK by historic racer Nigel Hulme and Cobra expert Rod Leach.
Le Mans Coupés Ltd 2007 to date
Approx 20 made (UK)

SUPERFORMANCE GRAND SPORT

Latest replica from Hi Tech Automotive of South Africa is a gorgeous recreation of the Corvette Grand Sport from the '60s. Available in turnkey minus form alongside fully-builts.
Le Mans Coupés Ltd 2010 to date
Approx 1 made (UK)

SUPERFORMANCE SHELBY DAYTONA COUPÉ

Glorious Shelby Daytona Coupé, licenced by Carroll Shelby and designed by the 1960s original's designer Peter Brock. Early cars had Roush-prepared V8 engines, although the Mk2s from 2008 had GM LS units. Absolutely superb, complete with air conditioning. Sold in the UK in fully-built and turnkey minus guises.
Le Mans Coupés Ltd 2002 to date
Approx 15 made (UK)

SUPERSNAKE

Created by Robin Hood Engineering founder Richard Stewart in 2007, after he had sold the RHE marque. The Supersnake was his take on a modern-day interpretation of the Cobra that also had elements of 'Big' Healey in the mix. Based on floorpan of Ford Mondeo Mk2 (albeit the monocoque is shortened by 15in) and utilises much of the donor.

Sold to Wheal Plenty, Cornwall-based Peninsula Sports Cars run by Paul Featherstone-Harvey in 2008, who began marketing the kit again in early 2011.
Richard Stewart 2006–8
Peninsula Sports Cars 2011 to date
Approx 2 made

SURF BUGGY

Created by Belgian Dirk Tinck as a one-off, but when he swapped it for a Manta Ray (*qv*) the guru of the beach buggy, James Hale, stepped in and brought the moulds, calling it the Surf. Based on a VW Beetle floorpan chopped by 12in.
GT Mouldings 2005–8
Approx 3 made

SUTOL 23

Appearing in 1989, the excellent Sutol (which is *Lotus* spelt backwards) was the brainchild of racer and businessman Murray Lewis, from Darlaston, who had previously been racing a Westfield X1 in the 750 Motor Club's Kit Car Challenge series.

Kits were priced from £2,200 which bought you an aluminium-clad spaceframe chassis and as-per-original double wishbones with Sutol's own uprights (a Formula Ford option was available), with the car based on Triumph running gear, with mid-mounted engine, although customers could opt for Ford Crossflow, YB VW Beetle or even Alfasud engines, mated to a Hewland Mk9 transaxle.
Sutol Motorsport 1990–92
Approx 14 made

SV2000

Also known as the Bugrat, this off-road style road-legal kit car was based on the Škoda Estelle and came from Vince Wright of RV Dynamics.
RV Dynamics 1998–2006
Approx 14 made

SWIFT DAYTONA

V12-powered Ferrari Daytona replica that appeared once at Stoneleigh in 1988 and no more.
Swift Classics 1988
Approx 1 made

SWIFT KJ280

A superb if expensive (try a £12,500 kit price in 1983!) Ford Granada-based, aluminium-bodied traditional roadster underpinned by a backbone chassis from the pencil of John Swift of Barnsley.
Swift Classics 1983–85
Approx 5 made

SYLVA AUTOKITS

Jeremy Phillips was an apprentice structural design draughtsman in Southampton for a company called Dibben Structural Engineers. After a couple of years in Canada he was working as a self-employed draughtsman and building an Arkley SS in his spare time, as was his near neighbour Nick Green, later of NG Cars, who at the time was an agent for John Britten of Arkley.

The Arkley build had well and truly ignited a fire and Phillips fancied creating his own car and a traditional roadster appealed, but Mr Green had already got there first with his recently launched TA, so something more modern was called for.

He adopted the name Sylva, Latin for woodland, for his own company, inspired by the nearby New Forest. His first car was the Star, which appeared in 1981.

Jeremy Phillips will go down in UK kit car history as one of the most gifted and innovative designers ever. A genius.

SYLVA FURY – *see Fury*

SYLVA J15

Hailing from Jeremy Phillips is the diminutive J15 two-seater that made its debut in 2009 and follows the traditional Sylva philosophy of superb handling, light weight and value for money. With a pleasing shape and echoes of all manner of classic '60s sports racers. Power comes from a variety of Ford engines such as Zetec Blacktop, with the whole ensemble underpinned by a delicate yet highly effective spaceframe chassis.
Sylva Autokits 2009 to date
Approx 15 made

SYLVA J16

A revised version of the Riot (*qv*), which was notable by being 80mm wider across the chassis, thus giving a larger cockpit. Otherwise, the car is identical mechanically to the Riot, which it replaced in April 2011.
Sylva Autokits 2011 to date
Approx 15 made

SYLVA JESTER

The aim with the quirky Jester was to get back to basics. Inspired by the beach buggy boom of the early '70s, the Jester ticked all the boxes. It's the only Sylva not designed solely by Jeremy Phillips, with input coming from Huw MacPherson. One thing is for sure. The little car, based on Fiesta Mk1, handles like a deity, just like all Sylvas in fact. Was originally going to be called the *Jesta*.

Taken over in 2002 by Mike Phillips of Harlequin Autokits, who came up with a slightly revised front end and windscreen frame that effectively made it a Mk2. When in 2005 Mike, an engineer, became busy with other things the project was shelved along with Raffo Cars' Belva (*qv*) and Belvetta (*qv*).

Resurrected in 2005 by Sylva Autokits agent Stingray Motorsport, run by Steve Knee, who came up with a Ford Ka donor option.
Sylva Autokits 1999–2002
Harlequin Autokits 2002–5
Stingray Motorsport 2005-10
Approx 160 made

SYLVA LEADER

Encouraged by his sister, who had moved to Lincolnshire a few years before, Jeremy Phillips upped sticks and moved east. His first Lincolnshire-based Sylva was the improved Leader, which for a time ran alongside the Star. Though it was clearly inspired by the former model it featured 'softened' styling and an all-fibreglass body, although the donor remained Vauxhall Viva. It was named after a sailing dinghy (sailing being a passion of Jeremy's).

Project taken over in 1987 by Robley Motors run by Rob and Shirley Andrews, a petrol station and general garage repair business in Worthen, Staffordshire.

John Jones of JP Autocraft of Stourport was the last custodian of the Leader and its older sister, the Star. Out of the blue the moulds turned up for sale in 2011.
Sylva Autokits 1984–85
Swindon Sportscars 1985–87
Robley Motors 1987–91
JP Autocraft 1992
Approx 150 made

SYLVA MOJO

A really big change for Sylva came with the Mojo, which was Phillips' first mid-engined car and a refreshingly bold move, proving that he's always been a brave designer and never afraid to push his boundaries.

Front suspension consisted of Ford Fiesta items and Sylva bespoke parts, while at the rear there was a de Dion arrangement. Power came from a variety of Ford engines.
Sylva Autokits 1998–2002
Approx 50 made

SYLVA MOJO 2

Appearing in 2002, the Mojo 2 was more than just a simple breathe over. It had a reshaped nose with further revisions behind the front wheel area. Under the skin, it had a revised rear end now featuring wishbones rather than a de Dion arrangement, with new engine mountings, wheelbase increased by 25mm, and a narrower track front and rear. In addition the front suspension now featured double wishbones and Sierra uprights rather than the Fiesta items of the Mk1. Taken over by Matthew Beardshaw of Meggt Ltd in 2008, and then Typhoon of Thorney, Cambridgeshire in 2011..
Sylva Autokits 2002–8
Meggt Ltd 2008-11
Typhoon Sportscars 2011 to date
Approx 85 made

SYLVA PHOENIX – *see Phoenix*

SYLVA PHOENIX Mk2 – *see Phoenix Mk2*

SYLVA RIOT

A jewel-like little car that harked back to Formula Junior days, although it was very much a Sylva product. Originally known as the R1ot after the Yamaha bike engine that powered it, although this was modified to Riot after the introduction of Ford engines. Superceded by the larger J16 in 2011.
Sylva Autokits 2004 –11
Approx 100 made

SYLVA STAR

The highly-rated Star was designer Jeremy Phillips' first model. A spaceframe chassis underpinned a steel-panelled centre section with fibreglass front and rear sections. Donor vehicle was either Vauxhall Viva or Chevette. Passed  to Swindon Sportscars in 1985 and Robley Motors in 1987, after which it ended up with Stourport-on-Severn-based John Jones and his JP Autocraft operation for a short time. Moulds turned up for sale unexpectedly in late 2011.

Sylva Autokits 1982–85
Swindon Sportscars 1985–87
Robley Motors 1987–91
JP Autocraft 1992
Approx 70 made

SYLVA STRIKER Mk1

1985 saw the launch of the iconic Striker, inspired by Jeremy Phillips' admiration for Colin Chapman. He based the car on the tried and tested Star/Leader principle and set about creating a suitable Lotus Seven-inspired body for it. The  first one was built for Jeremy's brother, Mark, and had a Leader chassis, Vauxhall front end, Ford rear and a Mazda Rotary engine pulled from a stricken RX3. This was the only Mk1.

Sylva Autokits 1985
Approx 1 made

SYLVA STRIKER Mk2

As far as the consumer was concerned however, the first Striker 'proper' was the Mk2 based on Escort Mk2. Along with the Caterham Seven it was the most successful kit car ever in competition, although this  diminutive Lotus Seven-inspired roadster is a serious challenger on the Queen's highway too.

Sylva Autokits 1985–2005
Raw Striker Ltd 2005–10
Raw Engineering 2010 to date
Approx 650 made

SYLVA STRIKER Mk3

 In 1988, a stripped-out budget version of the Striker was called for and it became a separate model on the Sylva price list, known as the Mk3. Came with a torque tube rear axle, outboard front dampers, Vauxhall subframes and wishbones and was based around the Vauxhall Chevette.

Sylva Autokits 1988–90
Approx 60 made

SYLVA STRIKER Mk4

Based on Striker Mk2 chassis the Mk4 had an all-enveloping body and was inspired by a pub chat with a group of friends, who persuaded Jeremy to create a paean to his favourite car of all time – the Lola Mk1. The result, later renamed the Phoenix (*qv*), went on to enjoy much race success like its Striker brother. A revised Sylva Phoenix Mk2 (*qv*) appeared in 1999.

Project passed in 2003 to Ian Gray of Ilkeston-based Stuart Taylor Motorsport, who acquired both the original version and the revised Mk2. He retained the Mk2 but sold the original Phoenix to Ian Boulton, a print finisher from Cheshire, who chose the name Cyana Sportscars for his new company. Cyan is an ink colour used in printing. Cyana also developed a Mazda MX-5-based version called the MX500.

However, Boulton concentrated on his printing operation and the project passed to one of his customers, Rob Johnston of Newcastle-under-Lyme, in 2008, who along with Anton Landon enjoyed a fair bit of racing success in the 750 Motor Club's Kit Car Championship.

Sylva Autokits 1988–99
Stuart Taylor Motorsport 2003–5
Cyana Sportscars 2005–8
Rob Johnston Chassis Engineering 2008 to date
Approx 70 made

SYLVA STYLUS

The Stylus was the GT Sylva with doors and a practical boot and was actually designed as a tourer by Jeremy Phillips, who sold around 20 examples.

Sold on to former National Health Service executive Peter Powell, who had been a customer of Phillips before buying the project. Originally based in Woking, Surrey, before moving to Llanidloes in mid-Wales. Erstwhile SSC employee Tim Benbow acquired the project in 2003 and changed the company name to Stylus Sportscars.

Sylva Autokits 1994–96
Specialist Sports Cars 1996–2003
Stylus Sports Cars 2003–7
Approx 75 made

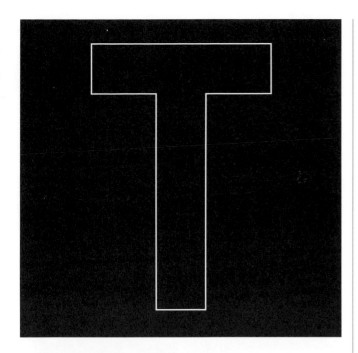

T6 LE MANS SPITFIRE

A Triumph-based replica of a Le Mans class-winning Spitfire variant made by Huddersfield-based Graham Pearce.
T6 Motorsport Ltd 2005–7
Approx 2 made

T&A PREDATOR

Early '90s Cobra replica made very briefly in Peterborough.
T&A Sportscars 1990
Approx 2 made

TA PHANTOM

The Phantom featured a revised '60s Ashley Laminates body, complete with an MGB windscreen. TA Design & Development were based in Wakefield, West Yorkshire, and run by Trevor Jones and Andy Williamson.
TA Design & Development 1990–91
Approx 2 made

TA SPIRIT

Started life as a one-off special called *Ynot*. Based on a mixture of Ford Cortina Mk3 and Escort Mk2 parts.
TA Design & Development 1990–91
Approx 3 made

TALON

Graham Brewer's Talon Sportscars of Christchurch, Dorset, took over the rights to the Neville Trickett-designed GP Talon (*qv*) (he also made the Eagle +2 (*qv*) under license for a time) and embarked on an ambitious plan to convert this Beetle-engined stalwart to front engine configuration, something it was never designed for. As a result they didn't do much with it, making one definitely and probably a second example before Leeds-based Allan Ballard took over. The car remained VW Beetle-based, although Ballard also came up with a Ford Cortina-based version known as the Talon F4.
Talon Sports Cars 1987–89
Talon Sports Cars Ltd 1989–91
Approx 6 made

TALON

Modern sports car designed by Jeff Ashton and had associations with the Avelle GT (*qv*) offered by James Hodds' Motion Car Developments.
SV Engineering 2001–2
Approx 2 made

TALON

Not really a kit car, but a great, fun conversion that transformed an old bedraggled Metro into a ripsnorting road rocket. Came from Talon Sports Cars run by Dudley Shearman and Gareth Cole based (originally) at the former GTM Cars workshop in Sutton Bonington, Leicestershire. Shearman was a long-time ex-GTM employee and marque expert.

Company now a Hawk Cars build agent, with Shearman being in sole control, although Shearman's co-director is Hawk boss, Gerry Hawkridge, who was a customer for the Talon Metro.
Talon Sport Cars 2005–7
Approx 10 made

TARA V8

Designed by well-known kit and industrial designer Tony Claydon in the early eighties, and was apparently almost taken on by Aston Martin. In 1989 Tony decided to offer the car in kit form. Used a backbone chassis by Southern Roadcraft.
Centrepoint Racing 1989–90
Approx 3 made

TAYDEC Mk2

Originally a sports-racer designed
by Tommy Clapham in 1971, and
discovered by West Yorkshire
designer John Suckling in
1997. He put the car back into
production in 2004.
Atlas (Kly) Ltd 2004–9
Approx 5 made

TDK MINI

Formerly the famous Maguire Mini, acquired by Mini racer Dave
Kimberley from Coventry, who also took over the FRA Mini (*qv*).
TDK Racing 2007 to date
Approx 5 made

TEAC RV-2/RV-4 – *see Eagle RV*

TEAC SS S3R – *see Eagle SS*

TEAL TYPE 35

After buying an American VW
Beetle-based Type 35 replica, ex-
Daimler engineer Ian Foster, who
was at the time running a brake
specialist outfit called Trafford
Brake Services, heavily revamped
it to suit his purposes.

After he'd finished, it featured a
twin-rail chassis and had a Morris Marina donor. Former Pan-Am marketing
man Mike Alderson helped with initial promotion work for the project. Car
also featured a GRP body, with Morris Marina front suspension and live rear
axle. Power was B-series 1,800cc or Triumph Straight-Six.

The Teal brand was taken over by Foster's friend Bob Jones
in 1986. A trained panel-beater before becoming an AA man,
Jones liked the chassis but felt that the car deserved an aluminium
body rather than GRP, while he also went for 18in wire wheels. He
developed the original chassis into a semi-spaceframe and Dicky
Dawes of Classic Car Panels, who made the Tri-Pacer (*qv*) three-
wheeler, started making the bodies.

The Teal T35 also used Viva components, with a variety of engines
suitable. The Triumph straight-six was a popular choice. The Teal T35
visually replicated the Bugatti Type 35B, the supercharged 2,261cc
racer.

Norman Durban, a customer of Bob Jones, bought the project in
1997 and moved production to Surrey, where it remained until Teal ceased
trading in 1999. Durban acquired only the T35 and T35B (Jaguar power
with transmission tunnel mods) projects, not the T59 and Tourer.
Teal Cars (Ian Foster) 1984–86
Teal Cars (Bob Jones) 1986–97
Teal Cars (Norman Durban) 1997–99
Approx 200 made

TEAL TYPE 35 TOURER

A step too far for the purists – a
Type 35 with an extra pair of
seats, and a full four-seater!
Teal Cars 1988–97
Approx 3 made

TEAL TYPE 44

A tasteful replica of the Bugatti
Type 44 from Bob Jones-era Teal
Cars.
Teal Cars 1988–89
Approx 1 made

TEAL TYPE 59

Originally made by Projects of
Distinction and sold under the
GPB brand name. Acquired by
Teal in 1991. Had a folded steel
centre monocoque with tubular
subframes front and rear, with
double wishbones on the front, a
five-link rear axle and a Jaguar XK
engine. Ended up at Vincent Hurricane makers, Caburn Engineering,
from 2009.
GPB 1989–91
Teal Cars 1991–97
Caburn Engineering 2009 to date
Approx 3 made

TECHNIC 550

Technic Ltd was based in Andover and run by Barrie Martin, an
aeronautical engineer. In the early '80s he had been based in America
and imported many Reynard FF1600 cars, as well as GP RSK and
Madison kits. Following his return to the UK he founded Technic Ltd
in 1989. In 1997 he was joined by Porsche fanatic and historic racer
Mike Walker, and the company name changed to Martin & Walker
relocating to an industrial unit at Thruxton circuit.

The 550 was the first and best-selling Technic product. First
demonstrator had a Vauxhall twin-cam engine and used Beetle
mechanicals but had a separate spaceframe chassis.
Technic Ltd 1987–97
Martin & Walker 1997 to date
Approx 160 made

TECHNIC GT COUPÉ

A hardtop version of the Porsche 356 Coupé that offered practicality and a nice build level. Not many customers agreed, the majority preferring the traditional convertible version. Based like the company's Speedster on VW Beetle floorpan and mechanicals.
Martin & Walker 1998 to date
Approx 6 made

TECHNIC GTS

A close approximation of the glorious Porsche 904 based on a 911 donor, weighing just 650kg. Available fully-built only. Most of these were exported to America.
Martin & Walker 1996 to date
Approx 30 made

TECHNIC SPEEDSTER

Speedster kit based on VW Beetle floorpan and mechanicals. The company made Ford-based chassis' for Moss Cars for a time in the early nineties.
Martin & Walker 1997 to date
Approx 40 made

TEMPEST SPORTS

Created by Teal founder Ian Foster and ex-TVR chief engineer John Box. A diminutive two-seater based on Reliant Kitten mechanicals. When Box was still working at TVR, he had evaluated the Stevens Cipher for the Blackpool manufacturer. Following a two-year gap project was taken over in 1992 by Thoroughbred Projects, who made the car until 1997. There then followed a four-year hiatus before Liverpudlian Steven Campbell came on to the scene in 2001 and offered it until 2003. John Melody took over in 2006 and he made several upgrades, including a disc brake conversion. Joe Mason of Reliant Spares acquired the project in late 2011.
Tempest Cars 1987–90
Thoroughbred Projects 1992–97
Tempest Cars 2001–3
Tempest Cars 2006-10
Reliant Sports 2011 to date
Approx 15 made

TEMPEST VANTIQUE

In 1988 John Box and Ian Foster came up with a commercial van version of the Tempest called the Vantique, based on the same Reliant mechanicals. The vehicle was underpinned by a Reliant Fox rolling chassis including 850cc engine, to which Tempest added 8in to the wheelbase, while also moving the engine back by the same distance. A 1½in square-tube spaceframe was added as a kind of framework. The front section and rear mudguards were glassfibre, with the bonnet and 'van' section made from aluminium. A 6cwt payload could be carried. Fully built examples cost from £10,000 in 1990.
Never really caught on.
Tempest Cars 1988–92
Thoroughbred Projects 1992–97
Approx 2 made

TERRIER MARK 2 1172

Len Terry was the man behind the Terrier marque. He was also known back in the day for being Colin Chapman's right-hand man at Lotus in the early days. His company Terrier Car & Engineering Company was based at Thornwood, Essex.

The Mark 1 was available for a whole host of proprietary bodyshells of the day, but 'proper' Terrier kit supply came with the Mark 2 of 1958, which was a highly competitive machine on the racetrack. Brian Hart won the 1172 Championship in 1958 in one and for a time held several circuit lap records.

It had a very effective multi-tube spaceframe chassis with double wishbone front and a live rear axle at the rear, with stressed body panels, and was available as a kit for £440, or as a comprehensive package including Ford 105E engine for £550.

Terry later moved to Peter Pellandine's Falcon Shells operation as technical director, and both the Falcon Sports (*qv*) and Peregrine (*qv*) models sported the Mark 2's chassis.
Terrier Car & Engineering Company Ltd 1957–58
Approx 45 made

THRUXTON GT200

Appearing for the first time at Stoneleigh in May 2011, the Thruxton GT200 hails from Cornish-based JWE Motorsport, run by Jim Walker, a car builder of real note and the man responsible for some very fine GTM builds over the years. The car is evocative of, but not a replica of, a Healey 3000, based on BMW E36/E46 mechanicals, weighing in at around 600kg. Kits were priced at £3,995 on launch.
JWE Motorsport 2011 to date
Approx 2 made

HIT KIT

TICI

The TiCi (pronounced *titchy*) was the work of Anthony Hill from Sutton-in-Ashfield, Nottinghamshire, a former furniture design lecturer at Loughborough College of Art, based in Shepshed. The first prototype of this diminutive little vehicle appeared in 1969 (although it was originally conceived back in 1966), when it was a 72in microcar with power coming from Triumph Daytona 500cc bike engine.

The slightly larger (89in) and now Mini-based production version was announced in 1972, using Mini front subframe and rear-mounted A-series engine. Hill cleverly enlisted the help of luminaries such as Stirling Moss and BRM sponsor Raymond Mays to publicise the car. C5 creator Sir Clive Sinclair was one of the first customers, as was the drummer from Showaddywaddy, Romeo Challenger. Hill, perhaps optimistically, described the TiCi as a 'City Sprint Commuter Car', although it was pretty rapid thanks to its ultra-light weight. Of the 40 made, twelve were exported (six to Spain and six to Japan). Ultimately, it was the introduction of VAT in 1973 that killed it.
TiCi Sales Ltd 1972–73
Approx 40 made

TIFOSI SS

Hailing from Chulmleigh, Devon-based Star Motor Company, the SS is a faithful reproduction of the original Sebring Sprite, successfully manufactured and campaigned by John Sprinzel in the early sixties. The SS is supplied as a complete bodyshell in primer that is ready to

accept the mechanicals from any MG Midget or Austin Healey Sprite. Rear suspension is the later semi-elliptical arrangement, while the bodyshells are built using brand new steel monocoques. Star absorbed by Quantam in late 2011.
Star Motor Company 2011
Quantum Sports Cars 2011 to date
Approx 25 made

T.I.G.E.R

A short-lived ambitious creation from ex-Tyrrell F1 ground-effect pioneer Chris Humberstone. The name stood for Turbine Intercooled Ground Effect Roadster. The wedge-shaped car had Renault 2.7-litre V6 power. Bonkers, bonkers, bonkers.
Cartel 1983
Approx 1 made

TIGER RACING

Founded by Jim Dudley, who for many years ran VW specialists Volkshouse from his base in Plumstead, South London, as well as being a diehard Lotus fan. A true family firm, with Jim's wife Sue, son Paul and daughter Laura all involved in the day-to-day running of the operation. A cracking company, makers of honest-to-goodness products, with one of the most loyal followings around.

The BARC run a Tiger race series with three classes, dedicated to Tiger's products.

TIGER AVIATOR

Launched towards the end of 2009 the Aviator is a different take on the Lotus Seven theme and was designed by Simon Keys, who was also responsible for the V-Storm (*qv*).
Tiger Racing 2009 to date
Approx 10 made

TIGER AVON

Project bought from Avon Coachworks (when known as the Avon Sprint (*qv*)), run by Leon Sansom, and heavily revised by Tiger. Was powered by Rover K-series engine when made by Phoenix but soon amended to Ford by Tiger.

So good was Tiger's transformation that Jim Dudley wrote a book for Veloce Publishing called *How to Build a Tiger Avon*.

A Mk2 version with all-new body was announced in early 2011, with lowered floors, wider wheel arches and revised scuttle panel among the changes, yet still retaining the family resemblance, and based on Ford mechanicals.
Tiger Racing 2001 to date
Approx 800 made

TIGER B6

A Super Six powered by bike engines, usually Kawasaki ZX-9 or Suzuki GSX-R1000.
Tiger Racing 1999–2000
Approx 10 made

TIGER CAT E1/SUPERCAT/CAT XL

Tiger's first budget model went extremely well from the time it was released in 1998. Based on Ford Sierra. The Supercat featured alternative nosecone and also higher spec, while Cat XL featured larger dimensions. Tiger sold around 800 of this family of kits.

Acquired by SouthWays Automotive of Fareham, Hampshire, run by ex-British Aerospace engineer Steve Dunford and Paul Buckthorpe in 2010, who have enthusiastically developed the model further.
Tiger Racing 1998–2010
SouthWays Automotive 2010 to date
Approx 810 made

TIGER CUB

Appeared in 1996 and was a budget version of the Super Six, although featured Ford Sierra MacPherson strut rear suspension. Body supplied with two-pack paint finish rather than in gelcoat.
Tiger Racing 1992–95
Approx 8 made

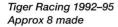

TIGER D-TYPE

Tiger acquired the former Stardust D-type (*qv*), subsequently Le Mans D-type (*qv*) replica from David Yoxall in 1999 and made one demonstrator to test the market, but didn't proceed with it. Sold to Lightning Sports Cars
Tiger Racing 1999–2000
Approx 1 made

TIGER HS6

Announced in early 2011, the HS6 is a superb take on the Lotus VI theme, with aluminium centre section and GRP wings. Unusually for Tiger Racing this model featured Triumph Herald or Spitfire running gear, although it used a separate Tiger-made steel chassis.
Tiger Racing 2011 to date
Approx 10 made

TIGER GTA

Announced on the eve of the National Kit Car Motor Show at Stoneleigh in 2011, the GTA (Grand Tourer Avon) has a fully-enveloping body designed around the company's Avon spaceframe chassis.
Tiger Racing 2011 to date
Approx 10 made

TIGER HUNTSMAN

Created in 1988 originally as a one-off by Graham Smith, powered by Alfa 1.5 flat four. Tiger Racing acquired the project in summer 1997 but didn't do very much with it and subsequently sold it on.
Tiger Racing 1997
Approx 1 made

TIGER LM

Tiger's Jim Dudley purchased the 250 LM project from Barry Sheppard at Rawlson in Dover and concentrated on the two-seat version, although they also acquired the 2+2.
Tiger Racing 1989–90
Approx 3 made

TIGER R6/R10

A lightweight version of the Super Six that appeared in 1999 and further pushed Tiger's track abilities. A popular choice for trackdays.

Renamed R10 in 2011, which denotes a switch to Kawasaki ZX-10 engine.
Tiger Racing 1999 to date
Approx 100 made

TIGER RS6

GRP-bodied version of the ZR6 (see below) with Duratec power.
Tiger Racing 2007 to date
Approx 5 made

TIGER STORM

Originally appeared in 1997 but had a revamp and was relaunched in 1999. Based on a Super Six chassis in 1½in square tube. Tiger's idea of a modern-day Lotus Elan.
Tiger Racing 1997, 1999–2001
Approx 5 made

TIGER SUPER SIX

It's probably fair to say that the Super Six is the car that put Tiger Racing on the specialist car map and is considered by many to be their classic model. Highly capable Lotus Seven-inspired sports car that was usually powered by Ford engines, although used several VW Golf parts too.
Tiger Racing 1991–2007
Approx 400 made

TIGER Z100

Mental twin bike-engined Lotus
Seven-inspired sports car
that at one time in 2001 held
the 0–60mph world record at
3.1 seconds. Project was a
collaboration with Z Cars.
Tiger Racing 2001–2
Approx 4 made

TIGER ZR6

Aluminium-bodied Lotus Seven-inspired sports car that featured
power from Duratec HE engine.
Tiger Racing 2008 to date
Approx 8 made

TIGRESS

Made in Dunbar, Lothian, and one
of the few Scottish kit cars. Not
the prettiest 2+2 ever, with weird
forward-hingeing, scissor-type
doors, with VW Beetle windows
and running gear. Brainchild
of Raymond Craig, an ex-RAF
engineer.
Autocult 1983–85
Approx 2 made

TILER TRIKE

Mini-based trike made in West Sussex, which utilised engine,
subframes and a variety of other mechanicals from the donor. Created
by Kevin Champion, never produced.
Tiler Car Company 1999–2000
Approx 1 made

TIPO 16 – *see Belva*

TIPO 17 – *see Belvetta*

TKH VENOM – *see Venom*

TMC COSTIN

Frank Costin had a design for a Lotus Seven rival, with a lightweight
spaceframe chassis and Rose-jointed suspension. At the time he was
working for a Republic of Ireland-based engineering company tasked
with producing an airport fire tender that he had designed.

Also working at this company was Peter Thompson, who liked the
sound of Costin's sports car and along with his brothers Val, Sean
and Anthony, gave up his job to set up Thompson Manufacturing
Company (TMC) in Castlebridge, County Wexford. They concentrated
fully on the TMC costing and employed nine staff.

The capable little car had an aluminium and glassfibre body and
based on Vauxhall Chevette running gear using the donor's 1,256cc
engine, although others, such as Ford Crossflow, CVH and Cosworth
BDR, could also be used.

A little gem; typical of Costin's skills. The operation sadly went bust
in 1987, which was a shame because the spaceframe chassis was a
work of art and was later purchased by American sports and racing
car manufacturer Panoz to underpin one of their cars.
Thompson Manufacturing Company 1983–87
Approx 39 made

TMC SCOUT – *see Scout*

TOMCAT

Not to be confused with the later Onyx Tomcat (*qv*). This one was
designed by a chap called Alan Hardy, from Nottingham. First
announced in 1986, it was a mid-engined sports coupé which
ultimately appeared at the Stafford Show in 1993, although it didn't
actually enter production.
Hardy Racing Organisation 1986, 1993–94
Approx 1 made

TOMCAT

Beefy and capable Range
Rover-based off-roader that was
originally made by Drew Bowler.
When he launched his fully-
built Wildcat project the Tomcat
moved to Skellingthorpe company
Tomcat Motorsport, run by Steve
Wells.
Bowler Engineering 1995–98
Tomcat Motorsport 1998 to date
Approx 120 made

TONIQ-R

Designed by University of Huddersfield design students Will Baxter, Colin Williams, Paul Philpot and Angus Fitton (now of *Car* magazine) and first shown as a concept at the Donington Show of 2002. Original prototype had a Westfield chassis but this was altered when the marketing for the project was taken over in 2004 by Stuart Taylor MotorSport, who underpinned the car with an STM Loco chassis.

Colin Williams then took over sole control and formed Toniq Ltd, working closely with Derek and Tris Elliston, who marketed the car more prominently.

The project was then moved to Cornwall under the control of Adrenaline Motorsport before moving again, to chassis-makers supreme Caged, who displayed a revised version of the car at Stoneleigh in 2009. It then became an Adrenaline Motorsport project outright in summer 2009 and was rebranded and revised as the Adrenaline CB, although after that company ceased trading in late 2009 it reverted to Toniq Ltd again, with Colin Williams in full control.

Stuart Taylor Motorsport 2002–4
Adrenaline Motorsport 2006–9
Adrenaline Motorsport 2009
Approx 17 made
Toniq Ltd 2004–6
Caged 2009
Toniq Ltd 2009 to date

TORERO S

Naz Maniscalschi and Bill Glazier were the men behind Mitcham-based Parallel Designs, although Glazier left within a couple of years. Naz had a background in car restoration and mechanics, learning his trade on top-end cars, and always had a love for exotic Italian sports cars, so it was a logical move for him to create his own replica of the Lamborghini Diablo.

Parallel Designs 2000 to date
Approx 75 made

TORNADO CARS

Bill Woodhouse and Anthony Bullen were the men behind the Tornado marque based in Rickmansworth, Hertfordshire, in an old polythene manufacturing factory.

The pair decided it would be a good idea to market a really sensible, affordable *special*. Not only did they achieve this aim, but proved it could be done for under £200, including the cost of the donor. The company built good cars, employed around 60 people at their height, and it was a shame that they hit financial problems and went into liquidation in 1963.

Later that year, well-known racing driver of the day, John Bekaert, acquired the marque and continued production of the Talisman, and also a new non-kit model a styling/tuning exercise for the Fiat 600 called the Tornado-Fiat 600D GT. By the end of 1964 a chap called Bert Wood bought the company.

Wood had sound ideas and wanted to relocate to a larger factory, although never did quite decide where that would be and remained in situ! Sadly, Tornado production didn't start again and the company became synonymous with crash repairs, which they continued with until closing their doors for good in 1986.

TORNADO BODYSHELL

Bill Woodhouse and Anthony Bullen were the men behind the original Tornado marque. Woodhouse decided that it would be a good idea to market a really sensible, buildable kit. Not only did he achieve his aim but also he proved that it could be done for under £200, including the cost of the donor. The company built good cars and it was a shame that they hit financial problems and went into liquidation in 1963.

Their first product was a bodyshell for specials builders of the late '50s.
Tornado Cars 1957–58
Approx 200 made

TORNADO M6 GTR

Created from scratch by Alan Sheldon, based initially on VW Beetle components and then its own spaceframe chassis, based around Renault V6, Rover V8 or small block Ford V8 power.
Tornado Sports Cars 1984–89, 1997–2002
Approx 30 made

TORNADO RAPTOR

A beefy larger dimensioned take on the Lotus Seven theme from Tornado Sports Cars, based on a triangulated spaceframe chassis with V8 power.
Tornado Sports Cars 1999-2008
Approx 50 made

TORNADO TALISMAN

This 2+2 marked a new direction for Bill Woodhouse's Tornado Cars, and was available in kit form or as a fully-built car. The ladderframe chassis had coil springs all round, with a live rear axle and Herald front suspension. The Talisman used an exclusive-to-Tornado Ford Classic, Cosworth-tuned engine. Bill Woodhouse was one of the most under-rated men to ever grace the kit car industry, and a gentleman to boot. A very clever man.
Tornado Cars 1961–64
Approx 196 made

TORNADO TEMPEST

Similar in concept to the company's Typhoon but adapted so it could accept engines such as the Ford Anglia 110E (OHV 997cc), BMC 'B' series and Triumph units. It also had rack and pinion steering and Herald front suspension.
Tornado Cars 1960–62
Approx 17 made

TORNADO THUNDERBOLT

An ambitious project, the Thunderbolt. It had a beefed-up and widened chassis so that it could accept Triumph TR3a or Ford Consul mechanicals.
Tornado Cars 1960
Approx 1 made

TORNADO TS40

Tornado Sports Cars had been making their M6 GTR replica since 1984, but this was joined – and ultimately superseded – by a GT40 replica from 1989. Underpinned by a spaceframe chassis, although a monocoque option was introduced in 2010. Power comes from Ford V8 and a Renault UN1 transaxle with internals modified to suit their requirements by Tornado's Andrew Sheldon, who initially worked with his dad, Alan, but then on his own.
Tornado Sports Cars 1989 to date
Approx 950 made

TOWNEND 581

Brothers Geoff and Peter Townend produced this two-seater bodyshell. It cost £108 with doors, panels and lights fitted. The hardtop cost £20 extra. It was designed for the 7ft 6in Ford 8 and 10 wheelbase, but could be altered to fit any chassis.
Townend Engineering 1958–62
Approx 60 made

TR REPLICA

Grand Illusions of Penn, Wolverhampton, briefly offered a range of TR2/TR3/TR3A replicas in 1991.
Grand Illusions 1991–92
Approx 2 made

TRAC 100

Created by Terry Rawlins of TRAC services of Colchester who had learnt his craft at Alf Hagon Motorcycles back in the day.

Terry's company – Terry Rawlins Auto Components – supplied all manner of parts, such as windscreen frames and brightwork for a variety of classics and kit cars. They had also restored a good amount of original Jaguar SS100s and with the potential for restorations running out, Terry acquired a stock of components that he decided to use on his own TRAC SS100 replica.

The project was subsequently taken over by Roger Williams, ex-Wilhire, via his Sufolk Jaguar concern.
Trac Services 1991–95
Approx 10 made

TORNADO TYPHOON

Although not to everyone's taste, the Typhoon was a sophisticated car for its time. Underpinned by a simple ladderframe, the fibreglass was of good quality while it had coil sprung rear suspension and split axle front. Donor vehicle was the Ford 8 or 10 range with the E93 sidevalve engine. There were DHC, coupé, four-seater and estate versions available. The body cost £130 and the chassis £70. A bargain.
Tornado Cars 1957–62
Approx 353 made.

TRACER

A William Towns design very far ahead of its time when it was unveiled in 1986.
Interstyl 1986
Approx 1 made

TRACKSTAR

Came from RS Jigtec and several were sold before that company ceased trading. Next appeared at Len Swan's Wildmoor MTC in 2005 before it was sold to an Asian company in 2006.
RS Jigtec 2001–3
Wildmoor Motor Traction 2005–6
Approx 6 made

TRAKKA TROUPER

A replica of the Renault Rodeo utility vehicle from Salford-based CL Cars, based on unmodified Renault 4 mechanicals.
CL Cars Ltd 1984
Approx 1 made

TRAMP

Richard Oakes had been working at Davrian for 14 months the day he was sent off to Brixham, Devon, to mend a crashed Davrian and ended up working for industrial fibreglass company Western Laminates, run by Roger Talbot, whose normal line of work was milk tanks, FF1600 bodies and panels for Davrian. While there Richard came up with one of the few British-created beach buggy kits.

Beautifully made, it didn't look like a revised GP, as many beach buggies of the day did. Another bonus was that it was also road-legal, based on an unmodified VW Beetle floorpan. A sizeable chunk of the Tramp buggies produced were sold by the company's agents, The Bespoke Buggy Company of south-west London. The project sold quickly initially, but Oakes went off to concentrate on his Nova project (*qv*) in late 1970 and within a year the company went into liquidation.
Western Laminates 1970–71
Approx 70 made

TRANSFORMER HF2000

Collaboration between Gerry Hawkridge, Colin Artus (who had bought one of the first BRA 427s that Gerry had done, and *Motor Sport* magazine journalist Gordon Cruickshank, who had been at university with Steve Murkett (who had a BRA 289 kit, like Gerry). They decided to come up with a paean to Lancia's legendary Stratos. Gerry used Roger Perry's original car and drawings to help him get the correct dimensions.

Very successful product and a superb one at that. Went on to become the Hawk HF (*qv*) when Gerry later set up Hawk Cars.
Transformer Cars 1984–90
Approx 250 made

TRANTOR

Possibly the only tractor kit ever made. Idea conceived by Stuart Taylor and Graham Edwards, with a prototype built in 1973, although the first production model didn't appear until 1978. Could be said to have been the inspiration for the JCB Fastrac range. Trantor name came from 'Transport Tractor'. The company was based in Lancashire.

A Series II arrived in 1983 that had more power (96bhp) but a reduced top speed. Taken over by Indian company HMT in 2003.
Trantor 1978–2003
Approx 100 made

TRI-PACER

Lovely three-wheeler from aluminium artisan Dicky Dawes. Based on Citroën 2CV floorpan and mechanicals. Could be had with a pair of close-coupled wheels instead of a single, when it was known as the Austin Somerset.
Classic Car Panels 1996–2001
Approx 18 made

TRIAD SPORT/WARRIOR

Basically an updated version of the Mosquito (*qv*) with new chassis, revised one-piece GRP body and exterior-mounted spare wheel. The Malvern-based company was run by friends Rick Jones and Ian Bowse, who offered two versions of the Triad – the Sport (nine made) and the Warrior Sprint (three made).
Malvern Autocraft 1993–98
Approx 12 made

TRIBUTE COUPÉ

A body conversion inspired by a very desirable coupé and based on Toyota Supra Mk IV. Hailing from Wareham-based Tribute Automotive, the Coupé was launched at the National Kit Car Motor Show at Stoneleigh in May 2011.The man behind the project is Chris Welch, a devout petrolhead and hot rod enthusiast and builder by profession.

Tribute Automotive 2011
Approx 1 made

TRIDENT

Superb single-seater in the style of a 1960s Formula Ford racer. Created by John Sims before being taken over by FF1600 guru Peter Alexander.

Trident Cars 2002–3
PA Motorsport 2003 to date
Approx 3 made

TRIDENT CARS

The original Trident was a model for TVR with styling by Trevor Fiore (real name *Frost*). TVR, owned at that time by Grantura Plastics, had gone into liquidation and Bill Last of Viking Performance, a TVR dealer and familiar with the specialist car scene, purchased the last of three Trident prototypes, a convertible, with the intention of productionising it. However, he commissioned Trevor Fiore to come up with a Trident 2+2 Fastback, which was 5in longer and 2½in wider than the intended TVR version. It was this car that he offered in fully-built and kit form.

Although the Trident was one of the prettiest cars of its day, the company folded in 1974, caused in no small part by the American emission regulations that strangled exports there.

The company was revived in 1976 under Bill Last's Viking Performance fibreglass division, albeit on a smaller scale, but it died again in 1978.

At the Motor Show in October 1998 a company called PB Design, run by Phil Bevan, relaunched the Trident marque with a new model called the *Ventura*. By 2001 Bevan had moved on and another new Trident was launched by Bill Chubb with a new model called the *Iceni*, which was only available fully-built with V8 power although later was converted to electric power.

TRIDENT TYCOON

The Tycoon used not only a Triumph TR6 chassis but its engine too, and revised Venturer styling.

Trident Cars 1971–73
Approx 6 made

TRIDENT VENTURER

The 1960s Trident operation aimed high and people often forget that their cars were available in kit form. The Venturer was produced by Viking Performance and Trident Cars boss Bill Last, originally based on Austin Healey 3000 chassis but soon switched to Triumph TR6, with power coming from Ford 3.0-litre V6.

An alternative version called the Clipper (30 sold), powered by a small block Ford V8 was also on the Trident price list, although this wasn't available in kit form. Last had acquired 30 V8 engines, at a discount, after they were ordered but not paid for by TVR.

Trident Cars 1969–74
Approx 49 made

TRIFID

Quirky yet well-built little three-wheeler from Mark Brook and Phil Wells. Featured a cut-down Mini floorpan and mechanicals with a narrowed subframe at the rear. Superlegerra construction (basically steel tubes covered in sheet steel).

Brookwell 1994
Approx 4 made

TR1KE

The tR1ke was created by Stuart Mills of MEV in 2008. A three-wheeler with a spaceframe front section, with Yamaha R1 engine and rear wheel, with drive coming via bike chain. Acquired by Road Track Race Ltd of Nottingham in 2009, run by Paul Holmes and Liam Wilkinson. The latter revised the styling in 2009.

Mills Extreme Vehicles 2008–9
Road Track Race Ltd 2009 to date
Approx 100 made

TRIKING

Tony Divey, based in Marlingford, Norfolk, was a former draughtsman at Lotus and also a Morgan trike enthusiast, who one day decided to create his own updated take on the theme complete with a backbone spaceframe chassis and Moto Guzzi V-twin engine. It remains possibly the most complete all-round three-wheeler ever made, along with the Buckland B8.

When asked once why he called the car Triking, Divey replied: 'Well you go "biking" on two wheels, so why not "triking" on three?' Sublime. Taken over by erstwhile employee Alan Layzell of Hingham when Tony retired.

Triking Cyclecars 1979–2009
Triking Sports Cars 2009 to date
Approx 187 made

TRILUX

The Trilux was a replica of a Morgan Supersports Aero from the 1920s. Very nicely put together and rated as one of the best three-wheelers ever made. Components from Citroën Ami, Renault 12 and Morris Marina.

Trilux 1986
Approx 1 made

TRIMINI

Very closely related to Robert Moss' Mosquito (*qv*), itself inspired by Tony Greenwood's fiendish three-wheeler of 1971 and similarly Mini-based. Man behind the project was Kim Argyle.

Argyle 1971–72
Approx 3 made

TRIO

Created by Ken Hallett of Dorset, the Trio was a three-wheeler sold in plan form, although he did sell a few chassis kits. Based around Mini mechanicals and A-series power. There were two instruction manuals – one for the chassis and one for the body. Chassis was an

80mm x 40mm box section, with a ply-skinned aluminium body with GRP bonnet and wings.

Trio Cars 1993–2000
Approx 25 plan sets sold and five chassis kits

TRIPOS R81

Originally created as a one-off by Laurie Abbott. Company put together by a consortium consisting of architects Ray Baum and Rodney Gordon and businessmen Martin Bunting and Peter Brow.

Its looks didn't appeal to everyone but the Tripos was one of the finest handling cars ever made. The prototype was based on Alfa Romeo mechanicals before perennial ace kit car set-up engineer Bob Egginton of ASD revised it around Ford components. The car's spaceframe was made from 1in tube. Cobretti was its final resting place.

Tripos R&D 1984–92
Cobretti 1992–98
Approx 6 made

TRITON

Locost-inspired sports car from company run by Mark Bean. Passed to Deanfield Motorsport.

Triton Sports Cars 2001–3
Approx 25 made

TRIUNE

Short-lived (stillborn) three-wheeler that had a four-wheeled sister called the Pharos (*qv*).

CDM 1983
Approx 1 made

TROLL T6

Superb little trials car from a Minehead-based company run by Peter James. James went through six incarnations of the car from 1978, with the T6 'F' being the later, and kit, version. Kits cost £5,314 with fully-built cars from £14,887. Power was Ford Crossflow. Project was

subsequently taken over by Westfield specialist Terry Nightingale of Essex, although he was so busy selling secondhand Westfields that nothing happened with the Troll.

Troll Engineering Company Ltd 1987–92
Terry Nightingale Autocraft Ltd 1995–99
Approx 31 made

TURNER 803 SPORTS

The Turner marque was named after its founder John 'Jack' Turner, who became a car manufacturer after making himself a *special* and being asked for replicas. It survived until 1966, when the company went into voluntary liquidation due to Jack's illness.

The Austin A30-based 803 Sports was the first commercially available Turner model, with the 803 part of its name denoting its 803cc engine. All based on a tube steel ladderframe chassis. Jack Turner passed away in early 2011, aged 94.
Turner Sports Cars (Wolverhampton) Ltd 1955–57
Approx 105 made

TURNER 950 SPORTS

The 950 Sports succeeded the 803 (see preceding entry) in 1957 and was pretty much identical except that it had slight modifications around the rear bodywork, while biggest change was the switch to the Austin A35's 948cc engine.

Turner Sports Cars (Wolverhampton) Ltd 1957–59
Approx 166 made

TURNER GT

A complete revamp for the GT of 1961, which Jack Turner introduced as a safeguard in case the Sports suddenly lost popularity. A stylish fixed-head, the GT featured Ford power and a fibreglass monocoque but sadly only a few were made.
Turner Sports Cars (Wolverhampton) Ltd 1961–65
Approx 10 made

TURNER SPORTS MkI

Jack Turner's new Sports model of 1959 became the biggest-selling Turner model of all, with pleasing body revisions and a variety of possible engine fitments including A35 and Coventry Climax 1,098cc.
Turner Sports Cars (Wolverhampton) Ltd 1959–60
Approx 160 made

TURNER SPORTS MkII

Pretty much identical to the MkI, the MkII added Ford Sidevalve and Pre-Crossflow power options.
Turner Sports Cars (Wolverhampton) Ltd 1960–63
Approx 160 made

TURNER SPORTS MkIII

The MkIII of 1963 could be instantly identified by its bonnet scoop and revised rear lights.
Turner Sports Cars (Wolverhampton) Ltd 1963–66
Approx 72 made

TUSCAN

Bedfordshire-based TI Motors was run by Tim Ivory. Budget-orientated Cobra replica that used Ford Cortina suspension at the front and Capri rear suspension, modified to accept coil over dampers. Power usually came from Ford V6 or Rover V8.
TI Motors 1985–87
Approx 35 made

TVR ENGINEERING

TVR's history is well documented in a whole host of books, so we'll keep it brief here; suffice to say that until 1973 they were very much a kit car producer.

Founded in 1957 in his home town of Blackpool by Trevor Wilkinson, who was a serial *specials* builder even before starting his company, which was originally known as Trevcar Motors before the name was changed to TVR (from 'TreVoR') in 1958.

We'll only focus on the models that were available in kit form here, but for the sake of completeness here's the others made until 1973 that were turnkey-only:
Griffith 200 (1963–64 – approx 124 made)
Griffith 400 (1964–65 – approx 300 made)
Tuscan V8 (1967–70 – approx 73 made)

TVR 1300

Triumph Spitfire-engined budget model. Had 2500M chassis.
TVR Engineering 1971–72
Approx 15 made

TVR 1600M

With its Crossflow 1,600cc engine the 1600M was aimed at the UK market. When the company was looking for a budget model in 1975 the 1600M was reintroduced for a couple of years.
TVR Engineering 1972–73, 1975–77
Approx 148 made

TVR 1800S Mk3

The 1800S Mk3 of 1964 came with a revised body style, including 'ban-the-bomb' rear lights from the Ford Cortina Mk1, and MGB B-series power. After TVR went bankrupt in 1965 incoming saviour Martin Lilley introduced a Mk4 version.
TVR Engineering 1964–67
Approx 128 made

TVR 1800S Mk4

The first of the Martin Lilley era TVRs was effectively the same as the Mk3 but featured an improved interior along with several other options.
TVR Engineering 1966–67
Approx 78 made

TVR 2500

Similar to the TVR 1300 but had engine from the Triumph TR6 (*qv*).
TVR Engineering 1971–72
Approx 385 made

TVR 2500M

Primarily intended for the American market although also available in the UK. Available as a kit until 1973 and the introduction of VAT.
TVR Engineering 1972–77
Approx 947 made

TVR 3000M

Visually, and under the skin, the same as the 1600M and 2500M, but featured Ford Essex V6 engine. Kits were available until 1973.
TVR Engineering 1972–79
Approx 654 made

TVR GRANTURA Mk1

The Grantura was the first proper TVR and featured a backbone chassis, Ford Consul windscreen and Austin Healey brakes.
TVR Engineering 1957–60
Approx 100 made

(Photo courtesy LAT)

TVR GRANTURA MkII

(Photo courtesy LAT)

The Grantura MkII had distinctive little 'bulges' over each wheel arch plus the addition of rear fins. Ford Classic 1,340cc was the standard engine choice.
TVR Engineering 1960–62
Approx 400 made

TVR GRANTURA MkIII

With the introduction of the MkIII came a brand new chassis and several other improvements, including independent suspension all round.
TVR Engineering 1962–64
Approx 90 made

TVR TUSCAN V6

Sister car to the beefy Tuscan V8 but unlike its brother was available in kit form.
TVR Engineering 1969–71
Approx 101 made

TVR VIXEN S1

The Vixen was the first model on which Martin Lilley's Ford influences started to show, with the switch from MGB to Ford power.
TVR Engineering 1967–68
Approx 117 made

TVR VIXEN S2

Vixen Series 2 featured the Tuscan chassis.
TVR Engineering 1968–70
Approx 438 made

(Photo courtesy LAT)

TVR VIXEN S3

Just a few detail changes for the S3.
TVR Engineering 1970–72
Approx 168 made

TVR VIXEN S4

New chassis for the Vixen S4 came from the 2500M and gave it a wider track.
TVR Engineering 1972–73
Approx 23 made

TWM

Terry Wrenn, formerly of Convair, set up TWM in Muskham Road, Newark, to sell bodyshells and a full kit package based around Austin A35 with a 'shell very similar to the Nickri Alpine (*qv*). Deluxe package could be had with a Downton-tuned engine. Bodies cost £85 in 1959.
TWM Engineering Company Ltd 1959–61
Approx 20 made

TWR LM GT40 BE

Trevor Williams imported the South African-made Bailey Edwards GT40 replica to the UK from 2010.
TWR Replicas 2010 to date
Approx 1 made (UK)

TWR LM 017 BE

Another Bailey Edwards product imported by TWR Replicas and this one was a glorious evocation of Porsche's legendary 917.
TWR Replicas 2010 to date
Approx 1 made (UK)

TWR LMSCF XJ13

Superb replica of the Jaguar XJ13, made in America by Sports Car Factory and imported to the UK by TWR Replicas.
TWR Replicas 2010 to date
Approx 3 made (UK)

TWR LM220C

Created by Berkshire-based TWR Replicas, run by Trevor Williams, the company wasn't connected with the late Tom Walkinshaw's TWR concern. The car is a replica of Jaguar's XJ220C and is a racer for the road with few concessions to comfort. Power comes from either Jaguar Supercharged V8 or V12.
TWR Replicas 2011 to date
Approx 1 made

TX TRIPPER

Air Vice Marshal Don 'Pathfinder' Bennett's son Torix was in bed recovering from an ulcer when he came up with the swoopy Tripper, although the Spanish agent wasn't particularly happy because 'Tripper' means gonorrhoea in Castilian, apparently! Oops.

The project lay dormant for 12 years until being resurrected in 1983, but by then its time had passed.

In spring 1971 a Herald-based kit cost £740 and a Ford version £845.
Technical Exponents 1970–71
Tripper Cars (Isleworth) 1983–84
Tripper Cars (Bangor) 1985–86
Approx 85 made

TYPE 48 CORSA SPYDER –
see HDS Warrior/Defender

TYPHOON VALDRIS

Appearing in autumn 2009 this Ford Mondeo-based kit was clearly inspired by the KTM X-BOW. Came from Stuart Elliott of Cambridgeshire, who had previously created the Shadow Le Mans (*qv*). Incidentally, a Valdris is a dagger.

Withdrawn from sale after KTM objected to it being too close in shape to their own X-BOW.
Typhoon Sportscars 2009–2010
Approx 1 made

TYTAN

MNR announced this pretty trackday-orientated car in summer 2005. They didn't do very much with it and it was sold to Mark Butler of Doncaster, who renamed it the Wolf (*qv*). Sold to a German company in 2009.
MNR Ltd 2005-7
MBR Racing 2007-9
Approx 5 made

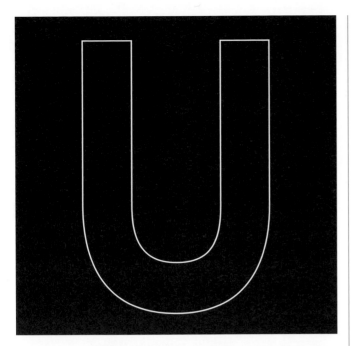

UFO BUGGY

A bonkers-looking VW Beetle-based beach buggy, offered from 1970 by Sibson Road, Birstall, Leicestershire-based company, with kits priced at £150 for road use or £130 if used off-road on the drag strip. A chap called Javan Swift was behind the UFO, and his advertising strapline was 'for your actual do-it-yourself-in-the-least-possible-time-Astro nut'. Hmm.

Swift Motor Components 1970–71
Approx 7 made

UFO DOODLEBUG

Along with the beach buggy the VW Beetle 'hot rod' conversion was also popular in the early seventies. Javan Swift sold this kit from his base in Birstall, Leicestershire, alongside his beach buggy package, although his sales mantra for the Doodlebug was more than a little distasteful by today's standards; 'Ask your dad if Hitler drove him off the beaches in this one', which appeared in his *Hot Car* magazine adverts of 1971. Hmm.

Swift Motor Components 1970–71
Approx 15 made

ULTIMA Mk1

Lee Noble and his dad Tony were both inspired by Colin Chapman. Lee had acquired a Lotus Europa Twin Cam, restored it and then raced it. In the mid-'80s he noticed the 750 Motor Club's Kit Car Challenge series and wasn't impressed! So he decided to build his own car to have a crack at it. The Ultima was the result.

The original prototype was built in Lee's garage, but he wasn't completely satisfied with the styling and revamped it into the Mk2 version, while also making a few other alterations. The Mk1 had a Renault 30 front end. The Mk1 demo/racer (registered NUT 612P) dominated the Kit Car series of 1986 and 1987, until it was effectively banned after other racers complained that it was too fast!

Kitdeal/Noble Motorsport 1985–86
Approx 12 made

ULTIMA Mk2

The Mk2 remained a one-off and featured a fabricated front end and bespoke double wishbones and push-rods and Rover V6 power.

Kitdeal/Noble Motorsport 1986–87
Approx 1 made

ULTIMA Mk3

Next logical step for the Ultima and the definitive Noble Ultima model, with a variety of revisions and upgrades. Lee Noble sold 13 Mk3s, but by 1992 he was concentrating on a variety of other projects. He therefore sold the rights to the Ultima Mk2 and Mk3 to Ted Marlow, a racer of note in the 750 Motor Club's Kit Car Challenge series in his potent Dutton V6 before graduating to an Ultima. He also ran an engineering company that had sponsored the race series, and in 1992 set up a new company called Ultima Sports with his son Richard, based in Long Itchington, Warwickshire, before moving to larger premises in Hinckley in 1993. Ted and Richard continued to sell the Mk3 before coming up with their all-new Ultima Sports (*qv*) model.

Incidentally, the last two Noble chassis (12 and 13) were purchased by McLaren as test mules for the F1 model. Number 12, nicknamed Albert, was used for testing a new gearbox, while 13, known as Edward, was used for testing the then new BMW V12 engine.

The aim of Ted and Richard's company was to produce a kit-form affordable supercar, with no rusty donor parts and using fine engineering, with cues taken from the buildability of model radio controlled cars.

Ted came up with a host of revisions, settling on Chevy V8 engines as standard, as were Porsche G50 transaxles, while they aimed their Ultimas at the roadgoing market and made subtle changes to the body to reflect this. Superb.

Kitdeal/Noble Motorsport 1987–92
Ultima Sports 1992–93
Approx 50 made

A
B
C
D
E
F
G
H
I
J
K
L
M
N
O
P
Q
R
S
T
U
V
W
X
Y
Z

ULTIMA CAN-AM

The Can-Am replaced the Spyder model in 2001. Featured a whole raft of enhancements over the outgoing model including the ability to convert from minimalist wind deflector to full glass windscreen in minutes.

Ultima Sports 2001 to date
Approx 350 made

ULTIMA GTR

Arriving in 1999, the staggeringly capable GTR replaced the Sports, which itself had replaced the Mk3. Again designed in-house, Ultima had moved to bigger premises in Hinckley in 1998, and set about improving every element of the existing car, with increased downforce and designed with the then new SVA requirements in mind. Standard engine fit is now GM LS-series units, delivering up to 720bhp.

The GTR is a true world-class supercar and has set countless world records, starting in 2004 with the 0–100–0mph record. On another record attempt at the Nürburgring, top sports car driver Tom Coronel described the GTR as the fastest and most powerful road car he'd ever driven. Stunning.

Ultima Sports 1999 to date
Approx 300 made

ULTIMA SPORTS

After acquiring the Ultima Mk3 project and selling a decent number of them, Ted Marlow with his son Richard set about creating an evolution of the Mk3. They had made several upgrades to the Mk3, making it their own, and aiming it mainly at the roadgoing market.

Meanwhile, the all-new Sports replaced the Mk3 in 1993 and was soon available in left-hand drive form – a shrewd move, as export sales proved strong. Ultima designed the Sports in-house and it was a natural development of the previous model. It went on to sell in very good numbers.

Ultima Sports 1993–99
Approx 200 made

ULTIMA SPYDER

Once Ultima had established their Sports model, Ted Marlow came up with a convertible version. Using the original Noble Ultima Spyder as inspiration, the car was completely revamped into an equally stunning package as the Sports, featuring an

innovative door design. It was based around Rover V8 and Renault UN1 transaxle, although a Chevy V8 installation was available from 1994. The car benefited from being wind-tunnel tested at MIRA, quite unusual for a kit car.

Ultima Sports 1993–2001
Approx 250 made

ULTIMINI

Milestone Motorsport, run by Ken Polkinghorne and based in Truro, was the company behind the former DFR Falcon silhouette Mini spaceframe kit. Two different body styles were available – Clubman and round front end.

Milestone Motorsport Engineering 2005–8
Approx 5 made

UNICORN

Quirky clubman's car with aluminium body, Marina donor and church hall-spec plastic seats with the metal legs removed. Blee Motors was based in Killingsworth, Tyne & Wear, and run by Dave Brooks, Richard Martin and John Woolatt.

Blee Motors 1986–87
Approx 1 made

UNICORN

After the failure of the four-wheeled Unicorn, Blee Motors came up with the two-wheeled kit-bike version, devised by BA Industrial Design man John Woolatt, with design from a chap called Dave Brooks. This Unicorn was a very pleasing thing, with a

Yamaha FJ900-style 'lateral frame concept', although the donor bike was the eighties despatch rider's beloved Suzuki GS500, a good enough choice as it was rugged and could take lots of punishment, featuring a twin overhead camshaft, four-stroke engine. Despite lots of box ticks this Unicorn was another non-starter.

Blee Motors 1988–89
Approx 3 made

UNIPOWER GT

Arguably the greatest kit car ever? Certainly the king of the Mini-based cars, without doubt.

A meeting at Goodwood in the mid-'60s would lead motor racing enthusiasts Ernie Unger and Val Dare-Bryan to create the Unipower GT, which was built in the workshop of racing driver Roy Pierpoint (later to market the GP Buggy). The diminutive Mini-based GT, powered by a 998cc engine, was sold through the Universal Power Drives company of Tim Powell and launched at the Racing Car Show of 1966.

After around 60 sales, at the end of 1968 Powell sold the project to another racing driver and enthusiast, Piers Weld-Forrester (a cousin of the Queen, no less), and production continued under the UWF (Unger Weld Forrester) banner until 1970, when, despite a full order book, production ceased. A true great.

Universal Power Drives 1966–68
UWF 1968–70
Approx 75 made

URBANIZER – *see Bandit*

UVA (UNIQUE VEHICLE & ACCESSORY CO)

Company founded in December 1981 by Alan Arnold and Terry Lee, who specialised in importing VW Beetle tuning equipment from the USA, from the likes of EMPI and BugPack. Alan spent two years thoroughly researching the kit car market. Didn't have the finances to develop their own car, so imported the Montage from America.

Arnold had previously autocrossed an Austin A30 and was ACSMC class E hillclimb champion in 1970 in a modified Lotus Seven, although a big shunt at Brands Hatch ended his racing career. Had been responsible for marketing STP oil treatment in the UK and also worked for Link Hanson Ltd and CBS brakes.

In 1985 they started bringing the Montage GT – a Veedub-based McLaren M6 replica – to the UK, which they offered in standard guise or, from 1986, in their own Rover V8-powered version. UVA even marketed the Reliant SS1 for a time.

Alan Arnold was also a leading light in the SMMT's SCMG (Specialist Car Manufacturer's Group), and for a time from the mid-'80s UVA were one of the UK's foremost kit car manufacturers, a fact that is often forgotten. Also a leading competitor and supporter of the SCORR championship in the '80s. The company was initially based in Alan Arnold's garage but soon moved to a modern unit in Newbury, before finally settling in Whitchurch in 1990 when times got hard for the company. Ex-Ford development engineer Gwyn Parry came on board and the company name changed to TAG (Terry, Alan and Gwyn) Automotive, with a further change to Laser Cars in 1992 when only Terry was left. And that was it for this once industry-leading firm. It all ended a bit messily, sadly.

UVA BAJA BUG

Baja treatment for a Beetle which at one stage was selling 20 units per month.
Unique Vehicle & Accessory Co 1982–91
TAG Automotive 1991–92
Laser Cars 1992–95
Approx 15 made

UVA FUGITIVE F20

Inspired by the American Baja desert racers. Tubular spaceframe with VW Beetle running gear.
Unique Vehicle & Accessory Co 1984–91
TAG Automotive 1991–92
Laser Cars 1992–95
Approx 500 made

UVA FUGITIVE F30

Mid- rather than rear-mounted VW engine, usually Rover V8.
Unique Vehicle & Accessory Co 1985–91
Approx 4 made

CAN AM

Possibly the first of the so-called exo cars some 12 years before the Ariel Atom. Based on Fugitive F40 chassis modified for mid-mounted Rover V8 power. Certainly made jaws drop when it appeared in 1986, on account of both its looks and its outrageous performance. UVA said that it was for customers who didn't like the cycle-style wings of the F30. Monster.
Unique Vehicle & Accessory Co 1986–91
Approx 12 made

UVA FUGITIVE F40

Four-seat version of the F20.
Unique Vehicle & Accessory Co 1985–91
Approx 7 made

UVA M6GTR

Having imported the VW Beetle-based Manta Montage to the UK, before long, UVA boss Alan Arnold set about redesigning the car to accept V8 power, complete with GRP monocoque.
Unique Vehicle & Accessory Co 1985–91
Approx 15 made

UVA MONTAGE

Made by Manta Cars in the USA, the Montage was a VW Beetle-based replica of the McLaren M6. At £3,895 kits were quite expensive when launched in the UK.
Unique Vehicle & Accessory Co 1984–86
Approx 7 made (UK)

UVA SHOGAN

Based on VW Beetle, from the door jambs back the body was replaced with an estate type section. UVA had intended to import an American kit called the *Vandetta*, but weren't happy with it so they devised their own version.
Unique Vehicle & Accessory Co 1985–91
Approx 15 made

A
B
C
D
E
F
G
H
I
J
K
L
M
N
O
P
Q
R
S
T
U
V
W
X
Y
Z

V8 STEALTH

Bikers' emporium Trike Tek of Brighton was responsible for this one.
Trike Tek 1998–2003
Approx 15 made

V-DUB ROADSTER

Another to join the early seventies passion for hot-rodded VW Beetles. This one came from a Crystal Palace-based company. Kits cost just £34 and the customer could choose from two widths of front cycle wing. Not around for long.
Roadster Components 1971
Approx 3 made

V-STORM

One of the so-called 'exo-cars', with exposed chassis rails. Pleasing design by Simon Keys with power from Aprilia V-Storm bike engine, although other bike fitments are possible. Company based in Oldham, Lancashire, and run by Simon Dickens. Launched a new Subaru Impreza-powered version in late 2009.
SDR Sportscars 2008 to date
Approx 45 made

VALLEY GAS 32 COUPÉ

Newbury-based hot rod specialists Valley Gas Speedshop launched their own 32 Coupé bodyshell package in 2010 priced from £2,724, with a basic chassis package at £924. The shell comes with doors, boot-lid and dash panel pre-fitted and in a choice of gelcoat colours.
Valley Gas Speedshop 2010 to date
Approx 10 made

VAN CLEE MUNGO/LAND RANGER/ EMMET/RUSLER

Citroën Mehari replica originally produced in Belgium from 1978 before Northern Irish company Van Clee Motors marketed it in the UK from 1983. Based on Citroën 2CV, naturally enough, either with a new floorpan or the donor item and an extremely clever four-wheel-drive system that utilised two 2CV gearboxes. Dutton Cars was the force behind the kit, selling about 20 of them.
Van Clee Motors 1983–92   *Dutton Cars 1992–94*
Approx 30 made

VANITY

Period van from EG Autocraft, hailing from the mind of Emillio Garcia, featuring a sheet alloy and GRP body.
EG Autocraft 1990–91
Approx 4 made

VARIO

Formerly the Manx (*qv*), taken over by Alan Fereday and relaunched in 2000, with involvement from kit car journalist and author, Iain Ayre. A spaceframe chassis underpinned the car with Fiat Uno mechanicals, replacing the original's Citroen 2CV underpinnings. Had a slight revision including addition of 4in width and use of donor windscreen and exhaust system.
Fereday Cars 2000–2
Approx 3 made

VELENO

Had its origins in the Searcher 1 which then became the Lyncar (*qv*). Taken over by the late Keith Kirk, who revised the Lyncar heavily. He dispensed with the aluminium monocoque and created a spaceframe chassis for it, designed to accept Ford Granada parts and Ford V6 power.

Kirk devised two versions: one based on Toyota MR2 Mk2 with a spaceframe chassis, and a version that used a mid-mounted V8 with wishbones all round.

Fully built examples were known as the Predator. After Kirk passed away the Auto Speciali projects were in limbo for a short while before Vindicator Cars took over the marketing of them in 2010.
Auto Speciali 2006–10   *Vindicator Cars 2010 to date*
Approx 4 made

VENOM

Was also known as the TKH Venom, but the first part of the name was dropped in 1986 when the company morphed into Venom Cars. This Countach replica was the first of the dimensionally correct copies of the Lamborghini that started a frenzy. Based on GTD chassis. Company based in Old Trafford, Manchester, and run by a chap called Gary Thompson, who later turned up as part of Mirage Replicas.
TKH Venom Services 1985–86
Venom Cars Ltd 1986–87
Approx 27 made

VERANTI CONVERTIBLE

Created by the Royale Motor Company founder John Barlow.
Veranti Motor Company 2003–8
Approx 40 made

VERANTI COUPÉ

Appeared in 2008 and like the original Convertible version (see previous entry) was based on Toyota MR2 Mk2. Designed by John Barlow.
Veranti Motor Company 2008
Approx 3 made

VIKING

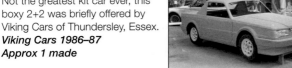

Not the greatest kit car ever, this boxy 2+2 was briefly offered by Viking Cars of Thundersley, Essex.
Viking Cars 1986–87
Approx 1 made

VIKING 380/SSR

Although not a replica of the Jaguar SS100, the Viking was obviously inspired by that car and designed by Peter Morris and his business partner Craig Hinton. Top-spec saw an aluminium body with box-section chassis and Jaguar XJ6 parts. The partners fell out, so there were two versions of this car for a time. Hinton's Leaping Cats operation, based in Blaby, Leicestershire, had already made a top quality C-type replica and called their version the 380 SSR.
Classis Cars of Coventry (aka Viking Cars) 1980-82
Leaping Cats 1982-83
Approx 8 made

VIKING DRAGON FIRE

Welsh-based operation – nothing to do with Viking of Thundersley – run by a chap who had previously created a tin opener that took all the sharp edges off! He also sold his own range of go-karts and hovercraft. Was originally the Charger (*qv*) and then the MDB Saratoga (*qv*).
Viking Sports Cars 1987–88
Approx 1 made

VIKING DRAGON FLY

Was originally known as the Charger 2 and then MDB Saturn.
Viking Sports Cars 1987–88
Approx 1 made

VIKING MINISPORT

Formerly the Peel Trident Mini (*qv*) and made on the Isle of Man before coming under the control of Bill Last's Viking Performance. Mini donor parts including front and rear subframes and windscreen, fibreglass body and a square tube chassis.
Peel Engineering 1966
Viking Performance 1966
Approx 23 made

A
B
C
D
E
F
G
H
I
J
K
L
M
N
O
P
Q
R
S
T
U
V
W
X
Y
Z

VINCENT BROOKLANDS

Mechanically very similar to the Vincent MPH (see below) and also created by Martin Vincent. For a brief time it was known as the Sports. Differed by having cycle wings and a folding 'fly' windscreen.

Followed the same production path as the MPH and has been produced by Dwornik Engineering since 1987.
Vincent Cars 1983–84
Swindon Sportscars 1984–87
Dwornik Engineering 1987 to date
Approx 6 made

VINCENT HURRICANE

The first model from Henley-based Martin Vincent, who sold his motorcycle courier business in 1982 and set about creating the Hurricane with his brother Robin. It was based on Triumph Spitfire/GT6, with windscreen sourced from the former. A very clever concept, as back in the early '80s Spitfires and GT6s were anything but collectible. Martin Vincent went on to become a motoring journalist and edited *Japanese Performance* magazine for a time.

Later moved to John Ingram's Domino concern, which made the bodies for Vincent, before being taken over by Les Stuart of Solihull for a short time before finally coming to rest at Caburn Engineering of Burgess Hill, run by Andy Hitchings, where it has resided ever since.
Vincent Cars 1982–87
Domino Cars 1987–91
Vincent Engineering/Glassfibre Mouldings 1991–95
Caburn Engineering 1995 to date
Approx 65 made

VINCENT MPH

The MPH is a replica of the 1934 Riley MPH. In 1993 it was also known briefly as the *Rallye*. The original version was a real peach of a traditional roadster, with a 'rat' rod look to it, being basic in style. It was underpinned by a ladderframe chassis that provided the basis for Ford Escort Mk2 donor parts and a fibreglass body and flowing wings, with aluminium bonnet. Front suspension was sourced from Triumph Herald/Vitesse.

Project moved to Swindon Sportscars in 1984 where it resided for around three years. Among other modifications they introduced short 'doorlets' to the body.

Erstwhile Swindon employee Toni Dwornik subsequently took the project over in 1987 and soon moved from Chiseldon, Wiltshire, to Peterborough. He set about revising and enhancing the product with a Mk3 version that had many upgrades including revised suspension and cast aluminium radiator surround, while he also enlarged the doors that Swindon had introduced.

As a skilled engineer, Dwornik has worked for a variety of top race teams in the UK and USA over the years, which has meant that occasionally the MPH and its sister, the Brooklands model, have taken a back seat, although they've never stopped being available. Toni moved to Headington, Oxfordshire, in 2008.
Vincent Cars 1982–84
Swindon Sportscars 1984–87
Dwornik Engineering 1987 to date
Approx 100 made

VINDICATOR CONCEPT COUPÉ

The first model from Vindicator Cars, founded by Roger Lea, was a two-seater coupé with Bond Bug-type roof operation.
Vindicator Cars 1989–91
Approx 1 made

VINDICATOR FAMILY

A rare four-seat kit car based on the company's Sprint model with revised chassis and bodywork.
Vindicator Cars 2003 to date
Approx 20 made

VINDICATOR F4

A solicitor approached the Vindicator boss John Butler with the idea for his dream car and asked him to make it a reality. The result is the F4, clearly inspired by the F4 Phantom fighter jet and based on Ford Mondeo. Wild and wacky looks certainly attract attention.
Vindicator Cars 2008 to date
Approx 1 made

VINDICATOR SHADOW

Originally launched at Stoneleigh in 1995 before being revamped for a relaunch in 1997.
Vindicator Cars 1995, 1997 to date
Approx 10 made

VINDICATOR SPRINT

Vindicator's most popular model. Underpinned by a spaceframe chassis from 1994. Company taken over by John Butler and Alan Taylor in 1999, with the former taking sole control when Taylor left a short while after. They moved to Lomax's former base in Halesowen in 2004. An honest-to-goodness kit car.
Vindicator Cars 1991 to date
Approx 150 made

VINDICATOR SR

Heavily revised version of the company's Concept Coupé that shared just one part with the original – the windscreen frame.
Vindicator Cars 1991
Approx 1 made

VINDICATOR VULCAN

A more track-orientated two-seater brother of the company's Shadow.
Vindicator Cars 1998 to date
Approx 6 made

VISCOUNT TC

A very close approximation of the Burlington Arrow, albeit made from fibreglass rather than plywood, offered for a couple of years by a Bury St Edmunds company and based on Triumph Herald/Vitesse mechanicals.
Viscount Motors 1985–86
Approx 10 made

VISTA MPH Mk1

First product from Dewsbury company Asquith Brothers, run by former Lucas and Ford test engineer Mike Fox, was this recreation of the Riley MPH using Riley mechanical parts and featuring an aluminium body. Cost from £40,000 to build. They'll still make one to special order for you…
Asquith Brothers Ltd 1985–99
Approx 6 made

VISTA MPH Mk2/Mk3

This was a Ford Sierra-based version of Asquith's superb MPH replica. It was half the price of the standard Riley-based version, and was also easier to build. Offered from 1989. The Mk2 used standard Pinto engine from the Sierra, while the Mk3 utilised the later DOHC unit.

Based on a spaceframe chassis and featured identical external dimensions to the standard Vista. Came with independent suspension all round and featured aluminium body with GRP wings and boot panel. Cost from £20,000 to build. Again, they'll still make one to special order.
Asquith Brothers Ltd 1989–99
Approx 30 made

VISTA PENNY

Next project for Asquith after the Vista MPH (see above) was the Vista Penny, a four-wheeled evocation of the Bond Bug but powered by a monstrous 170bhp Yamaha R1 engine.
Asquith Brothers Ltd 1999 to date
Approx 4 made

VOLKSPARTS ROADSTER

A traditional roadster kit based on Beetle floorpan and mechanicals from a Basingstoke VW specialist.
Volksparts 1973–74
Approx 2 made

A B C D E F G H I J K L M N O P Q R S T U V W X Y Z

VOLKSROD

Doncaster businessman and 'father' of the British buggy movement, Warren Monks, ran a double glazing company called Window Change, and along with his secretary Edna Gardom, was the first to launch a beach buggy in the UK. It was launched in September 1967 at the St Leger race meeting at Doncaster Racecourse, beating GP to market by just seven days!

Like many others, he was inspired by a buggy he'd seen in an American magazine, but rather than import one, he created his own using some of his contacts in the car and GRP trades.

Volksrod was taken over by Hartsdale Services, run by David Taylor in 1970, although Edna Gardom was retained to run the buggy side of the business. Ironically, Taylor knew nothing of the beach buggy business when he bought the window company, but before long was concentrating solely on Volksrod!

In 1971 Edna Gardom bought the rights to Volksrod and ran the company until 1977, when her son Trevor took over.

A very successful UK buggy, and at various times during the seventies they could count Coca Cola, John Player and pop group New Seekers among their customers.

Came to rest with Wellingborough-based Whitlee Engineering in 1984, run by John Whitworth and Andrew Leach, who got off to a shaky start, especially with glassfibre quality, before enlisting the help of ace laminators R&W Mouldings, who sorted things out.

When Leach departed in 1990, Whitworth carried on with input from employee Jeff Copson, who successfully drag-raced a MkV called 'Midnight Racer', changing the company name to Whitworth Engineering. In the summer of 1991, Stuart Hopewell joined the team and stayed until 1995, while laminating was under control of Premier Mouldings.

Sales had slowed down but the Volksrod was still available, and when Copson left in 1999, the name again changed – this time to John Whitworth Motor Services, trading from smaller premises.

In 2002 Hopewell returned on a part-time basis, and one of his first tasks was to hastily rescue the Volksrod moulds after Premier went bust, while also setting up his own Volkswagen restoration and repair company, STUVW.

VOLKSROD MkI

The MkI, based on a VW Beetle floorpan chopped by 13in, appeared in 1968. Like many of the early '70s buggies it was marginal at best as far as headlight height and legality was concerned.

Volksrod 1968–70
Approx 20 made

VOLKSROD MkII

Basically a revised and smoothed-out MkI, featuring integral headlamps and a wider windscreen. Made its debut at a VW show in Belgium in 1969. The MkII required the customer to chop 13½in from the standard Beetle floorpan. A MkII FL long-wheelbase version on unmodified Beetle floorpan (94½in) was also introduced.

Volksrod (Hartsdale Services) 1970
Approx 250 made

VOLKSROD MkIII

Revised bonnet, deeper sides and returned edges on the GRP body distinguished the MkIII, while the Beetle floorpan now required a 14in chop. Top fibreglass laminators Specialised Mouldings were also by now making the bodies and Volksrod's half-page adverts of the day trumpeted their new 'super-shine bodies'!

Edna Gardom acquired full control from 1971, with her son, Trevor, taking over the running of the company in 1979. They then concentrated solely on buggy production, dispensing with their windows business. To help cope with production they moved to larger premises in Askern, North Yorkshire. Ownership switched to Whitlee Engineering in 1996.

Volksrod Concessionaires (UK) Ltd 1970–84
Whitlee Engineering 1984–90
Whitworth Engineering 1990–91
Approx 120 made

VOLKSROD MkIV

The MkIV was basically a long-wheelbase version of the MkIII. It remains in production.

Volksrod Concessionaires (UK) Ltd 1971–84
Whitlee Engineering 1984–90
Whitworth Engineering 1990–95
J.E. Whitworth Motor Services 1995 to date
Approx 70 made

VOLKSROD MkV

In 1984 John Whitworth and Alan Lee had formed Whitlee Engineering to take over the rights to the well-known Volksrod marque in 1984, although by 1990 Whitworth was in sole control. The MkV was his first all-new Volksrod model, and although based on the MkIII shell it did feature some body mods such as no headlights, having a 'flat' front wing.

Whitworth Engineering 1991–93
Approx 25 made

VOLKSROD MkVI

Back to headlights for the MkVI, although it was a comedy of errors really, as a Portuguese villa-rental company had ordered 10 complete cars, but specified the old-style faired-in headlights. However, somewhere down the line there was a mix-up between Whitworth and the laminators; the former specifying 7in apertures, although the mould featured 5in gaps.

None of this really mattered anyway, because the Portuguese operation didn't order anything in the end and there were just two Mk6s produced.

Whitworth Engineering 1993
Approx 2 made

VOLKSROD MkVII

Similar in style to the MkVI with the same 14in Beetle floorpan chop required.. Main difference concerned the headlights again, which dispensed with the Volksrod tradition of Fiat 500 items for stock 5¾in units.

J.E. Whitworth Motor Services 2009 to date
Approx 3 made

VOODOO

One of the great kit cars that got away. Originally conceived as a private project for creators John Arnold and Geoff Neale, who wanted to build a car each. However, after being displayed at the British Motor Show of 1971 on the *Weekend Telegraph* newspaper stand a financial backer came along who wanted them to offer it for commercial sale.

No donor as such but used a Hillman Imp Sport 998cc engine with several Vauxhall Viva components. Bonkers opening canopy top featured a windscreen from a Chevron B16.

In 1973, with the project progressing nicely and Normandale Products of Stratford-upon-Avon in place to sell kits, the double blow of the backer withdrawing funding and the tragic death of John Arnold in a road accident spelled the end of the project.

In the early eighties, Geoff Neale planned a resurrection that featured a monocoque, larger dimensions, a replacement windscreen for the Chevron B16 item used on the original, and a new donor package. Ultimately though, this came to nothing.

Graham Boulter of Hollywood – that's West Midlands, not California! – acquired the project in 2007 and intends to resurrect it.

Normandale Products 1971–73
Voodoo Sportscars 2007 to date
Approx 3 made

VORTEX – *see Fiero Factory Venom*

VORTEX GTR – *see Phantom/Vortex GTR*

VORTEX V2

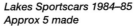

Second model from Chris Greville-Smith, designer of the successful Phantom Race Cars and Vortex Automotive GT3. The Lotus Seven-inspired sportscar made its debut at the Stoneleigh Kit Car Show of May 2011, with the demonstrator powered by a Ford Duratec Ecoboost engine delivering 300bhp, which when coupled to fine engineering and light weight meant performance was superb. Greville-Smith had previously been a designer at manufacturers such as Land Rover, Ford and Jaguar.

Vortex Automotive 2011 to date
Approx 2 made

VOYAGER I

A 1930s-inspired traditional roadster hailing from Lopton, near Cockermouth, Cumbria – company run by Andrew McClellan. The Voyager I was based on VW Beetle mechanicals complete with rear engine, and prior to its launch was the subject of much hype, with such claims in *Alternative Car* magazine as 'the component car that doesn't look like a kit car'. However, when launched at Stoneleigh in 1984 things clearly didn't go as expected, as the car was swiftly withdrawn for a rethink, and reappeared as the Voyager Sports (see next entry) shortly afterwards.

Lakes Sportscars 1984
Approx 1 made

VOYAGER SPORTS

Very quickly replaced the Voyager I. A hasty revamp after the 1984 Stoneleigh Show saw it switched to Vauxhall Viva mechanicals and therefore a front engine, with revisions to the bodyshell too.

Lakes Sportscars 1984–85
Approx 5 made

VPR

Dodge replica based on an aluminium chassis and bespoke suspension components, with some Ford Granada parts also used. Created by Colin Herd of Fife.

VPR Cars 1999–2004
Approx 3 made

VULTURE

Bromley-based company run by Malcolm and Peter Craker, who ran a family-owned garage business (Holmesdale Motor Traders) offering general repairs and car sales. Malcolm was the inspiration behind the Vulture, and got involved in buggy building after seeing GP co-director, Pierre du Plessis,

autocrossing a GP Buggy at Puttenden Manor, Kent. He promptly went out and bought a GP Buggy with a Corvair 2.3-litre engine, but then revised this to create his own offering, the Vulture, which had a shortened Beetle floorpan of 78½in, with kit prices at £170. The Vulture was actually very good, and had a unique perimeter reinforcement frame. Adverts urged customers to 'Get your claws into one'.

In 1971 the company came under the control of Michael Jeffs of Peterborough-based Vulrod Motors, who reduced the kit price to £135. Ironically, Jeffs had previously acquired the well-known Manta Ray that had appeared on the front cover of the debut issue of *Custom Car* magazine and was at the time languishing with Roberts Brothers' circus! He ceased making the Vulture in late 1972, although it did go on to form the basis of the Kingfisher Kombat (qv) from 1983.

Holmesdale Motor Traders 1970–71
Vulrod Motors 1971–72
Approx 120 made

W7DE

As the name suggests, the W7DE is a wider version of GTS Tuning's Panther (*qv*) and is based on either Ford Sierra or BMW E34 5-series, being called the BMW-7DE when based on the latter.
GTS Tuning 2003-10
Approx 50 made

WAM DB3S

Beautiful replica of the Aston Martin DB3S, of which 31 originals were made between 1953 and 1956. Coachbuilder and Aston expert Bill Monk created this one. Only available in kit form for a short time.
Bill Monk Classic Cars 1998 to date
Approx 11 made

WAM FIAT FORMULA SPORT

1970s Formula 1-inspired Fiat X1/9-based car. Chassis rails doubled up as coolant pipes, with small drop-down doors, transparent hood and tandem seating arrangement. Available in kit form (£7,907) or fully-built from £14,450.
Bill Monk Classic Cars 1997–98
Approx 1 made

WATFORD CHEETAH

Ex-Tornado Cars employees BJ Millar, Ken Hynder and Joe Bound ran this company located opposite Benskins Brewery in Watford High Street. It's probably unsurprising, given their circumstances, that the Cheetah looked a lot like the Tornado Typhoon.

Watford's primary business was supplying Ford-based tubular chassis with IFS from the Triumph Herald donor. The Cheetah used this chassis with independent suspension all round, and for its day the shell was pretty sophisticated, although the chassis was said to be a crude and flawed copy of the Tornado item.

They also made the FT chassis for Ford 8 or 10. The body cost around £130 and the chassis £70. The company ceased trading in 1961.
Watford Sports Cars 1959–61
Approx 25 made

WASP

Off-road rail-type device marketed by Wasp Engineering of Boston, Lincolnshire, run by Geordie McAvoy.
Wasp Engineering 1991–93
Approx 4 made

WATLING GT/GT DELUXE

Not as well known as some of its contemporaries, the Watling had a 'TVR-meets-E-type-meets-Marcos-look' about it and came from a pretty well-regarded St Albans company that specialised in racing car preparation and making boats and caravans in addition to car chassis.

The Watling GT kit cost £330 in 1960, with a convertible body option at just £230. It came with Watling's own ladderframe chassis and was quite advanced for its time, as items such as steering and pedals were adjustable. Comprehensive kit packages with Ford E93A engine supplied cost £550.
Watling Works 1959–61
Approx 70 made

WATSON'S MINI

Created in 1983 by Geoff Watson of Wakefield, West Yorkshire, a man with a serious pedigree in UK rallying. Usually featured a Rover K-series or Honda VTEC engine. Nicely made and enjoys a fine reputation.
Watson's Rally 1983 to date
Approx 75 made

WEBB'S WONDER – *see Hudson Free Spirit*

WESTBOURNE MODEL Y

A Ford Model Y replica offered by a Hampshire company run by ex-Jago employee Tony Puttick.
Westbourne Fender Works
1979–84
Approx 20 made

WESTFIELD SPORTS CARS

Founded in 1982 by Chris Smith, who'd previously run the Green Street Garage in Smethwick and had been buying and selling classic cars. Racing had always been a passion and Smith had raced a Chevron B8 as an engineer straight out of university in 1968, then did Modsports. The company name came from Chris' home, Westfield House, located in Armitage, Staffordshire. Subsequently moved to Netherton and finally to their current base in Kingswinford in 1985.

First car was an Eleven built for an American customer but not subsequently delivered to him, followed by a small batch of Lotus 23 replicas.

Well-known Lotus specialist and good friend of Smith's Paul Matty purchased the second Eleven chassis and had the car built by Doug and Mick Arthur of Midas Metalcraft.

The Smith family sold the company in 2006 to the Potenza Group, run by Frank Turner, with his son Julian installed as managing director. Chris Smith subsequently set up Chevron Cars, producing continuation B8 and B16 models.

WESTFIELD 23B

Requested by an American customer, a small batch of five cars was produced, complete with Lotus twin-cam engines and bodies produced by Peter Denty Racing.
Westfield Sports Cars 1982
Approx 6 made

WESTFIELD ELEVEN/XI

Westfield's first model, hailing from Lotus enthusiast Chris Smith, based at Westfield House in Dudley, hence the company name. His close friend and fellow Lotus expert Paul Matty encouraged him to create a replica of the delicate XI. Made around 140 the first time round, followed by another 100 from 2004.
Westfield Sports Cars 1982-86/2004-9
Approx 240 made

WESTFIELD FW400

Not available as a kit, the FW400 was designed by former Lotus Formula 1 designer Martin Ogilvie, and was a revised SEi body style that had a 190bhp Rover K-series VHPD engine and a rear-mounted Hewland Mk9 gearbox. The company now offer elements of the body in their standard SE kit packages.
Westfield Sports Cars 1998–2000
Approx 32 made

WESTFIELD GRAND PRIX MIDGET

Short-oval Midget racers have been popular since the '60s, but with open regulations and no one manufacturer offering cars Westfield decided to get involved and acquired the design of Cheltenham-based Martin Lyon. The Midget was shaped like a scaled-down Vanwall. Kit prices were from £3,000 in 1996.
Westfield Sports Cars 1996–97
Approx 12 made

WESTFIELD MEGA-BIRD

A Westfield SEi powered by Honda Super Blackbird bike engine.
Westfield Sports Cars 1999–2007
Approx 50 made

WESTFIELD MEGA-BLADE

A hugely popular Honda
Fireblade-powered Westfield SEi.
Westfield Sportscars
1999 to date
Approx 450 made

WESTFIELD MEGA-BUSA

The daddy! A Westfield SEi powered by Suzuki Hayabusa engine.
Bonkers performance.
Westfield Sports Cars 1999 to date
Approx 30 made all types

WESTFIELD SE/SEi

After litigation with Caterham Cars (see Westfield Seven S3 entry),
Westfield was forced to come up with revised styling for its basic
model. This was carried out by Roger Tucker of RT Designs.
Featured a GRP body and a defined bonnet waistline that gave it
identity. Originally known as the SE, complete with live rear axle, but
introduction of IRS (devised by Richard Jenvey) saw it switch to SEi
designation. Various special editions over the years including low
budget SP and SDV versions of 1994 and 2004 respectively.
Westfield Sports Cars 1987 to date
Approx 9,000 made

WESTFIELD SEiGHT

Rover V8-powered fire-breathing
version of the SE model. Original
version had a 240bhp Rover unit,
soon replaced by a 280bhp John
Eales-prepared unit. Switched
to BMW V8 power for a time in
the early 2000s, before switching
back to Rover V8.
Westfield Sports Cars 1986–2008
Approx 450 made

WESTFIELD SEVEN

Chris Smith's third and most
prolific model was a superb
replica of the Lotus Seven S1,
with a spaceframe chassis and
aluminium body with fibreglass
wings. His mechanic of the day,
Ian Gribbon, is credited with
encouraging him to create the car.
Westfield Sports Cars 1983–86
Approx 132 made

WESTFIELD SEVEN S3

Forever known as the 'pre-lit' (pre-litigation) cars in reference to the fact
that Caterham Cars objected to the styling. Basically a Lotus Seven
Series Three replica that resulted in litigation and a restyle for the range.
Westfield Sports Cars 1986–88
Approx 604 made

WESTFIELD SPORTS

Ford-based version of the Westfield Eleven (*qv*) with a lengthened
chassis and 1,600cc CVH-power. Replaced the Eleven from 1990.
Not a replica, but still managed to evoke the Lotus Eleven. Featured a
25mm square-tube spaceframe chassis, with double unequal-length
wishbones and Ford Cortina uprights, while the customer could
choose from live, five-link or independent rear suspension set-ups.
Westfield Sports Cars 1990–92
Approx 3 made

WESTFIELD SPORTS 2000/SS

The forerunner to the XTR range (see below) made some 14 years later, this car made its debut at the Kit Cars & Specials Action Day at Castle Combe in 1985. It featured a front-mounted Lotus twin-cam engine mated to a Ford Type 9 gearbox, Escort live rear axle with trailing arms and a Panhard rod. Roadgoing versions were to use Alfasud engines.
Westfield Sports Cars 1987–88
Approx 3 made

WESTFIELD TOPAZ/XEI

A sports coupé from Westfield that appeared at Stoneleigh in 1994, although work had originally begun in 1986, with the concept actually displayed at Stoneleigh in 1988. Roger Tucker had created six styling exercises and the Topaz was the one chosen.
Westfield Sports Cars 1988, 1994
Approx 1 made

WESTFIELD TRA/TRZ

Originally created as a one-off by Swiss customer Daniel Tirrez and known as the TRA (Tirrez Racing Automobiles), using a Mini silhouette bodyshell, based on a Westfield SE chassis cut in half, with power from a Suzuki GSX-R1100 engine. Chris Smith liked the concept and took it over, producing a batch of 22 for a one-make race series in France and revising the name to TRZ.
Westfield Sports Cars 1991
Approx 22 made

WESTFIELD XTR2

Trackday-orientated sports car from Westfield. Power came from a mid-mounted Suzuki Hayabusa engine, with Quaife torque-biasing limited slip differential and a triangulated spaceframe.
Westfield Sports Cars 2001 to date
Approx 100 made

WESTFIELD XTR4

A slightly revised version of the XTR2 that was powered by an Audi 1.8T engine.
Westfield Sports Cars 2003–9
Approx 20 made

WESTFIELD ZEI

Not available as a kit, this model is included here for completeness' sake. Euro crash-tested and a small volume type approved vehicle, it could be officially sold in a variety of European countries and was available in three guises: ZEi-powered by 1.8-litre Zetec E; ZEi 130 powered by a 2-litre 130bhp Zetec; and the really rapid ZEi 220 powered by a turbocharged Cosworth YB 2-litre, delivering, er, 220bhp.
Westfield Sports Cars 1991–95
Approx 250 made

WESTLITE

Ford Pop-based GRP bodyshell from the *specials* era. Kits cost £100, with windscreen £18 extra.
Westpole Motors 1959–61
Approx 20 made

WH IMP

If you thought the Toniq-R (*qv*) was the first of the kit cars designed by university students, then think again. Warwick University students Richard Haste and Tony Whitehead were responsible for the low-slung, two-seat, Hillman Imp-based WH Imp!
WH Design 1970
Approx 3 made

WHARFEDALE

A period van based on Ford components with a body made from Medite (plywood) and offered by White Rose Vehicles of Gillingham, Kent, who marketed the former John Cowperthwaite plan-built wooden-bodied kits – the Husky, Midge and Locust.
White Rose Vehicles 1996–2001
Approx 14 made

WHITBY WARRIOR

Crewe-based Whitby Engineering's main business was making ice cream vans. Their Warrior was Mini-based, unsurprisingly, with a whole variety of body styles for the customer to choose from, including pickup and estate. The company was run by Stuart Whitby, who after three years dropped the Warrior and concentrated on his main business, satisfying the demands of Mr Whippy!
Whitby Engineering 1983–86
Approx 18 made

WHITFIELD SERAPH – *see Seraph*

WILD BLOOD BRESCIA

Stillborn Austin A35-based Bugatti Brescia replica.
Wild Blood 1983
Approx 1 made

WILD BLOOD TYPE 55

Stillborn Bugatti Type 35 replica, from a short-lived Cheltenham-based operation.
Wild Blood 1983
Approx 1 made

WILLEEP RUGGER – *see Rugger*

WIZARD OF RODS BEETLE SALOON

Revised body conversion for the VW Beetle in oval rear window or Baja style, offered by self-proclaimed 'Wizard of Slough' Pete Cheeseman.
Wizard Roadsters 1997–98
Approx 12 made

WIZARD OF RODS BEETLE DELIVERY VAN

Beetle van, in a nutshell. Rear half of Beetle body removed and replaced by a bespoke back end.
Wizard of Rods 1987–94
Wizard Roadsters 1994–98
Approx 18 made

WIZARD OF RODS ROADSTER

Californian-style Beetle conversion. Original Beetle body chopped and beefed-up, or could be had in 'California' style.
Wizard of Rods 1987–94
Wizard Roadsters 1994–98
Approx 150 made

WIZARD OF RODS SUPER COUPÉ

Pete Cheeseman Beetle-based, Willy's Coupé-inspired creation, that had originally come to the UK via rodder-supreme Chris Boyle, under his Everyday Vehicles banner, before it moved to Rodshop.
Wizard of Rods 1987–94
Wizard Roadsters 1994–98
Approx 35 made

WIZARD OF RODS WINDJAMMER

Created in 1980 by Chris Boyle of 34 Corner fame under the Everyday Vehicles banner. Later passed to Pete Cheeseman's Wizard of Rods. Basically a Beetle with the roof removed and a targa-style top added.
34 Corner 1984–87
Wizard of Rods 1987–94
Wizard Roadsters 1994–98
Approx 50 made

WMC BUG

Michael and Gary Webster, based in Braishfield, Hampshire, were the men behind the WMC Bug. Gary owned Bond Bug number 38 plus the remains of a rolled example, and they also acquired a set of original moulds for the Tom Karen-designed Bug. Initially they produced a four-wheeled version, and excellent it was too. Due to public demand they then went on to offer the traditional three-wheeler in kit form for a while. A convertible Sports version was also offered but they made only one of these, while the standard fixed-head was interestingly called the 'Normal'!

Mini subframe on front to enable four-wheel configuration, which was 8in longer than the original three-wheeler and ran on 10in front wheels with 12in at the rear. Just four made of the standard body style before they packed up.

Webster Motor Company 1990–91
Approx 5 made

WOLF

Formerly known as the Tytan (*qv*) before being acquired by Mark Butler, who fitted his demo with Audi V8 engine.
MBR Racing 2007–9
Approx 1 made

WOLFE

A trackday/racer kit with a flowing body from Tony Gaunt of Belper, Derbyshire. Used a Sylva Riot (*qv*) chassis.
Wolfe Sports & Racing 2009 to date
Approx 2 made

WRAGG SINGLE SEATER

A glorious Austin 7 Twin-Cam replica created by a chap called Alan Wragg, of Sherwood Restorations of Blidworth, Nottinghamshire. Wragg's car replicated the Jamieson works racers of the early thirties and he built a dozen of them in the late seventies. He was tragically killed during an avalanche in Glencoe in 1988.
Sherwood Restorations 1978–82
Approx 12 made

WYVERN

Unique when launched in 1983, as it was the first Vauxhall Viva-based kit car and components from the HB, HC, Magnum and Firenza could be used, so engines therefore included 1,256cc, 1,599cc, 1,759cc, 1,975cc and 2,279cc, while the company could supply alternative mounts to accommodate the Ford Crossflow engine. A proper 2+2 with a strong steel box-section chassis. Very highly rated for its high quality. Described in the company's literature of the day as 'providing a new suit of clothes to transform that paragon of pedestrian motoring, the Vauxhall Viva, into something special'. Kits cost £1,660 in May 1985.

Maker JC Composites of Hereford was run by Gerry Johnson and ex-boat builder and Dateline Marine employee Brian Cook, who sold 35 kits in their first year of trading. Passed to Michael Matchen of Hawk Associates in autumn 1985 who introduced a Ford Escort Mk2 version.
JC Composites Ltd 1983–85
Hawk Associates 1985–86
Approx 105 made

XANTHOS TYPE 90

Devon-based Lotus expert Henry Twomes created this Lotus 23 replica. Incidentally, Xanthos was one of two horses (Balios being the other) that pulled Achilles' chariot. Featured a delicate round tube spaceframe chassis, proper period suspension, a Hewland Mk9 transaxle and a four-piece GRP body. Taken over by Honiton-based Nigel Silverthorn, before he ceased trading, leaving his erstwhile GRP makers Stuart Pease & Co holding the rights.

South West Replicas 1990–95
Xanthos Sports Cars 1995–2001
Xanthos Cars 2001–6
Stuart Pease & Co 2006 to date
Approx 45 made

XENER

A very short-lived F355 replica based on Toyota MR2 from Birmingham-based Prestige Projects UK, run by John Sembi.
Prestige Projects UK 2003
Approx 3 made

XR355

Ferrari F355 body conversion kit based on Toyota MR2, briefly available in the UK from an Irish company based in County Kildare.
Xotic Replicas 2006–8
Approx 15 made

XR360

Ferrari F360 body conversion based on Peugeot 406.
Xotic Replicas 2006–8
Approx 20 made

XR DIABLO

Lamborghini Diablo replica body conversion kit for Toyota MR2.
Xotic Replicas 2007–8
Approx 3 made

XR-GT

Interesting Scottish (Auchterarder, Perthy & Kinross) conversion kit for Ford Fiesta Mk2, designed by industrial designer Neale Woolfall. The company was run by publisher/author Peter Hingston.
Easybuild Projects Ltd 1996–97
Approx 1 made

XR XRR

Conversion kit to turn a P38 (Mk2) Range Rover into an L322 lookalike.
Xotic Replicas 2007–8
Approx 5 made

YAK YEOMAN

Utility-type kit.
Manchester Garages 1979–84
Approx 7 made

YKC BERLINETTA

Like its sister Roadster (see below), the Berlinetta went north in 1993 and became a YKC product. Steve Himsworth and co concentrated on the Roadster before launching the all-new Romero in 1998. Had wind-up windows and a removable hardtop.
YKC Sportscars 1993–98
Approx 150 made

YKC IMOLA

A Ford Sierra-based variant of the YKC Romero, distinguished by its revised front wings.
YKC Sportscars 1999–2004
Approx 20 made

YKC JULIETTA

Another pretty take on the YKC Romero theme, and again Ford Sierra-based. Became an Aquila Sportscars product in 2004.
YKC Sportscars 1999–2004
Aquila Sportscars 2004–7
Approx 40 made

YKC MILLE MIGLIA

A variant of the YKC Romero based on Ford Sierra and equipped with fly-screens. Had semi-monocoque box-section chassis.
YKC Sportscars 1999–2004
Approx 10 made

A B C D E F G H I J K L M N O P Q R S T U V W X Y Z

YKC PACE

Developed from the Richard Ashby-designed Street Rat (*qv*) that Martin Griffin had marketed for a time.
YKC Sportscars 2002–4
Approx 3 made

YKC RAIDER

A big, beefy Rover V8-powered trackday car devised by Don Burt that retained some of the traditional YKC styling characteristics in a larger overall package.
YKC Sportscars 1999–2004
Approx 2 made

YKC ROADSTER

Developed from the Marina-based Marlin Roadster (*qv*). Elvington-based YKC, originally known as Yorkshire Kit Cars, was an agent for Marlin for several years before acquiring this project outright in 1993. Steve Himsworth, Clive Gamble and team redeveloped the car to run on Ford Sierra mechanicals. The Roadster was superseded by the introduction of the Romero in 1998.

YKC Sportscars 1993–2004
Approx 500 made

YKC ROMERO

Arriving in 1998, the all-new Romero was a very nice Ford Sierra-based development of the Roadster model. The Romero spawned the similarly styled Imola, Julietta and Mille Miglia variants.

YKC Sportscars 1998–2004
Approx 80 made

YORK 427

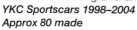

Jaguar-based Cobra replica that was around for about five minutes.
York Engineering 1980
Approx 1 made

Z CARS MINI CONVERSION

Bike-power – sometimes two at a time – for the Classic Mini. Superb.
Z Cars Ltd 2000 to date
Approx 350 made

Z CARS MONTE CARLO

GRP-bodied Mini silhouette with full spaceframe chassis from ex-policeman Chris Allanson, a man with a huge pedigree in grasstrack racing and also developer of the famed twin-engined Tiger Z100 (*qv*). Monster performance and superb build quality.
Z Cars Ltd 2004 to date
Approx 30 made

ZAGAROFF – *see Silhouette GS70*

ZEALIA

Lightweight E-type recreation, although not a kit car in the true sense of the word. Similar to the products made by Lynx and Proteus and of very high quality, complete with aluminium body. Created by Brian Wilkinson, the founder of Safety Devices and previously involved with the Broadspeed XJ6 and TWR XJS racers. Kits priced at £16,000.

Zealia 1996–99
Approx 15 made

ZEEMAX CS MINI

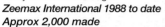

One of the many styling packages for the Mini and a variety of other cars from the pen of well-known automotive stylist Barry Perman. This one has been widely copied. Barry invented it though.

Zeemax International 1988 to date
Approx 2,000 made

ZERO

First product from father and son team, Terry and Leigh Whiteman, from Lytham St Anne's. Its 'Noddy-inspired' styling was not for everyone but it was fun and handled quite well, despite its relatively low power output from the donor Fiat 126.

Once the Whitemans were ready with their all-new Car Craft Cyclone (*qv*) they couldn't service two models so sold the Zero to Pete Magatti of the Fiat Recycling Centre in South Norwood, who traded as the Sun Motor Company.

Car Craft 1992–94
Sun Motor Company 1994–97
Approx 20 made

ZERO

First product from post-Robin Hood Great British Sportscars, run by Ian Rowley and Richard Hall. Ford-based, available in a variety of kit options including comprehensive and could be powered by a wide range of engines including Ford Duratec HE. Hall took over completely in 2010 and was joined by Keith Bird as co-director soon afterwards.

In October 2010, the company announced a wider (40mm) version called the Chubster (*qv*) and a BMW donor option, too.

Great British Sportscars 2007 to date
Approx 500 made

ZETA – *see Seta*

ZETTA 300

The 1953 Isetta bubble car was created by fridge manufacturer Renzo Rivolta, later of ISO cars fame. From 1957 to 1964 it was made under license in the UK at a Brighton factory, at a peak rate of 175 per week! The skids were put on bubble car popularity by the launch of the Minis in 1959.

Bubble car specialists Rick Edwards and Dave Chapman of Preston-based Tri-Tech Autocraft launched their replica, called the Zetta, in 1997. Very nicely made with a steel ladderframe chassis, Bedford Rascal front suspension (same track as the Isetta) and power from a 250cc Honda Super Dream four-stroke engine, although a 400cc upgrade option was available. Drive was by chain, with an in-house fabricated rear-swinging arm. Body of unstressed GRP. Very highly regarded.

Tri-Tech Automotive 1996–2001
Approx 17 made

ZIGCLAIR

One of the ultimate kits-that-got-away, a beautifully made Riley MPH-inspired roadster based on MGB mechanicals. Never made production, sadly.

Zigclair 1981
Approx 1 made

ZITA ZS

The Zita ZS was the brainchild of Tony Chappell, Chris Faulkener and Dick Weed from their base in Langley, Buckinghamshire. Came about because Faulkener didn't like the Mini Jem kit he was building so started his own project. Based on VW Beetle, it featured a Vauxhall Viva windscreen with pleasing fibreglass body, though before sales could get going the partners fell out, leaving Faulkener in sole control. It all come to nothing, ultimately.

FWC Cars 1971–72
Approx 2 made

ZONTA

An innovative Smart ForTwo-based version of the Rocket (*qv*) created by MEV's Stuart Mills. The Rocket also came under the control of this Nottingham-based company, which was part of the Smarts'R'Us operation, in 2009 who changed their name to Road Trace Race soon after.

Road Track Race Ltd 2007 to date
Approx 15 made

ZYNTECH – *see Reeves Revera*

Hole's 'Hall of Fame' Heroes

In this list I pay tribute to some people who would be founding members of the UK Kit Car Industry Hall of Fame should there ever be one. Some need no introduction and are obvious choices, while others are more than a little unsung. Here's my attempt to get them in the spotlight!

I salute every single one of you…

Dennis Adams – Along with brother Peter, he was responsible for the best Marcos creations, while they also did the Probe. Those two facts alone gain him automatic entry. Dennis later turned his hand to Rotrax, Dakar and Adam Roadster too.

Ken Attwell – The man who had the foresight to create the first proper GT40 replica, via his KVA operation.

Les Ballamy – Back in the fifties, most cars handled like pigs, but Leslie Ballamy, changed all that (along with Derek Buckler) via his LMB operation with his range of upgraded chassis and suspension parts.

Paul Banham – Prolific designer, who eschewed fripperies and glitz, didn't really like kit cars but sold lots of innovative kits in the late nineties/early noughties.

Tony Bostock – The daddy of kit car journalism, first in *Car Mechanics* in 1958, and then *Hot Car* in the 70's.

John Britten – A super gentleman and fine racer in the sixties. The man behind the Arkley SS.

Chris Boyle – Another rod man at heart, Chris nevertheless came up with lots of kit ideas over the years, including Wizard of Rods and Street Beetle that begat the Chesil, of course.

Derek Buckler – The 'daddy' of the UK's kit car industry. Simple as that, plus a superb character to boot. If he liked your car you got a bonnet badge, if not…

Richard Butterfield – Included here because as a very young man he created the first ever Mini-based kit car, at his dad's garden centre in Essex. The car? The Butterfield Musketeer.

Nick Butler – Not really a kit car designer, but took the Jago hot rod concept a stage further and developed it. Created some innovative and stunning vehicles over the years, plus he also offered two of his rods in kit form for a time in the late seventies. A lovely bloke.

Colin Chapman – No need for explanation!

Ray 'The Rodfather' Christopher – After establishing himself as arguably the UK's best-known rod builder, he later went on to sell a lot of GT40 replicas via his GT Developments operation. Possibly also the only rod/kit maker to earn a living as a professional wrestler too!

Adrian Cocking – ex-DJ Sportscars sales manager and founder of LR Roadsters, sold lots of Cobra, D-type and Daytona kits in the eighties and another real character.

Frank Costin – Legendary designer, served his time at the de Havilland Aircraft Company. Created the first Marcos and a whole raft of other cars including the Amigo and TMC Costin. Also supplied the 'Cos' part of Marcos…

Peter Coxhead – The nicest man I ever met in the kit car industry as well as being the most respected kit car journalist. Much missed mentor…

Tony Divey – Smashing chap, completely passionate about his beloved Triking. Rightly so, because it is the best three-wheeler ever.

Pierre du Plessis – South African who co-founded GP with John Jobber and the instigator of the legendary GP Buggy.

Tim Dutton – People can say what they like about Tim Dutton, but he changed the world of kit cars forever with his Dutton Cars operation, in volume terms and also the way they were sold.

Paul Emery – Belongs in the sixties box marked 'Jem Marsh' and 'Chris Lawrence', a skilled engineer and engine tuner. Also marketed his own range of cars for a time…

Peter Filby – Without Filby I wouldn't have written this book or written about kit cars at all. His writings were the catalyst for the latter day kit car movement. Respect.

Martin Foster – The best kit car magazine editor I ever saw. Edited *Kit Car, Kit Cars & Specials* and also *Custom Car* magazines over the years. Martin had the edge…

John Frayling – Another ex-Lotus man, who created several cars including the superb Clan Crusader.

Bernard Friese – The designer of the superb range of Gilbern models after the fateful day he met butcher Giles Smith.

Gordon Geskell – Included here because he had the foresight to think of turning a humble Mini into a limousine, with the Beauford, way back in the mid-eighties. He and his missus, Hillary, are lovely people.

Nick Green – MG enthusiast who established his own NG Cars marque and sold lots of traditional roadster style kits.

Gerry Hawkridge – No one makes replicas like Mr Hawkridge.

James Hale – The beach buggy 'guru'.

Bill Hines – A lovely, lovely bloke, responsible for the wonderful Dunsmore marque.

John Ingram – In an industry not short of skilled glassfibre laminators, the late John Ingram is arguably THE best ever; his company made bodies for many leading kit car makers in the eighties. Also co-founded the Domino marque.

George Jeffrey – No glamour for dear old George. He doggedly ploughed a furrow for many years back in the sixties, producing a range of racing cars, before entering the kit car industry with his J4 and J5 models. Two of the finest handling kits ever made. Deserved more success. Unsung hero.

Geoff Jago – Do not underestimate Geoffrey Jago's importance to the UK's specialist car industry. Revered for his pioneering efforts establishing the hot rodding movement in the UK, selling thousands of rods and parts, he went on to to sell a couple of thousand Jago Geep/Sandero kits. A gentleman of the first order.

John Jobber – The driving force behind GP Projects/Speedshop/ Concessionaires etc etc, and one of the shrewdest operators the kit car industry has ever seen.

Chris Lawrence – True character and a skilled engineer, responsible for the Deep Sanderson range among a whole host of other achievements. His book, *Morgan Maverick* is a superb read.

Brian Luff – Ex-Lotus man, Luff was behind several designs including the wonderful Status Minipower.

Jem Marsh – A legend. Marcos founder, character and one of the few survivors of the halcyon sixties period for the specialist car industry. Maverick – and one of the funniest men I have ever met. If Jem thinks you're an idiot he'll tell you!

Graham Nearn – After acting as a Lotus agent for many years, he had the foresight to take over the Lotus Seven, creating his own Caterham Cars operation to sell it. Top drawer. Specialist Car Industry legend.

Lee Noble – Redoubtable Leicestershire lad who has penned some of the greatest specialist cars ever, starting with the Ultima. Calls a spade a very heavy lifting implement!

Richard Oakes – Probably THE greatest specialist car designer ever. Humble origins as a go-fer at Davrian in the late sixties has led to a stream of top kit car designs, from Nova to Blackjack Zero, taking in the Beaver and the GTM Libra.

Peter Pellandine – Another of the founding fathers of the UK kit car industry, responsible for Ashley, Falcon and a whole raft of other designs spanning many, many years.

Jeremy Phillips – Responsible for some of the GREATEST kit cars ever designed, via his Sylva marque. Top bloke, too. A genius

Roland Sharman – Behind one of the best-selling UK beach buggies, in the Bugle, and included here for his indomitable spirit in continuing to market the car, despite going into liquidation several times. A believer.

Giles Smith – Ex-butcher who wanted his own sportscar. Met Bernard Friese one day in a shop and they ended up creating the legendary Gilbern Cars operation.

Chris Smith – Founder of the Westfield marque. A shrewd businessman, top driver and producer of some superb kit cars. Always worth listening to.

Professor Anthony 'Tony' Stevens – Designer of the best kit car you've never heard of, the Stevens Cipher. A great car…

Richard Stewart – Founder of the legendary Robin Hood Sports Cars operation, Richard ploughed his own furrow and revelled in it. Initially sold Ferrari Daytona replicas but then made his mark, earning his place in history by selling thousands of affordable Lotus Seven-inspired kitcars. Demands respect…

Den Tanner – Changed the face of the traditional roadster with his inexpensive Bulldog kit and then did the same for the Cobra replica with his Sumo package. Tanner had the Midas touch and demands respect, not least for the volume of kits he sold.

William Towns – Top designer, with Aston Martin DBS and angular seventies Lagonda on his résumé, plus all manner of other stuff including street furniture, clothing, Guyson E12, GS Europa and the Hustler range. Much missed.

Neville Trickett – Legendary designer behind the MiniSprint, Opus, Siva and many GP Projects designs.

Keith Waddington – Co-founded Ashley Laminates with Peter Pellandine and doggedly continued running the operation when Pellandine went off to set up Falcon Design.

Ivor Walklett – All the Walklett brothers, founders of Ginetta Cars, deserve to be included here, but Ivor was the stylist of some legendary specialist cars, including G4, G12, G15 and G21. A lovely man.

Nigel Whall – Changed the public's perception of three-wheelers via his Lomax range. Had the secret ingredient because although they weren't pretty there was something about them (obviously) as he sold thousands…

Bill Woodhouse – Another pioneer from the industry's early days, and his Tornado marque helped raise the quality of the products of the day. A very, very nice man to boot.

Top Sellers

I'm putting my neck on the block with this list, and will attempt to put kit cars sales into a form of league table in terms of volume. Kit car makers are notorious for fish jokes in that a minnow can turn into a huge Great White Shark when it comes to quoting sales figures, so please take these with a pinch of salt.

In addition, some of the fifties/sixties *specials* makers sold their bodyshells in huge numbers, with the majority not being completed, plus of course, sales records for that period are sketchy at best. We've done our best to guesstimate possible numbers.

It's impossible in some cases, where a manufacturer has made several models, to give specific figures, so you'll see a maker's name and the legend 'all types' where this is the case.

Finally, some have inevitably had to be listed twice or more, such as in the case of Lotus, who of course offered several of their road car models in component form pre-1973 and the advent of VAT, so, you'll see the Seven listed under Caterham and Lotus separately.

I've done my level best to make this list somewhere near accurate but you'll need to bear the above in mind, as it's not intended to be a 'written in stone' listing.

Lotus (all types)	21,142
Caterham Seven	13,500
Westfield (all types)	11,400
Robin Hood (all types)	10,000+
Lotus Elan (all types)	9158
Dutton Cars (all types)	8500
Lotus Europa (all types)	8345
TVR (all types until 1973)	4289
GP Buggy	4200
Spartan	4000
Lotus Europa S2	3615
Lomax 223	3500
Lotus Europa Special	3500
Pilgrim Sumo	3500
Tiger Racing (all types)	3400
Dutton Sierra (all types)	3200
Dutton Phaeton (all types)	3100
Lotus Elan S4	3000
DJ Sportscars DAX Cobra (all types)	3000
Scamp (all types)	3600
Lotus Elan S3	2650
Ginetta Cars	2621 +109 NON kit
NG Cars/Pastiche (all types)	2533
Gentry	2500
Pilgrim Bulldog	2200
Rochdale (all types)	2100

Jago Sandero/Geep	2100
Marlin/YKC Roadster	2075
Edwards Bros EB 50/60	2000
Beauford (all types)	1800
Marcos (all types until 1991)	1765 +310 NON kit
JBA Falcon (all types)	1700
GP Super Buggy/Alpine	1600
Lotus Europa Twin-Cam	1580
Dutton Melos (all types)	1500
Falcon Shells Mk3	1500
LR Roadsters RAM SC	1500
GP Spyder	1500
Lotus Elan Sprint	1353
Gilbern Cars (all types)	1350
Lotus Seven (all types)	1310
Mini Marcos (all types)	1270
Mini Marcos (all types)	1260
Lotus Elan S2	1250
Rickman (all types)	1250
MK Indy	1250
Locust (all types)	1225
NG TF	1200
Prova Countach	1200
Sheldonhurst (all types)	1190
RW Kitcars Karma (all types)	1145
Quantum (all types)	1125

Eagle RV	1105
Arkley SS	1100
Ultima Sports (all types)	1100+
NG TF	1010
Merlin (all types)	1000
Tornado TS40	1000
Roadhog	1000
Falcon Shells Mk2	1000
Moss Malvern/Roadster	1000
Fiero Factory/Euro/AS Euro 427	1000
Lotus Elite	998
Fury	950
GP Madison (all types)	920
Jago Model T	900
Extreme Sportscars (all types)	900
Lotus Elan S1	900
Kougar Sports	800
TVR Grantura (all types)	800
Bugle Buggy	871
Tornado Cars (all types)	764
GTM Rossa (all types)	750
Andersen Cub	750
TVR Vixen (All types)	746
Dutton B+/B-Type/Malaga	700
Cox/GTM/Primo Coupé	700
NCF Diamond (all types)	700
Elva (all types)	700
Turner Sports Cars (all types)	673
Lotus Europa S1	650
Striker (Sylva/Raw) (all types)	650
Marlin/YKC Berlinetta	650
NCF Blitz	650
Minijem	650
GT Developments GTD40	637
Charger 1 & 2 (MBC/DAX/MDB/Viking)	610
Eagle SS	610
Ginetta G15	610
Burlington Arrow/Berretta	600
Southern Roadcraft/Madgwick SRV8	600
Jago Model B	600
Ginetta G4 (all types)	600
Davrian (all types)	580
UVA (all types)	575
Lomax 224	550
Dakar	520
Ranger Automotive (all types)	510
Falcon Shells Caribbean	505
UVA Fugitive (all types)	503
Ashley Laminates 750	500
Volksrod (all types)	500
Banham 130 Spyder	500
Lightspeed Panels Magenta (all types)	500
Microplas Stiletto	500

Nova	500
Chesil	500
BRA 289	480
Nickri Laminates	475
Quantum 2+2	470
Covin Performance (all types)	467
BRA CV3	460
JZR	450
Lotus VI	426
Rat Buggy	420
NG TA	410
Jimini	400
KVA GT40 Mk1	400
Microplas Mistral	400
NG TC	400
Country Volks Buggy	400
Fiero Factory F282	400
Fiero Factory MR3 SS	400
DNA Automotive (all models)	400
Pembleton (all types)	380
EPC Hustler Buggy	375
Gardner Douglas GD427	375
Hustler Interstyl	369
GRS Tora	360
Grinnall Scorpion	350
Lotus Seven S3	350
Loco (STM/Aries)	350
Mallock U2	350
Hawk HF Series	350
Clan Crusader	350
Elva Courier Mk2	350
Freestyle (ABS/TH/Funbuggies)	325
Pilgrim Speedster	310
Renegade Buggy	310
UVA (all types)	309
Manta Ray Buggy	305
Midas Bronze/Coupé	305
MEV/RTR Rocket	300+
AK 427	300
Shark Buggy	300
Ashley Laminates 11/2	300
Autotune Aristocat	300
Banham Sprint	300
Banham Superbug	300
Deon/JH Classics	300
Falcon Shells Competition	300
Fairthorpe Electron Minor	300
Hawk 289 Series	300
GP LDV	280
Banham X21/X99	250
Caterham CSR	250
Triple C Challenger	250
Lotus Seven S1	245

Where were they based?

As a footnote to the main text of the book I thought it would be rather nice to give a county-by-county listing of where kit car manufacturers are/were based. It's not an exhaustive list, but does give a fascinating insight into hot beds of kit car activity.

ENGLAND

AVON

BATH
Hampshire Classics 1987–2000

BRISTOL
AED International Ltd 1983–84
AVA Cars 1990–91
CH Automotive 1998–2000
Evolution Sports Cars 1997–99
GS Cars 1975–80
HSP Motors 1970–72
ISH Car Company 1998–2000
Motorstyle 1984–85
Opus Cars 1966–70
Seraph Cars 1985–87
Spectre Designs 1994

TIMSBURY
Avon Coachworks 1996–99

BEDFORDSHIRE

BEDFORD
ARA Racing 2004–6
Midas Racing Services 1998
TI Motors 1985–87

HITCHIN
Heritage Engineering 1988–99

IVINGHOE ASTON
Broomstick Cars 1993–99

LEIGHTON BUZZARD
Classic Chassis Services 2007-2010

LITTLE STAUNTON
Costin Drake Technology 1970–72

LUTON
Dante Engineering 1956–59
Grannd Performance Mouldings 1995–96 (moved to Galway)
Speedex Castings & Accessories 1958–62

SANDY
Carisma Engineering 1989–92

BERKSHIRE

CAVERSHAM
Buckler Cars 1947–65

CROWTHORNE
Nomad Sales 1979–83

LAMBOURN
Dovetail Plastics 1985–88

NEWPORT
Unique Vehicle Accessories (UVA) 1982–90

READING
Aquarius Beach Buggies 1969–71
Robert Mandry Scamps 1969–87

SLOUGH
Lyncar Engineering 1990
MDB Cars 1986

WINDSOR
RGS Automobile Components 1953–62

WOKINGHAM
FibreFab 1970–81

BUCKINGHAMSHIRE

AYLESBURY
Crendon Replicas 1991 to date

BEACONSFIELD
Chassis Works 1994–2007

CADMORE END
Bohanna Stables 1975–77

CHALFONT ST PETER
Fairthorpe Cars 1957–67

HIGH WYCOMBE
Embeesea Cars/MBC Cars 1977–84
Kellforms Woodmasters 2004 to date

IVER HEATH
Seaspray Buggies 1971

LANGLEY
FWC Cars 1971–72

MARLOW
Bohanna Stables 1976–78
Dart Cars 1991

MILTON KEYNES
EBM Sportscars 1999–2001
K Sportscars 2008 to date
Lynx AE 2005 to date

PRINCES RISBOROUGH
GP Developments 1993–94
GP Projects 1994–2002
Steaney Developments 1982–86

WOOBURN GREEN
Britton Hazelgrove 1987

CAMBRIDGESHIRE

ELY
Fordham Engineering 1983–84
Omatic 2001–2

NEWMARKET
LR Roadsters 1986–93

PETERBOROUGH
AK Sportscars 1997 to date
Antique Automobiles 1971
Ferranté Cars 1984–85
Luego Sports Cars 2002–5
Oldham & Crowther Engineering 1984–88
Radical Sportscars 2005 to date
Ron Champion 1998–2002
Ronart Cars 1984 to date
Sports Car Services 1986–88
T&A Sportscars 1990
Trident Autovet 1985–86
Vulrod Motors 1971–72

ST NEOTS
Frenette 1991–92

THORNEY
Tiger Racing 1999 to date

THREE HOLES
Rodbodys 2005 to date
Sebring International 1995 to date

WHADDON
Morford Motor Company 1993–99

WHITTLESEY
Spyder Engineering 1985 to date

WISBECH
Shadow Auto Styling 2005–6
Typhoon Sports Cars 2009 to date

CHANNEL ISLANDS

JERSEY
Brian Luff Ltd 1980–81
Replica Car Imports 1980

CHESHIRE

CREWE
Whitby Engineering 1983–86

HAZEL GROVE
Cox & Co 1967–71
Heerey Engineering 1971–72

KNUTSFORD
Lomas Motorsport 1971–73

NORTHWICH
Christopher Neil Sportscars 1984–89

RUNCORN
Cyana Cars 2005–8
DRK 1984–98

SANDBACH
PK Manufacturing 1981–84
Sandbach Replica Cars 1981–82

WARRINGTON
Dragon Sportscars 2003–5
Evolution Sportscars 2005–6
Limited Edition Sportscars 1984–85
ShawSpeed 2003–6

CLEVELAND

MIDDLESBROUGH
Cartune 1971–73

CORNWALL

BODMIN
The Thousand Workshop 1983–84

CALLINGTON
Imperial Motor Company 1996–97

CAMBORNE
Moko Component Cars 1984–85

HAYLE
Ottercraft 1987–93

HELSTON
Blackjack Cars 1996 to date
GP Technical 2002–4
Javan Sports Cars 2005–9

LAMORNA
Evergreen Motor Company
1994–99

LISKEARD
TJ Overlanders 1985–92

NEWLYN COOMBE
Latham Sports Cars 1983–88

NEWQUAY
Adrenaline Motorsport 2006–9
Nova Developments 1994–97
Toniq Ltd 2009 to date

PORTHLEVEN
AC Auto Replicas 1992

REDRUTH
Cornish Classic Cars 1985–87

ST AUSTELL
Car Craft Clinic (Triple C)
1984–87
JWE Motorsport 2011 to date

ST COLUMB MAJOR
GV Plastics Fibreglass Products
1983–85

TINTAGEL
B&S Horton 1986

THREEMILESTONE
Alternative Autos 1985–86
Peninsula Sports Cars 2008 to
date

TORPOINT
ACM Ltd 1981–83

TRURO
Milestone Motorsport 2005 to
date

WEST LOOE
Excalibur Cars 1985–92

WHEAL PLENTY
Peninsula Sportscars 2010 to date

CUMBRIA

CARLISLE
Graham Autos (Glassfibre) Ltd
1984

LOPTON
Lakes Sports Cars 1984

SALTHOUSES
Fellpoint 1975–77

WORKINGTON
Shado Designs 1996

DERBYSHIRE

ASHBOURNE
Legendary Sports Cars 1994–98

CHESTERFIELD
Chesterfield Motor Spares 1994
Highfield Automotive 1993
Spire Sportscars 2005 to date
Kestrel Cars 1984–86

DERBY
A.G. Thorpe Developments 1979–85

GREAT LONGSTONE
Keith Cars 1989–96

ILKESTON
Aries Motorsport 2007 to date
Stuart Taylor Motorsport 1998–2007

RIPLEY
Stingray Motorsport 2007 to date

SWADLINCOTE
Square One Developments 1992–95

DEVON

BRIXHAM
Western Laminates 1970–71

CHULMLEIGH
Tifosi Devon/Star Motor Company
2006 to date

CREDITON
Marlin Cars 1992 to date

DARTMOUTH
Foulkes Developments 1981–85

EXETER
E-Zee Automotive 1990–93
Murtaya Sports Cars 2010 to date

EXMOUTH
Eurocat 1991

HOLSWORTHY
Malone Car Company 1998 to date

HONITON
Brooke Cars 2002 to date
Hoppa Street Buggies 2007 to date
MDA GT40 UK 2000–8
Xanthos Cars 2001–6

KINGSBRIDGE
AIMS 1991–92
Fergus Engineering 1986–87
Quantum Heritage 2010 to date
Quantum Sports Cars 2001–10
Quantum Sports Cars 2010 Ltd 2010
to date

NEWTON ABBOT
Exe Marine 1976–78

OKEHAMPTON
Custom Glassfibre 1978–80
Devon Moulding Company 1979

PAIGNTON
South West Engineering (CRC)
1991–2000
Stimulator Cars 1988–97

PLYMOUTH
Classic Motors 1984–86
Devon Moulding Company/Termtrend
1978
Invicta Cars 1982–84
Marlin Engineering 1979–92

SEATON
South West Replicas/Xanthos Sports
Cars 1990–2001

SOUTH BRENT
Phoenix Automotive 2011 to date

WRANGATON
RJH Sportscars & Panels 2000–7

DORSET

BLANDFORD FORUM
Siva Motor Company 1970–76

BOURNEMOUTH
Everyday Vehicles 1981–82

BRIDPORT
Loxton Laminates 1986–88
Trio Cars 1993–2000

BURTON BRADSTOCK
Chesil Motor Company 1993 to date

CHRISTCHURCH
Street Beetle 1990–91
Talon Sportscars 1987–89

FERNDOWN
MR2 Kits 2011 to date

GILLINGHAM
Protoflight 1984–85

PIDDLETRENTHIDE
Chevron Cars 1990–98

POOLE
Bay Area Rods 2005 to date
Broadbest Ltd 1987–88
Dooster 2001–4
Gaia Cars 1998–2002
Griffin Design 1975–79
GT Developments 1985–2000
Ray's Rods 1973–76
SuperStratos 2000 to date

PORTLAND
Bilmar Engineering 1971–72

RINGWOOD
Auto Build Services 1989–94
Brightwheel Replicas 1984–89
Classic Replicas 1989–2002
Classic Sportscars 2006–9
Prestige Sports Cars 1994–95
Sculptural Engineering 1999–2001

SHAFTESBURY
JH Classics 1993–94

SHERBORNE
S.E. Hamblin Ltd 1958–61

STURMINSTER NEWTON
Zero Racing 1999–2000

VERWOOD
Marlborough Cars 1985–86

DURHAM

CROSSGATE MOOR
J.J. Calver 1991
Pit Performance Vehicles 1988–89

HARTLEPOOL
HE-Fibreglass 1972–76
Saturn Sports Cars 2009 to date

TOW LAW
NCF Motors 1998 to date

WASHINGTON
Clan Cars 1971–74

ESSEX

BASILDON
Fibresports 1969 to date

BENFLEET
Furore Cars 2006 to date

BILLERICAY
Centrepoint Racing 1989–90

BRADWELL
MDV Specialist Engineering 2004–6

BRAINTREE
Asquith Motor Carriage Company
1981–84

BRIGHTLINGSEA
Perry Automotive Developments
1981–85

BURNHAM-ON-CROUCH
T5 Developments 2002–7

CHELMSFORD
Auriga Design 1993–2000

Bugle Buggies 2003 to date
Essex Proto Conversions 1970–72

CLACTON-ON-SEA
Daytona Classics 1986–89
Italia Sports Cars 2007 to date
Martin Automobiles 1986–96

COLCHESTER
Trac Services 1991–95

DAGENHAM
BMS Automotives 2000

DANBURY
Candy Apple Cars 1991–2000

EAST HANNINGFIELD
Deetype Replicas 1974–81

GRAYS
Sheen Engineering 1969–71

GREAT YELDHAM
Hunnable Holdings 1984–97

HARLOW
DJ Sportscars/DAX 1979 to date
Unique Autocraft 1981–93

HORNCHURCH
Apollo Cars 1971–72

LEIGH-ON-SEA
EJS Products 1971–72
Ranger Automotive 1972–76

LEYTONSTONE
Convair Developments 1955–59
Nordec Engineering 1959–60

LOUGHTON
Ashley Laminates 1955–62

MALDON
Claydon Hamilton Automotive Design
1995–98
Graham Hathaway Engineering 1989
to date
PB2 (Paintbox) 1998

NAZEING
Butterfield Engineering 1961–63

RAYLEIGH
Eurosport (UK) 1990–92

ROMFORD
Nickri Laminates 1958–61

SAFFRON WALDEN
Automotive Design Technology 1991

SHOEBURYNESS
Mercury Motorsport 1993–98
RS Automotive 1998–91

SOUTHEND-ON-SEA
Americar 1971–72
Calvy Car Company 1983–84
KaRa Sports Cars 1992–93
Merlin Cars 1980
Nova Kit Cars 1990–91
Paris Cars 1985–2003
Thoroughbred Cars 1980–84

SOUTH WOODHAM FERRERS
Beaver Coach Works 1991–92
Covin Performance Mouldings 1984–91

THUNDERSLEY
Viking Cars 1986–87

WALTHAM ABBEY
Falcon Shells 1957–64

WESTCLIFF-ON-SEA
Lynx Cars 1991–93

WEST MERSEA
DARE Engineering 1991 to date

WITHAM
Ginetta Cars 1962–73, 1977–89
Ram Automotive 1994–98

GLOUCESTERSHIRE

CHELTENHAM
Cotswold Kit Cars 2001–2
Spyders Inc 2004 to date
Wild Blood 1983

CINDERFORD
Land Ranger 4x4 2006–7

GLOUCESTER
Formula 27 Sportscars 1991–92
Harlequin Autokits 2000 to date
MR2 Kits 2002 to date

NAILSWORTH
Lomax Cars 1984–86
Mumford Engineering 1973–78,
1983–99

THRUPP
Formula 27 Sportscars 1992–2002

TIRLEY
OM Sportscars 2005 to date

WHITMINSTER
Specialist Performance Mouldings
1991–93

HAMPSHIRE

ALDERSHOT
JB Developments 1972–76
Seagull Cars 1984

ASH VALE
Dragonfly Cars 1984–86

BASINGSTOKE
BM Car Things 1971–72
Country Volks 1987–93
Hampshire Classics 1987
Volksparts 1973–74

BOTLEY
Jimini Automobiles 1990–93
Southern GT 2005 to date

BRAISHFIELD
Webster Motor Company
1990–91

DIBDEN PURLIEU
Gaia Cars 1994–1997

EAST MEON
Findhorn Cars 2002 to date

FORDINGBRIDGE
Dorset Motor Services 1990–92

HARTLEY WINTNEY
Fereday Cars 2000–4

HAYLING ISLAND
Audy Marine 1977–79

HOOK
Dragonfly Cars 1981–84

LYMINGTON
NG Cars 1979–89
Sylva Autokits 1981–82

NEW MILTON
Rickman Bros Engineering Ltd
1987–90
Rickman Developments
1991–92

PORT SOLENT
Stimson Design 2003 to date

PORTSMOUTH
Automotive Concepts 1987–88
Brace Engineering 1998–2000
HRB Automotive 2007–8
Self Fit Ltd 1970–71

SOUTHAMPTON
Automotive Design & Development
1971–74
Domino Cars 1986–2008
Highton Motors 1984

SOUTHSEA
Nouveau Developments 1981–83

SPARSHOLT
Lainston Investment Services
1973

THRUXTON
Martin & Walker 1997 to date
Thruxton Sports Cars 2001–4

TITCHFIELD
Classic Cars of Titchfield 1992–94

WESTBOURNE
Barrian Cars 1971–73
Westbourne Fender Works 1979–84

WHITCHURCH
Nimbus Projects 1984–87
Unique Vehicle Accessories (UVA) 1990–92

HEREFORDSHIRE

HEREFORD
BDN Sportscars 2004 to date
JC Composites 1983–85
Malvern Autocraft 1993–98
Raw Striker Ltd 2001 to date

HERTFORDSHIRE

ARKLEY
John Britten Garages 1970–87

BISHOP'S STORTFORD
Auto Kraft Shells 1959–62

CHESHUNT
Lotus Engineering 1959–66

HARPENDEN
Allard Replicas 1994–97

RICKMANSWORTH
Micron Plastics 1955–59
Tornado Cars Ltd 1960–64

SHENLEY
Ken Sheppard Customised Sports Cars 1965–67

ST ALBANS
Watling Works 1959–61

WATFORD
356 Sports 2004–6
Handmade Cars (Allora) 1985–89
Motorville 1987–89
Watford Sports Cars 1959–61

ISLE OF WIGHT

COWES
Island Plastics 1999–2001
Roca Engineering 1989
Skodek Engineering 1967–68

RYDE
Frogeye Car Company 1985–2000

KENT

BIGGIN HILL
Mirage Developments 1977–82

CANTERBURY
GTS Tuning 2001 to date

CRANBROOK
BGH Geartech (Fury) 2007 to date
Peterworth Trucks 1998–2000

DARTFORD
Panic Motor Sport 2004–6

DOVER
Banham Conversions 2002–4
Liberta Cars 1972
Rawlson Ltd 1982–84

EDENBRIDGE
Eldon Autokits 1996–99

FAVERSHAM
GTS Tuning 2001 to date

GILLINGHAM
White Rose Vehicles 1995–2000

HARRIETSHAM
Replicar Imports 1981–85

HAYES
Piper Cars 1967–71

HEADCORN
Lightning Motor Company 2001–6

HOO
Tyler Industrial Mouldings 1995–98

LENHAM
Lenham Sports Cars 1969–71

LONGFIELD
GTS Tuning 2005–8
HMS 1990–91

MAIDSTONE
Automotive Systems Developments (ASD) 1983–99
Blaze Motorsport 2006 to date
GKD Sports Cars 2006 to date
Leighton Cars 2001 to date
Speedwell Replica Cars 2008 to date

MARDEN
Aeon Sportscars 2003 to date
Fisher Sportscars 1995–2005

MARGATE
RS Motorsport 2009 to date

ORPINGTON
GCS Cars 1993–2000

PADDOCK WOOD
Eldon Autokits 1993–96

RAMSGATE
Rally Replicas 2009 to date

ROCHESTER
Banham Conversions 1997–2002

SANDHURST
Gravetti Engineering 1983-85

SHEERNESS
Minotaur Cars 1993, 1998–2006

STAPLEHURST
LDD Conversions 1976–80
NF Auto Developments 1995 to date

TONBRIDGE
Tyler Industrial Mouldings 1994–98

TUNBRIDGE WELLS
Speedsters 1992–93

WHITSTABLE
Replicar Imports 1991–92

WILMINGTON
Dakar Cars 1991–2002

LANCASHIRE

ACCRINGTON
Automotive Design & Development 1974–75

BEWBURGH
Rhino Engineering 1995–96

BLACKPOOL
Grantura Plastics 1969–70
Race & Rally Replicas 2007
SEM Cars 1989–91
Top Hat Coachworks 1987
TVR 1948–73

BLACKBURN
Bradley Motor Company 1990–96
Sports Cars & Specials 1987
Rally Legend Replicas 2011 to date
Panache Cars Ltd 1985–87

BOLTON
Copycats/Proteus 1982–2001
Masterco Engineering 1991–93
TriSport 1990

BURNLEY
Evans Hunter Sports Cars 1993–94
Reincarations 2009 to date

CHORLEY
Kirk Sportscars 2004–7

COLNE
Shepherd Developments 1985–86

DARWEN
Devlin Cars 1992
Panache Kit Cars 1983–87
Prova Designs 1989–2002

LANCASTER
PACE 1990–92

LEIGH
Lemazone 1984–87

LYTHAM ST ANNE'S
Car Craft Engineering 1988–2006

MANCHESTER
Beaujangles Sales Ltd 1971–73
Boom Trikes 2002 to date
Conan Cars 1986–88
Cybertech Developments 1992
GT Developments (GTD) 1983–85
JBF 1991
Kingfisher Mouldings 1982–86
Manchester Garages 1979–84
Spring Vale Motor Services 1998–2001
TKH Venom Services 1986

OLDHAM
Autobodies 1958–60
D&H Fabrication Techniques 1978–79
David Boler Engineering 1971–74
JMA Automotive 2004 to date
Minisport 2008 to date
SDR Sports Cars 2008 to date
Sherpley Car Company 1997–2003

PRESTON
Alto Component Cars 1994–97
Mill Auto Conversions 2006 to date
Ribble Publishers 1984–86
Reflex Cars 1992
Royale Motor Company 1991–2001
Specframe Vehicle Company 1983–85
Tempest Cars 2006 to date
Tri-Tech Automotive 1998–2002

RISHTON
Autotune (Rishton) Ltd 1983 to date
IJF Engineering 1992–2000

ROCHDALE
Rochdale Motor Panels & Engineering 1946–73

SALFORD
CL Cars Ltd 1984

SOUTHPORT
Beach Buggies of Southport 1971–72
Europa Engineering 1992 to date
Raffo Cars 1980–2000

STANDISH
GB Racing Sports 1988–90
JBA Engineering 1981–2005

STOCKPORT
Paul Haigh Autos 1971–72

WHALLEY
Bradley Motor Company 1990–96

WIGAN
Beauford Cars 1985–96
Imperial Motor Company 2009
to date
JZR Vehicle Restorations 1989–98,
2000 to date
Regent Motor Company 2006–8
Veranti Motor Company 2003–6

LEICESTERSHIRE

BARWELL
RMB Motors 1973–89
SP Motors/TP Motors 1997–2001
TM Motors 1989–97

BLABY
Leaping Cats 1982–83

BIRSTALL
UFO Cars 1970–71

BRUNTINGTHORPE
PYK 1986

GADDESBY
Dooster 2004–8

HINCKLEY
RIDEcars 2005–6
Ultima Sports 1988 to date

KIRKBY MALLORY
Classic Carriage Company
1993–94

LEICESTER
Dezina Cars 1993–97
Midtec Sports Cars 1991–97

MELTON MOWBRAY
Dakar 4x4 Design & Conversions
2002 to date
Pike Automotive 1987–89
RW Kitcars 1983–2000

REMPSTONE
CVC Ltd 1987

SUTTON BONINGTON
GTM Cars 1980–2003

SYSTON
Berkeley Car Company
1991–96

LINCOLNSHIRE

BOSTON
DC Supercars 2003 to date
Wasp Engineering 1991–93

GAINSBOROUGH
Alpha Centura Cars 2005
TH Engineering 2001–3

GRIMSBY
Lovel Cars UK 1999–2000
Onyx Sports Cars 1990 to date

HORNCASTLE
GT40 Supercars 2007 to date

LINCOLN
MI6 Cars 2010 to date

MARKET RASEN
ABS Motorsport 1990 to date

SCAMBLESBY
Sylva Autokits 1982 to date

SCUNTHORPE
Ginetta Cars 1989–93

SKELLINGTHORPE
Tomcat Motorsport 1998 to date

SLEAFORD
AT Fraser Ltd 1971–72

SOUTH WILLINGHAM
Emmbrook Engineering 1971–75

SPALDING
Evante Cars (Vegantune) 1983–91
Import Export 1983–85
Kelvedon Motors 1987

WILLOUGHTON
Lomax Cars 1983

EAST LONDON

BARKING
Concordette Developments 1960–62
Douglas Car Company 1991–98

BOW
Convair Developments 1955–56

CHINGFORD
LR Roadsters 1984–86

HACKNEY
Pell Abrahams Broadcasting
Company 1970–71

PLAISTOW
Dovercourt 1981–83

NORTH LONDON

HORNSEY
Lotus Engineering 1952–59

KENSAL RISE
Treacy Ltd 1969–72

ST JOHN'S WOOD
Rugger Agency 1981–83

SOUTH LONDON

BECKENHAM
American Speed Specialties 1991–95

BRIXTON
Mr Ed's Specialised Auto Designs
1980

BROMLEY
Fiorano 2005 to date
Homesdale Motor Traders 1970–71
Powerspeed 1970–71
Super Accessories 1958–63

CHARLTON
DG Motor Services 1997–2002

CLAPHAM
Davrian Developments 1967–83

CLERKENWELL
Group Six Sportscars 1972–77

CROYDON
Elva Cars (1961) Ltd (Trojan)
1961–65
Hand Crafted Cars 1998–2003
Markham-Peasey Laminated Plastics
Ltd 1960–61
Mr Ed's Specialised Auto Designs
1979–80

GREENWICH
Heron Plastics 1962–67

LEWISHAM
Grand Prix Metalcraft 1971–73

MITCHAM
Parallel Designs 2000 to date

PENGE
Klasse Chassis 1994

PLUMSTEAD
Tiger Racing 1989–99

SOUTH NORWOOD
Eagle Autos 1971–73
Hooper Design Services 1991–2000
Lurastore 1993–95
Reed Engineering 2001–5
Zero Engineering 1995–2004

STREATHAM

Eagle Autos 1971–73
Mr Ed's Specialised Auto Designs
1978–79, 1980–82
Ricketts of Streatham 1972
Markham-Peasey Laminated Plastics
Ltd 1958–61

VAUXHALL
Design Dynamics 1971–74

WALLINGTON
PB Motors 1988–93

WANDSWORTH
Asquith Motor Company
1987–2003
Sabre Sportscars 2009 to date

WEST NORWOOD
American Speed Specialties
1995–2000

WEST LONDON

CHISWICK
Kustom Buggies 1971–72

FULHAM
Bugle Automotive Traction &
Manufacturing Company of London
1970–72

KENSINGTON
Ayrspeed 1994–98
Lynx Cars 1974–76

KEW
Cambridge Engineering 1958–67

MERSEYSIDE

BIRKENHEAD
Sarronset 1983–85

HAYDOCK
Cartell 1988–89

LIVERPOOL
Andersen Motor Company 1985–
2003

ST HELENS
Regent Motor Company 2008 to date

MIDDLESEX

ASHFORD
Mutant 4x4 2009 to date

BRENTFORD
Aerotech Engineering 1997
GP Speedshop 1966–68

EDMONTON
1-6-2 Engineering 1983–86

HAMPTON
Action Automotive 2003 to date

HANWORTH
GP Speedshop 1968–72

HENDON
Coupés/Sun Carriage Company
1993–2001

HESTON
Skyspeed 1969–72

ISLEWORTH
GP Concessionaires 1972–93
Tripper Cars 1983–84

RUISLIP
C.L. Hollier Services 1989
Edge Sportscars 2004 to date

SHEPPERTON
Ainsworth Engineering 1972–73
JB Sportscars 1999–2001
Nelson Motors 1989–94
RJB Electronics 1976–77

NORFOLK

BARNHAM BROOM
Birchall Automotive 1984–88

EAST DEREHAM
Mike King 1971–72
Pallandine Engineering

FAKENHAM
Neville Wynes Fibreglass Products
Ltd 1990–2001

FRETTENHAM
Renegade Speedsters 2008 to date

HARLESTON
Pellandine Engineering 1990–92

HETHEL
Lotus Engineering 1966 to date

HINGHAM
Triking Sports Cars 2009 to date

KING'S LYNN
East Coast Manx 2003–7
Flatlands Engineering 2004 to date
Force 4 Engineering 1991–92

MARLINGFORD
Triking Cyclecars 1978–2007

NEW BUCKENHAM
Brian Luff 1976–77

Motors Marianne 1973–74
Status Company 1974–75
Status Motors 1971–73

NORTH BUDDENHAM
Neville Wynes Fibreglass 1988–90

NORWICH
Brian Luff 1985–86
Brooke Motor Company 1991–93
Encore Cars 1992–97
GT Supercars 2008 to date
Hudson Component Cars 1990–99
JBA Motors 2011 to date
Status Company 1971

STOKE FERRY
C.L. Hollier Services 1989–93

WYMONDHAM
Atlantis Motor Company
1982–86
Kamala Cars 2001 to date
PSR Fabrications 1990–93

NORTHAMPTONSHIRE

CORBY
Challenger Cars 1987–93
Midas Cars 1979–89
Silhouette Cars 1987–88

CREATON
Image Sports Cars 2005 to date

KETTERING
Concept Developments 1973–77
Odyssis Designs 1997–98

NORTHAMPTON
Cygnet Cars 1982–84
Kit Car Workshop (Fury) 2005–7
Shapecraft 1985 to date

SILVERSTONE
Firefox 2000

WELLINGBOROUGH
DG Motor Services 1982–2000
KMB Autosports 1976–80
Mirage Replicas 1988–2002
Whitworth Engineering 1984 to
date

NORTHUMBERLAND

CORNHILL-ON-TWEED
Northlight Sportscars 2003–4

MORPETH
Vortex Developments 1985

NINEBANKS
Foers Engineering 2007 to date

ROTHBURY
Kingfisher Motors 1982–84

NOTTINGHAMSHIRE

BLIDWORTH
Sherwood Restorations 1978–82

BOUGHTON
Great British Sportscars 2008 to date

HUCKNALL
Gemini Cars 1991–98
Griffon Motors 1985–89

LONG BENNINGTON
Gardner Douglas Sportscars 1990
to date

LONG EATON
Red Line Minis 2008 to date

MANSFIELD
Mills Extreme Vehicles 2005 to date

MANSFIELD WOODHOUSE
Great British Sportscars 2007–8
Robin Hood Engineering 1985–2007

NEWARK
Luego Sportscars 2005–7
Reeves Developments 1985–88,
1996
TWM Engineering Company 1959–61

NOTTINGHAM
Beardalls of Nottingham 1971–73
Dragonfly Cars 1994–95
Durow Cars 1986–94
Easom Engineering 1993, 1997
Road Track Race 2006 to date
Tomcat Cars 1986

PINXTON
Spartan Cars 1973–95

TOTON
Dragonfly Cars 1994–95

WEST STOCKWITH
Markham Street Rods 2005 to date

WORKSOP
MK Engineering 1998–2006
RoadRunner Racing 2006–10

OXFORDSHIRE

ABINGDON
Rapid Productions 2003

BANBURY
Magnum Engineering 2007 to date
Simmons Design 1990–92

BICESTER
Brooke Kensington 1996–2002
Latham Sports Cars 1988–90
Reynard Racing Cars 2009 to
date

CHALGROVE
Amplas 1984–85

CHINNOR
Racecorp 1991–93

CLANFIELD
Alternative Cars 2003 to date

HENLEY
Vincent Cars 1982–87

KIDLINGTON
Mosquito Cars 1976–77

LITTLE CLANFIELD
Jeffrey Cars 1972–74

OXFORD
Concept Car Company 1993–97

SHILTON
Jeffrey Racing Cars 1971–72

WITNEY
Ikon Car Craft 2005

RUTLAND

UPPINGHAM
East Coast Manx 2007 to date

SHROPSHIRE

BRIDGNORTH
Squire Sports Cars Company
1988–93

CRAVEN ARMS
Summerfield Car Company
1992–94

TELFORD
Astron Motors 1984–85
Delkit GRP 1984–85

SOMERSET

CHARD
Aspire Kit Cars 2010 to date

COTFORD ST LUKE
Billy Bob's Buggy Shop 2005 to date

CRICKLADE
High Performance Mouldings
1972–75

MINEHEAD
Troll Engineering Company Ltd
1987–92

SEAVINGTON ST MICHAEL
MiniXevo 2007 to date

RADSTOCK
CSA Character Cars 1987

TAUNTON
Classic Replicas UK Ltd 2001 to date
Nostalgia Cars 1998 to date

WELLINGTON
Funbuggies 2002–8

WESTON-SUPER-MARE
Nyram Cars 1987
Stanbury Design Services 1983–86

WINSHAM
Rhino Trikes 2003 to date

YEOVIL
AWE Engineering 1990–98

STAFFORDSHIRE

ARMITAGE
Westfield Sports Cars 1983–85

BIDDULPH
Beauford Cars 2002 to date

BURTON-ON-TRENT
A.G. Thorpe Developments
1983–84

CANNOCK
Advico 2011 to date

HALFPENNY GREEN
L&R 1993–2002

LICHFIELD
Adrian Wood Engineering 1978

SLEIGHFORD
Minari Engineering 1990–99

STAFFORD
Home Builts 1983–84
Lightning Sportscars 1984–85
Longton Avante Cars 1982–87
Radnall Brothers 1968–70

STOKE-ON-TRENT
Blitzworld 2006 to date
EB Bros (Staffs) 1959–64
Le Mans Sportscars 1994–97

TAMWORTH
Autobarn Fabrications 1984–90
Reef Engineering 1981–83

WORTHEN
Robley Motors 1987–91

SUFFOLK

BURY ST EDMUNDS
De Havilland Motor Company 2011
to date
Suffolk Sportscars 1996 to date
Viscount Motors 1985–86

BUXHALL
AB Performance 2010 to date

FRAMLINGHAM
Cottage Classics 2002

IPSWICH
Beccles Robotics and Automotive
Developments 1988
Elmsett Road Racing 1989–98
IPS Developments 1992-95
Stan Daniels 1987–88
Viking Performance 1966

STOWMARKET
The Countach Company 1993

WOODBRIDGE
Ginetta Cars 1957–62, 1973–77

SURREY

BISLEY
Teal Cars 1997–99

CARSHALTON BEECHES
CTR Developments 1971–72

CATERHAM
Caterham Cars 1973 to date

CHERTSEY
Scorhill Motors 1991–96

EGHAM
Classic Roadsters 2005 to date

EPSOM
NG Cars 1993–2000

FARNHAM
Peerhouse Cars 1983–84
Ridgway Road Garage 1965–67

GUILDFORD
LMB 1959–63

HASLEMERE
Scorhill Motors 1988–96

KINGSTON UPON THAMES
The Robert Peel Company
1964–65

MORDEN
Cobretti 1999 to date

NEW ADDINGTON
Phoenix Cars 1997–99
Spyder 550 Motors Ltd 2005–9

PURLEY
Arkon Developments 1971

REIGATE
Altair Engineering 2001–5

WALLINGTON
Cobretti 1989–99

WEST MOLESEY
C&D Automarine 1970–71

WHYTELEAFE
Nordec Engineering 1960–61

EAST SUSSEX

BATTLE
S&J Motors 1984–88

BEXHILL -ON-SEA
Elva Engineering 1958–61
Minion Motors 1983–85

BODIAM
Andrew Gardner Cars 2000

CAMBER SANDS
W. West Engineers 1967–69

DITCHLING
Aero Cycle Cars 2003 to date

EASTBOURNE
Imperial Specialist Vehicles 1985–87

FRANT
Hawk Cars 1990 to date
Transformer Cars 1984–90

HASTINGS
Cradley Motor Works 2002 to date

HAWKHURST
Invicta Replicas 1985

HOOE
Hooe Garage 1972–74

HURSTMONCEUX
Jackal Cars 1995–98

NORTHIAM
Lynx Cars 1976–80

ROBERTSBRIDGE
Auto Marine Developments 1980–88
Steve Smith 1981–83

RYE
Boxer Cars 1986–87
Camber Cars/Checkpoint Ltd 1967

ST LEONARD'S ON SEA
Auto Elite 1998–2003
Cradley Motor Works 2003 to date
Lynx Cars 1980 to date

UCKFIELD
Kougar Cars 1976–94

WEST SUSSEX

ARUNDEL
MF Cawley 1984

BILLINGSHURST
ACT Engineering 1994

BOGNOR REGIS
Bezzi Cars 1983–88
Deauville Cars 2001 to date
Regis Automotive 1991–94
Rico Cars 1996–2000

BOLNEY
The Novus Group 2000–1

BRIGHTON
2CV Heaven 2005–6
Heritage Motor Cars (Europe) 1992
Noovoh Developments 1976–81
Pilgrim Cars 1985–87
(Southern) Roadcraft 1985–99
Trike Tek 1998–2003

CHICHESTER
Alba Automotive 1997
Jago Automotive 1969 to date
Rodding Scene 1971–73
Speed Buggys 1970–71
Tiler Car Company 1991–92

CRAWLEY
Razor Sports Cars 2007 to date
Roadtech 2003–7

FONTWELL
Dutton Sports Ltd 1970–71

GOODWOOD
JPR Cars 1986–97
Langridge Developments 1984–86

HAYWARDS HEATH
Minos Cars 2000–2

HENFIELD
Mackintosh Design Ltd 1987–91

HORSHAM
Budge's Buggies 1987–89
Pulsar Sportscars 2004–5
Volkscare & Custom 1976–87

LAVANT
Khaleej Cars 1998–2001

LITTLEHAMPTON
Amphijeep 1989 to date

PAGHAM
Madgwick Cars 1999 to date

PORTSLADE
GT Mouldings 1981–2007

ROWFANT
Scamp Motor Company 1987–2002

SAYERS COMMON
Specialist Automotive 2007 to date

SHOREHAM
Ricardo Engineering (Foers Ibex)
2005–7

SMALL DOLE
Pilgrim Cars 1987 to date

STORRINGTON
Eagle Cars 1981–99

TANGMERE
Dutton Cars 1971–73
Motorspeed/MFE 1984–88

WORTHING
Dutton Cars 1973–93
Hacker Cars 1991–2000
Retroforza 2005–6

TYNE & WEAR

KILLINGSWORTH
Blee Motors 1986–87

NEWCASTLE UPON TYNE
Cheetah Cars 1983–86
DC Kit Cars 1986–87
FRA Car Company 2002–8
NCF Motors 1985–90
Sagesse Motor Company 1990–91
The Toyshop 1997–2002

NORTH SHIELDS
Northern Car Kits 1986–87

SOUTH SHIELDS
A1 Autocraft 2005–9
Tornado Products 1989–92

WALLSEND
Sabre Cars 1984–86

WARWICKSHIRE

BOURTON ON DUNSMORE
Meggt 2008 to date

COMPTON VERNEY
Interstyl 1974–89
Magnum Engineering 1987–2006
Ultima Sports 1987–89

NUNEATON
Gentry Motors 2008 to date

RYTON ON DUNSMORE
Dunsmore Motor Traction 1984–96

STRATFORD-UPON-AVON
Stinger Cars 1984–86
TPC 1985–88

STRETTON-ON-DUNSMORE
Dunsmore Motor Traction
1984–96

WARWICK
WH Design 1970

WEST MIDLANDS

BILSTON
Martyni Sportscars 1999–2008

BIRMINGHAM
Archer's Garage 1993 to date
BS Sportscars 1988–89
Croy Glassfibre Products 1977–79
Cybertech Cars 1992–93
DNA Automotive 2007 to date
Doon Buggies 2001 to date
Eland Meres 1981–83
Falcon Design 1984–91
GB Restorations 1992–96
GL Enterprises 1992
Kingfisher Kustoms 1979 to date
KMR Buggies 2003 to date
Procomp Motorsport 1999 to date
Prestige Projects UK 2003
Range Over Kits 2007 to date

BRIERLEY HILL
Auto Body Craft 1971–73
Brockmore Classic Replicas Ltd
1993–94

COVENTRY
AF 2004–5
Auto Forge Automobiles 1987–90
Classic Cars of Coventry 1980–82
Dunlop Systems & Design 2008 to
date
Phantom Automotive/Virago 1998
to date
RDM Automotive 2003–8
TDK Racing 2008 to date

DARLASTON
Sutol Motorsport 1990–92

HAGLEY
Vindicator Cars 1990–2004

HALESOWEN
De Novo Kits 1990–92
Lomax Cars 1986–2002
RS Jigtec 2001–3
Vindicator Cars 2004 to date

HOLLYWOOD
Voodoo Sportscars 2007 to date

KINGSWINFORD
Auto Body Craft 1969–71
Replicator Sportscars 2008
to date
Sports Power Drive 1999–2001
Westfield Sports Cars 1985 to
date

SMALL HEATH
GB Motors 1971–77

SOLIHULL
Concept Developments 1977–78
Monkspath Garage 1959–61
The Sun Motor Company 1987–88

STOURBRIDGE
A. Evans Mouldings 1979–81
Quantum Sports Cars 1987–2001

SUTTON COLDFIELD
GTD Supercars 2000–4

WALSALL
Squire Sports Car Company 1986–88

WOLVERHAMPTON
Grand Illusions 1991–92
Martyni Sportscars 2000–8
Turner Sports Cars 1955–66

WILTSHIRE

BRADFORD-ON-AVON
Adams Brothers/Roadsters
1970–71, 1986–94
Marcos Sales 1965–81

CHIPPENHAM
Simod Design 1998 to date

CHISELDON
Dwornik Engineering 1991–92

CORSHAM
SportCycle 2002–3

DILTON PEWSEY
Auto Milan 1994–2000

FROME
AVA Cars 1986–87
Classic Car Panels

MARLBOROUGH
AF 1969–80

MELKSHAM
Roman Kit Cars 2003–5

MERE
Gravetti Engineering 1983–86
GE Engineering plc 1987–89

SALISBURY
Edward Waddington Motors
1984–85
Factory Five Racing UK 2007
to date
Leopard Craft 1991

SWINDON
Swindon Sportscars 1986–91

TEFFONT MAGNA
Planet Engineering 2007 to date

TROWBRIDGE
MR Developments 1982–83

WARMINSTER
Dri-Sleeve Car Company 1970–71

WESTBURY
Fibreglass Applications 1975–78
Le Mans Sportscars 1995–98
Marcos Cars 1963–2003
Phoenix Automotive 1997–99

WORCESTERSHIRE

ABBERLEY
P.A. Needham Engineering (Shelsley
Cars) 2000–7

BAYTON
Gregori Sportscars 1998–2002
Pembleton Motor Company 2002 to
date

BEWDLEY
Lomax Cars 1986–92

BROMSGROVE
Autech Classic Cars 1985–88
Pro-Motive 2006 to date
Wildmoor Motor Traction
2005–6

EVESHAM
Imola Cars 1991
Minus Cars (224) 2005 to date
Realm Engineering 2000 to date

FLADBURY
Liege Motor Company 1995 to date

HARTLEBURY
Kennedy Design 1984–86

HEIGHTINGTON
Grinnall Cars 1988 to date

KIDDERMINSTER
Adam's Buggies 2008 to date
Calvy Motors 1992–95
Hi-Tech Engineering 1988–91
Tornado Sportscars 1985 to date

MALVERN
Mead & Tomkins (Malvern Autocraft)
1992–95

OMBERSLEY
Midland Classic Restorations 2010
to date
Peter May Engineering 1987 to date

REDDITCH
Alternative Vehicle Centre 1985–90
AM Specialist Cars 1996 to date
Auto Services 1988–91
Auto Speciali 2004–10
Fiero Factory 1998 to date
Legend Motor Company 1997–2001
Projects of Distinction 1993–95
Sandwood Automotive 1984
SP Engineering 1985
SPM (Lakeside Carriage Company)
1993–2002

STOULTON
Primo Designs 1995–2001

STOURPORT
JP Autocraft 1992

EAST YORKSHIRE

ALDBROUGH
Z Cars 1996 to date

BEVERLEY
CCT Kit Cars Ltd 2005–7

BRIDLINGTON
Classic Automotive Reproductions
1983–84

DINNINGTON
Houghton Coldwell 1969–70

DRIFFIELD
Kaig Motors 2002–3

GOOLE
Phoenix Automotive 1983–86

HOLME-on-SPALDING MOOR
Knight Motorsport Services 2008 to
date

HULL
Dominator Sports Cars 2004–5
Extreme Sports Cars 2001 to date
Roadrunner Racing 2010 to date

SCARBOROUGH
Harris Great Marques 1998–2005

NORTH YORKSHIRE

ELVINGTON
YKC (Yorkshire Kit Cars) 1992–2005

HARROGATE
Margin Sports Cars 1999–2001
MNR Ltd 2004 to date

RAWDON
Dragsport 1972

SKIPTON
Carson Automotive Engineering
1991–2000
Guyson International 1974–77
Litton Cars 1989–91

SOUTH YORKSHIRE

BARNSLEY
AGM Sports Cars 2002 to date
BWE Sportscars 1994 to date
Carlton Automotive 1984–95
Kit Cars International 1984–85
Lightspeed Panels 1972–86
S&R Sports Cars 1984–85
Swift Cars Ltd 1983–85

DONCASTER
Beribo Replica Automobiles
1981–95
MBR Racing 2005–8
Volksrod 1968–84

ROTHERHAM
Deltech Engineering 1990–97
Foers Engineering 1982–2007
MK Engineering 1997 to date
MK Sportscars 2002 to date
Pastiche Cars 1987–91
RoadRunner Racing 2010 to date
T&J Sportscars 1990–94

SHEFFIELD
Avalon Automotive 1990
Coldwell Engineering & Racing
1967–69
Ginetta Cars 1993–2006
Ian Birks 1995
JC Autopatterns 1985–87
MAC#1 Motorsports 2002 to date
MC Cars 1984–89
Moss Motor Company 1981–85
Real Life Toys 1991–95
Sector Three Engineering
1999–2000
Sheffield Beach Buggy Co
1970–71

WEST YORKSHIRE

BATLEY
Albo Engineering 1993–99

BRADFORD
FRS Sports Cars 2011 to date
Javelin Sports Cars 2007–8
Nova Cars 1977–79
Pell Engineering 1995–2004
Revelation Motorsport 2007 to date

DEWSBURY
Asquith Motors 1985 to date
Dewsbury Kit Cars 1990–91
Nova Cars 1979–82

HUDDERSFIELD
Early Ford Store 1989–94
T6 Motorsport 2005–7

KEIGHLEY
Capricorn Cars 1985

LEEDS
Rhino Buggies UK 2004
Talon Sports Cars 1989–91

MIRFIELD
Nova Sports Cars 1982–90

OSSETT
Roy Kelly Classics 1999 to date

PONTEFRACT
Vintage Motor Company

WAKEFIELD
KD Kit Cars 1991–96
S&R Sports Cars 1985–86
TA Design & Development 1990–91
Watson's Rally 1983 to date

ISLE OF MAN

PEEL
Peel Engineering 1953–66

WALES

ANGLESEY/SIR FON

BRYNSIENCYN
Island Classics 1983

GAERWEN
Esargi Ltd 2010 to date

LLANGEFNI
Island Classics 1983
Ranger 1984–85

BLAENAU GWENT

TREDEGAR
MDB Cars 1986–87

BRECKNOCKSHIRE/
SIR FRYCHEINIOG

BRIDGEND
Métisse Cars 1995–2009

CARMARTHENSHIRE/
SIR GAERFYRDDIN

AMMANFORD
Amalfi Cars 1997–2000

LLANELLI
Arrow Spyder Ltd 1989–91
EG Autocraft 1987–89
PKA Marketing 1987
Skorpion Car Company
1986–87

CEREDIGION/
CEREDIGION

ABERYSTWYTH
Northern Car Kits 1987–88

BRYNMAER
Hillcrest Classics 1987–88

CEREDIGION
Forzari Developments
1996–97

LAMPETER
Reflex Cars 1986–89

PONTERWYD
De Novo Kits 1986–90

PONTRHYDFENIGAID YSTRAD
MEURIG
Darrian Cars 1985 to date

DENBIGHSHIRE/
SIR DDINBYCH

DYSERTH
Classic Performance Cars 1994–95

RHYL
Classic Performance Cars 1994–95

WREXHAM
Listair Cars 1985–86

FLINTSHIRE/
SIR FFLINT

FLINT
BRA Motor Works 1996–2005

SARN
Penguin Speed Shop 2011 to date

GLAMORGAN/ MORGANNWG

CAERPHILLY
Sethera Cars 1989

CARDIFF
Ram Automotive 1993–94

FERNDALE
Viking Sports Cars 1986–88

MERTHYR TYDFIL
Automotive Engineering &
Manufacturing 1987–88

MONMOUTHSHIRE/ SIR FYNWY

MAGOR
MGP Restorations 1990–96

NEWPORT
Amalfi Sportscars 1994–2000
Buckland Cars 1983–99

PEMBROKESHIRE/ SIR BENFRO

MILFORD HAVEN
Hensen Automotive 1983–85

PEMBROKE
Sherpley Motor Company
2004–7

ST DAVID'S
MCR Race Cars 2008 to date

POWYS

LLANIDLOES
Specialist Sports Cars 1999–2004
Stylus Sports Cars 2004–2008

RADNORSHIRE/ SIR FAESYFED

TORFAEN
LC Developments 2003–7

SWANSEA

HENDREFOILAN
KVA 1982–94

VALE OF GLAMORGAN

LLANTWIT FARDRE
Gilbern Cars 1960–74

WREXHAM

BANGOR-ON-DEE
Tripper Cars 1985–86

RHONDDA CYNON TAFF
Formula Cars 1992

WREXHAM
Dash Sportscars 1985–92
Libra Cars 1985–92
Listair Cars 1985–87

SCOTLAND

ABERDEENSHIRE

ABERDEEN
Luego Sportscars 2007–2011
North East Fibreglass 1971–78

AYRSHIRE

AYR
W.T. Nugent (Engineering) 1971–72

BEITH
FES 1988–89

GLENGARNOCK
Esteem Motor Company 1994

DUMFRIESSHIRE

DUMFRIES
Deanfield Motorsport 2001–5

NEWTOWN ST BOSWELL
Challenger Automotive Developments
1993
Reiver Motor Car Company 1993

LANARKSHIRE

BLANTYRE
Haldane Developments 1987–91

EAST KILBRIDE
Haldane Developments 1991–94

GLASGOW
Rotor Motive 1998–2001

MIDLOTHIAN/ EDINBURGH

EDINBURGH
Challenge Motorsport Engineers 2005
Caledonian Probe Motor Company
1972

PERTHSHIRE

AUCHTERARDER
Easybuild Projects 1996–97

ROXBURGHSHIRE

JEDBURGH
Genie Cars 1988–92

WEST LOTHIAN/ LINLITHGOW

LIVINGSTONE
Rallye Cars 1990

NORTHERN IRELAND

COUNTY ANTRIM

LISBURN
Corry Cars 1983–85

COUNTY DOWN

NEWTOWNARDS
Clan Cars (NI) 1982–87